READINGS FOR
EXPERIMENTAL
PSYCHOLOGY

READINGS FOR EXPERIMENTAL PSYCHOLOGY

CHARLES L. SHERIDAN

University of Missouri
and Veterans Administration Hospital
Kansas City, Missouri

HOLT, RINEHART AND WINSTON, INC.
New York   Chicago   San Francisco · Atlanta
Dallas   Montreal   Toronto   London   Sydney

Copyright © 1972 by Holt, Rinehart and Winston, Inc.
All rights reserved
Library of Congress Catalog Card Number: 77-140653
ISBN: 0-03-079500-1
Printed in the United States of America
2 3 4 5   090   9 8 7 6 5 4 3 2 1

Preface

I have been teaching experimental psychology on an undergraduate level for several years, and I have often wished that there was a convenient way to give students access to some important background readings. From time to time, I have found exciting articles in which one or more important points had been exceptionally well made, articles which provided a particularly impressive demonstration of the power of experimental psychology or which described research strategy and tactics that might serve as effective models for the student with aspirations toward becoming an experimentalist. I have sometimes made copies of these articles available to my students and have generally been gratified by their enthusiastic reception. I have now put together a collection of such articles in a reasonably systematic fashion (an article, like a person, usually has far too many facets to allow simple categorization), and the present volume of readings is the end product.

What are the emphases of this collection? Most important is the emphasis on the *power* of experimental psychology. It would be hard to imagine a discipline that has greater potential for solving many of today's problems than does experimental psychology. The methods currently in vogue for solving society's problems cannot begin to compare with those of the experimentalist. Claims made without real evidence, hypotheses and hunches wrongly elevated to the status of "fact," uncontrolled observation, pseudo-explanation, wishful thinking and sundry other hopeless methods still prevail. Application of experimental methods, though difficult, would soon drive out these useless—even harmful—techniques. Even the solid techniques of naturalistic observation cannot compare with experimental methods, since it is only through experiment that we can identify controlling variables, and only by knowing the variables which control a behavioral phenomenon can we modify it.

Humanitarian students tend to be impatient with experimental methods, and to make the flight to "real people." But it seems to me that the true humanitarian must have the patience and discipline to apply truly effective methods to the solution of human problems. Without the self-checking imposed by experimental method, intended benificence may prove quixotic, and altruism may become little more than a subtle form of "ego-trip."

In the past, experimental psychology has seldom met the well-intentioned student halfway. Experimentalists typically have worked in the belief that some day their little collection of facts might be of use to someone, but few of them have given any serious attention to such matters. There is nothing wrong with "pure" research (I do it myself), but there is plenty of room in psychology for those of a more practical bent. I hope that some of the present readings will show such pragmatists what there is to be gained from experimental approaches to the problems which interest *them*.

A second major emphasis of this collection is that it is methodological. Where specific experiments are described, it is to illustrate a point of method. To understand experimental psychology is to understand how to apply certain methods. The content which "fleshes out" experimental psychology comes from the human questions, much refined, which the experimentalist brings to the field of interest.

A third emphasis is on the problems confronted by experimental psychology. A review of the literature reveals that, in article after article, we are told that our strategies are inadequate, that our methods of evaluating data reliability have led to a "crisis" in psychology, that our selection of experimental subjects is mere "bad habit," that our methods and our problems "pass each other by." Yet we tend to ignore these problems especially in the undergraduate curriculum. I think it is time we prepared students to face the problems squarely and to *do* something about them in the future.

I hope that this collection of readings will convey to students some feeling for the excitement of experimental psychology—an appreciation of its vast potential coupled with a realization that it is a field full of challenges. It is a tool which we have scarcely begun to put to its maximum use. Let these readings be an invitation to many who have not yet chosen their life's work to join us in the task ahead.

Charles L. Sheridan

Kansas City, Missouri

Contents

READINGS FOR EXPERIMENTAL PSYCHOLOGY

ONE
On Being a Scientist

From The Life and Letters of Charles Darwin

Charles Darwin

The stringent procedures of experimental psychology are often very difficult for the student to follow. Why should anyone bother submitting himself to the discipline of experimental method? Throughout the history of human thought, men have neglected to undergo such discipline because they believed that knowledge could be acquired reliably in other ways. We all have heard stories of the medieval reliance on authority—of medieval scholars debating the number of teeth in a horse's mouth endlessly without taking the trouble to look (unless "looking" might take the form of looking the answer up in Aristotle). We laugh at our ancestors, but often still use methods of gaining knowledge which are no more reliable than theirs. Today we continue to rely on intuition—for example, the clinical intuition of psychotherapists—common sense, unsystematic observation, authoritative claims, and so forth. Newspapers and magazines are full of so-called "behavioral facts" that have no solid basis.

Most people simply have no idea how often their intuitions or commonsense judgments are wrong. It is very common for mere hypotheses to be taken as facts. Anyone who has done real scientific work—especially experimental work—has had the opportunity to see how often seemingly impeccable hypotheses prove to be wrong when submitted to adequate procedures of evaluation. Even the greatest of scientists working in his area of expertise learns, upon testing his judgments, that most of them are very much in need of correction. Presumably, those who do not submit themselves to such scientific checking procedures never have the opportunity to discover the inadequacies of their initial hypotheses, and go on regarding them as facts.

The following brief passage from Darwin illustrates how a very great scientist regarded his unchecked judgments.

From my early youth I have had the strongest desire to understand or explain whatever I observed,—that is, to group all facts under some general laws. These causes combined have given me the patience to reflect or ponder for any number of years over any unexplained problem. As far as I can judge, I am not apt to follow blindly the lead of other men. I have steadily endeavoured to keep my mind free so as to give up any hypothesis, however much beloved (and I cannot resist forming one on every subject), as soon as facts are shown to be opposed to it. Indeed, I have had no choice but to act in this manner, for with the exception of the Coral Reefs, I cannot remember a single first-formed hypothesis which had not after a time to be given up or greatly modified. This has naturally led me to distrust greatly deductive reasoning in the mixed sciences. On the other hand, I am not very sceptical,—a frame of mind which I believe to be injurious to the progress of science. A good deal of scepticism in a scientific man is advisable to avoid much loss of time, but I have met with not a few men, who, I feel sure, have often thus been deterred from experiment or observations, which would have proved directly or indirectly serviceable.

In illustration, I will give the oddest case which I have known. A gentleman (who, as I afterwards heard, is a good

Reprinted from F. Darwin (Ed.), *The life and letters of Charles Darwin*, New York: D. Appleton & Co., 1898, pp. 83–84.

local botanist) wrote to me from the Eastern counties that the seed or beans of the common field-bean had this year everywhere grown on the wrong side of the pod. I wrote back, asking for further information, as I did not understand what was meant; but I did not receive any answer for a very long time. I then saw in two newspapers, one published in Kent and the other in Yorkshire, paragraphs stating that it was a most remarkable fact that "the beans this year had all grown on the wrong side." So I thought there must be some foundation for so general a statement. Accordingly, I went to my gardener, an old Kentish man, and asked him whether he had heard anything about it, and he answered, "Oh, no, sir, it must be a mistake, for the beans grow on the wrong side only on leap-year, and this is not leap-year." I then asked him how they grew in common years and how on leap-years, but soon found that he knew absolutely nothing of how they grew at any time, but he stuck to his belief.

After a time I heard from my first informant, who, with many apologies, said that he should not have written to me had he not heard the statement from several intelligent farmers; but that he had since spoken again to every one of them, and not one knew in the least what he had himself meant. So that here a belief—if indeed a statement with no definite idea attached to it can be called a belief—had spread over almost the whole of England without any vestige of evidence.

2

Last Will and Testament

Ivan Petrovich Pavlov

Experimental psychologists dislike leaving any behavioral questions to speculation, intuition, or any other unscientific procedure. Yet, when it comes to the issue of the scientist's behavior *as scientist,* there is little scientific information on which to rely. Today it is not possible to point to a book or review article giving general scientific information concerning which scientific behaviors will yield success. There are exceptional areas—such as the area of experimenter bias—in which such research has been done, but, by and large, scientists must rely on mere lore (or philosophy) when instructing the beginner in good scientific procedures. The following passages from I. P. Pavlov are typical of what is available to us. There are also a number of interesting books available on how to do good research. See, for example, Beveridge (1950), Platt (1962), Selye (1964), Wilson (1952), or Bachrach (1962). Keep in mind that although these are the best we have, most assertions made in works of this kind are not supported by the quality of evidence scientists demand in their specialized areas.

What would I wish for the youth of my fatherland who devote themselves to science?

First of all—Consistency. I can never speak without emotion of this most important condition for fruitful, scientific work. Consistency, consistency, and still more consistency. From the very begin-

Reprinted from *Conditioned reflexes and psychiatry* (trans. W. H. Gantt), New York: International Publishers, 1941, pp. 189–190.

ning of your work train yourselves to be strictly systematic in amassing knowledge.

Learn the ABC's of science before attempting to ascend its heights. Never reach for the next step without having mastered the preceding one.

Never attempt to cover up the gaps in your knowledge by even the most daring conjectures and hypotheses. No matter how the colourings of this bubble may please your eye, it will inevitably

5

burst leaving you with nothing but confusion.

Train yourselves to discretion and patience. Learn to do the manual labour in science. Study, compare, and accumulate facts.

No matter how perfect a bird's wing, it could never raise the bird aloft if it were not supported by air. Facts are the air of the scientist. Without them you will never be able to soar. Without them your "theories" are useless efforts.

Yet, while studying, experimenting, observing, try not to stop only at the surface of facts. Do not become an archivist of facts. Try to penetrate the mystery of their origin. Seek persistently the laws governing them.

Second, modesty. Never think that you already know everything. No matter in what high esteem you are held always have the courage to say to your self: "I am ignorant."

Don't allow yourself to be overcome by pride. On account of pride you will be stubborn where it is necessary to be conciliatory; you will reject useful advice and friendly assistance; you will lose your sense of objectivity.

In the group which I am called upon to direct, atmosphere is everything. We are all harnessed to one common cause and everyone furthers it to the best of his strength and ability. Frequently we can not distinguish what is mine and what is thine, but through this our common cause only gains.

Third, passion. Remember, science requires your whole life. Even if you had two lives to give it would still not be enough. Science demands of man effort and supreme passion.

Be passionate in your work and in your quests.

Our fatherland opens broad vistas to scientists, and we must truthfully say science is being generously introduced into the life of our country. Extremely generously.

What is there to say about the position of a young scientist in our country? It is perfectly clear. To him is given much, but of him much is demanded. And it is a matter of honour for the youth, as well as for all of us, to justify those great hopes which our fatherland places in science.

TWO
The Nature of Experimental Psychology

3
From Remembering

Frederic C. Bartlett

Experimental scientists are set off from other scientists by their use of rigorous control procedures involving manipulation of the environment. An important option is available to them, however, with respect to when certain controls shall be introduced. The experimentalist can choose either to introduce maximal control from the very outset, or to use a strategy of "deliberate confounding." The immediate introduction of heavy control has been the traditional ideal, but there are certain advantages in deliberate confounding. With deliberate confounding an experimenter is more likely to be able to deal with complex phenomena directly instead of by reasoning from simple principles.

Ebbinghaus (1885), in his studies on memory, used a classic analytic strategy. He reduced the verbal materials to be memorized to what he regarded as their simplest possible form. He used nonsense syllable lists, supposedly free of associations. In so doing, he originated a tradition of nonsense syllable learning studies which remains vigorous even today. Yet it is sometimes difficult to see how to apply the principles derived from nonsense syllable learning studies to more complex learning tasks. Bartlett adopted the deliberate confounding strategy. He worked with more complex materials than did Ebbinghaus.

With a deliberate confounding strategy an experimenter manipulates a whole complex of independent variables simultaneously, and he does this knowingly. When he finishes his experiment, he cannot say which of the clustered variables produced any effects on the dependent variable he may have observed. But it is possible for him to proceed to introduce the controls necessary to attain this information. If it should happen that the entire cluster of variables failed to produce effects of interest, then there might be little point in proceeding to the analytic phase of the experiment, and having run the deliberately confounded study will have saved a great deal of time and effort. As Anderson (1966) has pointed out, the history of most research areas in psychology has been one of starting out less analytical and becoming more and more analytical with respect to controlling variables.

In the following article Bartlett makes a number of interesting observations on strategies for experimenting in psychology. His discussion of the use of nonsense syllables is of special interest, but his attitude toward statistical procedures is also very interesting, and has a distinctly modern ring to it. The success of the strongly analytic approach to psychology cannot be questioned. Experimenters have typically introduced heavy control immediately, and there have been great successes using this kind of strategy (see, for example, the Miller article in this book). However, it is refreshing to see an alternative strategy so nicely articulated.

EXPERIMENT IN PSYCHOLOGY

1. Its Beginnings

No doubt there is a sense in which it is true to say that experiment in psychology is "at least as old as Aristotle,"[1] but certainly it can claim no great age as a method of *systematic* exploration of human reactions. This is a matter of some significance; for it means that, before experiment was systematically applied in psychology, the experimental method had already a long history of development in other realms, upon which the early experimenters in psychology built both their aims and their methods. All the pioneers in experimental psychology were trained either in physics or in physiology. Their influence, both for good and for ill, still remains stamped upon the accepted methods of the psychological laboratory. Further, as was natural at the time, they were often men of a strong philosophic bent. Gustav Theodor Fechner, who is

Reprinted from *Remembering*, New York and London: Cambridge University Press, 1932, pp. 1–11.
[1] Myers, *Text-Book of Experimental Psychology*, Cambridge 1911, p. 1.

usually regarded as the founder of experimental psychology, was, in fact, concerned mainly to establish a pan-psychic view of the Universe. The tendency to use psychological experiment chiefly as a buttress to some all-embracing philosophical theory is one that has clung to experimental psychology ever since its earliest days, and has provided the critics of this branch of science with many of their most potent modes of attack.

Fechner took his degree in medicine, but turned soon to physics and mathematics. In developing his methods he built upon the work of E. H. Weber, the physiologist, and had the close cooperation of A. W. Volkmann, who was Professor of Comparative Anatomy at Leipzig. Helmholtz, equally and even more deservedly renowned as one of the great pioneers of experimental psychology, was also trained in medicine, but was before everything else a physicist. Wundt, the first man definitely to set before himself the ideal of a science of experimental psychology, was by training a physiologist. Hering, who often gets less credit than he deserves for his influence in certain directions upon the development of psychological research, was a physiologist. Side by side with these men were others whose interests were more theoretical and speculative. Stumpf, also trained in medicine, was mainly interested in music and philosophy, and G. E. Müller, who had a very great and important influence upon the development of psychophysics, and in many other directions also, had a philosophical background.

It is no wonder, then, that experimental psychology began, either with direct studies of special sensorial reactions, or with attempts to determine a measure of relation between physical stimuli and various apparently simple forms of resulting human reaction or human experience. And it is equally no matter for surprise that views of wide import and theoretical basis were speedily developed. Moreover, it is easy to see why attempts have constantly been made to control variations of response and experience by known variations of stimuli, and to explain the former in terms of the latter; and why it has been thought that reactions must be reduced to their "simplest" form and studied in isolation from the mass of responses to which, in everyday life, they are related. Yet, even if we keep within the limits of special sense investigation, the tendency to overemphasise the importance of stimulus-determination and the ideal of simplification by isolation of reaction raise profound psychological difficulties. These become still more apparent as the experimental method pushes on to deal with more highly complex human responses.

2. Its Development

It was inevitable that, once the experimental method was introduced, it should sooner or later extend its appli-cation into all fields of psychological study. As every psychologist knows, the first laboratory of experimental psychology was founded by Wundt in 1879. At that very time, Ebbinghaus was trying to find a way to apply Fechner's exact methods to a study of the "higher mental processes," and particularly to memory. He succeeded to his own satisfaction and in 1885 published the essay *Über das Gedächtnis*, which even now is often characterised as one of the greatest advances ever made by experimental psychology. His ideals were the simplification of stimuli and the isolation of response. He secured the first by using nonsense syllables as his memory material, and the second, he curiously thought, followed immediately.

It is worth considering in some detail what Ebbinghaus actually achieved. He realised that if we use continuous passages of prose or of verse as our material to be remembered, we cannot be certain that any two subjects will begin on a level. Such material sets up endless streams of cross-association which may differ significantly from person to person. It is an experiment with handicaps in which the weighting is unknown. Provided the burden of explanation has to be borne by the stimulus, this is obviously a real difficulty; for the stimuli have every appearance of varying from one person to another in ways incalculable and uncontrollable. There appears an easy way of overcoming this obstacle. Arrange material so that its significance is the same for everybody, and all that follows can be explained within the limits of the experiment itself. Since the experimental conditions are both known and readily analysable, the explanations can be expressed definitely and with the greatest possible certainty. Now, thought Ebbinghaus, with great ingenuity, if all the material initially signifies nothing, all the material must signify the same for everybody. Moreover, any variable significance that becomes apparent in the course of the experiment must be explained by the course of the experiment.

In reality, the experiments are much less easy than was assumed by Ebbinghaus. Any psychologist who has used them in the laboratory knows perfectly well that lists of nonsense syllables set up a mass of associations which may be very much more odd, and may vary more from person to person, than those aroused by common language with its conventional meaning. It is urged that this is no serious drawback, since it may be countered by a routine uniform exposure of the syllables and the inculcation of a perfectly automatic attitude of repetition in the learner; so that, with time and patience, each subject learns to take the nonsense syllables solely for what they are in themselves.

Once more the remedy is at least as bad as the disease. It means that the results of nonsense syllable experiments begin to be significant only when very special habits of reception and repetition have been set up. They may then, indeed, throw some light upon the mode of establishment and the control of such habits, but it is at least doubtful whether they can help us to see how, in general, memory reactions are determined.

The psychologist, of all people, must not stand in awe of the stimulus. Uniformity and simplicity of structure of stimuli are no guarantee whatever of uniformity and simplicity of structure in organic response, particularly at the human level. We may consider the old and familiar illustration of the land-scape artist, the naturalist and the geologist who walk in the country together. The one is said to notice and recall beauty of scenery, the other details of flora and fauna, and the third the formations of soils and rock. In this case, no doubt, the stimuli, being selected in each instance from what is present, are different for each observer, and obviously the records made in recall are different also. Nevertheless, the different reactions have a uniformity of determination, and in each case spring from established interests. If we were to put rock sections before all three people, the differences would still persist and might very likely be greatly exaggerated. Uniformity of the external stimulating conditions is perfectly consistent with variability of determining conditions, and stability of determinants may be found together with variability of stimuli.

So far as the stimulus side of his method goes, Ebbinghaus's work is open to the following criticisms:

(a) It is impossible to rid stimuli of meaning so long as they remain capable of arousing any human response.

(b) The effort to do this creates an atmosphere of artificiality for all memory experiments, making them rather a study of the establishment and maintenance of repetition habits.

(c) To make the explanation of the variety of recall responses depend mainly upon variations of stimuli and of their order, frequency and mode of presentation, is to ignore dangerously those equally important conditions of response which belong to the subjective attitude and to predetermined reaction tendencies.

Ebbinghaus's "great advance" involves serious difficulties if we consider only the stimulus side of his experimental situation; but when we examine also the theory of isolation of response underlying his method, still greater trouble arises. It is assumed that simplification of the stimulus secures simplification of the response. Then it appears to be assumed that this simplification of response is equivalent to isolation of response. Finally, it seems often to be assumed—though this is not a necessary implication of the method—that when we know how the isolated response is conditioned we can legitimately conclude that it is determined in this same manner when it is built with others into more complex forms of reaction.

It is always extremely difficult to say what, from the psychological point of view, constitutes simplicity of response. Sometimes we take the "simple" response to be one that comes early in an order of development, as when we say that perceiving is "simpler" than thinking, or that touch reactions are "simpler" than visual. Obviously, nonsense syllables do not give us simplicity of response in this sense, for nobody dreams of laboriously learning to connect long strings of meaningless material until he enters the psychological laboratory, and by this time he must have arrived at some maturity, though perhaps he has achieved no great discretion.

Sometimes we mean that the "simple" response is one that the agent can say practically nothing about, except that it has occurred. This is a slippery criterion, for some subjects find practically nothing to say about any response, while others seem to be able to make every reaction the subject of long analytical discussion. Certainly, nonsense material reactions stand in no favoured position in this respect amongst the mass of memory responses of daily life.

Sometimes we call a response "simple" when it is isolated, cut off from the simultaneous functioning of other responses with which it is normally integrated. This seems to be the kind of "simplicity" that the nonsense material type of experiment has in mind. For instance, Myers, commenting favourably upon the use of these methods, says that by employing meaningless syllables "we have been able to eliminate associations by meaning, and to arrive at the conditions affecting the sheer retentivity and reproducibility of a presentation, and to determine the number and course of the associations which are formed among the members of a series of such objects. It is true that the conditions laid down may depart somewhat widely from those which obtain in daily life. But only from such simple beginnings can psychological knowledge advance beyond that stage which had already been reached before the application of experiment."[2] That is to say, in our experiments we want to deal with *pure* memory, or with recall uncontaminated by any of the related functions with which it is accompanied in daily life.

There is, however, only one way of securing isolation of response, and that is by the extirpation or paralysis of accompanying functions. This is one of the perfectly legitimate methods of the physiologist. It can be argued that the psychologist, who is always claiming to deal with the intact or integrated organism, is either precluded from using this method, or at least must employ it with the very greatest caution. However this may be, it is certain that such isolation is not to be secured by simplifying situations or stimuli and leaving as complex

[2]Myers, *op. cit.* p. 144.

an organism as ever to make the response. What we do then is simply to force this organism to mobilise all its resources and make up, or discover, a new complex reaction on the spot. The experimental psychologist may continue the responses until he has forced them into the mould of habit. When he has done that they have lost just that special character which initially made them the objects of his study.[3]

The third assumption, that when we have studied isolated reactions we can at once conclude that they operate in just this manner and with just these conditions as partial constituents of more complex responses, is less important. Undoubtedly Ebbinghaus, and to a greater extent many of his imitators, made this assumption. And not a few of the assertions made about recall on the basis of this assumption are no doubt correct, just because, as we have seen, the method nowhere approaches its vaunted "simplicity." But the study of isolated reactions has a value in and for itself, and though its conclusions must be generalised with great caution, they often yield hints with regard to integrated response that could not easily be obtained in any other way.

I have dealt at this length with the nonsense syllable experiments, partly because they are generally regarded as occupying a supremely important place in the development of exact method in psychology, and partly because the bulk of this book is concerned with problems of remembering studied throughout by methods which do not appear to approach those of the Ebbinghaus school in rigidity of control. But most of what

[3]For a brilliant illustration of this point see Sir Henry Head, *Aphasia and Kindred Disorders of Speech*, Cambridge 1926.

has been said could be applied, with the necessary change of terminology and reference, to the bulk of experimental psychological work on perceiving, on imaging, on feeling, choosing, willing, judging and thinking. In it all is the tendency to overstress the determining character of the stimulus or of the situation, the effort to secure isolation of response by ensuring simplicity of external control. The methods of the great physical and physiological pioneers, often brilliantly successful in the study of special sense reactions, and in the elucidation of certain psychophysical problems, have overspread the whole of psychological science. Yet all the while new problems, most of them concerned with conditions of response that have to be considered as resident within the organism—or the subject—itself have been forcing themselves to the front, and it is more than time that their implications were explicitly stated.

3. Statistical Developments

The "father of experimental psychology" in England was Francis Galton. A brilliant and original investigator, a man of independent mind and position, he possessed a thoroughly good general biological training, together with a wide range of interests. He was as convinced as anybody could be that, whenever possible, science must deal with quantities, and at the same time his thoroughly humanistic outlook impressed upon him that in all psychological experiments there must be a mass of conditions imperfectly controlled, and incapable of being varied one at a time. He thought he saw a way out of the difficulty by adopting a statistical treatment of observational and experimental results. Such treatment gives, not, indeed, the mode of determination of the individual reaction, but a picture of trends of response and of their interrelations. Since the measures which express these trends and their relations sum up in shorthand fashion the results of a very large number of cases, it may be assumed that they are free from the accidental limitations of the individual instance, and that they state, within limits that may also be statistically indicated, conclusions that hold good over the whole field of investigation.

Largely by direct influence, but probably in part also because Galton's outlook contains something that is peculiarly attractive to the English temperament, the methods initiated by him have become very widely used in English psychology, and have been greatly developed by his successors.[4] In fact statistical method has profoundly influenced psychological investigation everywhere throughout the world. The earlier belief, that experimental psychology might easily be made to yield ideal experimental situations, has almost wholly disappeared.

This, needless to say, has its own drawbacks. Statistical methods are, in a way, scientific makeshifts. They are devices for handling instances in which numerous conditions are simultaneously operating. They do not show how all these conditions are related, and by themselves they throw no light upon the nature of the conditions. To get any indication of these matters we still have to rely upon whatever experimental pre-arrangement of conditions is possi-

ble, and upon what can be learned from careful observational study of the instances upon which we are at work.

Thus, as Yule says: "The very fact that the experimenter is compelled to use statistical methods is a reflection on his experimental work. It shows that he has failed to attain the very object of experiment and exclude disturbing causes. He should ask himself at every stage: 'Are these disturbing causes really inevitable? Can I in no way eliminate them, or reduce their influence?' . . . In any case it should always be the aim of the experimenter to reduce to a minimum the weight of statistical methods in his investigations."[5] On looking over any fair sample of the immense bulk of work upon applied statistics in contemporary experimental psychology, a questioning mind will find it impossible to avoid the conviction that a very large number of investigators care little about the arrangement or observation of the conditions of those reactions which they are studying, providing only that they can obtain large numbers of reactions and treat them statistically.

This is just the opposite error to that of the Ebbinghaus type of experiment. There we find a naïve belief in the complete efficiency of external circumstances to produce any sort of desired reaction. Here, at its worst, we find an equally naïve belief in the value of counting, averaging and correlating responses, even though the investigator ceases to worry about the variability of their determining conditions. The first may lead to unwarrantable optimism, but the

[4] Especially, as all the psychological world knows, in the extremely important work of Prof. C. E. Spearman.

[5] Medical Research Council, *Industrial Health Research Board Special Report Series*, No. 28, p. 5. It would be a most excellent thing if this essay could be put into the hands of every biological research student at the beginning of his career.

second seems to me to give up the psychological ghost altogether.

If statistical applications in the field of psychology are to have any value whatsoever, they must be both preceded by and also supplemented by observation and interpretation, and the more exact these can be made the better. We may take one of the illustrations used by Yule. The marriage rate of a country depends upon a large number of conditions, of which the state of trade and industry are suspected to form one group. That these economic considerations are relevant is in no way initially proved by statistics. It is first suggested on the ground of common observation and knowledge. The statistician then treats the available data on both sides by his special methods, and demonstrates that the curve for the marriage rate "shows a series of oscillations or waves which rather closely reflect the general cyclical movement in trade and industry."[6] The waves, both of marriage rate and of imports and exports, are isolated, and the ordinate of the marriage rate wave is correlated with the ordinate of the trade wave of its own year and of the years immediately preceding and following. It then at once appears that the difference of phase between the two waves is small, the waves of the marriage rate lagging slightly behind those of the trade rate.

At this point interpretation comes in once more. If postponements of marriage depend solely upon the industrial conditions of the year in which they take place, it can be shown that the marriage rate wave ought to be considerably in advance of that of the trade curve. Yule was able to demonstrate that the statistics are consistent with "the simple assumption that postponements are proportional to the average conditions in the given year together with the four or five preceding years."

In this instance interpretation comes in at two points: first, to set the whole investigation going; and second, to check and direct the initial results of the investigation. At both points the interpretation rests directly upon human observation. If these considerations apply in the field of vital statistics, they are even more markedly true of the use of statistics in psychology, where very often, in spite of all the difficulties, it certainly is possible to confine and control observation to a greater or less degree. From beginning to end the psychological statistician must rely upon his psychology to tell him where to apply and how to interpret his statistics.

In this book there will be no statistics whatever. This must not be held to imply any disrespect for one of the most powerful tools which the psychologist can use. It is merely because an attempt is being made to deal with a field of research in which suspected relations must be made as definite as possible before it can become fruitful to collect and correlate masses of results. "Nothing," says C. S. Myers, "is more important than that the experimental psychologist should be well grounded in the theory and practice of statistical measurement. But at the same time nothing is more important than that he should know when and how to use this psychological knowledge and skill, employing them not merely mechanically and automatically, but with due regard to psychological conditions."[7]

[6]Yule, op. cit. pp. 13–14.

[7]"Psychological Cautions in the use of Statistics," Zeit. f. angewandte Psychologie, XXXVI, 82–6.

4. Experiment in Psychology

The task of the experimentalist in psychology is particularly difficult, not merely because of the multiplicity of conditions which are in all cases simultaneously operative, but also because the two great groups of these conditions often seem to work in opposing directions. "The conditions in psychological experiment are the internal conditions of the individual (or 'subject') on the one hand, and the conditions of his environment on the other."[8] Now, as we have seen, stability of the latter is perfectly consistent with great variability of the former, and it is equally true that variability of the latter may be accompanied by stability of the former. Hence no amount of careful control of the uniformity of the external conditions alone will ensure an unchanging and known determination of response. This should be clear the moment we consider that psychological reactions are merely one class of the whole group of biological responses which have grown up to meet the needs of a constantly changing external environment. Thus the external environment may remain constant, and yet the internal conditions of the reacting agent—the attitudes, moods, all that mass of determining factors which go under the names of temperament and character—may vary significantly. These, however, are precisely the kind of determinants which are pre-eminently important for the psychologist. For example, many experiments involve the subject in repeated reactions to a uniform simple situation. Obviously those responses which come late in the series are determined in various ways by those which come earlier, and it is this type of determination with which the psychologist is often directly concerned. Again, the external conditions may vary, and the description of the responses evoked may vary, yet the mode of determination of the responses may remain substantially the same. For example, the sportsman describing a game, the politician giving an account of some current controversy of State, the musician talking about a concert, are all dealing with very diverse material, and no doubt their ways of fulfilling their task would appear very different to the observer. Yet their selection, criticism, arrangement and construction of material may be quite strictly comparable, because they are the work of internal determining factors belonging to the same order.

It follows that while experimental psychology has to arrange external conditions with an eye to uniformity and control, the experimenter should never hesitate to break this external uniformity in the interests of stability of response. It follows also that there is little use in counting, averaging and correlating responses, unless a great amount of preliminary work has been done to elucidate the most likely directions in which to seek to establish connexions between conditions and reaction.

The only type of problem that the experimentalist can tackle is the problem of conditions. Here is a source of confusion in psychology from which other sciences have been free. Very often indeed the psychologist has to accept the verbal report of his subject as material on which to build his hypotheses. Such reports may contain terms like: "percept," "image," "idea," "memory," "thought"; and almost at once a tendency may arise to discuss the status of

[8] Myers, *op. cit.* p. 2.

all of these in some completed structure of knowledge, and the validity of the information that they seem to give about some kind of external reality. Such discussion very rapidly passes beyond the limits of experimental science. It inevitably raises questions as to the nature of these items of reported content of mental processes. It asks, for example: "What is the nature of the image? How, itself appearing as object, is it related to a so-called external object? Can the 'meaning' which it carries be accepted as having objective justification?" But the experimentalist must confine himself to asking: "Under what conditions does that kind of response which we call imaging occur, and what are the functions of the 'image' in relation to the particular mode of reaction which is being studied?" In thus restricting himself, he is casting, or should cast, no reflection upon the other problems set by the epistemologist. They may be more important, as they certainly are more difficult, even than his own.

Current Trends in Experimental Psychology

B. F. Skinner

This and the following paper are properly put together as a pair. In both of them Skinner discusses and gives a stirring defense of experimental psychology. In this article he explains what experimental psychology is, taking care to distinguish between "science" and "experimental science," stresses the need for an adequate theory of behavior—this, despite the fact that Skinner is supposed to be antitheoretical—and defends experimental psychology against a variety of objections. In the paper that follows he rejects various tempting alternatives to laboratory research and stresses the value of experimental psychology in solving man's problems. Hopefully, these papers will be of value to those who are so eager to solve mankind's pressing problems that they run the risk of adopting useless methods for solving them.

There is a familiar caricature of the experimental psychologist which runs something like this: He is first of all an apparatus man, who spends a good share of his time tinkering with sundry pieces of equipment which never quite work to his satisfaction. He investigates only problems which he calls appropriate to the laboratory. He cannot study learning as part of the complex and subtle interplay of behavior and environment in everyday life, so he confines himself to the memorizing of meaningless words presented with clocklike regularity in a standard aperture. He cannot bring love or hate or envy into the laboratory, so he investigates reactions to garter snakes and pistol shots. The only strong motives he knows are his own, for his subjects perform merely to oblige him or because they are required to do so as part of a course they are taking. (In an exceptional case, if he "has a grant," they may

Reprinted from *Current trends in psychology,* Pittsburgh: University of Pittsburgh Press, 1958, pp. 223–241.

be paid seventy-five cents an hour.) He remains an experimental psychologist only so long as his problems have no practical value; that is how he stays pure. If his field suddenly becomes important for industry or the public weal, then be becomes an industrial or applied psychologist and does the whole thing over again in no time at all with better and more expensive apparatus. He works only with amenable subjects—that is to say, with subjects in whom no one is really interested: white rats or dogs or human beings who have stepped out of their normal lives and into a laboratory frame as standard organisms.

The picture is not as amusing as it may seem. Parts of it are perhaps too close to the truth to be funny, and whether justified or not the general tone is disturbing. It supports a conviction, which most of us have reached on the strength of other evidence, that experimental psychology is passing through a critical phase in its history, and that it is under close and not always sympathetic scrutiny. Psychologists who take a broader interest in the affairs of men have grown impatient with their experimental colleagues, if not openly critical. They often appear to resent the historical seniority of the experimental field and the prestige which seniority has engendered. The experimental psychologists themselves have grown uncertain of their scientific position. Their confidence has been shaken, and desertions from the ranks occur more and more frequently.

This does not mean that a great deal of what may properly be called experimental psychology is not still going on, or that the results are not duly published in the journals. It would be possible to write a paper on "Current Trends in Experimental Psychology" by describing the latest improvements in techniques, by reporting the most important recent advances, and so on, and such a paper would not suffer from any shortage of material. But the important issue is the survival of the field itself, or at least its ultimate position with respect to other branches of the science. This ought to have first claim upon our attention.

The very definition of experimental psychology is in doubt. It is always easy to overemphasize some incidental or superficial feature. For example, there is no reason why we should suppose that experimental psychology is concerned with a special subdivision of human behavior. At one time, it is true, experimentalists were dedicated to a limited subject matter, particularly the fields of sensory processes, reaction times, and certain limited learning situations, but this is no longer so. Experimentation is now common in every field of human behavior. Nor is the experimental psychologist any longer distinguished by the fact that he uses apparatus. It is characteristic of him that he is not satisfied to observe behavior with his eyes and ears alone, but must connect his subjects to amplifiers and recorders of one sort or another. Characteristically, too, he does not take the environment simply as he finds it, but modifies it in various ways with various ingenious devices. He was once almost alone in these practices, but virtually every sort of investigator now adopts them from time to time. The use of apparatus may improve an experiment, but it must not be confused with experimentation itself. It is possible to be an experimentalist without using apparatus at all. It is also not true that experimental psychology necessarily deals with something less than the whole man in something less than the real world. To simplify the material of a science is one of the purposes of a laboratory, and simplification is worthwhile whenever it does not actually falsify. But the experimental psychologist has no corner on simplification. The psychoanalytic couch is a simplified world, and so is any test situation.

Since the experimental psychologist is no longer distinguished by a special field of research, or by his technical equipment, or by laboratory simplification, still another historical distinction must be given up: his statements are not necessarily more reliable than those of anyone else. At one time this might have been regarded as the essential difference. Experimental psychology stood for precision versus casual observation, for experimental validation versus general impression, for fact versus opinion. Most of what was said about human behavior in education, public affairs, industry, letters, and so on, was on the other side. The experimental psychologist was distinguished by the fact that one could trust his statements, no matter how limited their application. Elsewhere one expected nothing more than casual or philosophical discourse. But this is no longer true. Statements of comparable validity are characteristic of most of the fields represented in this conference and may be found in other and still larger spheres of human behavior. Rigorous definition, careful measurement, and validation no longer comprise a sufficient criterion; and even the consolation that the experimental psychologist was at least first to take these matters seriously will not suffice for a current definition.

We can make some progress toward delimiting a field of experimental psychology which is not merely an historical accident by looking more closely at the word *experimental.* In psychology, as in any science, the heart of the experimental method is the direct control of the thing studied. When we say, "Let us try an experiment," we mean, "Let us do something and see what happens." The order is important: we do something first and then see what happens. In more formal terms we manipulate certain "independent variables" and observe the effect upon a "dependent variable." In psychology the dependent variable, to which we look for an effect, is behavior. We acquire control over it through the independent variables. The latter, the variables which we manipulate, are found in the environment. We manipulate them when we stimulate an organism, when we alter conditions of motivation or learning, and so on. The great majority of psychological experiments can be reduced to this form. There may be variations on the theme: in sensory psychology, for example, we may wish to see how far we can change the environment *without* changing behavior, as when we study difference limens. But the basic pattern of control remains the same.

This is a narrow definition of an experimental science. It does not identify "experimental" with "scientific." Physics, chemistry, physiology, and genetics are experimental sciences in this sense. Astronomy, geology, and taxonomical biology would not generally qualify. This is no reflection upon the latter. We are merely classifying them according to methodology. The classification is worth making because the psychologist is more likely to find common problems and common solutions among sciences which have the same formal structure.

One interesting consequence of defining experimental psychology as a branch of the science in which we control the variables which govern behavior is that we thus exclude most investigations using correlational methods. It may be possible to prove the existence of a functional relation of the sort here in question by running a correlation between some aspect of behavior and some aspect of the environment, but if we are able to manipulate the aspect of the environment, letting it take different values at different times, we can get a much more complete account of the relation. The experimental control or elimination of a variable is the heart of a laboratory science, and, in general, it is to be preferred to manipulation through statistical treatment. It is not a question of a choice of methods, however. The two approaches represent different scientific plans and lead to different results. It is curious that our definition should single out the kind of result which has been traditionally accepted as characteristic of the field of experimental psychology. A possible explanation of why it does so will appear later.

A line drawn between functional and correlational analyses will run approximately along the accepted boundary between pure and applied psychology. If this were not an accident we might seize upon it in order to replace the distinction between the useful and the useless—a distinction which is not exactly flattering to the pure scientist. But the agreement is rough and accidental. Correlational techniques have been extensively used in pure research, and the reason they have dominated the science of psychology in its application to education, industry, public affairs, and elsewhere is not that the processes to be dealt with in those fields are of any special nature, but that is has generally been impossible to give an account of relevant factors in any other way.

The special problem of the applied psychologist is a practical one. He must gain control of certain relatively complex material—if not directly, as in the laboratory, then indirectly and frequently after-the-fact through statistical procedures. He is not confronted with any special sort of psychological fact for which a special method is required. The preference for correlational techniques in applied psychology may therefore change. It has been true of technology in general that as the basic engineering problem is solved, as the applied scientist gains control of his material, the connection with pure or laboratory science is strengthened. Common methods and common terms can be adopted. Something of this sort may be expected in psychology as engineering control is improved.

It is a familiar complaint that the kind of control possible in the laboratory is impossible in the world at large. The argument is that we cannot modify a natural environment in subtle ways or measure normal unhampered behavior to thousandths of a second. The complaint is especially loud with respect to the laboratory study of animal behavior. The fact that sciences like physiology, embryology, and genetics are very largely concerned with the study of animals and yet yield results constantly applied to men is dismissed as beside the point. Even though behavioral processes may be essentially similar in man and rat, it is argued that men cannot be similarly controlled, and that the results of the animal laboratory are therefore worthless when applied to the larger problems of human behavior.

This position is bound to grow weaker

as the applied sciences grow stronger. It is not true that human behavior is not controlled. At least we cannot proceed very far as scientists on that assumption. To have a science of psychology at all, we must adopt the fundamental postulate that human behavior is a lawful datum, that it is undisturbed by the capricious acts of any free agent—in other words, that it is completely determined. The genetic constitution of the individual and his personal history to date play a part in this determination. Beyond that, the control rests with the environment. The more important forces, moreover, are in the social environment, which is manmade. Human behavior is therefore largely under human control.

Except for the trivial case of physical restraint or coercion, the control is, of course, indirect. It follows the general pattern of altering a dependent variable by manipulating the independent variables. Now, there are many cases in which the independent variables are freely manipulable with respect to human behavior. In the nursery, in certain types of schools, in corrective and penal institutions the degree of control may be very great. Although there are certain legal and ethical restrictions, the kind of manipulation characteristic of the laboratory is quite feasible. Elsewhere—in education, industry, law, public affairs, and government—the control is not so likely to be lodged in a single person or agency. Here, the basic engineering problem is to acquire control. But we must remember that the problem has frequently been solved—perhaps as often as not to our sorrow.

Since human behavior is controlled—and controlled, moreover, by men—the pattern of an experimental science is not restricted in any way. It is not a matter of bringing the world into the laboratory, but of extending the practices of an experimental science to the world at large. We can do this as soon as we wish to do it. At the moment psychologists are curiously diffident in assuming control where it is available or in developing it where it is not. In most clinics the emphasis is still upon psychometrics, and this is in part due to an unwillingness to assume the responsibility of control which is implied in guidance and counseling. Most personnel psychologists still obtain men with desired capacities or personalities by selecting them from a larger population rather than by creating them through training and guidance. In education we design and redesign our curricula in a desperate attempt to provide a liberal education while steadfastly refusing to employ available engineering techniques which would efficiently build the interests and instill the knowledge which are the goals of education. In some curious way, we feel compelled to leave the active control of human behavior to those who grasp it for selfish purposes: to advertisers, propagandists, demagogues, and the like.

This diffidence in accepting control has had far-reaching consequences. It is doubtless to some extent responsible for the continued effort to analyze behavior into traits, abilities, factors, and so on. The end result of such a program is a description of behavior in terms of aspect rather than process. It is a static rather than a dynamic description, and again it is primarily correlational rather than functional. No one doubts the value of investigating relations between ability and age, intellect and socioeconomic status, emotionality and body type, and so on. The results may have important engineering applications. But so far as the single individual is concerned, we do not then proceed to *alter* age, or body type, or socio-economic status. Relations of this sort may make us more skillful in using the instruments of control already in our possession, but they do not help us to acquire new instruments. No matter how satisfactorily we may demonstrate the reality of abilities, traits, factors, and so on, we must admit that there is little we can do about them. They give us an aspect description of behavior which may have a practical value in classifying or selecting the members of a group, but they do not carry us very far toward the control of the behavior of the individual. That control requires techniques which are peculiarly experimental in nature, according to the present limited definition, and we may therefore anticipate that as soon as applied psychology emphasizes active control, the experimental pattern will emerge.

Our definition of the experimental field is therefore not yet complete, since it does not exclude the applied interest in functional control. But a final distinction can now be made. It concerns the use to which the control is put. What the experimental psychologist is up to when he is being essentially experimental is distinguished from other fields of psychology by the fact that he has a special goal. We need not blush to express this in rather general terms. The experimental psychologist is fundamentally interested in *accounting for* behavior, or *explaining* behavior, or in a very broad sense *understanding* behavior. If these are synonymous expressions I have been redundant and I apologize. If each carries its own special shade of

meaning, then all three, taken together, will come nearer to an adequate statement. In any event, we must try to be more precise.

We do not understand a thing simply by becoming familiar with it. Nor is it enough to be able to describe it, no matter how specific or subtle our terms may be. We make some progress toward understanding anything when we discover how it is related to other things, especially to antecedent events. This is what the layman means by cause and effect, and the satisfaction which he feels when he discovers the cause of an event is probably not to be distinguished from the satisfaction which the scientist takes in demonstrating a functional relationship. The discovery that the environment, in acting upon the organism, could be regarded as a causal agent in the direction and control of behavior, and the realization that it was therefore possible to dispense with fictitious inner controls marked the beginning of a science of behavior. This was as much the spirit of the sensory analysis of mind begun by the British Empiricists as it was the spirit of Descartes and the later analysts of action.

But the cataloguing of functional relationships is not enough. These are the basic facts of a science, but the accumulation of facts is not science itself. There are scientific handbooks containing hundreds of thousands of tabulated facts—perhaps the most concentrated knowledge in existence—but these are not science. Physics is more than a collection of physical constants, just as chemistry is more than a statement of the properties of elements and compounds. There is no better proof of this than the failure of simple fact-collecting to inspire the scientific worker. Most of the facts entered in our scientific handbooks are virtually hack work. Some were collected in the course of more rewarding scientific pursuits, but the tables are filled out only by the type of man who might otherwise be found collecting stamps or old coins. There is no more pathetic figure in psychology today than the mere collector of facts, who operates, or thinks he operates, with no basis for selecting one fact as against another. In the end, he is usually to be found doing something else, or perhaps nothing at all.

Behavior can only be satisfactorily understood by going beyond the facts themselves. What is needed is a theory of behavior, but the term *theory* is in such bad repute that I hasten to explain. Psychology has had no worse theories than any other science, but it has had them more recently, and they have suffered in the light of our improved understanding of scientific method. No one today seriously uses a fictional explanation as a theory, but all sciences have done so at one time or another. That mercury stands at a certain height in a barometer because nature abhors a vacuum to exactly that extent, or that certain bodies move because they are possessed by a *vis viva,* or that a substance burns by giving off phlogiston are the kinds of theories whose demise marks the progress of a science. They are the sort of hypotheses which Newton refused to make, and most scientists have followed his example. But Newton himself demonstrated the value of a proper scientific theory.

A theory, as I shall use the term here, has nothing to do with the presence or absence of experimental confirmation. Facts and theories do not stand in opposition to each other. The relation, rather, is this: theories are based upon facts; they are statements about organizations of facts. The atomic theory, the kinetic theory of gases, the theory of evolution, and the theory of the gene are examples of reputable and useful scientific theories. They are all statements about facts, and with proper operational care they need be nothing more than that. But they have a generality which transcends particular facts and gives them a wider usefulness. Every science eventually reaches the stage of theory in this sense.

Whether particular experimental psychologists like it or not, experimental psychology is properly and inevitably committed to the construction of a theory of behavior. A theory is essential to the scientific understanding of behavior as a subject matter. But if we are to consider the current status of experimental psychology rather than its destiny, we must admit that it is at the moment in the midst of theoretical chaos. This is, in fact, the explanation of the present crisis. Many experimentalists obviously lack motivation and direction and find it difficult to impart either one to their students. Many of them have lost interest and are turning to other fields. This is not due to any lack of financial support. Our universities can still win out against industrial offers when that is the only thing at issue. Nor is it a question of the support of research, although many universities have not fully understood their responsibility in generating as well as imparting knowledge. The real difficulty is that the experimental psychologist is unable to do anything with the facts he has accumulated, and he sees no reason to accumulate any more. He lacks a professional goal.

Part of this difficulty can be traced to the fact that the two great explanatory systems which have held the psychological field for a hundred years are no longer paying their way. They have lost their power to integrate and illuminate the facts of the science and to inspire and motivate the scientific worker. The only research to which they now lead is a sort of desperate patchwork to keep the theories intact, and this is unsatisfying.

One of these explanatory theories is the notion of a controlling mind. From our modern vantage point the essentially fictional nature of this explanation is clear. It is on a par with the abhorred vacuum or the *vis viva* or phlogiston. Most of us like to feel that the ghost has been laid, and that we are free of mentalistic explanations. But the inner man, constructed of such stuff as dreams are made on, still flourishes. At least half the textbooks in psychology still talk about mental life, and few are successful in convincing the student that this can be reduced to the stuff which is dealt with in the physical sciences. In psychiatry the score would be almost a hundred to one in favor of an appeal to psychic determiners of behavior. Psychoanalysis has assigned names to at least three of these inner men, and it is the exceptional psychoanalyst who is willing to regard them as physical entities.

We cannot break away from these hoary practices simply by resolving to avoid theory altogether. We need a better theory. But this will be of a different sort and cannot be reached by patching up an old model. One current practice, for example, is to make the inner man more respectable by stripping him of what we may call his personification. He no longer exists as a complete person, but only as small fractions of his old self—as wants, drives, attitudes, interests, and so on. It is the exceptional writer who convincingly defines terms of this sort in a nonmentalistic way; and even if an operational re-definition is successful, the old theory may leave its mark in the structure surviving.

The other current explanatory theory flourishes with greater prestige and presumably in more robust health. This is the physiological theory of behavior. The inner man is given neurological properties, with a great gain in scientific respectability. Psychiatry becomes neuropsychiatry, and psychology the study of the nervous system. It is difficult to attack this theory without seeming to criticize the physiological psychologist, but no criticism is involved. There are many precedents in the history of science for borderline disciplines. To integrate the facts of two sciences is an interesting and profitable endeavor. Eventually, we may assume, the facts and principles of psychology will be reducible not only to physiology but through biochemistry and chemistry to physics and subatomic physics. But this reduction is undoubtedly a long way off. The current theoretical practice which is objectionable is the use of a hypothetical neural structure, the conceptual nervous system, as a theory of behavior. The neurological references introduced into such a theory, like references to mental states, interfere with free theory building, and they produce a structure which is not optimal for the organization of behavioral facts.

The traditional physiological theory, too, eventually fails to motivate the psychologist. Valid neurological explanations of important psychological laws are not arrived at with a very rewarding frequency, and the investigations which they inspire have a tendency to lead to such a jumble of details that the original plan is lost sight of. We are all familiar with the type of graduate student who comes to study psychology full of enthusiasm for a science of behavior, who climbs the physiological family tree through Berkeley, Hume, Wundt, and the moderns, and finds himself studying some detailed physiological mechanism. His motivation eventually flags when he sees that his current activities have only the most tenuous connection with his original interest in human behavior. Such a case history is only a scale model of the history of experimental psychology. No matter how critically we may now view the original program of a science of mind, we must admit that a great driving force was lost when the nervous system had to be brought in. Instead of the basic psychophysical relation, the object of research became the operation of specific physiological mechanisms. Generalized brain theories of the Gestalt variety and dimensional analyses of consciousness are efforts to bring together again the fragments of a science of mind, and to add something of theoretical interest to the study of the physiology of end-organs. But the spark has been lost.

If we try to put these two great explanatory systems in good scientific order through operational re-definition, we only succeed in dealing the *coup de grâce*. We can, of course, define "mind" in behavioral terms, and we can set up a conceptual nervous system for the representation of behavioral facts, leaving the specification of the actual neural properties until some later date. But in this way we eliminate all the explanatory force of the theories. An operational definition is possible in every case, but it does not necessarily lead to a satisfactory theoretical construct. Whatever its success, it spoils the explanatory fun.

The appeal to what we may call naive physiologizing, like the appeal to psychic determiners, is made in an attempt to explain behavior by shifting to a different level of observation. These are "outside" theories, which account for one thing by pointing to something which is going on somewhere else at the same time. For this reason they cannot fill the need for a theory of behavior, no matter how carefully they may be extended or repaired. What is emerging in psychology, as it has emerged at some point in the history of most sciences, is a theory which refers to facts at a single level of observation. The logic of this is simple enough. We begin with behavior as a subject matter and devise an appropriate vocabulary. We express the basic protocol facts of the science in the terms of this vocabulary. In the course of constructing a theory we may invent new terms, but they will not be invented to describe any new sort of fact. At no time will the theory generate terms which refer to a different subject matter—to mental states, for example, or neurones. It is not the purpose of such a theory to explain behavior by turning to "outside" determiners.

The real achievement of such theory building is not easy to demonstrate because of the present confused condition in psychology. There is no generally accepted theory of behavior which will serve as an example. But the situation is not quite hopeless. A scientific theory is never fully subscribed to by all the practitioners of a science; if it were, there would be no further need for scientific effort. And while no explicit theory in experimental psychology today has more than a handful of adherents, in practice most psychologists respect certain underlying assumptions which constitute the beginning of an implicit theory. We realize how extensive this implicit theory is when we observe non-psychologists dealing with the same subject matter and see how they repeatedly violate our assumptions. We have, then, something to begin with by way of actual theoretical practice. We may also get a plausible glimpse of the future, for some of the features of an effective theory can be inferred from the nature of behavior as a subject matter and from comparable theories in other fields. It should, therefore, also be possible to evaluate the present status of psychology with respect to theory construction.

The first step in building a theory is to identify the basic data. It may be easy or difficult, depending upon the science. It was relatively easy, for example, to decide what events were to be taken into account in the Copernican theory of the solar system. Astronomers had observed the positions of the planets at given times; the theoretical problem was to relate these facts, not to identify them. In genetics, on the other hand, it is relatively difficult to discover what characteristics of an organism are valid genetic units. Psychology faces an even more difficult problem: what are the parts of behavior and environment between which orderly relations may be demonstrated?

The layman has little difficulty in analyzing the behavior of himself and his fellow men. He breaks it into discrete acts. He may report, for example, that someone "watched a car until it passed out of sight." The statement conveys useful information at the level of casual discourse, but is it necessarily a valid scientific description? The language of the kitchen may be of no use to the chemist, though the cook finds it meaningful enough. Anyone who has tried to analyze pursuit behavior knows the problem involved in orienting the eyes toward a moving object, and very much more than that is covered by the word *watch*. And when the layman, with what seems like breathless daring, reports that someone "chose to remain silent," he stakes out a field which might suffice for a lifetime of research. The statement may be quite effective for practical purposes, but it will not necessarily suffice for a scientific description. For what is "choice"? Even the behavior involved in choosing between simple objects like cigarettes or neckties is complex enough. But what is happening when one "chooses to remain silent"? And in what sense is remaining silent to be regarded as behavior at all?

In practice psychologists define "response" in many ways—from muscle twitch to telic effect. In the latter case they present the physiologist with the baffling problem of how two responses executed by different parts of the body can be mutually replaceable in a lawful physiological train of events. It is a common current practice to dodge the problem by accepting some practical measure of behavior, often limited to a particular measuring device, such as "maze performance" or some arbitrary criterion of "success." The physiologist has also been appealed to, but in vain, since an indication of the presence or absence of activity in a particular effector is of little help.

We cannot continue to leave the problem unsolved if we are to construct an effective theory. It may be that the notion of a unit of response is at fault and that a final statement will reflect the fluidity and continuity of behavior as a whole. This would require more powerful analytical tools, but it may be necessary. A further requirement must also be recognized; it is not the mere form of behavior which we undertake to predict but rather its occurrence. Expressions like "reaction tendency" or "excitatory potential" have attempted to take account of this fact. The end term in a theory of behavior, in short, is the probability of action.

In the companion problem of the environment, the layman again shows an enviable talent, for he describes and analyzes the environment with no hesitation whatsoever. The world to him is simply a collection of *things*. But his success gives the case away. He has analyzed the environment in terms of its practical importance. This is justifiable for his purposes; and in so far as various aspects of the environment have common practical consequences for everyone, the lay vocabulary might even be adopted for scientific use. But a complete scientific account must go back to properties of the environment which are effective before any consequences have been felt, and it must account for the process by which consequences alter the effectiveness of these properties.

Current practices are again diverse. Some psychologists, as in psychophysics, deal with stimuli one dimension at a time. Others, at the other extreme, refer to the "total situation"—an expression which seems safe because it can scarcely overlook anything, but which is unpleasantly vague. Our present knowledge of the physiology of the receptors offers little if any help in deciding upon an effective practice.

Since we have not clearly identified the significant data of a science of behavior, we do not arrive well prepared at the second stage of theory building, at which we are to express relations among data. Observed relations of this sort are the facts of a science—or, when a sufficient degree of generality has been reached, its laws. The general form of the laws of behavior can be inferred from the nature of our program, but examples are not very abundant among the achievements to date. A weakness at the first stage of theory construction cannot be corrected at the second. In psychophysics the stimulus is defined rigorously, if not very comprehensively, and an arbitrary definition of response seems to suffice. Consequently, some generality at the second stage has been achieved. In the field of learning, on the other hand, we have collected thousands of separate learning curves, but they represent changes in hundreds of different aspects of behavior in hundreds of different situations. As a result, we have no valid general expressions for learning processes. This is characteristic of most of the facts of experimental psychology, and the next step in the construction of a satisfactory theory is therefore very difficult.

This step—at the third stage in theory building—can be exemplified by a simple example from the science of mechanics. Galileo, with the help of his predecessors, began by restricting himself to a limited set of data. He proposed to deal with the positions of bodies at given times, rather than with their color or hardness or size. This decision, characteristic of the first stage in building a theory, was not so easy as it seems to us today. Galileo then proceeded to demonstrate a relation between position and time—the position of a ball on an inclined plane and the time which had elapsed since its release. Something else then emerged—namely, the concept of acceleration. Later, as other facts were added, other concepts appeared—mass, force, and so on. Third-stage concepts of this sort are something more than the second-stage laws from which they are derived. They are peculiarly the product of theory-making in the best sense, and they cannot be arrived at through any other process.

There are few, if any, clear-cut examples of comparable third-stage concepts in psychology, and the crystal ball grows cloudy. But the importance of the stage is indicated by the fact that terms like *wants, faculties, attitudes, drives, ideas, interests,* and *capacities* properly belong there. When it is possible to complete a theoretical analysis at this stage, concepts of this sort will be put in good scientific order. This will have the effect of establishing them in their own right. At present they need external support. Some of them, like wants and attitudes, come to us trailing clouds of psychic glory, and a wisp or two of the psychic can usually be detected when they are used. Other concepts, like drives and motives, borrow physiological support in certain favorable cases. Still others, like abilities and traits, have been made respectable through correlational analyses, which give them the status of "individual differences." Although most psychologists think of an ability as something which has meaning in the behavior of a single individual, current techniques of measurement find it necessary to make use of the position of the individual in a population. Magnitudes are assigned to the abilities and traits of the individual in terms of his relation to the

group rather than through direct measurement. A proper theory at this stage would characterize the behavior of an individual in such a way that measurement would be feasible if he were the only individual on earth. This would be done by determining the values of certain constants in equations describing his behavior—clearly a third-stage enterprise.

From all of this should emerge a new conception of the individual as the locus of a system of variables. Fortunately for psychology it has been possible to deal with behavior without a clear understanding of who or what is behaving, just as it seems to be possible to deal with personality without defining "person." The integrity or unity of the individual has been assumed, perhaps because the organism is a biological unit. But it is quite clear that more than one person, in the sense of an integrated and organized system of responses, exists within one skin. The individual proves to be no more undividable than the atom was uncuttable. Many sorts of metaphorical schemes have been devised to represent this fact. A single personality may be regarded as moving about from one level of consciousness to another, or personalities may be frankly multiple. A proper theory must be able to represent the multiplicity of response systems. It must do something more: it must abolish the conception of the individual as a doer, as an originator of action. This is a difficult task. The simple fact is that psychologists have never made a thoroughgoing renunciation of the inner man. He is surreptitiously appealed to from time to time in all our thinking, especially when we are faced with a bit of behavior which is difficult to explain otherwise.

Eventually we may expect the main features of a behavioral theory to have physiological significance. As the science of physiology advances, it will presumably be possible to show what is happening in various structures within the organism during particular behavioral events, and the theoretical systems of the two sciences may also be seen to correspond. An example of this rapprochement is the way in which facts and principles of genetics arrived at from the study of the characteristics of parents and offspring are seen to correspond to facts and principles of cell structure. The science of genetics has already reached the stage at which it is profitable to investigate both subject matters at the same time. Terms which originally described relations between the characteristics of parents and offspring may now carry additional cytological references.

A similar day may come in psychology. That is up to the physiologist and the physiological psychologist. But the eventual correspondence should not be allowed to obscure the present need for a behavioral theory. The hypothetical physiological mechanisms which inspire so much research in psychology are not acceptable as substitutes for a behavioral theory. On the contrary, because they introduce many irrelevant matters, they stand in the way of effective theory building. There is a tendency in some quarters to admit this while insisting upon compensating advantages. It is argued that the solidity of the nervous system gives it the strength to dispossess psychic fictions which a purely behavioral theory may lack. It is also thought to be a necessary intellectual crutch —an ever-present help in time of theoretical need. Many people cannot think

of the origination of an act without thinking of a motor center. They cannot conceive of learning without thinking of changes in synaptic resistance or some other protoplasmic change. They cannot contemplate a derangement of behavior without thinking of damaged tissue. Moreover, it is often pointed out that the histories of other sciences show many examples of theories which, under a proper operational analysis, would have been found to contain unwarranted references to other kinds of data but which made it possible to think more effectively about relevant data than would have been possible with a purely conceptual scheme. But this remains to be proved. It is not necessarily true that physiological theories have in the long run directed the energies of psychologists into the most profitable channels. An enlightened scientific methodology should enable us to improve upon the practices exemplified by the history of science. In any event an independent theory of behavior is not only possible, it is highly desirable, and such a theory is in no sense opposed to physiological speculation or research.

Because of the unhappy fate of so many psychological theories of the past, a sound theory of behavior must work itself out against a weight of indifference and even active opposition. Very few psychologists understand the nature of such a theory or are aware that it has a counterpart in most established sciences. Many of them deny the possibility of a respectable theory. It is encouraging to recall, however, that a good tentative theory has usually proved to be autocatalytic; a demonstration of what can be done, even within a limited sphere, draws attention to theory-building, and the process is accelerated.

There is usually no need to justify a theory of behavior when its potentialities are made clear, for these are very great. Consider the case of the social sciences, for example. The current practice of the sociologist is either to express his facts and theories without referring to individual behavior at all, or to construct a psychology of his own—devoting at least an introductory chapter (if not an entire treatise) to the motives and habits which lead men to live together and behave together as they do. The sociologist may or may not agree that the behavior of the group is to be predicted from a study of the psychology of the individual, but he has no hesitation in using the behavior of the individual to expound, if not to explain, sociological facts. The economist, whether professional or professorial, faces the same alternatives. Either he must state laws and make predictions without mentioning human behavior, or he must devise a special psychology to explain the activities of the great-grandchildren of Adam Smith's "economic man." It is the exceptional economist who does not account for facts about goods or money or labor or capital by pointing to what men will typically do under certain circumstances. Similarly, the political scientist, whether or not he hopes to derive the principles of government or the characteristics of political struggles from psychology, usually continues to talk about some species of "political man," to whom he assigns just the motives and capacities needed to account for his political facts.

Whatever his field, the social scientist does not currently find in the science of psychology a conceptual scheme with which he can talk about human behav-ior consistently and effectively. Economic man, political man, the group mind—these are crude explanatory fictions which need to be replaced by a sound behavioral theory. That such a theory need not be essential to a true social science is beside the point. There is no question that it would be enormously helpful.

There is a greater need for such a theory in those broad fields of human endeavor in which rigorous scientific practices are not yet feasible. For example, a widespread critical examination of our educational practices is currently in progress. This is basically a program of psychological engineering. Yet it is being projected and carried through with a quite unrealistic conception of human behavior. Ancient theories of the nature of man recur again and again with their familiar cant—"an integrated view of life," "a sense of personal responsibility," "a capacity to experience and understand life as a related whole," "the development of the mind," and so on. Educators are not wholly to blame, for we have not yet put forth a workable conception of human behavior suitable for their purposes.

Our legal system, to take another example, is based upon an even older form of the traditional theory. It is becoming more and more difficult to reconcile our modern conception of man and society with the legal notion of personal responsibility, of a will capable of conscious motion and dominated from time to time by ideas, feelings, and influences. But an alternative theory is apparently not yet in workable form.

The lack of an adequate understanding of human behavior is most cruelly felt in the field of government and world affairs. We are faced with the disheartening spectacle of hundreds of men of good will drawing up blueprints for the world of the future, while making assumptions about human nature which most of us know to be invalid. Two world wars have not been fought over anything as simple as world trade or boundaries. We are in transition from one conception of man to another and to an effective understanding of the possible relationships which may exist between men. We have paid a terrible price for knowledge which could conceivably be acquired through the peaceful and profitable methods of science, and as yet we have little to show for it. A great deal may depend upon whether we can reach in the near future a workable theory of human behavior.

One important role of a scientific theory of behavior, then, is to replace the theories which now pervade our thinking, which are part of our everyday speech, which influence all our dealings with our fellow men, and which stand in the way of applying the methods of science to human affairs. As everyone knows, many technical procedures which would improve our practices in education, law, politics, and so on are now available. The contribution which the science of psychology can make in these matters is very great. Psychologists have been powerful advocates of an objective attitude and will undoubtedly continue to insist that the methods of science be applied to human behavior and human society wherever possible. If we are to talk about behavior, let us be precise. If we are to insist that two facts are related, let us prove the relation. Psychology can offer better ways of describing and measuring behavior, better methods of guaranteeing the validity of statements, and so on. But

nothing of this sort is any longer exclusively a psychological contribution. The main task is to make these technical contributions felt, to put them into the hands of the people who need them; and we can do this only when we make it clear that a science is more than method, more than facts. The most important contribution that psychology can make today is a workable theory of behavior in the present sense—a conception of man which is in accord with all the facts of human behavior and which has been crucially tested in the experimental laboratory. Only an effective and progressive theory of behavior can bring about the proper change in attitude which will make it possible to apply the methods of science to human affairs in every field.

The survival of the traditional conception of man as a free and responsible agent is an excellent example of the general principle[1] that a theory is never overthrown by facts, but only by another theory. There are facts which have been well established for centuries which are incompatible with the traditional theories of human behavior, and these theories move about in the modern world in a welter of contradiction. But their proponents work busily to patch them up, and somehow they survive. A new interpretation here, a conspiracy of silence there, and the trick is turned; and this will continue to be so until a new and effective theory is worked out.

We cannot remedy the situation by mere dialectic. We need to arrive at a theory of human behavior which is not only plausible, not only sufficiently convincing to be "sold" to the public at large, but a theory which has proved

[1] Pointed out by President Conant of Harvard University in the *American Scientist,* January 1947.

its worth in scientific productivity. It must enable us, not only to talk about the problems of the world, but to do something about them, to achieve the sort of control which it is the business of a science of behavior to investigate. The superiority of such a theory will then be clear and we shall not need to worry about its acceptance.

The important trend in experimental psychology, then, is toward a satisfactory theory of behavior. Perhaps we should not be surprised at this, since the field was defined in such a way that it would necessarily be true. But the field had to be defined in that way. Experimental psychology is more than a tradition; it is more than an assemblage of practices and interests passed along from generation to generation without respect to a changing world. A tradition needs to be reviewed and justified, and this is especially true in experimental psychology, where it has been easy to lose the main theme. The trend, then, is toward a clarification of this theme, toward a sort of self-realization. The experimental psychologist is not using method for method's sake. He is not following an interest to which he has been led by indulging in one idle curiosity after another. He does not seize upon a field of research because the practical-minded have left it untouched. In so far as he is behaving as an experimental psychologist, he is trying to understand behavior. In this work he must discover and collect facts, and he must construct an adequate theory.

A clear realization of this aim should be helpful. There is nothing wrong with experimental psychology which a clear-cut objective will not cure. The development of an effective theory of behavior is ideal for this purpose. The science of experimental psychology will presumably remain in the hands of the professors. Critical issues in applied fields may lead to important contributions to theory; methods will be devised and facts discovered in industry, education, the clinic, and so on, which are relevant to a central science. But the husbanding of facts, the sifting of information from all fields of human behavior, the special study of questions which are theoretically crucial, and the working out of a satisfactory conceptual system will presumably remain the function of the psychologists in our universities. This is still so, at least, in older sciences with much more extensive technological applications. It is appropriate, too, that a concern for theory in this sense should remain closely associated with instruction.

But the academic psychologist is limited in the time and facilities available for research, and at the moment he may be rather bewildered by, if not envious of, the glittering technical advantages of his erstwhile colleagues. In theory-construction, however, he finds a field which is not only exclusively his own, but one in which he can experiment effectively and to some purpose with relatively limited resources. He will not need to confine himself to facts which have been neglected by those who can experiment more efficiently. He will be able to explore key positions of the greatest importance. The *experimentum crucis* is his field, and in it he may usually rest content with one subject for every hundred studied by his applied colleagues and with one chronoscope or pursuitmeter or cathode-ray oscillograph in place of dozens.

This is not a gesture of escape. It is not a conclusion that the grapes are sour. The experimental psychologist is above all a scientist, and this is the proper field of science—the discovery and ordering and understanding of nature. This is Faraday and Maxwell rather than the laboratories of General Electric or Westinghouse. It is Mendel and T. H. Morgan rather than an agricultural breeding station. It is Pasteur and Koch rather than research laboratories of great pharmaceutical houses. This is good company. To understand human behavior in the sense in which any part of nature is understood by science is truly an exciting and satisfying goal.

5

The Flight from the Laboratory

B. F. Skinner

An experimental psychologist sometimes invites a man into a laboratory, asks him to memorize a list of nonsense syllables or learn to keep a pointer on a moving target, and sends him on his way quite unaware that he will be asked to come back later for a second series of observations. The experiment will not succeed unless he is ignorant of the future test. I do not know whether the originator of these conferences was conducting such an experiment ten years ago, but I can now report what it feels like to be invited back for the second session. It is mainly a feeling of regret. If, when I was preparing my earlier paper, I had known that I would be asked to compare my prediction of trends in experimental psychology with a decade of actual historical fact, I should have confined myself to statements which could have been more easily twisted to accommodate the eventualities. I should have prepared a much more palatable dish of humble pie.

It is obvious now, after the fact, that

Reprinted from *Current trends in psychological theory*, Pittsburgh: University of Pittsburgh Press, 1958, pp. 242–257.

the trends I described were scarcely more than my hopes for the future of experimental psychology. Possibly my behavior could be defended as a gesture appropriate to the intellectual climate of 1947. Experimental psychology was then at the nadir of its popularity. Graduate students were turning to social, personal, clinical, and applied psychology in ever-increasing numbers, and defections from the ranks among older men were common. The practical contributions which experimental psychologists had made during World War II had not offset a growing impatience with their stubborn dedication to seemingly unimportant aspects of human behavior. But was there not a bright spot on this murky horizon? If the history of science were any guide, an effective psychology would eventually develop a central conception of human behavior which not only would be fundamentally "right" in the sense of enabling us to *understand* behavior, whatever that might mean, but would generate powerful techniques having important applications in every field of human affairs. No theory of behavior had yet come close to that achievement. Psychoanalysis was the only discipline which had spread beyond its original boundaries, and it had gone no further than some of the social sciences and literary criticism. Elsewhere—in government, economics, religion, education, and all the natural sciences—provincial theories of human behavior were eked out by the tattered theory which had been bequeathed to the English language by a long line of outmoded philosophies. It was as if each of the technologies of physical science had its own scientific conception of nature—as if specialists in synthetic fibers used one theory of molecular structure, pharmacologists another, and biochemists still another, while the layman carried on with a commonsense view of the structure of matter untouched by any of these technical treatments. Such a state of affairs was far from satisfactory. After all, it was the same man who was of interest to psychologists, political scientists, theologians, psychotherapists, economists, educators, literary critics, and scientific methodologists. Why should there be a different theory of human behavior in each case?

Into this power vacuum, it seemed to me, experimental psychology must eventually move. A general theory of human behavior was needed, and only an experimental science could supply it. Separate technologies of behavior could temporize with particular theories, but the special control of variables attainable only in laboratory experimentation would ultimately supply the account which, being in closest accord with the actual properties of the human organism, would be most useful in every field of human affairs. The close check with reality characteristic of experimental analysis would be most likely to expose the fictional entities which had played so devastating a role in what passed for psychological explanation and would permit us to escape from the inaccessible, hypothetical constructs emerging from statistical analyses. This extrapolation of the history of science was intended to give the experimental psychologist a broader horizon. In pointing out the potential significance of an effective theory of human behavior and the special place of a laboratory science in developing such a theory, I was trying to alter the contingencies of reinforcement of my colleagues in the hope of stemming what seemed to be a perpetually ebbing tide.

It is tempting to argue that this proved, indeed, to be an actual trend. It is possible that theories of behavior derived from the clinic or from field studies, rather than from the laboratory, are on the wane. A strict Freudian psychology, for example, is no longer stoutly defended. Certain general points have been made—in some sense we are all Freudians—but the facts and principles which have been salvaged can be stated in relatively non-technical language. Even the patient under therapy is no longer likely to be burdened with technical references to the structure and function of the psyche. Experimental psychologists are not responsible for this change, but if the common heritage of psychoanalysis is to be put in good scientific order, if an effective technology is to be more than a general understanding of the motives and emotions of oneself and one's fellow men, experimental psychologists will play an important role. The Freudian dynamisms can be subjected to experimental analysis, and the resulting changes in definition reveal the experimental method at work.[1] The Freudian explanatory system seldom traces the causal linkage far enough. We do not really explain "disturbed behavior" by attributing it to "anxiety" until we have also explained the anxiety. The extra step required is in the spirit of an experimental science: it is a search for a manipulable variable rather than a verbal explanation. Psychoanalysis itself has identified some of the conditions which must be changed in order to modify behavior in psychotherapy, and to bring about other behavioral effects, but its methodology is not adapted to the manipulation and control of these conditions. In contrast, experimental psychology is becoming more and more successful in dealing with the variables to which one must eventually turn for a full account of behavior and for effective control.

There are other signs of a change. The layman's way of talking about behavior, deeply entrenched in our everyday vocabulary though it is, has lost ground. It is viewed with greater uneasiness by those who use it. Ten years ago the physiologist, neurologist, or pharmacologist whose research involved behavior was likely to set up his own experiments and to describe his results in non-technical terms. He now accepts the experimental psychologist as a specialist to whom he must turn for help. To take a very different example, the lay terminology is now more often used with apologies (or in quotation marks) by political scientists. The ultimate danger of arguing from historical analogy, and of predicting or recommending courses of action by deducing theorems from axiomatic principles or governmental stereotypes, is more likely to be recog-

nized. The ideological use of the work of Pavlov by Soviet propagandists has little to recommend it, but we probably make the same mistake when we counter by expressing contempt for techniques of government based on conditioned reflexes. In the long run all this will have a salutary effect if it leads us to ask whether a more adequate science of behavior may not be relevant to the design of governmental practices. A conception of human behavior will eventually prove workable, not because it fits a momentary predilection for a philosophy of government, but because it survives the test of experimental analysis.

Somewhere between the extremes of physiology and government lies a third bit of evidence for a possible trend. Educational psychologists have long been devotees of research, but the pattern of a laboratory science has not been closely followed. Their experiments have seldom come to grips with the behavior of the individual student in the act of learning. On the other hand, the experimental psychology of learning, though once a staple in textbooks on education, has been receiving less and less attention. But we have learned a great deal about learning in the past decade. A proposal to put this to use in education was made at an earlier conference in this series. The principles of an experimental analysis are now being extended to the field of verbal behavior, and it is inconceivable that the results will not be used to improve instructional procedures. And with fabulous results. Enough has already been done to justify the prediction that what is now learned by the average college student will someday be learned in half the time with half the effort.

There is, then, evidence of a renais-

[1] See *Science & Human Behavior.*

sance in experimental psychology which might be attributed in part to a realization of the potential contribution of the experimental method. But it does not warrant the claim that I correctly predicted a major trend. A general theory of human behavior in this sense has appealed to only a "happy few." As one can easily discover by glancing at the tables of contents of our journals, experimental psychology as a whole has not shown much change. Very little current research is reported in the frame of reference of a comprehensive theory. Nor has the point of view of an experimental analysis yet reached far afield. Many social sciences remain untouched, and among natural scientists there is almost complete ignorance of the promise and achievement of the scientific study of behavior. Dr. Neils Bohr, one of the most distinguished living physicists, recently discussed certain issues in psychology as follows:

Quite apart from the extent to which the use of words like "instinct" and "reason" in the description of animal behavior is necessary and justifiable, the word "consciousness," applied to oneself as well as to others, is indispensable when describing the human situation. . . . The use of words like "thought" and "feeling" does not refer to a firmly connected causal chain, but to experiences which exclude each other because of different distinctions between the conscious content and the background which we loosely term ourselves. . . . We must recognize that psychical experience cannot be subjected to physical measurements and that the very concept of volition does not refer to a generalization of a deterministic description, but from the outset points to characteristics of human life. Without entering into the old philosophical discussion of freedom of the will, I shall only mention that in an objective description of our situation the use of the word "volition"

corresponds closely to that of words like "hope" and "responsibility," which are equally indispensable to human communications.[2]

These terms and issues would have been at home in psychological discussions fifty years ago. (Indeed, one commentator mentioned the similarity of Dr. Bohr's views to those of William James.)

How shocked Dr. Bohr would be if a distinguished psychologist were to discuss modern problems in physical science in terms which were current at the beginning of the century! Psychology in general, and experimental psychology in particular, is still a long way from providing a conception of human behavior which is as readily accepted by those who deal with men as the views of physics are accepted by those who deal with the physical world. And psychologists themselves are not doing much about it.

I therefore return to the attack. (In doing so I assert my membership in a species distinguished by the fact that, at least when psychotic, its members sometimes fail to show extinction.). . . But I shall not doggedly repeat my exhortations or promises of a decade ago. It is evidently not enough to strengthen the scientific behavior of psychologists by giving them a glimpse of an exciting future. Fortunately, as one achievement of the intervening decade, the problem can now be attacked with a better brand of behavioral engineering. I propose to analyze the behavior of psychologists. Why are they not currently developing the pure science of human behavior from which such tremendous technological advances would certainly flow? How are we to explain

[2]Bohr, N. *Atomic physics and human knowledge.* New York, 1958.

the continuing flight from the experimental field? Where have the experimental psychologists gone, and what are they doing instead? And why? And, above all, what steps can be taken to remedy the situation? Such questions clarify the engineering task which faces us if we are to *produce* the trend in experimental psychology which I insist upon predicting.

So stated, the problem has an analogy in a type of experiment which is growing in importance in the experimental analysis of behavior. When we have studied the performances generated by various contingencies of reinforcement in a single arbitrary response, we can move on to two or more concurrent responses. Instead of one lever to be pressed by a rat or one key to be pecked by a pigeon, our experimental space now frequently contains two or three levers or keys, each with its own set of reinforcing contingencies. In the present experiment, we are to account for the fact that psychologists have stopped pressing the experimental lever and have turned to other available manipulanda. To explain this two questions must be asked: (1) What has happened to the reinforcing contingencies on the experimental lever? and (2) What contingencies compete so effectively elsewhere? Once these questions have been answered, we can proceed to the engineering task of increasing the relative effectiveness of the experimental contingencies. It would probably be unfair to do this by attacking competing conditions, for any source of scientific zeal should be respected, but it is possible that some of the reinforcements responsible for activity on other levers can be made contingent upon the response in which we are primarily interested.

Some deficiencies in the rewards of the experimental psychologist were analyzed in my earlier paper. All sciences undergo changes in fashion. Problems lose interest even though they remain unsolved. In psychology many green pastures have been glimpsed on the other side of the experimental fence. The very success of a science may force it to become preoccupied with smaller and smaller details, which cannot compete with broad new issues. The philosophical motivation of the pioneers of a "mental science" has been lost. Although idealism is evidently still a fighting word in some parts of the world, dualism is no longer a challenging issue in American psychology. Classical research on the relation between the psychic and the physical has been transmuted into the study of the physiological and physical actions of end-organs. This is a scientific step forward, but an important source of inspiration has been left behind.

Some of the most effective rewards contingent upon experimental practice have been inadvertently destroyed in another way. We owe most of our scientific knowledge to methods of inquiry which have never been formally analyzed or expressed in normative rules. For more than a generation, however, our graduate schools have been building psychologists on a different pattern of Man Thinking. They have taught statistics in lieu of scientific method. Unfortunately, the statistical pattern is incompatible with some major features of laboratory research. As now taught, statistics plays down the direct manipulation of variables and emphasizes the treatment of variation after the fact. If the graduate student's first result is not significant, statistics tells him to increase the size of his sample; it does not tell him (and, because of self-imposed restrictions on method, it cannot tell him) how to achieve the same result by improving his instruments and his methods of observation. Bigger samples mean more work, the brunt of which the young psychologist may have to bear. When he gets his degree (and a grant), he may pass the labor on to someone else, but in doing so he himself loses contact with the experimental organism he is studying. What statisticians call experimental design (I have pointed out elsewhere that this means design which yields data to which the methods of statistics are appropriate) usually generates a much more intimate acquaintance with a calculating machine than with a behaving organism. One result is a damaging delay in reinforcement. An experiment may "pay off" only after weeks of routine computation. A graduate student who designs an experiment according to accepted statistical methods may survive the ordeal of the calculating room by virtue of his youthful zeal, but his ultimate reinforcement as a scientist may be so long deferred that he will never begin another experiment. Other levers then beckon.

The psychologist who adopts the commoner statistical methods has at best an indirect acquaintance with the "facts" he discovers—with the vectors, factors, and hypothetical processes secreted by the statistical machine. He is inclined to rest content with rough measures of behavior because statistics shows him how to "do something about them." He is likely to continue with fundamentally unproductive methods, because squeezing something of significance out of questionable data discourages the possibly more profitable step of scrapping the experiment and starting again.

Statistics offers its own brand of reinforcement, of course, but this is often not contingent upon behavior which is most productive in the laboratory. One destructive effect is to supply a sort of busy work for the compulsive. In the early stages of any inquiry the investigator often has to weather a period of ignorance and chaos during which apparent progress is slight, if not lacking altogether. This is something he must be taught to endure. He must acquire a kind of faith in the ultimate value of ostensibly undirected exploration. He must also learn to be indifferent to the criticism that he is not getting anywhere. If he has accepted funds in support of his research, he must learn to tolerate a gnawing anxiety about the annual report. At such times statistics offers consoling comfort and, what is worse, an all-too-convenient escape-hatch. How simple it is to match groups of subjects, devise a crude measure of the behavior at issue, arrange for tests to be administered, and punch the scores into IBM cards! No matter what comes of it all, no one can say that work has not been done. Statistics will even see to it that the result will be "significant" even if it is proved to mean nothing.

The intention of the statistician is honorable and generous. He wants the experimental scientist to be sure of his results and to get the most out of them. But, whether or not he understands the essence of laboratory practice, his recommendations are often inimical to it. Perhaps against his will, he has made certain essential activities in good laboratory research no longer respectable. The very instrument which might have made an experimental science more rewarding has, instead, all but destroyed its basic features. In the long run the psychologist has been deprived of some of his most profitable, and hence eventually most reinforcing, achievements.

The resulting flight from the laboratory can be stopped by pointing to alternative methods of research. If all psychologists are to be required to take courses in statistics, they should also be made familiar with laboratory practices and given the chance to behave as scientists rather than as the robots described by scientific methodologists. In particular, young psychologists should learn how to work with single organisms rather than with large groups. Possibly with that one step alone we could restore experimental psychology to the vigorous health it deserves.

But it will be worthwhile to examine the competing contingencies. Psychologists have fled from the laboratory, and perhaps for good reason. Where have they gone?

THE FLIGHT TO REAL PEOPLE

Laboratories can be dull places, and not only when furnished with calculating machines. It is not surprising that psychologists have been attracted by the human interest of real life. The experimental subject in the laboratory is only part of a man, and frequently an uninteresting part, while the whole individual is a fascinating source of reinforcement. Literature flourishes for that reason. Psychologists have long since learned to borrow from the literary domain. If a lecture flags, or a chapter seems dull, one has only to bring in a case history and everything literally "comes to life." The recipe is so foolproof that the lecture or test which consists of nothing but case histories has been closely approximated. But in resorting to this device for pedagogical or therapeutic effect psychologists have

themselves been influenced by these reinforcers; their courses of action as scientists have been deflected. They often recognize this and from time to time have felt the need for a special theory of scientific knowledge (based, for example, on empathy or intuition) to justify themselves. They seldom seem to feel secure, however, in the belief that they have regained full citizenship in the scientific commonwealth.

The reinforcements which flow from real people are not all related to, on the one hand, an intellectual conviction that the proper study of mankind is man or, on the other, the insatiable curiosity of a Paul Pry. In a world in which ethical training is widespread, most men are reinforced when they succeed in reinforcing others. In such a world personal gratitude is a powerful generalized reinforcer. We can scarcely hold it against psychologists that, like other men of good will, they want to help their fellow men—either one by one in the clinic or nation by nation in, say, studies of international good will. We may agree that the world would be a better place if more men would concern themselves with personal and political problems. But we must not forget that the remedial step is necessarily a short-term measure and that it is not the only step leading to the same goal. The lively prosecution of a science of behavior, applied to the broad problem of cultural design, could have more sweeping consequences. If such a promising alternative is actually feasible, anyone who is capable of making a long-term contribution may wisely resist the effect of other consequences which, no matter how important they may be to him personally, are irrelevant to the scientific process and confine him to short-term remedial action. A classical example from another field is Albert Schweitzer. Here is a brilliant man who, for reasons we need not examine, dedicated his life to helping his fellow men—one by one. He has earned the gratitude of thousands, but we must not forget what he might have done instead. If he had worked as energetically for as many years in a laboratory of tropical medicine, he would almost certainly have made discoveries which in the long run would help—not thousands—but literally *billions* of people. We do not know enough about Schweitzer to say why he took the short-term course. Could he not resist the blandishments of gratitude? Was he freeing himself from feelings of guilt? Whatever his reasons, his story warns us of the danger of a cultural design which does not harness some personal reinforcement in the interests of pure science. The young psychologist who wants above all to help his fellow men should be made to see the tremendous potential consequences of even a small contribution to the scientific understanding of human behavior. It is possibly this understanding alone, with the improved cultural patterns which will flow from it, which will eventually alleviate the anxieties and miseries of mankind.

THE FLIGHT TO MATHEMATICAL MODELS

The flight from the experimental method has sometimes gone in the other direction. If the human being studied in the laboratory has been too drab and unreal for some, he has been just the opposite for others. In spite of our vaunted control of variables, the experimental subject too often remains capricious. Sometimes he is not only warm but, as baseball players say, too hot to handle. Even the "average man," when captured in the statistical net, may be unpleasantly refractory. Some psychologists have therefore fled to an ivory image of their own sculpturing, mounted on a mathematical pedestal. These Pygmalions have constructed a Galatea who always behaves as she is supposed to behave, whose processes are orderly and relatively simple, and to whose behavior the most elegant of mathematical procedures may be applied. She is a creature whose slightest blemish can be erased by the simple expedient of changing an assumption. Just as political scientists used to simplify their problems by talking about an abstract Political Man, and the economists theirs by talking about Economic Man, so psychologists have built the ideal experimental organism—the Mathematical Model.

The effect of this practice on so-called learning theory has been pointed out elsewhere. . . . Early techniques available for the study of learning—from the nonsense syllables of Ebbinghaus, through the problem boxes of Thorndike and the mazes of Watson, to the discrimination apparatuses of Yerkes and Lashley—always yielded learning curves of disturbing irregularity. In experiments with these instruments an orderly change in the behavior of a single organism was seldom seen. Orderly processes had to be generated by averaging data, either for many trials or many organisms. Even so, the resulting "learning curves" varied in a disturbing way from experiment to experiment. The theoretical solution to this problem was to assume that an orderly learning process, which always had the same properties regardless of the particular features of a given experiment, took place somewhere inside the organism. A given result was accounted for by making a distinction between learning and performance. Though the performance might be chaotic, the psychologist could continue to cherish the belief that learning was always orderly. Indeed, the mathematical organism seemed so orderly that model builders remained faithful to techniques which consistently yielded disorderly data. An examination of mathematical models in learning theory will show that no degree of disorder in the facts has placed any restriction on the elegance of the mathematical treatment.

The properties which (to drop to a two-dimensional figure of speech) make a paper doll[3] more amenable than a living organism are crucial in a scientific account of behavior. No matter how many of the formulations derived from the study of a model eventually prove useful in describing reality (remember wave-mechanics!), the questions to which answers are most urgently needed concern the correspondence between the two realms. How can we be sure that a model is a model of *behavior?* What *is* behavior, and how is it to be analyzed and measured? What are the relevant features of the environment, and how are they to be measured and controlled? How are these two sets of variables related? The answers to these questions cannot be found by constructing models. (Nor is a model likely to be helpful in furthering the necessary empirical in-

---

[3]The reference, of course, is to the well-known song by Johnny S. Black, in which the lyricist expresses his preference for "a paper doll to call his own" rather than a "fickle-minded real live girl."

quiry. It is often argued that some model, hypothesis, or theory is essential because the scientist cannot otherwise choose among the facts to be studied. But there are presumably as many models, hypothesis, or theories as facts. If the scientific methodologist will explain how he proposes to choose among them, his answer will serve as well to explain how one may choose among empirical facts.)

What sort of behavioral engineering will reduce the rate of responding to the mathematical lever and induce distinguished psychologists to get back to the laboratory? Two steps seem to be needed. First, it must be made clear that the formal properties of a system of variables can be profitably treated only after the dimensional problems have been solved. The detached and essentially tautological nature of mathematical models is usually frankly admitted by their authors, particularly those who come into experimental psychology from mathematics, but for the psychologist these disclaimers are often lost among the integral signs. Secondly, the opportunity to be mathematical in dealing with factual material should be clarified. To return to the example of learning theory, the psychologist should recognize that with proper techniques one can *see learning take place,* not in some inner recess far removed from the observable performance of an organism, but as a change in that performance itself. Techniques are now available for the experimental analysis of very subtle behavioral processes, and this work is ready for the kind of mathematical theory which has always been productive at the proper stage in the history of science. What is needed is not a mathematical model, constructed with little regard for the fundamental dimensions of behavior, but a mathematical treatment of experimental data. Mathematics will come into its own in the analysis of behavior when appropriate methods yield data which are so orderly that there is no longer any need to escape to a dream world.

THE FLIGHT TO THE INNER MAN

Experimental psychology has suffered perhaps its greatest loss of manpower because competent investigators, beginning with a *descriptive* interest in behavior, have passed almost immediately to an *explanatory* preoccupation with what is going on inside the organism. In discussing this flight to the inner man I should like to believe that I am whipping a dead horse, but the fact remains that human behavior is still most commonly discussed in terms of psychic or physiological processes. A dualistic philosophy is not necessarily implied in either case for it may be argued, on the one hand, that the data of physics reduce at last to the direct experience of the physicist or, on the other, that behavior is only a highly organized set of biological facts. The nature of any real or fancied inner cause of behavior is not at issue; investigative practices suffer the same damage in any case.

Sometimes, especially among psychoanalysts, the inner men are said to be organized personalities whose activities lead at last to the behavior of the organism we observe. The commoner practice is to dissect the inner man and deal separately with his traits, perceptions, experiences, habits, ideas, and so on. In this way an observable subject matter is abandoned in favor of an inferred. It was Freud himself who insisted that mental processes could occur without "conscious participation" and that, since they could not always be directly observed, our knowledge of them must be inferential. Much of the machinery of psychoanalysis is concerned with the process of inference. In the analysis of behavior we may deal with *all* mental processes as inferences, whether or not they are said to be conscious. The resulting re-definition (call it operational if you like) conveniently omits the mentalistic dimension. At the same time, however, the explanatory force is lost. Inner entities or events do not "cause" behavior, nor does behavior "express" them. At best they are mediators, but the causal relations between the terminal events which are mediated are inadequately represented by traditional devices. Mentalistic concepts may have had some heuristic value at one stage in the analysis of behavior, but it has long since been more profitable to abandon them. In an acceptable explanatory scheme the ultimate causes of behavior must be found *outside* the organism.

The *physiological* inner man is, of course, no longer wholly inferential. New methods and instruments have brought the nervous system and other mechanisms under direct observation. The new data have their own dimensions and require their own formulations. The behavioral facts in the field of learning, for example, are dealt with in terms appropriate to behavior, while electrical or chemical activities occurring at the same time demand a different conceptual framework. Similarly, the effects of deprivation and satiation on behavior are not the same as the events seen through a gastric fistula. Nor is emotion, studied as behavioral predisposition, capable of being analyzed in terms appropriate to pneumographs and electrocardiographs. Both sets of facts, and their appropriate concepts, are important—but they are *equally* important, not dependent one upon the other. Under the influence of a contrary philosophy of explanation, which insists upon the reductive priority of the inner event, many brilliant men who began with an interest in behavior, and might have advanced our knowledge of that field in many ways, have turned instead to the study of physiology. We cannot dispute the importance of their contributions, we can only imagine with regret what they might have done instead.

If we are to make a study of behavior sufficiently reinforcing to hold the interest of young men in competition with inner mechanisms, we must make clear that behavior is an acceptable subject matter in its own right, and that it can be studied with acceptable methods and without an eye to reductive explanation. The responses of an organism to a given environment are physical events. Modern methods of analysis reveal a degree of order in such a subject matter which compares favorably with that of any phenomena of comparable complexity. Behavior is not simply the result of more fundamental activities, to which our research must therefore be addressed, but an end in itself, the substance and importance of which are demonstrated in the practical results of an experimental analysis. We can predict and control behavior, we can modify it, we can construct it according to specifications— and all without answering the explanatory questions which have driven investigators into the study of the inner

man. The young psychologist may contemplate a true science of behavior without anxiety.

THE FLIGHT TO LAYMANSHIP

Experimental psychology has also had to contend with what is in essence a rejection of the whole scientific enterprise. In a recent review of a study of the psychological problems of aging, the reviewer comments upon "a tendency in psychological thought which is returning to prominence after some years of relative disfavor. The statements have a certain refreshing directness and 'elegance' in their approach to the study of human behavior. The sterile arguments of so-called 'learning theory,' the doctrinaire half-truths of the 'schools,' the panacea treatments of 'systems,' and the high-sounding, empty technical terms often found in psychological writings are conspicuous by their absence." No one will want to defend "*sterile* arguments," "half-truths," "panaceas," or "*empty* technical terms," no matter what their sources, but the force of the passage is more than this. The author is rejecting all efforts to improve upon the psychology of the layman in approaching the problems of the aged. And many psychologists agree with him. "Enough of the lingo of the laboratory!" the argument runs. "Enough of clinical jargon! Enough of frightening equations! A plague on all your houses! Let us go back to commonsense! Let us say what we want to say about human behavior in the well-worn but still useful vocabulary of the layman!" Whether this is a gesture of fatigue or impatience, or the expression of a desire to get on with practical matters at the expense of a basic understanding, it must be answered by anyone who defends a pure science. It would be easier to find the answer if experimental psychology had moved more rapidly toward a helpful conception of human behavior.

Some progress has been made in proving the superiority of scientific concepts over those of traditional usage. Consider, for example, two psychological accounts written in the vulgar tongue. First, a sample in the field of emotional behavior:

The emotional temper of the type of juvenile delinquent just mentioned is as extraordinary as it is well-known. Far from being naturally peaceful, sympathetic, or generous, men who are excluded from the society of their fellow men become savage, cruel, and morose. The wanton destructiveness of the delinquent is not due to sudden bursts of fury, but to a deliberate and brooding resolve to wage war on everything.

The second has to do with intellect. It is an explanation of how a child learns to open a door by depressing a thumb-latch and pushing against the door with his legs.

Of course the child may have observed that doors are opened by grownups placing their hands on the handles, and having observed this the child may act by what is termed imitation. But the process as a whole is something more than imitative. Observation alone would be scarcely enough to enable the child to discover that the essential thing is not to grasp the handle but to depress the latch. Moreover, the child certainly never saw any grownup push the door with his legs as it is necessary for the child to do. This pushing action must be due to

an originally deliberate intention to open the door, not to accidentally having found this action to have this effect.

Both passages make intelligible points and would conceivably be helpful in discussing juvenile delinquency or the teaching of children. But there is a trap. Actually the heroes of these pieces were not human at all. The quotations are slightly altered passages from Romanes' *Animal Intelligence,* published about seventy-five years ago. The first describes the behavior of the prototype of all delinquents—the Rogue elephant. The "child" of the second was a cat—possibly the very cat which set Thorndike to work to discover how animals do, indeed, learn to press latches.

The experimental analysis of behavior has clearly shown the practical and theoretical value of abandoning a commonsense way of talking about behavior and has demonstrated the advantages of an alternative account of emotion and intelligence. That is to say, it has done this for cats, rats, pigeons, and monkeys. Its successes are only slowly reaching into the field of human behavior—not because we any longer assume that man is fundamentally different but in part because an alternative method of analysis is felt to be available because of the scientist's membership in the human species. But the special knowledge resulting from self-observation can be given a formulation which preserves intact the notion of the continuity of species. Experimental methods can be applied first to the behavior of the Other One, and only later to the analysis of the behavior of the scientist himself. The value of this practice is demonstrated in the consistency of the resulting account and the effectiveness of the resulting technological control.

It is not difficult to explain the strength of traditional concepts. Many of those who discuss human behavior are speaking to laymen and must adapt their terms to their audience. The immediate effect of the lay vocabulary also gains strength from its deep intrenchment in the language. Our legal system is based on it, and the literature of ideas is couched in it. Moreover, from time to time efforts are made to rejuvenate the philosophical systems from which it came. Aristotle, through Thomas Aquinas, still speaks to some students of behavior. The very fact that Aristotle's psychology, scarcely modified, can be seriously championed in behavioral science today shows how little it has done to advance our understanding. Aristotelian physics, chemistry, and biology have enjoyed no such longevity. We may look forward to the early demise of this sole survivor of Greek science.

A return to the lay vocabulary of behavior cannot be justified. The move is a matter of motivation, competence, or the accessibility of goals. These are all irrelevant to the long-term achievement of a scientific account of behavior. No doubt, many pressing needs can still be most readily satisfied by casual discussion. In the long run, however, we shall need an effective understanding of human behavior—so that, in the example cited, we shall know the nature of the changes which take place as men and women grow old and shall, therefore, be in the most favorable position to do something about them. To reach that understanding we must recognize the limitations of the remedial patchwork which emerges from commonsense discussion and must be willing to resort to experiments which quite possibly involve complicated techniques and to theoretical treatments quite possibly expressed in difficult terms.

CONCLUSION

We have glanced briefly at four *divertissements* in the growth of a science of human behavior. Real Men, Mathematical Men, Inner Men, and Everyday Men—it would be a mistake to underestimate their seductive power. Together they constitute a formidable array of rival suitors, and to groom the Experimental Organism for this race may seem a hopeless enterprise. But he has a chance, for in the long run he offers the greatest net reinforcement to the scientist engaged in the study of behavior. I doubt whether this fact will affect many of those who have already flown from the laboratory, but I am not speaking to them. A story about William James is appropriate. James was much in demand as a lecturer and one day discovered that he was scheduled to address a ladies' literary society in a suburb of Boston. He set off to keep his appointment after having picked up from his desk the first lecture which came to hand. It happened to be a lecture he had prepared for one of his Radcliffe classes. His audience, in contrast, was composed of elderly New England matrons. James was reading his paper, possibly thinking of other things, when to his horror he heard himself saying, ". . . and so, my fair young friends. . . ." He looked out upon a sea of startled faces and—failing utterly in this pragmatic test of a psychologist—

blurted out, "I should explain that this lecture was written for a very different audience."

I wish I could say, and also with more tact, what audience *this* lecture was prepared for. No matter how strong my conviction that we are close to an effective science of human behavior, with all which such a science implies, I do not expect to recapture the interest and enthusiasm of those who have fled from the laboratory to pleasurable dalliance elsewhere. But some of you, I hope, are not yet committed. For you the possibility of an adequate theory of behavior, in the sense in which any empirical science leads eventually to a theoretical formulation, together with its enormous technical potential, may be enough to tip the balance. And if such of you there be, I look to you to restore to experimental psychology the energy, enthusiasm, and productivity which characterized it in an earlier epoch.

We are living in an age in which science fiction is coming true. The thrilling spectacle of man-made satellites has turned our eyes toward outer space.

What we shall find there only time will tell. Meanwhile, we are confronted by far more important problems on the surface of the earth. A possible solution is in the spirit of another kind of science fiction: the eighteenth-century utopian dream of Perfectionism with its basic contention that, if human nature is determined by environment and if environment can be changed, human nature can be changed. Like an artificial satellite or a rocket to the moon, this was once a foolish dream. But science moves forward at a breathless pace. We may shortly be designing the world in which men will henceforth live. But how is it to be designed, and to what end? These are difficult questions, to which nothing short of an effective science of man will provide the answers. The methods of science no longer need verbal defense; one cannot throw a moon around the earth with dialectic. Applied to human behavior, the same methods promise even more thrilling achievements. That prospect will, I still believe, determine the trend in experimental psychology in the years to come.

THREE
Operationism

A Measurement Approach to Psychotherapy

Joel Greenspoon and Lawrence Simkins

The following article is exceptional in its articulate expression of the operationist approach to psychology. The authors make a sharp distinction between data and theory, and they argue that data should be defined by appeal to operational definitions. This means that the basic facts must be defined by providing a description of the ways in which they are measured. Greenspoon and Simkins feel that the muddled state of contemporary research on psychotherapy would be greatly improved if their "measurement approach" were to be used.

Although written in the context of research on psychotherapy, the viewpoint expressed in the article has application to the rest of psychology—and even beyond. It is a point of view which, though in a less fully articulated form, has long been regarded as fundamental to scientific psychology. Several of the key positions taken in the article have come under very critical scrutiny in recent times. The notion that there can be a clear line of demarcation between data and theory, and that theory is somehow superimposed on "raw facts," is one of these positions. Opponents have argued that facts do not exist independently of theories. Theories actually transform facts and, in one sense, help to create them (see Hanson, 1965 and the article by Polanyi included in the present book).

A second point, to which many clinical psychologists will react, is that the measurement viewpoint seems to "impose severe limitations on the size of the behavior unit." The psychotherapy research cited as exemplary by Greenspoon and Simkins deals with behaviors whose interest value is questionable (for example, "length of utterance" of the patient). This seems to be a case of the negative correlation between rigor and interest value so well described by Seeman and Marks in Article

21. Fortunately, there seems to be some hope of combining rigor and interest value, as we hope the remaining readings will show.

In a recent attempt to distill areas of agreement among the various therapeutic orientations, Rogers (1963) was somewhat distressed to find very little agreement. In this article he makes the following comment:

[If I] were to close my paper at this point, a one sentence summary would be "The field of psychotherapy is a mess." Therapists are not in agreement as to their goals or aims in therapy. They are in deep disagreement as to the theoretical structure which would contain their work. They cannot agree as to what constitutes failure. They diverge sharply in their views as to the promising directions for the future. It seems as though the field is completely chaotic and divided.

Why is Professor Rogers so distressed about the status of psychotherapy? Perhaps one of the reasons is that there is very little agreement among various therapeutic positions in terms of the constructs used to describe the basic events of psychotherapy, including the characteristics of the therapists, the patient, and the interaction between these two people. Rogers had initially assumed that the therapists were all talking about the same phenomena, but merely attaching different words or labels to these events. However he later came to the conclusion that the differences run much deeper; that not only are the labels different, but the referents are also different. Thus it appears that the same label may be applied to different events and different labels to the same event. It

Reprinted from *Psychological Record*, 1968, **18**, 409–423, by permission of the authors and publisher.

is extremely difficult, if not impossible, to make any meaningful comparisons among different types of psychotherapy unless the events are described in a common data language. Different constructs involving different sets of measurement operations have been introduced into the psychotherapy literature, with no way of establishing the relationship between one construct and another. It is the purpose of this article to provide a workable set of criteria and to examine some of the measurements commonly made in psychotherapy to determine if they meet these criteria. Our major thesis is that more careful attention to definition and measurement operations may provide a basis for creating some order in the chaos that Rogers has so aptly described.

DATA AND THEORETICAL LANGUAGE CONSTRUCTS

Before getting deeply involved in some of the problems of measurement in psychotherapy, we shall present a position on measurement which will provide the criteria which will guide our evaluation of measurement in psychotherapy. Our position on measurement is designed to provide criteria for the introduction of a term into the data language of the science. This does not mean that it is the only set of criteria that can be used. However, the value of this, or any, set of criteria is determined by several conditions. One of these conditions is the clarity and specificity, i.e., lack of ambiguity, of the data language. Professor Rogers has already indicated that there is considerable confusion about the events that are investigated in psychotherapy research. Since the data language is the language used to specify the independent and dependent variables, the value of a set of criteria for the introduction of terms into the data language may be reflected in the rigor, precision and reliability of the functional relationships that are developed.

The first issue that must be resolved, however, is a realization of the difference between a construct introduced as part of the data language and one intended as part of the theoretical language. Different criteria must be used in each of these two situations. The data language refers to the language that is used to describe the events that are dealt with by the investigator or therapist, or as Turner (1965, p. 189) has pointed out, "We initially speak of the data language, the observation language, the factual language. This is the language of the observables, of the dependent and independent variables as stated in formal expressions of empirical relationships." These events are frequently referred to, in one form or another, as stimulus events and response events. This language, the data language, should not reflect the theoretical biases of the investigator, but should be capable of being used effectively by any investigator. The data language essentially establishes the events subject to investigation, whether conducted in the laboratory or in the clinic. Any confusion about the events described in the data language cannot help but be compounded when efforts are made to account for the events. Confusion at the data language level can lead to nothing but greater confusion at the theoretical level.

The theoretical language, on the other hand, refers to the constructs that are developed to explain or account for the events that are described by the data language. At the theoretical level there will be and should be considerable variability in the constructs that are devised to account for the events. The major factor with respect to the theoretical constructs is that they relate in some consistent, reliable, and specifiable way to the events described in the data language.

The primary concern of this paper will be with the criteria for the introduction of constructs into the data language. We are proposing that all data language constructs be defined in terms of measurement operations. This position in no way places any limitations on the theoretical constructions that are developed to account for the events. It means that there may be an increased probability that all psychotherapists would use a common language to describe the events under observation. For reasons which will be discussed shortly, many frequently used constructs such as aggression, empathy, and reinforcement would be excluded from the data language. However, this does not mean that such constructs need be excluded from the theoretical language.

DEFINITION AND DATA LANGUAGE CONSTRUCTS

Psychologists of many different persuasions have tended to agree that the most rigorous and precise method of introducing constructs into the data language is through the use of operational definitions, (Boring, 1945; Bridgman, 1945; Feigel, 1945; Skinner, 1945). Unfortunately, psychologists seem to make use of several varieties of operational definitions, all of which have been called operational definitions. The different conceptualizations of operational definitions can produce constructs that differ markedly. We believe it is possible to classify the different types of operational definitions into three major categories: (*a*) verbal procedural operational definitions; (*b*) equivocant operational definitions; and (*c*) measurement oriented operational definitions.

The verbal procedural operational definition is one that includes verbal statements about what the researcher is doing which does not necessarily have a mensurational concomitant. The definition of a reinforcing stimulus as the introduction of a stimulus following a response that increases the frequency of that response is an example of the verbal procedural operational definition. This definition of a reinforcing stimulus is frequently referred to as an operational definition though there are no specified quantitative concomitants of this set of operations. One characteristic of this kind of verbal procedural definition is its reliance on a specified outcome, consequence or effect. It is necessary to collect the data before it is possible to determine if the requirements of the definition have been met. If you obtain the prescribed effect, then you have, in this illustration a reinforcing stimulus.

In other words, a "reinforcing" stimulus does not have a mensuration concomitant. One cannot denote a "reinforcing" stimulus. A reinforcing stimulus is defined in terms of the relationship between object (e.g., food) and the effect it has on the organism under investigation. Ordinarily relationships

between events are empirical or theoretical, not definitional.

It may be contended that the measurement of light is dependent on the reaction of a meter. Actually, the reaction of the meter is the measurement of light. Moreover, the meter is not the object of investigation, but the organism is the object of investigation in the case involving the reinforcing stimulus. The situation for psychology might be altered if one were able to construct or design the standard organism as Hull (1943) once suggested, although this solution is beset with numerous difficulties.

Equivocant operational definitions are frequently used by psychologists. The concept of equivocation was originally discussed by H. M. Johnson.

Scientific method requires a distinction between equivocance and equivalence. For two objects to be equivocant they need only bear the same name; for them to be equivalent (with respect to a particular function) they must be capable of interchange without altering any set of relations which are to be considered. The fallacy of treating two objects as equivalent because they bear the same name is called equivocation [1928, p. 238].

An example may clarify Johnson's conceptualization of equivocation. It might be found that the GSR is equal to some function of the intensity of electric shock. So far, so good! The intensity of the electric shock can be measured and the magnitude of the GSR can be measured and an empirical functional relationship can be established. The next step involves equating the GSR with another construct, frequently called emotion. Since, according to this procedure, GSR and emotion are identical, it is reasonable to follow through and state that emotion is equal to some function of the intensity of electric shock. Now it may be argued that there is nothing wrong with these procedures. Is it not permissible for a psychologist, or anyone else for that matter, to utilize any words that he desires so long as he defines them? And hasn't emotion been defined as the GSR? The answer would have to be in the affirmative, except that there are now two sets of words, GSR and emotion, applied to the same measurement. One of these sets of words can be eliminated.

However, by some unspecified but apparently shifty verbal footwork the GSR becomes some function of emotion. It isn't quite clear how this functional relationship has evolved, but it is one that almost inevitably evolves. It is not uncommon to find that the GSR is referred to as an index of emotion. We may ask how it is possible to determine that the GSR is an index of emotion since there is no independent measurement of emotion. The only measurement involved in this particular chain is the GSR. Therefore, it seems preferable not to consider emotion as a data language construct but as a theoretical construct.

The third method of introducing constructs into the data language is by the use of measurement operational definitions. This approach assumes a synonymity of measurement and definition. That is, the measurement operations constitute the operational definition of the construct. Moreover, this conceptualization includes as measurement the operations which are used to establish the class of events under consideration. It is necessary to construe this set of operations as measurement since it establishes the unit on which other measurement may be performed.

For example, the operations that are used to establish the events to be called hitting or striking comprise measurement because they establish the criteria of the unit of behavior under observation. This analysis is comparable to including the operation for the establishment of the inch or second as the unit in the measurement of length or time. Since these units are so commonplace and well established, we find it easy to forget about the operations that are used to create them.

By considering the operations involved in the creation of the units of behavior as measurement, we are able to limit these units to what the individual under observation is doing. It requires the investigator or psychotherapist to spell out precisely the criteria that he is using to create the class or classes of events with which he will deal. It also requires that all criteria used must be reducible to denotative (pointing at) operations as a last resort in creating the unit that is being used. This approach, with its emphasis on denotation as a critical feature of operationism, would limit the data language to constructs considered observable and consequently measurable. There is nothing inherent in this position that dictates or determines the size of the class events with which the investigator or therapist will work. The particular subject matter under investigation will probably be a major determinant of the particular unit or unit size. Unfortunately, some psychologists persist in looking for *the* unit of behavior. Such endeavors are as appropriate as seeking the physical dimensions of consciousness, which R. C. Davis (1953) noted was comparable to sending out a polar expedition to find Santa Claus, and has about the same probability of success.

SOME RELEVANT HISTORY

At this point it may be advantageous to examine some of the constructs commonly used in psychotherapy and psychotherapy research. A brief summary of some of the milestones in psychotherapy research may provide a better understanding of some of the difficulties that have been encountered.

Eysenck (1952), in what is now regarded as a classical study, attempted to examine the effectiveness of psychotherapy. His survey covered approximately 7000 neurotic patients from a variety of clinical settings. One of his more dramatic findings was that the improvement rate for patients treated by psychoanalysis was 44%, while those treated by therapists with an eclectic orientation was 64%. On the other hand, the improvement rate of patients treated custodially or by general practitioners was 72%. Eysenck's initial statement of these results was that there appeared to be an inverse relationship between recovery and psychotherapy. The implication was made that psychotherapy hinders recovery, or at best, has no effect on recovery rate. In any event, his data showed that roughly two-thirds of neurotic patients will recover or improve to a marked extent within two years of the onset of their illness whether or not they are treated by means of psychotherapy.

Subsequent to Eysenck's study, Levitt (1957) conducted a similar survey in which he attempted to assess the effectiveness of psychotherapy on "neurotic" children. His survey also showed that approximately two-thirds of the patients at the close of treatment and approximately three-quarters of the patients on follow-up showed improvement. However, approximately the same percentages were found in the control groups. Thus Levitt's findings are similar to those of Eysenck to the extent that there was a failure to support the view that psychotherapy is effective with "neurotic" children.

Upon the publication of Eysenck's results, a great deal of furor was precipitated and the battle lines were drawn between the believers and non-believers in the powers of psychotherapy. The believers took the position that psychotherapy was too complex and too unique to be reduced to experimental or statistical analysis. The extreme non-believers used Eysenck's results to reinforce their preconceptions regarding psychotherapy as being a form of faith healing. The aroused reactions to the Eysenck study were without foundation because there was very little basis upon which to conclude much of anything. At best, both the Eysenck and Levitt studies represent a failure to reject the null hypothesis. A positive statement that psychotherapy is not effective is equally unwarranted. The only statement that can be made is that the effectiveness of psychotherapy has not been demonstrated.

Many of the criticisms of the Eysenck study were legitimate. Rosenzweig (1954) systematically attacked Eysenck's study pointing to many uncontrolled variables. Bergin (1963), in discussing the Eysenck study and others of this nature, notes that it is unusual to find independent pre-, post-, and follow-up measures, as well as the equivalent treatment and non-treatment groups all in the same study. That Eysenck failed to control many variables or that his research design was faulty is appropriate criticism but, nevertheless, is like putting the proverbial cart before the horse. In order to "control" variables, one must first be able to identify and define the unit and measurement operations for that variable. The Eysenck study as well as many of the so-called "outcome" research investigations in psychotherapy, has failed to give sufficient attention to measurement operations. The unit of measurement in both the Eysenck and Levitt studies was "improvement" or "recovery." In most instances, the behavioral referents of these terms are not specified. Since both studies were actuarial, in which samples were drawn from a variety of clinics, the definition of improvement, as well as its measurement operations, probably varied from clinic to clinic. Once again, the terms "improvement" and "recovery" are not basic data language. Thus, the answer to the question as to whether psychotherapy produces "improvement" may have to wait until the behavior referent(s) of improvement have been specified as well as a set of operations for the definition and measurement of the units of behavior involved. For example, if improvement refers to a change in behavior, then operations for the measurement of that behavior, as well as a criterion of change, have to be specified. Therefore, we have to know how the behaviors are to be measured and how much change has to occur before the specifications established for "improvement" have been met. Under the present circumstances, whether a patient "improves" or "deteriorates" may well depend upon the definition of these variables, their measurement operations, and the conditions under which these measurement operations take place. In lieu of these considerations, it is not very surprising that Eysenck was unable to give us a definitive answer about the effectiveness of psychotherapy, or that Rogers was unable to find very many areas of agreement between the various psychotherapeutic approaches.

AN EXAMINATION OF PSYCHOTHERAPY

Turning now to psychotherapy, it would appear that we are interested in the extent to which the behavior of the therapist (independent variable) is related to changes in behavior of the patient (dependent variable). Operations for the measurement of each of them have to be established to determine the functional relationship between these two sets of variables. The variables in both instances are behavior. It is recommended that we use measurement operations to define our unit of behavior. However, typically in psychotherapy research, neither independent nor dependent variables are developed from a basic data language. If they were, many independent and dependent variables would be specified in terms of the measurement operation rather than the vague and ambiguous language that is commonly used. Response classes used in therapy research are usually quite broad, and the members composing the class may be relatively dissimilar. For example, hostility may be defined in terms of the specific content of verbal emission, a rise in vocal amplitude, frowning, sneering, looking away from the therapist, etc. To consider all of these behavioral events as hostility and to consider hostility as a data language construct could result in some anomalies, the most critical of which is the possibility that a given independent variable may have a different effect on each of these behavioral events. That is, an independent variable may result in an increase in the frequency of occurrence of one of these behavioral events and a decrease in the frequency of occurrence of another of these behavioral events. This situation would make it difficult to relate the particular independent variable to hostility. This result, however, would not be so confusing if we limited the relationship to the independent variable and the particular behavioral event.

SOME MEASUREMENT PRACTICES IN PSYCHOTHERAPY

Let us look at some of the measurement practices in contemporary psychotherapy research to determine to what extent they meet the criteria of measurement. One frequently employed measurement technique in psychotherapy has been to use rating scales. This technique has been widely used to measure "empathy." Upon reviewing the literature, we find that both the definition and measurement scale of this construct vary from investigator to investigator. As an example, Barrett-Lennard (1962, p. 3) defines understanding as follows:

Degree of empathetic understanding is conceived as the extent to which one person is conscious of the immediate awareness of another . . . it is an experiencing of the consciousness "behind" another's outward communication but with continuous awareness that this consciousness is originating and proceeding in the other.

The operations for the measurement of this construct consist of a series of statements presented to the client that he rates on a six point scale. An example would be the statement, "He (the therapist) tries to see things through my eyes." The client then either responds $+1$, $+2$, $+3$, reflecting the degree of intensity with which he would agree with the statement, or -1, -2, -3, reflecting intensity of disagreement with the statement. The client is requested to complete this questionnaire during different sessions. Another procedure is to have the therapist complete the scale. The items are identical except for a suitable change in pronouns.

Rogers (1957) outlines what he considers to be the six necessary and sufficient conditions for constructive personality change in psychotherapy. The conditions he lists are theoretical constructs. Whether or not these conditions are necessary, sufficient, or irrelevant to personality change may very well depend on the behaviors related to these constructs, the operations by which these behaviors are measured, and the overall structure of the theory. One of the necessary conditions according to Rogers (p. 96) is: "That the therapist experiences an empathetic understanding of the client's internal frame of reference and endeavors to communicate this experience to the client."

Truax (1961) provides measurement operations for the constructs that Rogers had proposed in order to test some of Roger's theoretical conceptions. Truax proposes the term "accurate empathy," the accuracy of the therapist's responses to the patient's feelings or experiences. The adjective "accurate" suggests some criteria which the therapist's behavior approximates. Degrees of accuracy could then be measured in terms of deviation from these criteria. Unfortunately, we were unable to find any specific reference to such criteria. From additional statements, it might be inferred that the criteria have to do with some behavior of the patient, but the behavior was never specified. Truax goes on to elaborate: (p. 10)

A low level of accurate therapist's empathy is when the therapist is no longer "with" the patient, but he is off on a tangent of his own; when he has misinterpreted what the patient is feeling or experiencing; when he is responding to a feeling that is expected of the patient, but is not currently a feeling of the patient . . .

A nine-point rating scale is used for the measurement of accurate empathy. In a subsequent report (Truax and Carkhuff, 1965) a description of the scale is given. At the lowest stage, for example, ". . . the therapist seems completely unaware of even the most conspicuous of the client's feelings. . . ." At the highest stage, (stage 9,) the therapist ". . . unerringly responds to the client's full range of feelings in their exact intensity . . . [p. 120]."

The definitions of empathy proposed by Barrett-Lennard and Truax do not constitute adequate operational definitions. Empathy is a theoretical construct. The definitions use the vernacular and are not data language constructs, according to the criteria that we have proposed. Terms such as "conscious," "immediate awareness," "therapist no longer 'with' the patient," suffer all the ambiguities of the vernacular since the behaviorial referents have not been specified. Furthermore, since both Barrett-Lennard and Truax use slightly different verbal definitions and meas-

urement scales of empathy, we have no way of knowing in what way Barrett-Lennard's empathy is related to Truax's empathy since the functional relationship between these two different definitions and measures of empathy have not been established. Consequently, legitimate comparisons of results from different investigations cannot be made. The psychotherapy literature is replete with references to the construct of empathy. There are almost as many different measurement operations as there are definitions, but all referring to the same construct.

Our earlier discussion concerning verbal procedural definitions is quite relevant to both the Barrett-Lennard and Truax investigations. Despite the differences in measurement operations, both investigators define empathy in terms of the relationships between two people and as a characteristic of the therapist. In the Truax studies the judges made their evaluations on both the therapists' and the clients' behavior. If empathy is alleged to be a characteristic of the therapist, it would appear that we are unable to denote an empathetic therapist any more than we are able to denote a reinforcing stimulus. We do not know whether or not we have an empathetic therapist until we have observed the behavioral reactions of the client. If empathy is to refer to some relationship between therapist and client, then it would be desirable to know precisely what behaviors were emitted and what conditions are necessary to produce this relationship.

If we continue to infer characteristics of the therapist's behavior from the effect it produces on the client, then we are never going to be able to develop any systematic relationship between client and therapist behaviors because the relationship is built into the definition. The tautology becomes evident when it is considered that the only statement that can be made is that empathetic therapists are those whose patients report favorable experiences, whereas therapists' patients who report unfavorable experiences lack empathy. We can say nothing about what classes of therapist behavior are related to these different experiences by the patient.

Truax's scale of empathy, as do all rating scales, raises some additional measurement considerations. The descriptions of each of the points on this nine point continuum were based on behavioral observations. The difficulty with the scale is that the reader does not know what these behaviors were. Furthermore, since these nine points supposedly represent discriminably different behaviors, from a measurement viewpoint the question can be raised as to the necessity of making the assumption that these nine classes of behavior fall along a unidimensional scale. Thus, changes in the patient are assumed to be a function of the changes in the therapist's position on the scale. In order to determine the functional relationship between amount of empathy and behavioral change in the patient, it would be necessary to have the therapist systematically change his behavior in the nine ways described by the scale, and then determine in what manner the differences in his behavior are related to changes in the behavior of the patient.

Another consideration in the development of a scale is that the unit of the scale should be defined in terms of some set of operations. As far as can be determined, no set of operations is performed in the establishment of the basic unit

that is involved in this scale. As such, it is difficult to determine what is meant by the different points on the scale. If the descriptions on the empathy scale do refer to classes of behavior emitted by the therapist in the presence of the patient, then we are in a position to ascertain directly in what manner these different behaviors are related to patient behavior without first going through the process of developing a "psychological" scale.

Although rating scales have definite limitations, other measures that have been employed in psychotherapy research are also not without problems. Two of the most widely used measures have been psychological tests and the Q sort. The Q sort has been used as a measure of some of the constructs that have evolved from client centered therapy. At the initiation of therapy the client is given a number of cards containing a series of statements. He is requested to sort these cards along a continuum that varies from most to least characteristic of himself. Usually the continuum is on an all point scale (0–10) and there is an additional restriction that the number of cards has to be placed along the 11 points to conform to a normal distribution. The client may be asked to sort the cards so that the statements reflect the type of person he is at present. This sort is referred to as the "real self" or "self as is." He is then asked to sort the cards once again, this time in a manner describing the type of person that he would like to be. This sort is referred to as the "ideal self." The procedures are then again carried out at the termination of therapy. The results of such investigations (e.g. Butler & Haigh, 1954) show a low correlation between the real and ideal sorts at the initiation of therapy, but a much higher correlation at the end of therapy. The results are then interpreted to mean that the effects of therapy were to produce a change in the client's experiences or preceptions of himself so that there is more congruence between the way he is and the way he would like to be.

Let's look at the behavior that is being measured. The behavior consists of sorting cards. The stimuli or independent variables are both the statements printed on the cards and the investigator's instructions to either "sort the cards as they describe you today," or "sort the cards as you would like to be." However, the changes in the client's card sorting behavior from the beginning to the end of therapy are attributed to a third class of independent variables that we know nothing about: the behaviors or manipulations of the therapist. In other words, there have been no systematic functions established between the behaviors of the therapist and the card sorting behaviors of the client. To make matters worse, although the investigators in these studies operationally define constructs like the "ideal self" in terms of the card sorting behavior of the client, this behavior is discussed in terms of the individual's perceptions or experience of himself. The card sorting behavior is treated as an indirect measure of perceptual experience. Through some kind of magical tour de force, the results of the investigation are discussed in terms of the relationship of one unknown set of variables (the therapist's behavior or what goes on in psychotherapy) and another unknown set of variables (the patient's perceptions of himself.)

The use of psychological tests as measures of behavior can be criticized along lines similar to that of the Q sort. Many of these criticisms and much wasted effort could have been avoided had psychologists heeded the warning of H. M. Johnson (1928) concerning the dangers of response equivocation. Many of our psychological tests represent the measurement of behavioral indicants. Thus anxiety can be measured in terms of the operations performed on the Taylor Manifest Anxiety Scale. However, this test behavior is treated as though it were related to some hypothetical state of the organism. The term "anxiety" now refers both to a behavior that we have measured and to a state of the organism that we have not measured. Changes in the test behavior supposedly parallel changes in the hypothetical state. Essentially, we have an epiphenomenon.

A test can be used as a measure of another variable provided the functional equivalence between the two variables has been established. For example, physicists can use temperature to determine the amount of pressure without directly measuring pressure under certain conditions because the functional relationship between temperature and pressure has already been established. In order to establish this function it was necessary to develop independent measures for both temperature and pressure, and systematically manipulate one of these variables to determine the effect on the other.

If one wishes to employ tests as measures in psychotherapy, it is first necessary to establish the functional relationship between the behavior(s) of the therapist and the test behavior of the patient. Once this function has been established, then we could use the tests to make statements about what the therapist is doing. It is rather curious that psychologists would rather use a presumed indirect measure of behavior in order to evaluate the effects of the therapeutic interaction when these behaviors can be measured directly. We would think a therapist would be more interested in the behaviors the client emits in his presence and outside the therapy situation than his card sorting behavior or his responses to TAT pictures. Tests could serve a useful purpose, for example, if we knew what the functional relationship was between the patient's test behaviors and the types of behaviors he engages in outside the therapy situation. If these functions were known, then the therapist would be in a position to derive information from the test on how the subject was behaving outside of therapy. These types of basic functions have not been determined, but one might suspect that, in lieu of the notoriously low validity coefficients, particularly in the case of projective techniques, the prospects of using tests in this fashion seem rather remote.

It appears as though psychotherapeutic practices and research suffer from an overdose of reality testing. That is, there are many constructs used in psychotherapy that are assumed to have an existence independent of any specifiable set of measurement operations. The constructs have been used in discussing psychotherapy, and the efforts of recent years have been devoted to devising ways and means of providing some quantitative characteristics of these constructs. Though it is easy to understand how this situation has arisen, the evidence does not warrant continuation of this practice. In addition to the questionable value of this procedure, it has tended to contribute heavily to the chaos and confusion in the area of psychotherapy.

The position that we have advanced is that psychotherapy research could proceed in a more systematic fashion if more careful attention is given to the definition and measurement of behavior. It behooves the investigators to specify what events he is measuring and the conditions under which the measurement operations take place. We have suggested denotation as one criterion for specifying the unit of measurement. Many of the constructs that are measured in contemporary psychotherapy research do not meet this criterion.

In order to obtain agreement by denotation it may be necessary to impose severe limitations on the size of the behavior unit and to rigorously specify the conditions under which the measurement operations are made. We believe this is necessary in order to produce a data language that is reliable not only in terms of inter-observer agreement but also in terms of replication of these operations by independent investigators. Behaviors such as smiling, nodding, level of vocal intensity, and eye movement may be more subject to denotation and hence reliable than are hostility, frustration, and empathy. Once we have established our unit(s) of behavior(s), then additional operations can be performed such as counting the frequency of that unit. One might ask, for instance, in what manner is rate of smiling by the therapist related to some behavior of the client? Assuming that there is a functional relationship, and that such a function is reliable, we may still find ourselves in disagreement at a theoretical level but at least we can agree and communicate at a data language level. We would not wish to imply that therapy research along the lines that we have suggested has not been performed. Certainly the work of Matarazzo and his associates (1962, 1963) would closely approximate the measurement criteria that have been suggested. The results of their investigations demonstrate a systematic function between duration of therapist utterance and duration of patient utterance. Vocal utterance was measured by the Chapple Interaction Chronograph. The independent variable was therapist's utterance duration which was systematically varied in order to study how this was related to the dependent variable which was the utterance duration of the client's speech. The virtue of their studies is that the behavior of the therapist is defined independently of the client's behavior. The behavioral measures were defined in terms of a set of physical measurement operations and one can denote the beginning and end of vocal utterance.

Although the Matarazzo investigations have been singled out as an example of the type of study which is in line with our proposals, other investigators, (e.g. Kanfer, 1959, 1960) have also proceeded along similar lines. While the theoretical merits of such investigations may be subject to debate, this is not the concern of this paper. It is our contention that, at our present stage of development, psychotherapy does not lack theoretical alternatives. There is, however, a paucity of reliable functional relationships.

Our analysis has led us to conclude that many of the difficulties in psychotherapy and psychotherapy research are a function of an inadequate data language. We have indicated that a rigorous, measurement-oriented approach to the data language of psychotherapy should result in a consistent, reliable, and precise description of the events of psychotherapy. We have tried to provide a set of criteria for the introduction of constructs into the data language that would reduce the ambiguities that are present in currently used data language. We have also recognized the arbitrariness of the data language that is used. However, we believe that the arbitrariness should be subject to some check, and we suggest that a most important check on the arbitrariness we have proposed is a reduction in the ambiguity of the data language which should, therefore, result in a more precise specification of independent and dependent variables. This increased precision with its concomitant mensurational properties or characteristics should allow for the development of consistent and reliable functional relationships. Moreover, a clear-cut distinction is made between data language and theory language that should reduce the probability of introducing theoretical constructs into the data language. One of the consequences of this distinction may be the development of a more adequate, useful set of theoretical constructs.

REFERENCES

Barrett-Lennard, G. T. 1962. Dimensions of therapist responses as causal factors in therapeutic change. *Psychol. Monogr.*, **76**, No. 43 (Whole No. 562).

Bergin, A. E. 1963. The effects of psychotherapy: Negative results revisited. *J. Counsel. Psychol.*, **10**, 244–250.

Boring, E. G. 1945. The use of operational definitions in science. *Psychol. Rev.*, **52**, 243–245.

Bridgman, P. W. 1945. Some general principles of operational analysis. *Psychol. Rev.*, **52**, 246–249.

Butler, J. M., & Haigh, G. V. 1954. Changes in the relation between self-concept and ideal concepts consequent upon client-centered counseling. In C. R. Rogers & R. F. Dymond (Eds.). *Psychotherapy and personality change.* Chicago: University of Chicago Press.

Davis, R. C. 1953. Physical psychology. *Psychol. Rev.*, **60**, 7–14.

Eysenck, H. J. 1952 The effects of psychotherapy: An evaluation. *J. Consult. Psychol.*, **16**, 319–324.

Feigl, H. 1945. Operationism and scientific method. *Psychol. Rev.*, **52**, 250–259.

Hull, C. L. 1943. *Principles of behavior.* New York: Appleton-Century Crofts.

Johnson, H. M. 1928. Some fallacies underlying the use of psychological tests. *Psych. Rev.*, **35**, 328–337.

Kanfer, F. 1959. Verbal rate, content and adjustment rating in experimentally structured interviews. *J. abnorm. soc. Psychol.*, **58**, 305–311.

Kanfer, F. 1960. Verbal rate, eyeblink, and content in structured psychiatric interviews. *J. abnorm. soc. Psychol.*, **61**, 341–347.

Levitt, E. E. 1957. The results of psychotherapy with children: An evaluation. *J. Consult. Psychol.*, **21**, 189–196.

Matarazzo, J. D., Hess, H. F., & Saslow, G. 1962. Frequency and duration characteristics of speech and silence behavior during interviews. *J. clin. Psychol.*, **18**, 416–426.

Matarazzo, J. D., Wertman, M., Saslow, G., & Wiens, A. 1963. An interviewer influence on durations of interviewer speech. *J. verb. learn. and verb. Behav.*, **1**, 451–458.

Rogers, C. R. 1957. The necessary and sufficient conditions of therapeutic personality change. *J. Consult. Psychol.*, **21**, 95–103.

Rogers, C. R. 1963. Psychotherapy today, or where do we go from here? *Amer. J. Psychotherapy*, **17**, 5–16.

Rosenzweig, S. A. 1954. A transvaluation of psychotherapy; A reply to Hans Eysenck. *J. abnorm. soc. Psychol.*, **49**, 298–304.

Skinner, B. F. 1945. The operational analysis of scientific terms. *Psychol. Rev.*, **52**, 270–277.

Truax, C. B. 1961. The process of group psychotherapy. *Psychol. Monogr.*, **75**, No. 14 (Whole No. 511).

Truax, C. B., & Carkhuff, R. R. 1965. Experimental manipulation of therapeutic conditions. *J. Consult. Psychol.*, **29**, 119–124.

Turner, M. B. 1965. *Philosophy and the science of behavior.* New York: Appleton-Century-Crofts.

7

Logic and Psychology

Michael Polanyi

For a very long time most experimental psychologists assumed that the correct philosophy of science was logical positivism. They assumed that theoretical statements in a science must be reducible to observation statements. Thus, for example, such tough-minded theorists as Hull and Spence went to great lengths to show that their theoretical constructs, such as "habit" and "drive," boiled down, upon analysis, to "nothing but" measurement operations such as trials to extinction or hours of deprivation. This led to Skinner's rejection of theory (Skinner, 1950) on the grounds that the theoretical constructs added nothing but confusion to the issues. If such constructs are nothing but symbols for measurement operations, why not deal with the measurement operations directly? Certainly this would save the scientist from the dangers of reifying the constructs.

The positivistic view of science was incorporated into psychology for a rather odd reason. Most of the time, scientists adopt a philosophy for pragmatic reasons—because that philosophy helps them to function as scientists. For example, operationism helped physicists to deal with specific theoretical problems such as those entailed in relativity theory. It makes sense to adopt a philosophical theory that facilitates scientific practice. But psychology adopted the positivistic approach primarily in what appears to have been an attempt to mimic physical sciences. The helpfulness of this approach to the practicing experimental psychologist is questionable.

In recent times many philosophers of science have made devastating critiques of the positivistic approach. Even leading positivistic philosophers have shifted in the direction of a pragmatic rather than a positivistic approach (see, for example, White, 1963). What if a theoretical system that was not reducible to "data language" or "measurement operations" just happened to result in a highly successful model of the behavior we wish to understand? What if such a theoretical model led to highly successful prediction and control of behavior? Would we reject the model because our positivistic theory said that it failed to meet somewhat arbitrary criteria? Hardly. We would be far more likely to be pragmatic about the matter. As Craik (1943) pointed out, we use our intellects largely to create *models* of the environment. Models commonly have the advantage of being easier to manipulate than the system of interest itself. If I want to build a bridge, one way to do it is to keep building bridges and watching them fall down until I finally make a successful one. But it would be far better if I had a model for bridge building which I could manipulate in my room at home or in my office. The model could be of cardboard, of plastic, or could take the form of equations written on paper or of a computer program. In any case, what I want is a useful model. This is what the scientific enterprise is about— making successful models for the universe. The positivistic position seems to imply that the only successful models will be those which meet positivistic criteria; but no one has ever demonstrated anything like that. In fact, it has been argued that successful scientific theories quite generally fail to meet such criteria (see, for example, Toulmin, 1953).

In the following article, Polanyi gives some very striking arguments against the view that theoretical statements must be reducible to data statements. There are many cases in which we can function effectively at a perceptual or conceptual level without being at all aware of the elements on which our percepts or concepts are based. Polanyi shows this in some very interesting ways. For opposing viewpoints, see Caws (1969) and Zaffron (1970).

I am happy to have this opportunity to put before you thoughts about the nature of scientific knowledge which I have pursued for some time past. My starting point dates back to my book, *Science, Faith and Society* (Polanyi, 1946). Upon examining the grounds on which science is pursued, I saw that its progress is determined at every stage by indefinable powers of thought. No rules can account for the way a good idea is found for starting an inquiry, and there are no firm rules either for the verification or

Reprinted from *American Psychologist,* 1968, **23**, 27–43, by permission of the author and the American Psychological Association. Expanded version of invited address presented at the meetings of the American Psychological Association, Washington, D.C., September 1967.

the refutation of the proposed solution of a problem.

This speculation may sound similar to much of what is often heard today. We are told that the teachings of science claim only to be probable but also to be merely tentative, ever open to refutation by adverse evidence. But this is not true. We bet our lives on the certainty of science every day, be it in medicine or engineering; in fact, nothing is more certain in our world than the established results of science. My point is that the *absence of strict criteria* on which to base our acceptance of science merely shows that our confidence in scientific knowledge *is based on nonstrict criteria.* Science is grounded, and is firmly grounded, on the kind of indefinable insights which the current view of science regards as mere psychological phenomena, incapable of producing rational inferences.

I believe, therefore, that any attempt to eliminate nonstrict modes of inference—or even to reduce them to insignificance—must be misleading. Such attempts have hampered philosophy and damaged our scientific methods. Later I shall give some examples of such cases.

My main task will be to survey the nonstrict rules of inference—in other words, the informal logic—on which science rests. This nonstrict logic will be seen to rest to some extent on psychological observations not hitherto accepted as the foundations of scientific inference. In these informal elements of science we shall recognize the *indeterminacy of scientific knowledge,* and I shall start by describing *three closely linked kinds of such indeterminacy.* The *first* indeterminacy lies in the *indeterminate content* of scientific knowledge. We shall find a *second* indeterminacy in the fact that the *coherence* which makes us accept a discovery to be true can be only *vaguely defined,* and a third indeterminacy will be seen when we find that the *data* on which a discovery ultimately rests *are not fully identifiable.*

THREE INDETERMINACIES OF KNOWLEDGE

All knowledge has an indeterminate content whenever it bears on reality. I shall show this to be scientific knowledge. It was Copernicus who claimed for the first time that science can discover new knowledge about fundamental reality, and this claim triumphed in the Copernican revolution. But recently—

for the past 80 years or so—the claim of science to know reality has been shaken by a positivist critique which condemned such claims as metaphysical. But I myself agree with Copernicus. In my opinion it is impossible to pursue science without believing that it can discover reality, and I want to reestablish here this belief in reality, although the resurrected idea of reality will, admittedly, look different from its departed ancestor.

It is not easy, of course, to say exactly what Copernicus believed when he persistently maintained, against heavy opposition, that his system was not merely a new computing device, but was a true image of the planets circling the sun. But it will become clear what he meant if we first look at the way the successors of Copernicus—for example, Kepler—relied on the reality of the heliocentric system. The three laws discovered by Kepler were based on the reality of the Copernican system: He was able to discover these laws only because he accepted it *as a fact* that the earth goes round the sun.

Whenever we believe in the reality of a thing, we expect that the thing will manifest itself in yet unknown ways in the future. But notice also that the laws by which Kepler confirmed the reality of the heliocentric system were very different from anything Copernicus himself might have expected. The elliptic planetary paths of Kepler conflicted sharply with the basic beliefs of Copernicus. Yet it remains true that Kepler's discoveries confirmed Copernicus' claim that his system was real, which shows that a claim to reality is essentially indeterminate. Affirmations of reality in nature always have a widely indeterminate content.

This fact brings us to our next point, which is the indefinable character of the signs by which we recognize reality in nature. The vagueness of the signs pointing to reality can be seen in the work of Copernicus. Copernicus claimed that his theory was an image of reality because it had a coherence that was lacking in the Ptolemaic system, and the principle of this argument was sound because it is the coherence of a thing that makes us attribute reality to it. We commonly recognize its coherence at a glance by merely looking at a real thing. I look at my right hand as I move it about in front of me, and I see a thousand rapidly changing clues as one single, unchanging object moving about at changing distances, presenting different sides at variable angles and in variable light. The integration of innumerable, rapidly changing particulars makes us see a real object in front of us.

Solid objects are deemed to be real inasmuch as they suggest another side not visible at the moment and also a hidden interior—and, moreover, they promise to last for some time, possibly colliding with other things and affecting them in one of an infinite number of possible ways. Such are the typical indeterminacies of a real thing.

By pointing at coherence as a token of reality, Copernicus made an essential contribution to the method on which empirical science was to be established. Science was to him (like perception) a way of seeing reality, and was what the theory of Copernicus meant to his successors who developed it further up to Newton's day. It is indeed what the body of science is to the scientist to this day: He sees in science an aspect of reality which as such is an inexhaustible source of new and promising problems. Natural science continues to bear fruit, because it offers us an insight into external reality.

These views of science and of its belief in reality were put forward about 20 years ago in my *Science, Faith and Society* (Polanyi, 1946). Since then I found welcome support for regarding science as an extension of perception when I became acquainted with the great work of Whewell (1890), written nearly a century before. Speaking of Kepler's discovery of the elliptic path of the planet Mars, Whewell wrote:

To hit upon the right conception is a difficult step; and when the step is once made, the facts assume a different aspect from what they had before: that done, they are seen in a new point of view; and the catching of this point of view is a special mental operation, requiring special endowments and habits of thought. Before this, the facts are seen as detached, separate, lawless; afterwards they are seen as connected, simple, regular; as parts of a general fact, and thereby possessing new relations, before unseen [p. 254].

Whewell knew well that he was dissenting here from the Baconian theory of induction; he fiercely attacked Mill's development of this theory, which was nevertheless to dominate the conception of scientific theory for many years afterward. Whewell held that Baconian enquiry can succeed only when guided by dawning insight. And in describing the act of insight, he reveals its kinship to the way our eyes, sharpened by native gifts and by special training, make out the true nature of a puzzling spectacle before us.

In the passage here quoted, Whewell also anticipates another part of my theory. He says that, by becoming parts of a comprehensive entity, the facts acquire new relations, hitherto unseen. I think he speaks here of a true coherence in nature, the inexhaustible implications of which are felt in its bearing on reality.

My view of coherence in science owes much to Gestalt psychology, but I go beyond Gestalt when speaking of *true* coherence in nature. A tendency to good closure is only a *clue to coherence;* it does not establish *true coherence.* Take the famous ambiguous picture representing either a vase or two opposing profiles. As we shift from one way of seeing it to the other, we either see the vase as a real body and the rest of the picture as empty background, or we see, on the contrary, the profiles as real bodies and the space between them as empty. We can observe here a sensory quality indicating coherence as well as the reality of coherence. But since this sensory quality can be shifted at will between two mutually exclusive alternatives, it does not *establish* a true coherence.

The way a judgment of true coherence is arrived at can be seen when a jury faces a serious and difficult decision. The jurors may see a pattern of circumstances pointing to the accused. But it is always conceivable that this pattern may be due to chance. How unlikely a chance should they admit to be possible? Or what degree of coincidence should be considered not to be reasonably believable? No rule can decide this. The decision must be arrived at under the discipline of a grim personal responsibility. It must rely on an ultimate power of the mind, on which the scientist too must ultimately rely for establishing a true coherence in nature.

This concludes my sketch of two major indeterminacies introduced by Copernicus into the foundation of sci-

ence. I pass now to a third kind of indeterminacy that is intrinsic to all empirical knowledge, and hence also to science.

I have spoken of the numberless items that contribute to my seeing my hand in front of me. They are known to us mainly by observing the various deficiencies caused by cutting out these several items. I can cut out marginal clues by looking at my hand through a blackened tube and observing that this makes my hand appear to swell up when brought nearer to my eyes. We can observe that the action of our eye muscles contributes clues to our vision by the application of drugs which increase the effort of contracting the muscles, and hence makes objects look smaller. Afflictions of the inner ear cause the whole spectacle before us to lose its balance; and there is ample evidence that past experiences, which we can hardly recall, affect the way we see things.

Perception thus establishes an observation of external facts without formal argument and even without explicitly stating the result; I hope to eventually show that science, too, is based on such nonexplicit knowing. But first I must set out the general structure of such knowing and expose the new indeterminacies introduced by it into empirical knowledge.

Consider the act of viewing a pair of stereoscopic pictures in the usual way, with one eye on each of the pictures. Their joint image might be regarded as a whole, composed of the two pictures as its parts. But we can get closer to understanding what is going on here if we note that, when looking through a stereo viewer, we see a stereo image at the focus of our attention while we are aware of the two stereo pictures in some peculiar nonfocal way. We seem to look through these two pictures, or past them, while we look straight at their joint image. We are indeed aware of them only as guides to the image on which we focus our attention. I can describe this relationship of the two pictures to the stereo image by saying that the two pictures function as *subsidiaries* to our seeing their *joint* image which is their joint meaning. This is the typical structure of tacit knowing which I shall now describe in some detail.

The grounds of all tacit knowing are items—or particulars—like the stereo pictures of which we are aware in the act of focusing our attention on something else, away from them. This I call the *functional relation* of subsidiaries to the focal target, and we may also call it a *from-to relation*. Moreover, I can say that this relation establishes a *from-to knowledge* of the subsidiaries, as linked to their focus. Tacit knowing is a from-to knowing. Sometimes it will also be called a from-at knowing, but this variation will be only a matter of convenience.

It will not be difficult to demonstrate the indeterminacies inherent in from-to knowledge, but I want first to add some other features to the structure of from-to knowledge. A characteristic aspect of from-to knowledge is exemplified by the change of appearance which occurs when the viewing of a pair of stereo pictures transforms these into a stereo image. A stereo image has a marked depth and also shows firmly shaped objects not present as such in the original stereo pictures. It therefore shows a novel sensory experience created by tacit knowing. Such *phenomenal transformation* is a characteristic feature of from-to knowing. I have already actually mentioned such a case when I spoke of the sensory quality of coherence in nature.

A moment ago I anticipated another feature of from-to knowing when I said that the stereo image is the *joint meaning* of the stereo pictures. The subsidiaries of from-to knowing bear on a focal target; in my view, whatever a thing bears on may be called its meaning. Thus the focal target on which they bear is the meaning of the subsidiaries. We may call this an act of sense giving and recognize it as the *semantic aspect* of from-to knowing.

A few examples will help to make us familiar with these three aspects of tacit knowing: the functional, the phenomenal, and the semantic. I could cite here the cases of visual perception and of scientific discovery, which are my main interest in this exposition, but they have complications which I wish to avoid for a time.

Take, as a simpler case, the from-to structure of the act of reading a printed sentence. The sight of the printed words guides our focal attention away from the print to a focal target that is its meaning. We have here both the *function* of from-to knowing and its *semantic* aspect. Its *phenomenal* aspect is also easy to recognize; it lies in the fact that a word in use *looks different* from what it would be like to someone who met it as a totally foreign word. The familiar use of a word, which is our subsidiary awareness of it, renders it, in a way, bodiless, or, as it is sometimes described, transparent.

Another example—and one that will help us later to understand visual perception—is the case of tactile cognition: of using a probe to explore a cavity, or a stick to feel one's way in the dark.

Such exploration is a from-to knowing, for we attend subsidiarily to the feeling of holding the probe in the hand, while the focus of our attention is fixed on the far end of the probe, where it touches an obstacle in its path. This perception is the function of tacit knowing and is accompanied by particularly interesting *phenomenal transformation.* The sensation of the probe pressing on fingers and palm, and of the muscles guiding the probe, is lost, and instead we feel the point of the probe as it touches an object. And, in addition to the functional and the phenomenal, the probing has, of course, a *semantic* aspect. For the information we get by feeling the point of the instrument is its meaning to us: It tells us what it is that we are observing by the use of the probe.

This use of probes may remind us of the fact that all sensation is assisted by some, however slight, skillful performance, the motions of which are performed with our attention focused on the intended action so that our awareness of the motions is subsidiary to the performance. From-to structure includes all skillful performances, from walking the street to walking a tightrope, and from tying a knot to playing a piano. More about this later.

We now have enough material to uncover the indeterminacies inherent in from-to knowing. We have a very obvious indeterminacy before us in the case of stereo vision. The three-dimensional depth of the stereo image has its basis in the differences between the two stereo pictures, that is to say, the differences due to the fact that the pictures are taken at points a few inches apart. These tiny differences are not noticeable by simple inspection, and even if we used powerful methods for measuring them, we would find them difficult to itemize since they extend all over the surface. We see, then, how readily our subsidiary awareness picks up and embodies in the focus of our attention items of evidence that we should never notice directly and might indeed find difficult to identify even if we searched for them. This demonstration should suffice to make it clear that the *grounds* of from-to knowledge may often be *unspecifiable.*

Let me stop here for a moment and recall the indeterminacy of all knowledge bearing on reality and the indeterminacy due to the impossibility of giving a precise rule for establishing true coherence in nature. We have now added, as a third indeterminacy of empirical knowledge, the fact that we may not know on what grounds we hold our knowledge to be true.

But let us realize that we could turn this deficiency into a flourish. Instead of deploring that a statement about external reality has an indeterminate content, we could take pride in the fact that we can thus *see beyond established facts;* instead of regretting that we cannot define the quality of coherence in nature, we could be gratified at the capability of *feeling* such subtle, virtually invisible, signs of reality. Far from being embarrassed by our incapacity to state all the grounds on which empirical knowledge rests, we could insist on the recognition of our powers to *know far more than we can tell.* These faculties are indeed those that we *shall* claim once we have accepted tacit knowing as a legitimate and, in fact, indispensable source of all empirical knowledge. But we must realize the whole depth of our tacit commitments before we can make them so firmly our own. For this, let me show yet further aspects of our tacit knowledge.

THE TACIT TRIAD

The structure of tacit knowing includes a conjoint pair of constituents. Subsidiaries exist as such by bearing on the focus to which we are attending from them. In other words, the functional structure of from-to knowing includes jointly a subsidiary "from" and a focal "to" (or "at"). But this pair is not linked together of its own accord. The relation of a subsidiary to a focus is formed by the act of a person who integrates one to the other. And so the from-to relation lasts only so long as a person, the knower, sustains this integration.

This is not merely to say that if we no longer look at a thing, we shall cease to see it. There is a specific action involved in dissolving the integration of tacit knowing. Let me describe this action.

We have now seen three centers of tacit knowledge: first, the subsidiary particulars; second, the focal target; and third, the knower who links the first to the second. We can place these three things in the three corners of a triangle. Or we can think of them as forming a triad, controlled by a person, the knower, who causes the subsidiaries to bear on the focus of his attention.

We can then say that the knower integrates the subsidiaries to a focal target—or that the subsidiaries have a meaning to the knower which fills the center of his focal attention, and that hence the knower can dissolve the triad by merely looking differently at the subsidiaries. The triad will disappear if the knower shifts his focal attention away from the focus of the triad and fixes it on the subsidiaries.

For example, if, instead of looking at the stereo pictures through the viewer, we take them out and look at them directly, we lose sight of their joint appearance on which we had focused before. Or if we focus our attention on a spoken word and thus see it as a sequence of sounds, the word loses the meaning to which we had attended before. Or again, we can paralyze the performance of a skill by turning our attention away from its performance and concentrating instead on the several motions that compose the performance.

These facts are common knowledge, but their consequences for the theory of tacit knowledge are remarkable. For the facts confirm our view that we can be aware of certain things in a way that is quite different from focusing our attention on them. They prove the existence of two kinds of awareness that are mutually exclusive, a *from-awareness* and a *focal awareness*. They also confirm that in the from-awareness of a thing we see a meaning of it, a meaning which is wiped out by focusing our attention *on* the thing, which will face us then in itself, in its raw bodily nature. The dual nature of awareness is made manifest here as the sense deprivation involved in substituting one kind of awareness for another.

Suppose, then, that it is possible, at least in principle, to identify all the subsidiaries of a triad; however elusive they may be we would still face the fact that anything serving as a subsidiary ceases to do so when focal attention is directed on it. It turns into a different kind of thing, deprived of the meaning it had in the triad. Thus subsidiaries are—in this important sense—essentially unspecifiable. We must distinguish, then, between two types of the unspecifiability of subsidiaries. One type is due to the difficulty of tracing the subsidiaries—a condition that is widespread but not universal—and the other type is due to a sense deprivation which is logically necessary and in principle absolute. This adds a fourth, and quite fundamental, indeterminacy to the grounds on which empirical knowledge rests.

I hope that if this analysis convinces us of the presence of two very different kinds of awareness in tacit knowing, it will also prevent us from identifying these two different kinds of awareness with a difference between conscious and unconscious awareness. Focal awareness is, of course, always conscious, but subsidiary awareness, or from-awareness, can have all levels of consciousness; it can range from a subliminal level to a fully conscious level. What makes awareness subsidiary is its functional character, and I shall therefore claim the presence of subsidiary awareness even for functions inside our body at levels completely inaccessible to experience by the subject. This claim will be particularly important for the theory of visual perception.[1]

---

[1]What I call "subsidiaries" include "subceived stimuli" (see Polanyi, 1966, pp. 7–9). Wall and Guthrie (1959, pp. 205–210) have shown that conditioning to shock syllables persists without reinforcement for subliminal presentation, but is extinguished for subliminal presentation when extinguished for supraliminal presentation. They note the parallelism between the subceived stimulus and the Freudian unconscious.

TACIT INFERENCE

Subsidiaries function as such by being integrated to a focus on which they bear. This integration is the tacit act of a person and can be valid or mistaken. Perception can be true or mistaken and so can our judgment of coherence, whether in deciding on the facts of a legal case or when perceiving coherence in nature. To arrive at such conclusions may be called an *act of tacit inference,* but such inferences differ sharply from drawing conclusions by an explicit deduction.

Piaget (1950) has described the contrasts between a sensorimotor act like perception and a process of explicit inference. Explicit inference is reversible: We can go back to its premises and go forward again to its conclusions, and we can rehearse this process as often as we like. This is not true for perception. For example, once we have seen through a visual puzzle, we cannot return to an ignorance of its solution. This holds, with some variations, for all acts of tacit knowing. We can go back to the two pictures of a stereo image by taking them out of the viewer and looking at them directly, but this completely destroys the stereo image. When flying by airplane first started, the traces of ancient sites were revealed in fields over which generations of country folk had walked without noticing them. But once he had landed, the airman could no longer see them either.

In some cases sense deprivation is incomplete. Thus we can concentrate on the sound and the action of our lips and tongue in producing a word, and this will cause us to lose the meaning of the word although the loss can be instantly made good by casting the mind forward for using the word once more in saying something. The same is true for a pianist who paralyzes his performance by intensely watching his own fingers: He can promptly recover their skillful use by attending once more to his music. In these instances the path to the integrated relation—which may have originally taken months of labor to extablish—is restored from its abeyance in a trice, while at the same moment the sight of the sense-deprived particulars is lost.

Explicit inference is very different; no such breaking up and rediscovery takes place when we recapitulate the deduction of the theorem of Pythagoras. Once this basic distinction between explicit inference and tacit integration is clear, it throws new light on a 100-year-old controversy. In 1867 Helmholtz offered to interpret perception as a process of unconscious inference, but this theory was generally rejected by psychologists, who pointed out that optical illusions are not destroyed by demonstrating their falsity. Psychologists had assumed, quite reasonably, that "unconscious inference" had the same structure as a conscious explicit inference. But if we identify "unconscious inference" with tacit integration, we have a kind of inference that is not damaged by adverse evidence, as explicit inference is. This difference between a deduction and an integration lies in the fact that deduction connects two focal items, the premises and consequents, while integration makes subsidiaries bear on a focus. Admittedly there is a purposive movement in a deduction—which is its essential tacit coefficient—but the deductive operation can be mechanically performed while a tacit integration is

intentional throughout and, as such, can be carried out only by a conscious act of the mind. Brentano (1942, orig. publ. 1874) has taught that consciousness necessarily attends to an object, and that *only* a conscious mental act can attend to an object. My analysis of tacit knowing has amplified this view of consciousness. It tells us not only that consciousness is intentional, but also that it always has roots *from which* it attends to its object. It includes a tacit awareness of its subsidiaries.

Such integration cannot be replaced by any explict mechanical procedure. In the first place, even though one can paraphrase the cognitive content of an integration, the sensory quality which conveys this content cannot be made explicit. I have already illustrated this fact much earlier by pointing to the quality of coherence in nature, but all of my examples of tacit knowing can be used to demonstrate it.

The irreducibility of tacit integration can be observed more fully for practical knowing. I could point to our incapacity to control directly the several motions contributing to a skillful performance—even such a familiar act as using our limbs. But these cases are perhaps too common to impress the imagination. So I shall take instead the example of finding one's way with inverting spectacles. It is virtually impossible to get about while wearing inverting spectacles by following the instruction that what—in the case of right-left inversion—is seen on the right is actually on the left, while, conversely, things seen on the left are on the right. The Austrian psychologist, Heinrich Kottenhoff (1961), however, has shown that continued efforts to move about while wearing inverted spectacles produce a novel quality of feeling and action by integrating the inverted sights to appropriate sensorimotor responses, so that the subject again finds his way about. This reintegration can be performed only subsidiarily; and explicit instruction to reintegrate sights and sensorimotor responses would be quite meaningless.

I have often quoted the case of the cyclist, but it still teaches its lesson here. We cannot learn to keep our balance on a bicycle by taking to heart that, to compensate for an imbalance, we must take a curve of which a radius is proportional to the square of the bicycle's velocity over the angle of imbalance. Such knowledge is totally ineffectual unless it is known tacitly.

The way in which particulars are picked up and assimilated as subsidiaries will be extensively dealt with in the section on scientific discovery. But we may anticipate one of its aspects, pointed out by Konrad Lorenz (1967) who arrived independently at the view that science is based on a gestaltlike integration of particulars. He demonstrated that the speed and complexity of tacit integration far exceeds the operations of any explicit selection of supporting evidence. I have recently (Polanyi, 1967b) developed this idea further by showing that the serial behavior demonstrated by Lashley (1951) in the production of a spoken sentence can be understood by considering that tacit knowing can pick up simultaneously a whole set of data and combine them in a meaningful spoken sequence.

An integration established in this summary manner will often override single items of contrary evidence. It can only be damaged by new contradictory facts if these items are absorbed in an alternative integration which disrupts the one previously established. In Ames's skew-room experiment the illusion of a boy taller than the man persists so long as the evidence of the room's skew shape is slight, but the illusion is instantly destroyed if a shift of the observer's position or a tapping of the ceiling makes the skewness of the room more manifest. This fact effectively competes, then, with the hitherto established integration and destroys it.

David Hume has taught that, when in doubt, we must suspend judgment. This theory might apply to conclusions derived on paper which can be manipulated at will—at least on paper. Our eyes continue to see a little boy taller than a grown man although we know this to be false, so long as no feasible alternative integration is presented to the imagination. But if an alternative is presented, and this perception happens to be true, a new perception will take place and correct our errors. Helmholtz could have answered his opponents on this score, but he would have had to admit that his "unconscious inferences" were very different from conscious inferences.

INDWELLING

There is yet another important aspect of tacit knowing which should be included here. In all examples of tacit knowing that I have given, the focal target which forms the meaning of the subsidiaries is placed some distance away from them. Most striking, perhaps, was the displacement of meaning when the sensations of hand and muscles holding a probe were displaced to the far end of the probe. The displacements of the focal target invariably went in the same direction, namely, away from us. And if one tries to construct a triad, the focus of which points in the opposite direction—so that the meaning of the subsidiaries would lie on our side of them—this proves impossible.

The most important displacement of meaning is found in visual perception; I mention perception here only to explain why meaning produced by tacit knowing is always displaced outward. Our senses point into external space and our actions, too, are, as a rule, projected outward; so the objects of our conscious attention lie predominantly outward from us. Our muscles, our sense organs, our nervous system, are experienced as they perform their functions of noticing and interpreting things outside and manipulating them for our own purposes. One is aware of the body subsidiarily as it performs these functions, while focal observation of one's own body is only superficial. We may look focally at our hands and feet, but even so our subsidiary awareness of them predominates: One still feels them to be part of the body. This is what the from-knowledge of the body feels like to us: It amounts to awareness of living in one's own body.

Having identified the feeling of being in one's body with from-knowledge of the body, one can look upon all from-knowledge as akin to the sense of being in one's body. *In this sense, then, to make something function subsidiarily is to interiorize it, or else to pour one's body into it.* The fact that we do feel probes and tools to be part of the body bears out this parallelism. Any integration of things which makes them bear on our focal interest can be regarded as an indwelling of these things.

We may say that our own existence, which we experience, and the world that we observe are interwoven here. Bodily being, by participating subsidiarily in one's perceptions and actions, becomes a being in the world, while external observations and projects subsidiarily involving one's own bodily feelings become, up to a point, a self-transformation, an existential choice. And this involves our cultural framework. Every time we rely on our traditional grounds in forming a judgment, we somewhat modify their meaning, and on these lines a creative act can renew our grounds extensively. Copernicus, for example, radically changed the grounds of empirical judgment, and since then the grounds of scientific judgment have been further modified repeatedly.

This adds yet another indeterminacy to the four I have previously mentioned. Applied to science, our fifth indeterminacy consists of the existential choices involved in modifying the grounds of scientific judgment.

But something even more vital follows from formulating tacit knowing as an act of indwelling. It deepens our knowledge of living things. Biology studies the shapes of living things and the way they grow into these shapes from germ cells; it describes the organs of plants and animals and explains the way they function; it explores the motor and sensory capacities of animals and their intelligent performances. These aspects of life are controlled by biological principles. Morphology, embryology, physiology, psychology all study the principles by which living beings form and sustain their coherence and respond in ever new ways to an immense variety of novel circumstances. The ways in which animals, such as cattle or dogs or men, coherently control their bodies form a comprehensively functioning system. Any chemical or physical study of living things that is irrelevant to these workings of the organism forms no part of biology.

We therefore recognize and study the coherence of living things by integrating their motions—and any other normal changes occurring in their parts—into our comprehension of their functions. *We integrate mentally what living beings integrate practically.* Chess players rehearse a master's game to discover what he had in mind. Generally we share the purpose of a mind by indwelling its actions. This is my answer to the great question: How do we know another mind?

SOME SIGNS OF A DEFICIENCY

I shall now show, as I promised, how philosophic thought and the methodological principles of science have been misguided by not having a clear knowledge of tacit knowing. I shall take as my examples, first, the knowledge of other minds; second, universal terms; third, principles of explanation; and fourth, empirical generalization.

Knowledge of Other Minds

Up to a point, Gilbert Ryle (1949) has argued about our knowledge of other minds as I have done here. He strikingly demonstrated that we do not get to know the workings of another mind by a process of inference; we are following them (p. 61), but since he had no conception of tacit knowing, he concluded that body and mind are "not two things [p. 74]," "not tandem operations [p. 46]," and that accordingly "most intelligent performances are not clues to the mind; they are those workings [p. 58]."

This theory I shall reject; the theory of tacit knowing also tells us that we do not know another mind by a process of inference, but nevertheless it retains the dualism of mind and body. It says that the body seen focally is one thing, while the body seen subsidiarily points to another thing; these two different things are the body and the mind. More about this later.

Merleau-Ponty (1962), writing some years before Ryle, anticipated his premises by declaring: "I do not understand the gestures of others by an act of intellectual interpretation . . . [p. 185]," to which he added a little further on: "The act by which I lend myself to these spectacles must be recognized as irreducible to anything else [p. 185]."

This teaching anticipated the existential commitment present in tacit knowledge, but did so without recognizing the triadic structure which determines the functions of this commitment—the way it establishes our knowledge of a valid coherence. The contrast between explicit inference and an existential experience imbued with intentionality is not sufficient for defining the structure and workings of tacit knowing. We are offered an abundance of brilliant flashes without a constructive system.

The philosophy of behaviorism does not contest the duality of body and mind,[2] but it assumes that all mental performances can be fully specified without referring to any mental motives. Could this be true? Consider an analogy. All textbooks of physiology refer to organs and the function of organs, and in spite of frequent solemn declarations

[2]See, for example, B. F. Skinner (1964, p. 79).

that such teleological conceptions are unnecessary and indeed objectionable, no one has yet published a textbook of physiology that does not speak of organs and their functions. For the biological functions of organs can be known only as coherent wholes. This also applies, of course, to the motions forming a skillful performance, or an act of intelligence; these can be identified only as parts of their meaningful combination. To describe, as behaviorists claim to do, workings of the mind without relying on the guidance of mental motives is as impossible as it is to describe physiological events occurring in an organ without being guided by the observation of its coherent physiological functions.

To some extent behaviorism succeeds in claiming the impossible, because our knowledge of the mind's coherence is so stable that any isolated workings of the mind will instantly evoke their underlying mental motives which the isolated workings are supposed to replace. In my book, *Personal Knowledge* (Polanyi, 1958, pp. 370–371) I have described how the behaviorist psychology of learning achieves such a semblance of its program. To begin with, the performance is favored by limiting the enquiry to the crudest forms of learning. These much simplified cases can then be plausibly described in objectivist terms, but even so they can be shown to apply to the actual process of learning only because their meaning is tacitly understood by their bearing on the mental events covertly kept in mind. One thus succeeds in using objectivist terms which are, strictly speaking, meaningless, as effective paraphrases for the mentalistic terms which they are supposed to eliminate.

Noam Chomsky's (1959) critique of B. F. Skinner's (1957) *Verbal Behavior* presents many illustrations of such behaviorist paraphrasing. Apparently objective terms, like stimulus, control, response, and so on, are so used that their ambiguity covers the mental terms which they are supposed to replace. Chomsky shows that either you use these objectivist terms literally—and then what is said is obviously false and absurd—or you use them as substitutes for the terms which they are supposed to eliminate—and then you do not say anything else than what you would have said in mentalist terms.

The same criticism applies to the mechanical simulation of tacit knowing. A tacit integration can only be superficially paraphrased by a computer, and such paraphrases succeed by evoking the mental qualities which they claim to enact.

Universal Terms

The mere fact that biology deals with classes of plants and animals involves indeterminacies which, for centuries past and up to this day, philosophers have tried in vain to eliminate.

Plato and his school were the first to be troubled by the fact that *in applying our conception of a class of things, we keep identifying objects that are different from one another in every particular.* If every man is clearly distinguishable from any other man and we yet recognize each of them as a man, what kind of "man" is the one by reference to whom all these men are recognized? He cannot be both fair and dark, young and old, nor brown, white, black, and yellow all at once: but neither can he have any one of these alternative properties, nor indeed any particular property whatever. Plato concluded that the general idea of man refers to a *perfect man* who has no particular properties, and of whom individual men are imperfect copies, corrupted by having such properties.

The Platonic idea of man, however, embodies the incompatibility of identifying different individuals, instead of eliminating it. An attempt to avoid this fallacy was made about 900 years ago by Roscellinus in the idea of nominalism. According to this doctrine, the word "man" is but the name for a collection of individual men. But the indeterminacy reappears once more, when we ask how to justify the labeling of a collection of different individuals by the same name, and how, moreover, we can continue to label in a constant fashion, as time goes on, any number of further individuals differing in every particular from any individual thus labeled before, and yet can continually exclude a vast number of other individuals as not belonging to the class we have labeled.

Perhaps it is no wonder that another 700 years later Kant (1929) should have declared that the way our intelligence forms and applies the conception of a class of particulars "is a skill so deeply hidden in the human soul that we shall hardly guess the secret trick that Nature here employs [p. A141]."

Yet, in the present age of philosophy, in 1945 F. Waismann attempted to answer the question deemed insoluble by Kant. He pointed out that general terms have an "open texture," which admits differences in the instances to which it applies. But this merely shifts the question, for to ascribe "open texture" to a word is merely to imply that among an indefinitely extending series of different objects the word properly applies to some objects and not to the rest. The question how this is done remains open, exactly as before.

No wonder that the more incisive reappraisal of the old quandary by W. V. O. Quine[3] (1960, 1967) led him back to the conclusion reached by Kant: that the grounds on which instances are assigned to an empirical category of objects are inscrutable.

Yet the speculations of two and a half millennia, striving to eliminate the indeterminacy involved in subsuming a presumed instance of a class to that class, seem to have been misguided. This indeterminacy is irreducible, but its comprehension is safely controlled by tacit integration.

Tacit knowing commonly integrates groups of particulars to their joint meaning. Members of a class like a species, a family, a language—or members of any other group properly denoted by a single universal term—possess a joint meaning. Moreover, the meaning of a class is an aspect of reality for it points to yet unrevealed joint properties of its members. If the joint appearance of disparate members of a class in the conception of a class should need support by analogy, I would think once more of a binocular sight uniting two slightly different images in a single image of a different sensory character; or of the fact that the way we see an object integrates, among many other events in the body, innumerable memories beyond con-

---

[3]In his contribution to the Symposium on Logic and Psychology at the Convention of the American Psychological Association in 1967, Quine ascribed the identification of specimens of a class to undefined native powers, and also showed that the general features of a class cannot be empirically demonstrated. He regards this as an instance of the inscrutability of the categoricals. Cf. Quine (1960, p. 60f).

scious recollection; or of a metaphor fusing two disparate ideas in a powerful joint meaning or, again, of the way we instantly understand a novel chain of words conveying a joint meaning we have never before encountered.

Principles of Explanation

Once we have fully realized the structure of the tacit triad, the recognition and acceptance of its functions become irresistible. I shall demonstrate this by discussing the way in which we produce a scientific explanation. Our capacity to look for an explanation depends on our propensity to be puzzled. But to be puzzled implies a judgment. For example, most physicists believe today that is is nonsensical to be puzzled by the fact that one radium atom decomposes today and another perhaps 50 years later, since there can be no explanation for this. Some scientists, however, oppose this view and this opposition implies a fundamental difference of opinion. Furthermore, it is useless to be puzzled by events which, although they may be explicable in principle, are not ripe for explanation, or are not worth the trouble of explaining them. There are many variations of the advisability of being puzzled. In any case, a scientific explanation must serve to dispel puzzlement.

Relief from puzzlement, however, may be attained by other means than that of explanation, and such cases throw light on explanation itself. Suppose we are puzzled by the way an intricate piece of machinery is constructed and the way it works, or by the layout of a building in which we keep losing our way. What we are seeking here is an understanding of the machine or the building—an insight into them, but not an explanation. Such insight is a partic-

ular type of tacit integration that I have not yet mentioned. Its subsidiary items are the particulars of the complex entity—the machine, or the rooms in the building—and when we integrate these particulars and thus bring out their joint meaning, their puzzling aspect is transformed into a lucid image. This process is the insight that relieves our puzzlement.

Such insight is in general not an image that can be seen on a sheet of paper. For it often serves to illuminate a spatial arrangement of opaque objects, like complex machines and buildings. The anatomy of a complex living thing, or a complex arrangement of geological strata, or a complex atomic arrangement in crystals, may also be baffling and can be understood only by an act of insight. But any plane aspect can give only a fragmentary view of such systems and only by combining such aspects in the imagination can a three-dimensional understanding of the aggregate be achieved. Such insight is a purely mental fact, like any other focal target, comprising a large number of subsidiaries. Such insight differs, however, from all the focal targets (like those of stereo vision, reading a sentence, exploration of a cavity, etc.) that I have mentioned before, in that this focal target does not lie away from the subsidiaries, but coincides in our imagination with the spectacle of the aggregate of which it is our insight. It signifies that the imaginative probing of a puzzling aggregate has established in it an intelligible coherence.

If this coherence can be formulated in explicit terms, it can amount to the kind of discovery exemplified by Whewell in the discovery of Kepler's planetary laws. But its area can be extended also in the opposite direction, down to the level of animal intelligence as in the classic experiments of Wolfgang Köhler on the powers of insight in chimpanzees. The chimpanzee, presented with a string slung doubly across a rod, realized that the string could not be disengaged by pulling at its end, but first must be unwound. Returning to human thought, we note that biology frequently starts with the question, "How does it work?" much as we start when we try to understand complex machinery. Furthermore, I have shown previously that we understand living things, the functioning of their organs, and the working of their intelligence, by indwelling them, which is also an act of insight. Similar insight is involved in taxonomy which orders biological specimens much as X-ray crystallography does in establishing the space group to which a crystalline specimen belongs.

Thus the establishment of coherence has many forms, some tacitly known, others explicitly formulated, some in common use and others forming part of science.

This brings us back to the subject of scientific explanation. One possibility for extending the recognition of coherence in nature consists in subsuming a natural law within a more general law of which it is a special case. This procedure has been singled out by modern philosophers from J. S. Mill (1943) to Carl G. Hempel (Hempel, 1964; Hempel & Oppenheim, 1948) and Ernest Nagel (1961) as constituting the scientific explanation of natural phenomena. But thus to limit the study of a wide area to the analysis of a fragment of it obscures the subject. Michael Scriven (1962) has criticized this analysis of explanation, and has suggested that concepts condemned by many logicians "as psychological not logical"—for exam-

ple, understanding, belief, judgment—might have to be returned to circulation. My account of relief from puzzlement by the spreading of coherence extends Scriven's criticism. To define the explanation of an event as its subsumption under a general law leaves unexplained its capacity to relieve puzzlement and isolates it from numerous other, more fundamental, acts which have this capacity. Explanation must be understood as a particular form of insight.

The consequences of striving for strictness are similar here to those arising in the case of behaviorism. The actual subject matter is restricted to a fragment found suitable for formalization. This formalization, if carried out strictly, would produce a result that has no bearing on the subject matter, but by calling it an "explanation" one imbues it with the memory of that informal act of the mind which it was supposed to replace.

Such a denial of mental powers avoids its ultimate consequences by borrowing the qualities of the very powers it sets out to eliminate. I have called this a pseudosubstitution. A pseudosubstitution is a gesture of intellectual self-destruction that is kept within safe bounds by its inconsistency. I have mentioned this practice in my critique of behaviorism and of the simulation of tacit integration by computers; our culture is pervaded by such false intellectual pretenses.

Empirical Generalization

If the orthodox theory of scientific explanation is misleading, the treatment of empirical generalization is equally so. Without going into detail, I may point out here three major errors which have resulted from the attempt to define empirical validity by strict criteria. First, since no formal procedure could be found for having a good idea from which to start on an enquiry, philosophers virtually abandoned the attempt to understand how this is done. Second, having arrived at the conclusion that no formal rule of inference can establish a valid empirical generalization, it was denied that any such generalization could be derived from experimental data—while ignoring the fact that valid generalizations are commonly arrived at by empirical enquiries based on *informal* procedures. Third, it was claimed that a hypothesis is strictly refutable by a single piece of conflicting evidence—an illusory claim, since one cannot formally identify a contradictory piece of evidence.

I established these mistakes in *Science, Faith and Society* (Polanyi, 1946) and also developed there some ideas about the informal powers which guide the pursuit of science and provide criteria for accepting its results. Underlying these ideas was the assumption that science was based on our powers to discern coherence in nature. This discernment is what sight and other senses do on the physiological level in the act of perception and I generalized these powers to include scientific discovery. I said that "the capacity of scientists to guess the presence of shapes as tokens of reality differs from the capacity of our ordinary perception only by the fact that it can integrate shapes presented to it in terms which the perception of ordinary people cannot readily handle [p. 24]."

Since that was written, I have tried to pursue systematically the kinship of perception and scientific discovery. Among earlier writers I relied for my work on Poincaré (1908), Hadamard

(1945), and Polya (1945), and confirmation of my position came later in the works of philosophers criticizing the hypothetico-deductive method. Fuller confirmation was to be found in the admirable *Harvard Case Histories in Experimental Science* directed by J. B. Conant (1957). The work in Thomas S. Kuhn's (1962) book *The Structure of Scientific Revolutions* brought further confirmation of my views in detail, and the analysis of science by Leonard K. Nash (1963) in *The Nature of the Natural Sciences* has combined my own views with those of other authors in a presentation of science as an insight into the nature of reality. A few years ago I experienced the wonderful surprise of finding my basic assumptions anticipated by Whewell. I have illustrated this previously in a quotation in this paper.

VISUAL PERCEPTION

In my earlier section on "Indwelling" I have moved fast over a wide range of subjects. I have described how meaning is displaced outward because we have no effective focal awareness of the body; next I explained the feeling we have of being in our body and included in this feeling our from-awareness of other subsidiaries, so that finally we arrived at recognizing how we know another mind. Carrying these results forward, we can now undertake to describe visual perception as a case of tacit knowing and then use this result for defining the way the mind controls the body.

Let me spell out first how visual perception is to be interpreted as tacit knowing. Think once more of a beam of light coming from an object and entering my eyes. The responses to the

beam occur in my eyes, and in the muscles adjusting my eyes as well as those sustaining the position of my head, and they also include events in my inner ear and the effects of memories, some vivid and others not consciously recalled. These responses function as subsidiaries which I integrate to form the sight of the object; *the object as I see it is the meaning I give to the responses the object evokes in my body.*

There are three points in this theory of perception that may present difficulties, and each of these difficulties will bring up a long-standing problem of visual perception. I hope to resolve these problems by aligning the structure of visual perception with that of other cases of from-to knowledge having very different content.

The first difficulty may be found in the radical transformation of sensory qualities involved in seeing things outside in their colors and shapes as being at a particular distance and in a particular motion, and in seeing them also as a particular kind of object. For these qualities are totally different from those of the internal bodily responses of which they are supposed to be the meaning. But we may answer that such far-reaching transformations are quite common in from-to knowing. For example, the meaning of most spoken words in no way resembles the sound of the words from which we attend to this meaning of them.

Second, we may find it difficult to assume that the meaning of events inside one's body can be seen outside at some distance from one. We have seen, however, other nonvisual displacements of meaning in the case of probes and tools, and there is much experimental material showing that events generated inside the body, not capable of being experienced in themselves, may be made to evoke conscious expectations of events outside the body.

Third, one may think it difficult to accept that we should claim to be subsidiarily aware, in terms of our visual perception, of bodily events—for example, events inside the labyrinth—which we cannot experience in themselves at all. Let me say, therefore, once more that when I speak of my "subsidiary awareness" of something, I do not describe an awareness of it in the usual sense; I merely refer to the *function* of an event in affecting my awareness of its meaning, as observed at the focus of my attention. When understood in this way—which is the way I defined it from the start—subsidiary awareness will be found and accepted at all levels of consciousness.

The three difficulties I mentioned are thus disposed of, but we are still left with an important problem. Just how far should we go in tracing the responses of the body to a beam of light and including them as subsidiaries of our visual perception? For my part I can see no reason for halting our pursuit of the responses affecting visual perception at the point where they generate neural traces entering the cortex. I shall say that we are subsidiarily aware of these neural traces. And this step actually involves no extension of the perceptual mechanism accepted previously, since we can see nothing with our eyes detached from the brain. To integrate extracortical responses of the body to the sight of an object means, therefore, also to integrate their cortical traces to this sight.

Moreover, this completion of our scheme solves an important problem.

Cortical traces spread simultaneously along many lines that have no anatomical link to any single point of the brain, and thus the unity of consciousness has no representation in the brain structure. Both Sherrington and Eccles have pointed out this fundamental gap in the equivalence of brain and consciousness. The theory of perception as tacit knowing necessarily ascribes to consciousness such powers of integration which may be taken to secure the unity of conscious experience, in spite of the unconnectedness of its cortical traces.

In my explanation of visual perception as a from-to knowledge of bodily responses to a beam of light, I have relied on experimental data in which such bodily responses were recorded. We must yet ask how these two different aspects of perception—the somatic and the mental—have been established, and this will necessarily raise the problem of body and mind.

We can formulate the mind-body dualism as the disparity between the experience of a subject observing an external object like a cat, and a neurophysiologist observing the bodily mechanisms by which the subject sees the cat. The experience of the two is very different. The subject sees the cat, but does not see the mechanism he uses in seeing the cat, while, on the other hand, the neurophysiologist sees the mechanism used by the subject, but does not share the subject's sight of the cat.

Admittedly, the neurophysiologist is aware of the subject's mind seeing the cat, for up to a point he shares the subject's mind by indwelling its external workings. He sees the subject as a sentient thinking fellow man and can understand his response to the sight of the cat; for example, he can follow the subject's description of the cat. And, of course, on his part, the subject can understand the description of his own neural mechanism, although he himself cannot observe it.

But the fact remains that to see a cat differs sharply from a knowledge of the mechanism of seeing a cat. They are a knowledge of quite different things. The perception of an external thing is a from-to knowledge. It is a subsidiary awareness of bodily responses evoked by external stimuli, seen with a bearing on their meaning situated at the focus of our attention. The neurophysiologist has no experience of this integration, he has an at knowledge of the body with its bodily responses at the focus of his attention. These two experiences have a sharply different content, which represents the viable core of the traditional mind-body dualism. "Dualism" thus becomes merely an instance of the change of subject matter due to shifting one's attention from the direction on which the subsidiaries bear and focusing instead on the subsidiaries themselves.

Current neurophysiology is based on a parallelism of body and mind as two aspects of the same thing. This theory is false; but it is plausible, because body and mind are closely connected. The mind relies for its actions on the body, and since to our modern thinking matter appears more substantial than mind, it seems reasonable to assume that the body altogether determines mental actions.

I must contradict this, however briefly, by defining the actual relation of body and mind. Some principles—for example, those of physics—apply in a variety of circumstances. These circumstances are not determined by the principles in question; they are its boundary conditions, and no principle can deter-mine its own boundary conditions. When there is a principle controlling the boundary conditions of another princi-ple, the two operate jointly. In this rela-tion the first can be called the higher, the second the lower principle.

Mental principles and the principles of physiology form a pair of jointly operating principles. The mind relies for its workings on the continued operation of physiological principles, but it con-trols the boundary conditions left un-determined by physiology. This lends substance to my conclusion derived from the structure of tacit knowing, that body and mind are profoundly different singly, and not two aspects of the same thing.[4]

This disposes of mechanical deter-minism. If mind and body were two aspects of the same thing, the mind could not conceivably do anything but what the bodily mechanism prescribed. But the existence of two kinds of aware-ness—the focal and the subsidiary—distinguishes sharply between the mind as a from-to experience and the sub-sidiaries of this experience when seen

focally as a bodily mechanism. Though rooted in the body, the mind is free in its actions—exactly as our common sense knows it to be free.[5]

THE PURSUIT OF SCIENCE

By now we have collected enough evi-dence demonstrating the powers of tacit knowing. In returning, therefore, to the foundations of science which were to be the main subject of this paper, I shall expand our view of tacit knowing in the direction of its *dynamics*. This will include science in the making, from the sighting of a problem to the claiming of discov-ery.

I have previously described how we can wipe out the meaning of a word by attending directly to its physical details. Such loss of meaning can be made good by casting the mind forward to the act of saying something in which the word will have to be included with its proper meaning.

This illustrates a basic principle of tacit dynamics. The casting forward of an intention is an act of the imagina-tion. It is only the imagination that can direct our attention to a target that is as yet unsupported by subsidiaries. Al-though the lost meaning of a word is in recent memory, when our imagina-tion sallies forth seeking to restore it, this meaning is not yet present. But the imagination must feel that this lost

---

[4]My theory of irreducible levels goes back to my *Personal Knowledge* (Polanyi, 1958) and has since been developed further in a number of stages, a survey of which is to be found in my book, *The Tacit Dimension* (Polanyi, 1966). See also my paper, "Life Transcending Physics and Chemistry" (Polanyi, 1967a). An application of the theory to the body-mind relation is to be found in my paper, "The Structure of Conscious-ness" (Polanyi, 1965).

F. S. Rothschild (1958, 1962) anticipated my conclusion that the mind is the meaning of the body. His writings extend back to 1930. They are summarized in *Das Zentralnervensystem als Symbol des Erlebens*, with a briefer summary in English in 1962 (see references). He has developed this idea widely in neurophysiology and psychiatry, where I am not competent to follow him.

[5]The fact that we cannot predict what a person will do if we tell him what he would have done if we had not told him of our prediction does not disprove the deterministic character of a mechan-ical model of man. If predictability is to represent our capacity for accounting for the behavior of a system, the system must remain closed until we have verified our prediction.

meaning is available if it is to start on an action which will require the use of the word in its restored meaning. For only by thrusting in a feasible direction can the imagination succeed in evoking a lost meaning.

I shall now develop further this kind of imaginative action. Our intention of saying something normally evokes our verbal expression of it. Modern linguistics, however, has shown that most of our speech consists of sentences we have never before used; they are composed for the first time on this occasion. Yet when we start uttering such a sentence, we are as a rule confident that we shall find the words we need and bring them out in the order expressing our thought. We can speak as we do because we feel that many thousands of words are available for our novel purposes, and we can trust the powers of our imagination, bent on this purpose, *to evoke from these available resources the implementation of our purpose.*

To listen to speech and understand novel sentences is a similar action. Our imagination moves ahead of a novel text before us, trusting itself to evoke an understanding of it, and it commonly does so by evoking and combining available meanings that will match the meaning of the unprecedented sentences before us.

This is, in essence, also the way the imagination works on its major tasks. It is the way it works in search of discovery. The scientist's imagination does not roam about casting up random hypotheses to be tested by him. He starts by thrusting forward ideas he feels to be promising because he senses the availability of resources that will support them—and his imagination then goes on to hammer away in directions felt to be plausible, bringing up material that has a reasonable chance of confirming these guesses.

The scientific imagination, achieving discovery, passes through a typical life cycle. The claim of Copernicus that his system was real declared a vision of boundless unknown implications. For 60 years this vision remained quiescent. Then Kepler's imagination transformed the vision of Copernicus into a new and dynamic anticipation. He brushed aside as unreal Copernicus's fantastic system of epicycles and set out to find laws reflecting the mechanical foundations of the heliocentric order. His triumph offered a new becalmed vision to the imagination. Thus ended a life cycle.

When the imagination goes into action to start a scientific enquiry, it not only becomes more intense, but also more concrete, more specific. Although the target toward which it thrusts is yet empty, it is seen to lie in a definite direction. It represents a particular problem vaguely pointing but still always pointing to a hidden feature of reality. Once the problem is adopted, its pursuit will rely on a particular range of resources that are felt to be available in a particular direction. These resources will include the amount of labor and money needed for the quest. No problem may be undertaken unless we feel that its possible solution would be worth the probable expense.

These strangely perceptive anticipations are not arrived at either by following rules, or by relying on chance; nor are they guaranteed by a wealth of learning. Yet their practice is common and indeed indispensable; no scientist can survive in his profession unless he can make such anticipations with a reasonable degree of success. For this goal he needs exceptional gifts. But his gifts, although exceptional, are of the same kind as underlie the mere use of speech, and are actually found at work in every deliberate human action. They are intrinsic to the dynamics of all from-to knowledge, down to the simplest acts of tacit knowing.

In science the path from problem to discovery can be lengthy. The enquiry having been launched, the imagination will continue to thrust forward, guided by a sense of potential resources. It batters its path by mobilizing these resources, occasionally consolidating some of them in specific surmises. These surmises will then tentatively fill, up to a point, the hitherto empty frame of the problem.

It is a mistake to think of heuristic surmises as well-defined hypothetical statements which the scientist proceeds to test in a neutral and indeed critical spirit. Hunches often consist essentially in narrowing down the originally wider program of the enquiry. They may be most exciting, and may indeed turn out later to have been crucial, yet they are mostly far more indeterminate than the final discovery will be. The range of their indeterminacy lies at some point between that of the original problem and of its eventual solution.

Besides, the relation of the scientist to his surmises is one of passionate personal commitment. The effort that led to a surmise committed every fiber of his being to the quest; his surmises embody all his hopes.

The current theory that ignores the mechanism of tacit knowing must ignore and indeed deny such commitments. The tentativeness of the scientist's every step is then taken to show that he is uncommitted. But every step made in

the pursuit of science is *definitive,* definitive in the vital sense that it definitely disposes of the time, the effort, and the material resources used in making that step. Such investments add up with frightening speed to the whole professional life of the scientist. To think of scientific workers cheerfully trying this and trying that, calmly changing course at each failure, is a caricature of a pursuit consuming a man's whole person. Any questing surmise necessarily seeks its own confirmation.

You might expect me to conclude by showing how a problem is eventually resolved by the discovery of a coherence in nature, the hidden existence of which has first been sighted in a problem and which had become increasingly manifest by its pursuit. I must, however, first introduce another factor, the identification of which we owe to Henri Poincaré. In a classic essay included in *Science et Méthode* (1908) he described two stages in the way we hit upon an idea that promises to solve a scientific problem. The first stage consists in racking one's brains by successive sallies of the imagination, while the second, which may be delayed for hours after one has ceased one's efforts, is the spontaneous appearance of the idea one has struggled for. Poincaré says that this spontaneous process consists in the integration of some of the material mobilized by thrusts of the imagination; he also tells us that these thrusts would be useless but for the fact that they are guided by special anticipatory gifts of the scientist.

It seems plausible to assume, then, that two faculties of the mind are at work jointly from the beginning to the end of an enquiry. One is the deliberately active powers of the imagination, and the other a spontaneous process of integration, which we may call *intuition*. It is intuition that senses the presence of hidden resources for solving a problem and which launches the imagination in its pursuit. And it is intuition that forms there our surmises and which eventually selects from the material mobilized by the imagination the relevant pieces of evidence and integrates them into the solution of the problem.

But, you may ask, what about the measurements, computations, and algebraic formulae used in the pursuit and formulation of science? These are, of course, essential, but I have dealt with them when showing that the use of language is a tacit operation, both in our spoken language and in our understanding of it when spoken by others. The same applies to all other explicit thought; it can be developed and understood only by a tacit operation and it is thus based throughout on tacit knowing. All knowledge is either tacit or rooted in tacit knowing.

To sum up, I call "logic" the rules for reaching valid conclusions from premises assumed to be true. Currently logic seems to be defined instead as the rules for reaching strict conclusions from strict premises. I think we should reject this definition. No strict rules can exist for establishing empirical knowledge. Most people know this, but would urge us to accept strictness as an unattainable ideal for which to strive. But this is to turn a blind eye on tacit knowing, in which alone lies our capacity for acquiring empirical knowledge.

Our age prides itself on its unflinching frankness in calling a spade a spade and worse than that. But for all this bluntness, we are strictly Victorian when it comes to mentioning the mind, acknowledging its autonomous actions and its indeterminate range of knowing—even though all the power and beauty of thought relies on these tacit faculties.

I think we should drop these intellectual fictions, for there are reasonable alternatives that are much nearer the truth.

REFERENCES

Brentano, F. *Psychologie vom empirischem Standpunkt.* (Reprint of 1874 ed.) Leipzig: Oskar Kraus, 1942.

Chomsky, N. Review of B. F. Skinner, *Verbal behavior. Language,* 1959, **35,** 26–58.

Conant, J. B. *Harvard case histories in experimental science.* Cambridge: Harvard University Press, 1957.

Hadamard, J. *The psychology of invention in the mathematical field.* Princeton: Princeton University Press, 1945.

Helmholtz, H. von. *Handbuch der Physiologischen Optik.* Leipzig: L. Voss, 1867.

Hempel, C. G. Scientific explanation. In *Forum philosophy of science series.* Washington, D.C.: United States Information Agency, Voice of America, 1964. (Pamphlet)

Hempel, C. G., & Oppenhelm, P. Studies in the logic of explanation. *Philosophy of Science,* 1948, **15,** 135–178.

Kant, I. *Critique of pure reason.* (Trans. by N. Kemp-Smith) New York: St. Martin's Press, 1929.

Kottenhoff, H. Was ist richtiges Schen mit Umkehrbrillen und in welchem Sinne stellt sich das Sehen um? In *Psychologia Universalis.* Vol. 5. Meisenheim am Glan: A. Hain, 1961.

Kuhn, T. S. *The structure of scientific revolutions.* Chicago: University of Chicago Press, 1962.

Lashley, K. S. The problem of serial behavior. In L. A. Jeffress (Ed.), *Cerebral mechanisms in behavior. The Hixon symposium.* New York: Wiley, 1951.

Lorenz, K. Gestalt perception as fundamental to scientific knowledge. *General Systems,* 1967, **7,** 37–56.

Merleau-Ponty, M. *Phenomenology of perception.* London: Routledge, 1962.

Mill, J. S. *System of logic, ratiocinative and inductive.* Vol. 1. London: Parker, 1943. Pp. 450–505.

Nagel, E. *The structure of science.* New York: Harcourt, Brace & World, 1961.

Nash, L. K. *The nature of the natural sciences.* Boston: Little, Brown, 1963.

Piaget, J. *Psychology of intelligence.* New York: Harcourt, Brace, 1950.

Poincaré, H. *Science et méthode.* Paris: Flammarion, 1908.

Polanyi, M. *Science, faith and society.* London: Oxford University Press, 1946. (Reprinted: Chicago: University of Chicago Press, 1964).

Polanyi, M. *Personal knowledge.* Chicago: University of Chicago Press, 1958. (Rev. ed., New York: Harper Torchbooks, 1964.)

Polanyi, M. The structure of consciousness. *Brain,* 1965 (Part 4), 799–810.

Polanyi, M. *The tacit dimension.* New York: Doubleday, 1966. (Reprinted: London: Routledge, 1967.)

Polanyi, M. Life transcending physics and chemistry. *Chemical and Engineering News,* 1967, **45,** No. 35. (a)

Polanyi, M. Sense-giving and sense reading. *Philosophy,* 1967, **42,** 301. (b)

Polya, G. *How to solve it.* Princeton: Princeton University Press, 1945.

Quine, W. V. O. *Word and object.* Cambridge: M.I.T. Press, 1960.

Quine, W. V. O. In S. Koch (Chm.), Logic and psychology. Symposium presented at the meeting of the American Psychological Association, Washington, D.C., September 1967.

Rothschild, F. S. *Das Zentralnervensystem als Symbol des Erlebens.* Basel and New York: S. Karger, 1958.

Rothschild, F. S. Laws of symbolic mediation in the dynamics of self and personality. *Annals of the New York Academy of Sciences,* 1962, **96,** 774.

Ryle, G. *The concept of mind.* London: Hutchinson, 1949.

Scriven, M. Explanation, prediction and laws. In *Minnesota Studies in the Philosophy of Science.* Vol. 3. Minneapolis: University of Minnesota Press, 1962.

Skinner, B. F. *Verbal behavior* New York: Appleton-Century-Crofts, 1957.

Skinner, B. F. Behaviorism at fifty. In T. W. Wann (Ed.), *Behaviorism and phenomenology.* Chicago: University of Chicago Press, 1964.

Waismann, F. Verifiability. *Proceedings Aristotelian Society Supplement,* 1945, 19.

Wall, H. W., & Guthrie, G. M. Extinction responses to subceived stimuli. *Journal of General Psychology,* 1959, **60,** 205–210.

Whewell, W. *Philosophy and discovery.* (Quoted text written in 1856) London: John W. Parker, 1890.

FOUR
Psychophysics

8

Detection Theory and Psychophysics

John A. Swets

The application of decision theory to psychology has resulted in a theory of signal detection which has revolutionized psychophysics and which is having a very broad impact on psychology as a whole. The methods of psychophysics have always been applied broadly in psychology, so it is to be expected that any methodological change that occurs in psychophysics will influence the rest of psychology. It is presumably for this reason that the theory of signal detection has come to receive great emphasis in many of the newer textbooks in psychology.

   With the theory of signal detection, the old concept of "threshold" is abandoned. The threshold fails to get at the purely sensory limitations it was intended to delineate. Thresholds change as a function of non-sensory variables, such as "expectations" or signal probability or the consequences of hits and false alarms. The theory of signal detection is designed to extract the purely sensory limitations from limitations imposed by these other variables. In the following article, Swets provides a relatively simple summary of the meaning and impact of the theory of signal detection.

I am particularly pleased to discuss the application in psychophysics of the general theory of signal detection at a symposium commemorating Fechner's founding work. Although this effort is in part a theoretical and experimental critique of Fechner's principal concepts

Reprinted from *Psychometrika*, 1961, **26**, 49–63, by permission of the author.

and methods, which indicates that they should be replaced, I suspect that he would have welcomed it warmly—in fact, that he would have been among the first to recognize the value of these new tools had they become available in his time. I suspect this on the basis of his interest in Bernoulli's early ideas about statistical decision ([3], p. 284), and in the notion of subthreshold, or "negative," sensations ([3], p. 293)—two central concepts in the psychophysical application of the theory of signal detectability.

The theory of signal detectability (henceforth called TSD) was developed most fully in the years 1952–1954 by Peterson, Birdsall, and Fox (35) at the University of Michigan, and by Van Meter and Middleton (55) at the Massachusetts Institute of Technology. At the same time, although working apart from TSD, Smith and Wilson (39) at the Massachusetts Institute of Technology and Munson and Karlin (33) at the Bell Telephone Laboratories were conducting psychoacoustic experiments that demonstrated the relevance of the theory to human observers; their experimental results led them to suggest a similar theory of the human detection process. Meanwhile, Tanner and Swets (52, 53) were making a formal application of TSD in the field of vision.

Since then, other general discussions and reviews similar to this one have appeared; I should mention the 1955 paper by Swets, Tanner, and Birdsall (47) that includes a complete review of the data collected in vision; the 1956 paper by Tanner, Swets, and Green (54) that includes several studies in audition; Green's (22) exposition in the current series of tutorial articles in the *Journal of the Acoustical Society;* and Licklider's chapter (30) in the series edited by Koch for the American Psychological Association. The present discussion is distinguished from the first three of these in that it is not tutorial, detailed, nor documentary. The statistical and psychophysical bases of the work are not considered here, and no data are presented.

In this sense, the present discussion is most like Licklider's. Its only advantage is that of time—it comes three years later and is based on three times as many papers.

It will be helpful to emphasize at the outset (as Green [22] has suggested) that TSD is a combination of two distinct theoretical structures: (i) statistical decision theory, or the theory of statistical inference, as developed principally by Wald (59) who built upon the earlier work of Neyman and Pearson (34), and (ii) the theory of ideal observers, initiated by Siegert (see 29). In TSD, statistical decision theory is used to treat the detection task as a decision process, specifically, as an instance of testing statistical hypotheses. This enables TSD to deal effectively with the long-standing problem in psychophysics of the control and measurement of the *criterion for signal existence* that is employed by the observer. The theory of ideal observers makes it possible to relate the level of the detection performance attained by a real observer to the mathematically ideal detection performance. The mathematical ideal is the upper limit on the detection performance that is imposed by the environment. This limit is stated in terms of measurable parameters of the signal and of the masking noise for a variety of types of signal and noise. It is often instructive, as we shall see, to consider the nature of the discrepancy between observed and ideal performance.

We have used TSD as a framework for the experimental study of sensory systems. The framework role suggests itself for the theory, because the theory specifies the nature of the detection process, and it defines the experimental methods that are appropriate, given its conception of the detection process. TSD is also, to a limited extent, but to a far larger extent than is generally recognized, a "substantive" theory of vision and audition. We have examined the correspondence between the human observer's detection process and the process described by the theory. The methods that the theory prescribes have been compared with others available. We have examined some substantive implications of the theory and have applied the theory and methods to other substantive problems.

I shall discuss, in turn, how the decision-theory aspects and the ideal-observer concepts of TSD have been applied to human behavior, with an emphasis on theory and experimental method. Unfortunately, the time available will permit only a slight admixture of substantive results. I shall concentrate on the simplest detection task, mentioning only briefly extensions of the theory and experimental procedures to more complex perceptual tasks.

DECISION ASPECTS OF SIGNAL DETECTION

As I have noted, the decision-theory part of TSD impressed us strongly at our first acquaintance because it gave promise of dealing with a difficult problem in psychophysics—namely, the determination of the dichotomy between the observer's positive and negative reports, between stimuli he reports he does and does not see or hear, etc. To state the problem otherwise, it is the definition of the observer's criterion for making a positive response. Let us review briefly just how TSD deals with this problem.

The Fundamental Detection Problem and the Concept of the Likelihood Ratio

I shall first define a particular detection problem, a very simple one—in terms of TSD, the fundamental detection problem. The observer is instructed to attend to a certain class of physical events (perhaps visual or auditory) that the experimenter generates during a specified interval of time, and to make a report following the interval about these events. Coincident with the specified observation interval, presumably, is some (neural) activity of the relevant sensory system. This activity forms the sensory basis, a part of the total basis, for the observer's report. This *sensory response,* as we shall call it for the moment (meanwhile noting that the sensory activity coincident with the specified temporal interval need not be entirely a response to the physical events produced by the experimenter), may be *in fact* either simple or complex, it may have many dimensions or few, it may be qualitative or quantitative, it may be anything—the exact, or even the general, nature of the actual sensory response is of no concern to the application of the theory.

Only two assumptions are made about the sensory response. One is that the sensory response that occurs in the presence of a given signal is *variable.* In particular, the response is perturbed by random interference or "noise"—noise produced inadvertently by the experimenter's equipment for generating stimuli, or deliberately introduced by the experimenter, or inherent in the sensory system. It is assumed that some noise, whatever its origin, is always present. Thus the sensory response will vary over time in the absence of any signal, as well as vary from one presentation to the next of what is ostensibly the same signal. In the fundamental detection problem, the observation interval contains either the noise alone, or a specified signal and the noise. The observer's report is limited to these two classes of stimulus events—he says "Yes" (the interval contained the specified signal) or "No" (the interval did not contain the specified signal, i.e., it contained noise alone). Note that he does not say whether or not he *heard* (or *saw*) the signal—but whether or not, under the circumstances, he prefers the decision that it was present to the decision that it was absent.

The second assumption made about the sensory response is that, whatever it may be in fact, it may be represented (insofar as it affects the observer's report) as a *unidimensional* variable. In particular, the observer is assumed to be aware of the probability that each possible sensory response will occur during an observation interval containing noise alone, and also during an observation interval containing a signal in addition to the noise. He is assumed to base his report on the ratio of these two quantities, the *likelihood ratio*. The likelihood ratio derived from any observation interval is a real, nonzero number and may thus be represented along a single dimension.

The Likelihood Ratio Criterion

According to TSD, following statistical decision theory, the observer's report following an observation interval will depend upon whether or not the likelihood ratio measured in that interval exceeds some critical value of the likelihood ratio, some *criterion*. The criterion (or decision rule) is presumed to be established by the observer in accordance with his detection goal and the relevant situational parameters. For example, if his goal is to maximize the expected value of his decisions, i.e., to maximize his total payoff over several trials in which each of the four possible decision outcomes has a value associated with it, then his criterion will depend on these values and on the *a priori* probability that a signal will occur on a given trial. Statistical decision theory prescribes the optimal criterion for any values assumed by this set of parameters. (We shall discuss shortly the relationship between the optimal criterion and the criterion used by the human observer.) The observer may try to achieve any of a number of other detection goals, and there will be, in general, a different optimal criterion corresponding to each goal. The criterion under each of these goals, i.e., under each definition of optimum, can be expressed in terms of the likelihood ratio (35, 59). (It can be shown that the optimal criterion is defined equally as well on any monotonic function of the likelihood ratio—the number corresponding to the criterion will differ, but the decisions will be the same.)

We next consider a probability defined on the variable likelihood ratio, in particular, the probability that each value of the likelihood ratio will occur with each of the classes of possible stimulus events, noise alone, and signal plus noise. We have, therefore, two probability distributions. The one associated with signal plus noise will have a greater mean—indeed, its mean is assumed to increase monotonically with increases in the signal strength. If the observer follows the procedure described (i.e., if he reports that the signal that was specified is present whenever the likelihood ratio exceeds a certain criterion, and that noise alone is present whenever it is less than this criterion) then, from the fourfold stimulus-response matrix that results, we can extract two independent, quantitative measures—a measure of the observer's criterion and a measure of his sensitivity.

The Operating Characteristic

The important concept here is the *operating characteristic* (OC). Suppose we induce the observer to change his criterion from one set of trials to another. Suppose for each criterion we plot the proportion of *Yes* reports made when noise alone was present (the proportion of false alarms). Then as the criterion varies, we trace a single curve (running from 0 to 1.0 on both coordinates) showing the proportion of hits to be a nondecreasing function of the proportion of false alarms. This curve describes completely the successive stimulus-response matrices that are obtained, since the complements of these two proportions are the proportions that belong in the other two cells of the matrix. The particular curve generated in this fashion depends upon the signal and noise parameters and upon the observer's sensitivity. The point on this curve that corresponds to any given stimulus-response matrix represents the criterion employed by the observer in generating that matrix.

We have found that, to a good approximation, the OC curves produced by human observers correspond to theoretical OC curves based on normal probability distributions (47, 54). (This is an empirical fact; it is not necessary to make in advance any particular assumptions about the form of the probability distributions in order to use the OC analysis.) These OC curves have the convenient property of being characterized by a single parameter: the difference between the means of the signal-plus-noise and noise-alone distributions divided by the standard deviation of the noise distribution. This parameter has been called d'. Further, the slope of the curve at any point is equal to the value of the likelihood ratio criterion that produces that point. Thus, to repeat, from any stimulus-response matrix, one can obtain two independent measures: one an index of the sensitivity of the observer to the particular signal and noise used, the other an index of his criterion.

The Experimental Invariance of d'

It has been shown experimentally, in both vision (47) and audition (54), that the measure d' remains relatively constant with changes in the criterion. Thus, TSD provides a measure of sensitivity that is practically uncontaminated by attitudinal or motivational variables, i.e., by variables that might be expected to affect the observer's criterion.

It has also been shown that the measure d' remains relatively invariant over different experimental procedures. Specifically, we have compared estimates of d' obtained from the Yes–No procedure (i.e., the fundamental detection problem) with estimates of d' obtained from a forced-choice procedure. Under forced-choice, n temporal intervals were defined on each trial, exactly one of which contained the signal; the observer selected one of the n intervals. The probability of a correct response as a function of d' can be calculated by using the empirical OC curve or by making some assumptions about the form of the probability distributions. We have calculated this probability as a function of d', under the assumptions that the probability distributions are normal and of equal variance. The relations between the probability of a correct response and d', for several different numbers of alternatives in a forced-choice trial, have been tabulated (15).

For both vision (52) and audition (41) the estimates of d' from the Yes–No procedure and from the four-interval forced-choice procedure are very nearly the same. We have further found remarkably consistent estimates of d' from forced-choice procedures with 2, 3, 4, 6, and 8 intervals (41). Also, the rating procedure in which the observer chooses one of *several* categories of certainty about the presence of a signal in a *single* interval yields OC curves (or estimates of d') in both vision (42) and audition (14), that are indistinguishable from those obtained with the Yes–No procedure. These results are particularly fortunate since, as Licklider has pointed out, they represent "a break in the trend . . . to regard the results of a psychophysical test as meaningless except in relation to the procedure of the test" ([30], p. 73). It is evidently possible to have one rather than many psychophysical sciences.

The Observer's Criterion and the Optimal Criterion

I have mentioned earlier that we would return to a brief discussion of the relationship of the observer's criterion to the criterion specified as optimal by statistical decision theory. Let us note, first, that TSD can be a useful tool in analyzing psychophysical data if it is merely the case that the observer controls a criterion (in terms of the likelihood ratio or some monotonic function of the likelihood ratio), whether or not his criterion bears any relationship to the optimal one. We have worked with the expected-value definition of the optimal criterion (in which the optimal criterion is a function of the *a priori* probability of signal occurrence and the values associated with the decision outcomes) simply because the manipulation of these parameters is a convenient and effective way of inducing the observer to change his criterion in a psychophysical experiment. This manipulation enables us to trace an empirical OC curve. Strictly speaking, whether or not the observer adjusts his criterion in terms of these variables in everyday life is of no concern in the laboratory. Neither are we concerned with subjective probabilities or the linearity of the utility of money. We are, of course, interested in the result we observed: the observer's successive criteria in our experiments were highly correlated with the optimal expected-value criteria, that is, the human observer is capable of approximating the optimal criterion. Even though our experimental situation is artificial in this respect, the result teaches us something about the observer's capabilities.

I should quickly add that it is difficult to compare the observer's criterion and the optimal criterion in more than a correlational sense. The reason for this is that the function relating the expected value to the criterion is very flat: any criterion within a very wide range (a range of as much as 0.40 in false-alarm rate) will result in a payoff that is at least 90 per cent of the maximum payoff possible. Nonetheless, the fact that our observers respond to a change in *a priori* probabilities or decision values by setting a new criterion—the fact that they can adopt successively and repeatedly as many as five criteria showing a perfect rank-order correlation with the optimal criteria—has made it possible to achieve in our experiments what Graham has called "a quantification of the instruction stimuli" ([18], p. 868). Egan (who has been successful in controlling the criterion with such verbal instructions as "lax," "moderate," and "strict" [see 14]) is now preparing to examine, in more detail than was done previously, the relationship between the observer's criterion and various definitions of the optimal criterion, i.e., the relationship between quantitative instruction stimuli and quantitative estimates of the resulting criterion (10).

IMPLICATIONS FOR PSYCHOPHYSICAL METHODS

I would now like to return to the proposition that TSD provides a framework for the study of sensory systems, in particular, that it specifies the experimental procedures that may be properly used given its conception of the nature of the detection process.

Perhaps the most salient procedural implications of TSD are those concerned with the use of catch trials (trials containing noise alone) and the treatment of positive (Yes) responses made on those trials. As I have remarked, when we first became acquainted with TSD, it was apparent that the theory would be val-

uable in psychophysics because it spoke forth eloquently on exactly those conceptual and procedural problems that many of us believed to be handled inadequately in classical psychophysics. Licklider has expressed our discomfiture very aptly: "More and more, workers in the field are growing dissatisfied with the classical psychophysical techniques, particularly with the method of 'adjustment' or 'production' that lets the listener attend to the stimulus for an unspecified length of time before deciding that he can 'just hear it' and with the methods of 'limits' and 'constants' (in their usual forms) that ask the listener to report 'present' or 'absent' when he already knows 'present.' It is widely felt that the 'thresholds' yielded by these procedures are on such an insecure semantic basis that they cannot serve as good building blocks for a quantitative science" ([30], p. 75).

It is simply not adequate to employ a few catch trials, enough to monitor the observer, and then to remind him to avoid false-positive responses each time one is made. This procedure merely serves to drive the criterion up to a point where it cannot be measured, and it can be shown that the calculated threshold varies by as much as 6 db as the criterion varies in this unmeasurable range. Precision is also sacrificed when highly trained observers are employed along with the untestable assumption that they do maintain a constant high criterion. Even if all laboratories should be fortunate enough to have such observers, the figure of 6 db is a reasonable estimate of the range of variation among "constant criterion" observers in different laboratories. To be sure, for some problems, this amount of variability is not bothersome; for others, however, it is.

Experiments have also shown that the use of enough catch trials to provide a good estimate of the probability of a false-positive response will again leave one far short of the precision attainable—if this estimate is used to correct the data on signal trials for spurious positive responses on the grounds that these responses are independent of sensory-determined positive responses. Suffice it to say here that several experimenters, in a number of different experiments in different laboratories, have failed to find any evidence for the independent existence of a sensory threshold, a threshold that is independent of the probability of a false-positive report. We find *response* thresholds aplenty—any criterion used by the observer is such—but no measurable *sensory* thresholds. Of course, the validity of the various classical procedures depends directly on the validity of the concept of a sensory threshold.

In view of a large collection of data, it seems to me to be only reasonable (1) to add enough noise in psychophysical experiments (a background of some kind) to bring the noise to a level where it can be measured, (2) to manipulate the response criterion so that it lies in a range where it can be measured, (3) to include enough catch trials to obtain a good estimate of this response criterion, and (4) to use a method of analysis that yields a measure of sensitivity that is independent of the response criterion. This prescription will stand, I believe, until such time that it becomes possible to demonstrate that all traces of noise can be eliminated from a sensory experiment. The only other qualifying remark I would make is a positive one: we can forgo estimating the response criterion in a forced-choice experiment. Experi-

ence has shown that we can reasonably view the observer as choosing the interval having the greatest "sensory response" associated with it, without regard to any criterion. For this reason, the forced-choice procedure is a highly desirable procedure for use in purely sensory studies.

THE THEORY OF IDEAL OBSERVERS

The portion of TSD that pertains to the optimal or ideal performance in the sense of detectability, or sensitivity, rather than the decision criterion, is known as the theory of ideal observers. This theory gives, for several types of signal and noise, the maximum possible detectability as a function of the parameters of the signal and noise (35). Under certain assumptions, this relationship can be stated precisely. We have regarded the case of the "signal specified exactly" (in which everything about the signal is known, including its frequency, phase, starting time, duration, and amplitude) as a useful standard in psychoacoustic experiments. In this case, the maximum d' is equal to $\sqrt{2E/N_0}$ in which E is the signal energy, or time integral of power and N_0 is the noise power in a one-cycle band. Recently, an ideal observer applicable to visual signals has also been developed (51).

We believe that a theory of ideal performance is a good starting point in working toward a descriptive theory. Ideal theories involve few variables, and these are simply described. Experiments can be used to uncover whatever additional variables may be needed to describe the performance of real observers. Alternatively, experiments can be used to indicate how the ideal theory can be degraded, i.e., to identify those functions of which the ideal detection device must be deprived, in order to describe accurately real behavior. Measures can be defined to describe the real observer's efficiency; Tanner and Birdsall (50) have, for example, described the efficiency measure η as used in the expression

$$d'_{obs} = \eta \sqrt{2E/N_0}$$

in which the value of d' is that observed experimentally. They have suggested that substantive problems may be illuminated by the computation of η for different types of signals and for different parameters of a given type of signal. The observed variation of this measure should be helpful in determining the range over which the human observer can adjust the parameters of his sensory system to match different signal parameters. (He is, after all, quite proficient in detecting a surprisingly large number of different signals.) This variation should also be helpful in determining which parameters of a signal the observer is not using, or not using precisely, in his detection process.

The human observer, of course, performs less well than does the ideal observer in the great majority of, if not in all, detection tasks. The interesting question, one that usually turns out to be a heuristic question, concerns not the amount but the nature of the discrepancy that is observed. The next few paragraphs illustrate how asking this question led to information about certain substantive issues in audition and vision.

We find that the human observer performs less well than the ideal observer defined for the case of the "signal specified exactly." That is, the human observer's "psychometric function" (the proportion of correct positive responses as a function of the signal energy) is shifted to the right. Further, the slope of the human observer's function is greater than that of the ideal function for this particular case—a result sometimes referred to as low-signal suppression. Let us consider three possible reasons for these discrepancies.

First, the human observer may well have a *noisy decision process*, whereas the ideal decision process is noiseless. For example, the human observer's criterion may be unstable. If he vacillates between two criteria, the resulting point of his OC curve will be on a straight line connecting the points corresponding to the two criteria; this average point falls below the OC curve (a curve with smoothly decreasing slope) on which the two criteria are located. Again, the observer's decision axis may not be continuous—as far as we know, it may be divided into a relatively small number of categories. This possibility has not been studied intensively.

A second likely reason for the deviation from ideal is the *noise inherent in the human sensory systems.* We have attempted to estimate the amount of internal noise (including noise in the decision process and in the sensory system) in two ways: by examining the decisions of an observer over several presentations of the same signal and noise (on tape) (46), and by examining the correlation among the responses of several observers to a single presentation (2, 23). Both Egan and Green (10, 24) are continuing this line of work with taped presentations.

A third, and favored, possibility is *faulty memory.* This explanation is favored, *a priori,* because it easily accounts not only for the shift of the human's psychometric function but also for the greater slope of his function. The reasoning proceeds as follows: if the detection process involves some sort of tuning of the receptive apparatus, and if the observer's memory of the characteristics of the incoming signal is faulty (these characteristics being amplitude, frequency, starting time, duration, phase in audition, and location in vision), then the observer is essentially confronted with a signal not specified exactly, but specified only statistically. He has some uncertainty about the incoming signal. When we introduce some uncertainty into our calculations of the psychometric function of the ideal detector (35), we find that performance falls off as uncertainty increases, and that this decline in performance is greater for weak signals than strong ones. That is, a family of theoretical uncertainty curves shows progressively steeper slopes coinciding with progressive shifts to the right. This is intuitively proper—the accuracy of knowledge about signal characteristics is less critical for strong signals, since strong signals carry more information about these characteristics with themselves. For visual (51) and auditory data (22) the slopes are fitted well by the theoretical curve that corresponds to uncertainty among approximately 100 orthogonal signal alternatives. It is not difficult to imagine that the product of the uncertainties about the time, location, and frequency of the signals used in these experiments could be as high as 100.

It is possible to obtain empirical corroboration of this theoretical analysis of uncertainty due to faulty memory. This is achieved by providing various aids to memory within the experimental proce-dure. (Tanner [48] has used this technique in auditory studies; Green [22] has replicated his results in audition, and Green and Swets [28] have obtained similar results in visual studies.) In these experiments, the memory for frequency is made unnecessary by introducing a continuous tone or light (a carrier) of the same frequency as the signal, so that the signal to be detected is an increment in the carrier. This procedure also eliminates the need for phase memory in audition and location memory in vision. In further experiments, instead of a continuous carrier, a pulsed carrier (one that starts and stops along with the signal) is used in order to make memory for starting time and duration unnecessary. In all of these experiments a forced-choice procedure is used, so that the memory for amplitude beyond a single trial can also be considered irrelevant. In this way, all of the information thought to be relevant may be contained in the immediate situation. Experimentally, our observers' psychometric functions show progressively flatter slopes as we introduce more and more memory aids in this way. In fact, when all of the aids mentioned above are used, the observer's slope parallels that for the ideal observer without uncertainty, and it is as little as 3 db from the ideal curve in absolute value.

EXAMPLES OF SUBSTANTIVE PROBLEMS STUDIED IN THIS FRAMEWORK

I shall simply list some other examples of substantive problems in vision and audition that have been studied within the framework of TSD. A way of treating one set of related problems follows directly from statistical theory. These are problems in which the observation is expanded in one way or another: (i) the observation interval is lengthened, (ii) the number of observations preceding a decision is increased, (iii) the number of signals presented in a given interval is increased, or (iv) the number of observers concentrating on the same signal is increased. From statistical theory, the distribution of the sum of n random variables with the same mean and variance has a mean equal to n times the mean and a variance equal to n times the variance. Since the measure of detectability d' is equal to the mean of the hypothetical probability distribution that is due to the signal (we can consider the mean of the noise distribution to be zero) divided by the standard deviation (the square root of the variance), we would predict that, as the number of signals or observations is increased, the measure d' will increase as the square root of the number. Or we might think in terms of the result in statistics that the standard deviation of the estimate of a population mean decreases as the square root of the number of samples, and be led to the same prediction. Experiments in audition have shown d' to increase, within certain limits, as $\sqrt{t}$, where t is the duration of a tone-burst signal in white noise (26), and to increase as $\sqrt{n}$, where n is the number of tonal components of a complex signal (up to 16) (27), or the number of observation intervals preceding a decision (up to five) (46), or the number of observers (up to three) (2).

A persistent favorite among the substantive problems in audition that have been studied experimentally in this setting is the problem of frequency analysis, or the problem of the critical band. Fletcher's (17) original experiment, in which the width of the band of noise that masked a tonal signal was varied systematically, has been repeated with signals of a specified duration and with a different type of analysis (54). A variety of other procedures has been used in the attack on this problem, including signals of uncertain frequency (7, 20, 46, 54, 56, 57), complex signals compounded of several frequencies (21, 27, 31), and signals consisting of a band of noise (19). Other studies of substantive problems that were guided by TSD include studies of reaction time (45), physiological recording (16), and some aspects of color vision (40).

EXTENDED APPLICATIONS TO MORE COMPLEX PROBLEMS

I have spoken, so far, primarily about simple detection procedures (Yes–No and forced-choice procedures involving a single, specified observation interval) employing single, simple signals (a tone burst in white noise, or a spot of light on a larger uniform background). I should at least mention some of the areas in which extensions of the basic theory have been applied to somewhat more complex problems.

The theory has been applied to the recognition or identification process as well as to the detection process: to the recognition of one of two frequencies (49), and to problems requiring both detection and recognition (43). Very recently, following Anderson's (1) work in statistics, some preliminary attempts have been made to deal with the recognition of one of a large number of signals and thus to move closer to some significant problems in perception (25, 32).

Following Wald's (58) developments in sequential analysis, we have studied the problem of deferred decision (44). In this problem, the observer decides after each observation interval whether to make a terminal decision (Yes or No) or to request another observation before making a terminal decision. Values and costs are assigned to the possible outcomes of a terminal decision, and a fixed cost is assessed for each additional observation that is requested. This deferred decision paradigm, it will be recognized, represents another way of striking out in the direction of realism. We have examined in this way the trading relationship that commonly exists in perceptual tasks between time and error. In a similar vein, the theory has recently been extended to handle the case of detection in which the observation interval is not specified for the observer— the so-called vigilance, or low-probability watch, problem (13).

Still another more complex area of research that has received extensive study is that of speech communication. Many of the techniques employed in studies with simple signals have been used with success here, including operating characteristics, confidence ratings, repetition of items, deferred decisions, and analyses in terms of the degree of uncertainty that exists (4, 5, 6, 8, 9, 11, 12, 36, 37, 38).[1]

[1] A scheme for organizing the rather extensive bibliography of this paper (and other related publications) may be helpful. As it happens, an organization is most effectively accomplished in terms of personalities. After the original applications of TSD, Tanner, Green, and I have gone somewhat separate ways. Tanner's efforts have been directed principally toward an examination of the role of models in experimental studies and toward applications of the concept of the ideal observer; Green has concentrated on substantive problems in audition, especially the problem of frequency analysis; I have been primarily concerned with the decision process and with applications of the theory to psychophysical tasks that are less idealized than those studied initially. Egan, Pollack, and Clarke have employed the theory in studying various problems in speech communication and have contributed a number of studies dealing with methodological problems.

REFERENCES

1. Anderson, T. W. *An introduction to multivariate statistical analysis.* New York: Wiley, 1958.
2. Birdsall, T. G., and Swets, J. A. Unpublished work.
3. Boring, E. G. *A history of experimental psychology.* (2nd ed.). New York: Appleton Century-Crofts, 1950.
4. Carterette, E. C. Message repetition and receiver confirmation of messages in noise. *J. acoust. Soc. Amer.,* 1958, **30,** 846–855.
5. Clarke, F. R. Confidence ratings, second-choice responses, and confusion matrices in intelligibility tests. *J. acoust. Soc. Amer.,* 1960, **32,** 35–46.
6. Clarke, F. R. Constant-ratio rule in speech communication. *J. acoust. Soc. Amer.,* 1957, **29,** 715–720.
7. Creelman, C. D. Detection of signals of uncertain frequency. *J. acoust. Soc. Amer.,* 1960, **32,** 805–809.
8. Decker, L., and Pollack, I. Confidence ratings and message reception for filtered speech. *J. acoust. Soc. Amer.,* 1958, **30,** 432–434.
9. Egan, J. P. Monitoring task in speech communication. *J. acoust. Soc. Amer.,* 1957, **29,** 482–489.
10. Egan, J. P. Personal communication.
11. Egan, J. P., and Clarke, F. R. Source and receiver behavior in the use of a criterion. *J. acoust. Soc. Amer.,* 1956, **28,** 1267–1269.
12. Egan, J. P., Clarke, F. R., and Carter-

ette, E. C. On the transmission and confirmation of messages in noise. *J. acoust. Soc. Amer.*, 1956, **28**, 536–550.

13. Egan, J. P., Greenberg, G. Z., and Schulman, A. I. Detection of signals presented at random time. *J. acoust. Soc. Amer.*, 1959, 31, 1579. (Abstract).

14. Egan, J. P., Schulman, A. I., and Greenberg, G. Z. Operating characteristics determined by binary decisions and by ratings. *J. acoust. Soc. Amer.*, 1959, **31**, 768–773.

15. Elliott, P. B. Tables of d'. Tech. Rep. No. 97, Electronic Defense Group, Univ. Michigan, 1959.

16. Fitz Hugh, R. The statistical detection of threshold signals in the retina. *J. gen. Physiol.*, 1957, **40**, 925–948.

17. Fletcher, H. Auditory patterns. *Rev. mod. Phys.*, 1940, **12**, 47–65.

18. Graham, C. H. Visual perception. In S. S. Stevens (Ed.), *Handbook of experimental psychology.* New York: Wiley, 1951.

19. Green, D. M. Auditory detection of a noise signal. *J. acoust. Soc. Amer.*, 1960, **32**, 121–131.

20. Green, D. M. Detection of a pulsed sinusoid of uncertain frequency. Unpublished paper.

21. Green, D. M. Detection of multiple component signals in noise. *J. acoust. Soc. Amer.*, 1958, **30**, 904–911.

22. Green, D. M. Psychoacoustics and detection theory. *J. acoust. Soc. Amer.*, 1960, **32**, 1198–1203.

23. Green, D. M. Unpublished work.

24. Green, D. M. Personal communication.

25. Green, D. M., and Birdsall, T. G. The effect of vocabulary size on articulation score. Tech. Rep. No. 81, Electronic Defense Group, Univ. Michigan, 1958.

26. Green, D. M., Birdsall, T. G., and Tanner, W. P., Jr. Signal detection as a function of signal intensity and duration. *J. acoust. Soc. Amer.*, 1957, **29**, 523–531.

27. Green, D. M., McKey, M. J., and Licklider, J. C. R. Detection of a pulsed sinusoid in noise as a function of frequency. *J. acoust. Soc. Amer.*, 1959, **31**, 1446–1452.

28. Green, D. M., and Swets, J. A. Unpublished work.

29. Lawson, J. L., and Uhlenbeck, G. E. *Threshold signals.* New York: McGraw-Hill, 1950. Ch. 7.

30. Licklider, J. C. R. Three auditory theories. In S. Koch (Ed.), *Psychology: a study of a science.* Vol. 1. New York: McGraw-Hill, 1958.

31. Marill, T. Detection theory and psychophysics. Tech. Rep. No. 319, Research Laboratory of Electronics, Mass. Inst. of Tech., 1956.

32. Marill, T., and Green, D. M. Statistical recognition functions and the design of pattern recognizers. *IRE Trans. on Electronic Computers,* (in press).

33. Munson, W. A., and Karlin, J. E. The measurement of the human channel transmission characteristics *J. acoust. Soc. Amer.*, 1956, **26**, 542–553.

34. Neyman, J., and Pearson, E. The testing of statistical hypotheses in relation to probabilities. *Proc. Cambridge Phil. Soc.*, 1933, **29**, 492–510.

35. Peterson, W. W., Birdsall, T. G., and Fox, W. C. The theory of signal detectability. Inst. Radio Engrs. *Trans. Professional Group on Information Theory,* 1954, *PGIT-4,* 171–212.

36. Pollack, I. Message repetition and message reception. *J. acoust. Soc. Amer.*, 1959, **31**, 1509–1515.

37. Pollack, I. Message uncertainty and message reception. *J. acoust. Soc. Amer.*, 1959, **31**, 1500–1508.

38. Pollack, I., and Decker, L. R. Confidence ratings, message reception, and the receiver operating characteristic. *J. acoust. Soc. Amer.*, 1958, **30**, 286–292.

39. Smith, M., and Wilson, E. A. A model for the auditory threshold and its application to the multiple observer. *Psychol. Monogr.*, 1953, **67**, No. 9 (Whole No. 359).

40. Swets, J. A. Color vision. Quarterly Progress Rep., Research Laboratory of

Electronics, Mass. Inst. of Tech., April 15, 1960.

41. Swets, J. A. Indices of signal detectability obtained with various psychophysical procedures. *J. acoust. Soc. Amer.,* 1959, **31,** 511–513.

42. Swets, J. A. Unpublished work.

43. Swets, J. A., and Birdsall, T. G. The human use of information, III: decision-making in signal detection and recognition situations involving multiple alternatives. Inst. Radio Engrs. *Trans. Information Theory,* 1956, *IT–2,* 138–165.

44. Swets, J. A., and Green, D. M. Sequential observations by human observers of signals in noise. In C. Cherry (Ed.) *Information theory.* London: Butterworths Scientific Publications, 1961.

45. Swets, J. A., Schouten, J. F., and Lopes-Cardozo, B. On the span of attention, in preparation.

46. Swets, J. A., Shipley, E. F., McKey, M. J., and Green, D. M. Multiple observations of signals in noise. *J. acoust. Soc. Amer.,* 1959, **31,** 514–521.

47. Swets, J. A., Tanner, W. P., Jr., and Birdsall, T. G. The evidence for a decision-making theory of visual detection. Tech. Rep. No. 40, Electronic Defense Group, Univ. Michigan, 1955. This material, slightly revised, will appear as: Decision processes in perception, *Psychol. Rev.,* in press.

48. Tanner, W. P., Jr. Memory. (Mimeo.)

49. Tanner, W. P., Jr. Theory of recognition. *J. acoust. Soc. Amer.,* 1956, **28,** 882–888.

50. Tanner, W. P., Jr., and Birdsall, T. G. Definitions of d' and η as psychophysical measures. *J. acoust. Soc. Amer.,* 1958, **30,** 922–928.

51. Tanner, W. P., Jr., and Jones, R. C. The ideal sensor system as approached through statistical decision theory and the theory of signal detectability. In Minutes and Proceedings of the Armed Forces-NRC Vision Committee meeting, held at Washington, D.C., November, 1959.

52. Tanner, W. P., Jr., and Swets, J. A. A decision-making theory of visual detection. *Psychol. Rev.,* 1954, **61,** 401–409.

53. Tanner, W. P., Jr., and Swets, J. A. The human use of information, I: signal detection for the case of the signal known exactly. Inst. Radio Engrs. *Trans. Professional Group on Information Theory,* 1954, *PGIT–4,* 213–221.

54. Tanner, W. P., Jr., Swets, J. A., and Green, D. M. Some general properties of the hearing mechanism. Tech. Rep. No. 30, Electronic Defense Group, Univ. Michigan, 1956.

55. Van Meter, D., and Middleton, D. Modern statistical approaches to reception in communication theory. Inst. Radio Engrs. *Trans. Professional Group on Information Theory,* 1954, *PGIT–4,* 119–145.

56. Veniar, F. A. Effect of auditory cue on discrimination of auditory stimuli. *J. acoust. Soc. Amer.,* 1958, **30,** 1079–1081.

57. Veniar, F. A. Signal detection as a function of frequency ensemble, I. *J. acoust. Soc. Amer.,* 1958, **30,** 1020–1024; II. 1075–1078.

58. Wald, A. *Sequential analysis.* New York: Wiley, 1947.

59. Wald, A. *Statistical decision functions.* New York: Wiley, 1950.

FIVE
The Reliability and Generality of Data

9

The Test of Significance in Psychological Research

David Bakan

Many scientists have the attitude that the statistical method of scientific induction is *the* method of induction. This attitude is reflected in many experimental psychology textbooks that are dedicated entirely to an elaboration of statistically oriented experimental designs. Ideally, statistical methodology would indeed be the whole of scientific methodology. We have to make judgments about the reliability and generality of data, and we have the option of making them either systematically or unsystematically—of making the nature and bases of our decisions explicit or of leaving them nonexplicit. It is always better to have such matters explicit in order to avoid muddling of various sorts. The idea behind statistical procedures is to make the inductive process explicit. Fisher, the great statistician, regarded statistics as an "analytic account" of induction in general.

Yet there is a great deal of discontentment over the present status of statistical procedures, especially concerning the ways in which the test of significance is normally used by psychologists. Bakan, in the following article, even goes so far as to say that there is a crisis in psychology as a result of the misuse of tests of significance. This does not mean that such tests do not have their uses; it simply means that the way in which psychologists normally use significance tests is not legitimate. Bakan does a superb job of describing these abuses.

That which we might identify as the "crisis of psychology" is closely related

Reprinted from *Psychological Bulletin*, 1966, **66**, 423–437, by permission of the author and the American Psychological Association.

to what Hogben (1958) has called the "crisis in statistical theory." The vast majority of investigations which pass for research in the field of psychology today entail the use of statistical tests of significance. Most characteristically, when a psychologist finds a problem he wishes to investigate he converts his intuitions and hypotheses into procedures which will yield a test of significance; and will characteristically allow the result of the test of significance to bear the essential responsibility for the conclusions which he will draw.

The major point of this paper is that the test of significance does not provide the information concerning psychological phenomena characteristically attributed to it; and that, furthermore, a great deal of mischief has been associated with its use. What will be said in this paper is hardly original. It is, in a certain sense, what "everybody knows." To say it "out loud" is, as it were, to assume the role of the child who pointed out that the emperor was really outfitted only in his underwear. Little of that which is contained in this paper is not already available in the literature, and the literature will be cited.

Lest what is being said in this paper be misunderstood, some clarification needs to be made at the outset. It is not a blanket criticism of statistics, mathematics, or, for that matter, even the test of significance when it can be appropriately used. The argument is rather that the test of significance has been carrying too much of the burden of scientific inference. Wise and ingenious investigators can find their way to reasonable conclusions from data because and in spite of their procedures. Too often, however, even wise and ingenious investigators, for varieties of reasons not the least of which are the editorial policies of our major psychological journals, which we will discuss below, tend to credit the test of significance with properties it does not have.

LOGIC OF THE TEST OF SIGNIFICANCE

The test of significance has as its aim obtaining information concerning a characteristic of a *population* which is itself not directly observable, whether for practical or more intrinsic reasons. What is observable is the *sample*. The work assigned to the test of significance is that of aiding in making inferences from the observed sample to the unobserved population.

The critical assumption involved in testing significance is that, if the experiment is conducted properly, *the characteristics of the population have a designably determinative influence on samples drawn from it,* that, for example, the mean of a population has a determinative influence on the mean of a sample drawn from it. Thus if P, the population characteristic, has a determinative influence on S, the sample characteristic, then there is some license for making inferences from S to P.

If the determinative influence of P on S could be put in the form of simple logical *implication,* that P implies S, the problem would be quite simple. For, then we would have the simple situation: if P implies S, and if S is false, P is false. There are some limited instances in which this logic applies directly in sampling. For example, if the range of values in the population is between 3 and 9 (P), then the range of values in any sample must be between 3 and 9 (S). Should we find a value in a sample of, say, 10, it would mean that S is false; and we could assert that P is false.

It is clear from this, however, that, *strictly speaking,* one can only go from the denial of S to the denial of P; and not from the assertion of S to the assertion of P. It is within this context of simple logical implication that the Fisher school of statisticians have made important contributions—and it is extremely important to recognize this as the context.

In contrast, approaches based on the theorem of Bayes (Bakan, 1953, 1956; Edwards, Lindman, & Savage, 1963; Keynes, 1948; Savage, 1954; Schlaifer, 1959) would allow inferences to P from S even when S is not denied, as S adding something to the credibility of P when S is found to be the case. One of the most viable alternatives to the use of the test of significance involves the theorem of Bayes; and the paper by Edwards et al. (1963) is particularly directed to the attention of psychologists for use in psychological research.

The notion of the null hypothesis[1] promoted by Fisher constituted an advance *within this context* of simple logical implication. It allowed experimenters to set up a null hypothesis complementary to the hypothesis that the investigator was interested in, and provided him with a way of positively confirming his hypothesis. Thus, for example, the investigator might have the hypothesis

that, say, normals differ from schizophrenics. He would then set up the *null hypothesis* that the means in the population of all normals and all schizophrenics were *equal*. Thus, the rejection of the null hypothesis constituted a way of *asserting* that the means of the populations of normals and schizophrenics *were different*, a completely reasonable device whereby to affirm a logical antecedent.

The model of simple logical implication for making inferences from S to P has another difficulty which the Fisher approach sought to overcome. This is that it is rarely meaningful to set up any simple "P implies S" model for parameters that we are interested in. In the case of the mean, for example, it is rather that P has a determinative influence on the *frequency* of any specific S. But one experiment does not provide many values of S to allow the study of their frequencies. It gives us *only one* value of S. The *sampling distribution* is conceived which specifies the relative frequencies of all possible values of S. Then, with the help of an adopted *level of significance,* we could, *in effect,* say that S was false; that is, any S which fell in a region whose relative theoretical frequency under the null hypothesis was, say, 5% would be *considered* false. If such an S actually occurred, we would be in a position to declare P to be false, still within the model of simple logical implication.

It is important to recognize that one of the essential features of the Fisher approach is what may be called the *once-ness* of the experiment; the inference model takes as critical that the experiment has been conducted *once*. If an S which has a low probability under the null hypothesis actually occurs, it is taken that the null hypothesis is false.

---

[1] There is some confusion in the literature concerning the meaning of the term null hypothesis. Fisher used the term to designate any exact hypothesis that we might be interested in disproving, and "null" was used in the sense of that which is to be nullified (cf., e.g., Berkson, 1942). It has, however, also been used to indicate a parameter of zero (cf., e.g., Lindquist, 1940, p. 15), that the difference between the population means is zero, or the correlation coefficient in the population is zero, the difference in proportions in the population is zero, etc. Since both meanings are usually intended in psychological research, it causes little difficulty.

As Fisher (1947, p. 14) put it, why should the theoretically rare event under the null hypothesis actually occur to "us"? If it does occur, we take it that the null hypothesis is false. Basic is the idea that "the theoretically unusual does not happen to me."[2] It should be noted that the referent for all probability considerations is neither in the population itself nor the subjective confidence of the investigator. It is rather in a hypothetical population of experiments all conducted in the same manner, but *only one of which is actually conducted.* Thus, of course, the probability of falsely rejecting the null hypothesis if it were true is exactly that value which has been taken as the level of significance. Replication of the experiment vitiates the validity of the inference model, unless the replication itself is taken into account in the model and the probabilities of the model modified accordingly (as is done in various designs which entail replication, where, however, the total experiment, including the replications, is again considered as *one* experiment). According to Fisher

(1947), "it is an essential characteristic of experimentation that it is carried out with limited resources [p. 18]." In the Fisher approach, the "limited resources" is not only a making of the best out of a limited situation, but is rather an integral feature of the inference model itself. Lest he be done a complete injustice, it should be pointed out that he did say, "In relation to the test of significance, we may say that a phenomenon is experimentally demonstrable when we know how to conduct an experiment which will rarely fail to give us statistically significant results [1947, p. 14]." However, although Fisher "himself" believes this, it is *not* built into the inference model.[3]

DIFFICULTIES OF THE NULL HYPOTHESIS

As already indicated, research workers in the field of psychology place a heavy burden on the test of significance. Let us consider some of the difficulties associated with the null hypothesis.

1. The a Priori Reasons for Believing that the Null Hypothesis is Generally False Anyway

One of the common experiences of research workers is the very high frequency with which significant results are

---

[2] I playfully once conducted the following "experiment": Suppose, I said, that every coin has associated with it a "spirit"; and suppose, furthermore, that if the spirit is implored properly, the coin will veer head or tail as one requests of the spirit. I thus invoked the spirit to make the coin fall head. I threw it once, it came up head. I did it again, it came up head again. I did this six times, and got six heads. Under the null hypothesis the probability of occurrence of six heads is $(\frac{1}{2})^6 = .016$, significant at the 2% level of significance. I have never repeated the experiment. But, then, the logic of the inference model does not really demand that I do! It may be objected that the coin, or my tossing, or even my observation was biased. But I submit that such things were in all likelihood not as involved in the result as corresponding things in most psychological research.

[3] Possibly not even this criterion is sound. It may be that a number of statistically significant results which are *borderline* "speak for the null hypothesis rather than against it [Edwards et al., 1963, p. 235]." If the null hypothesis were really false, then with an increase in the number of instances in which it can be rejected, there should be some substantial proportion of more dramatic rejections rather than borderline rejections.

obtained with large samples. Some years ago, the author had occasion to run a number of tests of significance on a battery of tests collected on about 60,000 subjects from all over the United States. Every test came out significant. Dividing the cards by such arbitrary criteria as east versus west of the Mississippi River, Maine versus the rest of the country, North versus South, etc., all produced significant differences in means. In some instances, the differences in the sample means were quite small, but nonetheless, the *p* values were all very low. Nunnally (1960) has reported a similar experience involving correlation coefficients on 700 subjects. Joseph Berkson (1938) made the observation almost 30 years ago in connection with chi-square:

I believe that an observant statistician who has had any considerable experience with applying the chi-square test repeatedly will agree with my statement that, as a matter of observation, when the numbers in the data are quite large, the *P*'s tend to come out small. Having observed this, and on reflection, I make the following dogmatic statement, referring for illustration to the normal curve: "If the normal curve is fitted to a body of data representing any real observations whatever of quantities in the physical world, then if the number of observations is extremely large—for instance, on an order of 200,000—the chi-square *P* will be small beyond any usual limit of significance."

This dogmatic statement is made on the basis of an extrapolation of the observation referred to and can also be defended as a prediction from *a priori* considerations. For we may assume that it is practically certain that any series of real observations does not actually follow a normal curve *with absolute exactitude* in all respects, and no matter how small the discrepancy between the normal curve and the true curve of observations, the chi-square *P* will be small if the sample has a sufficiently large number of observations in it.

If this be so, then we have something here that is apt to trouble the conscience of a reflective statistician using the chi-square test. For I suppose it would be agreed by statisticians that a large sample is always better than a small sample. If, then, we know in advance the *P* that will result from an application of chi-square test to a large sample, there would seem to be no use in doing it on a smaller one. But since the result of the former test is known, it is no test at all [pp. 526–527].

As one group of authors has put it, "in typical applications . . . the null hypothesis . . . is known by all concerned to be false from the outset [Edwards et al., 1963, p. 214]." The fact of the matter is that *there is really no good reason to expect the null hypothesis to be true in any population.* Why should the mean, say, of all scores east of the Mississippi be *identical* to all scores west of the Mississippi? Why should any correlation coefficient be *exactly* .00 in the population? Why should we expect the ratio of males to females be *exactly* 50:50 in any population? Or why should different drugs have *exactly* the same effect on any population parameter (Smith, 1960)? *A glance at any set of statistics on total populations will quickly confirm the rarity of the null hypothesis in nature.*

The reason why the null hypothesis is characteristically rejected with large samples was made patent by the theoretical work of Neyman and Pearson (1933). The probability of rejecting the null hypothesis is a function of five factors: whether the test is one- or two-tailed, the level of significance, the standard deviation, the amount of deviation from the null hypothesis, *and the number of observations.* The choice of a one- or two-tailed test is the investigator's; the level of significance is also based on the choice of the investigator; the standard deviation is a given of the situation, and is characteristically reasonably well estimated; the deviation from the null hypothesis is what is unknown; and the choice of the number of cases in psychological work is characteristically arbitrary or expeditious. Should there be any deviation from the null hypothesis in the population, *no matter how small*—and we have little doubt but that such a deviation usually exists—a sufficiently large number of observations will lead to the rejection of the null hypothesis. As Nunnally (1960) put it,

if the null hypothesis is not rejected, it is usually because the *N* is too small. If enough data are gathered, the hypothesis will generally be rejected. If rejection of the null hypothesis were the real intention in psychological experiments, there usually would be no need to gather data [p. 643].

2. Type I Error and Publication Practices

The Type I error is the error of rejecting the null hypothesis when it is indeed true, and its probability is the level of significance. Later in this paper we will discuss the distinction between *sharp* and *loose* null hypotheses. The sharp null hypothesis, which we have been discussing, is an exact value for the null hypothesis as, for example, the difference between population means being precisely zero. A loose null hypothesis is one in which it is conceived of as being *around* null. Sharp null hypotheses, as we have indicated, rarely exist in nature. Assum-

ing that loose null hypotheses are not rare, and that their testing may make sense under some circumstances, let us consider the role of the publication practices of our journals in their connection.

It is the practice of editors of our psychological journals, receiving many more papers than they can possibly publish, to use the magnitude of the *p* values reported as one criterion for acceptance or rejection of a study. For example, consider the following statement made by Arthur W. Melton (1962) on completing 12 years as editor of the *Journal of Experimental Psychology,* certainly one of the most prestigious and scientifically meticulous psychological journals. In enumerating the criteria by which articles were evaluated, he said:

The next step in the assessment of an article involved a judgment with respect to the confidence to be placed in the findings— confidence that the results of the experiment would be repeatable under the conditions described. In editing the *Journal* there has been a strong reluctance to accept and publish results related to the principal concern of the research when those results were significant at the .05 level, whether by one- or two-tailed test. This has not implied a slavish worship of the .01 level, as some critics may have implied. Rather, it reflects a belief that it is the responsibility of the investigator in a science to reveal his effect in such a way that no reasonable man would be in a position to discredit the results by saying that they were the product of the way the ball bounces [pp. 553–554].

His clearly expressed opinion that nonsignificant results should not take up the space of the journals is shared by most editors of psychological journals. It is important to point out that I am not advocating a change in policy in this connection. In the total research enterprise where so much of the load for making inferences concerning the nature of phenomena is carried by the test of significance, the editors can do little else. The point is rather that the situation in regard to publication makes manifest the difficulties in connection with the over-emphasis on the test of significance as a principal basis for making inferences.

McNemar (1960) has rightly pointed out that not only do journal editors reject papers in which the results are not significant, but that papers in which significance has not been obtained are not submitted, that investigators select out their significant findings for inclusion in their reports, and that theory-oriented research workers tend to discard data which do not work to confirm their theories. The result of all of this is that "published results are more likely to involve false rejection of null hypotheses than indicated by the stated levels of significance [p. 300]," that is, published results which are significant may well have Type I errors in them far in excess of, say, the 5% which we may allow ourselves.

The suspicion that the Type I error may well be plaguing our literature is given confirmation in an analysis of articles published in the *Journal of Abnormal and Social Psychology* for one complete year (Cohen, 1962). Analyzing 70 studies in which significant results were obtained with respect to the power of the statistical tests used, Cohen found that power, the probability of rejecting the null hypothesis when the null hypothesis was false, was characteristically meager. Theoretically, with such tests, one should not often expect significant results even when the null hypothesis was

false. Yet, there they were! Even if deviations from null existed in the relevant populations, the investigations were characteristically not powerful enough to have detected them. This strongly suggests that there is something additional associated with these rejections of the null hypotheses in question. It strongly points to the possibility that the manner in which studies get published is associated with the findings; that *the very publication practices themselves are part and parcel of the probabilistic processes on which we base our conclusions concerning the nature of psychological phenomena.* Our total research enterprise is, at least in part, a kind of scientific roulette, in which the "lucky," or constant player, "wins," that is, gets his paper or papers published. And certainly, going from 5% to 1% does not eliminate the possibility that it is "the way the ball bounces," to use Melton's phrase. It changes the odds in this roulette, but it does not make it less a game of roulette.

The damage to the scientific enterprise is compounded by the fact that the publication of "significant" results tends to stop further investigation. If the publication of papers containing Type I errors tended to foster further investigation so that the psychological phenomena with which we are concerned would be further probed by others, it would not be too bad. But it does not. Quite the contrary. As Lindquist (1940, p. 17) has correctly pointed out, the danger to science of the Type I error is much more serious than the Type II error—for when a Type I error is committed, it has the effect of stopping investigation. A highly significant result appears definitive, as Melton's comments indicate. In the 12 years that he edited the *Journal of Experimental Psychol-*

ogy, he sought to select papers which were worthy of being placed in the "archives," as he put it. Even the strict repetition of an experiment and not getting significance in the same way does not speak against the result already reported in the literature. For failing to get significance, speaking strictly within the inference model, only means that that experiment is inconclusive; whereas the study already reported in the literature, with a low p value, is regarded as conclusive. Thus we tend to place in the archives studies with a relatively high number of Type I errors, or, at any rate, studies which reflect small deviations from null in the respective populations; and we act in such a fashion as to reduce the likelihood of their correction.

PSYCHOLOGIST'S "ADJUSTMENT" BY MISINTERPRETATION

The psychological literature is filled with misinterpretations of the nature of the test of significance. One may be tempted to attribute this to such things as lack of proper education, the simple fact that humans may err, and the prevailing tendency to take a cookbook approach in which the mathematical and philosophical framework out of which the tests of significance emerge are ignored; that, in other words, these misinterpretations are somehow the result of simple intellectual inadequacy on the part of psychologists. However, such an explanation is hardly tenable. Graduate schools are adamant with respect to statistical education. Any number of psychologists have taken out substantial amounts of time to equip themselves mathematically and philosophically. Psychologists as a group do a great deal

of mutual criticism. Editorial reviews prior to publication are carried out with eminent conscientiousness. There is even a substantial literature devoted to various kinds of "misuse" of statistical procedures, to which not a little attention has been paid.

It is rather that the test of significance is profoundly interwoven with other strands of the psychological research enterprise in such a way that it constitutes a critical part of the total cultural-scientific tapestry. To pull out the strand of the test of significance would seem to make the whole tapestry fall apart. In the face of the intrinsic difficulties that the test of significance provides, we rather attempt to make an "adjustment" by attributing to the test of significance characteristics which it does not have, and overlook characteristics that it does have. The difficulty is that the test of significance can, especially when not considered too carefully, do *some* work; for, after all, the results of the test of significance *are* related to the phenomena in which we are interested. One may well ask whether we do not have here, perhaps, an instance of the phenomenon that learning under partial reinforcement is very highly resistant to extinction. Some of these misinterpretations are as follows:

1. Taking the p Value as a "Measure" of Significance

A common misinterpretation of the test of significance is to regard it as a "measure" of significance. It is interpreted as the answer to the question "How significant is it?" A p value of .05 is thought of as less significant than a p value of .01, and so on. The characteristic practice on the part of psychologists is to compute, say, a *t*, and then "look up" the significance in the table, taking the *p* value as a *function of* t, and thereby a "measure" of significance. Indeed, since the *p* value is inversely related to the magnitude of, say, the difference between means *in the sample*, it can function as a kind of "standard score" measure for a variety of different experiments. Mathematically, the *t* is actually very similar to a "standard score," entailing a deviation in the numerator, and a function of the variation in the denominator; and the *p* value is a "function" of *t*. If this use were explicit, it would perhaps not be too bad. But it must be remembered that this is using the *p* value as a *statistic descriptive of the sample alone,* and does not automatically give an inference to the population. There is even the practice of using tests of significance in studies of total populations, in which the observations cannot by any stretch of the imagination be thought of as having been randomly selected from any designable population.[4] Using the *p* value in this way, in which the statistical inference model is even hinted at, is completely indefensible; for the single function of the statistical inference model is making inferences to populations from samples.

The practice of "looking up" the *p* value for the *t,* which has even been advocated in some of our statistical handbooks (e.g., Lacey, 1953, p. 117; Underwood, Duncan, Taylor, & Cotton, 1954, p. 129), rather than looking up the *t* for a given *p* value, violates the inference model. The inference model is based on the presumption that one

---

[4] It was decided not to cite any specific studies to exemplify points such as this one. The reader will undoubtedly be able to supply them for himself.

initially adopts a level of significance as the specification of that probability which is too low to occur to "us," as Fisher has put it, in this one instance, and under the null hypothesis. A purist might speak of the "delicate problem . . . of fudging with a posteriori alpha values [levels of significance. Kaiser, 1960, p. 165]," as though the levels of significance were initially decided upon, but rarely do psychological research workers or editors take the level of significance as other than a "measure."

But taken as a "measure," it is only a measure of the sample. Psychologists often erroneously believe that the *p* value is "the probability that the results are due to chance," as Wilson (1961, p. 230) has pointed out; that a *p* value of .05 means that the chances are .95 that the scientific hypothesis is correct, as Bolles (1962) has pointed out; that it is a measure of the power to "predict" the behavior of a population (Underwood et al., 1954, p. 107); and that it is a measure of the "confidence that the results of the experiment would be repeatable under the conditions described," as Melton put it. Unfortunately, none of these interpretations are within the inference model of the test of significance. Some of our statistical handbooks have "allowed" misinterpretation. For example, in discussing the erroneous rhetoric associated with talking of the "probability" of a population parameter (in the inference model there is no probability associated with something which is either true or false), Lindquist (1940) said, "For most practical purposes, the end result is the same as if the 'level of confidence' type of interpretation is employed [p. 14]." Ferguson (1959) wrote, "The .05 and .01 probability levels are descriptive of our degree of confidence [p. 133]." There is little question but that sizable differences, correlations, etc., in *samples*, especially samples of reasonable size, speak more strongly of sizable differences, correlations, etc., in the population; and there is little question but that if there is real and strong effect in the population, it will continue to manifest itself in further sampling. However, these are inferences which *we* may make. They are outside the inference model associated with the test of significance. The *p* value within the inference model is only the value which we take to be as how improbable an event could be under the null hypothesis, which we judge will not take place to "us," in this one experiment. *It is not a "measure" of the goodness of the other inferences which we might make.* It is an a priori condition that we set up whereby we decide whether or not we will reject the null hypothesis, not a measure of significance.

There is a study in the literature (Rosenthal & Gaito, 1963) which points up sharply the lack of understanding on the part of psychologists of the meaning of the test of significance. The subjects were 9 members of the psychology department faculty, all holding doctoral degrees, and 10 graduate students, at the University of North Dakota; and there is little reason to believe that this group of psychologists was more or less sophisticated than any other. They were asked to rate their degree of belief or confidence in results of hypothetical studies for a variety of *p* values, and for *n*'s of 10 and 100. That there should be a relationship between the average rated confidence or belief and *p* value, as they found, is to be expected. What is shock-

ing is that these psychologists indicated substantially greater confidence or belief in results associated with the larger sample size for the same *p* values! According to the theory, especially as this has been amplified by Neyman and Pearson (1933), the probability of rejecting the null hypothesis for any given deviation from null and *p* value *increases* as a function of the number of observations. The rejection of the null hypothesis when the number of cases is small speaks for a more dramatic effect in the population: and if the *p* value is the same, the probability of committing a Type I error remains the same. Thus one can be more confident with a small *n* than a large *n*. The question is, how could a group of psychologists be so wrong? I believe that this wrongness is based on the commonly held belief that the *p* value is a "measure" of degree of confidence. Thus, the reasoning behind such a wrong set of answers by these psychologists may well have been something like this: the *p* value is a measure of confidence; but a larger number of cases also increases confidence; therefore, for any given *p* value, the degree of confidence should be higher for the larger *n*. The wrong conclusion arises from the erroneous character of the first premise, and from the failure to recognize that the *p* value is a function of sample size for any given deviation from null in the population. The author knows of instances in which editors of very reputable psychological journals have rejected papers in which the *p* values and *n*'s were small on the grounds that there were not enough observations, clearly demonstrating that the same mode of thought is operating in them. Indeed, rejecting the null hypothesis with a small n is indicative of a strong deviation from null in the population, the mathematics of the test of significance having already taken into account the smallness of the sample. Increasing the n increases the probability of rejecting the null hypothesis: and in these studies rejected for small sample size, that task has already been accomplished. These editors are, of course, in some sense the ultimate "teachers" of the profession; and they have been teaching something which is patently wrong!

2. Automaticity of Inference

What may be considered to be a dream, fantasy, or ideal in the culture of psychology is that of achieving complete automaticity of inference. The making of inductive generalizations is always somewhat risky. In Fisher's *The Design of Experiments* (1947, p. 4), he made the claim that the methods of induction could be made rigorous, exemplified by the procedures which he was setting forth. This is indeed quite correct in the sense indicated earlier. In a later paper, he made explicit what was strongly hinted at in his earlier writing, that the methods which he proposed constituted a relatively *complete* specification of the process of induction:

That such a process induction existed and was possible to normal minds, has been understood for centuries; it is only with the recent development of statistical science that an analytic account can now be given, about as satisfying and complete, at least, as that given traditionally of the deductive processes [Fisher, 1955, p. 74].

Psychologists certainly took the procedures associated with the t test, F test, and so on, in this manner. *Instead* of having to engage in inference themselves, they had but to "run the tests" for the purpose of making inferences, since, as it appeared, the statistical tests were analytic analogues of inductive inference. The "operationist" orientation among psychologists, which recognized the contingency of knowledge on the knowledge-getting operations and advocated their specification, could, it would seem, "operationalize" the inferential processes simply by reporting the details of the statistical analysis! It thus removed the burden of responsibility, the chance of being wrong, the necessity for making inductive inferences, from the shoulders of the investigator and placed them on the tests of significance. The contingency of the conclusion upon the experimenter's decision of the level of significance was managed in two ways. The first, by resting on a kind of social agreement that 5% was good, and 1% better. The second in the manner which has already been discussed, by not making a decision of the level of significance, but only reporting the p value as a "result" and a presumably objective "measure" of degree of confidence. But that the probability of getting significance is also contingent upon the number of observations has been handled largely by ignoring it.

A crisis was experienced among psychologists when the matter of the one-versus the two-tailed test came into prominence; for here the contingency of the result of a test of significance on a decision of the investigator was simply too conspicuous to be ignored. An investigator, say, was interested in the difference between two groups on some measure. He collected his data, found that Mean A was greater than Mean B in the sample, and ran the ordinary two-tailed t test; and, let us say, it was not significant. Then he bethought himself. The two-tailed test tested against *two* alternatives, that the population Mean A was greater than population Mean B and vice versa. But then, he really wanted to know whether Mean A was greater than Mean B. Thus, he could run a one-tailed test. He did this and found, since the one-tailed test is more powerful, that his difference was now significant.

Now here there was a difficulty. The test of significance is not nearly so automatic an inference process as had been thought. It is manifestly contingent on the decision of the investigator as to whether to run a one- or a two-tailed test. And somehow, making the decision *after* the data were collected and the means computed, seemed like "cheating." How should this be handled? Should there be some central registry in which one registers one's decision to run a one- or two-tailed test before collecting the data? Should one, as one eminent psychologist once suggested to me, send oneself a letter so that the postmark would prove that one had pre-decided to run a one-tailed test? The literature on ways of handling this difficulty has grown quite a bit in the strain to somehow overcome this particular clear contingency of the results of a test of significance on the decision of the investigator. The author will not attempt here to review this literature, except to cite one very competent paper which points up the intrinsic difficulty associated with this problem, the *reductio ad absurdum* to which one comes. Kaiser (1960), early in his paper, distinguished between the *logic* associated with the test

of significance and other forms of inference, a distinction which, incidentally, Fisher would hardly have allowed: "The arguments developed in this paper are based on logical considerations in statistical inference. (We do not, of course, suggest that statistical inference is the only basis for scientific inference) [p. 160]." But then, having taken the position that he is going to follow the logic of statistical inference relentlessly, he said (Kaiser's italics): "*we cannot logically make a directional statistical decision or statement when the null hypothesis is rejected on the basis of the direction of the difference in the observed sample means* [p. 161]." One really needs to strike oneself in the head! If Sample Mean A is greater than Sample Mean B, and there is reason to reject the null hypothesis, in what other direction can it reasonably be? What kind of logic is it that leads one to believe that it could be otherwise than that Population Mean A is greater than Population Mean B? We do not know whether Kaiser intended his paper as a *reductio ad absurdum*, but it certainly turned out that way.

The issue of the one- versus the two-tailed test genuinely challenges the presumptive "objectivity" characteristically attributed to the test of significance. On the one hand, it makes patent what was the case under any circumstances (at the least in the choice of level of significance, and the choice of the number of cases in the sample), that the conclusion is contingent upon the decision of the investigator. An astute investigator, who foresaw the results, and who therefore pre-decided to use a one-tailed test, will get one p value. The less astute but honorable investigator, who did not foresee the results, would feel obliged to use a two-tailed test, and would get another p value. On the other hand, if one decides to be relentlessly logical within the logic of statistical inference, one winds up with the kind of absurdity which we have cited above.

3. The Confusion of Induction to the Aggregate with Induction to the General

Consider a not atypical investigation of the following sort: A group of, say, 20 normals and a group of, say, 20 schizophrenics are given a test. The tests are scored, and a t test is run, and it is found that the means differ significantly at some level of significance, say 1%. What inference can be drawn? As we have already indicated, the investigator could have insured this result by choosing a sufficiently large number of cases. Suppose we overlook this objection, which we can to some extent, by saying that the difference between the means in the population must have been *large enough* to have manifested itself with only 40 cases. But still, what do we know from this? The *only* inference which this allows is that the mean of all normals is different from the mean of all schizophrenics in the populations from which the samples have presumably been drawn at random. (Rarely is the criterion of randomness satisfied. But let us overlook this objection too.)

The common rhetoric in which such results are discussed is in the form "Schizophrenics differ from normals in such and such ways." The sense that both the reader and the writer have of this rhetoric is that it has been justified by the finding of significance. Yet clearly it does not mean *all* schizophrenics and *all* normals. All that the test of significance justifies is that *measures of central tendency of the aggregates* differ in the populations. The test of significance has *not* addressed itself to anything about the schizophrenia or normality which characterizes *each* member of the respective populations. Now it is certainly possible for an investigator to develop a hypothesis about the nature of schizophrenia *from which he may infer* that there should be differences between the means in the populations; and his finding of a significant difference in the means of his sample would add to the credibility of the former. However, that 1% which he obtained in his study bears only on the means of the populations, and is not a "measure" of the confidence that he may have in his hypothesis concerning the nature of schizophrenia. There are *two* inferences that he must make. One is that of the sample to the population, for which the test of significance is of some use. The other is from his inference concerning the population to his hypothesis concerning the nature of schizophrenia. The p value does not bear on this second inference. The psychological literature is filled with assertions which confound these two inferential processes.

Or consider another hardly atypical style of research. Say an experimenter divides 40 subjects at random into two groups of 20 subjects each. One group is assigned to one condition and the other to another condition, perhaps, say, massing and distribution of trials. The subjects are given a learning task, one group under massed conditions, the other under distributed conditions. The experimenter runs a t test on the learning measure and again, say, finds that the difference is significant at the 1% level of significance. He may then say in his report, being more careful than the psychologist who was studying the difference between normals and schizophrenics (being more "scientific" than his clinically-interested colleague), that "the mean in the population of learning under massed conditions is lower than the mean in the population of learning under distributed conditions," feeling that he can say this with a good deal of certainty because of his test of significance. But here too (like his clinical colleague) he has made *two* inferences, and not one, and the 1% bears on the one but not the other. The statistical inference model certainly allows him to make his statement for the population, but only for *that* learning task, and the *p* value is appropriate only to that. But the generalization to "massed conditions" and "distributed conditions" beyond that particular learning task is a second inference with respect to which the *p* value is not relevant. The psychological literature is plagued with any number of instances in which the rhetoric indicates that the *p* value does bear on this second inference.

Part of the blame for this confusion can be ascribed to Fisher who, in *The Design of Experiments* (1947, p. 9), suggested that the mathematical methods which he proposed were exhaustive of scientific induction, and that the principles he was advancing were "common to all experimentation." What he failed to see and to say was that after an inference was made concerning a population parameter, *one still needed to engage in induction* to obtain meaningful scientific propositions.

To regard the methods of statistical inference as exhaustive of the inductive inferences called for in experimentation is completely confounding. When the test of significance has been run, the necessity for induction has hardly been completely satisfied. However, the research worker knows this, in some sense, and proceeds, as he should, to make further inductive inferences. He is, however, still ensnarled in his test of significance and the presumption that *it* is the whole of his inductive activity, and thus mistakenly takes a low *p* value for the measure of the validity of his *other* inductions.

The seriousness of this confusion may be seen by again referring back to the Rosenthal and Gaito (1963) study and the remark by Berkson which indicate that research workers believe that a large sample is better than a small sample. We need to refine the rhetoric somewhat. Induction consists in making inferences from the particular to the general. It is certainly the case that as confirming particulars are added, the credibility of the general is increased. However, *the addition of observations to a sample is,* in the context of statistical inference, *not the addition of particulars* but the modification of what is one particular in the inference model, the sample aggregate. In the context of statistical inference, it is not necessarily true that "a large sample is better than a small sample." For, as has been already indicated, obtaining a significant result with a small sample suggests a larger deviation from null in the population, and may be considerably more meaningful. Thus more particulars are better than fewer particulars on the making of an inductive inference; but not necessarily a larger sample.

In the marriage of psychological research and statistical inference, psychology brought its own reasons for accepting this confusion, reasons which inhere in the history of psychology. Measurement psychology arises out of two radically different traditions, as has been pointed out by Guilford (1936, pp.

5 ff.) and Cronbach (1957), and the matter of putting them together raised certain difficulties. The one tradition seeks to find propositions concerning the nature of man in *general*—propositions of a general nature, with each *individual a particular* in which the general is manifest. This is the kind of psychology associated with the traditional experimental psychology of Fechner, Ebbinghaus, Wundt, and Titchener. It seeks to find the laws which characterize the "generalized, normal, human, adult mind [Boring, 1950, p. 413]." The research strategy associated with this kind of psychology is straightforwardly inductive. It seeks inductive generalizations which will apply to *every* member of a designated class. A single particular in which a generalization fails forces a rejection of the generalization, calling for either a redefinition of the class to which it applies or a modification of the generalization. The other tradition is the psychology of individual differences, which has its roots more in England and the United States than on the continent. We may recall that when the young American, James McKeen Cattell, who invented the term *mental test*, came to Wundt with his own problem of individual differences, it was regarded by Wundt as *ganz Amerikanisch* (Boring, 1950, p. 324).

The basic datum for an individual-differences approach is not anything that characterizes *each* of two subjects, but the *difference between them*. For this latter tradition, it is the *aggregate* which is of interest, and not the general. One of the most unfortunate characteristics of many studies in psychology, especially in experimental psychology, is that the data are treated as aggregates while the experimenter is trying to infer general propositions. There is hardly an issue of most of the major psychological journals reporting experimentation in which this confusion does not appear several times; and in which the test of significance, which has some value in connection with the study of aggregates, is not interpreted as a measure of the credibility of the general proposition in which the investigator is interested.

The distinction between the aggregate and the general may be illuminated by a small mathematical exercise. The methods of analysis of variance developed by Fisher and his school have become techniques of choice among psychologists. However, at root, the methods of analysis of variance do not deal with that which any two or more subjects may have in common, but consider only *differences between* scores. This is all that is analyzed by analysis of variance. The following identity illustrates this clearly, showing that the original total sum squares, of which everything else in any analysis of variance is simply the partitioning of, is based on the literal difference between each pair of scores (cf. Bakan, 1955). Except for *n*, it is the only information used from the data:

$$\sum_{i=1}^{n} (X_i - \bar{X})^2 = \frac{1}{2}\left[\frac{(X_1 - X_2)}{1}\right]^2$$
$$+ \frac{2}{3}\left[\frac{(X_1 - X_3) + (X_2 - X_3)}{2}\right]^2$$
$$+ \cdots + \frac{n-1}{n}$$
$$\left[\frac{(X_1 - X_n) + \cdots + (X_{n-1} - X_n)}{n-1}\right]^2.$$

Thus, what took place historically in psychology is that instead of attempting to *synthesize* the two traditional approaches to psychological phenomena, which is both possible and desirable, a syncretic combination took place of the methods appropriate to the study of aggregates with the aims of a psychology which sought for general propositions. One of the most overworked terms, which added not a little to the essential confusion, was the term "error," which was a kind of umbrella term for (at the least) variation among scores from different individuals, variation among measurements for the same individual, and variation among samples.

Let us add another historical note. In 1936, Guilford published his well-known *Psychometric Methods*. In this book, which became a kind of "bible" for many psychologists, he made a noble effort at a "Rapprochement of Psychophysical and Test Methods" (p. 9). He observed, quite properly, that mathematical developments in each of the two fields might be of value in the other, that "Both psychophysics and mental testing have rested upon the same fundamental statistical devices [p. 9]." There is no question of the truth of this. However, what he failed to emphasize sufficiently was that mathematics is so abstract that the same mathematics is applicable to rather different fields of investigation without there being any necessary further identity between them. (One would not, for example, argue that business and genetics are essentially the same because the same arithmetic is applicable to market research and in the investigation of the facts of heredity.) A critical point of contact between the two traditions was in connection with scaling in which Cattell's principle that "equally often noticed differences are equal unless always or never noticed [Guilford, 1936, p. 217]" was adopted as a fundamental assumption. The "equally often noticed differences" is, of course, based on aggregates. By means of this assumption, one could collapse the distinction between the two areas of investigation. Indeed, this is not really too bad if one is alert to the fact that *it is* an assumption, one which even has considerable pragmatic value. As a set of techniques whereby data could be analyzed, that is, as a set of techniques whereby one could *describe* one's findings, and then make inductions about the nature of the psychological phenomena, that which Guilford put together in his book was eminently valuable. However, around this time the work of Fisher and his school was coming to the attention of psychologists. It was attractive for several reasons. It offered advice for handling "small samples." It offered a number of eminently ingenious new ways of organizing and extracting information from data. It offered ways by which several variables could be analyzed simultaneously, away from the old notion that one had to keep everything constant and vary only one variable at a time. It showed how the effect of the "interaction" of variables could be assessed. But it also claimed to have mathematized induction! The Fisher approach was thus "bought," and psychologists got a theory of induction in the bargain, a theory which seemed to exhaust the inductive processes. Whereas the question of the "reliability" of statistics had been a matter of concern for some time before (although frequently very garbled), it had not carried the burden of induction to the degree that it did with the Fisher approach. With the "buying" of the Fisher approach the psychological research worker also bought, and then overused, the test of significance, employing it as the measure of the significance, in the largest sense of the word, of his research efforts.

SHARP AND LOOSE
NULL HYPOTHESES

Earlier, a distinction was made between sharp and loose null hypotheses. One of the major difficulties associated with the Fisher approach is the problem presented by sharp null hypotheses; for, as we have already seen, there is reason to believe that the existence of sharp null hypotheses is characteristically unlikely. There have been some efforts to correct for this difficulty by proposing the use of loose null hypotheses; in place of a single point, a region being considered null. Hodges and Lehmann (1954) have proposed a distinction between "statistical significance," which entails the sharp hypothesis, and "material significance," in which one tests the hypothesis of a deviation of a stated amount from the null point instead of the null point itself. Edwards (1950, pp. 30–31) has suggested the notion of "practical significance" in which one takes into account the meaning, in some practical sense, of the magnitude of the deviation from null together with the number of observations which have been involved in getting statistical significance. Binder (1963) has equally argued that a subset of parameters be equated with the null hypothesis. Essentially what has been suggested is that the investigator make some kind of a decision concerning "How much, say, of a difference makes a difference?" The difficulty with this solution, which is certainly a sound one technically, is that in psychological research we do not often have very good grounds for answering this question. This is partly due to the inadequacies of psychological measurement, but mostly due to the fact that the answer to the question of "How much of a difference makes a difference?" is not forthcoming outside of some particular practical context. The question calls forth another question, "How much of a difference makes a difference *for what?*"

DECISIONS VERSUS ASSERTIONS

This brings us to one of the major issues within the field of statistics itself. The problems of the research psychologist do not generally lie within practical contexts. He is rather interested in making assertions concerning psychological functions which have a reasonable amount of credibility associated with them. He is more concerned with "What is the case?" than with "What is wise to do?" (cf. Rozeboom, 1960).

It is here that the decision-theory approach of Neyman, Pearson, and Wald (Neyman, 1937, 1957; Neyman & Pearson, 1933; Wald, 1939, 1950, 1955) becomes relevant. The decision-theory school, still basing itself on some basic notions of the Fisher approach, deviated from it in several respects:

1. In Fisher's inference model, the two alternatives between which one chose on the basis of an experiment were *reject* and *inconclusive*. As he said in The Design of Experiments (1947), "the null hypothesis is never proved or established, but is possibly disproved, in the course of experimentation [p. 16]." In the decision-theory approach, the two alternatives are rather *reject* and *accept*.

2. Whereas in the Fisher approach the interpretation of the test of significance critically depends on having one sample from a *hypothetical* population of experiments, the decision-theory approach conceives of, is applicable to, and is sensible with respect to numerous repetitions of the experiment.

3. The decision-theory approach added the notions of the Type II error (which can

be made only if the null hypothesis is accepted) and power as significant features of their model.

4. The decision-theory model gave a significant place to the matter of what is concretely lost if an error is made in the practical context, on the presumption that accept entailed one concrete action, and reject another. It is in these actions and their consequences that there is a basis for deciding on a level of confidence. The Fisher approach has little to say about the consequences.

As it has turned out, the field of application par excellence for the decision-theory approach has been the sampling inspection of mass-produced items. In sampling inspection, the acceptable deviation from null can be specified; both accept and reject are appropriate categories; the alternative courses of action can be clearly specified; there is a definite measure of loss for each possible action; and the choice can be regarded as one of a series of such choices, so that one can minimize the overall loss (cf. Barnard, 1954). Where the aim is only the acquisition of knowledge without regard to a specific practical context, these conditions do not often prevail. Many psychologists who learned about analysis of variance from books such as those by Snedecor (1946) found the examples involving log weights, etc., somewhat annoying. The decision-theory school makes it clear that such practical contexts are not only "examples" given for pedagogical purposes, but actually are essential features of the methods themselves.

The contributions of the decision-theory school essentially revealed the intrinsic nature of the test of significance beyond that seen by Fisher and his colleagues. They demonstrated that the methods associated with the test of significance constitute not an assertion, or an induction, or a conclusion calculus, but a decision- or risk-evaluation calculus. Fisher (1955) has reacted to the decision-theory approach in polemic style, suggesting that its advocates were like "Russians [who] are made familiar with the ideal that research in pure science can and should be geared to technological performance, in the comprehensive organized effort of a five-year plan for the nation." He also suggested an American "ideological" orientation: "In the U.S. also the great importance of organized technology has I think made it easy to confuse the process appropriate for drawing correct conclusions, with those aimed rather at, let us say, speeding production, or saving money [p. 70]."[5] But perhaps a more reasonable way of looking at this is to regard the decision-theory school to have explicated what was already implicit in the work of the Fisher school.

CONCLUSION

What then is our alternative, if the test of significance is really of such limited appropriateness as has been indicated? At the very least it would appear that we would be much better off if we were to attempt to *estimate* the magnitude of the parameters in the populations; and recognize that we then need to make other inferences concerning the psychological phenomena which may be manifesting themselves in these magnitudes. In terms of a statistical approach which is an alternative, the various methods associated with the theorem of

[5] For a reply to Fisher, see Pearson (1955).

Bayes which was referred to earlier may be appropriate; and the paper by Edwards et al. (1963) and the book by Schlaifer (1959) are good starting points. However, that which is expressed in the theorem of Bayes alludes to the more general process of inducing propositions concerning the nonmanifest (which is what the population is a special instance of) and ascertaining the way in which that which is manifest (which the sample is a special instance of) bears on it. This is what the scientific method has been about for centuries. However, if the reader who might be sympathetic to the considerations set forth in this paper quickly goes out and reads some of the material on the Bayesian approach with the hope that thereby he will find a *new basis for automatic inference,* this paper will have misfired, and he will be disappointed.

That which we have indicated in this paper in connection with the test of significance in psychological research may be taken as an instance of a kind of essential mindlessness in the conduct of research which may be, as the author has suggested elsewhere (Bakan, 1965), related to the presumption of the non-existence of mind in the subjects of psychological research. Karl Pearson once indicated that higher statistics were only common sense reduced to numerical appreciation. However, that base in common sense must be maintained with vigilance. When we reach a point where our statistical procedures are substitutes instead of aids to thought, and we are led to absurdities, then we must return to the common sense basis. Tukey (1962) has very properly pointed out that statistical procedures may take our attention away from the data, which constitute the ultimate base for any inferences

which we might make. Robert Schlaifer (1959, p. 654) has dubbed the error of the misapplication of statistical procedures the "error of the third kind," the most serious error which can be made. Berkson has suggested the use of "the interocular traumatic test, you know what the data mean when the conclusion hits you between the eyes [Edwards et al., 1963, p. 217]." We must overcome the myth that if our treatment of our subject matter is mathematical it is therefore precise and valid. Mathematics can serve to obscure as well as reveal.

Most importantly, we need to get on with the business of generating *psychological* hypotheses and proceed to do investigations and make inferences which bear on them; instead of, as so much of our literature would attest, testing the statistical null hypothesis in any number of contexts in which we have every reason to suppose that it is false in the first place.

REFERENCES

Bakan, D. Learning and the principle of inverse probability. *Psychological Review,* 1953, **60,** 360–370.

Bakan, D. The general and the aggregate: A methodological distinction. *Perceptual and Motor Skills,* 1955, **5,** 211–212.

Bakan, D. Clinical psychology and logic. *American Psychologist,* 1956, **11,** 655–662.

Bakan, D. The mystery-mastery complex in contemporary psychology. *American Psychologist,* 1965, **20,** 186–191.

Barnard, G. A. Sampling inspection and statistical decisions. *Journal of the Royal Statistical Society* (B), 1954, **16,** 151–165.

Berkson, J. Some difficulties of interpretation encountered in the application of the chi-square test. *Journal of* the American Statistical Association, 1938, **33**, 526–542.

Berkson, J. Tests of significance considered as evidence. *Journal of the American Statistical Association*, 1942, **37**, 325–335.

Binder, A. Further considerations on testing the null hypothesis and the strategy and tactics of investigating theoretical models. *Psychological Review*, 1963, **70**, 101–109.

Bolles, R. C. The difference between statistical hypotheses and scientific hypotheses. *Psychological Reports*, 1962, **11**, 639–645.

Boring, E. G. *A history of experimental psychology*. (2nd ed.) New York: Appleton-Century-Crofts, 1950.

Cohen, J. The statistical power of abnormal-social psychological research: A review. *Journal of Abnormal and Social Psychology*, 1962, **65**, 145–153.

Cronbach, L. J. The two disciplines of scientific psychology. *American Psychologist*, 1957, **12**, 671–684.

Edwards, A. L. *Experimental design in psychological research*. New York: Rinehart, 1950.

Edwards, W., Lindman, H., & Savage, L. J. Bayesian statistical inference for psychological research. *Psychological Review*, 1963, **70**, 193–242.

Ferguson, L. *Statistical analysis in psychology and education*. New York: McGraw-Hill, 1959.

Fisher, R. A. *The design of experiments*. (4th ed.) Edinburgh: Oliver & Boyd, 1947.

Fisher, R. A. Statistical methods and scientific induction. *Journal of the Royal Statistical Society* (B), 1955, **17**, 69–78.

Guilford, J. P. *Psychometric methods*. New York: McGraw-Hill, 1936.

Hodges, J. L., & Lehman, E. L. Testing the approximate validity of statistical hypotheses. *Journal of the Royal Statistical Society* (B), 1954, **16**, 261–268.

Hogben, L. *The relationship of probability, credibility and error: An examination of the*

contemporary crisis in statistical theory from a behaviourist viewpoint. New York: Norton, 1958.

Kaiser, H. F. Directional statistical decision. *Psychological Review*, 1960, **67**, 160–167.

Keynes, J. M. *A treatise on probability*. London: Macmillan, 1948.

Lacey, O. L. *Statistical methods in experimentation*. New York: Macmillan, 1953.

Lindquist, E. F. *Statistical analysis in educational research*. Boston: Houghton Mifflin, 1940.

McNemar, Q. At random: Sense and nonsense. *American Psychologist*, 1960, **15**, 295–300.

Melton, A. W. Editorial. *Journal of Experimental Psychology*, 1962, **64**, 553–557.

Neyman, J. Outline of a theory of statistical estimation based on the classical theory of probability. *Philosophical Transactions of the Royal Society* (A), 1937, **236**, 333–380.

Neyman, J. "Inductive behavior" as a basic concept of philosophy of science. *Review of the Mathematical Statistics Institute*, 1957, **25**, 7–22.

Neyman, J., & Pearson, E. S. On the problem of the most efficient tests of statistical hypotheses. *Philosophical Transactions of the Royal Society* (A), 1933, **231**, 289–337.

Nunnally, J. The place of statistics in psychology. *Education and Psychological Measurement*, 1960, **20**, 641–650.

Pearson, E. S. Statistical concepts in their relation to reality. *Journal of the Royal Statistical Society* (B), 1955, **17**, 204–207.

Rosenthal, R., & Gaito, J. The interpretation of levels of significance by psychological researchers. *Journal of Psychology*, 1963, **55**, 33–38.

Rozeboom, W. W. The fallacy of the null hypothesis significance test. *Psychological Bulletin*, 1960, **57**, 416–428.

Savage, L. J. *The foundations of statistics*. New York: Wiley, 1954.

Schlaifer, R. *Probability and statistics for busi-*

ness decisions. New York: McGraw-Hill, 1959.

Smith, C. A. B. Review of N. T. J. Bailey, *Statistical methods in biology. Applied Statistics,* 1960, **9,** 64–66.

Snedecor, G. W. *Statistical methods.* (4th ed.; orig. publ. 1937) Ames, Iowa: Iowa State College Press, 1946.

Tukey, J. W. The future of data analysis. *Annals of Mathematical Statistics,* 1962, **33,** 1–67.

Underwood, B. J., Duncan, C. P., Taylor, J. A., & Cotton, J. W. *Elementary statis-*

tics. New York: Appleton-Century-Crofts, 1954.

Wald, A. Contributions to the theory of statistical estimation and testing hypotheses. *Annals of Mathematical Statistics,* 1939, **10,** 299–326.

Wald, A. *Statistical decision functions.* New York: Wiley, 1950.

Wald, A. *Selected papers in statistics and probability.* New York: McGraw-Hill, 1955.

Wilson, K. V. Subjectivist statistics for the current crisis. *Contemporary Psychology,* 1961, **6,** 229–231.

10

The Speed of the Nerve Impulse

Hermann von Helmholtz

The following paper is a great classic describing the first measurement of the velocity of nerve impulses. Before Helmholtz did his research it was believed that the conduction velocity of nerves could not be measured because it was equal to the velocity of light. In fact, it was Helmholtz's own teacher, Johannes Mueller, who expounded that view. Considering how difficult it is for a student to break away from traditions that are taken for "established fact," it is very impressive that Helmholtz set out to take such measurements. Equally striking is his ingenuity in using the limited electrical apparatus available to him in order to take such refined measures. Very important, too, was the great meticulousness with which he established the reliability of his measures. Helmholtz used statistical procedures, replication, and multiple measurement in order to establish reliability. The article by Stoyva and Kamiya in the present book illustrates the value of multiple measurement in permitting psychologists to deal with concepts incapable of description by a single measurement operation. Here we see an additional advantage. If an experimenter wishes to be confident of the reliability of his data, he can hardly do better than to measure the same phenomenon in a variety of ways.

The duration of the twitch of an animal muscle is ordinarily only a small fraction of a second, except for a longer lasting, weak after-effect. Since our senses are not capable of immediate perception of single time elements of such short duration, we must use more artificial methods to observe and measure them. Two of these especially are to be considered here. In the first, the events whose time intervals one wishes to find out are recorded by a suitable mechanism on a surface which moves with even speed. The time intervals appear on it as proportional space differences and can be measured by the latter. Ludwig has already used this method

Reprinted from Dagobert D. Runes (Ed.), *A treasury of world science,* New York: Philosophical Library, 1962, pp. 438–447.

for physiological purposes in order to show the fluctuations of blood pressure in the arteries and of atmospheric pressure in the pleural cavity. The other, essentially different, method of measuring time is the one proposed by Pouillet. The duration is here measured by the effect which a force of known intensity has produced during this interval. Pouillet has a galvanic current act on a resting magnet. The beginning and end of the current correspond exactly to the beginning and end of the interval to be measured; the magnitude of arc of the excursions which the magnet performs is, then, proportional to the duration to be measured. . . .

The foundation of Pouillet's method for measuring small time intervals is as follows: the time during which a galvanic current of known intensity from a coil has affected a magnet can be calculated exactly from its changed movement. Up to the present, one cannot anticipate a lower limit of time divisions measurable in this way, since one can increase at will the intensity of the acting current and the magnitude of its effect on the magnet by increasing the electromotor cells and the windings on the coil. But a limitation is imposed in the application of this procedure; namely, one must know how to cause the beginning and end of the supposed current, which from now on we shall call the time-measuring one, to coincide exactly with the beginning and end of the mechanical process the duration of which is to be measured. In the experiments to be described here the time-measuring current started at the moment when an instantaneous electric shock passed through the muscle or its nerve, and stopped when the circuit within which it circulated was interrupted by the contraction of the muscle. At the same time one could determine exactly the tension which the muscle had to develop in order to be able to separate the conductive metals from each other. The duration of the time-measuring current to be calculated is therefore identical with the time which elapses between the stimulation of the muscle, or of its nerve, and the moment at which its tension reaches a certain magnitude. . . .

In making measurements of the time which elapses between the stimulation of the nerve and the lifting of the overweight by the muscle, one finds that the time depends upon the point on the nerve at which one applies the electrical shock; the time is the longer, the longer the portion of the nerve between the stimulated point and the muscle. The experiment . . . can be repeated any number of times, by placing two of the four conducting wires, about two to three lines apart, on the nerve close to where it enters the muscle, and the two others, just as far apart, on the pelvic part of the nerve. I found it to be of advantage to move this second place not quite to the transected end of the sciatic plexus, but approximately to the place where the strands of this plexus combine to form the trunk of the sciatic nerve, because the extreme cut ends become inefficient relatively fast. Depending on whether one connects the first or the second pair of the leads with the induction coil, either the nerve point closer to the muscle, or the more distant one, will be affected by the current. Comparative measurements, which incidentally are carried out like those previously discussed, prove that the deflections of the magnet by the time-measuring current are on the average from 5–7 dial parts larger when the more distant point of the nerve is stimulated than the one closer to the muscle.

Apparently this difference cannot be caused by any of the formerly discussed sources of error, which are based on the mechanical and electrical occurrences in our measuring procedure, because all of these affect the experiments involving stimulation of the distant or near nerve point equally. Rather occurrences inside of the nerve itself must be the cause. . . .

We must . . . make sure that the intensity of stimulation is the same at both places. If this is so, then experiments show that whatever places on the nerve are stimulated, corresponding energy stages will follow each other at like time intervals, but the time between each of these energy stages (and the stimulation) is larger by a definite amount, as the stimulated spot is further away from the muscle. Therefore, if we express by curves the rise and fall of energy for two different nerve points, then the curve corresponding to the stimulation of the more distant point is congruent with the other, but between its starting point and the point corresponding to the moment of stimulation, here lies a larger part of the abscissa. From the nature of the time lapse which the muscle exhibits following stimulation we can draw conclusions concerning the course of the corresponding processes in the nerve which are mostly still unknown. . . . Now, since duration and strength of the stimulating electric current are exactly the same in both stimulated places the retardation of the effect must be due to the fact that a certain time elapses until it has spread from the more distant spot to the muscle. These experiments, therefore, enable us to find out the rate of propagation of the impulse in the

motor nerves of the frog, provided that we understand by impulse those processes in the nerve, which develop in it as a result of an external *stimulus.*

As long as the physiologists thought that nerve action could be ascribed to the propagation of an imponderable or psychic principle, it would have appeared incredible that the speed of this current should be measurable within the short distances of the animal body. At present we know from the investigations on the electromotor properties of nerves by Du Bois-Reymond, that the activity by which the conduction of an impulse is mediated is at least closely associated with, perhaps even essentially caused by, a changed arrangement of their material molecules. Accordingly, the conduction in the nerve would belong to the group of propagated molecular effects of ponderable bodies, to which, *e.g.,* belongs sound conduction in air and in elastic substances or the discharge of a tube filled with an explosive mixture. Under these circumstances, it is no longer surprising to see that the rate of conduction is not only measurable but as we shall see, even very moderate. Incidentally, the impossibility of observing time intervals of this kind in the daily perceptions of our own body, or in physiological experiments on muscle twitches must not surprise us, since the intervals which we may be sure that we observe between sensations involving the nerve fibers of our different sense organs are not much smaller than a second. One will recall that the most experienced astronomers differ by a full second in the comparative observation of visual and acoustic perceptions. . . .

From the greater number of my experimental series, all of which gave the same result, with more or less exactness,

I shall present herewith those which seem to be the most reliable on account of their extent or the correspondence of their single observations. For stimulation, we have invariably used currents which brought about maximum excitation. This was controlled by simultaneously observed elevations expressed in millimeters.

The series are arranged according to different plans. In some of them, all observations are made with the same or only two different overweights, in order to get as extensive figures as possible for the calculation of the essential time interval. For these I have calculated the means of the time-lapse between stimulation and muscle reaction for both points on the nerve, the difference between these means which corresponds to the rate of conduction in the nerve, and finally, in order to evaluate their exactness, the probable errors of all these values according to the rules of probability.

In other experimental series, the overweights have been exchanged as often as possible in order to prove that the delay is the same, for different degrees of muscle energy, provided one stimulates from the more distant point on the nerve, but the form of the energy increase is not altered. Obviously, the few experiments made with each overweight cannot furnish such exact values for differences due to nerve conduction as would longer series; therefore the individual means for these differences often vary considerably. However, the larger and smaller values are distributed entirely irregularly, and those for different overweights do not differ more from each other than those for the same overweight in successive observations. It follows that the magnitude of the differ-

ence does not depend noticeably on the amount of overweight, as is so definitely the case when the deflections of the magnet increase by decrease of the stimulation.

Finally, the rate of propagation of the nerve impulse was calculated after each experimental series. To do this, one must know the length of the traversed nerve piece, that is, the distance between the terminals at the two stimulated nerve places closest to the muscle. Unfortunately this length is very uncertain on account of the great extensibility of the nerve. If the nerve is not stretched, its fibers are bent in an undulating fashion; in order to measure its length I have always stretched it to such an extent that the transverse satin-like striations of its surface disappeared, on the assumption that the fibers would then run approximately straight. But a few millimeters are then always left to one's own discretion. Incidentally, it would not yet pay to devise an improved measuring technique since the inaccuracies of the time measurements are relatively much greater than those of the length measurements. Therefore it is not surprising that the established values of the rate of conduction still differ considerably from each other. . . .

EXPERIMENTAL SERIES X

Done on December 29 with the muscles of a frog kept for four months. Through the more distant point on the nerve is sent a stronger current, generated with the coils touching each other, and through the nearer point a weaker current with a distance between the coils of $2\frac{1}{2}$ cm. After each two observations the muscle is reset.

**Measurements of the Time-lapse of the Twitch of Animal* Muscles and
of the Rate of Propagation of the Nerve Impulse**

Number	Overweight	Lift	Difference of Deflection on Stimulation of	
			Further	Nearer
			Nervepoint	
1	20 gr.	1.19	100.09	
2		1.22	96.15	
3		1.22		93.92
4		1.15		97.19
5		1.10	97.70	
6		1.10	104.33	
7		1.17		93.87
8		1.12		92.27
9		1.15	106.43	
10		1.15	101.74	
11		1.12		98.00
12		1.17		98.60
13		1.12	96.81	
14		1.10	103.99	
Mean			100.98	95.64
Probable error of the mean			±0.86	±0.66
The same of the single observation			±2.42	±1.61
Duration of the time in sec. from stimulation to lifting			0.02437	0.02307
Probable error of the same			±0.00020	±0.00016
Time difference due to propagation			0.00130 ± 0.00027	
Rate of propagation			30.8 ± 6.4†	

* *I.e.,* skeletal.
† *I.e.,* meters/sec.

A. Right muscle—nerve length 40 mm., deflection before 116.09, after 112.45, mean 114.27.

The values found for the rate of propagation between 11 and 21° C. are therefore:

a) from series IX, X, and XI.

$$24.6 \pm 2.0$$
$$30.8 \pm 6.4$$
$$32.0 \pm 9.7$$
$$31.4 \pm 7.1$$
$$38.4 \pm 10.6$$

From these one finds by the method of least squares as most probable mean: 26.4 [meters/sec.].

b) from series XII, XIII, and XIV.

$$29.1$$
$$25.1$$
$$26.9$$
Mean $\overline{27.0}$

Finally, I summarize the results of the present investigations: I) If animal (skeletal) muscle, or its nerve, is stimulated by a momentary electric shock, a short time passes during which its elastic tension does not change noticeably; then it gradually rises to a maximum, and just as gradually falls again. The contraction of animal muscle differs from that which occurs in organic (visceral), nonrhythmically reaction muscle, after a relatively short stimulation, only in that its single phases pass much more rapidly.

If two different points of a motor nerve are stimulated by a momentary stimulus and if the magnitude of the stimulations is the same for both, then the time-lapse of the subsequent muscle twitch, is also the same; however, if the more distant point on the nerve has been stimulated, all of the muscle twitch stages occur later by an equal amount. From this, we conclude that the conduction of the nerve impulse to the muscle requires a measurable time. . . .

In the first series of my investigations on the time relations of muscle and nerve activity I have proved by the electromagnetic method of measuring time, that the mechanical reactions of the muscle, following a nerve stimulation, set in later if the excitation has to pass a longer portion of the nerve before getting to the muscle. The method mentioned offers, in fact, the best guarantee where safe execution of exact measurements is desired, but it has the great disadvantage of yielding the said result only after extensive and tedious series of experiments, which on account of their long duration require an especially favorable condition of the frog preparation. The other graphic method of measuring time, the application of which has been mentioned before, is essentially one in which the muscle during twitching records the magnitudes of its contractions on a moving surface; this promised a much simpler and easier demonstration of the rate of propagation in the nerves, and, since this seemed to me sufficiently important, I undertook to follow up the matter in this way, and I was perfectly successful.

The procedure of the experiments, I have already briefly indicated in the previous paper. A pen which is raised by the twitching muscle draws a curve on a surface moving with uniform speed, the vertical coordinates of the curve are proportionate to the contractions of the muscle, the horizontal ones proportionate to the time. As a starting point of this curve we shall fix that point which corresponds to the moment of stimulation of the muscle or its nerve. Now, if we arrange for two curves to be drawn in succession, and if we take care that at the moment of stimulation the pen occupies always exactly the same point on the surface, then both curves will have the same starting point, and from the congruence or noncongruence of their individual parts one can observe whether or not the different stages of the mechanical muscle response have occurred, in both instances, at the same or a later time after stimulation. . . .

If the animal parts are rather vigorous and fresh, then the shapes of the double curve are all alike, at whatever nerve spot one may start the stimulation. Then, each drawing consists of two curves of congruent shape which are shifted in a horizontal direction with respect to each other by a certain amount as in Fig. 1, such that the curve which has been drawn upon stimulation of the nearer nerve spot, is also nearer to the starting point of stimulation. The curve *adefg* corresponds to the stimulation of the nearer nerve point, $a\delta\epsilon\varphi g$ to the one of the more distant nerve point . . .

When we look at the double curve Fig. 1 it is evident that both of the muscle twitches recorded have been entirely identical as to strength, duration, and course of the different stages

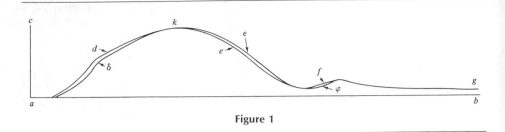

Figure 1

of contraction except that the one has started later after stimulation than the other one. Now, since the arrangement of the apparatus and the mechanical forces of the muscle have been exactly the same, the delay of the reaction in one instance can only have been derived from the longer time of propagation in the nerve. . . .

It is the great advantage of the described method that one can recognize immediately in each single drawing from the shape of the two curves whether the muscle has worked uniformly in both instances, whereas this fact could be deduced by the electromagnetic method of time measurement only from a long series of single experiments. As to the absolute value of the rate of propagation, the horizontal distances of the two curves cannot be measured with great accuracy; nevertheless, the values of that rate are about the same as in the former method. For instance, the horizontal distance in Fig. 1 is about 1 mm, the circumference of the cylinder corresponding to $\frac{1}{6}$ sec, is 85.7 mm, therefore the length of the abscissae is 514.2 mm per second. One mm corresponds therefore to $\frac{1}{514.2}$ sec. The length of the nerve involved in propagation was 53 mm, from which follows a rate of propagation of 27.25 m per sec. The most probable value from previous experiments was 26.4 m.

11
$N = 1$

William F. Dukes

It is customary in psychological research to assure the generalizability of findings by replicating them on a substantial number of subjects. The use of large numbers of subjects is characteristic of most statistically oriented psychologists. Those who use the "experimental analysis of behavior" techniques tend to use relatively small numbers of subjects. In the following article, Dukes shows how experiments done on only one experimental subject can be of value.

In the search for principles which govern behavior, psychologists generally confine their empirical observations to a relatively small sample of a defined population, using probability theory to help assess the generality of the findings obtained. Because this inductive process commonly entails some knowledge of individual differences in the behavior involved, studies employing only one subject ($N = 1$) seem somewhat anomalous. With no information about intersubject variability in performance, the general applicability of findings is indeterminate.

Although generalizations about behavior rest equally upon adequate sampling of both subjects and situations,

Reprinted from *Psychological Bulletin*, 1965, **64**, 74–79, by permission of the author and the American Psychological Association.

questions about sampling most often refer to subjects. Accordingly, the term "$N = 1$" is used throughout the present discussion to designate the *reductio ad absurdum* in the sampling of subjects. It might, however, equally well (perhaps better, in terms of frequency of occurrence) refer to the limiting case in the sampling of situations—for example, the use of one maze in an investigation of learning, or a simple tapping task in a study of motivation. With respect to the two samplings, Brunswik (1956), foremost champion of the representative design of experiments, speculated:

In fact, proper sampling of situations and problems may in the end be more important than proper sampling of subjects, considering the fact that individuals are probably on the whole much more alike than are situations among one another [p. 39].

As a corollary, the term $N = 1$ might also be appropriately applied to the sampling of experimenters. Long recognized as a potential source of variance in interview data (e.g., Cantril, 1944; Katz, 1942), the investigator has recently been viewed as a variable which may also influence laboratory results (e.g., McGuigan, 1963; Rosenthal, 1963).

Except to note these other possible usages of the term $N = 1$, the present paper is not concerned with one-experimenter or one-situation treatments, but is devoted, as indicated previously, to single-subject studies.

Despite the limitation stated in the first paragraph, $N = 1$ studies cannot be dismissed as inconsequential. A brief scanning of general and historical accounts of psychology will dispel any doubts about their importance, revealing, as it does, many instances of pivotal research in which the observations were confined to the behavior of only one person or animal.

SELECTIVE HISTORICAL REVIEW

Foremost among $N = 1$ studies is Ebbinghaus' (1885) investigation of memory. Called by some authorities "a landmark in the history of psychology . . . a model which will repay careful study [McGeoch & Irion, 1952, p. 1]," considered by others "a remedy . . . at least as bad as the disease [Bartlett, 1932, p. 3]," Ebbinghaus' work established the pattern for much of the research on verbal learning during the past 80 years. His principal findings, gleaned from many self-administered learning situations consisting of some 2,000 lists of nonsense syllables and 42

stanzas of poetry, are still valid source material for the student of memory. In another well-known pioneering study of learning, Bryan and Harter's (1899) report on plateaus, certain crucial data were obtained from only one subject. Their letter-word-phrase analysis of learning to receive code was based on the record of only one student. Their notion of habit hierarchies derived in part from this analysis is, nevertheless, still useful in explaining why plateaus may occur.

Familiar even to beginning students of perception is Stratton's (1897) account of the confusion from and the adjustment to wearing inverting lenses. In this experiment according to Boring (1942), Stratton, with only himself as subject,

settled both Kepler's problem of erect vision with an inverted image, and Lotze's problem of the role of experience in space perception, by showing that the "absolute" localization of retinal positions—up-down and right-left—are learned and consist of bodily orientation as context to the place of visual excitation [p. 237].

The role of experience was also under scrutiny in the Kelloggs' (1933) project of raising one young chimpanzee, Gua, in their home. (Although observations of their son's behavior were also included in their report, the study is essentially of the $N = 1$ type, since the "experimental group" consisted of one.) This attempt to determine whether early experience may modify behavior traditionally regarded as instinctive was for years a standard reference in discussions of the learning-maturation question.

Focal in the area of motivation is the balloon-swallowing experiment of physiologists Cannon and Washburn

(1912) in which kymographic recordings of Washburn's stomach contractions were shown to coincide with his introspective reports of hunger pangs. Their findings were widely incorporated into psychology textbooks as providing an explanation of hunger. Even though in recent years greater importance has been attached to central factors in hunger, Cannon and Washburn's work continues to occupy a prominent place in textbook accounts of food-seeking behavior.

In the literature on emotion, Watson and Rayner's study (1920) of Albert's being conditioned to fear a white rat has been hailed as "one of the most influential papers in the history of American psychology" (Miller, 1960, p. 690). Their experiment, Murphy (1949) observes,

immediately had a profound effect on American psychology; for it appeared to support the whole conception that not only simple motor habits, but important, enduring traits of personality, such as emotional tendencies, may in fact be 'built into' the child by conditioning [p. 261].

Actually the Albert experiment was unfinished because he moved away from the laboratory area before the question of fear removal could be explored. But Jones (1924) provided the natural sequel in Peter, a child who, through a process of active reconditioning, overcame a nonlaboratory-produced fear of white furry objects.

In abnormal psychology few cases have attracted as much attention as Prince's (1905) Miss Beauchamp, for years the model case in accounts of multiple personality. An excerpt from the Beauchamp case was recently included, along with selections from Wundt, James, Pavlov, Watson, and others, in a volume of 36 classics in psychology (Shipley, 1961). Perhaps less familiar to the general student but more significant in the history of psychology is Breuer's case (Breuer & Freud, 1895) of Anna O., the analysis of which is credited with containing "the kernel of a new system of treatment, and indeed a new system of psychology [Murphy, 1949, p. 307]." In the process of examining Anna's hysterical symptoms, the occasions for their appearance, and their origin, Breuer claimed that with the aid of hypnosis these symptoms were "talked away." Breuer's young colleague was Sigmund Freud (1910), who later publicly declared the importance of this case in the genesis of psychoanalysis.

There are other instances, maybe not so spectacular as the preceding, of influential $N = 1$ studies—for example, Yerkes' (1927) exploration of the gorilla Congo's mental activities; Jacobson's (1931) study of neuromuscular activity and thinking in an amputee; Culler and Mettler's (1934) demonstration of simple conditioning in a decorticate dog; and Burtt's (1932) striking illustration of his son's residual memory of early childhood.

Further documentation of the significant role of $N = 1$ research in psychological history seems unnecessary. A few studies, each in impact like the single pebble which starts an avalanche, have been the impetus for major developments in research and theory. Others, more like missing pieces from nearly finished jigsaw puzzles, have provided timely data on various controversies.

This historical recounting of "successful" cases is, of course, not an exhortation for restricted subject samplings, nor does it imply that their greatness is independent of subsequent related work.

FREQUENCY AND RANGE
OF TOPICS

In spite of the dated character of the citations—the latest being 1934—$N = 1$ studies cannot be declared the product of an era unsophisticated in sampling statistics, too infrequent in recent psychology to merit attention. During the past 25 years (1939–1963) a total of 246 $N = 1$ studies, 35 of them in the last 5-year period, have appeared in the following psychological periodicals: the *American Journal of Psychology, Journal of Genetic Psychology, Journal of Abnormal and Social Psychology, Journal of Educational Psychology, Journal of Comparative and Physiological Psychology, Journal of Experimental Psychology, Journal of Applied Psychology, Journal of General Psychology, Journal of Social Psychology, Journal of Personality, and Journal of Psychology.* These are the journals, used by Bruner and Allport (1940) in their survey of 50 years of change in American psychology, selected as significant for and devoted to the advancement of psychology as science. (Also used in their survey were the *Psychological Review, Psychological Bulletin,* and *Psychometrika,* excluded here because they do not ordinarily publish original empirical work.) Although these 246 studies constitute only a small percent of the 1939–1963 journal articles, the absolute number is noteworthy and is sizable enough to discount any notion that $N = 1$ studies are a phenomenon of the past.

When, furthermore, these are distributed, as in Table 1, according to subject matter, they are seen to coextend fairly well with the range of topics in general psychology. As might be expected, a large proportion of them fall into the clinical and personality areas. One cannot, however, explain away $N = 1$ studies as case histories contributed by clinicians and personologists occupied less with establishing generalizations than with exploring the uniqueness of an individual and understanding his total personality. Only about 30% (74) are primarily oriented toward the individual, a figure which includes not only works in the "understanding" tradition, but also those treating the individual as a universe of responses and applying traditionally nomothetic techniques to describe and predict individual behavior (e.g., Cattell & Cross, 1952; Yates, 1958).

In actual practice, of course, the two orientations—toward uniqueness or generality—are more a matter of degree than of mutual exclusion, with the result that in the literature surveyed purely idiographic research is extremely rare. Representative of that approach are Evans' (1950) novel-like account of Miller who "spontaneously" recovered his sight after more than 2 years of blindness, Rosen's (1949) "George X: The self-analysis of an avowed fascist," and McCurdy's (1944) profile of Keats.

RATIONALE FOR $N = 1$

The appropriateness of restricting an idiographic study to one individual is obvious from the meaning of the term. If uniqueness is involved, a sample of one exhausts the population. At the other extreme, an N of 1 is also appropriate if complete population generality exists (or can reasonably be assumed to exist). That is, when between-individual variability for the function under scrutiny is known to be negligible or the data from the single subject have a

TABLE 1   Total Distribution of $N = 1$ Studies (1939–1963)

Category	f	Examples
Maturation, development	29	Sequential development of prehension in a macaque (Jensen, 1961); smiling in a human infant (Salzen, 1963)
Motivation	7	Differential reinforcement effects of true, esophagal, and sham feeding in a dog (Hull, Livingston, Rouse, & Barker, 1951)
Emotion	12	Anxiety levels associated with bombing (Glavis, 1946)
Perception, sensory processes	25	Congenital insensitivity to pain in a 19-year-old girl (Cohen, Kipnis, Kunkle, & Kubzansky, 1955); figural aftereffects with a stabilized retinal image (Krauskopf, 1960)
Learning	27	Delayed recall after 50 years (Smith, 1963); imitation in a chimpanzee (Hayes & Hayes, 1952)
Thinking, language	15	"Idealess" behavior in a chimpanzee (Razran, 1961); opposite speech in a schizophrenic patient (Lafial & Ameen, 1959)
Intelligence	14	Well-adjusted congenital hydrocephalic with IQ of 113 (Teska, 1947); intelligence after lobectomy in an epileptic (Hebb, 1939)
Personality	51	Keats' personality from his poetry (McCurdy, 1944); comparison in an adult of P and R techniques (Cattell & Cross, 1952)
Mental health, psychotherapy	66	Multiple personality (Thigpen & Cleckley, 1954); massed practice as therapy for patient with tics (Yates, 1958)
Total	246	

point-for-point congruence with those obtained from dependable collateral sources, results from a second subject may be considered redundant. Some $N = 1$ studies may be regarded as approximations of this ideal case, as for example, Heinemann's (1961) photographic measurement of retinal images and Bartley and Seibel's (1954) study of entoptic stray light, using the flicker method.

A variant on this typicality theme occurs when the researcher, in order to preserve some kind of functional unity and perhaps to dramatize a point, reports in depth one case which exemplifies many. Thus Eisen's (1962) description of the effects of early sensory deprivation is an account of one quondam hard-of-hearing child, and Bettelheim's (1949) paper on rehabilitation a chronicle of one seriously delinquent child.

In other studies an N of 1 is adequate because of the dissonant character of the findings. In contrast to its limited usefulness in *establishing* generalizations from "positive" evidence, an N of 1 when the evidence is "negative," is as useful as an N of 1,000 in *rejecting* an asserted or assumed universal relationship. Thus Krauskopf's (1960) demonstration with one stopped-image subject eliminates motion of the retinal image as necessary for figural aftereffects; and Lenneberg's (1962) case of an 8-year-old boy who lacked the motor skills necessary for speaking but who could understand language makes it "clear that hearing oneself babble is not a necessary factor in the acquisition of understanding . . . [p. 422]." Similarly Teska's (1947) case of a congenital hydrocephalic, $6\frac{1}{2}$ years old, with an IQ of 113, is sufficient evidence to discount the notion that prolonged congenital hydrocephaly results in some degree of feeblemindedness.

While scientists are in the long run more likely to be interested in knowing *what is* than *what is not* and more concerned with how many exist or in what proportion they exist than with the fact that at least one exists, one negative case can make it necessary to revise a traditionally accepted hypothesis.

Still other $N = 1$ investigations simply reflect a limited opportunity to observe. When the search for lawfulness is extended to infrequent "nonlaboratory" behavior, individuals in the population under study may be so sparsely distributed spatially or temporally that the psychologist can observe only one case, a report of which may be useful as a part of a cumulative record. Examples of this include cases of multiple personality (Thigpen & Cleckly, 1954), unilateral color blindness (Graham, Sperling, Hsia, & Coulson, 1961) congenital insensitivity to pain (Cohen et al., 1955), and mental deterioration following carbon monoxide poisoning (Jensen, 1950). Situational complexity as well as subject sparsity may limit the opportunity to observe. When the situation is greatly extended in time, requires expensive or specialized training for the subject, or entails intricate and difficult to administer controls, the investigator may, aware of their exploratory character, restrict their observations to one sub-ject. Projects involving home-raising a chimpanzee (Hayes & Hayes, 1952) or testing after 16 years for retention of material presented during infancy (Burtt, 1941) would seem to illustrate this use of an N of 1.

Not all $N = 1$ studies can be conveniently fitted into this rubric; nor is this necessary. Instead of being oriented either toward the person (uniqueness) or toward a global theory (universality), researchers may sometimes simply focus on a problem. Problem-centered research on only one subject may, by clarifying questions, defining variables, and indicating approaches, make substantial contributions to the study of behavior. Besides answering a specific question, it may (Ebbinghaus' work, 1885, being a classic example) provide important groundwork for the theorists.

Regardless of rationale and despite obvious limitations, the usefulness of $N = 1$ studies in psychological research seems, from the preceding historical and methodological considerations, to be fairly well established. (See Shapiro, 1961, for an affirmation of the value of single-case investigations in fundamental clinical psychological research.) Finally, their status in research is further secured by the statistician's assertion (McNemar, 1940) that:

The statistician who fails to see that important generalizations from research on a single case can ever be acceptable is on a par with the experimentalist who fails to appreciate the fact that some problems can never be solved without resort to numbers [p. 361].

REFERENCES

Bartlett, F. C. *Remembering*. Cambridge, England: University Press, 1932.

Bartley, S. H., & Seibel, J. A further study

of entoptic stray light. *Journal of Psychology*, 1954, **38**, 313–319.

Bettelheim, B. H. A study in rehabilitation. *Journal of Abnormal and Social Psychology*, 1949, **44**, 231–265.

Boring, E. G. *Sensation and perception in the history of experimental psychology.* New York: Appleton-Century, 1942.

Breuer, J., & Freud, S. Case histories. (Orig. publ. 1895; trans. by J. Strachey) In J. Strachey (Ed.), *The standard edition of the complete psychological works of Sigmund Freud.* Vol. 2. London: Hogarth Press, 1955. Pp. 19–181.

Bruner, J. S., & Allport, G. W. Fifty years of change in American psychology. *Psychological Bulletin*, 1940, **37**, 757–776.

Brunswik, E. *Perception and the representative design of psychological experiments.* Berkeley: Univer. California Press, 1956.

Bryan, W. L., & Harter, N. Studies on the telegraphic language. The acquisition of a hierarchy of habits. *Psychological Review*, 1899, **6**, 345–375.

Burtt, H. E. An experimental study of early childhood memory. *Journal of Genetic Psychology*, 1932, **40**, 287–295.

Burtt, H. E. An experimental study of early childhood memory: Final report. *Journal of Genetic Psychology*, 1941, **58**, 435–439.

Cannon, W. B., & Washburn, A. L. An explanation of hunger. *American Journal of Physiology*, 1912, **29**, 441–454.

Cantril, H. *Gauging public opinion.* Princeton: Princeton Univer. Press, 1944.

Cattell, R. B., & Cross, K. P. Comparison of the ergic and self-sentiment structures found in dynamic traits by R- and P- techniques. *Journal of Personality*, 1952, **21**, 250–271.

Cohen, L. D., Kipnis, D., Kunkle, E. C., & Kubzansky, P. E. Observations of a person with congenital insensitivity to pain. *Journal of Abnormal and Social Psychology*, 1955, **51**, 333–338.

Culler, E., & Mettler, F. A. Conditioned behavior in a decorticate dog. *Journal of Comparative Psychology*, 1934, **18**, 291–303.

Ebbinghaus, H. *Über das Gedächtnis.* Leipzig: Duncker & Humblot, 1885.

Eisen, N. H. Some effects of early sensory deprivation on later behavior: The quondam hard-of-hearing child. *Journal of Abnormal and Social Psychology*, 1962, **65**, 338–342.

Evans, J. Miller. *Journal of Abnormal and Social Psychology*, 1950, **45**, 359–379.

Freud, S. The origin and development of psychoanalysis. *American Journal of Psychology*, 1910, **21**, 181–218.

Glavis, L. R., Jr. Bombing mission number fifteen. *Journal of Abnormal and Social Psychology*, 1946, **41**, 189–198.

Graham, C. H., Sperling, H. G., Hsia, Y., & Coulson, A. H. The determination of some visual functions of a unilaterally color-blind subject. *Journal of Psychology*, 1961, **51**, 3–32.

Hayes, K. J., & Hayes, Catherine. Imitation in a home-raised chimpanzee. *Journal of Comparative and Physiological Psychology*, 1952, **45**, 450–459.

Hebb, D. O. Intelligence in man after large removals of cerebral tissue: Defects following right temporal lobectomy. *Journal of General Psychology*, 1939, **21**, 437–446.

Heinemann, E. G. Photographic measurement of the retinal image. *American Journal of Psychology*, 1961, **74**, 440–445.

Hull, C. L., Livingston, J. R., Rouse, R. O., & Barker, A. N. True, sham, and esophageal feeding as reinforcements. *Journal of Comparative and Physiological Psychology*, 1951, **44**, 236–245.

Jacobson, E. Electrical measurements of neuromuscular states during mental activities: VI. A note on mental activities concerning an amputated limb. *American Journal of Physiology*, 1931, **96**, 122–125.

Jensen, G. D. The development of prehension in a macaque. *Journal of Comparative and Physiological Psychology*, 1961, **54**, 11–12.

Jensen, M. B. Mental deterioration following carbon monoxide poisoning. *Journal of Abnormal and Social Psychology*, 1950, **45**, 146–153.

Jones, Mary C. A laboratory study of fear: The case of Peter. *Journal of Genetic Psychology*, 1924, **31**, 308–315.

Katz, D. Do interviewers bias poll results? *Public Opinion Quarterly*, 1942, **6**, 248–268.

Kellogg, W. N., & Kellogg, Luella. *The ape and the child.* New York: McGraw-Hill, 1933.

Krauskopf, J. Figural after-effects with a stabilized retinal image. *American Journal of Psychology*, 1960, **73**, 294–297.

Laffal, J., & Ameen, L. Hypotheses of opposite speech. *Journal of Abnormal and Social Psychology*, 1959, **58**, 267–269.

Lenneberg, E. H. Understanding language without ability to speak: A case report. *Journal of Abnormal and Social Psychology*, 1962, **65**, 419–425.

McCurdy, H. G. *La belle dame sans merci. Character and Personality*, 1944, **13**, 166–177.

McGeoch, J. A., & Irion, A. L. *The psychology of human learning.* New York: Longmans, Green, 1952.

McGuigan, F. J. The experimenter: A neglected stimulus object. *Psychological Bulletin*, 1963, **60**, 421–428.

McNemar, Q. Sampling in psychological research. *Psychological Bulletin*, 1940, **37**, 331–365.

Miller, D. R. Motivation and affect. In Paul H. Mussen (Ed.), *Handbook of research methods in child development.* New York: Wiley, 1960, Pp. 688–769.

Murphy, G. *Historical introduction to modern psychology.* New York: Harcourt, Brace, 1949.

Prince, M. *The dissociation of a personality.* New York: Longmans, Green, 1905.

Razran, G. Raphael's "idealess" behavior. *Journal of Comparative and Physiological Psychology*, 1961, **54**, 366–367.

Rosen, E. George X: The self-analysis of an avowed fascist. *Journal of Abnormal and Social Psychology*, 1949, **44**, 528–540.

Rosenthal, R. Experimenter attributes as determinants of subjects' responses. *Journal of Projective Techniques*, 1963, **27**, 324–331.

Salzen, E. A. Visual stimuli eliciting the smiling response in the human infant. *Journal of Genetic Psychology*, 1963, **102**, 51–54.

Shapiro, M. B. The single case in fundamental clinical psychological research. *British Journal of Medical Psychology*, 1961, **34**, 255–262.

Shipley, T. (Ed.). *Classics in psychology.* New York: Philosophical Library, 1961.

Smith, M. E. Delayed recall of previously memorized material after fifty years. *Journal of Genetic Psychology*, 1963, **102**, 3–4.

Stratton, G. M. Vision without inversion of the retinal image. *Psychological Review*, 1897, **4**, 341–360, 463–481.

Teska, P. T. The mentality of hydrocephalics and a description of an interesting case. *Journal of Psychology*, 1947, **23**, 197–203.

Thigpen, C. H., & Cleckley, H. A case of multiple personality. *Journal of Abnormal and Social Psychology*, 1954, **49**, 135–151.

Watson, J. B., & Rayner, Rosalie. Conditioned emotional reactions. *Journal of Experimental Psychology*, 1920, **3**, 1–14.

Yates, A. J. The application of learning theory to the treatment of tics. *Journal of Abnormal and Social Psychology*, 1958, **56**, 175–182.

Yerkes, R. M. The mind of a gorilla. *Genetic Psychology Monographs*, 1927, **2**, 1–193.

SIX

Theory and Experiment
in Psychology

12

The Nature of
Scientific Theory

Clark L. Hull

The following account of the nature of scientific theory is in accord with a conventional view of the hypothetico-deductive nature of science. In this view, experimental work is done in order to test the implications of scientific theories. Deductions from theories become hypotheses capable of experimental test. This view of the relationship between theory and research was one almost universally held by experimental psychologists. It seems to be much less in favor today, with research ideas being tied only very loosely to theory if they are connected to theory at all. The subsequent article by Skinner expounds a view which seems currently to be much more in vogue.

THE TWO ASPECTS OF SCIENCE: EMPIRICAL AND EXPLANATORY

Men are ever engaged in the dual activity of making observations and then seeking explanations of the resulting revelations. All normal men in all times have observed the rising and setting of the sun and the several phases of the moon. The more thoughtful among them have then proceeded to ask the question, "Why? Why does the moon wax and wane? Why does the sun rise and set, and where does it go when it sets?" Here we have the two essential elements of modern science: the making of observations constitutes the empirical or factual component, and the systematic attempt to explain these facts constitutes the theoretical component. As science has developed, specialization, or division of labor, has occurred; some men have devoted their time mainly to the making of observations, while a smaller number have occupied themselves largely with the problems of explanation.

From *Principles of behavior* by Clark L. Hull. Copyright 1943. Reprinted by permission of the publishers, Appleton-Century-Crofts, Educational Division, Meredith Corporation.

During the infancy of science, observations are for the most part casual and qualitative—the sun rises, beats down strongly at midday, and sets; the moon grows from the crescent to full and then diminishes. Later observations, usually motivated by practical considerations of one kind or another, tend to become quantitative and precise—the number of days in the moon's monthly cycle are counted accurately, and the duration of the sun's yearly course is determined with precision. As the need for more exact observations increases, special tools and instruments, such as graduated measuring sticks, protractors, clocks, telescopes, and microscopes, are devised to facilitate the labor. Kindred tools relating to a given field of science are frequently assembled under a single roof for convenience of use; such an assemblage becomes a laboratory.

As scientific investigations become more and more searching it is discovered that the spontaneous happenings of nature are not adequate to permit the necessary observations. This leads to the setting up of special conditions which will bring about the desired events under circumstances favorable for such observations; thus experiments originate. But even in deliberate experiment it is often extraordinarily difficult to determine with which among a complex of antecedent conditions a given consequence is primarily associated; in this way arise a complex maze of control experiments and other technical procedures, the general principles of which are common to all sciences but the details of which are peculiar to each. Thus in brief review we see the characteristic technical development of the empirical or factual aspect of science.

Complex and difficult as are some of the problems of empirical science, those of scientific theory are perhaps even more difficult of solution and are subject to a greater hazard of error. It is not a matter of chance that the waxing and waning of the moon was observed for countless millennia before the comparatively recent times when it was at last successfully explained on the basis of the Copernican hypothesis. Closely paralleling the development of the technical aids employed by empirical science, there have also grown up in the field of scientific theory a complex array of tools and special procedures, mostly mathematical and logical in nature, designed to aid in coping with these peculiar difficulties. Because of the elementary nature of the present treatise, very little explicit discussion of the use of such tools will be given.

THE DEDUCTIVE NATURE OF SCIENTIFIC THEORY AND EXPLANATION

The term *theory* in the behavioral or "social" sciences has a variety of current meanings. As understood in the present work, a theory is a systematic deductive derivation of the secondary principles of observable phenomena from a relatively small number of primary principles or postulates, much as the secondary principles or theorems of geometry are all ultimately derived as a logical hierarchy from a few original definitions and primary principles called axioms. In science an observed event is said to be explained when the proposition expressing it has been logically derived from a set of definitions and postulates coupled with certain observed conditions antecedent to the event. This, in brief, is the nature of scientific theory and explanation as generally understood and accepted in the physical sciences after centuries of successful development (*1*, pp. 495–496).

The preceding summary statement of the nature of scientific theory and explanation needs considerable elaboration and exemplification. Unfortunately the finding of generally intelligible examples presents serious difficulties; because of the extreme youth of systematic behavior theory (*1*, p. 501 ff.; *2*, p. 15 ff.) as here understood, it is impossible safely to assume that the reader posesses any considerable familiarity with it. For this reason it will be necessary to choose all the examples from such physical sciences as are now commonly taught in the schools.

We can best begin the detailed consideration of the nature of scientific explanation by distinguishing it from something often confused with it. Suppose a naïve person with a moderate-sized telescope has observed Venus, Mars, Jupiter, and Saturn, together with numerous moons (including our own), and found them all to be round in contour and presumably spherical in form. He might proceed to formulate his observations in a statement such as, "All heavenly bodies are spherical," even though this statement goes far beyond the observations, since he has examined only a small sample of these bodies. Suppose, next, he secures a better telescope; he is now able to observe Uranus and Neptune, and finds both round in contour also. He may, in a manner of speaking, be said to explain the sphericity of Neptune by subsuming it under the category of heavenly bodies and then applying his previous empirical generalization. Indeed, he could have predicted the spherical nature of Nep-

tune by this procedure before it was observed at all:

All heavenly bodies are spherical.
Neptune is a heavenly body,
Therefore Neptune is spherical.

Much of what is loosely called explanation in the field of behavior is of this nature. The fighting propensities of a chicken are explained by the fact that he is a game cock and game cocks are empirically known to be pugnacious. The gregariousness of a group of animals is explained by the fact that the animals in question are dogs, and dogs are empirically known to be gregarious. As we have seen, it is possible to make concrete predictions of a sort on the basis of such generalizations, and so they have significance. Nevertheless this kind of procedure—the subsumption of a particular set of conditions under a category involved in a previously made empirical generalization—is not exactly what is regarded here as a scientific theoretical explanation.

For one thing, a theoretical explanation as here understood grows out of a problem, e.g., "What must be the shape of the heavenly bodies?" Secondly, it sets out from certain propositions or statements. These propositions are of two rather different kinds. Propositions of the first type required by an explanation are those stating the relevant initial or *antecedent conditions*. For example, an explanation of the shape of heavenly bodies might require the preliminary assumption of the existence of (1) a large mass of (2) more or less plastic, (3) more or less homogeneous matter, (4) initially of any shape at all, (5) the whole located in otherwise empty space. But a statement of the antecedent conditions is not enough; there must also be available a set of statements of *general principles* or rules of action relevant to the situation. Moreover, the particular principles to be utilized in a given explanation must be chosen from the set of principles generally employed by the theorist in explanations of this class of phenomena, the choice to be made strictly on the basis of the nature of the question or problem under consideration taken in conjunction with the observed or assumed conditions. For example, in the case of the shape of the heavenly bodies the chief principle employed is the Newtonian law of gravitation, namely, that every particle of matter attracts every other particle to a degree proportional to the product of their masses and inversely proportional to the square of the distances separating them. These principles are apt themselves to be verbal formulations of empirical generalizations, but may be merely happy conjectures or guesses found by a certain amount of antecedent trial-and-error to agree with observed fact. At all events they originate in one way or another in empirical observation.

The concluding phase of a scientific explanation is the derivation of the answer to the motivating question from the conditions and the principles, taken jointly, by a process of inference or reasoning. For example, it follows from the principle of gravitation that empty spaces which might at any time have existed within the mass of a heavenly body would at once be closed. Moreover, if at any point on the surface there were an elevation and adjacent to it a depression or valley, the sum of the gravitational pressures of the particles of matter in the elevation acting on the plastic material beneath would exert substantially the same pressure laterally as toward the center of gravity. But since there would be no equal lateral pressure originating in the valley to oppose the pressure originating in the elevation, the matter contained in the elevation would flow into the valley, thus eliminating both. This means that in the course of time all the matter in the mass under consideration would be arranged about its center of gravity with no elevations or depressions; i.e., the radius of the body at all points would be the same. In other words, if the assumed mass were not already spherical it would in the course of time automatically become so (*4*, p. 424). It follows that all heavenly bodies, including Neptune, must be spherical in form.

The significance of the existence of these two methods of arriving at a verbal formulation of the shape of the planet Neptune may now be stated. The critical characteristic of scientific theoretical explanation is that it reaches independently through a process of reasoning the same outcome with respect to (secondary) principles as is attained through the process of empirical generalization. Thus scientific theory may arrive at the general proposition, "All heavenly bodies of sufficient size, density, plasticity, and homogeneity are spherical," as a theorem, simply by means of a process of inference or deduction without any moons or planets having been observed at all. The fact that, in certain fields at least, practically the same statements or propositions can be attained quite independently by empirical methods as by theoretical procedures is of enormous importance for the development of science. For one thing, it makes possible the checking of results obtained by one method against those obtained by the other. It is a general assumption in scientific methodology that if everything entering into both procedures is correct, the statements yielded by them will never be in genuine conflict.

SCIENTIFIC EXPLANATIONS TEND TO COME IN CLUSTERS CONSTITUTING A LOGICAL HIERARCHY

This brings us to the important question of what happens in a theoretical situation when one or more of the supposed antecedent conditions are changed, even a little. For example, when considering the theoretical shape of heavenly bodies, instead of the mass being completely fluid it might be assumed to be only slightly plastic. It is evident at once, depending on the degree of plasticity, the size of the mass, etc., that there may be considerable deviation from perfect sphericity, such as the irregularities observable on the surface of our own planet. Or suppose that we introduce the additional condition that the planet revolves on its axis. This necessarily implies the entrance into the situation of the principle of centrifugal force, the familiar fact that any heavy object whirled around in a circle will pull outward. From this, in conjunction with other principles, it may be reasoned (and Newton did so reason) that the otherwise spherical body would bulge at the equator; moreover, this bulging at the equator together with the principle of gravity would, in turn, cause a flattening at the poles (4, p. 424). Thus we see how it is that as antecedent conditions are varied the theoretical outcome (theorem) following from these conditions will also vary. By progressively varying the antecedent conditions in this way an indefinitely large number of theorems may be derived, but all from the very same group of basic principles. The principles are employed over and over in different combinations, one combination for each theorem. Any given principle may accordingly be employed many times, each time in a different context. In this way it comes about that scientific theoretical systems potentially have a very large number of theorems (secondary principles) but relatively few general (primary) principles.

We note, next, that in scientific systems there are not only many theorems derived by a process of reasoning from the same assemblage of general principles, but these theorems take the form of a logical hierarchy: first-order theorems are derived directly from the original general principles; second-order theorems are derived with the aid of the first-order theorems; and so on in ascending hierarchical orders. Thus in deducing the flattening of the planets at the poles, Newton employed the logically antecedent principle of centrifugal force which, while an easily observable phenomenon, can itself be deduced, and so was deduced by Newton, from the conditions of circular motion. The principle of centrifugal force accordingly is an example of a lower-order theorem in Newton's theoretical system (4, p. 40 ff.). On the other hand, Newton derived from the bulging of the earth at its equator what is known as the "precession of the equinoxes" (4, p. 580), the fact that the length of the year as determined by the time elapsing from one occasion when the shadow cast by the winter sun at noon is longest to the next such occasion, is shorter by some twenty minutes than the length of the year as determined by noting the time elapsing from the conjunction of the rising of the sun with a given constellation of stars to the next such conjunction. This striking phenomenon, discovered by Hipparchus in the second century B.C., was first explained by Newton. The precession of the equinoxes accordingly is an example of a higher-order theorem in the Newtonian theoretical system.

From the foregoing it is evident that in its deductive nature systematic scientific theory closely resembles mathematics. In this connection the reader may profitably recall his study of geometry with (1) its definitions, e.g., point, line, surface, etc., (2) its primary principles (axioms), e.g., that but one straight line can be drawn between two points, etc., and following these (3) the ingenious and meticulous step-by-step development of the proof of one theorem after the other, the later theorems depending on the earlier ones in a magnificent and ever-mounting hierarchy of derived propositions. Proper scientific theoretical systems conform exactly to all three of these characteristics.[1] For example, Isaac Newton's *Principia* (4), the classical scientific theoretical system of the past, sets out with (1) seven definitions concerned with such notions as matter, motion, etc., and (2) a set of postulates consisting of his three famous laws of motion, from which is derived (3) a hierarchy of seventy-three formally proved theorems together with large numbers of appended corollaries. The

[1] The formal structure of scientific theory differs in certain respects from that of pure mathematics, but these differences need not be elaborated here; the point to be emphasized is that mathematics and scientific theory are alike in that they are both strictly deductive in their natures.

theorems and corollaries are concerned with such concrete observable phenomena as centrifugal force, the shape of the planets, the precession of the equinoxes, the orbits of the planets, the flowing of the tides, and so on.

SCIENTIFIC THEORY IS NOT ARGUMENTATION

The essential characteristics of scientific theory may be further clarified by contrasting it with argumentation and even with geometry. It is true that scientific theory and argument have similar formal or deductive structures; when ideally complete both should have their terms defined, their primary principles stated and their conclusions derived in an explicit and logical manner. In spite of this superficial similarity, however, the two differ radically in their essential natures, and it would be difficult to make a more serious mistake than to confuse them. Because of the widespread tendency to just this confusion, the distinction must be stressed. An important clue to the understanding of the critical differences involved is found in the objectives of the two processes.

The primary objective of argumentation is persuasion. It is socially aggressive; one person is deliberately seeking to influence or coerce another by means of a process of reasoning. There is thus in argumentation a proponent and a recipient. On the surface the proponent's objective often appears to be nothing more than to induce the recipient to assent to some more or less abstract proposition. Underneath, however, the ultimate objective is usually to lead the recipient to some kind of action, not infrequently such as to be of advantage to the proponent or some group with which the proponent is allied. Now, for the effort involved in elaborate argumentation to have any point, the proposition representing the objective of the proponent's efforts must be of such a nature that it cannot be substantiated by direct observation. The recipient cannot have made such observations; otherwise he would not need to be convinced.

Moreover, for an argument to have any coerciveness, the recipient must believe that the definitions and the other basic assumptions of the argument are sound; the whole procedure is that of systematically transferring to the final culminating conclusion the assent which the recipient initially gives to these antecedent statements. In this connection it is to be noted that systems of philosophy, metaphysics, theology, etc., are in the above sense at bottom elaborate arguments or attempts at persuasion, since their conclusions are of such a nature that they cannot possibly be established by direct observation. Consider, for example, Proposition XIV of Part One of Spinoza's *Ethic* (5):

Besides God no substance can be, . . .

The primary objective of scientific theory, on the other hand, is the establishment of scientific principles. Whereas argumentation is socially aggressive and is directed at some other person, natural science theory is aggressive towards the problems of nature, and it uses logic as a tool primarily for mediating to the scientist himself a more perfect understanding of natural processes. If Newton had been a scientific Robinson Crusoe, forever cut off from social contacts, he would have needed to go through exactly the same logical processes as he

did, if he were *himself* to have understood why the heavenly bodies are spherical rather than cubical. Naturally also, argumentation presupposes that the proponent has the solution of the question at issue fully in hand; hence his frequent overconfidence, aggressiveness, and dogmatism. In contrast to this, the theoretical activities of science, no less than its empirical activities, are directed modestly toward the gradual, piecemeal, successive-approximation establishment of scientific truths. In a word, scientific theory is a technique of investigation, of seeking from nature the answers to questions motivating the investigator; it is only incidentally and secondarily a technique of persuasion. It should never descend to the level of mere verbal fencing so characteristic of metaphysical controversy and argumentation.

Some forms of argumentation, such as philosophical and metaphysical speculation, have often been supposed to attain certainty of their conclusions because of the "self-evident" nature of their primary or basic principles. This is probably due to the influence of Euclid, who believed his axioms to be "self-evident truths." At the present time mathematicians and logicians have largely abandoned intuition or self-evidentiality as a criterion of basic or any other kind of truth. Similarly, scientific theory recognizes no axiomatic or self-evident truths; it has postulates but no axioms in the Euclidian sense. Not only this; scientific theory differs sharply from argumentation in that its postulates are not necessarily supposed to be true at all. In fact, scientific theory largely inverts the procedure found in argument: *whereas argument reaches belief in its theorems because of antecedent belief in its postulates, scientific theory reaches belief in its postulates to a considerable extent through direct or observational evidence of the soundness of its theorems (2, p. 7).*

THEORETICAL AND EMPIRICAL PROCEDURES CONTRIBUTE JOINTLY TO THE SAME SCIENTIFIC END

No doubt the statement that scientific theory attains belief in its postulates through belief in the soundness of its theorems will come as a distinct surprise to many persons, and for several reasons. For one thing, the thoughtful individual may wonder why, in spite of the admitted absence of self-evident principles or axioms, the basic principles of scientific systems are not firmly established at the outset by means of observation and experiment. After such establishment, it might be supposed, the remaining theorems of the system could all be derived by an easy logical procedure without the laborious empirical checking of each, as is the scientific practice. Despite the seductive charm of its simplicity this methodology is, alas, impossible. One reason is, as already pointed out (p. 3), that the generalizations made from empirical investigations can never be quite certain. Thus, as regards the purely empirical process every heavenly body so far observed might be spherical, yet this fact would only increase the probability that the next one encountered would be spherical; it would not make it certain. The situation is exactly analogous to that of the continued drawing of marbles at random from an urn containing white marbles and suspected of containing black ones also. As one white marble after another is drawn in an unbroken succession the proba-bility increases that the next one drawn will be white, but there can never come a time when there will not be a margin of uncertainty. *On the basis of observation alone* to say that all heavenly bodies are spherical is as unwarranted as it would be to state positively that all the marbles in an urn must be white because a limited random sampling has been found uniformly to be white.

But even for the sampling of empirical theory or experimental truth to be effective, the sampling of the different situations involved must be truly random. This means that the generalization in question must be tried out empirically with all kinds of antecedent conditions; which implies that it must be tested in conjunction with the operation of the greatest variety of other principles, singly and in their various combinations. In *very* simple situations the scientist in search of primary principles needs to do little more than formulate his observations. For example, it is simple enough to observe the falling of stones and similar heavy objects, and even to note that such objects descend more rapidly the longer the time elapsed since they were released from rest. But the moment two or more major principles are active in the same situation, the task of determining the rôle played by the one under investigation becomes far more difficult. It is not at all obvious to ordinary observation that the principle of gravity operative in the behavior of freely falling bodies is the same as that operative in the behavior of the common pendulum; ordinary falling bodies, for example, do not manifest the phenomena of lateral oscillation. The relation of gravity to the behavior of the pendulum becomes evident only as the result of a fairly sophisticated mathematical analysis requiring the genius of a Galileo for its initial formulation. But this "mathematical analysis," be it noted, is full-fledged scientific theory with *bona fide* theorems such as: the longer the suspension of the pendulum, the slower the beat.

In general it may be said that the greater the number of additional principles operative in conjunction with the one under investigation, the more complex the theoretical procedures which are necessary. It is a much more complicated procedure to show theoretically that pendulums should beat more slowly at the equator than at the pole than it is to deduce that pendulums with long suspensions should beat more slowly than those with short ones. This is because in the former situation there must be taken explicitly into consideration the additional principle of the centrifugal force due to the rotation of the earth about its axis.

At the outset of empirical generalization it is often impossible to detect and identify the active scientific principle by mere observation. For example, Newton's principle that all objects attract each other inversely as the squares of the distances separating them was a daring conjecture and one extending much beyond anything directly observable in the behavior of ordinary falling bodies. It is also characteristic that the empirical verification of this epoch-making principle was first secured through the study of careful astronomical measurements rather than through the observation of small falling objects. But the action of gravity in determining the orbits of the planets is even less obvious to ordinary unaided observation than is its rôle in the determination of the behavior of the pendulum. Indeed, this can be detected

only by means of the mathematics of the ellipse, i.e., through a decidedly sophisticated theoretical procedure, one which had to await the genius of Newton for its discovery.

Earlier in the chapter it was pointed out that the theoretical outcome, or theorem, derived from a statement of supposed antecedent conditions is assumed in science always to agree with the empirical outcome, provided both procedures have been correctly performed. We must now note the further assumption that if there is disagreement between the two outcomes there must be something wrong with at least one of the principles or rules involved in the derivation of the theorem; empirical observations are regarded as primary, and wherever a generalization really conflicts with observation the generalization must always give way. When the breakdown of a generalization occurs in this way, an event of frequent occurrence in new fields, the postulates involved are revised if possible so as to conform to the known facts. Following this, deductions as to the outcome of situations involving still other combinations of principles are made; these in their turn are checked against observations; and so on as long as disagreements continue to occur. Thus the determination of scientific principles is in considerable part a matter of symbolic trial-and-error. At each trial of this process, where the antecedent conditions are such as to involve jointly several other presumptive scientific principles, symbolic or theoretical procedure is necessary in order that the investigator may know the kind of outcome to be expected if the supposed principle specially under investigation is really acting as assumed. The empirical procedure is necessary in order to determine whether the antecedent conditions were really followed by the deductively expected outcome. Thus both theoretical and empirical procedures are indispensable to the attainment of the major scientific goal—that of the determination of scientific principles.

HOW THE EMPIRICAL VERIFICATION OF THEOREMS INDIRECTLY SUBSTANTIATES POSTULATES

But how can the empirical verification of the implications of theorems derived from a set of postulates establish the truth of the postulates? In seeking an answer to this question we must note at the outset that absolute truth is not thus established. The conclusion reached in science is not that the postulates employed in the derivation of the empirically verified theorem are thereby shown to be true beyond doubt, but rather that the empirical verification of the theorem has *increased the probability* that the next theorem derived from these postulates in conjunction with a different set of antecedent conditions will also agree with relevant empirical determinations. And this conclusion is arrived at on the basis of chance or probability, i.e., on the basis of a theory of sampling.

The nature of this sampling theory may be best explained by means of a decidedly artificial example. Suppose that by some miracle a scientist should come into possession of a set of postulates none of which had ever been employed, but which were believed to satisfy the logical criterion of yielding large

numbers of empirically testable theorems; that a very large number of such theorems should be deducible by special automatic logical calculation machines; that the theorems, each sealed in a neat capsule, should all be turned over to the scientist at once; and, finally, that these theorems should then be placed in a box, thoroughly mixed, drawn out one at a time, and compared with empirical fact. Assuming that no failures of agreement occurred in a long succession of such comparisons, it would be proper to say that each succeeding agreement would increase the probability that the next drawing from the box would also result in an agreement, exactly as each successive uninterrupted drawing of white marbles from an urn would increase progressively the probability that the next drawing would also yield a white marble. But just as the probability of drawing a white marble will always lack something of certainty even with the best conceivable score, so the validation of scientific principles by this procedure must always lack something of being complete. Theoretical "truth" thus appears in the last analysis to be a matter of greater or less probability. It is consoling to know that this probability frequently becomes very high indeed (*3*, p. 6).

THE "TRUTH" STATUS OF LOGICAL PRINCIPLES OR RULES

Despite much belief to the contrary, it seems likely that logical (mathematical) principles are essentially the same in their mode of validation as scientific principles; they appear to be merely invented rules of symbolic manipulation which have been found by trial in a great variety of situations to mediate the deduction of existential sequels verified by observation. Thus logic in science is conceived to be primarily a tool or instrument useful for the derivation of dependable expectations regarding the outcome of dynamic situations. Except for occasional chance successes, it requires sound rules of deduction, as well as sound dynamic postulates, to produce sound theorems. By the same token, each observationally confirmed theorem increases the justified confidence in the logical rules which mediated the deduction, as well as in the "empirical" postulates themselves. The rules of logic are more dependable, and consequently less subject to question, presumably because they have survived a much longer and more exacting period of trial than is the case with most scientific postulates. Probably it is because of the widespread and relatively unquestioned acceptance of the ordinary logical assumptions, and because they come to each individual investigator ready-made and usually without any appended history, that logical principles are so frequently regarded with a kind of religious awe as a subtle distillation of the human spirit; that they are regarded as never having been, and as never to be, subjected to the tests of validity usually applicable to ordinary scientific principles; in short, that they are strictly "self-evident" truths (3, p. 7). As a kind of empirical confirmation of the above view as to the nature of logical principles, it may be noted that both mathematicians and logicians are at the present time busily inventing, modifying, and generally perfecting the principles or rules of their disciplines (6).

SUMMARY

Modern science has two inseparable components—the empirical and the theoretical. The empirical component is concerned primarily with observation; the theoretical component is concerned with the interpretation and explanation of observation. A natural event is explained when it can be derived as a theorem by a process of reasoning from (1) a knowledge of the relevant natural conditions antedating it, and (2) one or more relevant principles called postulates. Clusters or families of theorems are generated, and theorems are often employed in the derivation of other theorems; thus is developed a logical hierarchy resembling that found in ordinary geometry. A hierarchy of interrelated families of theorems, all derived from the same set of consistent postulates, constitutes a scientific system.

Scientific theory resembles argumentation in being logical in nature but differs radically in that the objective of argument is to convince. In scientific theory logic is employed in conjunction with observation as a means of inquiry. Indeed, theoretical procedures are indispensable in the establishment of natural laws. The range of validity of a given supposed law can be determined only by trying it out empirically under a wide range of conditions where it will operate in simultaneous conjunction with the greatest variety and combination of other natural laws. But the only way the scientist can tell from the outcome of such an empirical procedure whether a given hypothetical law has acted in the postulated manner is first to deduce by a logical process what the outcome of the investigation *should* be if the hypothesis really holds. This deductive process is the essence of scientific theory.

The typical procedure in science is to adopt a postulate tentatively, deduce one or more of its logical implications concerning observable phenomena, and then check the validity of the deductions by observation. If the deduction is in genuine disagreement with observation, the postulate must be either abandoned or so modified that it implies no such conflicting statement. If, however, the deductions and the observations agree, the postulate gains in dependability. By successive agreements under a very wide variety of conditions it may attain a high degree of justified credibility, but never absolute certainty.

REFERENCES

1. Hull, C. L. The conflicting psychologies of learning—a way out. *Psychol. Rev.,* 1935, **42,** 491–516.
2. Hull, C. L. Mind, mechanism, and adaptive behavior. *Psychol. Rev.,* 1937, **44,** 1–32.
3. Hull, C. L., Hovland, C. I., Ross, R. T., Hall, M., Perkins, D. T., and Fitch, F. B. *Mathematico-deductive theory of rote learning.* New Haven: Yale Univ. Press, 1940.
4. Newton, I. *Principia* (trans. by F. Cajori). Berkeley: Univ. Calif. Press, 1934.
5. Spinoza, B. DE. *Ethic* (trans. by W. H. White and A. H. Stirling). New York: Macmillan Co., 1894.
6. Whitehead, A. N., and Russell, M. A. *Principia mathematica* (Vol. I). London: Cambridge Univ. Press, 1935.

13

A Case History in Scientific Method

B. F. Skinner

In the following selection, Skinner takes a view of scientific method not unlike that of Polanyi, only he does so from the standpoint of a behaviorist. He argues, just as Polanyi does, that science proceeds without formulated rules. Discoveries tend to occur serendipitously—while the scientist is looking for something else. However, it is doubtful that Skinner would be as skeptical as Polanyi of the possibility of someday discovering rules of scientific behavior. Skinner has far too much faith in the power of science for that.

    Skinner makes a number of other important points in this article. Several points characteristic of the Skinnerian approach are defended here, including critical evaluation of statistical methodology in psychology and an argument in support of the view that behavior is a useful subject matter in its own right without appeal to its physiological bases. More than anything, however, the article is valuable for the close view it gives us of the faltering first steps of a great scientist—a man whose work might revolutionize our society. It shows very strikingly how humble the beginnings of a great research enterprise can be. It seems a long way from rats in a runway to the possible transformation of an educational system, but Skinner has made the journey.

It has been said that college teaching is the only profession for which there is no professional training, and it is commonly argued that this is because our graduate schools train scholars and sci-

entists rather than teachers. We are more concerned with the discovery of knowl-

Address of the President at the Eastern Psychological Association meetings in Philadelphia, April, 1955.

(Some of the investigators mentioned in this article are now working at laboratories other than those indicated. *Ed.*)

Reprinted from *American Psychologist,* 1956, **11,** 221–233, by permission of the author and the American Psychological Association.

edge than with its dissemination. But can we justify ourselves quite so easily? It is a bold thing to say that we know how to train a man to be a scientist. Scientific thinking is the most complex and probably the most subtle of all human activities. Do we actually know how to shape up such behavior, or do we simply mean that some of the people who attend our graduate schools eventually become scientists?

Except for a laboratory course which acquaints the student with standard apparatus and standard procedures, the only explicit training in scientific method generally received by a young psychologist is a course in statistics—not the introductory course, which is often required of so many kinds of students that it is scarcely scientific at all, but an advanced course which includes "model building," "theory construction," and "experimental design." But it is a mistake to identify scientific practice with the formalized constructions of statistics and scientific method. These disciplines have their place, but it does not coincide with the place of scientific research. They offer *a* method of science but not, as is so often implied, *the* method. As formal disciplines they arose very late in the history of science, and most of the facts of science have been discovered without their aid. It takes a great deal of skill to fit Faraday with his wires and magnets into the picture which statistics gives us of scientific thinking. And most current scientific practice would be equally refractory, especially in the important initial stages. It is no wonder that the laboratory scientist is puzzled and often dismayed when he discovers how his behavior has been reconstructed in the formal analyses of scientific method. He is likely to protest that this is not at all a fair representation of what he does.

But his protest is not likely to be heard. For the prestige of statistics and scientific methodology is enormous. Much of it is borrowed from the high repute of mathematics and logic, but much of it derives from the flourishing state of the art itself. Some statisticians are professional people employed by scientific and commercial enterprises. Some are teachers and pure researchers who give their colleagues the same kind of service for nothing—or at most a note of acknowledgment. Many are zealous people who, with the best of intentions, are anxious to show the nonstatistical scientist how he can do his job more efficiently and assess his results more accurately. There are strong professional societies devoted to the advancement of statistics, and hundreds of technical books and journals are published annually.

Against this, the practicing scientist has very little to offer. He cannot refer the young psychologist to a book which will tell him how to find out all there is to know about a subject matter, how to have the good hunch which will lead him to devise a suitable piece of apparatus, how to develop an efficient experimental routine, how to abandon an unprofitable line of attack, how to move on most rapidly to later stages of his research. The work habits which have become second nature to him have not been formalized by anyone, and he may feel that they possibly never will be. As Richter (5) has pointed out, "Some of the most important discoveries have been made without any plan of research," and "there are researchers who do not work on a verbal plane, who cannot put into words what they are doing."

If we are interested in perpetuating the practices responsible for the present corpus of scientific knowledge, we must keep in mind that some very important parts of the scientific process do not now lend themselves to mathematical, logical, or any other formal treatment. We do not know enough about human behavior to know how the scientist does what he does. Although statisticians and methodologists may seem to tell us, or at least imply, how the mind works—how problems arise, how hypotheses are formed, deductions made, and crucial experiments designed—we as psychologists are in a position to remind them that they do not have methods appropriate to the empirical observation or the functional analysis of such data. These are aspects of human behavior, and no one knows better than we how little can at the moment be said about them.

Some day we shall be better able to express the distinction between empirical analysis and formal reconstruction, for we shall have an alternative account of the behavior of Man Thinking. Such an account will not only plausibly reconstruct what a particular scientist did in any given case, it will permit us to evaluate practices and, I believe, to teach scientific thinking. But that day is some little distance in the future. Meanwhile we can only fall back on examples.

Some time ago the director of Project A of the American Psychological Association asked me to describe my activities as a research psychologist. I went through a trunkful of old notes and records and, for my pains, reread some of my earlier publications. This has made me all the more aware of the contrast between the reconstructions of formalized scientific method and at least one case of actual practice. Instead of amplifying the points I have just made by resorting to a generalized account which is not available, I should like to discuss a case history. It is not one of the case histories we should most like to have, but what it lacks in importance is perhaps somewhat offset by accessibility. I therefore ask you to imagine that you are all clinical psychologists—a task which becomes easier and easier as the years go by—while I sit across the desk from you or stretch out upon this comfortable leather couch.

The first thing I can remember happened when I was only twenty-two years old. Shortly after I had graduated from college Bertrand Russell published a series of articles in the old *Dial* magazine on the epistemology of John B. Watson's Behaviorism. I had had no psychology as an undergraduate, but I had had a lot of biology, and two of the books which my biology professor had put into my hands were Loeb's *Physiology of the Brain* and the newly published Oxford edition of Pavlov's *Conditioned Reflexes*. And now here was Russell extrapolating the principles of an objective formulation of behavior to the problem of knowledge! Many years later when I told Lord Russell that his articles were responsible for my interest in behavior, he could only exclaim, "Good Heavens! I had always supposed that those articles had demolished Behaviorism!" But at any rate he had taken Watson seriously, and so did I.

When I arrived at Harvard for graduate study, the air was not exactly full of behavior, but Walter Hunter was coming in once a week from Clark University to give a seminar, and Fred Keller, also a graduate student, was an expert in both the technical details and the sophistry of Behaviorism. Many a time he saved me as I sank into the quicksands of an amateurish discussion of "What is an image?" or "Where is red?" I soon came into contact with W. J. Crozier, who had studied under Loeb. It had been said of Loeb, and might have been said of Crozier, that he "resented the nervous system." Whether this was true or not, the fact was that both these men talked about animal behavior without mentioning the nervous system and with surprising success. So far as I was concerned, they cancelled out the physiological theorizing of Pavlov and Sherrington and thus clarified what remained of the work of these men as the beginnings of an independent science of behavior. My doctoral thesis was in part an operational analysis of Sherrington's synapse, in which behavioral laws were substituted for supposed states of the central nervous system.

But the part of my thesis at issue here was experimental. So far as I can see, I began simply by looking for lawful processes in the behavior of the intact organism. Pavlov had shown the way; but I could not then, as I cannot now, move without a jolt from salivary reflexes to the important business of the organism in everyday life. Sherrington and Magnus had found order in surgical segments of the organism. Could not something of the same sort be found, to use Loeb's phrase, in "the organism as a whole?" I had the clue from Pavlov: control your conditions and you will see order.

It is not surprising that my first gadget was a silent release box, operated by compressed air and designed to eliminate disturbances when introducing a rat into an apparatus. I used this first in studying the way a rat adapted to a novel stimulus. I built a soundproof box containing a specially structured space. A rat was released, pneumatically, at the far end of a darkened tunnel from which it emerged in exploratory fashion into a well-lighted area. To accentuate its progress and to facilitate recording, the tunnel was placed at the top of a flight of steps, something like a functional Parthenon (Figure 1). The rat would peek out from the tunnel, perhaps glancing suspiciously at the one-way window through which I was watching it, then stretch itself cautiously down the steps. A soft click (carefully calibrated, of course) would cause it to pull back into the tunnel and remain there for some time. But repeated clicks had less and less of an effect. I recorded the rat's advances and retreats by moving a pen back and forth across a moving paper tape.

The major result of this experiment was that some of my rats had babies. I began to watch young rats. I saw them right themselves and crawl about very much like the decerebrate or thalamic cats and rabbits of Magnus. So I set

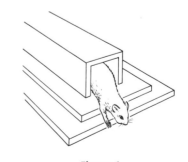

Figure 1

about studying the postural reflexes of young rats. Here was a first principle not formally recognized by scientific methodologists: When you run onto something interesting, drop everything else and study it. I tore up the Parthenon and started over.

If you hold a young rat in one hand and pull it gently by the tail, it will resist you by pulling forward and then, with a sudden sharp spring which usually disengages its tail, it will leap out into space. I decided to study this behavior quantitatively. I built a light platform covered with cloth and mounted it on tightly stretched piano wires (Figure 2). Here was a version of Sherrington's torsion-wire myograph, originally designed to record the isometric contraction of the *tibialis anticus* of a cat, but here adapted to the response of a whole organism. When the tail of the young rat was gently pulled, the rat clung to the cloth floor and tugged forward. By amplifying the fine movements of the platform, it was possible to get a good kymograph record of the tremor in this

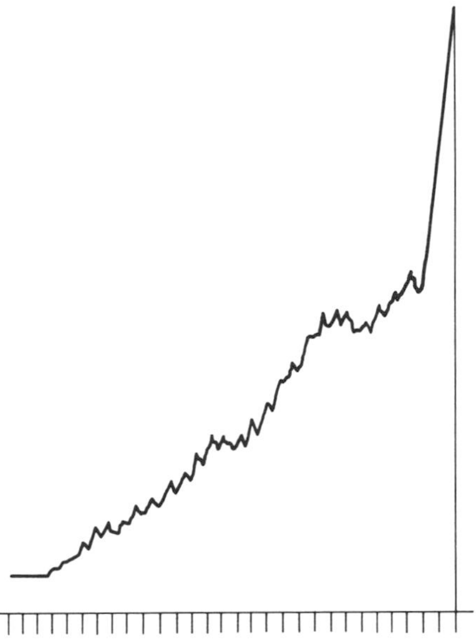

Figure 3

motion and then, as the pull against the tail was increased, of the desperate spring into the air (Figure 3).

Now, baby rats have very little future, except as adult rats. Their behavior is literally infantile and cannot be usefully extrapolated to everyday life. But if this technique would work with a baby, why not try it on a mature rat? To avoid attaching anything to the rat, it should be possible to record, not a pull against the substrate, but the ballistic thrust exerted as the rat runs forward or suddenly stops in response to my calibrated click. So, invoking the first principle of scientific practice again, I threw away the piano-wire platform, and built a runway, eight feet long. This was constructed of light wood, in the form of a girder, mounted rigidly on vertical glass plates, the elasticity of which permitted a very slight longitudinal movement (Figure 4). The runway became

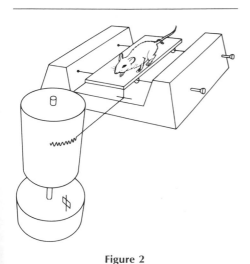

Figure 2

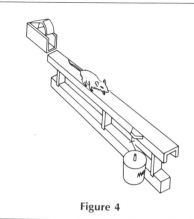

Figure 4

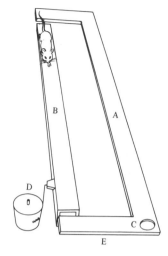

Figure 5

the floor of a long tunnel, not shown, at one end of which I placed my sound-less release box and at the other end myself, prepared to reinforce the rat for coming down the runway by giving it a bit of wet mash, to sound a click from time to time when it had reached the middle of the runway, and to harvest kymograph records of the vibrations of the substrate.

Now for a second uniformalized principle of scientific practice: Some ways of doing research are easier than others. I got tired of carrying the rat back to the other end of the runway. A back alley was therefore added (Figure 5). Now the rat could eat a bit of mash at point C, go down the back alley A, around the end as shown, and back home by runway B. The experi-menter at E could collect records from the kymograph at D in comfort. In this way a great many records were made of the forces exerted against the sub-stratum as rats ran down the alley and occasionally stopped dead in their tracks as a click sounded (Figure 6).

There was one annoying detail, how-ever. The rat would often wait an inordinately long time at C before starting down the back alley on the next run. There seemed to be no explanation for this. When I timed these delays with a stop watch, however, and plotted them, they seemed to show orderly changes (Figure 7). This was, of course, the kind of thing I was looking for. I forgot all about the movements of the substratum and began to run rats for the sake of the delay measurements alone. But there was now no reason why the runway had to be eight feet long and, as the second principle came into play again, I saw no reason why the rat could not deliver its own reinforcement.

A new apparatus was built. In Figure

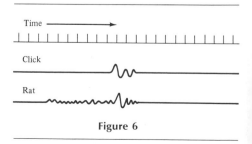

Figure 6

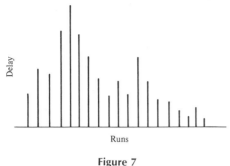

Figure 7

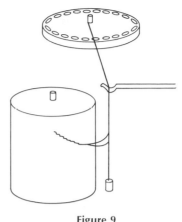

Figure 9

8, we see the rat eating a piece of food just after completing a run. It produced the food by its own action. As it ran down the back alley A to the far end of the rectangular runway, its weight caused the whole runway to tilt slightly on the axis C and this movement turned the wooden disc D, permitting a piece of food in one of the holes around its perimeter to drop through a funnel into a food dish. The food was pearl barley, the only kind I could find in the grocery stores in reasonably uniform pieces. The rat had only to complete its journey by coming down the home stretch B to enjoy its reward. The experimenter was able to enjoy *his* reward at the same time, for he had only to load the magazine, put in a rat, and relax. Each tilt

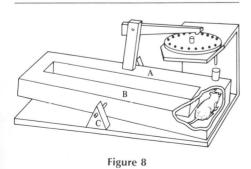

Figure 8

was recorded on a slowly moving kymograph.

A third unformalized principle of scientific practice: Some people are lucky. The disc of wood from which I had fashioned the food magazine was taken from a storeroom of discarded apparatus. It happened to have a central spindle, which fortunately I had not bothered to cut off. One day it occurred to me that if I wound a string around the spindle and allowed it to unwind as the magazine was emptied (Figure 9), I would get a different kind of record. Instead of a mere report of the up-and-down movement of the runway, as a series of pips as in a polygraph, I would get a *curve.* And I knew that science made great use of curves, although, so far as I could discover, very little of pips on a polygram. The difference between the old type of record at A (Figure 10) and the new at B may not seem great, but as it turned out the curve revealed things in the rate of responding, and in changes in that rate, which would certainly otherwise have been missed. By allowing the string to unwind rather than to wind, I had got my curve in an

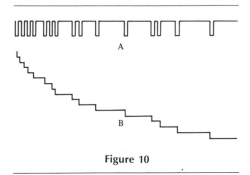

Figure 10

awkward Cartesian quadrant, but that was easily remedied. Psychologists have adopted cumulative curves only very slowly, but I think it is fair to say that they have become an indispensable tool for certain purposes of analysis.

Eventually, of course, the runway was seen to be unnecessary. The rat could simply reach into a covered tray for pieces of food, and each movement of the cover could operate a solenoid to move a pen one step in a cumulative curve. The first major change in rate observed in this way was due to ingestion. Curves showing how the rate of eating declined with the time of eating comprised the other part of my thesis. But a refinement was needed. The behavior of the rat in pushing open the door was not a normal part of the ingestive behavior of *Rattus rattus*. The act was obviously learned but its status as part of the final performance was not clear. It seemed wise to add an initial conditioned response connected with ingestion in a quite arbitrary way. I chose the first device which came to hand—a horizontal bar or lever placed where it could be conveniently depressed by the rat to close a switch which operated a magnetic magazine. Ingestion curves obtained with this initial response in the chain were found to have the same properties as those without it.

Now, as soon as you begin to complicate an apparatus you necessarily invoke a fourth principle of scientific practice: Apparatuses sometimes break down. I had only to wait for the food magazine to jam to get an extinction curve. At first I treated this as a defect and hastened to remedy the difficulty. But eventually, of course, I deliberately disconnected the magazine. I can easily recall the excitement of that first complete extinction curve (Figure 11). I had made contact with Pavlov at last! Here was a curve uncorrupted by the physiological process of ingestion. It was an orderly change due to nothing more than a special contingency of reinforcement. It was pure behavior! I am not saying that I would not have got around to extinction curves without a breakdown in the apparatus; Pavlov had given too strong a lead in that direction. But it is still no exaggeration to say that some of the most interesting and surprising results have turned up first because of similar accidents. Foolproof apparatus is no doubt highly desirable, but Charles Ferster and I in recently reviewing the data from a five-year program of research found many occasions to congratulate ourselves on the fallibility of relays and vacuum tubes.

I then built four soundproof ventilated boxes, each containing a lever and a food magazine and supplied with a cumulative recorder, and was on my

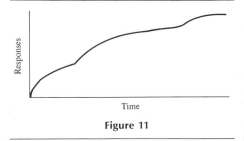

Figure 11

way to an intensive study of conditioned reflexes in skeletal behavior. I would reinforce every response for several days and then extinguish for a day or two, varying the number of reinforcements, the amount of previous magazine training, and so on.

At this point I made my first use of the deductive method. I had long since given up pearl barley as too unbalanced a diet for steady use. A neighborhood druggist had shown me his pill machine, and I had had one made along the same line (Figure 12). It consisted of a fluted brass bed across which one laid a long cylinder of stiff paste (in my case a MacCollum formula for an adequate rat diet). A similarly fluted cutter was then lowered onto the cylinder and rolled slowly back and forth, converting the paste into about a dozen spherical pellets. These were dried for a day or so before use. The procedure was painstaking and laborious. Eight rats eating a hundred pellets each per day could easily keep up with production. One pleasant Saturday afternoon I surveyed my supply of dry pellets, and, appealing to certain elemental theorems in arithmetic, deduced that unless I spent the rest of that afternoon and evening at the pill machine, the supply would be exhausted by ten-thirty Monday morning.

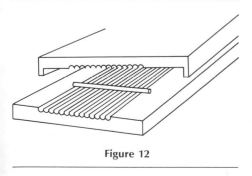

Figure 12

Since I do not wish to deprecate the hypothetico-deductive method, I am glad to testify here to its usefulness. It led me to apply our second principle of unformalized scientific method and to ask myself why *every* press of the lever had to be reinforced. I was not then aware of what had happened at the Brown laboratories, as Harold Schlosberg later told the story. A graduate student had been given the task of running a cat through a difficult discrimination experiment. One Sunday the student found the supply of cat food exhausted. The stores were closed and so, with a beautiful faith in the frequency-theory of learning, he ran the cat as usual and took it back to its living cage unrewarded. Schlosberg reports that the cat howled its protest continuously for nearly forty-eight hours. Unaware of this I decided to reinforce a response only once every minute and to allow all other responses to go unreinforced. There were two results: (a) my supply of pellets lasted almost indefinitely and (b) each rat stabilized at a fairly constant rate of responding.

Now, a steady state was something I was familiar with from physical chemistry, and I therefore embarked upon the study of periodic reinforcement. I soon found that the constant rate at which the rat stabilized depended upon how hungry it was. Hungry rat, high rate; less hungry rat, lower rate. At that time I was bothered by the practical problem of controlling food deprivation. I was working half time at the Medical School (on chronaxie of subordination!) and could not maintain a good schedule in working with the rats. The rate of responding under periodic reinforcement suggested a scheme for keeping a rat at a constant level of deprivation. The argument went like this: Suppose you reinforce the rat, not at the end of a given period, but when it has completed the number of responses ordinarily emitted in that period. And suppose you use substantial pellets of food and give the rat continuous access to the lever. Then, except for periods when the rat sleeps, it should operate the lever at a constant rate around the clock. For, whenever it grows slightly hungrier, it will work faster, get food faster, and become less hungry, while whenever it grows slightly less hungry, it will respond at a lower rate, get less food, and grow hungrier. By setting the reinforcement at a given number of responses it should even be possible to hold the rat at any given level of deprivation. I visualized a machine with a dial which one could set to make available, at any time of day or night, a rat in a given state of deprivation. Of course, nothing of the sort happens. This is "fixed-ratio" rather than "fixed-interval" reinforcement and, as I soon found out, it produces a very different type of performance. This is an example of a fifth unformalized principle of scientific practice, but one which has at least been named. Walter Cannon described it with a word invented by Horace Walpole: *serendipity*—the art of finding one thing while looking for something else.

This account of my scientific behavior up to the point at which I published my results in a book called *The Behavior of Organisms* is as exact in letter and spirit as I can now make it. The notes, data, and publications which I have examined do not show that I ever behaved in the manner of Man Thinking as described by John Stuart Mill or John Dewey or in reconstructions of scientific behavior by other philosophers of science. I never

faced a Problem which was more than the eternal problem of finding order. I never attacked a problem by constructing a Hypothesis. I never deduced Theorems or submitted them to Experimental Check. So far as I can see, I had no preconceived Model of Behavior—certainly not a physiological or mentalistic one, and, I believe, not a conceptual one. The "reflex reserve" was an abortive, though operational, concept which was retracted a year or so after publication in a paper at the Philadelphia meeting of the APA. It lived up to my opinion of theories in general by proving utterly worthless in suggesting further experiments. Of course, I was working on a basic Assumption—that there was order in behavior if I could only discover it—but such an assumption is not to be confused with the hypotheses of deductive theory. It is also true that I exercised a certain Selection of Facts but not because of relevance to theory but because one fact was more orderly than another. If I engaged in Experimental Design at all, it was simply to complete or extend some evidence of order already observed.

Most of the experiments described in *The Behavior of Organisms* were done with groups of four rats. A fairly common reaction to the book was that such groups were too small. How did I know that other groups of four rats would do the same thing? Keller, in defending the book, countered with the charge that groups of four were too *big*. Unfortunately, however, I allowed myself to be persuaded of the contrary. This was due in part to my association at the University of Minnesota with W. T. Heron. Through him I came into close contact for the first time with traditional animal psychology. Heron was interested in inherited maze behavior, inherited activity, and certain drugs—the effects of which could then be detected only through the use of fairly large groups. We did an experiment together on the effect of starvation on the rate of pressing a lever and started the new era with a group of sixteen rats. But we had only four boxes, and this was so inconvenient that Heron applied for a grant and built a battery of twenty-four lever-boxes and cumulative recorders. I supplied an attachment which would record, not only the mean performance of all twenty-four rats in a single averaged curve, but mean curves for four subgroups of twelve rats each and four subgroups of six rats each (3). We thus provided for the design of experiments according to the principles of R. A. Fisher, which were then coming into vogue. We had, so to speak, mechanized the latin square.

With this apparatus Heron and I published a study of extinction in maze-bright and maze-dull rats using *ninety-five* subjects. Later I published mean extinction curves for groups of twenty-four, and W. K. Estes and I did our work on anxiety with groups of the same size. But although Heron and I could properly voice the hope that "the possibility of using large groups of animals greatly improves upon the method as previously reported, since tests of significance are provided for the properties of behavior not apparent in single cases may be more easily detected," in actual practice that is not what happened. The experiments I have just mentioned are almost all we have to show for this elaborate battery of boxes. Undoubtedly more work could be done with it and would have its place, but something had happened to the natural growth of the method. You cannot easily make a change in the conditions of an experiment when twenty-four apparatuses have to be altered. Any gain in rigor is more than matched by a loss in flexibility. We were forced to confine ourselves to processes which could be studied with the baselines already developed in earlier work. We could not move on to the discovery of other processes or even to a more refined analysis of those we were working with. No matter how significant might be the relations we actually demonstrated, our statistical Leviathan had swum aground. The art of the method had stuck at a particular stage of its development.

Another accident rescued me from mechanized statistics and brought me back to an even more intensive concentration on the single case. In essence, I suddenly found myself face to face with the engineering problem of the animal trainer. When you have the responsibility of making absolutely sure that a given organism will engage in a given sort of behavior at a given time, you quickly grow impatient with theories of learning. Principles, hypotheses, theorems, satisfactory proof at the .05 level of significance that behavior at a choice point shows the effect of secondary reinforcement—nothing could be more irrelevant. No one goes to the circus to see the average dog jump through a hoop significantly oftener than untrained dogs raised under the same circumstances, or to see an elephant demonstrate a principle of behavior.

Perhaps I can illustrate this without giving aid and comfort to the enemy by describing a Russian device which the Germans found quite formidable. The Russians used dogs to blow up tanks. A dog was trained to hide behind a tree or wall in low brush or other cover. As a tank approached and passed, the dog ran swiftly alongside it, and a small magnetic mine attached to the dog's back was sufficient to cripple the tank or set it afire. The dog, of course, had to be replaced.

Now I ask you to consider some of the technical problems which the psychologist faces in preparing a dog for such an act of unintentional heroism. The dog must wait behind the tree for an indefinite length of time. Very well, it must therefore be intermittently reinforced for waiting. But what schedule will achieve the highest probability of waiting? If the reinforcement is to be food, what is the absolutely optimal schedule of deprivation consistent with the health of the dog? The dog must run to the tank—that can be arranged by reinforcing it with a practice tank— but it must start instantly if it is to overtake a swift tank, and how do you differentially reinforce short reaction times, especially in counteracting the reinforcement for sitting and waiting? The dog must react only to tanks, not to a refugee driving his oxcart along the road, but what are the defining properties of a tank so far as a dog is concerned?

I think it can be said that a functional analysis proved adequate in its technological application. Manipulation of environmental conditions alone made possible a wholly unexpected practical control. Behavior could be shaped up according to specifications and maintained indefinitely almost at will. One behavioral technologist who worked with me at the time (Keller Breland) is now specializing in the production of behavior as a salable commodity and has described this new profession in the *American Psychologist* (2).

There are many useful applications within psychology itself. Ratliff and Blough have recently conditioned pigeons to serve as psychophysical observers. In their experiment a pigeon may adjust one of two spots of light until the two are equally bright or it may hold a spot of light at the absolute threshold during dark adaptation. The techniques which they have developed to induce pigeons to do this are only indirectly related to the point of their experiments and hence exemplify the application of a behavioral science (4). The field in which a better technology of behavior is perhaps most urgently needed is education. I cannot describe here the applications which are now possible, but perhaps I can indicate my enthusiasm by hazarding the guess that educational techniques at all age levels are on the threshold of revolutionary changes.

The effect of a behavioral technology on scientific practice is the issue here. Faced with practical problems in behavior, you necessarily emphasize the refinement of *experimental* variables. As a result, some of the standard procedures of statistics appear to be circumvented. Let me illustrate. Suppose that measurements have been made on two groups of subjects differing in some detail of experimental treatment. Means and standard deviations for the two groups are determined, and any difference due to the treatment is evaluated. If the difference is in the expected direction but is not statistically significant, the almost universal recommendation would be to study larger groups. But our experience with practical control suggests that we may reduce the troublesome variability by changing the conditions of the experiment. By discovering, elaborating, and fully exploiting every relevant variable, we may eliminate *in advance of measurement* the individual differences which obscure the difference under analysis. This will achieve the same result as increasing the size of groups, and it will almost certainly yield a bonus in the discovery of new variables which would not have been identified in the statistical treatment.

The same may be said of smooth curves. In our study of anxiety, Estes and I published several curves, the reasonable smoothness of which was obtained by averaging the performances of 12 rats for each curve. The individual curves published at that time show that the mean curves do not faithfully represent the behavior of any one rat. They show a certain tendency toward a change in slope which supported the point we were making, and they may have appeared to justify averaging for that reason.

But an alternative method would have been to explore the individual case until an equally smooth curve could be obtained. This would have meant, not only rejecting the temptation to produce smoothness by averaging cases, but manipulating all relevant conditions as we later learned to manipulate them for practical purposes. The individual curves which we published at that time do not point to the need for larger groups but for improvement in experimental technique. Here, for example, is a curve the smoothness of which is characteristic of current practice. Such curves were shown in the making in a demonstration which Ferster and I arranged at the Cleveland meeting of the American Psychological Association (Figure 13). Here, in a single organism, three different schedules of reinforcement are yielding corresponding performances with great uniformity under appropriate stimuli alternating at

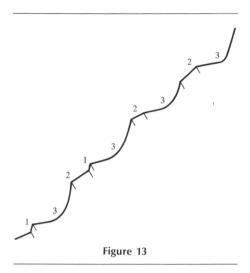

Figure 13

random. One does not reach this kind of order through the application of statistical methods.

In *The Behavior of Organisms* I was content to deal with the over-all slopes and curvature of cumulative curves and could make only a rough classification of the properties of behavior shown by the finer grain. The grain has now been improved. The resolving power of the microscope has been increased manyfold, and we can see fundamental processes of behavior in sharper and sharper detail. In choosing rate of responding as a basic datum and in recording this conveniently in a cumulative curve, we make important temporal aspects of behavior *visible*. Once this has happened, our scientific practice is reduced to simple looking. A new world is opened to inspection. We use such curves as we use a microscope, X-ray camera, or telescope. This is well exemplified by recent extensions of the method. These are no longer part of my case history, but perhaps you will permit me to consult you about what some critics have described as a *folie à deux* or group neurosis.

An early application of the method

to the behavior of avoidance and escape was made by Keller in studying the light aversion of the rat. This was brilliantly extended by Murray Sidman in his shock-avoidance experiments. It is no longer necessary to describe avoidance and escape by appeal to "principles," for we may *watch* the behavior develop when we have arranged the proper contingencies of reinforcement, as we later watch it change as these contingencies are changed.

Hunt and Brady have extended the use of a stable rate in the study of anxiety-producing stimuli and have shown that the depression in rate is eliminated by electro-convulsive shock and by other measures which are effective in reducing anxiety in human patients. O. R. Lindsley has found the same thing for dogs, using insulin-shock therapy and sedatives. Brady has refined the method by exploring the relevance of various schedules of reinforcement in tracing the return of the conditioned depression after treatment. In these experiments you *see* the effect of a treatment as directly as you see the constriction of a capillary under the microscope.

Early work with rats on caffeine and Benzedrine has been extended by Lindsley with dogs. A special technique for evaluating several effects of a drug in a single short experimental period yields a record of behavior which can be read as a specialist reads an electro-cardiogram. Dr. Peter Dews of the Department of Pharmacology at the Harvard Medical School is investigating dose-response curves and the types and effects of various drugs, using pigeons as subjects. In the Psychological Laboratories at Harvard additional work on drugs is being carried out by Morse,

Herrnstein, and Marshall, and the technique is being adopted by drug manufacturers. There could scarcely be a better demonstration of the experimental treatment of variability. In a *single* experimental session with a *single* organism one observes the onset, duration, and decline of the effects of a drug.

The direct observation of *defective* behavior is particularly important. Clinical or experimental damage to an organism is characteristically unique. Hence the value of a method which permits the direct observation of the behavior of the individual. Lindsley has studied the effects of near-lethal irradiation, and the effects of prolonged anesthesia and anoxia are currently being examined by Thomas Lohr in cooperation with Dr. Henry Beecher of the Massachusetts General Hospital. The technique is being applied to neurological variables in the monkey by Dr. Karl Pribram at the Hartford Institute. The pattern of such research is simple: establish the behavior in which you are interested, submit the organism to a particular treatment, and then look again at the behavior. An excellent example of the use of experimental control in the study of *motivation* is some work on obesity by J. E. Anliker in collaboration with Dr. Jean Mayer of the Harvard School of Public Health, where abnormalities of ingestive behavior in several types of obese mice can be compared by direct inspection.

There is perhaps no field in which behavior is customarily described more indirectly than psychiatry. In an experiment at the Massachusetts State Hospital, under the sponsorship of Dr. Harry Solomon and myself, O. R. Lindsley is carrying out an extensive program which might be characterized as a quantitative study of the temporal properties of psychotic behavior. Here again it is a question of making certain characteristics of the behavior visible.

The extent to which we can eliminate sources of variability before measurement is shown by a result which has an unexpected significance for comparative psychology and the study of individual differences. Figure 14 shows tracings of three curves which report behavior in response to a multiple fixed-interval fixed-ratio schedule. The hatches mark reinforcements. Separating them in some cases are short, steep lines showing a high constant rate on a fixed-ratio schedule and, in others, somewhat longer "scallops" showing a smooth acceleration as the organism shifts from a very low rate just after reinforcement to a higher rate at the end of the fixed interval. The values of the intervals and ratios, the states of deprivation, and the exposures to the schedules were different in the three cases, but except for these details the curves are quite similar. Now, one of them was made by a *pigeon* in some experiments by Ferster and me,

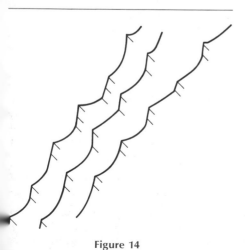

Figure 14

one was made by a *rat* in an experiment on anoxia by Lohr, and the third was made by a *monkey* in Karl Pribram's laboratory at the Hartford Institute. Pigeon, rat, monkey, which is which? It doesn't matter. Of course, these three species have behavioral repertoires which are as different as their anatomies. But once you have allowed for differences in the ways in which they make contact with the environment, and in the ways in which they act upon the environment, what remains of their behavior shows astonishingly similar properties. Mice, cats, dogs, and human children could have added other curves to this figure. And when organisms which differ as widely as this nevertheless show similar properties of behavior, differences between members of the same species may be viewed more hopefully. Difficult problems of idiosyncrasy or individuality will always arise as products of biological and cultural processes, but it is the very business of the experimental analysis of behavior to devise techniques which reduce their effects except when they are explicitly under investigation.

We are within reach of a science of the individual. This will be achieved, not by resorting to some special theory of knowledge in which intuition or understanding takes the place of observation and analysis, but through an increasing grasp of relevant conditions to produce order in the individual case.

A second consequence of an improved technology is the effect upon behavior theory. As I have pointed out elsewhere, it is the function of learning theory to create an imaginary world of law and order and thus to console us for the disorder we observe in behavior itself. Scores on a T maze or jumping stand hop about from trial to trial almost capriciously. Therefore we argue that if learning is, as we hope, a continuous and orderly process, it must be occurring in some other system of dimensions—perhaps in the nervous system, or in the mind, or in a conceptual model of behavior. Both the statistical treatment of group means and the averaging of curves encourage the belief that we are somehow going behind the individual case to an otherwise inaccessible, but more fundamental, process. The whole tenor of our paper on anxiety, for example, was to imply that the change we observed was not necessarily a property of behavior, but of some theoretical state of the organism ("anxiety") which was merely *reflected* in a slight modification of performance.

When we have achieved a practical control over the organism, theories of behavior lose their point. In representing and managing relevant variables, a conceptual model is useless; we come to grips with behavior itself. When behavior shows order and consistency, we are much less likely to be concerned with physiological or mentalistic causes. A datum emerges which takes the place of theoretical fantasy. In the experimental analysis of behavior we address ourselves to a subject matter which is not only manifestly the behavior of an individual and hence accessible without the usual statistical aids but also "objective" and "actual" without recourse to deductive theorizing.

Statistical techniques serve a useful function, but they have acquired a purely honorific status which may be troublesome. Their presence or absence has become a shibboleth to be used in distinguishing between good and bad work. Because measures of behavior

have been highly variable, we have come to trust only results obtained from large numbers of subjects. Because some workers have intentionally or unconsciously reported only selected favorable instances, we have come to put a high value on research which is planned in advance and reported in its entirety. Because measures have behaved capriciously, we have come to value skillful deductive theories which restore order. But although large groups, planned experiments, and valid theorizing are associated with significant scientific results, it does not follow that nothing can be achieved in their absence. Here are two brief examples of the choice before us.

How can we determine the course of dark adaptation in a pigeon? We move a pigeon from a bright light to a dark room. What happens? Presumably the bird is able to see fainter and fainter patches of light as the process of adaptation takes place, but how can we follow this process? One way would be to set up a discrimination apparatus in which choices would be made at specific intervals after the beginning of dark adaptation. The test patches of light could be varied over a wide range, and the percentages of correct choices at each value would enable us eventually to locate the threshold fairly accurately. But hundreds of observations would be needed to establish only a few points on the curve and to prove that these show an actual change in sensitivity. In the experiment by Blough already mentioned, the pigeon holds a spot of light close to the threshold throughout the experimental period. A single curve, such as the one sketched in Figure 15, yields as much information as hundreds of readings, together with the means and

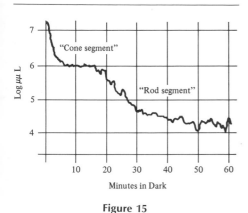

Figure 15

mouse was reinforced with a small piece of food after completing a short "ratio" of responses. The hypothalamic-obese mouse shows an exaggerated but otherwise normal ingestion curve. The hereditary-obese mouse eats slowly but for an indefinite length of time and with little change in rate. The gold-poisoned obese mouse shows a sharp oscillation between periods of very rapid responding and no responding at all. These three individual curves contain more information than could probably ever be generated with measures requiring statistical treatment, yet they will be viewed with suspicion by many psychologists because they are single cases.

It is perhaps natural that psychologists should awaken only slowly to the possibility that behavioral processes may be directly observed, or that they should only gradually put the older statistical and theoretical techniques in their proper perspective. But it is time to insist that science does not progress by carefully designed steps called "experiments" each of which has a well-defined beginning and end. Science is a continuous and often a disorderly and accidental process. We shall not do the young psychologist any favor if we agree

standard deviations derived from them. The information is more accurate because it applies to a single organism in a single experimental session. Yet many psychologists who would accept the first as a finished experiment because of the tables of means and standard deviations would boggle at the second or call it a preliminary study. The direct evidence of one's senses in observing a process of behavior is not trusted.

As another example, consider the behavior of several types of obese mice. Do they all suffer from a single abnormality in their eating behavior or are there differences? One might attempt to answer this with some such measure of hunger as an obstruction apparatus. The numbers of crossings of a grid to get to food, counted after different periods of free access to food, would be the data. Large numbers of readings would be needed, and the resulting mean values would possibly not describe the behavior of any one mouse in any experimental period. A much better picture may be obtained with one mouse of each kind in single experimental sessions, as Anliker has shown (1). In an experiment reported roughly in Figure 16, each

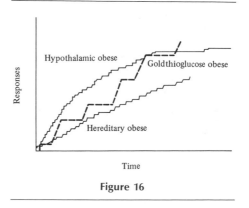

Figure 16

to reconstruct our practices to fit the pattern demanded by current scientific methodology. What the statistician means by the design of experiments is design which yields the kind of data to which *his* techniques are applicable. He does not mean the behavior of the scientist in his laboratory devising research for his own immediate and possibly inscrutable purposes.

The organism whose behavior is most extensively modified and most completely controlled in research of the sort I have described is the experimenter himself. The point was well made by a cartoonist in the Columbia *Jester* (Figure 17). The caption read: "Boy, have I got this guy conditioned! Everytime I press the bar down he drops in a piece of food." The subjects we study reinforce us much more effectively than we reinforce them. I have been telling you simply how I have been conditioned to behave. And of course it is a mistake to argue too much from one case history. My behavior would not have been shaped as it was were it not for personal characteristics which all psychologists fortunately do not share. Freud has had something to say about the motivation of scientists and has given us some in-

sight into the type of person who achieves the fullest satisfaction from precise experimental design and the intricacies of deductive systems. Such a person tends to be more concerned with his success as a scientist than with his subject matter, as is shown by the fact that he often assumes the role of a roving ambassador. If this seems unfair, let me hasten to characterize my own motivation in equally unflattering terms. Several years ago I spent a pleasant summer writing a novel called *Walden Two*. One of the characters, Frazier, said many things which I was not yet ready to say myself. Among them was this:

I have only one important characteristic, Burris. I'm stubborn. I've had only one idea in my life—a true *idée fixe* . . . to put it as bluntly as possible, the idea of having my own way. "Control" expresses it, I think. The control of human behavior, Burris. In my early experimental days it was a frenzied, selfish desire to dominate. I remember the rage I used to feel when a prediction went awry. I could have shouted at the subjects of my experiments, "Behave, damn you, behave as you ought!" Eventually I realized that the subjects were always right. They always behaved as they ought. It was I who was wrong. I had made a bad prediction.

(In fairness to Frazier and the rest of myself, I want to add his next remark: "And what a strange discovery for a would-be tyrant, that the only effective technique of control is unselfish." Frazier means, of course, positive reinforcement.)

We have no more reason to say that all psychologists should behave as I have behaved than that they should all be-

Figure 17

have like R. A. Fisher. The scientist, like any organism, is the product of a unique history. The practices which he finds most appropriate will depend in part upon this history. Fortunately, personal idiosyncrasies usually leave a negligible mark on science as public property. They are important only when we are concerned with the encouragement of scientists and the prosecution of research. When we have at last an adequate empirical account of the behavior of Man Thinking, we shall understand all this. Until then, it may be best not to try to fit all scientists into any single mold.

REFERENCES

1. Anliker, J. E. Personal communication.
2. Breland, K., and Breland, M. A field of applied animal psychology. *Amer. Psychologist,* 1951, **6,** 202–204.
3. Heron, W. T., and Skinner, B. F. An apparatus for the study of behavior. *Psychol. Rec.,* 1939, **3,** 166–176.
4. Ratliff, F., and Blough, D. S. Behavioral studies of visual processes in the pigeon. Report of Contract N5ori–07663, Psychological Laboratories, Harvard University, September 1954.
5. Richter, C. P. Free research versus design research. *Science,* 1953, **118,** 91–93.

SEVEN

The Influence of
Measurement Procedures
on Experimental Results

14

Free Behavior and
Brain Stimulation

José M. R. Delgado

In the following selection from Delgado's *Free Behavior and Brain Stimulation,* he reviews a variety of techniques which have been used to study the relationship of brain and behavior. He advocates the use of "free behavior" as a dependent variable. Of particular interest is a finding which has also come to the attention of other investigators—that the effects of an independent variable may change radically with a change in the method of measuring the behavior. In one experimental setting a brain stimulus may give rise to a simple movement of limited skeletal musculature. The same stimulus may be capable of producing a complex sequence of behaviors in a social context. The importance of the dependent measure in determining functional relationships has been observed in many settings outside the area of physiological psychology.

I. INTRODUCTION

Among the methods used to investigate the neurophysiological basis of behavior, perhaps the most direct and dramatic is electrical stimulation of the brain. Results are obtained immediately, are repeatable, and evoked and spontaneous responses often flow in close correlation

Reprinted from *International review of neurobiology,* Vol. 6, New York and London: Academic Press, 1964, 349–354.

with each other and with mutual dependence. In the last decade, methods for implantation of electrodes in the brain have multiplied and improved, and already a remarkable body of knowledge has accumulated on the effects of cerebral stimulation on autonomic reactions, conditioning, instrumental responses, self-stimulation, electrical activity and other important aspects (Brazier, 1960, 1961; Jasper *et al.,* 1958; Jasper and Smirnov, 1960; Roe and Simpson, 1958; Sheer, 1961a;

Simon *et al.,* 1961; Wolstenholme and O'Connor, 1958). We know that animals may seek or avoid excitation of specific cerebral regions, that direct stimulation of the brain may induce conditioning, may determine learning, and may evoke a wide variety of behavioral effects, such as tameness, ferocity, vocalization, sexual activity, stereotyped walking, changes in social hierarchy, and modification of food intake. Therapeutic implantation of electrodes in humans has made it possible to demonstrate that increases in friendliness, changes in output of words, inhibition of thoughts, hallucinations, fear, *deja vu,* memories, hostility, changes in sexual orientation and other effects may be evoked by direct stimulation of the brain (Higgins *et al.,* 1956; Ramey and O'Doherty, 1960; see also Section VI of Sheer, 1961a).

In spite of this impressive list of evoked phenomena, direct stimulation of the brain must be considered a crude method for the exploration of cerebral functions, and our understanding of the results is rather limited (Teuber, 1961). Reliability of evoked effects has been controversial (Penfield and Welch, 1949; Sherrington, 1947). Recently it was claimed that electrical stimulation produces little that resembles the normal (Cobb, 1961). Most studies have been descriptive without providing quantification of observed evoked effects, and, as stated by Carpenter (1960), "Clearly there is a need to progress from qualitative descriptions . . . to the formation of quantitative expressions which accurately represent behavior (and) social interactions. . . ." Long-term investigations are rare, and fatigability has been explored to only a limited extent. Little is known about interaction between spontaneous and evoked behavior, or about possible brief or permanent modifications of spontaneous behavior induced by brain stimulation. The influence of brain excitation on social behavior is an almost unexplored subject.

While observation of total behavior has been the purpose of field studies, which must be carried out under difficult and sometimes hazardous conditions, in the laboratory, where investigators may have animal colonies at their disposal day and night, they have chosen to observe only a few patterns of behavior for very short daily periods. In studies of rhesus groups in captivity (Brody and Rosvold, 1952; McDowell, 1953; Rosvold *et al.,* 1954; Mirsky, 1955; Mirsky *et al.,* 1957), observation periods were of only 10–60 minutes, and only one colony was studied for as much as 2 hours daily. The need for a thorough and objective collection of data on all forms of behavior has been mentioned by several authors (Klüver, 1933; Scott, 1958; Yerkes and Yerkes, 1935). The one author who attempted to record spontaneous normal group behavior (McDowell, 1953), commented that other investigators had selected particular monkey activities such as mating, and had neglected much of the "total behavior picture."

A series of recent methodological developments has made possible the continuous recording and the quantification of the total spontaneous behavior of animal colonies, providing a base line which may be compared with effects evoked by cerebral stimulation. In addition, the invention of transistors permits the construction of minute and practical instruments for the establishment of wireless two-way contact between animals and investigators, and allows stimulation of the brain in completely free animals. A review of methods, problems, results and possibilities is presented in this paper, which has the following specific aims: (*1*) to describe methodology for cinemanalysis, telerccording, and telestimulation in order to study free behavior during brain stimulation; (*2*) to demonstrate that spontaneous activities may be recorded, identified and quantified, allowing the systematic study of free and evoked behavior on both individual and social levels; (*3*) to discuss the types and significance of behavior evoked by brain stimulation in unrestrained subjects; and (*4*) to present a theory of "fragmental organization of behavior."

II. CONDITIONED REFLEXES, INSTRUMENTAL RESPONSES, AND FREE BEHAVIOR

Two of the classical techniques for the analysis of cerebral-behavior relations are conditioned reflexes and instrumental responses. As is well known, in conditioning, a normal reaction (e.g., salivary secretion), which responds to a normal stimulus (e.g., the sight of food), may be experimentally elicited by a neutral stimulus (the sound of a bell), if previously bell and food have been repeatedly paired. In the instrumental response, the animal learns a task (e.g., pressing a bar) in order to avoid an unpleasant sensation (e.g., electric shock), or to get a reward (e.g., food). A sensory cue such as a buzzer usually precedes the punishment or reward, and is able to evoke the learned response by itself.

Both of these methods yield results which are easy to quantify, and with many variants, they have been basic in our present knowledge of cerebral-behavioral relations. In recent years they have also been used in combination with electrical stimulation of the brain. However, in order to interpret and evaluate the results obtained with conditioning and with instrumental responses, the following considerations, which apply to one or both of these techniques, should be kept in mind: (*1*) A selection of experimental subjects is necessary, rejecting those who do not learn, or who have spontaneous behavior unsuitable for the test because they are noisy, destructive, distractible, or too lazy (*2*) Learning of a specific type of response is required; (*3*) The test explores one single type of learned behavior; (*4*) Usually the performance of the test is a "yes" or "no" proposition and in only a few cases is there a multiple choice. (*5*) The tests require the performance of acts which, in general, are not found in spontaneous life, such as lifting cups or pressing bars; (*6*) The tests are carried on with animals under restraint, or confined in small cages or special chairs; (*7*) The tests occupy only a short amount of time from the total span of the animal's life; and (*8*) Training and handling of the animals may modify their normal behavioral responses.

Another methodological approach for the investigation of cerebral-behavioral relations is the study of the continuous flow of spontaneous activities and the analysis of modifications induced by brain stimulation. This type of study may be called "*task-free*," because no specific performance is demanded of the animals, or "*free behavior*," because what the animals choose to do is observed, rather than what they do when confronted with instrumental tests. Usually the animals are free on a stage or inside a cage in the company of other animals. The term "free behavior" is probably the most descriptive, and will be used throughout this paper with the understanding that in some experiments, electrical stimulation of the brain may evoke a predictable response, leaving little freedom of choice to the animal. During spontaneous behavior, the animal is reacting to natural external or internal stimuli (Krushinskii, 1962). Brain stimulation is an experimental variable which may produce an effect by itself (evoked reaction), or may modify the free responses to natural stimuli. Both evoked and free behavior interact with each other (see Section IV, B). In the experimentation within behavioral spontaneity lie the merits and handicaps of this type of study. Most of the forementioned limitations inherent in conditioning and instrumental response techniques do not apply to the study of free behavior. It should be emphasized that, since the subjects are not expected to do a special task, there are no entrance requirements, and none are rejected from the experiment. As indicated by Nissen (1951), instrumental responses explore "what animals *can* do"—a specific type of learning, of adaptive behavior, and frequently leave "only one definite way of reaction open to the animal," (Katz, 1937), while spontaneous behavior shows what animals normally do in a situation of complete freedom of conduct. Each technique gives different and complementary types of information.

Laboratory life admittedly cannot be equated with life in the field, and the confinement of animals in cages may produce behavioral changes (Carpenter,

1942a; Clark and Birch, 1945; Grossack, 1953; Kinnaman, 1902; Scott, 1958; Yerkes and Yerkes, 1935; Zuckerman, 1932). However, the systematic study of brain stimulation would not be possible in the field. According to Lorenz (1950), it is easier to investigate behavior patterns in a cage than in the field because the absence of natural surroundings and releasing situations simplify the study. Maslow (1936) thinks that in the laboratory situation, we have "not so much the introduction of new factors, as the exclusion of many variables and uncontrollable factors."

III. STUDY OF FREE BEHAVIOR

Having the animals under some restraint is advantageous for the study of electrical activity of the brain, autonomic reactions, instrumental responses, and other effects. Restraint, however, imposes obvious handicaps because it inhibits behavior and makes impossible the display of a good number of individual and social activities. Stimulation of the same point may give different results in the animal with or without restraint. For example, in one monkey seated on a chair, excitation of the nucleus medialis dorsalis of the thalamus evoked movement of the head, restlessness, and vocalization; the same stimulation in the animal when free in the colony evoked a reliable sequence with head movement, walking, jumping, hanging on the wall, and walking back to the starting point. Most of the information discussed in the present paper refers to free-moving animals. The different degrees of experimental freedom in neurophysiological studies of awake subjects may be classified as follows:

Restrained animals

1. Body and limbs secured to a board. This method is useful mainly for recordings.

2. In a chair or harness. Dogs in Pavlovian experiments or monkeys in chairs (Lilly, 1958a; Mason, 1958). The animal has limited mobility and may feed himself (Fig. 5).

3. On a platform or stage, prevented from escape by a belt or collar and a chain, through which electrical connections may be attached (Bursten and Delgado, 1958).

Unrestrained animals

1. On an enclosed stage, in a small cage or an aquarium. Leads connect the animal with instruments, allowing considerable freedom of movement (Hess, 1932; Lilly, 1961; Olds, 1960).

2. Completely free—carrying its own stimulator or transmitter. Mobility limited by the size of the living quarters. Social studies are possible (Delgado, 1959b, 1962) (Figs. 1, 2, and others).

3. Field studies. The subject is completely free in natural habitat, carrying a harness with instrumentation and contact is established by radio or by programming mechanism (Craighead and Craighead, 1963).

In addition to animal studies, information about cerebral stimulation has been obtained from human patients who have electrodes implanted in their brains for diagnostic or therapeutic purposes for days or months (Bickford *et al.*, 1960; Delgado and Hamlin, 1958, 1960; Heath, 1954; Sem-Jacobsen, 1959; Sherwood, 1960; Spiegel and Wycis, 1963; also see Section VI of Sheer, 1961a). These studies have exceptional value because cerebral areas may be explored while the patient is comfortably sitting down in an armchair outside the operating room, and is reading, talking, or engaged in other spontaneous activities.

REFERENCES

Bickford, R. G., Dodge, H. W., Jr., and Uihlein, A. In *Electrical Studies on the Unanesthetized Brain* (Eds. E. R. Ramey and D. S. O'Doherty). New York: Harper (Hoeber), 1960, 214.

Brazier, M. A. B. *The Central Nervous System and Behavior.* New Jersey: Madison Printing Co., 1960.

Brazier, M. A. B. *Brain and Behavior,* Vol. 1, 1st Conference, Am. Inst. Biol. Sci., Washington, D.C., 1961.

Brody, E. B., and Rosvold, H. E. *Psychosomat. Med.,* 1952, **14,** 406–415.

Bursten, B., and Delgado, J. M. R. *J. Comp. and Physiol. Psychol.,* 1958, **51,** 6–10.

Carpenter, C. R. *Biol. Symposia.,* 1942a, **8,** 177–204.

Carpenter, C. R. Comments on Imanishi, K. *Current Anthropol.,* 1960, **1,** 402, 403.

Clark, G., and Birch, H. G. *Psychosomat. Med.,* 1945, **7,** 321–329.

Cobb, S. In *Electrical Stimulation of the Brain* (Ed. D. E. Sheer). University of Texas Press, Austin, Texas, 1961, 7–8.

Craighead, F. C., and Craighead, J. H. In *Bio-Telemetry* (Ed. L. Slater). New York: Pergamon Press, 1963, 133–148.

Delgado, J. M. R. *Electroencephalog. and Clin. Neurophysiol.,* 1959b, **11.** 591–593.

Delgado, J. M. R. *Proc. 1st Intern. Pharmacol. Congr., Stockholm.* New York: Pergamon Press, 1962, **8,** 265–292.

Delgado, J. M. R., and Hamlin, H. *Electroencephalog. and Clin. Neurophysiol.,* 1958, **10,** 463–486.

Delgado, J. M. R., and Hamlin, H. In *Electrical Studies on the Unanesthetized Brain* (Eds. E. R. Ramey and D. S. O'Doherty). New York: Harper (Hoeber), 1960, 133.

Grossack, M. *J. Psychol.,* 1953, **35,** 241–244.

Heath, R. G. (Ed.). *Studies in Schizophrenia. A Multidisciplinary Approach to Mind-Brain Relationships.* Harvard Univ. Press, Cambridge, Massachusetts, 1954.

Hess, W. R. *Beitrage zur Physiologie des*

Hirnstammes. I. Die Methodik der lokalisierten Reizung und Ausschaltung subkortikaler Hirnabschnitte. Thieme, Leipzig, 1932.

Higgins, J. W., Mahl, G. F., Delgado, J. M. R., and Hamlin H. *A.M.A. Arch. Neurol. Psychiat.,* 1956, **76**, 399–419.

Jasper, H. H., and Smirnov, G. D. (Eds.). The Moscow Colloquium on Electroencephalography of Higher Nervous Activity. *Electroencephalog. and Clin. Neurophysiol.* Suppl. 13, 1960.

Jasper, H. H., Proctor, L. D., Knighton, R. S., Noshay, W. C., and Costello, R. T. (Eds.) *Reticular Formation of the Brain,* Henry Ford Hosp. Intern. Symposium, Boston, Mass., Little, Brown, 1958.

Katz, D. *Animals and Men.* New York: Longmans, Green, 1937.

Kinnaman, A. J. *Am. J. Psychol.,* 1902, **13**, 98–148; 173–218.

Klüver, H. *Behavior Mechanisms in Monkeys.* Univ. of Chicago, Press, Chicago, Ill., 1933.

Krushinskii, L. V. *Animal Behavior: Its Normal and Abnormal Development,* Translation publ. by Consultants Bureau, New York (Russian ed.: Moscow Univ. Press, Moscow, 1960), 1962.

Lilly, J. C. *J. Appl. Physiol,* 1958a, **12**, 134–136.

Lilly, J. C. *Man and Dolphin,* 1961, Doubleday, Garden City, New York.

Lorenz, K. Z. *Symposia Soc. Exptl. Biol,* 1950, **4**, 221–268.

McDowell, A. A. *Am. Psychologist,* 1953, **8**, 395–396.

Maslow, A. H. *J. Genet. Psychol.,* 1936, **48**, 261–277.

Mason, J. W. *J. Appl. Physiol.,* 1958, **12**, 130–132.

Mirsky, A. F. *J. Comp. and Physiol.,* 1955, **48**, 327–335.

Mirsky, A. F., Rosvold, H. E., and Pribram, K. H. *J. Neurophysiol.,* 1957, **20**, 588–601.

Nissen, H. W. In *Comparative Psychology* (Ed. C. P. Stone). Prentice-Hall, Englewood Cliffs, New Jersey, 1951, 423.

Olds, J. In *Electrical Studies on the Unanesthetized Brain* (Eds. E. R. Ramey and D. S. O'Doherty). New York: Harper (Hoeber), 1960, 17.

Penfield, W., and Welch, K. *J. Physiol.* (London), 1949, **109**, 358–365.

Ramey, E. R., and O'Doherty, D. S. (Eds.). *Electrical Studies on the Unanesthetized Brain.* New York: Harper (Hoeber), 1960.

Roe, A., and Simpson, G. G. (Eds.). *Behavior and Evolution,* Yale Univ. Press, New Haven, Connecticut, 1958.

Rosvold, H. E., Mirsky, A. F., and Pribram, K. H. *J. Comp. and Physiol. Psychol.,* 1954, **47**, 173–178.

Scott, J. P. *Animal Behavior.* Univ. of Chicago Press, Chicago, Illinois, 1958.

Sem-Jacobsen, C. W. *Acta Psychiat. Scand.,* 1959, **34**, Suppl. No. 136, 207–213.

Sheer, D. E. (Ed.). *Electrical Stimulation of the Brain.* Univ. of Texas Press, Austin, Texas, 1961a.

Sherrington, C. S. *The Integrative Action of the Nervous System.* Cambridge Univ. Press, London and New York, 1947.

Sherwood, S. L. In *Electrical Studies on the Unanesthetized Brain* (Eds., E. R. Ramey and D. S. O'Doherty). New York: Harper (Hoeber), 1960, 374.

Simon, A., Herbert C. C., and Strauss, R. (Eds.). *The Physiology of Emotions.* Charles C Thomas, Springfield, Illinois, 1961.

Spiegel, E. A., and Wycis, H. T. (Eds.). Proc. Symp. Stereotaxic Surg., Philadelphia, Pennsylvania, 1961, *Confinia Neurol.* In press., 1963.

Teuber, H. L. In *Brain and Behavior,* Vol. 1, 1961, 393, 1st Conf. Am. Inst. Biol. Sci, Washington, D.C.

Wolstenholme, G. E. W., and O'Connor, C. M. (Eds.). *CIBA Foundation Symposium on the Neurological Basis of Behavior.* Boston Massachusetts., Little, Brown, 1958.

Yerkes, R. M., and Yerkes, A. W. In *A Handbook of Social Psychology* (Ed. C. A. Murchison). Oxford Univ. Press, London and New York, 1935, 973.

Zuckerman, S. *The Social Life of Monkeys and Apes.* Kegan Paul, London, 1932.

15

Direct Measurement of the Ways Children Know Language and Numbers

Joseph S. Edwards

We have said that experimental findings are heavily determined by the method of measurement. The Edwards article shows the implications of this in a particularly vivid way. Does Johnny know how to read? Does Jane know the alphabet? Does Jimmy know how to count? The answer to these seemingly simple questions depends on the method used for measuring reading, knowledge of the alphabet, and counting. In some instances, the child can name an object, for example, a ball, indicating that he has the response "ball" in his repertoire; he can also go get the ball when presented with the written word "ball"; yet, he cannot read the word *ball* in the sense of saying "ball" when presented with the printed word! One measure says that he can read and another measure says that he cannot. The measure that happens to be selected can have a profound influence on the educational fate of the child. That measurement procedures influence results is a fact of more than mere academic interest.

A full behavioral assessment of language must include an analysis of the ways in which symbols and objects are presented as well as the ways in which a person

This research was supported in part by PHS Training Grant HD 00183 from the National Institute of Child Health and Human Development to the Kansas Center for Research in Mental Retardation and Human Development. The effort of James Early, Maureen Mooney and particularly David Thomas made the research possible. Appreciation is also extended to Diane Edwards and Charles L. Sheridan for critically evaluating the manuscript. The author is now a faculty member of the psychology department of the University of Missouri at Kansas City.

This paper is dedicated to Ogden R. Lindsley, who taught me the value of direct measurements of human behavior.

responds to them. The result of such an assessment would be a functional analysis describing under what conditions symbols can be used. The function of language is its most essential aspect. Vygotsky (1962, p. 5) states the problem as, "A word without meaning is an empty sound, no longer a part of human speech." Bridgman (1927, p. 4) also points to a functional analysis when he states that, "For of course the true meaning of a term is to be found by observing what a man does with it, not by what he says about it." In the functional analysis described above, meaning is determined by the relationship between the method of presentation and the method of responding. Meaning becomes an experimental problem in an attempt to isolate the conditions under which symbolic events are functional.

An advantage of approaching meaning and language experimentally is that it may be possible to isolate deficits specific to the method of presentation, the method of responding, or both. Once a deficit has been specified, the procedures for remediation can be developed. Jaffe (1966) suggested that a common source of confounding language function is that visual and auditory presentations are typically not tested separately. It may well be that an individual has "auditory" language but not "visual" language; a fact not clarified if the two modalities are not tested separately.

Before a remedial procedure can be adequately tested, diagnostic procedures which pinpoint and record both skills and deficiencies with language must be developed. Schiefelbush (1969) strongly suggested that a functional analysis of the components of speech, language, and communication must be done if programs are to be adequately designed

for the study and remediation of these processes.

The present studies were conducted as a part of a diagnostic research program to accomplish the goals of precisely pinpointing language functions. The methods of presenting materials and the methods of responding were varied to determine the ways in which a word, symbol, or number had meaning.

METHOD

Subjects

Thirty children (ages 2–12 years) participated. Nineteen of these children were enrolled in either special education classes or a tutorial program for disadvantaged youth.

Materials

Language and number skills were assessed with a variety of materials. Alphabet materials consisted of the capital letter sample from the *Wide Range Achievement Test* (Jastak, Bijou, and Jastak, 1965) and all 26 capital letters of the alphabet mounted on 3-by-5 cards. Word-object materials were obtained from the *Peabody Picture Vocabulary Test* (Dunn, 1965) and the Dolch word series (Dolch, 1953). Addition problems whose answers summed to 10 or less were the arithmetic materials. There were 20 problems. A fifth grade text was used to study reading comprehension.

General Procedure and Experimental Design

In each study pennies were used to reinforce correct responses unless otherwise specified. At the beginning of each task the child was instructed that each correct answer would earn him some money. At the end of the task the number of correct answers was calculated and the child was paid on a ratio of three or four correct answers per penny.

The rate of correct responses, the rate of wrong responses, the total rate, and accuracy were recorded to describe each child's performance. Rate and accuracy are perhaps the most fundamental dimensions of symbolic responding (Edwards, 1969). With both of these data it is possible to pinpoint the specific deficits and skills of individual children. In addition, these recordings are sensitive to: (1) behaviors whose rate must be accelerated (rate building task), (2) behaviors which occur at an acceptable rate but which must be brought under appropriate environmental control (accuracy task), and (3) behaviors which have to be built or shaped and whose rate must be accelerated. These data have proven to be satisfactory measures for determining what type of behavioral skills and deficits individual children exhibit.

The methods of presentation involved a separate assessment of auditory input from visual input. The method of response included saying, finding, and writing. The schematic diagram below outlines the procedures by input-output modalities and the text describes the details of the procedures.

INPUT-OUTPUT SYSTEMS

Auditory	*Visual*	*None*
Listen—Find	Look—Find	. . . Find
Listen—Say	Look—Say	. . . Say
Listen—Write	Look—Write	. . . Write

Listen—Find: The experimenter says the symbol and the child selects the symbol he hears from an array of symbols spread out in front of him. This procedure assesses the child's ability to translate the auditory input into visual function. *Listen—Say:* The experimenter says the symbol and the child repeats orally the symbol he hears. This procedure crudely isolates any sensory problems in audition and precisely assesses whether the child can make the necessary speech sounds essential for a verbal language. *Listen—Write:* The experimenter says the symbol and the child writes what he hears on a sheet of paper. These three procedures enable an assessment of auditory skill relative to the responses of say, find, and write. This permits any response deficit to be isolated with respect to auditory stimuli. *Look—Find:* The child is shown a symbol from a deck of symbols and is asked to find the symbol that looks like the sample from an array of written symbols spread out in front of him. This procedure directly assesses visual function before more complicated procedures are introduced and insures that the child is able to match symbols visually. *Look—Say:* The symbol is presented to the child and he is asked to say what it is. This procedure assesses whether or not the child can say what he sees. This is the traditional oral reading assessment procedure. *Look—Write:* The symbol is presented and the child is to copy what he sees. This procedure assesses whether the child can reproduce what he sees and helps isolate listen-write and look-write skills and/or deficits. In all of these procedures, symbols were presented in a random order. *. . . Find:* Written symbols of the alphabet or number sequence are presented in a random array in front of the child. The child is instructed to point to the letters or numbers in the sequence that they should occur. . . . *Say:* The child is asked to say the alphabet or count from 1–50 without either visual or auditory symbol inputs. Verbal recall is assessed with this procedure. . . . *Write:* The child is asked to write the alphabet or the number sequence from 1–50 without either visual or auditory inputs. Written recall is assessed with this procedure. These nine procedures directly assess both stimulus and response skills and deficits and can be made appropriate to assessments of performance with a variety of curricula (colors, numbers, letters, words, objects, etc.).

RESULTS

Study 1. Look—Say: Alphabet Sample of the Wide Range Achievement Test vs the Full Alphabet Curriculum

Figure 1 presents the performance of two out of eight children on the *Wide Range Achievement Test* (WRAT) sample and full alphabet. The first child performed at a higher level of accuracy (81%) on the full alphabet than he did on the WRAT sample (46%). The second child performed at a lower level of accuracy (40%) on the full alphabet than on the WRAT sample (100%). The WRAT sample is unrepresentative of the performance skills of both children. The test results grossly underestimate the performance of the first child and overestimate that of the second child.

Four other children who performed perfectly on the full alphabet also performed perfectly on the WRAT. The other two children had lower levels of accuracy on the WRAT.

The range of response accuracy for the eight children's performance on both tasks was 0–60%. This large difference supports the suggestion that the WRAT sample is only representative of a child's performance when he performs the full alphabet perfectly. In addition, it should be noted that the time taken to administer the full alphabet in comparison to that taken for the WRAT averaged about 25 seconds longer.

Study 2. . . . Say vs. . . . Write: Differential Skill in Reciting Numbers as a Function of the Method of Responding

Figure 2 shows the performance of three out of eleven children who said (. . . say) and wrote (. . . write) the numbers 1–50 from memory. The first child said the number sequence less accurately than he wrote them indicating that the method of assessing his skill in counting critically determines the accuracy of his performance. The second and third children recited the number sequence perfectly on both procedures. These two children can recite the number sequence, and the procedure used is not a critical determinant of their accuracy. The total response rates of these three children clearly indicates that . . . write is a much slower rate performance than . . . say.

The median total response rate for the eleven children on the . . . say procedure was 85 numbers per minute whereas the median rate for . . . write was 12 numbers per minute. . . . Say is approximately 7 times faster than . . . write. Every child said the numbers faster than he wrote them and this effect occurred in spite of wide differences in response accuracy. Examination of the third child's performance in Figure 2

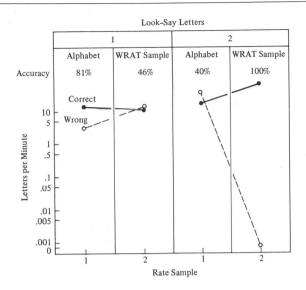

Figure 1   Differential skill in looking and saying capital letters of the alphabet as a function of a test sample.

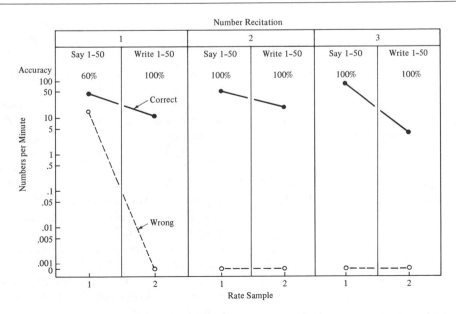

Figure 2   Number recitation skill as a function of the method of responding (saying vs. writing).

shows that he recites the numbers accurately in both procedures but the rate at which he writes the number (4 per min.) is 3 times lower than the median pupil's writing rate. A remedial program for this child would involve a detailed analysis of his writing performance. In contrast the performance of the first child clearly indicates a different remedial problem. His total response rate on both procedures approximates the median pupil's rate but the accuracy of his . . . say performance is much lower than his performance on the . . . write procedure. Remedial techniques for this child would attempt to determine methods for increasing his . . . say accuracy. If either the . . . say or the . . . write procedure had been used alone one would have come to opposite conclusions concerning this child's recitation skills.

Study 3. Look—Write: Differential Effects of the Method of Presenting Arithmetic Problems

This investigation sought to determine if the method of presenting arithmetic problems to children would affect their performance on addition problems. Five children, three of whom were enrolled in a special education class, participated.

Figure 3 presents three children's performance in adding number combinations which summed to 10 or less when number symbols ("2 + 2 = 4") and written number problems ("Two + Two = 4") were used. The overall accuracy of the first two children decreased when the problems were presented in written form. Both children performed perfectly when the problems were presented in symbol form. In contrast, the third child's performance indicates that

he cannot add numbers in either symbolic or written form. The deficit exposed with the first two children has nothing to do with arithmetic skill but concerns the way that the skill is assessed. The third child's performance indicates that he has minimal arithmetic skills. The focus of a remedial program for him would concern the instruction of addition before learning how to read and work written addition problems.

Study 4. Alphabet Assessment: Different Ways to Know the Letters

In this investigation the performance of: (1) 12 children was analyzed using 4 assessment procedures and (2) a young child's (age 2 years and 10 months) acquisition of 7 different ways to know the alphabet is described.

Four procedures, . . . say, look-say capital letters, look—write capital letters, and listen—write capital letters were used to assess 12 children's skill in using letters of the alphabet.

The order of highest overall response rates was: . . . say, look—say, look—write, and listen—write. The median accuracy across all procedures was 90% or greater.

In Figure 4 Paul's performance with capital letters of the alphabet is presented. Look—write capitals yielded the highest accuracy and listen—write capitals the lowest accuracy. The letters were more effective stimuli when Paul looked and wrote them than when he listened and wrote them. This difference is further indicated by comparing his performance in the look—say and look—write procedures.

Variations in the input procedures with a writing response are shown in

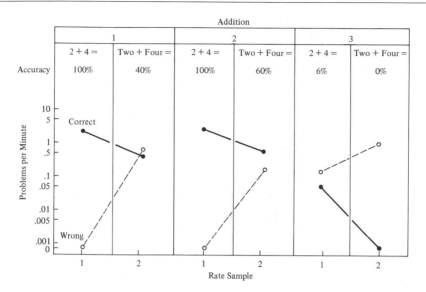

Figure 3 Performance on simple addition problems as a function of the method of presenting the problems (symbols vs. words).

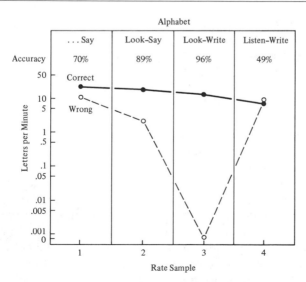

Figure 4 Differential performance of a boy under four different procedures for assessing alphabet skills.

rate samples 3 and 4. Auditory presentation of the letters produced the largest decrease in accuracy. The deficiency indicated involves a difficulty in reproducing letters that he hears. This deficiency, however, is not due to an inability to write the letters as demonstrated by the look-write procedure. In addition to showing Paul's relative skill with four ways of using the alphabet the overall rate at which he performed under the various conditions again corroborates the general finding that listen—write tasks take more time than any of the other procedures used here and that this area is the place where instruction is needed. This child's knowledge of the alphabet is a direct function of the procedures used to assess it.

Figure 5 presents performance rates and accuracy for a 2-year-and-10-month-old boy. Seven procedures were used to assess skill with capital letters of the alphabet in each of the 28 rate samples. Reinforcements for correct answers consisted of drinks of coke, praise, and mixed candy. Following the assessment sample in each session teaching periods were conducted in an attempt to improve this young boy's skill with the alphabet. The teaching involved drill with the procedures used in the assessments.

Inspection of the performance under the different procedures shows that this boy perfectly responded only in the listen—say procedure during the first rate sample. Acquisition to 100% accuracy was most rapid in the look—find, look—say, and . . . say procedures. In these procedures where 100% accuracy was obtained the order of highest overall response rates was: . . . say, listen—say, look—say, and look—find respectively. In procedures that required a written

response (. . . write, listen—write, and look—write) rate correct and accuracy were the lowest. In the look—write and listen—write procedures accuracy improved from levels lower than 10% to 62% by the last session. Performance in the . . . write procedure shows the smallest improvement.

In procedures which required a find or say response the rate of acquisition was faster than in procedures which required a written response. The early perfect performance exhibited in the listen-say procedure demonstrated that this young boy had the capability of saying all the letters of the alphabet. Rapid acquisition in the look—find procedure indicated that he had no difficulties in handling visual stimuli. Using visually presented letters, simple variation in the response from say or find to write in the look—write procedure shows that the deficit is in writing. Improvement in writing during the look—write procedure is paralleled by simultaneous improvements in accuracy in the listen—write and in the . . . write procedures respectively. . . .Write skills appear to be dependent upon skills present in the look—write and listen—write procedures. This boy's performance in the listen—write procedure was largely a function of deficiencies in writing whereas Paul's performance under this procedure (Fig. 4) was a function of other variables since he demonstrated he could perform the look—write procedure perfectly.

In addition, the order in which this young boy's performance improved indicates the relative difficulty of acquiring language skills with these seven procedures. Listen—say, look—find, and . . . say are skills acquired more rapidly than look—write, listen—write, and . . . write. This boy also had little or no

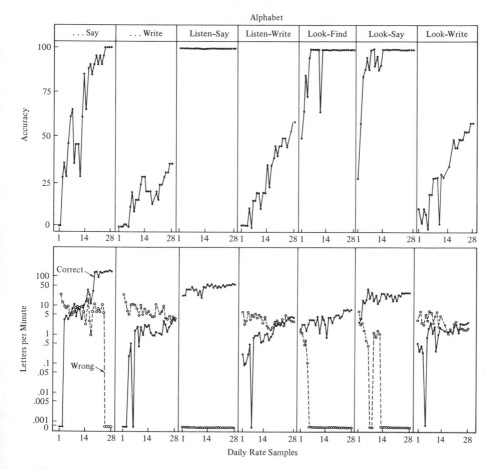

Figure 5   Acquisition of seven different alphabet skills by a young boy (2 years and 10 months).

difficulty with say and find responses. Difficulties with the writing response reflect his current level of motor coordination rather than specific difficulties with symbolic materials.

Study 5. How Do Children Know Words: Saying, Finding, Using

The results from three tasks are presented. The first task consisted of 25 words and their corresponding object pictures taken from the Dolch series. Three procedures: (1) look—say words, (2) look—say objects, and (3) look at word—find object were utilized to determine if eight pupils could use the words in these three ways.

Figure 6 summarizes the median accuracy and the response rates of eight pupils, four of whom were enrolled in a primary learning disability class and four who were enrolled in regular second and third grade classes. The data from both groups were combined since there

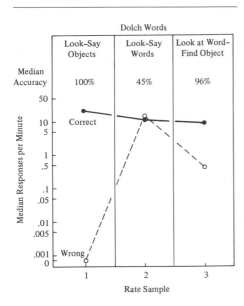

Figure 6 The performance of eight pupils shows that skill in oral reading (look-say words) does not accurately predict understanding of those words.

was no systematic relationship between the grade placement and performance. The median accuracy was highest for identifying the objects and lowest for looking and saying the words. The overall response rate was higher for reading the words and identifying the objects. The level of accuracy in look—say the words does not accurately predict whether any of the children could use the words to label a pictorial referent of the word. The deficiency exposed here concerns how written words are used as stimuli when two different methods of responding are provided.

The written words were not effective discriminative stimuli for producing accurate "look at the word and say" responses. However, a large number of these same words were effective discriminative stimuli when the children did

not have to look and say the word, but could respond to them with object pictures. Thus, the same event (written words) can have stimulus functions under one set of conditions and little or no function under other conditions. Remedial procedures based on this assessment would involve visually presented words to be orally read. The deficits of these children concern the method of responding to the written words, not their understanding of the meaning of the words.

The second task consisted of three procedures to assess performance on the *Peabody Picture Vocabulary Test* (PPVT). Since the PPVT provides norms to assess listen-to-the-word-and-find-the-picture levels of skill the cutoff points were utilized in this project so that an IQ score could be obtained in addition to an assessment of other language skills. The procedures were: (1) look—say words, (2) look at word—find object picture, and (3) listen to word—find object picture. Again, the procedures utilized here attempt to determine how children can use words. The procedures used in this task sought to isolate whether children would respond more effectively to words presented auditorally or visually as well as determine if they could say what the words were.

Figure 7 summarizes five pupils' performance. The overall rate of response was highest for look—say words and lowest for look at the word and find the object picture. The median accuracy was highest on the listen to the word and find the object picture procedure and lowest on look and say the words. Although the level of accuracy of these pupils is extremely low in the look—say word procedure these same pupils are capable of using written words to label

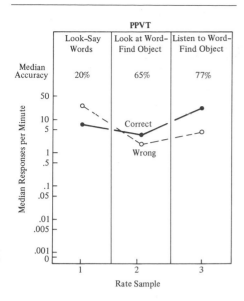

Figure 7 The performance of five pupils on three procedures to assess reading and understanding shows that every pupil understood words better auditorally than he did visually. This result was not accurately predicted by oral reading skills (look-say words).

pictures at a much higher level of accuracy.

The results from this task corroborate the findings using the Dolch words by showing that look at words and find the object pictures and listen to words and find object pictures are not always predicted by skill in look and say the words. In addition, every pupil did better on the listen to the word and find the object picture procedure than on the look at the word and find the object picture procedure. This result has consistently been found across all levels of accuracy and with three other tasks.

In two of the procedures used here responding was held constant (find the object picture) with variations made only in the method of presenting word

stimuli. In this way determinations of the ways a child can use words is assessed directly. The third procedure used written stimuli and an oral response. Comparing the performance of a child under this procedure with that obtained in looking at the word and finding the object helps separate performance deficits which are a function of looking and saying words from understanding the words. These different procedures appear to have exposed language usage skills with words that are often independent of whether a child can say the word he sees.

Figure 8 presents a replication of the previous task with the addition of four other procedures to assess eleven children's performance. The children were enrolled in a special tutorial program for disadvantaged youth. Performance on the first 75 questions of the PPVT was analyzed. The seven procedures were: look—say words, look—find words, listen—find words, listen—say words, listen—say object name, look at the word—find the object picture, and listen to the word—find the object picture.

The highest rate performance of these eleven children was on the listen—say word procedure, the listen—say object name procedure, and the listen to the word—find the object procedure. Performance accuracy was lowest in look—say the words and highest on the other procedures that involved the use of words alone. Looking at the word and finding the object picture was less accurate for every child than listening to the word and finding the object picture but performance on these two procedures was considerably more accurate than on the look—say word procedure.

Again, these data show that visually

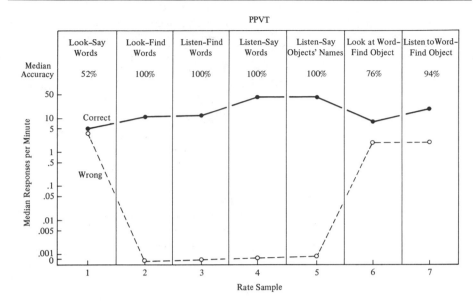

Figure 8 Performance rates and accuracy of eleven children under seven procedures for assessing word-object skills show that the major deficit involves oral reading skills (look-say words), not understanding the words (look-find words; listen-find words; listen-say words), the objects (listen-say object names), or the word-object relationships (look at word-find object picture; listen to word-find object picture).

presented words may have no function for one type of response but serve as an effective stimulus for another. Performance on the listen—find word, listen—say word, and listen—say object name procedures rule out the possibility of listening, or perceptual impairments as variables influencing the results. The median accuracy of the children clearly indicates that they can use words in written and auditory modes when they can listen and say the words and object names and find the visual duplicate of a sample stimulus. Performance difficulties by all children are evident when the words are presented visually and a say or find response is required (look—say words; look at word—find object picture). Understanding the words used here appears to be less of a problem than

training "look—say" the words skills. None of the pupils in this study could look and say the words better than he performed on the listen and find the word, listen and say the word, or listen and say the object name procedures. In addition, it was again found that all pupils performed at a higher level of accuracy when they listened to the words and found the object picture than when they looked at the word and found the object picture.

Study 6. Longitudinal Study in Reading Comprehension

Figure 9 presents Jerry's (9 years old) performance using four procedures for assessing his reading comprehension.

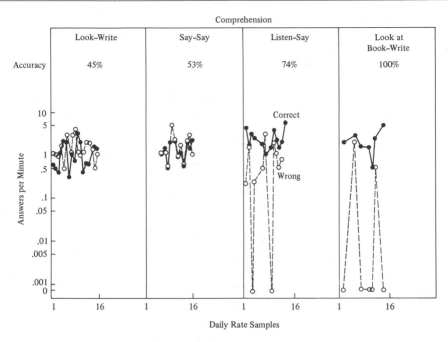

Figure 9   Performance of a boy on four comprehension assessment procedures shows that his skill is a function of the assessment procedures.

Look at the question and write the answer, say the question and say the answer, listen to the question and say the answer, and look at the book and write the answer were the procedures. The highest level of accuracy occurs when Jerry looks at the book and writes his answers. Looking at the questions and writing the answer and listening to the question and writing the answer produced the lowest levels of accuracy.

This chart shows that the method utilized to assess Jerry's understanding of the reading material critically determines the accuracy of his performance. Look at the question and write your answer and listen to the question and write your answer procedures if used independently of the other two procedures would have revealed the conclu-

sion that Jerry did not "understand" the material. His accuracy is too low. Jerry's deficiency, however, is largely a function of the method of asking him the questions. Comparisons of results from the listen to the question and write your answer procedure with say the question and say your answer procedure shows a difference of 21% in overall accuracy. The effective use of the reading materials was also determined by comparing his performance on the look at the question and write your answer procedure with look at the book and write your answer procedure. Accuracy in the latter procedure improved 55%. This result clearly shows the power of the method of presenting questions and the method of responding that are used with this child. Jerry's diagnosis was "slow reader," "had difficulties in comprehension," and "stutters." This classification appears to be too imprecise to pinpoint the exact deficiencies of Jerry's performance.

DISCUSSION AND SUMMARY

The procedures presented in this paper involved an assessment of language function by varying either the method of presenting the materials or the method of responding to those materials. Data were presented which showed that one method of presenting materials may serve as an effective stimulus with one type of response but have no function when a different response is required. Data also indicated that variations of the stimulus using the same response critically affected performance rates and accuracy. These results question the statements made by McCarthy and Kirk in discussing the experimental edition of the *Illinois Test of Psycholinguistic Abilities* format as:

To test pure decoding ability, only the mode of reception, auditory or visual, need be specified (i.e., it is irrelevant how the subject responds). To test encoding ability only the mode of response, vocal or motor, need be specified. To test association ability, or a combination of abilities simultaneously, the entire channel must be specified (1961, p. 3).

In contrast to the quote above, the data presented here show that input-output systems must be precisely specified to pinpoint and analyze language deficits. The procedures used here show that when language is defined in behavioral terms, experimental investigations of the ways language is used can be made directly. Skinner (1957) outlined a framework which provided new terms and definitions of potential behavioral functions of language. However, the major research emphasis has concerned the manipulation of vocal response rates in small animals and humans (e.g., Greenspoon, 1955; Lane, 1961; Salzinger and Waller, 1962). Very little emphasis has been placed on an analysis of how language is functional both as a stimulus and as a response (cf. Holz and Azrin, 1966).

Hively (1966) presented an experimental design similar to the one described in this paper. However, no data were presented to support the design. The present study has established a design and showed in what ways that design has sensitivity over other currently available methods (e.g. ITPA, PPVT). By varying the methods of presenting symbols and their referents, it is possible to directly record and separate skills and deficits. The procedures were shown to be maximally sensitive to pinpointing a particular deficit thus permitting precise remediation steps to be undertaken. In fact the same procedures can be used to analyze as well as teach, thus making it an economical package. Meaning and understanding become relevant insofar as a procedure identifies under what conditions language is functional for any particular person and subject matter. The development of specialized instructional methods to teach specific performance skills can be evaluated daily with the assessment procedures appropriate to that instruction.

Rates of responding (correct, wrong, total) and the overall accuracy of that responding provide maximally sensitive records for specifying performance skills and deficits. This combination of records permits a wide range of flexibility in analyzing the performance of single children as well as making comparisons across children and across procedures. Deficits which involve rate, accuracy, or both rate and accuracy can be precisely identified. Remedial programs based on these data could focus precisely on increasing specific dimensions of a behavior. Learning involves both rate and accuracy. Pinpointing the exact parameters of performance increases the precision of diagnostic methods and remedial procedures.

The following conclusions can be made from the studies conducted here: (1) a standardized test sample may or may not be representative of a person's performance, and it is not always possible to predict under what conditions representativeness is obtained, (2) typical reading assessments (look—say words) may not accurately predict a child's use of the word under other conditions, (3) the procedures used to assess reading comprehension can drastically alter performance rates and accuracy, (4) look at the word and find the object picture and listen to the word and find the object picture assessments showed that every child did better when he listened to the word and found the picture, (5) comparisons of performance on look and say words with look at the word and find the object picture revealed that every child could use more words than he could say, (6) alphabet assessments indicated that looking and saying letters and listening and writing the letters appear to be independent of a child's ability to orally recite the same letters, (7) the assessment of counting skills and addition showed that performance was critically affected by the

method of responding and the method of presenting the arithmetic problems, (8) assessments and instruction with seven alphabet procedures revealed that the procedures are sensitive to specifying performance skills and deficits in a young child and that the same procedures can be used as the instructional format, (9) the method of responding is clearly an important variable in curriculum analysis, and must be specified as precisely as the stimulation methods if we are to precisely analyze skills and deficits and suggest curriculum revisions functionally.

REFERENCES

Bridgman, P. W. *The logic of modern physics.* New York: MacMillan, 1927.

Dolch, E. W. *Match.* Champaign, Illinois: The General Press Publishers, 1953.

Dunn, L. M. *Peabody Picture Vocabulary Test.* Minneapolis: American Guidance Services, Inc. 1965.

Edwards, J. S. Precisely teaching children labeled learning disabled. Unpublished dissertation, University of Kansas, 1969.

Jaffe, J. The study of language in psychiatry: psycholinguistics and computational linguistics. In Arieti, S. (Ed.), *American Handbook of Psychiatry,* Vol. III. New York: Basic Books, 1966.

Jastak, J. F., Bijou, S. W., and Jastak, S. R. *Wide Range Achievement Test.* Wilmington, Delaware: Guidance Associates, 1965.

Greenspoon, J. The reinforcing effect of two spoken sounds on the frequency of two responses. *American Journal of Psychology,* 1955, **68**, 409–416.

Hively, W. A framework for the analysis of elementary reading behavior. *American Educational Research Journal,* 1966, **3**, 89–103.

Holz, W. C., and Azrin, N. H. Conditioning

human verbal behavior. In Honig, W. (Ed.), *Operant behavior: Areas of research and application.* New York: Appleton-Century-Crofts, 1966.

Lane, H. L. Operant control of vocalizing in chickens. *Journal of the Experimental Analysis of Behavior,* 1961, **4,** 171–177.

McCarthy, J. J., and Kirk, S. A. Experimental Edition, *Illinois Test of Psycholinguistic Abilities.* Urbana, Illinois: University of Illinois Press, 1961.

Salzinger, K., and Waller, M. B. The operant control of vocalization in the dog. *Journal of the Experimental Analysis of Behavior,* 1962, **5,** 383–389.

Schiefelbusch, R. L. Language functions of retarded children. *Folia Phoniatrica,* 1969, **21,** 129–144.

Skinner, B. F. *Verbal behavior.* New York: Appleton-Century-Crofts, 1957.

Vygotsky, L. S. *Thought and language.* Cambridge: The M.I.T. Press, 1962.

EIGHT

The Experimenter Effect

16

The Experimenter Effect

Buddy L. Kintz, Dennis J. Delprato, David R. Mettel, Carol E. Persons, and Robert H. Schappe

One of the few areas in which there is a considerable amount of research on doing research is that bearing on experimenter effects. The experimenter himself can be an influential variable determining the outcomes of his experiments, as the article shows.

It is significant that a problem which perplexed some of the most influential scientists of Germany in 1904 was resolved at that time, yet should contaminate psychological investigations of the present day, that is, the experimenter's influence on his subjects. The amazing horse of Mr. von Osten caused an uproar throughout all of Germany which Professor Stumpf and his co-workers, through meticulous investigation, demonstrated to be the result of the questioners' unintentional, involuntary cues utilized by the animal. This incident dramatically emphasized the stimulus value of "unconscious" cues emitted by an experimenter to his animal subjects. Even though questioners of "Hans" were

Reprinted from *Psychological Bulletin*, 1965, **63**, 223–232, by permission of the author and the American Psychological Association.

aware that this might be the explanation for his feats and were most careful in attempting to refrain from allowing him this advantage, the unconscious cues were still emitted until the situation was carefully analyzed and the specific variables controlled (Pfungst, 1911).

McGuigan (1963) states:

While we have traditionally recognized that the characteristics of an experimenter may indeed influence behavior, it is important to observe that we have not seriously attempted to study him as an independent variable [p. 421].

However, Stumpf with his careful, detailed measurements of questioners' cues began the study of the experimenter as an independent variable in 1904, but not until recently has this problem been considered by experimental psychologists for study (Cordaro & Ison, 1963; McGuigan, 1963; Rosenthal & Halas, 1962). Clinical psychologists have long led the way in this aspect of investigation. The personal effect of examiners upon patients' performance in clinical tests was initiated as an object of study 35 years ago (Marine, 1929). Yet, psychologists working in the laboratory have not been completely unaware of the implications of experimenter influence upon subjects.

Ebbinghaus (1913) in discussing the effects of early data returns upon psychological research stated:

it is unavoidable that, after the observation of the numerical results, suppositions should arise as to general principles which are concealed in them and which occasionally give hints as to their presence. As the investigations are carried further, these suppositions, as well as those present at the beginning, constitute a complicating factor which probably has a definite influence upon the subsequent results [pp. 28–29].

Pavlov, noting the apparent increase in learning ability of successive generations of mice in experiments on the inheritance of acquired characteristics, suggested that an increase in the teaching ability of experimenters may have, in fact, constituted the critical variable (Gruenberg, 1929, p. 327).

The foregoing yields some indication of the scope inherent in this phenomenon. However, response-induced bias is not the only data-affected result. A study in which experimenters (Es) recorded the frequency of contractions and head turns of planaria demonstrated that E's expectancy can dramatically influence the data obtained in this type of situation (Cordaro & Ison, 1963). In this case subject's (S's) re-

sponses were not affected, but highly statistically significant differences in number of reported responses were obtained for E's expecting a low frequency of response and for E's expecting a high frequency of response. In other words, Es saw (reported) what they expected to see.

Thus far we have seen that E may not only bias S's responses but also that this interpretation of S's responses may be biased. Because these effects are dependent upon E's knowledge of the hypothesis to be tested or his expectancy, one can readily propose that the solution to this problem would be, as is often the case, a simple matter of having research assistants (As) who are unaware of the hypothesis collect the data for E. In testing this suggestion, it was found that "a subtle transfer of cognitive events" existed, resulting in response bias (Rosenthal, Persinger, Vikan-Kline, & Mulray, 1963, p. 313). The authors state:

Our finding of a subtle transmission of E's bias to their As forces us to retract an earlier suggestion for the reduction of E bias (Rosenthal, 1963c). Our recommendation had been to have E employ a surrogate data collector who was to be kept ignorant of the hypothesis under test. The implication of the suggestion was simply not to have E tell A the hypothesis. It now appears that E's simply not telling A the hypothesis may not insure A's ignorance of that hypothesis [pp. 332–333].

It is the present authors' contention that wherever an experimenter-subject relationship exists, the possibility also exists for E to contaminate his data by one or more of a multitude of conveyances. It appears that experimental psychology has too long neglected the experimenter as an independent variable. By relating some of the findings of clinical and social psychologists, as well as the few experimental studies to date, it is hoped that experimental psychologists will no longer accept on faith that the experimenter is necessary but harmless. Implications for experimental, counseling, and testing psychology will also be considered.

RESEARCH FINDINGS

Nondifferentiated Effects

Research studies have been, on the whole, minimal in reporting differential results with regard to individual *E*s. In particular, this is true concerning careful discussion of the possible reasons for the differing data. It is, however, illustrative of the pervasiveness of experimenter effect to examine several of the studies which have shown a nondifferentiated experimenter influence.

Lord (1950) was interested in examining Rorschach responses in three different types of situations. Thirty-six *S*s took the Rorschach three times—once from each of three different female examiners. Of the Rorschach responses being considered for differences within *S*s, Lord found 48 to yield *t* tests significant at the .10 level. Of these, 27 were due to examiner differences.

In an interesting study on learning without awareness (Postman & Jarrett, 1952), 30 different *E*s—all students in advanced experimental psychology classes—were employed. The *S*s responded to 240 stimulus words with another word which came to mind. Half the *S*s were instructed to guess, and half were told, the "correct" principle of

answering, which was to give common associations as found in speaking and writing. Differences among *E*s were highly significant sources of data variance. Postman and Jarrett suggest that since complete universal uniformity of experimenter behavior is apparently impossible, the difficulty experienced in attempting to replicate results of other investigators is to be expected.

Using a verbal conditioning paradigm, Kanfer (1958) reinforced verb responses with a flashing light, under three different reinforcement schedules. Two *E*s were employed, with apparently little difference between them. In reinforcing *S*s, *E* simply was required to distinguish between verbs and nonverbs. A significant interaction was found between *E* and method. There was more frequent reinforcement of words for one schedule than for the others, the frequency varying with the *E*. Apparently, even the ability of an *E* to perform such a relatively elementary, objective task as judging whether a word is, or is not, a verb, is highly subject to individual differences.

A recent experiment (Severin & Rigby, 1963) investigated different patterns of digit grouping. An incidental finding from this study is pertinent here. In analyzing the variance of perfect memorizing, an *E* effect was found, significant at the .01 level. Further, this effect was largely due to only one of the four *E*s, since repetition of the analysis without this *E*'s data yielded no significant *E* difference.

An avoidance study using rats (Harris, Piccolino, Roback, & Sommer, 1964) was primarily concerned with the effects of alcohol on learning the avoidance response in a Miller-Mowrer shuttle box. Two teams, of two *E*s each, were employed. The alcohol did not produce differential results, but the different E teams did. It is likely that this outcome is due to differences in the handling of the animals by Es.

Personality

In discussing the differential effect of E upon S, Masling (1960) was writing with particular attention to projective testing. However, it seems logical to postulate that if sex and aspects of the examiner's personality (such as warmth or coldness) are causative of differential results in projective testing, the influence of these personal variables may also be felt in other, even objective, situations.

In attempting to assess effects of personality factors of experimenters in the experimental situation, McGuigan (1960) compared trait scores of Es on personality tests with dependent variable scores of Ss. He did not obtain any significant correlations, but noted several quite high ones that may indicate directional influences. For example, the more neurotic (Bl-N scale of the Bernreuter) the E, the poorer the performance of S.

The effect of E's personality upon Ss' performances had been investigated earlier (Sanders & Cleveland, 1953) using projective techniques. Nine Es took the Rorschach, which was scored blindly by two experienced clinical psychologists. The Es were then trained in administering the Rorschach, and each E gave it to 30 Ss. An attempt was made to deliberately standardize the questioning procedures used. After taking the Rorschach, each S filled out a questionnaire designed to elicit his attitudes about the particular E. Sanders and Cleveland found that overtly anxious Es (as indicated by their own Rorschach responses) tended to elicit more subject flexibility and responsiveness, while overtly hostile Es (again measured by their Rorschach responses) drew more passive and stereotyped responses and less of the hostile responses. The Ss' questionnaires indicated that Es who were most liked were those who had been rated low on anxiety and hostility.

The research just mentioned has been primarily interested in the effect of the personality of E, per se, on Ss' performances. One further study is especially interesting, as it tries to answer the pertinent question of whether E's personality and personal bias can interact. Rosenthal, Persinger, and Fode (1962) used 10 naive Es, who were biased to expect certain results. They found that agreement of final data and E bias were related to Es' scores on the MMPI scales, L, K, and Pt, but not to age or grade-point average.

The S-E personality interaction is dependent, of course, not only on the personality of E, but also to some degree on that of S. In one of the few studies designed to investigate this interaction, Spires (1960; cited in McGuigan, 1963) used a 2×2 design in a verbal conditioning paradigm, reinforcing a particular class of pronouns with the word "good." The Ss were divided into two groups, one of which had scored high on the Hy scale of the MMPI and one of which had scored high on the Pt scale. Each group was subdivided in half, receiving either a positive or a negative "set" ("this experimenter is warm and friendly" or "this experimenter is cold and unfriendly"). The high Hy-positive set group far surpassed the other three groups. The high *Hy*-negative set group performed the poorest. Thus, not only *E*'s personality, but *S*s' perception of this personality, can contribute to the *E* effect.

Investigation of *S*s' perception of *E* has been undertaken by two related studies (Rosenthal, Fode, Friedman, & Vikan-Kline, 1960; Rosenthal & Persinger, 1962). In the first experiment, *S*s were asked to rate *E* on a number of variables. In the second study, the experiment was not actually conducted, but only described, and *S*s were requested to imaginatively rate their imaginary *E*. Yet a correlation which was calculated between the ratings of the first and second studies yielded an *r* of .81. This would appear to support the hypothesis that naive *S*s, in particular, may have a kind of predetermined "set" about what a "typical" *E* is like—scientific, intelligent, etc.

Experience

Investigators with widely variant amounts of experience are busily conducting studies every day. Cantril (1944) stated that interviewers who are highly experienced show as much bias as those who are less experienced. In an experimental investigation, however, Brogden (1962) came to a different conclusion. Four *E*s each trained a group of rabbits and recorded the acquisition speed of a conditioned shock-avoidance response. The rabbits of the three experienced *E*s reached the learning criterion faster than the naive *E*'s rabbits. To further study this result, the naive *E* was required to run another group of rabbits to see whether his practice would produce more rapid conditioning in the second group. Another experienced *E* trained another group of *S*s to serve as a control measure. The data show both a significant *E* practice effect (for the naive *E* only) and a significant difference between *E*s.

Sex

Several studies have been concerned with investigating the manner in which results are influenced by *E* differences in sex. In a verbal conditioning study (Binder, McConnell, & Sjoholm, 1957), *S*s were reinforced for saying hostile words. Two clearly distinguishable *E*s were employed: one—a young, petite feminine girl; the other—a mature, large masculine male. Significantly more hostile words were emitted in the presence of the female *E*. It is conceivable that *S*s perceived the male *E* as being more hostile than the female *E*, in which case the results confirm Sanders and Cleveland's (1953) findings that hostile *E*s elicit fewer hostile responses from their *S*s than do other *E*s.

Sarason and Minard (1963) also found that sex and hostility significantly influenced *S*s' performances. Degree of contact between *S* and *E* and *E*'s prestige value (as perceived by *S*) also contributed significant effects. Sarason and Minard warn that ignoring these situational variables is hazardous research methodology.

In a very recent experiment investigating the sex variable, Stevenson and Allen (1964) show what is perhaps the most clear-cut demonstration of *S-E* interaction. Eight male and eight female *E*s each tested eight male and eight female *S*s in a simple sorting task. The mean number of responses was recorded at 30-second intervals. With either male or female *E*s, female *S*s made more responses than did male *S*s. However, all *S*s performed relatively better under an opposite-sexed *E*.

Expectancy Effect

Perhaps the component of experimenter effect which is the cause of greatest concern is that by which the *E* in some way influences his *S*s to perform as he has hypothesized. The reasons for concern about expectancy effect are that so little is known about it and so little research has been devoted to it. Only recently have systematic studies been conducted in this area.

Rosenthal and Fode (1963a) demonstrated the problem clearly in an experiment with two groups of randomly assigned animals. One group of six *E*s was instructed that its group of rats was "maze-bright" and a second group of six *E*s was instructed that its group of rats was "maze-dull." In a simple T maze, the maze-bright rats performed significantly better than the maze-dull rats.

In a similar study (Rosenthal & Lawson, 1964) investigators divided 38 *E*s into 14 research teams, each of which had one rat randomly assigned to it. Six of the teams were told that their rats were bred for dullness and the other eight were told that their rats had been bred for brightness. Seven experiments, including such tasks as operant acquisition, stimulus discrimination, and chaining of responses, were conducted. In seven out of eight comparisons (overall $p = .02$), difference in performance again favored *E*s who believed their *S*s to be bred for brightness. A factor which may have prompted the difference was that *E*s who believed their rats were bred

for brightness handled them more than *E*s who believed their rats were bred for dullness.

In both experiments cited, the question arises as to the sensitivity of the animals to attitudinal differences in *E*s transmitted through the tactual and sensory modalities. Further research is required to clarify the issue.

Modeling Effect

Modeling effect is defined (Rosenthal, 1963b) as a significant correlation between *E*'s performance and the performance of randomly assigned *S*s on the same task.

Graham (1960) divided 10 psychotherapists into two groups on the basis of their perception of movement in Rorschach inkblots. In the ensuing psychotherapeutic sessions, patients of the group of psychotherapists that perceived more movement in the inkblots saw a significantly greater amount of movement than the patients of the group of psychotherapists that had perceived less movement.

In the area of survey research the phenomenon of modeling has been reported in studies by Cantril (1944) and Blankenship (1940) who have found that interviewers elicit from their interviewees, at a probability greater than chance, responses which reflect the interviewers' own beliefs.

Rosenthal (1963b) reported eight experiments conducted to assess the existence and magnitude of experimenter modeling effect by employing the task of *S*s' rating a series of photographs of people on a scale of apparent successfulness and unsuccessfulness ranging from −10 to +10. Prior to each experiment, *E*s had rated the photos which were selected because in earlier ratings on the same scale they had yielded a mean value of zero. The resulting eight rank-order correlations between Es ratings and their Ss' ratings ranged from −.49 to +.65. Only the rho of +.65 was significantly different from 0 ($p < .001$), but the hypothesis of equality among the eight rhos was rejected using a chi-square test ($p < .005$).

Hammer and Piotrowski (1953) had three clinical psychologists and three interns rate 400 House-Tree-Person drawings on a 3-point scale of aggression. The degree of hostility which clinicians saw in the drawings correlated .94 with the evaluations of their personal hostility made by one of the investigators.

Early Data Returns Effect

Early data returns effect is the problem of the experimenter who is receiving feedback from his experiment through early data returns and who contaminates the subsequent data. The reasons why this occurs are unclear but some suggestions are that E's mood may change if the data are contrary to his expectations, or if the data are in agreement with his expectations, there is the possibility of heightening an existing bias. There is evidence (Rosenthal, Persinger, Vikan-Kline, & Fode, 1963) that this mood change in E, brought about by "good results," may lead him to be perceived by the Ss as more "likable," "personal," and more "interested" in their work and thereby influence their performance.

In the study by Rosenthal, Persinger, Vikan-Kline, and Fode (1963), three groups of four Es each had three groups of Ss rate the apparent success of people in photographs on a scale ranging from −10 to +10. The Es were instructed that Ss' mean rating would be about +5. In each of two experimental groups, two Ss were confederates of the investigator while in a control group all of the Ss were naive. One of the confederate pairs was instructed to give "good data" (in accord with E's expectations) and the other pair was instructed to give "bad data" (contrary to E's expectations). Ratings of all Ss were learned after several trials. It was hypothesized that the experience of having obtained good data would lead those Es to obtain "better" subsequent data while the experience of having obtained bad data would lead those Es to obtain "worse" data in relation to the control. Although neither experimental group differed significantly from the control group, the experimental groups were significantly different from each other. There was a further tendency for the effect of early returns to become more pronounced in the later stages of data gathering.

Griffith (1961) states clearly the effect of early data returns in an autobiographical documentary:

Each record declared itself for or against . . . (me) . . . (and) . . . (my) . . . spirit rose and fell almost as wildly as does the gambler whose luck supposedly expresses to him a higher love or reflection [p. 309].

Overview of Cues and Their Transmission

After discussing at some length the various experimenter effects, the question must certainly arise as to how the experimenter contaminates his data. What are these cues and how are they transmitted? Some suggestions have been made but it is necessary to look at evidence dealing directly with the problem. It was suggested earlier that in the case of laboratory animals it might be due to tactual and kinesthetic cues, but probably also involved are all of the sensory processes of the organism so that E inadvertently transmits cues by nearly everything that he does.

In dealing with humans, because of the probable lack of bodily contact, cues are transmitted verbally and/or visually. But "verbally" implies not only the words, but also the inflectional and dynamic processes of speaking.

The transmission of verbal cues was first dramatically demonstrated by Greenspoon (1955) who, by reinforcing plural nouns with "mmm-hmmm," was able to increase the frequency of emission of such words.

In a similar experiment, Verplanck (1955) was able to control the content of Ss' conversation by agreeing with some opinions and disagreeing with others. The results showed that every S increased in his rate of speaking opinions with reinforcement by agreement, and 21 out of the 24 Ss decreased their rate of opinion statements with nonreinforcement.

Rosenthal and Fode (1963b) conducted two experiments specifically designed to investigate the transmission of cues from E to his human Ss. The Ss were to rate the apparent success or failure of persons in photographs on a scale ranging from −10 to +10. All Es received identical instructions except that five of them were told that their Ss would probably rate the pictures at about +5 while the remaining Es were told their Ss would probably rate the pictures at about −5. Further, prior to the experiment, each E rated the pictures on the same scale as the Ss. Results showed that Ss for high-biased (+5) Es obtained significantly higher mean ratings than Ss of low-biased (−5) Es. Since Es were not permitted to say anything to Ss other than what was on the instruction sheet, the communication of bias must have been done by tone, manner, gesture, or facial expression. The second experiment designed to investigate this nonverbal transmission of cues was conducted in the same manner as the first with the exception that now, instead of E showing each photo to his Ss, each set of 10 photos was mounted on cardboard and labeled so that S could give his rating without Es' handling the photos. The results showed that elimination of visual cues from E to S did significantly reduce the effect of E's bias. It can be hypothesized then that visual cues play an important part in the phenomenon of E bias, but probably to a lesser degree than verbal cues.

Wickes (1956) also showed the import of visual cues by effectively using nodding, smiling, and leaning forward in his chair as reinforcement for certain responses given to inkblots by clients in psychotherapy sessions.

Considerable research is required to learn what the cues are, how they are transmitted, and how they can be controlled.

IMPLICATIONS OF THE EXPERIMENTER EFFECT

The preceding survey of the literature has revealed the existence of the experimenter effect in all aspects of psychology. Although the experimenter effect is generally recognized and perhaps paid lip service, it tends to be a forgotten skeleton in the research psychologist's closet. Comparison of a study by Postman and Jarrett (1952) with one by Spence (1964) provides an example.

Postman and Jarrett (1952) commented:

We have paid too little attention to the contributions made by variations in *E*s' behavior to the experimental results. The difficulty which many psychologists experience in repeating the results of other investigators may be due to our failure to attack systematically the role of differences among *E*s [p. 253].

Spence (1964), after examining various aspects of variability occurring in experiments using the Taylor Manifest Anxiety scale, says the following in concluding his discussion of the experimenter-subject interaction:

This is, nevertheless, a potentially important variable and should be investigated further, possibly by deliberately manipulating the behavior of *E* [p. 136].

It is clear from a comparison of these two statements that during the past 12 years the progress in examining and controlling the experimenter effect has been something less than spectacular. Thus, the objective of this portion of the present paper is to attempt to alter further research procedure by emphasizing the implications of the experimenter effect as it relates to the individual psychologist engaged in his varied activities.

Clinical Implications

Clinicians have long recognized the influence of the experimenter (therapist) upon the behavior of a subject (client).

In fact, the differing views existing in the clinical realm as to the most effective therapeutic procedure to utilize seem to have their origin in the clinician's conception of the role of the therapist in the therapeutic situation. For example, the psychoanalyst believes transference is essential if the client is to be led to adjustment, whereas the nondirective therapist strives to accompany the patient along the road to adjustment rather than to lead.

Even though clinicians not only recognize but argue over the implementation of the experimenter influence, they are not exempt from a thorough evaluation of the implications (some of which are discussed below) that the experimenter variable holds for the clinical field.

Perhaps a reevaluation of the experimenter variable will reveal that pseudo-differences exist among the effects of various psychotherapeutic techniques. Goldstein (1962) showed that clients who are rehabilitated by a particular technique may be more products of perceived therapist expectancies than of therapeutic techniques. An essentially different technique employed by a therapist expecting good results with his procedure can rehabilitate the client just as completely.

Considering the present state of sophistication in the clinical realm, it is not unreasonable to assume that therapist expectancies are likely to play a large part in client rehabilitation. Thus, the pseudoproblem may tend to thwart intensive searches for valid, operationally defined therapeutic procedures.

Other more specific clinical areas affected by *E-S* interaction would include the effect upon patients' Rorschach scores as a function of experimenter differences (Lord, 1950), the once-removed influence of the experienced clinician's effect upon a neophyte therapist's prognosis of a patient (Rosenthal, 1963c), the possibility that the therapist may be a contributing factor to the patient's failure to recover as the result of perceived negative therapist expectancy (Sanders & Cleveland, 1953), and the not-so-alluring possibility that patients receiving the stamp of rehabilitation have only adjusted to the wishes of the therapist and not necessarily to the emotional problems which brought them to the therapist originally (Verplanck, 1955).

These are important problems for practicing clinicians, and it is to their credit that they have recognized this, as evidenced by the increasing use of the team approach in diagnosing clients. Utilization of the team approach may be extended to therapy in order to reduce the negative aspects of the clinician-client interaction.

Such a team approach might involve the objective assignment of patients to therapists by means of a large-scale correlational determination of what therapist-patient "personality types" interact most effectively in the therapeutic situation. Of course, the determination of personality types still leaves us with all the previously mentioned E-S interaction problems, but nonetheless attempts at improvement can be made even if imperfect tools must be used.

Implications for the Field of Testing

The general field of testing which would include IQ tests, placement tests, reading readiness tests, aptitude tests, etc., is also beset with the problem of the experimenter variable. Even though there have been rigorous attempts at standardization of test items and procedures in this area, E or administrator of the test still influences the test taker in other subtle ways (Kanfer, 1958; Rosenthal, 1963a).

The implications of the experimenter effect in the testing area have many ramifications. It is questionable whether many tests have been proven sufficiently reliable and valid in their own right, and this problem is further complicated by the experimenter variable. Judgment of an individual's score on special abilities and IQ tests, etc., must not only be viewed in light of which test was used, but must also take into consideration the previously ignored variable of the specific administrator. In addition to knowing that a person achieved an IQ score of 105 on the Stanford-Binet and not the Wechsler, it is also necessary to know whether or not E was threatening, docile, friendly, anxious, or expected the test taker to be smart, dumb, score well, etc. (Binder, McConnell, & Sjoholm, 1957; McGuigan, 1963; Rosenthal, 1963a).

The administrator contamination problem may eventually be resolved by the application of machines to the administration of tests. At this time a more judicious selection of the hundreds of available tests on the part of administrators, using test results to guide their decision-making process, is essential. In addition, test results should be viewed with a more sophisticated, critical eye, with IQ and aptitude scores being considered as but some of many indices of performance. All persons using test scores must recognize the strong influence of E and make decisions accordingly.

Experimental Implications

The psychologist engaged in controlled experimentation should realize that he has failed to provide a control for himself. That this variable is disregarded is evidenced by Woods' (1961) investigation of 1,737 published experiments, of which 42%—45% involved multiple authorship. None of these ran an analysis of experimenter interaction.

One particular aspect of controlled experimental endeavor which has neglected the experimenter effect is learning-theory research. Much energy is expended on "crucial" experiments which ostensibly attempt to determine which of the conflicting theories of Hull, Tolmon, Guthrie, and others are correct. At the present time these crucial experiments have produced results which are generally inconclusive, except for establishing a high correlation between the theory an *E*'s results support and his theoretical position.

The experiments already reviewed provide a speculative base for partially explaining the conflicting results obtained by the supporters of various learning theories. As Rosenthal (1963c) has shown, experimenter bias is a powerful influence in the experimental situation. The *E* has many opportunities to influence, unintentionally, *S*s who have been brought into a very strange, highly structured situation. In view of this, it is not surprising—it should be expected—that *E*s favoring a particular learning theory would tend to obtain results favoring this same theory.

Results reported recently (Cordaro & Ison, 1963; Rosenthal & Fode, 1963a; Rosenthal & Halas, 1962) indicate that *E*s also affect the results of studies using

nonhuman *S*s. These findings further emphasize the possibility that the overlooked experimenter variable may have contaminated many crucial learning experiments.

This is not to suggest that being able to replicate studies and/or controlling the experimenter variable is the panacea for psychology's problems. But it can not be overemphasized that at the present time *E* is a powerful, yet much ignored, variable. It is a strange paradox that even many of the most adamantly scientific of psychologists have failed to control for the experimenter variable.

CONCLUSIONS

Future experimentation might prove more profitable if more rigorous communication could be established between researchers of differing points of view and theoretical orientations so that a system of research exchange might be established. This suggestion admittedly presents a multitude of problems, not the least of which would be that of authorship credit. Although this and many other problems would arise, they would not be insurmountable.

If research exchange were implemented, it might prove an effective means of controlling the experimenter effect and, in addition, bring scientific communication into the prepublication stage of research. This in itself might prove to be the most important contribution of all.

Other suggestions for control of the experimenter variable have been given previously by Rosenthal (1963c) and McGuigan (1963). These suggestions included counterbalancing of *E*s and the use of factorial designs which include the experimenter as a major independent variable. Fode (1960; cited in Rosenthal, 1963), as reported by Rosenthal (1963c), found that both visual and auditory cues influenced the behavior of *S*s. Thus, another suggestion involves the elimination of verbal and visual cues, including inflections of the voice, speaking peculiarities, gestures, etc., as transmitted to *S*s during the reading of instructions.

This paper, which began with a discussion of a horse and the subtlety of experimenter cues, has ranged far afield. We have seen that the experimenter effect exerts an insidious influence upon the relationship between counselor and client. Indeed, the more objective and nondirective the counselor, the greater the potential hidden effect. To be unaware of the relationship between counselor and client expectations is to lose much of the control that a counselor must maintain over the counseling situation. In the same way teachers must be aware that objective appraisal by their students is affected by the goals which the students believe their teachers have. And finally, but probably most important at this time, directors of laboratory research who use student *E*s, must be aware of the extremely great effect of their personal biases which can be perceived by the student *E*s and translated into practically any significant experimental effect.

REFERENCES

Binder, A., McConnell, D., & Sjoholm, N. A. Verbal conditioning as a function of experimenter characteristics. *Journal of Abnormal and Social Psychology*, 1957, **55**, 309–314.

Blankenship, A. B. The effect of the interviewer upon the response in a public opinion poll. *Journal of Consulting Psychology*, 1940, **4**, 134–136.

Brogden, W. J. The experimenter as a factor in animal conditioning. *Psychological Reports*, 1962, **11**, 239–242.

Cantril, H., & Research Associates. *Gauging public opinion*. Princeton, N. J.: Princeton Univer. Press, 1944.

Cordaro, L., & Ison, J. R. Psychology of the scientist: X. Observer bias in classical conditioning of the planarian. *Psychological Reports*, 1963, **13**, 787–789.

Ebbinghaus, H. *Memory: A contribution to experimental psychology*. (Orig. publ. 1885; trans. by H. A. Ruger & Clara E. Bussenius) New York: Teachers College, Columbia University, 1913.

Fode, K. L. The effect of non-visual and non-verbal interaction on experimenter bias. Unpublished master's thesis, University of North Dakota, 1960.

Goldstein, A. P. *Therapist-patient expectancies in psychotherapy*. New York: Pergamon Press, 1962.

Graham, S. R. The influence of therapist character structure upon Rorschach changes in the course of psychotherapy. *American Psychologist*, 1960, **15**, 415.

Greenspoon, J. The reinforcing effect of two spoken sounds on the frequency of two responses. *American Journal of Psychology*, 1955, **68**, 409–416.

Griffith, R. M. Rorschach water precepts: A study in conflicting results. *American Psychologist*, 1961, **16**, 307–311.

Gruenberg, B. C. *The story of evolution*. New York: Van Nostrand, 1929.

Hammer, E. F., & Piotrowski, Z. A. Hostility as a factor in the clinician's personality as it affects his interpretation of projective drawings. *Journal of Projective Techniques*, 1953, **17**, 210–216.

Harris, H. E., Piccolino, E. B., Roback, H. B., & Sommer, D. K. The effects of alcohol on counter conditioning of an avoidance response. *Quarterly Journal of Alcoholic Studies*, 1964, **25**, 490–497.

Kanfer, F. H. Verbal conditioning: Reinforcement schedules and experimental influence. *Psychological Reports,* 1958, **4,** 443–452.

Lord, E. Experimentally induced variations in Rorschach performance. *Psychological Monographs,* 1950, **64** (10, Whole No. 316).

McGuigan, F. J. Variation of whole-part methods of learning. *Journal of Educational Psychology,* 1960, **51,** 213–216.

McGuigan, F. J. The experimenter: A neglected stimulus object. *Psychological Bulletin,* 1963, **60,** 421–428.

Marine, E. L. The effect of familiarity with the examiner upon Stanford-Binet test performance. *Teachers College Contributions in Education,* 1929, **381,** 42.

Masling, J. The influence of situational and interpersonal variables in projective testing. *Psychological Bulletin,* 1960, **57,** 65–85.

Pfungst, O. *Der Kluge Hans.* (Orig. publ. 1905; trans. by C. L. Rahn) New York: Holt, 1911.

Postman, L., & Jarrett, R. F. An experimental analysis of learning without awareness. *American Journal of Psychology,* 1952, **65,** 244–255.

Rosenthal, R. Experimenter attributes as determinants of subjects' responses. *Journal of Projective Techniques,* 1963, **27,** 324–331. (a)

Rosenthal, R. Experimenter modeling effects as determinants of subjects' responses. *Journal of Projective Techniques,* 1963, **27,** 467–471. (b)

Rosenthal, R. On the social psychology of the psychological experiment: The experimenter's hypothesis as unintended determinant of experimental results. *American Scientist,* 1963, **51,** 268–283. (c)

Rosenthal, R., & Fode, K. L. The effect of experimenter bias on the performance of the albino rat. *Behavioral Science,* 1963, **8,** 183–189. (a)

Rosenthal, R., & Fode, K. L. Psychology of the scientist: V. Three experiments in experimenter bias. *Psychological Reports,* 1963, **12,** 491–511. (b)

Rosenthal, R., Fode, K. L., Friedman, C. J., & Vikan-Kline, L. L. Subjects'

perception of their experimenter under conditions of experimenter bias. *Perceptual and Motor Skills,* 1960, **11,** 325–331.

Rosenthal, R., & Halas, E. S. Experimenter effect in the study of invertebrate behavior. *Psychological Reports,* 1962, **11,** 251–256.

Rosenthal, R., & Lawson, R. A longitudinal study of experimenter bias on the operant learning of laboratory rats. *Journal of Psychiatric Research,* 1964, **2,** (2), 61–72.

Rosenthal, R., & Persinger, G. W. Let's pretend: Subjects' perception of imaginary experimenters. *Perceptual and Motor Skills,* 1962, **14,** 407–409.

Rosenthal, R., Persinger, G. W., & Fode, K. L. Experimenter bias, anxiety, and social desirability. *Perceptual and Motor Skills,* 1962, **15,** 73–74.

Rosenthal, R., Persinger, G. W., Vikan-Kline, L. L., & Fode, K. L. The effect of early data returns on data subsequently obtained by outcome-biased experimenters. *Sociometry,* 1963, **4,** 487–498.

Rosenthal, R., Persinger, G. W., Vikan-Kline, L. L., & Mulray, R. C. The role of the research assistant in the mediation of experimenter bias. *Journal of Personality,* 1963, **31,** 313–335.

Sanders, R., & Cleveland, S. E. The relation between certain experimenter personality variables and subjects' Rorschach scores. *Journal of Projective Techniques,* 1953, **17,** 34–50.

Sarason, I. G., & Minard, J. Interrelationships among subjects, experimenters, and situational variables. *Journal of Abnormal and Social Psychology,* 1963, **67,** 87–91.

Severin, F. T., & Rigby, M. K. Influences of digit grouping on memory for telephone numbers. *Journal of Applied Psychology,* 1963, **47,** 117–119.

Spence, K. W. Anxiety (drive) level and performance in eyelid conditioning. *Psychological Bulletin,* 1964, **61,** 129–140.

Spires, A. M. Subject-experimenter interaction in verbal conditioning. Unpublished doctoral dissertation, New York
University, 1960.

Stevenson, H. W., & Allen, S. Adult performance as a function of sex of experimenter and sex of subject. *Journal of
Abnormal and Social Psychology,* 1964, **68,**
214–216.

Verplanck, W. S. The control of the content
of conversation. *Journal of Abnormal and
Social Psychology,* 1955, **51,** 668–676.

Wickes, T. H. Examiner difference in a test
situation. *Journal of Consulting Psychology,*
1956, **20,** 23–26.

Woods, P. J. Some characteristics of journals
and authors. *American Psychologist,* 1961,
16, 699–701.

NINE

Selection of Experimental Subjects: Animal

17

The Snark Was a Boojum

Frank A. Beach

Experimental psychologists have attained a certain notoriety for their use of rats, especially albino rats, as experimental subjects. There is a widespread conviction that the behavior of rats cannot be generalized to the behavior of humans. The rat psychologist argues, on the other hand, that the most general principles of behavior apply to a wide range of species, and that such principles can therefore be discovered by doing research on almost any convenient experimental subject. If we are in search of those psychological principles which are general to, let us say, all mammals, then we are free to use any mammal in attempting to discover them. Convenience becomes the most important determinant of which species we will select. Many rat psychologists have taken the view that these most general principles must be discovered first, so their use of rats is justified.

To argue that the use of rats is justified is not the same as to argue that it is an optimal research strategy. Many psychologists feel that subject selection could be improved. Some argue that human subjects should receive most of our attention, and others maintain that a true comparative psychology, involving a variety of species, would be especially revealing.

In the article that follows, Beach presents a strong case for the enrichment of comparative psychology. At the time he wrote the article, comparative psychology seemed to be a dying field. Since then, largely owing to the work of the behavioral biologists known as ethologists, comparative psychology has revived, and it is still very much in the ascendancy today.

Presidential address delivered before the Division of Experimental Psychology of the American Psychological Association, September 7, 1949. Reprinted from *American Psychologist*, 1950, **5,** 115–124. Copyright 1950 by the American Psychological Association, and reproduced by permission.

Those of you who are familiar with the writings of Lewis Carroll will have recognized the title of this address as a quotation from his poem "The Hunting of the Snark." Anyone who has never read that masterpiece of whimsy must now be informed that the hunting party includes a Bellman, a Banker, a Beaver, a Baker and several other equally improbable characters. While they are sailing toward the habitat of their prey the Bellman tells his companions how they can recognize the quarry. The outstanding characters of the genus *Snark* are said to be its taste which is described as "meager but hollow," its habit of getting up late, its very poor sense of humor and its overweening ambition. There are several species of Snarks. Some relatively harmless varieties have feathers and bite, and others have whiskers and scratch. But, the Bellman adds, there are a few Snarks that are Boojums.

When the Baker hears the word, Boojum, he faints dead away, and after his companions have revived him he explains his weakness by recalling for their benefit the parting words of his Uncle.

If your Snark be a Snark, that is right:
Fetch it home by all means—you may
    serve it with greens
And it's handy for striking a light.

But oh, beamish nephew, beware of the
    day,
If your Snark be a Boojum! For then,
You will softly and suddenly vanish away,
And never be met with again!

Much later in the story they finally discover a Snark, and it is the Baker who first sights the beast. But by great misfortune that particular Snark turns out to be a Boojum and so of course the Baker softly and suddenly vanishes away.

Thirty years ago in this country a small group of scientists went Snark hunting. It is convenient to personify them collectively in one imaginary individual who shall be called the Comparative Psychologist. The Comparative Psychologist was hunting a Snark known as Animal Behavior. His techniques were different from those used by the Baker, but he came to the same unhappy end, for his Snark also proved to be a Boojum. Instead of animals in the generic sense he found one animal, the albino rat, and thereupon the Comparative Psychologist suddenly and softly vanished away. I must admit that this description is somewhat overgeneralized. A few American psychologists have done or are doing behavioral research that is broadly comparative. All honor to that tiny band of hardy souls who are herewith excepted from the general indictment that follows.

It is my aim, first, to trace the initial development and subsequent decline of Comparative Psychology in the United States. Secondly, I intend to propose certain explanations for the attitude of American psychologists toward this branch of the discipline. And finally I will outline some of the potential benefits that may be expected to follow a more vigorous and widespread study of animal behavior.

Instead of beginning with the uncritical assumption of a mutual understanding, let me define the basic terms that will be used. Comparative psychology is based upon comparisons of behavior shown by different species of animals including human beings. Comparisons between *Homo sapiens* and other animals are legitimate contributions to comparative psychology, but comparisons between two or more non-human species are equally admissible. Like any other responsible scientist the Comparative Psychologist is concerned with the understanding of his own species and with its welfare; but his primary aim is the exposition of general laws of behavior regardless of their immediate applicability to the problems of human existence. Now this means that he will not be content with discovering the similarities and differences between two or three species. Comparisons between rats and men, for example, do not in and of themselves constitute a comparative psychology although they may well represent an important contribution toward the establishment of such a field. A much broader sort of approach is necessary and it is the failure to recognize this fact that has prevented development of a genuine comparative psychology in this country.

PAST AND CURRENT TRENDS

The history of comparative behavior studies in America is reflected in the contents of our journals that are expressly devoted to articles in this field. They have been the *Journal of Animal Behavior* and its successor, the *Journal of Comparative and Physiological Psychology.* Animal studies have, of course, been reported in other publications but the ones mentioned here adequately and accurately represent the general interests and attitudes of Americans toward the behavior of non-human animals. I have analyzed a large sample of the volumes of these journals, starting with Volume I and including all odd-numbered vol-

umes through 1948. I have classified the contents of these volumes in two ways—first in terms of the species of animal used, and second in terms of the type of behavior studied. Only research reports have been classified; summaries of the literature and theoretical articles have been excluded from this analysis.

Types of Animals Studied

Figure 1 shows the number of articles published and the total number of species dealt with in these articles. The number of articles has tended to increase, particularly in the last decade; but the variety of animals studied began to decrease about 30 years ago and has remained low ever since. In other words, contributors to these journals have been inclined to do more and more experiments on fewer and fewer species.

Data represented in Figure 2 further emphasize the progressive reduction in the number of species studied. Here we see that the *Journal of Animal Behavior* contained nearly as many articles dealing with invertebrates as with verte-

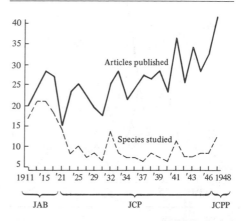

Figure 1 Number of articles published and variety of species used as subjects.

brates; but interest in invertebrate behavior fell off sharply after World War I and, as far as this type of analysis is capable of indicating, it never rose appreciably thereafter. The attention paid to behavior of invertebrates during the second decade of this century is also reflected in the policy of publishing annual surveys of recent research. Each volume of the *Journal of Animal Behavior* contains one systematic review devoted to lower invertebrates, another dealing with spiders and insects with the exception of ants, a third summarizing work on ants and a single section covering all studies of vertebrates.

Figure 2 shows that in the early years of animal experimentation sub-mammalian vertebrates, which include all fishes, amphibians, reptiles, and birds, were used as experimental subjects more often than mammals. But a few mammalian species rapidly gained popularity and by approximately 1920, more work was being done on mammals than on all other classes combined. Now there are approximately 3,500 extant species of mammals, but taken together they make up less than one-half of one percent of all animal species now living. A psychology based primarily upon studies of mammals can, therefore, be regarded as comparative only in a very restricted sense. Moreover the focus of interest has actually been even more narrow than this description implies because only a few kinds of mammals have been used in psychological investi-

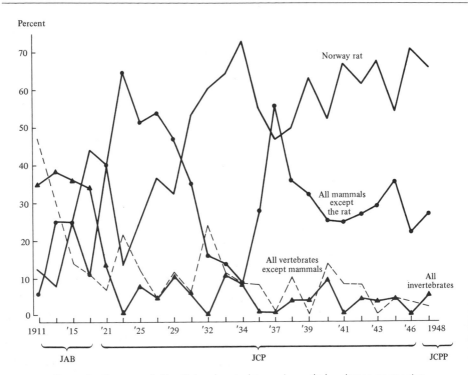

Figure 2 Percent of all articles devoted to various phyla, classes or species.

gations. The Norway rat has been the prime favorite of psychologists working with animals, and from 1930 until the present more than half of the articles in nearly every volume of the journal are devoted to this one species.

During the entire period covered by this survey the odd-numbered volumes of the journals examined includes 613 experimental articles. Nine percent of the total deal with invertebrates; 10 percent with vertebrates other than mammals; 31 percent with mammals other than the rat; and 50 percent are based exclusively upon the Norway rat. There is no reason why psychologists should not use rats as subjects in some of their experiments, but this excessive concentration upon a single species has precluded the development of a comparative psychology worthy of the name. Of the known species of animals more than 96 percent are invertebrates. Vertebrates below the mammals make up 3.2 percent of the total; and the Norway rat represents .001 percent of the types of living creatures that might be studied. I do not propose that the number of species found in a particular phyletic class determines the importance of the group as far as psychology is concerned; but it is definitely disturbing to discover that 50 percent of the experiments analyzed here have been conducted on one one-thousandth of one percent of the known species.

Some studies of animal behavior are reported in journals other than the ones I have examined but the number of different animals used in experiments published elsewhere is even fewer. The six issues of the *Journal of Experimental Psychology* published in 1948 contain 67 reports of original research. Fifty of these articles deal with human subjects

and this is in accord with the stated editorial policy of favoring studies of human behavior above investigations of other species. However, 15 of the 17 reports describing work on non-human organisms are devoted to the Norway rat.

During the current meetings of the APA, 47 experimental reports are being given under the auspices of the Division of Experimental Psychology. The published abstracts show that in half of these studies human subjects were employed while nearly one-third of the investigations were based on the rat.

Is the Experimental Psychologist going to softly and suddenly vanish away in the same fashion as his one-time brother, the Comparative Psychologist? If you permit me to change the literary allusion from the poetry of Lewis Carroll to that of Robert Browning, I will venture a prediction. You will recall that the Pied Piper rid Hamelin Town of a plague of rats by luring the pests into the river with the music of his magic flute. Now the tables are turned. The rat plays the tune and a large group of human beings follow. My prediction is indicated in Figure 3. Unless they escape the spell that *Rattus norvegicus* is casting over them, Experimentalists are in danger of extinction.

Types of Behavior Studied

I trust that you will forgive me for having demonstrated what to many of you must have been obvious from the beginning—namely, that we have been extremely narrow in our selection of types of animals to be studied. Now let us turn our attention to the types of behavior with which psychologists have concerned themselves.

Figure 3   Current position of many experimental psychologists.

Articles appearing in our sample of volumes of the journals can be classified under seven general headings: (1) conditioning and learning; (2) sensory capacities, including psychophysical measurements, effects of drugs on thresholds, etc.; (3) general habits and life histories; (4) reproductive behavior, including courtship, mating, migration, and parental responses; (5) feeding behavior, including diet selection and reactions to living prey; (6) emotional behavior, as reflected in savageness and wildness, timidity and aggressive reactions; and (7) social behavior, which involves studies of dominance and submission, social hierarchies, and interspecies symbiotic relations.

In classifying articles according to type of behavior studied I have disregarded the techniques employed by the investigator. It is often necessary for an animal to learn to respond differentially to two stimuli before its sensory capacities can be measured; but in such a case the article was listed as dealing with sensory capacity rather than learning. The aim has been to indicate as accurately as possible the kind of be-

havior in which the experimenter was interested rather than his methods of studying it.

It proved possible to categorize 587 of the 613 articles. Of this total, 8.6 percent dealt with reproductive behavior, 3.7 percent with emotional reactions, 3.2 percent with social behavior, 3.0 percent with feeding, and 2.8 percent with general habits. The three most commonly treated types of behavior were (1) reflexes and simple reaction patterns, (2) sensory capacities, and (3) learning and conditioning. Figure 4 shows the proportion of all articles devoted to each of these three major categories.

The figure makes it clear that conditioning and learning have always been of considerable interest to authors whose work appears in the journals I have examined. As a matter of fact slightly more than 50 percent of all articles categorized in this analysis deal with this type of behavior. The popularity of the subject has increased appreciably during the last 15 years, and only once since 1927 has any other kind of behavior been accorded as many articles per volume. This occurred in 1942 when the number of studies dealing with reflexes and simple reaction patterns was unusually large. The temporary shift in relative emphasis was due almost entirely to a burst of interest in so-called "neurotic behavior" or "audiogenic seizures."

Combining the findings incorporated in Figures 2 and 4, one cannot escape the conclusion that psychologists publishing in these journals have tended to concentrate upon one animal species and one type of behavior in that species. Perhaps it would be appropriate to change the title of our journal to read "The Journal of Rat Learning," but

there are many who would object to this procedure because they appear to believe that in studying the rat they are studying all or nearly all that is important in behavior. At least I suspect that this is the case. How else can one explain the fact that Professor Tolman's book *Purposive Behavior in Animals and Men* deals primarily with learning and is dedicated to the white rat, "where, perhaps, most of all, the final credit or discredit belongs." And how else are we to interpret Professor Skinner's 457-page opus which is based exclusively upon the performance of rats in bar-pressing situations but is entitled simply *The Behavior of Organisms?*

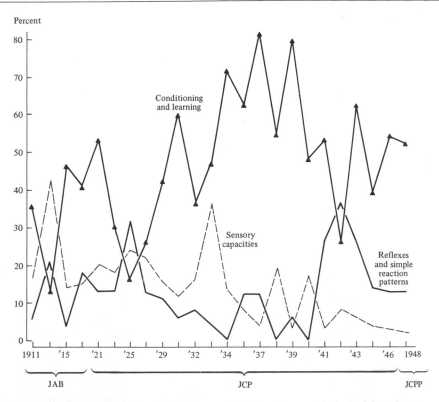

Figure 4 Percent of all articles concerned with various psychological functions.

INTERPRETATION OF TRENDS

In seeking an interpretation of the demonstrated tendency on the part of so many experimentalists to restrict their attention to a small number of species and a small number of behavior patterns, one comes to the conclusion that the current state of affairs is in large measure a product of tradition. From its inception, American psychology has been strongly anthropocentric. Human behavior has been accepted as the primary object of study and the reactions of other animals have been of interest only insofar as they seemed to throw light upon the psychology of our own species. There has been no concerted effort to establish a genuine comparative psychology in this country for the simple reason that with few exceptions American psychologists have no interest in animal behavior *per se*.

Someone, I believe it was W. S. Small at Clark University in 1899, happened to use white rats in a semi-experimental study. The species "caught on," so to speak, as a laboratory subject, and gradually displaced other organisms that were then being examined. Psychologists soon discovered that rats are hardy, cheap, easy to rear, and well adapted to a laboratory existence. Because of certain resemblances between the associative learning of rats and human beings, *Rattus norvegicus* soon came to be accepted as a substitute for *Homo sapiens* in many psychological investigations. Lack of acquaintance with the behavioral potentialities of other animal species and rapid increase in the body of data derived from rat studies combined to progressively reduce the amount of attention paid to other

mammals, to sub-mammalian vertebrates and to invertebrate organisms. Today the trend has reached a point where the average graduate student who intends to do a thesis problem with animals turns automatically to the white rat as his experimental subject; and all too often his professor is unable to suggest any alternative.

To sum up, I suggest that the current popularity of rats as experimental subjects is in large measure the consequence of historical accident. Certainly it is not the result of systematic examination of the available species with subsequent selection of this particular animal as the one best suited to the problems under study.

Concentration of experimental work upon learning seems to stem almost exclusively from the anthropocentric orientation of American psychology. Learning was very early accepted as embodying the most important problems of human behavior; and accordingly the majority of animal investigations have been concerned with this type of activity.

ADVANTAGES AND DISADVANTAGES OF CONCENTRATION

I have no wish to discount the desirable aspects of the course which experimental psychology has been pursuing. There are many important advantages to be gained when many independent research workers attack similar problems using the same kinds of organisms. We see this to be true in connection with various biological sciences. Hundreds of geneticists have worked with the fruitfly, *Drosophila*. And by comparing, combining, and correlating the results of their investigations, it has been possible to check the accuracy of the findings, to accelerate the acquisition of new data, and to formulate more valid and general conclusions than could have been derived if each worker dealt with a different species. Something of the same kind is happening in psychology as a result of the fact that many investigators are studying learning in the rat, and I repeat that this is a highly desirable objective.

Another valuable result achieved by the methods currently employed in experimental psychology is the massing of information and techniques pertaining to rat behavior to a point which permits use of this animal as a pedagogical tool. A recent article in the *American Psychologist* reveals that each student in the first course in psychology at Columbia University is given one or two white rats which he will study throughout the semester. This, it seems to me, is an excellent procedure. The beginning student in physiology carries out his first laboratory exercises with the common frog. The first course in anatomy often uses the dogfish or the cat as a sample organism. And college undergraduates learn about genetics by breeding fruitflies. But the usefulness of the rat as a standardized animal for undergraduate instruction, and the preoccupation of mature research workers with the same, single species are two quite different things.

Advanced research in physiology is not restricted to studies of the frog and although many geneticists may confine their personal investigations to *Drosophila,* an even larger number deals with other animal species or with plants. As a matter of fact, the benefits that students can derive from studying one kind of animal as a sample species must always stand in direct proportion to the amount of information research workers have gathered in connection with other species. The rat's value as a teaching aid in psychology depends in part upon the certainty with which the student can generalize from the behavior he observes in this one animal; and this in turn is a function of available knowledge concerning other species.

There is another obvious argument in favor of concentrating our efforts on the study of a single animal species. It is well expressed in Professor Skinner's book, *The Behavior of Organisms.*

In the broadest sense a science of behavior should be concerned with all kinds of organisms, but it is reasonable to limit oneself, at least in the beginning, to a single representative species.

I cannot imagine that anyone would quarrel with Skinner on this point and I am convinced that many of the psychologists currently using rats in their investigational programs would agree with him in his implicit assumption that the Norway rat *is* a "representative species." But in what ways is it "representative," and how has this "representativeness" been demonstrated? These questions lead at once to a consideration of the disadvantages of overspecialization in terms of animals used and types of behavior studied.

To put the question bluntly: Are we building a general science of behavior or merely a science of rat learning? The answer is not obvious to me. Admittedly there are many similarities between the associative learning of lower animals and what is often referred to as rôte learning in man. But the variety of organisms which have been studied, and the number of techniques which have been employed are so limited, it is difficult to believe that we can be approaching a comprehensive understanding of the basic phenomena of learning. It may be that much remains to be discovered by watching rats in mazes and problem boxes, but it is time to ask an important question. How close are we getting to that well-known point of diminishing returns? Would we not be wise to turn our attention to other organisms and to devise new methods of testing behavior before we proceed to formulate elaborate theories of learning which may or may not apply to other species and other situations.

Another very important disadvantage of the present method in animal studies is that because of their preoccupation with a few species and a few types of behavior, psychologists are led to neglect many complex patterns of response that stand in urgent need of systematic analysis. The best example of this tendency is seen in the current attitude toward so-called "instinctive" behavior.

The growing emphasis upon learning has produced a complementary reduction in the amount of study devoted to what is generally referred to as "unlearned behavior." Any pattern of response that does not fit into the category of learned behavior as currently defined is usually classified as "unlearned" even though it has not been analyzed directly. Please note that the classification is made in strictly negative terms *in spite of the fact that the positive side of the implied dichotomy is very poorly defined.* Specialists in learning are not in accord as to the nature of the processes involved, nor can they agree concerning the number and kinds of learning that may occur. But in spite of this uncertainty most "learning psychologists" confidently identify a number of complex behavior patterns as "unlearned." Now the obvious question arises: Unless we know what learning is—unless we can recognize it in all of its manifestations—how in the name of common sense can we identify any reaction as "unlearned"?

The fact of the matter is that none of the responses generally classified as "instinctive" have been studied as extensively or intensively as maze learning or problem-solving behavior. Data relevant to all but a few "unlearned" reactions are too scanty to permit any definite conclusion concerning the role of experience in the shaping of the response. And those few cases in which an exhaustive analysis has been attempted show that the development of the behavior under scrutiny is usually more complicated than a superficial examination could possibly indicate.

For example, there is a moth which always lays its eggs on hackberry leaves. Females of each new generation select hackberry as an oviposition site and ignore other potential host plants. However, the eggs can be transferred to apple leaves, and when this is done the larvae develop normally. Then when adult females that have spent their larval stages on apple leaves are given a choice of materials upon which to deposit their eggs, a high proportion of them select apple leaves in preference to hackberry. This control of adult behavior by the larval environment does not fit into the conventional pigeon-hole labeled "instinct," and neither can it be placed in the category of "learning." Perhaps we need more categories. Certainly we need more data on more species and more kinds of behavior.

Primiparous female rats that have

been reared in isolation usually display biologically effective maternal behavior when their first litter is born. The young ones are cleaned of fetal membranes, retrieved to the nest, and suckled regularly. However, females that have been reared under conditions in which it was impossible for them to groom their own bodies often fail to clean and care for their newborn offspring. Observations of this nature cannot be disposed of by saying that the maternal reactions are "learned" rather than "instinctive." The situation is not so simple as that. In some way the early experience of the animal prepares her for effective maternal performance even though none of the specifically maternal responses are practiced before parturition.

It seems highly probable that when sufficient attention is paid to the so-called "instinctive" patterns, we will find that their development involves processes of which current theories take no account. What these processes may be we shall not discover by continuing to concentrate on learning as we are now studying it. And yet it is difficult to see how a valid theory of learning can be formulated without a better understanding of the behavior that learning theorists are presently categorizing as "unlearned."

POTENTIAL RETURNS FROM THE COMPARATIVE APPROACH

If more experimental psychologists would adopt a broadly comparative approach, several important goals might be achieved. Some of the returns are fairly specific and can be described in concrete terms. Others are more general though no less important.

Specific Advantages

I have time to list only a few of the specific advantages which can legitimately be expected to result from the application of comparative methods in experimental psychology. In general, it can safely be predicted that some of the most pressing questions that we are now attempting to answer by studying a few species and by employing only a few experimental methods would be answered more rapidly and adequately if the approach were broadened.

Let us consider learning as one example. Comparative psychology offers many opportunities for examination of the question as to whether there are one or many kinds of learning and for understanding the rôle of learning in the natural lives of different species. Tinbergen (1942) has reported evidence indicating the occurrence of one-trial learning in the behavior of hunting wasps. He surrounded the opening of the insect's burrow with small objects arranged in a particular pattern. When she emerged, the wasp circled above the nest opening for a few seconds in the usual fashion and then departed on a hunting foray. Returning after more than an hour, the insect oriented directly to the pattern stimulus to which she had been exposed only once. If the pattern was moved during the female's absence she was able to recognize it immediately in its new location.

Lorenz's concept of "imprinting" offers the learning psychologist material for new and rewarding study. Lorenz (1935) has observed that young birds of species that are both precocial and social quickly become attached to adults of their own kind and tend to follow them constantly. Newly-hatched birds that are reared by parents of a foreign species often form associations with others of the foster species and never seek the company of their own kind. A series of experiments with incubator-reared birds convinced Lorenz that the processes underlying this sort of behavior must occur very early in life, perhaps during the first day or two after hatching, and that they are irreversible, or, to phrase it in other terms, that they are not extinguished by removal of reinforcement.

J. P. Scott's studies (1945) of domestic sheep reveal the importance of early learning in the formation of gregarious habits. Conventional learning theories appear adequate to account for the phenomena, but it is instructive to observe the manner in which the typical species pattern of social behavior is built up as a result of reinforcement afforded by maternal attentions during the nursing period.

The general importance of drives in any sort of learning is widely emphasized. Therefore it would seem worthwhile to study the kinds of drives that appear to motivate different kinds of animals. In unpublished observations upon the ferret, Walter Miles found that hunger was not sufficient to produce maze learning. Despite prolonged periods of food deprivation, animals of this species continue to explore every blind alley on the way to the goal box.

Additional evidence in the same direction is found in the studies of Gordon (1943) who reports that non-hungry chipmunks will solve mazes and problem boxes when rewarded with peanuts which the animals store in their burrows but do not eat immediately. Does this represent a "primary" drive to hoard food or an "acquired" one based upon learning?

Many experimentalists are concerned with problems of sensation and perception; and here too there is much to be gained from the comparative approach. Fring's studies (1948) of chemical sensitivity in caterpillars, rabbits and men promise to increase our understanding of the physiological basis for gustatory sensations. In all three species there appears to be a constant relationship between the ionic characteristics of the stimulus material and its effectiveness in evoking a sensory discharge. The investigations of Miles and Beck (1949) on reception of chemical stimuli by honey bees and cockroaches provide a test for the theory of these workers concerning the human sense of smell.

The physical basis for vision and the role of experience in visual perception have been studied in a few species but eventually it must be investigated on a broader comparative basis if we are to arrive at any general understanding of the basic principles involved. Lashley and Russell (1934) found that rats reared in darkness give evidence of distance perception without practice; and Hebb (1937) added the fact that figure-ground relationships are perceived by visually-naive animals of this species. Riesen's (1947) report of functional blindness in apes reared in darkness with gradual acquisition of visually-directed habits argues for a marked difference between rodents and anthropoids; and Senden's (1932) descriptions of the limited visual capacities of human patients after removal of congenital cataract appear to support the findings on apes. But the difference, if it proves to be a real one, is not purely a function of evolutionary status of the species involved. Breder and Rasquin (1947) noted that fish with normal eyes but without any visual experience are unable to respond to food particles on the basis of vision.

I have already mentioned the necessity for more extensive examination of those patterns of behavior that are currently classified as "instinctive." There is only one way to approach this particular problem and that is through comparative psychology. The work that has been done thus far on sexual and parental behavior testifies, I believe, to the potential returns that can be expected if a more vigorous attack is launched on a broader front.

We are just beginning to appreciate the usefulness of a comparative study of social behavior. The findings of Scott which I mentioned earlier point to the potential advantages of using a variety of animal species in our investigation of interaction between members of a social group. Carpenter's (1942) admirable descriptions of group behavior in free-living monkeys point the way to a better understanding of dominance, submission, and leadership.

One more fairly specific advantage of exploring the comparative method in psychology lies in the possibility that by this means the experimentalist can often discover a particular animal species that is specially suited to the problem with which he is concerned. For example, in recent years a considerable amount of work has been done on hoarding behavior in the laboratory rat. The results are interesting, but they indicate that some rats must learn to hoard and some never do so. Now this is not surprising since Norway rats rarely hoard food under natural conditions. Would it not seem reasonable to begin the work with an animal that is a natural hoarder? Chipmunks, squirrels, mice of the genus *Peromyscus,* or any one of several other experimental subjects would seem to be much more appropriate.

And now, as a final word, I want to mention briefly a few of the more general facts that indicate the importance of developing comparative psychology.

General Advantages

For some time it has been obvious that psychology in this country is a rapidly expanding discipline. Examination of the membership roles of the several Divisions of this Association shows two things. First, that the number of psychologists is increasing at a prodigious rate; and second that the growth is asymmetrical in the sense that the vast majority of new workers are turning to various applied areas such as industrial and clinical psychology.

It is generally recognized that the applied workers in any science are bound to rely heavily upon "pure" or "fundamental" research for basic theories, for general methodology and for new points of view. I do not suggest that we, as experimentalists, should concern ourselves with a comparative approach to practical problems of applied psychology. But I do mean to imply that if we intend to maintain our status as indispensable contributors to the science of behavior, we will have to broaden our attack upon the basic problems of the discipline. This will sometimes mean sacrificing some of the niceties of laboratory research in order to deal with human beings under less artificial conditions. It may also mean expanding the number of non-human species studied and the variety of behavior patterns investigated.

Only by encouraging and supporting a larger number of comparative investigations can psychology justify its claim to being a true science of behavior. European students in this field have justly condemned Americans for the failure to study behavior in a sufficiently large number of representative species. And non-psychologists in this country are so well aware of our failure to develop the field that they think of animal behavior as a province of general zoology rather than psychology. Top-rank professional positions that might have been filled by psychologically trained investigators are today occupied by biologists. Several large research foundations are presently supporting extensive programs of investigation into the behavior of sub-human animals, and only in one instance is the program directed by a psychologist.

CONCLUSION

If we as experimental psychologists are missing an opportunity to make significant contributions to natural science—if we are failing to assume leadership in an area of behavior investigation where we might be useful and effective—if these things are true, and I believe that they are, then we have no one but ourselves to blame. We insist that our students become well versed in experimental design. We drill them in objective and quantitative methods. We do everything we can to make them into first rate experimentalists. And then we give them so narrow a view of the field of behavior that they are satisfied to work on the same kinds of problems and to employ the same methods that have been used for the past quarter of a century. It would be much better if some of our well-trained experimentalists were encouraged to do a little pioneering. We have a great deal to offer in the way of professional preparation that the average biologist lacks. And the field of animal behavior offers rich returns to the psychologist who will devote himself to its exploration.

I do not anticipate that the advanced research worker whose main experimental program is already mapped out will be tempted by any argument to shift to an entirely new field. But those of us who have regular contact with graduate students can do them a service by pointing out the possibilities of making a real contribution to the science of psychology through the medium of comparative studies. And even in the absence of professorial guidance the alert beginner who is looking for unexplored areas in which he can find new problems and develop new methods of attacking unsettled issues would be wise to give serious consideration to comparative psychology as a field of professional specialization.

REFERENCES

1. Breder, C. M., and P. Rasquin. Comparative studies in the light sensitivity of blind characins from a series of Mexican caves. *Bulletin Amer. Mus. Natl. Hist.*, 1947, **89**, Article 5, 325–351.
2. Carpenter, C. R. Characteristics of social behavior in non-human primates. *Trans. N. Y. Acad. Sci.*, 1942, Ser. 2, 4, No. 8, 248.
3. Frings, H. A contribution to the comparative physiology of contact chemoreception. *J. comp. physiol. Psychol.*, 1948, **41**, No. 1, 25–35.
4. Gordon, K. The natural history and behavior of the western chipmunk and the mantled ground squirrel. *Oregon St. Monogr. Studies in Zool.*, 1943, No. 5, 7–104.
5. Hebb, D. O. The innate organization of visual activity. I. Perception of figures

by rats reared in total darkness. *J. gen. Psychol.*, 1937, **51,** 101–126.

6. Lashley, K. S., and J. T. Russell. The mechanism of vision. XI. A preliminary test of innate organization. *J. genet. Psychol.*, 1934, **45,** No. 1, 136–144.

7. Lorenz, K. Der Kumpan in der Umwelt des Vogels *J. f. Ornith.*, 1935, **83,** 137–213.

8. Miles, W. R., and L. H. Beck. Infrared absorption in field studies of olfaction in honeybees. *Proceed. Natl. Acad. Sci.*, 1949, **35,** No. 6, 292–310.

9. Riesen, A. H. The development of visual perception in man and chimpanzee. *Science,* 1947, **106,** 107–108.

10. Scott, J. P. Social behavior, organization and leadership in a small flock of domestic sheep. *Comp. Psychol. Monogr.*, 1945, 18, No. 4, 1–29.

11. Senden, M. v. *Raum- und Gestaltauffassung bei operierten Blindgeborenen vor und nach der Operation.* Leipzig: Barth, 1932.

12. Tinbergen, N. An objectivistic study of the innate behavior of animals. *Biblio. Biotheoret.*, 1942, **1,** Pt. 2, 39–98.

18

The Albino Rat: A Defensible Choice or Bad Habit?

Robert B. Lockard

Lockard's article is an attack on the widespread use of the albino rat as a subject in psychological experiments. Since the use of rat subjects has become deeply entrenched in tradition, it is well worthwhile to reevaluate the reasons for following the tradition. Otherwise we might indeed find ourselves victims of habit and tradition.

Lockard's argument centers on the evaluation of the representativeness of the albino rat. It is easy to show that albino rats are far from representative of mammals. They are in fact a rather peculiar species. Perhaps psychologists should consider a strategy that has been common in physiology and medicine—the strategy of using human subjects, and if this is impossible, then of searching the animal kingdom for characteristics most like man with respect to the organ of interest. In this way it should be possible to assure maximum generality of data.

The albino rat obviously occupies a prominent role in psychology: theories are tested upon it, students are trained with it, and generalizations are based upon it. If the albino rat had come into fashion as the consequence of deliberate

Reprinted from *American Psychologist,* 1968, **23,** 734–742. Copyright 1968 by the American Psychological Association, and reproduced by permission.

The preparation of this paper was greatly aided by Grant GB–5895 from the National Science Foundation.

and complete consideration of its merits in relation to scientific criteria, we could merely review periodically the wisdom of the choice and relax in the interim, secure in the belief that millions of man-hours and dollars were not being invested on a poorly chosen animal. However, the albino rat, which I shall call *albinus,* occupied the laboratory largely as the result of a chance chain of circumstances, described later. Though accidental, its dominance of laboratories, articles, and theories of the behavior of organisms has become a fact. Thus we are faced with a most serious problem, for if *albinus* is unsuitable or unique or misleading, so are many of the products of psychology. Just as any science scrutinizes its tools and methods for flaws which might affect its findings, it is time we had an analytical examination of our *albinus* and asked what it is and where it is leading or misleading us.

The albino rat, *Rattus norvegicus* var. *albinus*, is a domesticated variant of the Norway rat, *Rattus norvegicus*, also called the brown rat. To understand to what extent *albinus* is representative of "animals," whether it is a freak or a good sample from which to generalize, it is necessary to understand the relationship to the wild Norway, the Norway itself, and the known and probable effects of domestication.

FROM ASIA TO THE LABORATORY

The Norway rat is a native of eastern Asia (Walker, 1964, p. 904), normally inhabiting stream banks and other watery places. Great migrations probably occurred in ancient times, for there are descriptions of them "Making periodical visits in infinite multitudes to the countries bordering the Caspian Sea and swimming boldly over the rivers holding by one another's tails [Barrett-Hamilton & Hinton, 1916, p. 608]." "Rats" in the sense of pests entering human dwellings were unknown in Europe until the time of the Crusades (1095, 1147, and 1191), when the black rat, *Rattus rattus*, a south Asian rat, was introduced by returning caravans. *Rattus rattus* was probably the rat of the Pied Piper, though no other German records of *rattus* occur until

later. It quickly spread throughout Europe, became a formidable pest, and indirectly killed a quarter of the population with typhus and the black plague, which is transmitted to humans by rat fleas. Rat-borne disease has altered human destiny more than the doings of any single human famous in our histories (Zinsser, 1935). *Rattus rattus* became known as "the common rat" and gained worldwide distribution aboard ships of the early explorers. However, in about 1727, which was a "mouse year" in the Caspian region, hordes of *norvegicus* crossed the Volga and migrated westward. There may have been slightly earlier migrations, for a visit of the Russian fleet probably transported *norvegicus* to Copenhagen in 1716, and *norvegicus* may have been aboard the ship which transported the House of Hanover from Germany to England in 1714, giving rise to the eighteenth century political name, "Hanoverian rat." Early *norvegicus* colonies were established by Russian ships and wrecks in the Baltic regions; meanwhile, *norvegicus* dispersed overland, reaching Paris and most of low-altitude Europe by about 1750 and Switzerland by 1809. *Rattus norvegicus* also traveled by ship, reaching Greenland about 1780, eastern United States in 1775, and our Pacific coast about 1851.

In the later 1700s records of royal rat catchers often showed *Rattus rattus* and *Rattus norvegicus* inhabiting the same buildings, with *rattus* in the rafters, walls, and thatched roofs in accordance with its arboreal habits, and *norvegicus* in the basements and sewers. Rather quickly, however, the heavier and more pugnacious *norvegicus* displaced *rattus* throughout most of Europe and in northern latitudes connected by trade routes. *Rattus rattus* dwindled to isolated colonies except in warm climates, where *norvegicus* often seems unable to displace the established *rattus.* Though *norvegicus* became the dominant pest associated with man in a parasitic fashion, it also survives well in the wild in certain California valleys and on most islands, some of which have been devastated by the omnivorous *norvegicus,* which eats bird's eggs, most vegetation, and can even survive by eating marine debris after turning an island into a sterile rock.

Albino forms of *norvegicus* were noted in England in 1822 and 1858, and doubtlessly occurred elsewhere. From 1800 to 1870 rats were trapped and held in large numbers for the sport of rat baiting, popular in England and France. Up to 200 rats were put in a pit and a terrier freed among them, spectators betting upon the time taken to kill the last rat. Richter (1954) discussed records indicating that albinos were removed from the collections and kept for breeding and show purposes. The precise time and place of the origin of albino varieties is unknown, as is the question of single or multiple origin, but it is very likely that the first laboratory albinos came from the collections of animal fanciers. According to Richter (1954, 1959), the first laboratory use of albino rats was by Philipeaux (1856) in Paris. Rats were first used in breeding experiments by Crampe (1877–1885). H. H. Donaldson, a noted authority on rats, began using them in 1893 at the University of Chicago. The first psychological research with rats was by Steward (1898), Kline (1899), and Small (1900); see Miles (1930). Donaldson's colony at Chicago seems the basis for the influential experiments of Watson in 1903 and 1907, and the 1908 study of orien-

tation in the maze by Carr and Watson. Donaldson's *The Rat,* published in 1915 and revised in 1924, emphasized certain physiological similarities between rat and man and repeatedly stressed a formula for supposedly equating age between the two species. Donaldson's book and his colony, which was the basis of the stock at the Wistar Institute, were extremely influential for the widespread adoption of the rat in medical research. Although the Wistar Institute is now out of the rat business, a number of commercial suppliers now maintain colonies.

THE EFFECTS OF DOMESTICATION

The first laboratory albinos were probably not a representative sample of *norvegicus.* It is well known that trapping is not a random process, and Boice (1966) has pointed out that hungry, timid, small, scarred low social status *norvegicus* are the most likely to enter traps. The subsequent selection of "sports"—albinos and piebalds—from the rat pens introduced an additional bias, making the very start of the laboratory stock a somewhat unique group.

Later analysis of Crampe's breeding experiments of about 1880 showed that an albino female mated with a wild male transmitted to her offspring three mutant genes: c (albino), a (nonagouti), and h (hooded). When albino rats were brought from Europe by Donaldson and others about the turn of the century, they proved to be homozygous for these same three mutant genes. Some albinos supplied to W. E. Castle by H. H. Donaldson in 1903 were of this triple recessive type (Castle, 1947). The nonagouti, or black mutation, is accompanied by gentler behavior, and when these were mated with double recessive hooded rats and the offspring crossed with albinos, some homozygous triple recessives (cc, aa, hh) resulted. Most of today's albino rats are black and hooded, although the coat color cannot be expressed because of albinism, itself unrelated to tameness. Today's pigmented laboratory rats, like the hooded, do not differ much from *albinus* and will be lumped under that name.

In 1906, Donaldson transferred his albino colony to the Wistar Institute. Helen King became associated with him in a reenactment of the domestication of the wild *norvegicus* under controlled conditions. She published two extensive reports, the first in 1929 (King & Donaldson, 1929) after 10 generations of captive *norvegicus* and the second in 1939 (King, 1939) after 25 generations. Albinos were similarly bred and used as controls. The initial differences between captive *norvegicus* and the albinos were appreciable:

The wild Norway are more excitable and much more savage. They gnaw their cages. The body weight is less for a given body length, hence it is a slighter animal. The skeleton is relatively heavier, also the suprarenals (both sexes) and the testes and ovaries. The thyroid is of like weight, but the hypophysis distinctly lighter in both sexes. On the other hand, the brain and spinal cord are both heavier than in the Albino [King & Donaldson, 1929, p. 7].

Across 25 generations in captivity, the captive *norvegicus* changed. They became fatter, like *albinus*. Growth was accelerated, finally averaging 20% heavier than the first generation. The brain, thyroid, and suprarenals decreased in weight. The average length of reproductive period became 8 months longer than at

first. Fertility increased; Generation 1 had an average of 3.5 litters, whereas Generation 19 produced an average of 10.18 litters each. Even by the end of 10 generations in captivity the behavior had changed remarkably:

They had lost much of their viciousness and their fear of man; females rarely killed the young returned to the nest after being handled with bare hands; their nervous tension was distinctly less than that in animals of the earlier generations . . .; they made but little effort to escape when the door of the cage was opened or when the cage was cleaned. Rats of the later generations had not, however, overcome their aversion to the presence of strange individuals, and such intruders were killed as promptly as in the earlier generations [King & Donaldson, 1929, p. 67].

While an animal species is often thought of as a "type," such as the type specimen in a museum, a more fertile approach has been to consider individual animals as the morphological results of a sample of genes from the gene pool of the population. The animal is "made" from the genes in the sample. In this view, species differ not because they have different coat colors or types of teeth, but because the two gene pools differ. Rat and lizard gene pools probably contain a few, but just a few, of the same genes. *Rattus rattus* and *Rattus norvegicus* share a large number of genes, but not enough to produce viable fetuses. *Rattus norvegicus* and *albinus* have somewhat different gene pools and hence are somewhat different animals. But how different, and in what ways? Fortunately, the issue at hand is not the impossible task of a complete genetic analysis, but is an estimate of how unique *albinus* has become in matters of behavior and related sensory, endocrine, and nervous system function. A complete review would be lengthy indeed, but the following brief examples assembled from the writings of Richter, Robinson, and Barnett (except where noted) serve to illustrate how some of the known differences are expressed.

Wild or F_1 captive Norways have a complex social organization in which a number of specific behavioral displays operate. Tolman (1958, p. 229) once remarked that rats have little social life, partly true for *albinus*, which has lost a number of stereotyped behaviors. The "threat posture" is absent, and the "amicable" display of "crawling under" is gone. Fighting behavior in *albinus* is incomplete, immature, and rather harmless in character, resembling play. Placed together in a chamber and shocked, *norvegicus* pairs fight savagely while many *albinus* varieties do not. Intruders are killed by *norvegicus* but merely sniffed by *albinus*. Wild types show flight from man and violent struggling, attack, vocalization, and sometimes death when held; *albinus* has the remnant behavior of "backing away." Vocalization in *norvegicus* is common, with a fundamental of 400 cycles per second and other components at 200 and 4,400 cycles per second; albino mutants of wild *norvegicus* vocalized with a fairly pure fundamental of 2,800 cycles per second, and today's *albinus* is almost silent. Fits and convulsions in treadmills (Griffiths, 1956) and other situations common in various *albinus* strains are almost unknown in *norvegicus*. Activity during food deprivation is much greater in *norvegicus* than *albinus*. The killing of mice (which normally compete with rats within the habitat) was investigated by Karli (1956), who found that mice were killed by 70% of *norvegicus* but only by 12% of *albinus* types. Boice (1966) has noted a number of interesting differences: *norvegicus* mothers kept cleaner nests than *albinus*, removing fecal bolli to the front of the cage. When originally trapped, the wild *norvegicus* were obviously "agitated" but showed absolutely no defecation, a response common in *albinus* and allegedly indicative of "emotion." When watered, Boice's deprived F_1 *norvegicus* paused several times before approaching the water tube, then drank from a sideways posture; *albinus* waited at the watering place and drank head-on, without pauses. The "new object response" of neophobia of *norvegicus* is quite marked, leading to avoidance behavior, delays in feeding, "shyness," and reduction in food intake. This behavior is absent in *albinus*, which may briefly investigate, but "this has nothing in common with avoidance behavior in wild rats [Barnett, 1958]."

The endocrine system of *albinus* differs markedly from *norvegicus*, possibly qualitatively, in that the enlarged *albinus* pituitary may now perform substitute functions formerly sustained by the now diminutive adrenals, which may weigh $\frac{1}{10}$ as much as those of *norvegicus*. Albinos also have smaller preputials, liver, spleen, heart, kidneys, and brain; however, albinos have larger pituitaries, thymus, thyroid, parathyroids, and Peyer's patches. The substantial departure of the brain and endocrine system of *albinus* led Keeler (1947) to characterize *albinus* as hypoglandular. Robinson (1965) summarized the Keeler thesis:

The Wistar albino is to a great extent a quiet and tractable rat because of (1) a small brain which could interfere with alertness

(2) diminutive olfactory bulbs which could reduce much of the disturbing stimuli of the laboratory environment and (3) the reduced size of the adrenal glands which could have a depressing effect on violent reaction [p. 188].

The above collection of differences is but some fraction of the total, for only a few research efforts have aimed directly at the topic. However, the incomplete picture may be sketched in because the process of domestication, more properly called laboratorization in this case (Robinson, 1965, p. 417), is well understood in terms of its general outlines (Castle, 1947; Hale, 1962; Richter, 1954; Spurway, 1955). The phylogenetically established behaviors essential to survival in the wild are no longer kept intact in peak condition. Many, such as attack and flight from big species like man, intraspecific aggression, and strong pair bonds, are maladaptive in the new environment and are vigorously selected against. Phenotypes with these traits leave few progeny, and the genes responsible for the behavior decline in frequency and may vanish from the population. A great number of other genetically determined properties are subject to either low or neutral selection pressure; they are not disadvantageous, just unnecessary. There is little apparent reproductive advantage to keen sensory function, predator recognition, dietary preferences, digestive efficiency, heat-conserving nests, complicated burrows, or accurate behavioral periodicities. These sorts of functions, or characters, would more or less persist, but with greatly increased variability. Mutations affecting them would be preserved and accumulate in the gene pool. The net results would fall along a spectrum from

complete loss of the function through degenerate, incomplete, or inappropriate expression to apparent intactness, depending upon the specific case. On the other hand, the new environment is not merely a route to tame degeneracy; it makes various positive demands, vigorously selecting for genes favoring survival and differential reproduction in captivity, the new "natural habitat." Examples of the sorts of traits favored might be intraspecific "amiability," immediate acceptance of strangers, large litters, long reproductive period, year-round fertility, reduced mobility, tolerance of loud sounds and handling by humans, and possibly even such specific items as the ability to extricate feet stuck in $\frac{1}{2}$-inch wire mesh.

The overall result of the complex of genetic changes during domestication is like speciation; a new species forms, rapidly or slowly, depending upon severity of selection pressure, and resembles the wild parent species less and less with time. The greater the number of captive generations, the more different the new habitat; and the less the influx of the wild genotype, the less will be the overall resemblance to the wild form, as in cattle and dogs. The chihuahua, great dane, and poodle are largely the products of man, while their ancestors, wolf or jackal, are products of nature. The new habitat of *albinus* differs more from the wild one than the barnyards and pastures of most other domesticated animals differ from previous conditions; hence, one may expect *albinus* to be in the process of becoming one of the more extreme domestic animals, least related to its ancestors.

To complicate matters, there is not just one *albinus* population nor habitat; there are distinct colonies with little or no gene exchange and different selection pressures within each colony. Not only do nondeliberate practices alter the gene pool, but each breeder engages in unique practices based upon a mixture of folklore, science, and business economics. A casual glimpse leaves one with the impression of a stable "inbred" strain "just like" the famous parent stock; but commercial breeders select for what they think their customers fancy, such as resistance to respiratory disease. They also select for profit, such as countering the usual tendency of domestic animals to weigh more than wild by selecting small rats, for rats sell by the unit but eat by the pound. Breeding advertised as "random" is probably not, except where geneticists give the orders, and strains called "inbred" may be just as genetically heterogeneous as wild populations:

a population, long inbred, raised under laboratory conditions and homogeneous with respect to age, has a variability entirely comparable to a population existing under natural conditions, genetically diverse, and [with] a somewhat less uniform age distribution [Bader, 1956, quoted by Robinson, 1965, p. 440].

The rat types most popular with psychologists are neither genetically homogeneous, time-stable in genotype, nor genetically "understood." Robinson (1965), for example, stated:

the strain appellations Long-Evans, Osborne-Mendel, Slonaker, Sprague-Dawley and Wistar, to name a few of the more well-known designations in common usage, have little genetic meaning. The names indicate remote origin more than anything else, yet rats of these descriptions are employed extensively in laboratories. There is

nothing wrong in this, of course, provided the designation does not inadvertently obscure the genetic diversity inherent in the rats of the various colonies. Abundant evidence of such diversity has been presented in the foregoing chapters [p. 675].

In summary, *albinus* is not one rat, but many, depending upon the source. Types popular with psychologists are heterogeneous, with wide individual differences, in contrast to recognized strains designated by combinations of capital letters and numbers. The statistical properties of a colony's gene pool change with time, making last decade's data out of date—from animals no longer existent. And *albinus* is not *norvegicus;* it is rapidly evolving, and it is only a matter of time until it is recognized as a separate species. It is hardly a random sample from the population of "organisms"; it is more like a commercial product.

WHAT ABOUT NORVEGICUS?

By now, some readers will have been persuaded that *albinus* is unsuitable for their purposes and will be considering *norvegicus*. There are, however, a number of reasons that might persuade one differently. First, the anthropocentrically inclined will find that rodents are rather separated evolutionarily from primates, the latter having arisen from protoinsectivores (Davis & Golley, 1963, p. 129). Moles and shrews would be a bit closer. Second, murid rodents (Old World rats and mice, 100 genera, of which *Rattus* is one genus, with about 570 named forms) did not emerge until late Miocene, about 15 million years ago (Walker, 1964, pp. 869, 903). Rodents themselves evolved in Paleocene times, about 60 million years ago; thus murid rodents are newcomers. They are not some sort of preserved form of ancestral stock from which many other animals and their behavior evolved. One of the earliest known rodents, *Paramys,* was like a large squirrel (Colbert, 1955, p. 295). The oldest known group of living rodents is *Aplodontia,* called Sewellels or "Mountain Beavers," inhabiting the Northwest (Walker, 1964, p. 668). Third, rodents in general and *norvegicus* in particular are not "general" forms of animal, but are specialized:

It [*norvegicus*] has acquired accordingly a stouter and heavier body, a shorter tail, and its structure, in many points, has suffered modifications adapting it for burrowing, swimming, and the other activities incidental to its peculiar mode of living [Barrett-Hamilton & Hinton, 1916, p. 612].

Fourth, since *norvegicus* so very recently spread throughout the world from its eastern Asia habitat it is axiomatic that it is rapidly speciating. It may be that no other undomesticated mammal is undergoing such rapid genetic change in various newly inhabited regions. Thus data from captive *norvegicus* would be like a still snapshot of a moving process, an interesting document in the history of its change. Certain zoologists specifically interested in the processes of domestication and speciation have deliberately chosen *norvegicus* because of its unique history; but the very properties which make the rat valuable to them should serve as a warning to others wishing a preparation with temporal stability, unspecialized, with an evolutionary position allowing some generalization to subsequent animal groups.

THE PSYCHOLOGIST AND THE RAT

For sake of convenience I would like to distinguish two kinds of rat research: that involving learning and motivation and that concerned with what might be called the natural functions, such as sexual and maternal behavior; social behavior including dominance, displays, aggression, etc.; hoarding; diet selection and feeding behavior; sensory and physiological function; and so on. Learning will be discussed later; for the moment, consider the wisdom of studying some natural function in *albinus.*

For the biologist it would be automatic to presume that all structures and stable functions resulted from developmental processes coded in the genome of the individual, the "genetic instructions" themselves phylogenetically established by natural selection. The structures and functions are kept intact because "bad" genes causing unintactness are eliminated. The mechanisms of behavior resulting from this process are simply not going to remain unimpaired during the genetic change of domestication (see Lorenz, 1965, p. 99). Therefore, *albinus* is an indefensible choice not only in the realm of species-typical behaviors, but also for dietary and taste preferences (*albinus* may now eat whatever does not bite back), motivational mechanisms, and so on. Even in matters of growth, reproduction, endocrinology, nervous and sensory systems, disease, and drug response, the numerous instances of differences between strains, and between wild and domesticated rats, should convince any investigator that *albinus* is not the place to start looking for mechanisms nature has produced nor for analyzing how they work. It is at least a waste of time, if not outright folly, to experiment upon the degenerate remains of what is available intact in other animals. Psychology has enough embarrassing incidents such as "studying" antipredator responses to hawk shapes by domestic white leghorn chickens. Commercial pharmaceutical and other biological research using domestic forms is not undertaken with the blithe assumption that a given function is representative; the matter is carefully checked, and animals become characterized as "good for" one function and "atypical" for another.

If one rules out *albinus* because it is a poor carrier of phylogenetically acquired natural mechanisms, one is left with the problem of its suitability for the study of learning. Obviously *albinus* learns; why not use this tame convenient animal at least as a test run, to see if we can analyze how its learning process works? Its degenerate sensory, emotional, and natural behavior systems are not matters of concern, and are even assets in the laboratory, making it manageable and easily recaptured. Besides, a shift to other species would disconnect psychology from the vast literature and experience with *albinus*, undoing half a century of accumulated work.

There can be no doubt that differences between strains and between wild and domesticated rats have been found in a wide variety of learning situations; these have been reviewed by Robinson (1965, pp. 508–569). Psychologists, however, perhaps as a result of familiarity with the sequence stemming from Tryon's work, seem to dismiss the possibility of genetically determined differences in learning itself in favor of the belief that the differences are due to "emotional factors," mere physical differences, or sometimes to "parameters" or "constants" in equations. In addition, there seems to be the assumption that learning is a monolithic uniprocess, not a name for a collection of processes; that it is a completely general mechanism, not related to the animal's adaptive requirements; that the mechanism operates in the same qualitative way in whatever animal it is found, with "slow learners" or primitive forms manifesting a mere "rate parameter" difference; and that despite the degeneration of sensory input mechanisms, central mechanisms, and motor output, "the learning mechanism" has remained intact in *albinus*. Many animals had "the learning process," and *albinus* was the most convenient carrier, though itself superfluous.

A biological approach to learning supports quite a different set of views. To begin with, learning is not inherent in the physical world like gravitation; it occurs in organisms. For perhaps two billion years the Earth had no organisms, and no learning. Life appeared in the form of some self-reproducing molecule or aggregate; it diversified and proliferated over some two to three billion years, producing new adaptations to the environment during evolution. The first fish occurred about .3 billion years ago, then amphibians, then reptiles about .185 billion years ago. Some reptiles evolved mammalianlike adaptations, and then mammals appeared .06 billion years ago, occupying about the last 2% of life's history on earth. The unicellular life forms, and those which fermented or photosynthesized for a living, were not endowed with a full-blown learning mechanism. Learning evolved at some stage in evolution; it was an adaptive mechanism conferring a reproductive advantage. Those genes allowing it were reproduced in greater numbers each generation, finally typifying the first species able to profit in some way from experience. Just as the first photoreceptor was a simple thing countless evolutionary developments short of the vertebrate eye, the first learning mechanism was doubtlessly primitive. What it could do is yet unknown; perhaps it could briefly store a little sensory information or facilitate a motor neuron, but certainly it could not handle the Hampton Court maze. Like other structures and functions which evolved, learning no doubt responded to selection pressure like any other survival function, increasing in complexity and storage capacity by accumulating whatever fresh additions, novelties, and extensions increased the probability of reproduction.

Thus it is more probable that learning in mammals is a collection of evolved functions, not a monolithic uniprocess. It is probably not a completely general process qualitatively the same in rat, octopus, and bee, but strongly reflects idiosyncrasies of the adaptive requirements. It is also the case that functions of superficial resemblance actually evolved independently on different occasions; they occur in qualitatively different ways, such as flying in reptiles, birds, mammals, and insects. It is quite possible that learning independently evolved a number of times, creating superficial similarities but quite different underlying mechanisms, analogous but not homologous.

Perhaps the rat's most complex phenomenon is learning, as it involves the way the central nervous system regulates behavior. Because domestication allows an increase in genetic diversity and the accumulation of random mutations, these stand every chance of debilitating, gene by gene, the learning phenomenon. "The more complicated an adapted process, the less chance that a random change will improve its adaptedness [Lorenz, 1965, p. 12]." Furthermore, if learning in the rat is a collection of processes instead of a uniprocess, certain "items" in the collection will be lost, then more, as domestication proceeds. With selection pressure no longer keeping the functions intact, its parts will disintegrate in whatever sequence the supporting biology fails. "Shelter, food, and mates are provided without the individual making a move to fend for himself. Even an 'idiot' rat could flourish in such an environment [Robinson, 1965, p. 514]." If a uniprocess began to fail, it should remain qualitatively the same while declining in some quantitative index. But if a multiprocess disintegrated, not only would it change qualitatively, but different individuals—being random samples from a diverse gene pool—would be qualitatively different. Thus a group of *albinus* would produce appreciable variance in certain tasks—unnecessary variance, in fact, when viewed against another animal in a more intact state. Also, when a function begins to atrophy, it is probable that certain of its components fail first, being the most "difficult" to maintain by natural selection. Therefore, even if rat learning were completely analyzed, the result might be quite incomplete, lacking in aspects normally occurring in animals and providing an inaccurate and incomplete picture. The learning theorist using *albinus* must either claim disinterest in generality or admit subscription to the theory that the learning processes of *albinus* are not much different from those of "mammals in general." This theory would seem quite difficult to support.

One cannot prove that *albinus* is unsuitable for learning research; the facts necessary for this presume the complete comparative analysis of learning which the very concentration on *albinus* delays. Also, facts alone would probably not be enough, for *albinus* is so entrenched in its cozy new habitat that it has influential members of the host species emotionally committed to its continued welfare. One may, however, weigh the risks inherent in developing a natural science around an unnatural animal, one which was produced in its present form by the laboratorization process absolutely unique in natural history. The present *albinus* never before existed and will never again exist; the laboratory rats of next century will be quite different. One can imagine a sort of "schmoo" in a germ-free environment, surrounded by life-support systems and fitted with prosthetic devices, attended by technicians and still studied by scientists; its riddles of "the learning process" still unsolved, for continued survival in the new habitat favors a baffling learning process, one which is composed of pieces no longer harmoniously interlocking and which changes in time rapidly enough to make past findings discrepant, all the while producing enough variability to keep the entire enterprise confused.

ALTERNATIVES TO ALBINUS

1. Inbred rat strains meeting the definitions and recommendations of competent committees and of recognized genetic nomenclature could be used in place of popular types with "little genetic meaning." A table of 57 such rat strains is given in Robinson (1965, pp. 672–675), and the commercial availability of some of these and numerous inbred mouse strains is covered in the publication *Laboratory Animals: Part II. Animals for Research* (revised August 1966), available for $2.00 from National Academy of Sciences, 2101 Constitution Avenue, Washington, D. C. 20418. Use of inbred rat or mouse strains would be a concession to the rat habit having the virtue of reducing intraexperiment variability, clearly defining the animal, drawing from a population of genetic meaning and knowledge, and having a rate of genetic change less than that of commercial animals. The collection of problems associated with domestication would remain, as would those of phyletic position.

2. Similarly, the American Psychological Association could establish a special strain for laboratory studies of behavior, maintaining a complicated breeding system which preserved tameness, while maintaining a constant influx of genes from the wild type. Rigidly maintained procedures could eliminate temporal change and many of the problems of domestication, leaving principally the problems of phyletic position and lack of generality of findings.

3. Simpler forms abundant in nature, such as earthworms, fish, or frogs would overcome most of the *albinus* problems mentioned, as well as provide the distinct possibility that simpler forms have simpler mechanisms more likely to yield to analysis than complex ones.

4. For those rat runners who are really educational psychologists in disguise and who would like results broadly ap-

plicable to "higher mammals," principally humans, an animal in a better ancestral position than the offshoot rat should be selected. One possibility is the Solenodon, a primitive insectivore thought to resemble the basic stock from which a number of mammalian lines, including primates, evolved. An even more impressive candidate is the Tupaia (oriental tree shrew), a sort of living fossil transitional between insectivores and primates, from which the prosimians most probably evolved. It is a primitive placental, one of the most generalized of all living mammals. The Tupaia is diurnal, thus more suited for human daytime research habits than nocturnal animals. It is easily tamed and breeds throughout the year. (See Colbert, 1955, and index of Walker, 1964.) *Laboratory Animals,* mentioned above, lists five suppliers.

5. The approaches mentioned above presume the current strategy of focusing resources upon a single animal. Regardless of the species chosen, this approach risks mistaking the particular for the general. Beach (1950) has eloquently argued the case that concentration upon *albinus* provides too narrow a view of behavior, leading to a science of "rat learning" and neglecting most other behaviors. Behavioral science presumably aims to analyze and understand *all* behaviors of anything that behaves, taking a truly broad and scientific approach to the vast array of phenomena about us. Within this framework one's thinking changes from "What learning problem shall I study with *albinus?*" to "What problem in behavior is the most interesting and potentially significant, and which animal is best for its study?" Instead of thinking of various animals as "laboratory difficulties," one may

view them as natural preparations; there are squirrels with all-cone retinas, mammals with no corpus callosum, nocturnal animals, diurnal animals, animals which imprint and those which do not, fish with electric organs, raccoons with overdeveloped "hand areas" in the cortex, animals which stay still when hungry, animals with built-in stellar charts, bug detectors, mouse detectors, animals which can learn one thing but not another, and so on and on. These and many more natural preparations, achieved without surgery, are literally awaiting research; fewer than 1% of all species have a single behavioral paper. There is a best animal for every problem.

Chemistry made advances after the "practical" effort to transmute lead into gold was abandoned in favor of scientific curiosity of much broader scope, and we would be astonished if astronomers studied only Earth and applied false generalizations to the rest of the universe. Future historians of psychology may devote a few paragraphs to the *albinus* era, noting that progress was made only after getting some perspective and generality into the field by comparing results from different species, and avoiding atypical findings by abandoning unnatural animals.

REFERENCES

Barnett, S. A. Experiments on "neophobia" in wild and laboratory rats. *British Journal of Psychology,* 1958, **49,** 195–201.

Barrett-Hamilton, G. E. H., & Hinton, M. A. L. *A history of British mammals.* London: Gurney & Jackson, 1916.

Beach, F. A. The snark was a boojum. *American Psychologist,* 1950, **5,** 115–124.

Boice, R. The problem of domestication in the laboratory rat and a comparison of partially reinforced "discriminatory" and anticipatory licking in domestic and wild strains of *Rattus norvegicus*. Unpublished doctoral dissertation, Michigan State University, 1966.

Carr, H. A., & Watson, J. B. Orientation in the white rat. *Journal of Comparative Neurology and Psychology*, 1908, **18**, 27–44.

Castle, W. E. The domestication of the rat. *Proceedings of the National Academy of Science*, 1947, **33**, 109–117.

Colbert, E. H. *Evolution of the vertebrates*. New York: Wiley, 1955.

Crampe, H. Kreuzungen zwischen Wanderraten verschiedener Farbe. *Landwirthschaftliche Jahrbücher*, 1877, **6**, 385–395.

Davis, D. E., & Golley, F. B. *Principles in mammology*. New York: Reinhold, 1963.

Donaldson, H. H. *The rat: Data and reference tables*. (Rev. ed.) Philadelphia: Wistar Institute Memoir No. 6, 1924.

Griffiths, W. J. Diet selections of rats subjected to stress. *Annals of the New York Academy of Science*, 1956, **67**, 1–10.

Hale, E. B. Domestication and the evolution of behaviour. In E. S. E. Hafez (Ed.), *The behaviour of domestic animals*. London: Bailliere, Tindall & Cox, 1962.

Karli, P. The Norway rat's killing response to the white mouse: An experimental analysis. *Behaviour*, 1956, **10**, 81–103.

Keeler, C. E. Modification of brain and endocrine glands, as an explanation of altered behavior trends, in coat character mutant strains of the Norway rat. *Journal of the Tennessee Academy of Science*, 1947, **22**, 202–209.

King, H. D. Life processes in gray Norway rats during fourteen years in captivity. *American Anatomical Memoirs*, 1939, No. 17.

King, H. D., & Donaldson, H. H. Life processes and size of the body and organs of the gray Norway rat during ten generations in captivity. *American Anatomical Memoirs*, 1929, No. 14.

Kline, L. W. Methods in animal psychology. *American Journal of Psychology*, 1899, **10**, 256–279.

Lorenz, K. *Evolution and modification of behavior*. Chicago: University of Chicago Press, 1965.

Miles, W. R. On the history of research with rats and mazes. *Journal of General Psychology*, 1930, **3**, 324–337.

Philipeaux, J. M. Note sur l'extirpation des capsules survénales chez les rats albinos (*Mus rattus*). *Comptes Rendus de la Academie des Sciences* (Paris), 1856, **43**, 904–906.

Richter, C. P. The effects of domestication and selection on the behavior of the Norway rat. *Journal of the National Cancer Institute*, 1954, **15**, 727–738.

Richter, C. P. Rats, man and the welfare state. *American Psychologist*, 1959, **14**, 18–28.

Robinson, R. *Genetics of the Norway rat*. Oxford: Pergamon Press, 1965.

Small, W. S. An experimental study of the mental processes of the rat. *American Journal of Psychology*, 1900, **11**, 133–165.

Spurway, H. The causes of domestication: An attempt to integrate some ideas of Konrad Lorenz with evolution theory. *Journal of Genetics*, 1955, **53**, 325–362.

Steward, C. C. Variations in daily activity produced by alcohol and by changes in barometric pressure and diet, with a description of recording methods. *American Journal of Physiology*, 1898, **1**, 40–56.

Tolman, E. C. *Behavior and psychological man*. Berkeley: University of California Press, 1958.

Walker, E. P. *Mammals of the world*. Baltimore: Johns Hopkins Press, 1964.

Watson, J. B. Animal education. *Contributions of the Psychology Laboratory of the University of Chicago*, 1903, **4**, 5–122.

Watson, J. B. Kinaesthetic and organic sensations: Their role in the reactions of the white rat. *Psychological Review Monographs*, 1907, **8**(2, Whole No. 33).

Zinsser, H. *Rats, lice, and history*. Boston: Little Brown, 1935.

19

Pharmacological Differentiation of Allergic and Classically Conditioned Asthma in the Guinea Pig

Don R. Justesen, Edward W. Braun, Robert G. Garrison, and R. Brian Pendleton

The following article shows how a judiciously selected animal "model" was used to deepen our understanding of asthma as a behavioral problem. Justesen et al. were able to produce asthma in guinea pigs through classical conditioning procedures, and their investigations were then extended to an analysis of the neural pathways underlying conditioned and unconditioned asthma. Subsequent research by other investigators showed the applicability of the findings obtained with animal subjects to human asthma.

Allergic bronchial asthma is the most widespread of the genetically predisposed hypersensitivities that afflict a substantial segment of the human population (Raffel, 1961; Benack, 1967). As is true of its kindred reactions, urticaria

This article is based on an article of the same title published in *Science*, 1970, **170**, 864–866. Copyright 1970 by the American Association for the Advancement of Science.

and angioedema, asthma rarely develops spontaneously in infrahuman animals (Raffel, 1961); the paucity of "natural" animal preparations available for laboratory investigation may help explain why, after two millenia of clinical recognition and concern, there is neither prevention nor cure of asthma— only palliation or the hope of spontaneous remission (McGovern & Knight,

1967; Brown, 1965). Experimental allergic asthma is readily brought about, however, in the guinea pig. When sensitized by forced inhalation or systemic infusion of a foreign protein and later provocatively challenged by it, the animal exhibits a bronchoconstrictive reaction that resembles the clinical attack (Ratner, Jackson, & Gruehl, 1927; Ratner & Gruehl, 1929; Ratner, 1953; Kallos & Pagel, 1937). Moreover, several investigators have reported that the reaction is amenable to classical conditioning(Noelpp & Noelpp-Eschenhagen, 1951, 1952; Ottenberg, Stein, Lewis, & Hamilton, 1958). We report here studies bearing on the neuropharmacology of allergic and "learned" forms of experimental asthma; the aim was to shed additional light on *Cavia porcellus* as a model of the human asthmatic condition.

Prior investigators of conditional asthma in the guinea pig have relied upon gross visual observation to index an attack (Ottenberg et al., 1958). Since pilot work by us (Braun, Pendleton, Garrison, & Justesen, 1967) revealed that mere confinement of the animal in a small conditioning chamber evokes many of the behaviors used to index an attack—licking and chewing movements, pilomotor activity, and rapid, jerky movements of the limbs and body—we sought to develop a measure uncontaminated by irrelevant behaviors. The recourse was to whole-body plethysmography.[1]

A plethysmographic measure was contrived that was also to function as a classical conditioning chamber. We shall describe the measure and summarize the studies by which its twofold use was validated before addressing pharmacological experiments of primary interest.

Figure 1 is a photograph of one of several plethysmography/conditioning chambers used by us.[2] The hollow steel probe of a Statham P23BB pressure transducer is shown inserted through a rubber seal into the interior of a chamber fabricated from $\frac{1}{4}$ in. ($\sim$6 mm) sheet Plexiglas (internal dimensions in cm: $31 \times 15 \times 13$). The chamber's base and walls were formed into a single unit, a continuous recessed lip near the inside top providing a seat for a removable

---

[1] The "labored breathing" characterizing an asthma attack is due to increased airway impedance arising from congestion or constriction of the airway. Increased airway impedance will augment the positive intrapulmonic pressure that normally occurs during expiration and likewise augment the partial intrapulmonic vacuum that occurs during inspiration. The pressure *differential* between the

expiratory peak and the inspiratory peak of each respiratory cycle will thus be greater during an attack of asthma than when the airway is patent. One could measure the differential directly via intrapulmonic pressure sensing. However, to avoid the trauma and complications of surgery and chronic implantation, we based our measure upon the principle of indirect or whole-body plethysmography: an animal in an airtight chamber surrounded by a fixed volume of air will, in generating the intrapulmonic pressure differential, cause a simultaneous and inverse pressure change to occur in the airspace of the surround.

[2] Several chambers of the same internal dimensions and of the same or slightly differing equippage were used interchangeably during the experiments described in this paper. In later phases of our studies, when animals were being exposed to protein aerosol, thorough washing, rinsing, and drying of a chamber was necessary; availability of additional clean chambers permitted uninterrupted scheduling and execution of experiments. One of the chambers had portals for two nebulizers, another was equipped with metered vacuum as well as metered positive pressure inlet—to permit plethysmographic measurement *during* activation of a nebulizer—but the basic unit shown in Fig. 1 was employed throughout and was the simplest to construct and use.

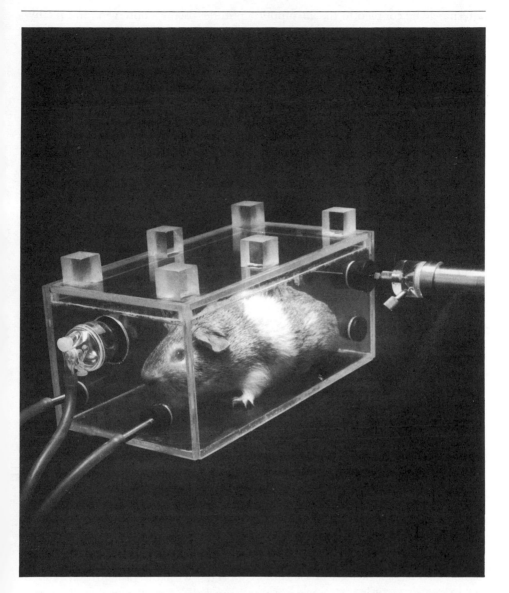

Figure 1 An 850 gram guinea pig is shown in a Plexiglas chamber by which whole-body plethysmograms were recorded during experimentally induced attacks of asthma. Twenty-five mm cubes of Plexiglas fused to the lid served as handles for easy removal and also supported a weight required to make the chamber airtight. Other equippage is explained in text.

lid. When the lid was in place and weighted by a standard concrete building block the chamber could be rendered airtight. Two rubber hoses made con-

nection with the chamber near the base; one was coupled to a filtered vacuum line; the other, to an air supply metered to provide 6–9 psi. A third hose could alternately be coupled to the air supply and was fitted to an Adrenomist nebulizer by which aerosolized solutions were introduced into the chamber. All three hoses were obtained from a stock of standard surgical tubing and were clamped shut with hemostats during recording of plethysmograms.

The output of the transducer was coupled to a Grass Model 6A1–A d–c bridge-and-amplifier unit, thence to a power amplifier and a wide-track ink-writing pen of a Grass Model 6–8–2 EEG–polygraph. The amplifying circuitry was calibrated to produce a vertical deflection of 1 cm/mm Hg.

Validation studies proceeded in two phases. In the first, we dosed adult guinea pigs with drugs known to cause and to counteract constriction of the airway (Koelle, 1965; Innes & Nickerson, 1965). Just before dosing an animal, a basal plethysmogram was recorded; it was invariably noted that low amplitude undulations[3] were generated in the ink-record, rise and fall of the pen being coincident with an animal's inspiratory and expiratory movements (see samples of basal recordings in Fig. 2). Each of five animals was then injected subcutaneously with 200 μg of Bethanol (urecholine Cl @ 5 mg/ml), subsequent three- to five-fold rises over basal am-

plitude being observed in plethysmograms (see Fig. 2a). Within 1–2 min of an observed rise, the air supply to the nebulizer and the vacuum return were activated, a 1:100 concentration of Isuprel (isopropylnorepinephrine) being introduced thereby into the chamber at a rate approximating 0.5 ml/min. After three minutes of exposure to the aerosolized Isuprel another plethysmogram was recorded. Amplitudes in all cases had returned to basal levels (see Fig. 2a).

The second phase of the validating studies involved induction of allergic asthma. Thirty-three experimentally naive guinea pigs ranging in weight from 350 to 750 g were assorted into one of four treatment conditions, one experimental and three control. The experimental condition was populated by 23 animals each injected intraperitoneally with 1 mg of 5X purified crystalline egg albumin (Nutritional Biochemical Co.) dissolved in 1 ml of distilled water. Ten to 14 days after the sensitizing treatment each animal was challenged for 3 min by an 800 mg% solution of the albumin in aerosolized form.[4] The three control conditions were respectively formed about: three animals in a sham-sensitization, sham-challenge sequence in which distilled water only was used; four sham sensitized animals later challenged by the protein; and three initially injected with the protein that later received sham challenge.

None of the ten controls generated noticeable change in plethysmographic amplitude while unequivocal rises were produced by 16 of the 23 experimental

---

[3]Amplitude of basal plethysmograms was highly consistent for a given animal and usually was higher in the case of heavier animals. Because of this interindividual variation—likely due in part to larger animals having a smaller net volume of air to respire when in the chamber and in part to varying capacity, elastance, or ambient patentability of airway tissues—absolute pressures were not employed as criteria of changed airway impedance. Instead, each animal served as its own control, its basal amplitude being used as a control reference for a plethysmogram generated during an experimental treatment.

[4]The mg% solution is a weight/volume concentration: i.e., an 800 mg% albumin solution contains 800 mg of the protein per 100 ml of distilled water.

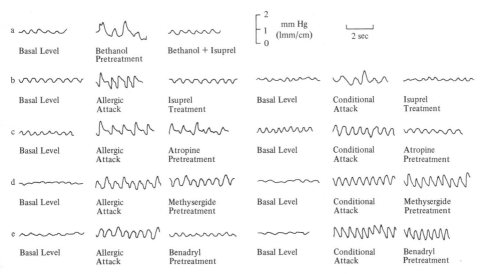

Figure 2 Ink records typifying control (basal) and experimentally modulated plethysmo-grams of guinea pigs. Segment *a* is a series of three ink recordings generated by a non-asthmatic animal; they reflect, from left to right: basal activity; response to an injection of Bethanol; and response to inhaled Isuprel a few minutes later. The triad of recordings to the reader's left in segments *b* through *e* are those respectively taken during basal measures, during allergic attacks, and during pharmacological treatment of the attacks. The corresponding triad of records to the reader's right reflect measures based upon classically conditioned attacks of asthma. Recordings from animals pretreated with meth-scopolamine are not presented in Figure 2 but closely resemble those of atropine treated subjects.

animals; during provocative challenge each of the other seven animals convulsed and were dying, presumably from anaphylactic shock, before a plethysmo-gram could be recorded. Surviving animals were not removed from the chamber but were exposed within 1–2 min of provocative challenge to a 3 min treatment by aerosolized Isuprel. Without exception, plethysmograms of experimental animals returned to basal levels (see Fig. 2*b*).

To summarize the validating studies: Bethanol is a powerful parasympatho-mimetic agent especially effective in producing bronchoconstriction (Koelle, 1965); Isuprel, a beta adrenergic com-pound that acts directly upon and re-laxes smooth muscle of the airway when inhaled as an aerosol (Innes & Nicker-son, 1965). The respective rise and fall of plethysmographic amplitude associ-ated with injection of the former and inhalation of the latter confirm the utility of the amplitudinal index of airway constriction. Additional confirmation was gained in finding that only animals undergoing appropriate sensitization and challenging treatments generated rises in amplitude—which rises, further-more, were reversed in all surviving ani-mals by the Isuprel.

Following execution of pilot studies aimed at optimizing experimental parameters[5] classical conditioning of the allergic asthma was attempted. The design of the conditioning experiment was the same as employed in the second validation study. Sixteen guinea pigs, including eight carried over from the validating studies, were selected for their reliability in responding with plethysmographically indexed attacks of asthma to three successive provocative challenges. Nine experimentally naive animals were given a sham or albumin sensitization treatment appropriate to their placement, three each, into one of the three control conditions. Weights of the animals ranged from 500 to 925 g; only males were used.

Each of the 25 animals was subjected to a daily block of six trials conducted at 45–60 min intervals. The first trial invariably consisted of a 3 min sham challenge that followed and was followed in turn by a 8–12 sec plethysmographic measure.[6] During each of the

five ensuing trials an animal was sham challenged by distilled water or challenged by the albumin solution as appropriate to its treatment condition. Challenges were presented for 3 min intervals and distilled water or an 800 mg% albumin solution was released into the chamber as an aerosol at 0.5–0.7 ml/min. Both the positive pressure and vacuum systems were activated during the interval of challenge. Upon cessation of a challenging treatment the nebulizer was inactivated by diverting its air supply to the chamber's air inlet. In concert with the vacuum line the inrush of fresh air served to flush aerosols from the chamber. The flushing was followed by a thorough washing of the chamber in distilled water, then in 95% ethanol, and then again in distilled water. In a similar attempt to control residual albumin, each animal upon completion of a trial was sponged with a clean, damp towel.

During intertrial intervals preceding the sixth daily trial, animals were individually housed in a small carrying cage and removed from the conditioning area to a darkened, quiet room—this, to control for the possibility of adventitious extinction occurring to hissing sounds emitted by the nebulizer during conditioning of other animals.

In the procedure as described, an experimental (and therefore sensitized) animal undergoing provocative challenge and generating a rise of plethysmographic amplitude would be exhibiting an unconditional asthmatic reaction (UR). Inhalation of the albumin constituted the unconditional

---

[5] While all albumin-injected guinea pigs studied by us have shown a strong—and often mortal—reaction to the initial provocative challenge, approximately half are completely desensitized by the time a second challenge is presented. The basis for the desensitization is unknown but has been reported by other investigators (Ratner et al., 1927; Ratner & Gruehl, 1929; Ratner, 1953; Ottenberg et al., 1958). We did find by reducing the concentration of the albumin solution from 800 to 300 mg% during the first provocative challenge that mortality was averted in all of 17 animals so treated. Subsequent challenges by the 800 mg% solution have invariably been well tolerated. Finally, all animals exhibiting allergic attacks to their second provocative challenge have continued to do so to subsequent provocations by the protein.

[6] Plethysmographic measures were kept short in duration since the accumulation of expired CO_2 in a closed chamber might have led to an artifactual constriction of the airway (Loofbourrow et al., 1957). We later observed a two fold increase in plethysmographic amplitude generated by an

---

experimentally naive, 450g animal in an airtight chamber—but only after seven minutes of continuous confinement.

stimulus (US) and all the other present-ments of a challenging treatment—hissing sounds of the nebulizer, visual and tactile properties of the aerosol, etc.—would collectively constitute the conditional stimulus (CS). Thus the initial sham challenge of a daily block of trials was the prime CS, the pre- and post-challenge plethysmograms respectively yielding a baseline and the measure of conditional responding (CR). Criterion for both URs and CRs was a rise in average peak amplitude of the plethysmogram at least 2.5 times an animal's basal level.[7]

Three of the 16 experimental animals exhibited criterional rises during the initial (sham) challenge on the second day of conditioning; seven, on the third day; and the remaining six, on the fourth. None of the control animals generated noticeable amplitudinal changes across the four day span.

When an experimental animal exhibited a CR it was given a series of sham challenges at 45–60 min intervals until a post challenge plethysmogram returned to the basal level. Resistance to extinction was moderate, CRs persisting from three to eight trials. On the day following the extinction measure each experimental animal was given five provocative challenges at 45–60 min intervals, then observed for plethysmographic amplitude following a single

sham challenge. All 16 animals exhibited recovery of the CR.

The relative ease of producing, extinguishing, and recovering the conditional asthmatic reaction having been demonstrated, we turned to experiments aimed at delineating nervous and humoral pathways participating in allergic and conditional attacks.[8] A minimum of two probes by each of several drugs was presented to a minimum of three different animals exhibiting as many allergic and conditional attacks. Probes were ordered across time and animals were selected for treatment so as to randomize the sequence of testing allergic and conditional reactions and to permit dissipation of drug effects before retesting. Each probe trial consisted of a sequence in which the basal plethysmogram was observed, test challenges presented (sham and/or provocative) to confirm viability of a conditional or allergic reaction[9] and then an animal was dosed with a drug and subjected to another sham or provocative challenge.

[7]Both URs and CRs occurred as essentially all-or-none rises in plethysmographic amplitude, the actual increment being three- to four-fold for most animals. The absence of graded levels, particularly during later extinction measures, may have been an artifact of our blocked-trials procedure and lengthy US and CS intervals; however, in similar but "on line" plethysmographic measures of human asthmatics the same all-or-none pressure increments have been observed (McFadden et al., 1969).

[8]One short-lived experiment involved sectioning of the vagus nerve bilaterally in four guinea pigs and unilaterally in two that were to serve as controls. Sections were made in the neck at a level a few mm caudad to the lower mandible. None of the four experimental animals recovered from anesthesia; both controls did. The guinea pig's apparent critical need for a bilaterally intact vagus prevented us from learning whether its fibers participate, as we suspect, in the conditional attack.

[9]An animal given a series of provocative challenges may concomitantly be developing a conditional attack; to control for such a dual occurrence when pharmacologically probing an allergic attack we always presented sham challenges priorly to ensure absence of a CR. Similarly, to control for the possibility that the CR had extinguished, when pharmacologically probing a conditional attack, a second sham challenge was always presented 1–3 days later, after dissipation of a drug, to vouchesafe the integrity of the CR.

If the plethysmographic amplitude recorded after the dosing fell to or nearly to the basal level an instance of positive control was noted; if the amplitude continued to be elevated, an instance of no control was noted. Finally, if an intermediate fall occurred, an instance of inconclusive control was noted. Instances of the three categories of pharmacological control are respectively coded as "+", "−", and "?" in the summary of conditions and findings presented in Table 1. The Table also presents routes, timing, and levels of dosing as well as pertinent pharmacological activity of drugs. Representative plethysmograms are presented in Fig. 2.

The rationale for selecting drugs was primarily based upon reference materials in Goodman and Gilman.[10] Briefly summarized: we anticipated that inhaled Isuprel as a relaxant of airway muscle would control both allergic and conditional attacks—it did; that a conditional attack, presumably parasympathetically mediated, would respond to cholinergic blocking agents possessing both central (atropine) and peripherally restricted (methscopolamine) sites of action—it did; and, finally that methysergide, a peripherally acting congener of LSD and a potent serotonin blocking agent, would control allergic attacks while the antihistamine Benadryl would not—these last expectations were strongly disconfirmed.

Immunologists are in general agreement that the atopic hypersensitivity is engendered when an allergen and specific antibody produced in a sensitized individual combine in some fixed-tissue locus. The combination is believed to result in the local release of an autacoid such as histamine or serotonin that irritates surrounding tissues. While histamine has long been implicated as an irritative principal responsible for the symptoms of urticaria and angioedema, its role as a major bronchoconstrictive trigger of human asthma has been denied and ascribed to other autacoids, particularly serotonin (cf. Douglas, 1965).

The failure of methysergide to control allergic attacks and the implication that histamine and not serotonin is the bronchoconstrictive trigger in the experimentally asthmatic guinea pig augurs for a strong species difference. While parsimony dictates such an interpretation, the Benadryl data compel consideration of an alternate possibility. Asthma in the human being, at least when resistant to antihistaminic premedication, may be the classically conditioned aftermath of earlier, intermittent provocations by an allergen. Perhaps allergenically released histamine is a bronchoconstrictive trigger in the early stages of asthma; perhaps, too, the dire emotional states usually attending the allergic attack are conditioned, their recurrence without the allergen serving to activate vagal or other parasympathetic pathways investing the muscle of the airway. If such conditioning does take place in the asthma patient, one would expect, e.g., that pretreatment by antihistamines would provide better control of asthma in pediatric than in adult patients. Similarly, one would expect cholinergic blocking agents and not antihistamines to control the adult's attack. In the light of this speculation we shall conclude

[10]We refer to Section IV, chapters 21 through 28, and Section V, chapters 29 and 30, in L. S. Goodman and A. Gilman, Eds., *The Pharmacological Basis of Therapeutics*, 3rd ed. (New York: Macmillan, 1965).

TABLE 1 Summary of conditions and effects of pharmacological treatments of allergic and classically conditioned attacks of asthma

Drug and Dose Level	Activity	Route, Timing of Admin. before Experimental Assessment (in min)	Number of Animals Tested (and Replications)	Control Exerted Over	
				Allergic Attack	Conditional Attack
Isuprel 1:100 concen.	Smooth Muscle Relaxant	Inhaled Aerosol (0)	4 (3)	+++ +++ +++ +++	+++ +++ +++ +++
Atropine 5 mg/kg	General Parasympathetic Blocker	Intraperitoneally (30)	3 (3)	--- --- ---	+++ +? + +++
Methscopolamine 8 mg/kg	Peripheral Parasympathetic Blocker	Intraperitoneally (30)	3 (3)	--- ---	+++ +++ ++?
Methysergide 10 mg/kg	Peripheral Serotonin Blocker	Intraperitoneally (120)	3 (3)	--- --- --? -	--- --- ---
Benadryl 1 mg/kg	Antihistamine	Intraperitoneally (30)	10 (2)	++ ++ ++ ++ ++ ++ ++ ++	--- --- --- --- --- ---

259

by noting findings recently published by McFadden and his colleagues (McFadden, Luparello, Lyons, & Bleecker, 1969). Increased airway impedance as measured by whole-body plethysmography was found to occur in 13 of 29 chronic-asthma patients when sham challenged by physiological saline. This psychogenic constriction of the airway—which was repeatedly but selectively occasioned when the patient was led to believe he was being challenged by *his* allergen—was selectively abolished, moreover, by controlled pretreatment with atropine.[11]

REFERENCES

Benack, R. T. *What is allergy?* Springfield, Ill.: Charles C Thomas, 1967; cf. Coca, A. F., & Cooke, R. A., *J. Immunol.,* 1923, **8,** 163.

[11] The data we report here were originally presented to members of the Division of Psychopharmacology at the Annual Meeting of the American Psychological Association in San Francisco on 1 September 1968. The paper is based in part upon the second author's M.D. thesis research performed in the Neuropsychology Laboratories for the Kansas University School of Medicine. Financial support was provided by the U.S. Veterans Administration and by a grant from the Kansas University Medical Center. We thank B. Ascough, E. B. Brown, D. C. Greaves, G. N. Loofbourrow, E. J. Walaszek, and E. L. Wike of the University of Kansas or its Medical Center for technical and material assistance. We are especially indebted to Prof. Harbans Lal, now of the University of Rhode Island, for helping us select and evaluate effects of the pharmacological probes. Mrs. Kay Wahl and Mr. Marvin Barsky prepared figure materials.

Braun, E. W., Pendleton, R. B., Garrison, R. G., & Justesen, D. R. *Sci. Proc. Amer. Psychiat. Assoc.,* 1967, **123,** 201.

Brown, E. A. In M. L. Hirt (Ed.), *Psychological and allergic aspects of asthma.* Springfield, Ill.: Charles C Thomas, 1965.

Douglas, W. W. In L. S. Goodman & A. Gilman (Eds.), *The pharmacological basis of therapeutics* (3rd ed). New York: Macmillan, 1965. Chap. 29, p. 621; chap. 30, p. 645.

Innes, I. R., & Nickerson, M. In L. S. Goodman & A. Gilman (Eds.), *The pharmacological basis of therapeutics* (3rd ed.). New York: Macmillan, 1965. Chap. 24, p. 498.

Kallos, P., & Pagel, W. *Acta Med. Scandinav.,* 1937, **91,** 292.

Koelle, G. B. In L. S. Goodman & A. Gilman (Eds.), *The pharmacological basis of therapeutics* (3rd ed.). New York: Macmillan, 1965. Chap. 23, p. 467.

Loofbourrow, G. N., Wood, W. B., & Baird, I. L. *Amer. J. Physiol.,* 1957, **191,** 411.

McFadden, E. R., Jr., Luparello, T., Lyons, H. A., & Bleecker, E. *Psychosom. Med.,* #2, 1969, **31,** 134–143.

McGovern, J. P., & Knight, J. A. *Allergy and human emotions.* Springfield, Ill.: Charles C Thomas, 1967.

Noelpp, B., & Noelpp-Eschenhagen, I. *Helv. Med. Acta.,* 1951, **18,** 142.

Noelpp, B., & Noelpp-Eschenhagen, I. *Int. Arch. Allergy,* 1952, **2,** 321; 1952, **3,** 108.

Ottenberg, P., Stein, M., Lewis, J., & Hamilton, C. *Psychosom. Med.,* 1958, **20,** 395.

Raffel, S. *Immunity.* New York: Appleton-Century-Crofts, 1961.

Ratner, B. *J. Allergy,* 1953, **24,** 316.

Ratner, B., & Gruehl, H. L. *Amer. J. Hyg.,* 1929, **10,** 236.

Ratner, B., Jackson, H. C., & Gruehl, H. L. *Amer. J. Dis. Child.,* 1927, **34,** 23.

TEN

The Selection of Experimental Subjects: Human

20

The Human Subject in Psychological Research

Duane P. Schultz

It would seem that the safety with which an experimenter can generalize to human subjects would be complete if experimenters simply adopted the expedient of using human subjects in their research. But there are actually many influences that tend to limit the generality of typical experimental findings obtained with human subjects. The following article summarizes them nicely, and also provides a discussion of some ethical issues surrounding the use of human subjects.

In recent years, a number of psychologists have focused their research attention on the fundamental technique of their science: the experimental method. Articles and books have told us of experimenter effects in behavioral research (Rosenthal, 1966), the social nature of psychological research (Friedman, 1967), demand characteristics (Orne, 1962), and a host of other variables that may be confounding the data we con-

Reprinted from *Psychological Bulletin*, 1969, **72**, 214–228. Copyright 1969 by the American Psychological Association, and reproduced by permission.

Preparation of this paper was supported by the Group Psychology Branch, Office of Naval Research, under Contract No. N00014–67–C–0131 (P001).

tinue to collect in such large quantities. We are warned, by the findings of this research on research, of the effect of unintended cues provided by our behavior, dress, speech, and commitment to a specific hypothesis; by the physical appearance of our laboratories; and by the general level of psychological research sophistication of the students who serve as our subjects. In short, this research suggests that the experimental situation may not be what we intend in our elaborately designed studies.

One essential aspect of the research process is the nature of the person who supplies our data: the human subject (usually known as the college sophomore). The common conception of the human subject seems to be that he (or, more aptly, it) functions as "a stimulus-response machine: you put a stimulus in one of the slots, and out comes a packet of reactions [Burt, 1962, p. 232]."

That such an image, no matter how devoutly believed, is totally incorrect and misleading, is a conclusion forced upon this researcher by his experience in personally "running" subjects in a 3-year program of research on small-group behavior. That experience, together with an awareness of the growing literature on the human subject, has led to some sobering and alarming implications.

A hint of the seriousness of this problem is provided in the form of an imaginary letter from a subject to an experimenter in which Jourard (1968) noted what subjects have told him about their laboratory experiences. The letter is disturbing for the subject says to the experimenter:

It's getting so I find it difficult to trust you. I'm beginning to see you as a trickster, a manipulator. . . . I lie to you a lot of the time. . . . When I don't lie, I will sometimes just answer at random, anything to get through with the hour, and back to my own affairs. . . . Did you ever stop to think that your articles, and the textbooks you write, the theories you spin—all based on your data (my disclosures to you)—may actually be a tissue of lies and half-truths (my lies and half-truths) or a joke I've played on you because I don't like you or trust you? That should give you cause for some concern [pp. 9, 11].

This is indeed cause for concern. The present paper looks critically at the human subject: what he was earlier in the history of psychology, what he is today, why his current image and role must change, and how such change might be brought about.

THE SUBJECT'S CHANGING ROLE IN PSYCHOLOGY'S HISTORY

The subjects (or, more properly, observers) who served in the laboratories of Wundt and Titchener bear little resemblance to today's subjects. First, they were either the psychologists themselves or psychologists-in-training (graduate students). As such, they were probably highly motivated in their roles as observers; surely, one would have had to be to perform the complex and time-consuming introspections required in that era. They were well trained for their task, having undergone long apprenticeships, and they knew exactly what to look for and what errors to avoid. Boring (1953) noted that observers in the Leipzig reaction experiments were required to perform some 10,000 introspective reactions before they were considered capable of providing data worthy of publication. Thus, the early subjects were highly skilled and motivated to pursue what Titchener called the "hard introspective labor."

It is interesting that the observers during this introspective era were sometimes referred to in journal articles as "reagents," which may be defined as any substance which, from its capacity for certain reactions, is used in detecting, examining, or measuring other substances (*Webster's New Collegiate Dictionary*, 1958, p. 704). This might suggest that a subject was considered to be of the nature of a chemical reagent: a constant which will elicit an invariant reaction from any substance or process to which it might be applied. It might be suggested, then, that subjects were thought of as rather like recording instruments, objectively noting the characteristics of their focus of observation.

This "machine view" of observers was noted by Titchener (1912) when he spoke of the technique of observing becoming mechanized through training and practice, so that observation was not a conscious process.

In speaking of this mechanism of habit, Titchener (1912) quoted Wundt as saying that *"In his attention to the phenomena under observation,* the observer in psychology, no less than the observer in physics, *completely forgets to give subjective attention to the state of observing* [p. 443]." Thus, we have an objective and detached observing mechanism who reports to the experimenter on the processes observed and attempts to mirror them accurately.

Could anyone be a reagent? Did everyone have this invariant capacity for certain reactions? The structuralists' answer was initially negative. Titchener (1895b) quoted Wundt as follows:

there are individuals who are entirely incapable of any steady concentration of the attention, and who will therefore never make trustworthy [reagents]. That should not be surprising. It is not everyone who has the capacity for astronomical or physical observation; and it is not to be expected either that everyone is endowed with the gifts requisite for psychological experimentation [p. 507].

Binet (1894) also noted that "the aptitude for introspection is not given to everyone; some possess it in high degree; these are the born psychologists [p. 18]."

It was thought, then, that there was a "disposition" (as Titchener called it) for psychological research. Precisely what constituted this disposition was never made explicit beyond describing it as specific habits, attitudes, and "characteristics of mind." Presumably,

however, a master introspectionist would recognize this ability.

By 1912, perhaps due to a shortage of "born psychologists," Titchener modified the requirement of a disposition for introspection, noting that "any normal person, coming to the task with goodwill and application, may understand and acquire [it] [p. 446]." Thus, a person could be trained to properly introspect. This training, Titchener argued, was similar to the kind of training required for reliable observations in biology or physics. In addition to the proper training, introspection required that the observers be in good health, free from anxiety and worry, and comfortable in their surroundings at the time of observation.

It was suggested previously that a subject was considered a constant eliciting an invariant reaction. If this were true, the research findings must have resulted in satisfyingly consistent data with no extreme scores to cause dismay. But surely Titchener's reagents, no matter how well trained and mechanized, could not have all produced highly similar reactions, considering the subjective nature of their task. It seems that they did not, but let us quote from Titchener on this point of data consistency.

In his famous reaction-time debate with James Mark Baldwin (1895–1896), Titchener noted that "The only results ruled out are those which are wholly irregular and inconstant [1895b, p. 507]." In one research report, Titchener noted that "Seven participants in this investigation were found to be incapable of reacting with any degree of constancy: their results were therefore not employed [1895a, p. 75]." Thus, out of the 10 reagents in this particular study, 7 gave inconsistent results, but the remaining 3 consistent reagents (no doubt "born psychologists") gave highly similar reaction times and so constituted the findings.

Small wonder that Baldwin engaged in such an active debate. In commenting on another Titchener study in which the results of six out of nine reagents were ruled out, Baldwin asked:

If one-third of mankind are to be taken to prove that a result is a universal principle, the rest being deliberately excluded because they cannot get the result that the one-third do, then what conclusions could not be proved in well-managed psychological laboratories [1896, p. 82]?

Baldwin favored the use of untrained and unpracticed observers, and the Titchener-Baldwin debate centering on the kinds of subjects to be used was really a debate between the older structuralist position and the newer American spirit of functionalism. Wundt and Titchener searched for general laws of the human mind and so the existence of individual differences among the reagents was, to them, a source of annoyance to be eliminated rather than investigated.

The functionalist spirit or attitude was able to accommodate the notion of individual differences; indeed, it fostered an active psychology of individual differences under the aggressive leadership of James McKeen Cattell. The functionalists were interested in studying the minds of untrained observers and so could turn to naïve subjects from the college and general populations. Earlier, a precursor of functional psychology, Sir Francis Galton, used naïve subjects from the general population in his famous anthropometric laboratory—and these subjects even paid for the privilege of being tested.

Thus, the functionalists' concern with individual differences brought about a change in the kind of human subject studied, from the trained and well-practiced professional of Titchener to the untrained and naïve amateur of Cattell and other functionalists.

There was another change taking place also, and that had to do with the decline of introspection with an attendant demotion in status of the human subject from observer to the one (or thing) observed. In the early years of this century, dissatisfaction was being expressed over introspection in this country (except, of course, at Cornell). For example, G. Stanley Hall said in 1910 that "formerly everyone supposed that self-observation . . . was the oracle and muse of philosophic studies. Now, however, . . . it is coming to be seen that this method gives us access to but a very small part of the soul [p. 621]." Hall urged the use of natural history methods involving careful observation and description of the actions of other people.

Even before John B. Watson and his behaviorist manifesto of 1913, there was a decided leaning among many American psychologists toward greater objectivity. At the functionalist base at the University of Chicago, much research was conducted in the early 1900s without recourse to introspection. Many of the subjects used in these studies were those most readily available—the graduate and undergraduate students.

Completing with a sharp finality the move away from introspection (of the classical variety) and toward the more exclusive use of the experimental observation of behavior was, of course, behaviorism. And it was this that brought about the total change of role of the human subject.

In classical introspection, the reagent

was the observer and the observed at the same time. It was the reagent who observed the subject matter (his own conscious experience). As Boring (1953) commented, the observer "has the responsibility for the correctness of his descriptions of conscious data [p. 184]." The observer, then, had a very important and responsible position. The experimenter set up the conditions and recorded the observations reported by the observer.

With behaviorism, this situation changed completely for Titchener's observer became Watson's subject. In other words, with behaviorism, the true observer is the experimenter who observes the responses of the subject to the conditions the experimenter has set up. Thus, the human subject was demoted in status—he no longer observed, he merely behaved and became the object of observation. And almost anyone can behave—children, the mentally ill, animals, and even the college sophomore!

This image of the subject-as-object is reinforced by the mechanomorphic tendencies of behaviorism whose model of man is that of an organic machine—an inanimate, determined, reacting, empty organism. The tendency to view subjects as mechanical objects to be poked, prodded, manipulated, and measured causes the experimenter-subject dyad to be of the order of Buber's I-It relationship. The relationship is not that of person-to-person, but rather that of person-to-thing, with its attendant tendencies of domination, manipulation, and control.

This detachment and separation between experimenter and subject

means looking at something that is not you, not human, not personal, something independent of you the perceiver. It is something

to which you are a stranger. . . . You the observer are, then, really alien to it, uncomprehending and without sympathy and identification [Maslow, 1966, p. 49].

In the same vein, Clark Hull suggested that we should consider "the behaving organism as a completely self-maintaining robot, constructed of materials as unlike ourselves as may be [1943, p. 27]."

Viewed in this manner, the sophomore in our laboratory is not a person, not an individual, but merely an anonymous, expendable object—and a sample object at that!

THE SUBJECT IN CONTEMPORARY PSYCHOLOGY

Bias in the Selection of Subjects

In reading our journals, one receives the distinct impression that the only kind of people of interest to psychologists are college students! If college students were truly representative samples of the population at large, there would be no problem in generalizing from the results of our studies. But (fortunately or unfortunately) they do differ in highly significant ways from the general population, and we cannot have a truly meaningful science of human behavior by studying such a restricted sample.

How biased in subject selection is our research? Smart (1966) examined the two largest journals of the American Psychological Association reporting research with human subjects: the *Journal of Abnormal and Social Psychology* (1962–1964, Volumes 64–67) and the *Journal of Experimental Psychology* (1963–1964, Volumes 65–68). The present author reviewed the same journals for the pe-

TABLE 1   Human Subject Sources in American Psychological Association Journals

Subjects	JEP[a] Smart	JEP Schultz	JASP[b] Smart	JPSP[c] Schultz
Introductory Psychology	42.2%	41.2%	32.2%	34.1%
Other college	43.5%	42.5%	40.9%	36.1%
Precollege	7.0%	7.1%	16.9%	18.5%
Special adult	7.3%	5.6%	9.4%	10.1%
General adult	0	0	0.6%	1.2%
All male	22.3%	19.3%	33.6%	26.7%
All female	6.0%	6.0%	10.8%	10.6%

[a] Journal of Experimental Psychology.
[b] Journal of Abnormal and Social Psychology.
[c] Journal of Personality and Social Psychology.

riod 1966–1967 (the *Journal of Personality and Social Psychology*,[1] Volumes 3–7, and the *Journal of Experimental Psychology*, Volumes 71–75), and the data from both surveys is contained in Table 1. Both surveys dealt only with nonpsychiatric subject groups.

Inspection of Table 1 reveals a striking degree of similarity between the two sets of data with a heavy concentration of college students as subjects. In addition to the great reliance on college students, both surveys revealed an overrepresentation of male subjects. The extremely small percentage of studies sampling the general adult population was particularly disturbing; none of the studies published in the *Journal of Experimental Psychology* during those years used a sample of the general population. Further, this author's survey found that in this journal, the nature of the subjects studied was not specified in 3.6% of the articles for the 2-year period. No mention could be found in these articles of where the subjects were obtained, who they were, or even if they were male or female. This certainly seems a serious omission in the reporting of research.

The fact that college students are our

primary focus of research has a number of important and sobering consequences. For example, approximately 80% of our research is performed on the 3% of the population currently enrolled in college (United States Department of Commerce, 1967). Regardless of how much our college enrollments may increase, college students most likely will never be truly representative of the total adult population, in terms of level of intelligence alone. Further, this pronounced emphasis on college students means that most of our research is conducted with a very young group, primarily ages 18–24.

Such students are probably at the peak of their learning and intellectual abilities and this could mean that many findings in learning, especially verbal learning, could be special to the college student with limited applicability to other groups [Smart, 1966, p. 119].

There is also the problem of social class representation for, as Smart noted, the college student population contains more upper-and middle-class people and fewer lower-class people than the general population.

There is a further biasing effect in

[1] One of the journals created by splitting *JASP*.

much of our psychological research that further limits the degree of generalizability of our findings. While some students are required to serve as subjects as a part of their course work, others voluntarily agree to serve. Those who do volunteer to serve as subjects do so for a variety of reasons. Orne (1962), Riecken (1962), and Rosenthal and Rosnow (1969) suggested several reasons, such as pay, course credit, the opportunity to learn something about oneself, and a desire to contribute to science. Among volunteers for a sensory deprivation experiment, Jackson and Pollard (1966) reported that 50% of the subjects said they volunteered out of curiosity, 21% for the money ($1.25 per hour), and only 7% in order to help science. Rosenthal and Rosnow noted that psychology majors appear to have a higher volunteer rate than nonpsychology majors.

Differences in actual task performance as a function of the reason for volunteering remain to be determined. It seems plausible to suggest that a subject volunteering in the hope of learning something about himself might perform differently than one volunteering for, say, course credit.

Are there any significant and meaningful differences between those who volunteer for psychological research and those who do not? Rosenthal (1965) summarized the extensive research on this problem and reported some disturbing findings. The rates of volunteering vary widely within the same university (10% to 100%), even when the same recruiter is issuing the same invitation to participate in the same experiment. However, Rosenthal did find certain situational variables that tend to increase the likelihood of volunteering.

These include (a) having only a relatively less attractive alternative to volunteering; (b) increasing the intensity of the request to volunteer; (c) increasing the perception that others in a similar situation would volunteer; (d) increasing acquaintanceship with, the perceived prestige of, and liking for, the experimenter; (e) having greater intrinsic interest in the subject matter being investigated; and (f) increasing the subjective probability of subsequently being favorably evaluated or not unfavorably evaluated by the experimenter (Rosenthal, 1965, p. 403).

Further, Rosenthal found that certain personal attributes were likely to be associated with a higher level of volunteering. He concluded that volunteers tend to have greater intellectual ability, interest, and motivation; greater unconventionality; lower age; less authoritarianism; greater need for social approval; and greater sociability (1965, pp. 403–404).

Thus, there is strong reason to suspect that in studies using only volunteer subjects, these subjects probably differ in various ways from those who do not volunteer. At the very least, this seems to violate the requirement of random sampling and thus places limitations on the statistical procedures used to analyze the data.

It might also be suggested that volunteers perform in the experimental situation in different ways than nonvolunteers as a function of their different personal characteristics. For example, Rosnow and Rosenthal (1966) reported exploratory research which suggested that volunteers, because of their greater need for social approval, were more highly motivated than nonvolunteers to verify the experimenter's hypothesis (or at least their interpretation of the hypothesis).

Another problem in the area of the volunteer subject is that some volunteers never show up for the experiment. The evidence suggests that in terms of personality test performance these "no shows" are more like nonvolunteers than volunteers who do show up. As a result, studies investigating volunteer-nonvolunteer differences are really comparing nonvolunteers with some unknown mix of true volunteers and other nonvolunteers. Thus, the results of volunteer-nonvolunteer comparisons may tend to underestimate differences between those who actually contribute data and those who do not.

And so we have the human subject who actually enters the laboratory and provides the data for our study of human behavior. He is primarily a male college student and is often enrolled in a psychology class. As least some of the time he will be a subject because he happened to be in class on the day volunteers were recruited or because his own personal characteristics and/or some aspect of the recruiting situation led him to volunteer. If a course requirement dictates that he serve as a subject, and if he has a choice among experiments, his own personal characteristics may lead him to choose one kind of experiment as opposed to another.

Are our subjects chosen at random? Are they representative of the general population, of the population of college students, of the population of college sophomores, or even of the sophomores of their own college? The answer to all of these questions, for much of our reported research, would seem to be a taunting and haunting No.

The Subject in the Laboratory

We now have our subject in the laboratory and are ready to instruct him in the experimental task. What is his set or attitude as he begins the experiment? Is he totally naïve with regard to psychological experimentation or does he approach the situation with certain predispositions and suspicions that can influence his task performance in ways not intended by the experimenter?

First, consider the attitudes of college students toward compulsory participation in experiments. Mention was made earlier of the policy of many psychology departments of requiring experimental participation as part of the introductory course. Gustav (1962) investigated the attitudes of 251 students at New York University toward their compulsory participation as subjects. At the time of this investigation, all students had participated in one experiment, though not all in the same study.

The results indicated that large numbers of required-service subjects may not be entering our laboratories with completely neutral feelings about the situation. Approximately 40% of the subjects expressed unfavorable attitudes, ranging from annoyance and irritation to fear and apprehension, toward their experiences as subjects, and 37% stated flatly that they would not have participated voluntarily. The remaining subjects reported more positive attitudes of great interest, enthusiasm, curiosity, and eagerness.

Argyris (1968) reported on an evaluation of the general psychology course by 600 undergraduates at a large university and noted that an overwhelming majority of the students focused on the course requirement of research participation. "The students were very critical, mistrustful, and hostile to the requirement. In many cases they identified how they expressed their pent-up feelings by 'beating the researcher' in such a way that he never found out . . . [p. 188]."

That such attitudes (either favorable or unfavorable) can influence the subjects' performance in a number of kinds of experimental tasks seems eminently possible. For example, those students who reported they were bored may well have performed the experimental task in a perfunctory fashion, going through the motions in order to get it over with as quickly as possible. Those who reported irritation at being required to serve might have deliberately distorted their responses in an attempt at revenge. The large number of subjects who reported apprehension and a fear of being measured and found wanting may have distorted results because of their high levels of tension and anxiety.

Holmes (1967) investigated the influence of performance in past experiments on performance in later experiments. It was found that subjects with a greater degree of experiment experience (more than six studies) tended to see the later experiment as more scientific and more valuable than those with low experience (one study). Further, the more experienced subjects made more of an attempt to cooperate with the experimenter but evidenced less interest in what the later experiment was about. Thus, subjects' perceptions of and behavioral intentions in experiments were influenced by their prior experience as research subjects.

One important requisite of psychological research is that the incoming subjects be naïve as to the nature and purpose of the experiment in which they are serving. With the large number of research studies being performed in the many universities with active graduate departments, the problem of subject naïveté may be assuming serious proportions.

With regard to specific experiments conducted over a long period of time, it seems very difficult to keep details of the experiment secret from potential future subjects. Despite out best intentions and attempts to secure pledges of secrecy, it seems that many subjects do talk about our research (in tones of ridicule or respect) to their fellow students. Even using signed pledges in connection with a well-established university honor code does not always prevent the arrival of new subjects who say, "Oh, I heard about this." Rokeach and Zemach (1966) suggested that highly interesting studies become so widely discussed and understood on a campus that the results are relatively useless. This is indeed a serious problem for long-term research projects.

On a more general level is the increasing sophistication of college students with regard to certain aspects of research methodology and attempts at deception. Surely many sophomores know by now that if they are given two questionnaires or tests with an activity or task in between, they are expected to change their answers on the second test.

As for deception, perhaps it is the researchers who are being deceived. Kelman (1967) noted that subjects "may not know the exact purpose of the particular experiment in which they are participating, but at least they know, typically, that it is *not* what the experimenter says it is [p. 6]." Brown (1965) asked: "Does any of our subjects ever believe us [p. 580]?" Orne (1962) noted that our attempts at concealing the true purpose of our studies are

so widely known in the college population that even if a psychologist is honest with the subject, more often than not he will be distrusted. As one subject pithily put it, "Psychologists always lie!" This bit of paranoia has some support in reality [pp. 778–779].

Argyris (1968) commented that subjects now come into the laboratory fully expecting to be deceived.

It would seem, then, that the subject does not enter the experiment as a tabula rasa but rather with a variety of positive and negative attitudes, expectations, and suspicions, any one of which can distort his performance. In some cases he knows the details of the specific experiment and, in many more cases, his sophistication with regard to laboratory techniques is such that the label, naïve, is a gross distortion of reality.

Performance in the Experimental Task

As we have seen, the subject brings certain attitudes and predispositions into the laboratory which may influence his behavior in the experimental task. The nature of his social interaction with the experimenter, as well as the conditions of the experiment, can also influence his behavior as a subject. His responses are being made not only to our manipulations of the independent variable, but to the host of cues Orne (1962) called demand characteristics of the experimental situation. These demand characteristics include

The rumors or campus scuttlebutt about the research, the information conveyed during the original solicitation, the person of the experimenter, and the setting of the laboratory, as well as all explicit and implicit communications during the experiment proper [p. 779].

The experimental situation is one of social interaction, but the relationship has some of the characteristics of a superior-subordinate one. When a subject has crossed the threshold of the laboratory, he has implicitly agreed to come under the control of the experimenter, to do whatever the experimenter asks on the basis of limited (and probably false) information, with little, if any, opportunity to ask questions. Perhaps the only other such one-sided relationships are those of parent and child, physician and patient, or drill sergeant and trainee.

Orne (1962) found, in several informal experiments, that people would tolerate high degrees of boredom and discomfort as long as the requests were phrased in terms of performing an experiment. For example, subjects were each given 2,000 sheets of paper filled with rows of random numbers and assigned a task that required 224 additions for each sheet of paper. The subjects' watches were taken away and they were cheered with the announcement that the experimenter would return "eventually." Orne noted that he gave up over 5 hours later but the subjects were still working.

Outside of the Army, where would we tolerate such an imposition? And yet our human subjects daily subject themselves to boredom, embarrassment, humiliation, fright, and, often, physical pain, because of the high degree of control in this situation.

The experimenter-subject relationship has a socially as well as historically defined character. As we have seen, the majority of subjects are college students. The experimenter, if not always a professor, is at least a deputy or representative of a professor (a graduate student). The experimenter is perceived by the subject as a member of the academic establishment that students are traditionally used to obeying; he represents another figure in the long line of those who have stood in loco parentis. As such, the experimenter

has responsibilities toward his students and is bound to protect as well as guide them . . . he is rational, serious and purposive. He may be eccentric; but he is not lunatic, a prankster or an idler. His behavior is explicable in terms of the scheme of motives, purposes, and norms that govern the academic community [Riecken, 1962, p. 29].

But there is more to the experimenter than just his membership in a superordinate group. He is also a *psychologist,* reputed to have uncanny skills and techniques to probe and prod and poke into our innermost workings, to find out things about us which we would rather keep secret.

Thus, the experimenter is a powerful figure to the subject. He represents control over the student by his membership in the academic establishment, and he has a certain mystique about him by virtue of his alleged unique power or ability to see all.

Further, there is a one-sided distribution of information in this relationship. The experimenter presents a certain amount of information about the task which the subject may or may not believe. The subject may suspect that some information is being withheld, but he is not allowed to question the experimenter about this suspicion. As Riecken (1962) suggested, the experimenter plays

a serious game with the subject, inviting the latter to behave under specified conditions but revealing neither what the experimenter regards as the "right answer" nor even the criteria by which a particular answer will be judged . . . "the right answer" remains the property of the master of these ceremonies until the program is over [pp. 30–31].

Riecken suggested that because of the inadequate and possibly misleading information given the subject, he may look for meaning and purpose in the situation and try to discern the "right" answer or "right" behavior. As suggested earlier, the subject may begin the experiment with certain preconceptions or suspicions and these may be sharpened or modified in the light of information received in the laboratory, for example, instructions, behavior of the experimenter, physical and social environment, and other demand characteristics. The subject may be continuously redefining the situation until the experiment is completed, trying to determine what is expected of him so that he may behave accordingly.

Several reasons have been suggested as to why subjects may make such efforts. Orne (1962), for example, suggested that most subjects in psychological experiments have such a high regard for the aims of science that they

tend to share (with the experimenter) the hope and expectation that the study in which they are participating will in some material way contribute to science. . . . Both subject and experimenter share the belief that whatever the experimental task is, it is important, and that as such no matter how much effort must be exerted or how much discomfort must be endured, it is justified by the ultimate purpose [p. 778].

The present author feels that such high and noble purpose can be attributed to only a minority of college student subjects. This is supported by the report of Jackson and Pollard (1966), cited previously, which found that only 7% of a group of volunteers gave as their motivation for volunteering a desire to help science. Perhaps even fewer nonvolunteers are concerned with making a contribution to science.

Orne (1962) did suggest that subjects were concerned about their own self-image as revealed by their task performance, but he felt that they were more concerned that their behavior serve to validate the experimenter's hypothesis and thus contribute to science.

Riecken (1962) felt that the subject attempted to uncover the rationale of the experiment for the purpose, not of contributing to science, but to present himself in the most favorable light—to "put his best foot forward." This seems a reasonable hypothesis, particularly if the experimenter is also the subject's instructor, or if he is particularly pleasant or charming or witty. Under these circumstances the subject might not only want to be thought well of by the experimenter but also might sincerely want to help the experimenter get "good" results, that is, the results the subject thinks the experimenter wants.

A third reason might be suggested for a subject's attempts to divine the nature of an experiment. He may want to foul up the experimenter's research by responding in the "wrong" way, in a manner opposite to what he thinks the experimenter wants—what Masling (1966) called "the screw you effect." As noted earlier, some subjects resent compulsory participation and so might wish to perpetrate revenge on the experimenter. Further, even some volunteer subjects may react in this way because the experimenter is their instructor, or because he is not pleasant, charming, or witty.

However, regardless of the reason for the subject's attempts to figure out the experiment, he does try to interpret it and responds according to his perception of the situation. Whether his perception is accurate or not is secondary to the fact that he is not a passive responder to the situation. He is an active participant in it, and this very activity changes the nature of the situation for him. His world, then, is not simply what the experimenter defines and presents to him. No matter how thoroughly we attempt to control and standardize the experimental situation, it is, in fact, neither controlled nor standardized to the subject. The resulting situation is one that is not intended and, more importantly, not known to the experimenter, and one that will vary among subjects.

Ethical Issues

Where is the line drawn between our responsibility to our discipline (and careers), and to those who enter our laboratories, willingly or unwillingly, to provide us with data? It seems that far too often, any concern for the well-being of our subjects is second to our interest in obtaining significance with clever new techniques of deception and probing. Perhaps this is something we really do not think about, or would prefer not to think about. Perhaps we are so used to the anonymity of subjects-as-objects and to their function as a mechanical source of data that we fail to recognize the need for concern about them as human beings.

The American Psychological Association has considered the problem of ethics in research. Principle 16, Research Precautions, of the "Ethical Standards of Psychologists" reads in part:

a. Only when a problem is of scientific significance and it is not practicable to investigate it in any other way is the psychologist justified in exposing research subjects . . . to physical or emotional stress as part of an investigation.
b. When a reasonable possibility of injurious aftereffects exists, research is conducted only when the subjects or their responsible agents are fully informed of this possibility and agree to participate nevertheless.
c. The psychologist seriously considers the possibility of harmful aftereffects and avoids them, or removes them as soon as permitted by the design of the experiment [American Psychological Association, 1963, pp. 59–60].

It is suggested that many of our experiments do involve potential emotional stress and that our subjects (volunteers and nonvolunteers) are rarely informed of this possibility. Further, we seldom bother to attempt to deal with any possible harmful aftereffects, for our interest in the subject ceases as soon as he leaves the laboratory. While there are exceptions to this seeming indifference to our subjects (and perhaps this is an important point in itself), they are indeed exceptions where they should be the rule.

Baumrind (1964) argued that researchers should insure that subjects do not leave the experimental laboratory more humiliated, insecure, or hostile than when they entered. This, she suggested, is part of the debt or obligation we have to our subjects in return for their participation in our many studies which manipulate, embarrass, and discomfort them.

Kelman (1967) expressed concern not only over the potentially harmful consequences of our experiments but also about the use of deception per se. He viewed such deception (even when there is little danger of harmful effects) as a violation of the basic respect and dignity to which every human being is entitled. Deception in the laboratory, he argued, is reinforcing an unfortunate trend in which man is increasingly considered as a manipulatable object and is therefore treated in a deliberate and highly systematic manner.

A further source of ethical concern relates to the invasion of privacy in cases where the subject is studied without his consent and/or where the data are not treated in full confidence. In our culture, the individual's right to privacy is being severely eroded to the point where it is cause for serious concern. In the laboratory, our subjects' inner feelings, fears, and fantasies are often exposed to view through deception and other techniques designed for such purposes. That we insist we are only interested in behavior may have no meaning to a subject who, through some overt action, feels that he has displayed cowardice, conformity, or some other characteristic he would rather not have displayed. "The right to privacy is the right of the individual to decide for himself how much he will share with others his thoughts, his feelings, and the facts of his personal life [Panel on Privacy and Behavioral Research, 1967, p. 536]."

Concern over the ethical use of human subjects in research has been increasing in recent years: In January 1966, the Panel on Privacy and Behavioral Research was appointed by the President's Office of Science and Technology; in July 1966, the United States

Public Health Service adopted regulations dealing with the rights and welfare of human subjects; and in May 1967, the American Psychological Association devoted an entire issue of the *American Psychologist* to various aspects of this problem.

The Panel on Privacy and Behavioral Research noted that while most research does not violate the individual's right to privacy, there are enough serious exceptions to justify increased attention to the problem. The Panel strongly urged that subject participation be on a voluntary and informed consent basis wherever possible and that researchers take every precaution necessary to guarantee the subjects' privacy and the absence of permanent physical or psychological harm.

The fact that the Public Health Service had to institute regulations designed to protect the welfare of human subjects perhaps attests to our own lack of concern for the problem. Those who would seek research support from that agency are now compelled to be sensitive to the issue.

CONCLUSIONS

The present paper has discussed several problems relating to the selection of human subjects and the kinds of situations and tasks to which those subjects are exposed. There are serious methodological implications of the former and both methodological and ethical implications of the latter. The situation is cause for serious and constructive alarm within psychology, for if our source of data is open to question then surely one can legitimately question the validity of that data.

We cannot continue to base some 80% of our human subject data on college students and still call our work a science of human behavior. We cannot continue to use statistical techniques which are predicated in part on the random sampling and assignment of subjects when this requirement is not being fully met. We cannot continue to design elaborate studies based on deception when we may be the only ones being deceived. Our population of naïve and trusting subjects is running low and we can no longer assume that all subjects will respond to our experiments in the manner in which we define those situations. Finally, we cannot continue to ignore the welfare, dignity, and privacy of our subjects.

What can be done about these matters? An important part of any attempted resolution of the problem is an active awareness of its existence. As mentioned earlier, greater attention is being paid in recent years to the nature of experimentation in psychology, and part of the focus of this research on research has been the human subject. What actual impact this new area of research will have on future studies remains to be seen.

However, it is not possible to find noticeable changes in the nature of most subject groups as reported in our journals; the great majority continue to be college students. Will any such change require external pressures such as those imposed by the Public Health Service? If journal editors and grant agency referees started requiring more representative and more randomly chosen subjects, or evidence of differences between volunteers and nonvolunteers, then the subject selection situation would change rather rapidly.

In the absence of any such pressures, such changes will probably be a long time in developing because it may well be true that the majority of the psychologists who design experiments do not participate in the actual subject selection or data collection. Rosenthal (1966) noted that there is

a trend for less highly selected experimenters to collect data for serious scientific purposes. Not only more and more graduate students are collecting behavioral data but undergraduates as well. . . . The young postdoctoral psychologist can hardly wait to turn the burdens of data collection over to *his* graduate student assistants [pp. 335, 364].

As a result, many who design the studies may not see, for example, the subtle as well as the distinct demand characteristics in operation, nor do we hear the comments of subjects as they enter and leave the laboratory. Hence, although we may read the relevant articles and be aware of the problem on an intellectual level, we may lack direct experience with subjects and so may not be sensitive to the problem on a more visceral or working level.

The solution to the selection problem is an obvious one; more effort must be made to sample the noncollege population. And, just as obviously, this is much more easily said than done. There are few, if any, logistical difficulties in using our captive college students but there are numerous such problems in obtaining a noncollege group to participate, particularly if the experiment requires such a group to come to the university campus to serve. For example, it took the author several weeks of telephone and mail contact to finally secure 50 United States Naval Reservists to come

to the laboratory to participate in an experiment. Even with these subjects, however, the problem of representativeness remains since they are a special group and not entirely representative of the general population. It is, nonetheless, a step in the right direction.

Smart (1966) suggested that more representative subject sampling could be accomplished through the establishment of large panels of subjects (necessarily volunteers) from the surrounding community; for example, industry, large clerical concerns, churches, and various other adult groups. This, of course, has the problem of using only volunteers, who may differ significantly from those who fail to volunteer. Also, these groups would not necessarily reflect the characteristics of the general population. Further, the subjects would probably have to be paid, presenting a problem for non-grant-supported research. These limitations   notwithstanding,   such groups would still supply data more generalizable than those supplied by the almost exclusive use of college students.

Rosenthal (1966) suggested that data collection centers or institutes be established with experiments being conducted by professionally trained data collectors. His concern is with the effects of the experimenter's behavior on the results of a study, and consequently he proposed standardized and thorough training for those whose sole task would be to collect data, such as a laboratory technician in medical research or an interviewer in survey research. The data collector would not be a scientist or scientist-in-training and hence would have no vested interest in the results. Rosenthal does suggest that pilot studies still be performed by the individual investigator and his assistants, as is now the case, but the large-scale research study would then be turned over to an institute, just as survey research is turned over to a data collection organization such as the National Opinion Research Center.

At first glance, this might seem farfetched but "one can already have surveys conducted, tests validated, and experimental animals bred to order. What is proposed here simply extends the limits of the kind of data that could become available on a contract basis [Rosenthal, 1966, p. 365]." (If one is skeptical of the need for the use of professional data collectors, one has only to read Rosenthal's account of the effects of the experimenter's hypotheses and behavior on the interpretation of his results.)

The use of such centers would facilitate the collection of data from more representative samples of subjects; adult subjects could be obtained and paid for their participation. It is not farfetched to envision mobile data-collection centers housed in truck vans, taking the experiment virtually anywhere to secure subjects. With this mobility, there could be even greater success in getting a subject sample that would approximate the general population.

It is recognized that these centers or institutes would be expensive to establish and maintain, but they have the potential of providing us with a meaningful science of behavior, a science based more on the real world and less on the college campus.

Thus, it is within the realm of possibility to change our selection procedures so as to bring into the laboratory subjects who are more representative of the general population than is now the case. The procedures are admittedly expensive, time-consuming, difficult, and probably frustrating, but there seems no question that they would provide more valid and generalizable data.

It is suggested, however, that even if all research in psychology utilized perfectly random and representative samples, the results would still be highly questionable (indeed, some would say virtually worthless) without basic changes in our experimental procedures. The increasing sophistication of subjects has been discussed with regard to experimentation and their growing suspicion of what we say and do to them in our laboratories. Subjects seem "wise" to what we are doing and prone to respond in terms of their own interpretation of the situation, attitude toward us, and feeling about being used as subjects. Surely these, and the ethical considerations discussed above, justify the charge that some change in our methods of collecting data is necessary.

But there is a third, more basic, important, and compelling reason for such a change—our model or image of man as an organic stimulus-response machine, an inanimate, determined, reacting, empty organism, is obsolete. The image of the human subject-as-object is no longer appropriate, if, indeed, it ever was.

The model of man adopted by early scientific psychology was quite naturally that of the prevailing climate of thought induced by the mechanistic philosophers. In the so-called (and so long dominant) Newtonian world view, the image of the universe as a great machine was extended to man, and concepts such as determinism and mechanistic causation were applied to human nature.

One aspect of Newtonian classical physics of particular relevance to observation and experimentation is the notion that nature constitutes a unique reality independent of man. Derived from this is the assumption that nature is objectively observable and independent of the observer. Thus, there developed a dichotomy between man and nature, inner world and outer world, observer and the observed. The observer is, as discussed earlier, detached, distant, aloof, and essentially different from what is being observed, be it the physical universe, the contents of consciousness, or the behavior of a subject.

This highly objective and detached spectator observation (by the experimenter) of a machinelike object (the subject) would be commendable, indeed necessary, if the underlying assumptions, that is, the Newtonian machine view of the universe and the consequent behaviorist machine view of man, were valid. But physics many years ago discarded this mechanical view, recognizing the ultimate subjectivity of all that which we would call objective, and that the very act of observing nature disturbs it, thus distorting or changing reality.

One important implication of this is the closing of the gap between the observer and the observed, and the change of focus of scientific inquiry from an independent and objectively knowable universe to man's observation of the universe. No longer the detached observer, the modern scientist is now cast in the role of participant-observer. The process of observation becomes an interaction, with both sides contributing to the observational transaction. There is no longer an independent fact and independent observer but rather an interaction and integration of the two in an observation.

Thus, a change in experimental technique is called for on empirical, ethical, as well as philosophical grounds. Let us examine two recently proposed experimental approaches in the light of these considerations.

One approach, suggested by Brown (1965) and Kelman (1967), among others, is that of role playing. Instead of deliberately concealing the nature and purpose of the experiment, these would be explained to the subject and his cooperation sought. The intent is for the subject to directly and actively involve himself in the experiment, and to conscientiously participate in the experimental task. In this approach, the subject hopefully would have a more positive attitude toward the experiment and the experimenter if he felt that he was sharing with the experimenter in a collaborative endeavor rather than being used as a guinea pig.

This technique eliminates the questionable practice of deception which, as discussed earlier, is frequently ineffective. The subject, in role playing, is not considered as merely a mechanical responder to stimuli but is much more of an acting participant. How effectively subjects will role play, of course, may depend on a number of variables including the degree of intrinsic interest of the task, the face validity of the instructions, and the subject's perception of and attitude toward the experimenter. Of course, the latter point is also a serious problem in current research techniques.

Role playing would seem to offer two advantages: the elimination of deception and the involvement of the subject as more of a direct participant in the data collection. It must be remembered that the subject is a direct and influencing participant in data collection whether we recognize or like it. Such being the case, it would seem appropriate to make active use of this participation rather than to pretend that it does not exist.

Another approach, suggested by Jourard (1968), involves the conducting of experiments with a mutual self-disclosure between the experimenter and the subject. Instead of the impersonal, detached, and distrustful relationship that is now often the case, Jourard suggests a greater openness and mutual knowing in the experimenter-subject dyad. The subject would be encouraged to report what the stimuli and his behavioral responses really mean to him. The experimenter, in turn, would explain what he thinks the subject's responses mean, and the subject asked to respond. Thus, both experimenter and subject would be open and revealing to one another.

This approach, too, eliminates the problem of deception, and it involves the subject as an active participant and collaborator, perhaps even more fully than role playing. It might be suggested, however, that the subject's degree of self-disclosure and openness would depend in large measure on the "personality" of the experimenter and that this factor could influence the subject's responses more than the independent variables involved in the experiment. Of course, as we have seen, the subject's perception of and attitude toward the experimenter affects his behavior in contemporary research, but this influence of the experimenter would seem to be greater when he is more intrusive and interacting in the experiment.

Of less importance, but still a consideration, is the fact that such an approach would be tremendously time-consuming in experiments requiring relatively large numbers of subjects. Further, it would be difficult to adapt this technique to group research involving interaction and intermember influence.

These reservations notwithstanding, the technique is an interesting one and does offer certain advantages including the potential for changing "the status of the subject from that of an anonymous *object* of our study to the status of a *person*, a fellow seeker, a *collaborator* in our enterprise [Jourard, 1968, p. 25]." Jourard and his students are performing very imaginative research to investigate the technique.

Both of these approaches have several points in common. They eliminate deception and "require us to *use* the subject's motivation to cooperate rather than to bypass it; they may even call for increasing the sophistication of potential subjects, rather than maintaining their naïveté [Kelman, 1967, p. 10]." They both involve the subject as an active participant in the research process (which he always was) rather than assuming him to be an inanimate, mechanical responder to stimuli (which he *never* was).

For the various reasons discussed herein, it seems imperative that psychology adopt a more realistic image of the human subject—one that reflects and incorporates both the newer thinking in philosophy of science and the results of our own research on research. If we are able to cast off our prejudices and long-ingrained habits of thought and practice in research, we might even advance to the point of discovering "what everyone else already knows, that one can usually understand a person's behavior much better if one tries to find out what he thought of the experiment and decided to do about it [Farber, 1963, p. 187]." Perhaps, then, the best way of investigating the nature of man is to ask him.

REFERENCES

American Psychological Association. Ethical standards of psychologists. *American Psychologist*, 1963, **18**, 56–60.

Argyris, C. Some unintended consequences of rigorous research. *Psychological Bulletin*, 1968, **70**, 185–197.

Baldwin, J. M. The "type-theory" of reaction. *Mind*, 1896, **5**, 81–90.

Baumrind, D. Some thoughts on ethics of research. *American Psychologist*, 1964, **19**, 421–423.

Binet, A. *Introduction à la psychologie expérimentale*. Paris: Alcan, 1894.

Boring, E. G. A history of introspection. *Psychological Bulletin*, 1953, **50**, 169–189.

Brown, R. *Social psychology*. New York: Free Press, 1965.

Burt, C. The concept of consciousness. *British Journal of Psychology*, 1962, **53**, 229–242.

Farber, I. E. The things people say to themselves. *American Psychologist*, 1963, **18**, 185–197.

Friedman, N. *The social nature of psychological research*. New York: Basic Books, 1967.

Gustav, A. Students' attitudes toward compulsory participation in experiments. *Journal of Psychology*, 1962, **53**, 119–125.

Hall, G. S. A children's institute. *Harper's Monthly Magazine*, 1910, cxx.

Holmes, D. S. Amount of experience in experiments as a determinant of performance in later experiments. *Journal of Personality and Social Psychology*, 1967, **7**, 403–407.

Hull, C. L. *Principles of behavior*. New York: Appleton-Century-Crofts, 1943.

Jackson, C. W., & Pollard, J. C. Some nondeprivation variables which influence the "effects" of experimental sensory deprivation. *Journal of Abnormal Psychology*, 1966, **71**, 383–388.

Jourard, S. M. *Disclosing man to himself*. Princeton, N. J.: Van Nostrand, 1968.

Kelman, H. C. Human use of human subjects: The problem of deception in social psychological experiments. *Psychological Bulletin*, 1967, **67**, 1–11.

Masling, J. Role-related behavior of the subject and psychologist and its effects upon psychological data. *Nebraska Symposium on Motivation*, 1966, **14**, 67–103.

Maslow, A. H. *The psychology of science*. New York: Harper & Row, 1966.

Orne, M. T. On the social psychology of the psychological experiment: With particular reference to demand characteristics and their implications. *American Psychologist*, 1962, **17**, 776–783.

Panel on Privacy and Behavioral Research. Privacy and behavioral research. *Science*, 1967, **155**, 535–538.

Riecken, H. W. A program for research on experiments in social psychology. In N. Washburne (Ed.), *Decisions, values and groups*. Vol. 2. New York: Pergamon Press, 1962.

Rokeach, M., & Zemach, R. The pledge to secrecy: A method to assess violations. Paper presented at the meeting of the American Psychological Association, New York, August 1966.

Rosenthal, R. The volunteer subject. *Human Relations*, 1965, **18**, 389–406.

Rosenthal, R. *Experimenter effects in behavioral research*. New York: Appleton-Century-Crofts, 1966.

Rosenthal, R., & Rosnow, R. L. The volunteer subject. In R. Rosenthal & R. L. Rosnow (Eds.), *Artifact in behavioral research*. New York: Academic Press, 1969.

Rosnow, R. L., & Rosenthal, R. Volunteer subjects and the results of opinion change studies. *Psychological Reports*, 1966, **19**, 1183–1187.

Smart, R. Subject selection bias in psychological research. *Canadian Psychologist,* 1966, **7a,** 115–121.

Titchener, E. B. Simple reactions. *Mind,* 1895, **4,** 74–81. (a)

Titchener, E. B. The type-theory of the simple reaction. *Mind,* 1895, **4,** 506–514. (b)

Titchener, E. B. Prolegomena to a study of introspection. *American Journal of Psychology,* 1912, **23,** 427–448.

United States Department of Commerce. *200 million Americans.* Washington, D.C.: United States Government Printing Office, 1967.

Watson, J. B. Psychology as the behaviorist views it. *Psychological Review,* 1913, **20,** 158–177.

Webster's new collegiate dictionary. Springfield, Mass.: G. & C. Merriam, 1958.

ELEVEN
Selection of Research Topics: The Choice between Rigor and Interest

21

The Behavior of the Psychologist at a Choice Point

William Seeman and Philip A. Marks

Experimental psychology has generally been identified with the meticulous analytic study of psychological "part processes" such as simple sensory processes or simple learning. Sometimes we lose sight of the fact that the experimental method is applicable to all aspects of psychology—that experimental psychology is a method rather than a content area. It is largely due to historical accident that simple processes have been given so much emphasis by experimental psychologists. Science has traditionally been analytic (elementalism, atomism), and it was natural for experimental psychologists to place great emphasis on analytic techniques. Furthermore, experimental psychology traces its origins to physiology, which naturally places emphasis on the functioning of organs rather than on the functioning of organisms. These factors were bound to lead to an early emphasis on piecemeal analysis, and early emphases have a way of jelling into traditions.

The result of the elementaristic tradition was that psychologists seemed to focus too much of their attention on minute problems, so that they were often accused of knowing "more and more about less and less." The study of vital human problems was given over to psychologists who had little feeling for scientific rigor. Psychologists seemed forced to choose between scientific rigor and immediate relevance to life. This dilemma is nicely expressed in the following article. In a very colorful way, Seeman and Marks point out that rigor alone cannot be the sole determinant of the value of psychological research. The "interest value" must also be taken into account. Rigor seems inversely related to interest value in the typical psychological experiment.

This is a story about a white rat who wanted to be a psychologist. His name was Herman. As Herman was at the upper end of the rat-intelligence continuum, and was, in fact, the very, very brightest member of a "bright" strain which had been developed over many generations, he was able to secure entrance to a graduate school.

One of the first things he learned (which he had, of course, known all along) was that there was a vast amount of experimental literature about the behavior of the white rat at a choice point. (To be sure, there were a few Skinnerians who occasionally had some unkind words to say about the T-maze as an instrument of experimentation, but in the main the maze was accepted as shedding light on the "dynamics" of choice behavior.) What surprised our white rat, Herman, however, was that very little knowledge was available about the behavior of the *psychologist* at a choice point. Except for a few major efforts, such as the Michigan study of clinical psychology students, there had not been much time available for the investigation of the investigative behavior of psychologists and of the choices involved therein. He did find that E. K. Strong had demonstrated quite a while back that professional choices were not likely to be wholly accidentally determined. And thinking about this it occurred to him (let us face it—our rat, Herman, had a taint of the "clinician" somewhere about him) that the psycho-

analysts might be right, and that it might be true, as Roy Schafer had said, "Interests themselves must be regarded as . . . expressions . . . of major dynamic trends." So he was not in the least surprised when he found that Strong and Tucker had demonstrated that four rather distinctive profiles could be derived respectively for surgeons, internists, pathologists, and psychiatrists. He would have been surprised if it were *not* so, if these different specialists were *not* "different kinds of people."

Then, in diligent pursuit of his course assignments, Herman began to read the long "methodological" discussions which dotted the pages of the *Bulletin,* the *Review,* and, to a lesser extent, the pages of some of the other journals. In a short time he was able to distinguish between "theory" and "meta-theory," although it must be admitted that he occasionally confused these with "methodological considerations." One thing he found: psychological theorizing being what it was, it seemed terribly easy for some psychologists to yield to the temptation of telling *other* psychologists what, as theorists and/or methodologists and/or meta-theorists, they *had* to do in order to remain members-in-good-standing of the "scientific" club. The rules of the game called "science" as they pertained to the domain called "behavior" were sometimes laid out with enviable precision, neatness, and order. The more our Herman thought about this, the more puzzled he became; puzzled, then worried, then haunted. He pursued an elusive idea and an elusive word—*choice.* It disrupted his chain of associations, became obsessively omni-

Reprinted from *American Scientist,* 1962, **50** (No. 4), 538–547, by permission of the authors and publisher.

present in his thoughts, and punctuated his dreams in a shamelessly unsymbolic and undisguised form. It seemed to him that there were a number of instances in which important but implicit choices were being made; instances in which it was not quite explicit, always, *that* there were choices being made. For example, he happened one day upon two graduate doctoral students who were just completing experiments, one on secondary reinforcement, the other on changes in the "self-concept" with psychotherapy. The student with the secondary-reinforcement problem was taunting the other with his lack of "rigor." Either you were rigorous, said the former, or you were not. If you were, you could call yourself a "scientist"; if you were not, you couldn't.

That evening Herman worked far into the night, digging deep into the philosophy of science. He read, he thought; he thought, he read, and then he thought harder and harder. The more he read and the deeper he immersed himself in thought, the more perplexed he became. It was clear that rigor was a great idea, as it was clear, most psychologists would agree, that any and every area of psychology ought to be made as rigorous as possible, although writers on projective techniques occasionally contrived to give a contrary impression. But he wondered why, if rigor were the absolutely exclusive criterion, the student had not done an experiment in classical mechanics! What looked like the beautiful precision and control of secondary reinforcement (like "rigor," in short) began to look like sloppy lack of controls as compared with the precision and rigor of classical physics. This particular experiment, as he recalled, had been executed in the absence of any knowledge

about the life history of the rat subjects before they had been purchased at the institute. And, being a white rat himself, he knew this might not be an irrelevant variable. It must be, then (so our Herman ruminated), that there was an element of *choice* here; the psychologist took what rigor he could get and took it in something he happened to be *interested* in. To the psychologist's credit it had to be said that rigor was largely devised, evolved, invented, or discovered as a result of blood, sweat, tears, thought, and the ingenuity of his efforts. All in all, considering the psychology of the investigator, it seemed to Herman that this constituted an interesting bit of behavior at a choice point. It made him sad, though, to think of the poor thanks the psychologist sometimes got for his efforts at rigor, for he remembered the graduate student in physics who had asked scornfully: "Tell me, are there any *laws* in psychology?"

Then, too, the methodological papers puzzled him in another way. He seemed to recall that somewhere MacFarlane had written that the centralist doctrine which was given substantial meaning by the work of Freud had somehow got distorted (in the projective techniques) into "Your unconscious is you." He wondered whether, comparably, the doctrine of operationism hadn't got distorted into "seeing is believing." Thus, in a discussion of intervening variables *versus* hypothetical constructs, he was informed that while one was permitted (if he *must*) to resort to hypothetical constructs, temporarily, he had nevertheless better cash these in at the earliest market opportunity for intervening variables. What looked like a methodological *must* to one psychologist seemed to Herman on closer examination, to be a doctrinal preference. If he were a clinician (which thank heavens, he was not!) he might even have said that this was an *interest* choice being smuggled in (quite unconsciously) as formal methodological doctrine. Such a methodological dictum, if adopted, would make it impossible to suggest that things might not, in fact, be what they seem, and that skimmed milk could conceivably masquerade as cream. It would, for example, make it impossible to say that observed behavior such as a persistent and hyperkinetic pursuit of women by a man could be a "defensive reaction-formation," a means of defending against "unconscious homoerotic impulses." He had read somewhere that Meehl had referred to this as sometimes giving the appearance of having a heads-I-win-tails-you-lose flavor. But here, too, there was a choice. Some psychologists might be made uncomfortable by the mere mention of such a possibility, and had every right to avoid it and to work in another theatre of operations. Those who elected to work this area would just have to be content with a little less rigor, less elegance, less precision, and perhaps a good deal more discouragement.

One October morn our Herman walked into his statistics course and sat down. The instructor was a well-known statistician with a widely-respected book in the field. He began the lecture (the instructor, that is) by announcing that he had spent the summer reading all the psychology journal articles he could (including the experimental journals) and these had depressed him. Of the whole lot, there were only two satisfactory papers; just two papers in which the researchers had been careful to see that all the assumptions underlying the

statistical procedures used were actually met by the data. The statistician then proceeded to present to the class as an illustrative instance a study which *did* meet the requirements. It was a study in tossing pennies. Now Herman had no objection to tossing pennies, and he certainly felt that people who enjoyed tossing pennies ought to be permitted to do so. (He had himself once made a brief but disastrous visit to Las Vegas and the roulette tables.) But as a white rat he had (he felt) a certain natural interest in the *human organism*. He thought that he should be permitted to choose between a precise estimate of something he was not the least interested in and a less precise estimate of something he passionately wanted to know.

Herman was made saddest of all by the constant guerilla warfare carried on by the "clinical" and "experimental" students. He thought the clinicians sometimes had a tendency to fuzziness about the "clinical method," "dynamics," and "clinical validation." He especially wondered what the latter might mean, and he counted seven different definitions of the word "dynamic." (On the other hand he had just read Gibson's seven different definitions of the word "stimulus.") But, thinking again in terms of choice and in the psychology of the investigator, it occurred to him that some of the more solid clinicians were making much the same *kind* of choice when they elected to research "countertransference," "identification," and "self-concept" in preference to secondary reinforcement, pursuit rotor tasks, and reactive inhibition —the same kind of choice as were those psychologists who elected to research secondary reinforcement, pursuit rotor tasks, and reactive inhibition in pref-

```
 1. MATHEMATICS . . . . . . . . . . . . . . . . . . . . STATISTICS
 2. H-CONSTRUCT . . . . . . . . . . . . . . . . . . . . I-VARIABLE
 3. ARISTOTLE . . . . . . . . . . . . . . . . . . . . . GALILEO
 4. S-O-R LAWS . . . . . . . . . . . . . . . . . . . . . S-R LAWS
 5. RORSCHACH . . . . . . . . . . . . . . . . . . . . . MMPI
 6. FACTOR ANALYSIS . . . . . . . . . . . . . . . . . . PSYCHOANALYSIS
 7. PSYCHOPHYSICS . . . . . . . . . . . . . . . . . . . BEHAVIORISTICS
 8. PREDICTION . . . . . . . . . . . . . . . . . . . . . EXPLANATION
 9. S-R LAWS . . . . . . . . . . . . . . . . . . . . . . R-R LAWS
10. LOGIC . . . . . . . . . . . . . . . . . . . . . . . . MEASUREMENT
11. CONSTRUCT VALIDITY . . . . . . . . . . . . . . . . CONCURRENT VALIDITY
12. HOCKHEIMER . . . . . . . . . . . . . . . . . . . . SEDLITZ
```

Figure 1   Qualifying examination.

erence to the capture probability of electrons, magnetic field, and hydrodynamics; all of which latter could, beyond all shadow of doubt, be stated with more exact and elegant mathematical precision and with greater generality than the "laws" of secondary reinforcement, pursuit rotor tasks, and reactive inhibition. At least it appeared to our rat that the same logic which would compel the psychologist to turn from the disturbing messiness and lack of controls in research on "countertransference," "identification," and the "self-concept" to the more rigorous controls of secondary reinforcement, pursuit rotor tasks, and reactive inhibition should compel the psychologist to turn from the messiness and lack of controls in research on secondary reinforcement, pursuit rotor tasks, and reactive inhibition to the more elegant, more general, more precise research on capture probability, magnetic fields, and hydrodynamics.

Troubled by this unprecedented and heretical view, Herman's advisor recommended that he (Herman) schedule his doctoral qualifying examination at once. Passively Herman acquiesced. The examination, reproduced in Figure 1, was given in three parts.

The instructions for each part were simple and straightforward, and were these.

Part I: "Select the member of each pair having the highest personal *interest* value"; Part II: "Select the member of each pair having the highest '*rigor*' value"; Part III: "Select the member of each pair having the highest *theory* value" (i.e., the one that is more theoretical than empirical).

Separate answer sheets were used for each part, and in no instance was Herman informed of the precise nature of the required tasks or permitted to see the instructions until he had completed the preceding part (e.g., he had to complete Part I before he could even be informed that there was to be a Part II, etc.). Herman's Interest, Rigor, and Theory scores are given in Figure 2.

Herman's advisor, and indeed his entire department, were extremely delighted with the results. A comparison of Herman's interests with his notions of rigor revealed a congruency of 75.0%—he was, so they reasoned, a rigorous-rat. A comparison of his inter-

Part I: Interest			Part II: Rigor			Part III: Theory	
A	B		A	B		A	B
1. (X)	( )		1. (X)	( )		1. (X)	( )
2. ( )	(X)		2. ( )	(X)		2. (X)	( )
3. ( )	(X)		3. ( )	(X)		3. ( )	(X)
4. (X)	( )		4. ( )	(X)		4. (X)	( )
5. ( )	(X)		5. ( )	(X)		5. (X)	( )
6. (X)	( )		6. (X)	( )		6. ( )	(X)
7. ( )	(X)		7. (X)	( )		7. ( )	(X)
8. (X)	( )		8. (X)	( )		8. ( )	(X)
9. (X)	( )		9. (X)	( )		9. (X)	( )
10. (X)	( )		10. (X)	( )		10. (X)	( )
11. ( )	(X)		11. (X)	( )		11. ( )	(X)
12. (X)	( )		12. (X)	( )		12. (X)	( )

Figure 2   Herman's interest, rigor, and theory scores.

ests with his notions of theory revealed a congruency of 66.7%—Herman was a theoretically-oriented-rigorous-rat. Yet, upon *Herman's* closer inspection, such results were, for him, scarcely cause for rejoicing. What saddened him was the state of affairs represented by his low rigor-theory item overlap (41.7%). He wondered how a theoretically-oriented-rigorous-rat like himself could have actually obtained a higher rigor-empirical percentage (58.3%). Was he conflicted? It occurred to him that quite possibly he was—that, being infra-human, of course he was—"I am," he mused, "a theoretically-oriented-rigorous-conflicted-rat!"

In his second year of graduate study Herman became fascinated with the problems presented by learning theory. After surveying the various theories as presented in Hilgard, he tackled reinforcement theory more systematically, studying Hull with great care. One night he fell asleep whilst ruminating over the problem of extinction and stimulus-response asynchronism. Suddenly, he sat bolt upright, waking from a dream in which he had been pursuing Hull's idea of developing a unit of habit strength, the "hab." Why not a unit of rigor—the "rig?" Well, why not? (The *definition* of rigor was, at least implicitly, very easy. It could be found in Mendelssohn's opening sentence in the paper "Probability Enters Physics": "Physics—or, if you like, experimental philosophy—is a philosophical method which differs from others in that it relies on rigorous quantitative relations between observations.")

In a burst of creative excitement and activity he burrowed into the works of Norbert Weiner and Anatol Rapaport: into cybernetics, into information theory, into James Miller's general systems theory. Armed with this constellation of information he then set to work building a machine, a rigometer, which like an ammeter or a voltmeter, would register values directly on a dial. In this manic burst of imaginative activity, Herman hardly ate or slept; it was too exciting. He knew that if the circuits could be made to reverberate properly, if enough circuits could be provided to obviate information overload, and if the programing mathematics could be mastered, the most complex theories and experimental designs could be fed into the machine and a precise measure of their rigor obtained in "rig" units.

At last the machine was ready. Would it work? With trembling paws and much trepidation Herman fed into the machine a number of theories: Newton's gravitational theory, Maxwell's and Boltzmann's equations expressing pressure and temperature of a gas as average energy of motion of gas molecules, Schrödinger's mathematical representation of de Broglie's theory of matter waves. The indicator swept over the face of the dial registering extraordinarily high values in "rigs." So far so good! Feeding in the various theories of learning, Herman saw the indicator move downward on the dial; lower and lower "rigs," as was to be expected. As he fed in the theories of transference and countertransference the dial plummeted ever lower. Herman was delighted. His rigometer was an indubitable success!

Nothing succeeds like success, and nothing breeds success more than the proliferation of previous success. Herman had run across some of Flesch's measures of readability and across some measures of interest. Why not, though, a more *precise* measure of interest, so that various problems could be assessed for their interest value? He decided to build another machine, an intometer, based upon certain statistical facts: The listed interests of the APA membership; the rated interest value of certain questions (e.g., How long does it take an ameba to locate food in a T-maze? How can we devise methods to prevent mutual annihilation by the hydrogen bomb? etc.); the nature and extent of subscriptions to professional journals; and a number of other variables. Only after he had completed this piece of apparatus did it occur to Herman to investigate the relationship between the rigor value (in "rigs") and the interest value (in "ints") of certain questions. What he found disturbed him not a little, and is presented in Figure 3.

He found that if he plotted on the abscissa the interest values of some of the problems randomly sampled from the universe of problems, and along the ordinate the rigor values of the tightest experimental designs which could be devised to study those problems—he found that an inverse relationship turned up. One could say either that high rigor problems had low interest values or that high interest problems had low rigor values as measured by the instrumentation. With this Herman was not at all happy.

But degree-getting is not a process

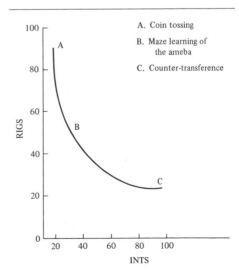

Figure 3 Relationship between rigor values (RIGS) and interest values (INTS) for a random sample of problems.

which waits on the personal happiness of the student, human or infra-human. The dissertation hurdle had now to be cleared. Herman selected as his problem "the prediction of daydreams in a gravitational field" and set up the problem in the following manner: He first surveyed a number of college samples to determine the incidence of certain daydreams types, and established with astonishingly high reliability (with rank-order correlations of the magnitude of .95) the incidence of these daydreams types under twenty-five separate conditions. This was a purely empirical study, involving nothing more than frequency counts of daydreams. The dissertation problem proper was designed to answer the question: What kinds of theories could maximally predict these twenty-five daydream frequencies? To answer this question Herman selected five physicists, five chemists, five zoologists, five physiologists, five learning theorists and five clinical psychologists, and asked each of these to select any available theory in his chosen domain. These theories were then fed into the rigometer and their mean value in "rigs" thus determined. The next step was to require each selected theory to deduce logically (i.e., predict) the daydream outcomes, and the total number of "hits" (successful predictions) was computed for the theories in the chosen domains described above. The results of the experimental procedure are presented in Figure 4.

Herman's committee confronted these experimental results with dismayed incredulity, and were thrown into pandemonium. (Notable exceptions to this reaction were to be observed in the committee member representing the philosophy of science and the honorary

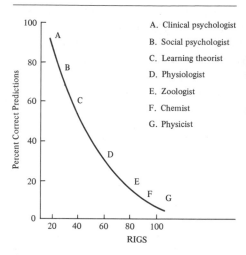

Figure 4 Relationship between rigor values (RIGS) and per cent of correct predictions of daydreams for a selected number of theories (correct predictions for all 25 daydreams would yield 100%; for 24 daydreams 96%, etc.)

committee member from physics, both of whom inspected the curve representing the results with imperturbable equanimity.) Having examined the experimental results with minute and corrosive care and being unable to locate any errors in the design, procedure, and data analysis, the committee members concluded that Herman's thesis was not quite cricket. It was simply inadmissible on logical-theoretical-methodological-meta-theoretical grounds, that any theory of lower rig value could effect more successful predictions in *any* scientific domain. Surely, to take any other position was to throw a wrench into the machinery of science.

However heretical the doctrine presented by our theoretically-oriented rigorous-conflicted-rat, that doctrine, he maintained, had its validity credentials firmly anchored to the experimental results of his thesis. His committee remained unimpressed and unconvinced.

Herman then confronted them with yet another piece of experimental evidence. This was a little problem he had worked out just for the fun of it, at the time he had done his major survey of daydreams. At that time he had asked the chairman of each of the following departments in the university graduate school to suggest a problem of current interest in his own domain. Indicated here are the departments and the problems set forth:

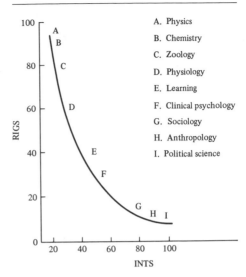

Figure 5 Relationship between interest values (INTS) and rigor values (RIGS) as a function of departmental problems.

A. Physics (The capture probability of electrons)

B. Chemistry (The molecular structure of crystals)

C. Zoology (Tonic labrinthinc reflexes of the crawdad)

D. Physiology (Muscle action potentials)

E. Learning (Gradient of secondary reinforcement)

F. Clinical psychology (Outcomes of psychotherapy)

G. Sociology (Delinquency prediction and control)

H. Anthropology (Cultural evolution of mankind)

I. Political science (Avoidance of mutual annihilation by the H-bomb)

The rig values attached to the methods of inquiry designed to investigate these questions are given in Figure 5.

Herman then challenged the committee to draw a line dividing the "scientific" from the "non-scientific" disciplines. (Naturally, to avoid contamination with respect to inter-rater agreement he politely requested them to do this independently.) The committee quite naturally refused to comply with such a highhanded request on the part of a graduate student, especially when he was infra-human. Herman then inquired whether the people at position A should expel from the scientific brotherhood (on the grounds of low rig value) all people at position E; or whether the people at position E should (on the same grounds) expel all people at position F; etc. The committee stared stonily and silently first at each other and then at Herman. *They* knew right from wrong, doctrinal sin from doctrinal truth. They politely but firmly suggested that such heretical doctrine (and such experimental results) could not be embraced under the rubric of "science." Equally firmly, they suggested Herman might be in the wrong school. Moreover, they left him no choice!

TWELVE
Research on Complex
Human Behavior:
I. Analog Research

22

War Hawks and Peace Doves: Alternate Resolutions of Experimental Conflicts

Marc Pilisuk, Paul Potter, Anatol Rapaport, and J. Alan Winter

In the preceding article, Seeman and Marks seem to take the view that nonrigorous theories may be better predictors of certain phenomena than rigorous theories. Their article epitomizes an attitude that is virtually universal though not often articulated among psychologists—the attitude that they must choose between rigor and relevance or "interest value" of research materials. Some investigators have done studies which strongly suggest that it may not be necessary to make such a choice. It may be possible to examine issues of immediate importance in situations of considerable complexity through rigorous, and even *experimental* methods.

The remaining articles in the present book have been selected to illustrate some methods for dealing fairly rigorously with problems which are vitally important to us *right now*. The article that follows involves a tactic of using an analog of the real situation of interest. Since the experimenters are dealing with warring behavior, it would be difficult—though perhaps not out of the question—to do otherwise. War games are used as analogs of real warring situations. The results are of some interest, especially with respect to the landslide effect of strategies which involve uncompromising attempts to maximize one's own gains at the expense of an opponent.

The use of analogs is not entirely satisfying. It may be an improvement over such methods as casual observation or interviewing, but it is always possible to doubt the adequacy of the analogy. An analog is always similar in some respects to the real situation, but it is different in other respects. When an investigator uses a game as the representative of love or war, or when, as is commonly done, an experimenter uses an animal analog of neurosis or some other human behavior of interest, we must always wonder whether some of the differences between the analog and the real situation change the findings in important ways. Whenever possible, an experimenter should work in authentic situations, thereby providing increased confidence in the generality of his data.

We have long been led to believe that there are sharp limitations on the experimental investigation of most human behaviors. The widespread use of rats in psychological research has customarily been justified by arguing that human subjects cannot be manipulated in the ways that are required. But it is quite possible that experimental psychologists have given up too easily. The rest of the articles in this book show that the persevering experimenter can find ways to study psychological phenomena which at first blush seem inaccessible to scientific investigation.

The two-person, two-choice Prisoner's Dilemma game offers the players an opportunity to demonstrate either trust, by choosing the cooperative (C) response, or suspicion, by choosing the defection (D) response (Deutsch, 1958). In the conventional experimental situation each of the players has an opportunity to make only the completely cooperative response or the completely defecting response. Cooperative responses when made by both players provide rewards to both. Defecting responses, if they are mutual, are detrimental to both players. The incentive to defect, however, derives from the nature of payoffs following asymmetrical choices by the pair members. When one player defects (chooses D) unilaterally while the second player chooses C, the defector is most highly rewarded and to the detriment of the cooperator. When the game is played without communication, rationality (in the strict sense of game theory) provides no solution consistent with the collective interests of the players.

The following example of a payoff matrix for a Prisoner's Dilemma game helps to demonstrate the nature of the dilemma:

Reprinted from *Journal of Conflict Resolution*, 1965, **9**, 491–508, by permission of the authors and publisher.

Research relating to this project was made possible by assistance from the following sources: National Science Foundation, grants G 99 and GS 586; National Institutes of Health, M–423801–02–03–04–05; and Sigma Xi, the Scientific Research Society of America. . . .

		Player A's Choices	
		C	D
Player B's	C	20, 20	40, −20
Choices	D	−20, 40	0, 0

In repeated trials of a game of this kind, a pair of players generally establishes a stable relationship. This relationship is characterized either by a lengthy succession of mutually beneficial outcomes (CC) or by a succession of mutually punishing or nonrewarding outcomes (DD). There are, of course, trials in which only one player tries to cooperate while his partner defects and gains at his expense. But the frequency of such asymmetrical behavior declines after a series of trials and pairs generally fall into either the cooperative pattern or the noncooperative, from which they depart only rarely (Rapoport, 1965; Pilisuk and Rapoport, 1963). The significance of this lock-in phenomenon lies in the degree to which the game presents a microsimulation of interpersonal behavior. Two individuals are obliged to make a series of behaviors which affect their partner's well-being as well as their own. Eventually, large numbers of these pairs develop a stable interaction pattern which defines them as a social unit.

What characteristics distinguish a cooperating pair of "Peace Doves" from a competing pair of "War Hawks"? Are their personalities different? Are the Doves in a pair more like each other than the members of Hawk pairs? Does the game environment, aside from such obvious experimental manipulation as changing the payoff matrix, affect the relative frequencies of Dove-like or Hawk-like outcomes? And, perhaps of greatest importance to the psychologist, is there a pattern of early play, a system of gestures and responses in the game itself, which so teaches the lesson of cooperation that it is productive of Doves rather than of Hawks?

The game designed to answer these questions is more complex than the two-choice game described previously. The new form permits each player a range of moves in every trial of the game so that his choice is no longer constricted to total cooperation or total defection but may vary from 0 to 20 units of cooperation, as may his partner's choice. The resultant 21 by 21 matrix of possible outcomes is so fixed as to contain the same basic paradox as the 2 by 2 game. Like the 2 by 2 game, the newer design produces its quota of Dove pairs, Hawk pairs, and some intermediary ("Mugwump") pairs.

The difference is that the newer game more closely approximates many actual situations where the choice is not whether to cooperate or not but rather what degree of cooperation to choose. Also, a versatile set of arms-race-simulating conditions, e.g., missile conversion, inspection, etc., are easily fitted to the game (Pilisuk and Rapoport, 1964). And most important, the added choice flexibility permits a more refined study of gestures and responses which may lead players to suspicion or to trust.

METHOD

A total of 128 male college students (64 pairs) participated as subjects in this study. The experimental room contained booths permitting up to three pairs of subjects to participate simultaneously while completely eliminating visual and verbal contact between pair members. Subjects who knew one another prior to the experimental session were not paired. Recruitment was from volunteers for paid psychological experiments.

Subjects first completed questionnaires used to assess self-acceptance and monetary risk performance. The characteristics of the game were then described to them and play began. Upon completion of games a brief strategy questionnaire was used to obtain subjective descriptions of strategies employed. After the experimental session was completed, subjects were asked to take home and complete the questionnaires which were used to assess tolerance for ambiguity, internationalism, and social risk preference. Upon receipt of completed take-home questionnaires, subjects were paid for their participation in the experiment, in amounts corresponding to their actual achievements in the game.[1]

[1]The tolerance for ambiguity measure is a six-point Likert-type scale containing the eighteen items relating to preferences for regularity or change, clarity or ambiguity, balance or asymmetry, etc. Nine items were selected from a pool of F scale correlate items which had been classified by their authors as measures of tolerance for ambiguity (Webster *et al.*, 1955). The remaining nine items were taken from a measure of tolerance for ambiguity reported in a study by O'Connor (1952). The F scale has been shown to predict noncooperation in simple non-zero-sum games. The authors suspected the "cognitive style" aspect of authoritarianism to be more relevant to game performance than the affective or attitudinal components and selected tolerance for ambiguity for measurement.

The self-acceptance measure was included in the battery to test the notion that acceptance of oneself might be instrumental to the development of trust for a partner. People who are less self-accepting tend also to be less accepting of others (Berger, 1952) and, perhaps, less willing to trust the other player in a non-zero-sum game. Fifty items were selected randomly, one-half of all those used in the Q-sort technique reported in Rogers and Dymond (1954). Actual discrepancies between self-image and ideal image were used.

The internationalism scale contained items from other attitude scales (Levinson, 1957; Samson and Smith, 1957) combined and modified to produce a set of questions which the authors felt might be appropriate for the population at hand. (Copies of the scale are available on request.) Because internationalism was shown to be related to non-zero-sum game behavior (Lutzker, 1960), we anticipated an even greater effect upon game behavior in games loaded with the semantic referents of the arms race.

Since monetary rewards were used in the game

When play began, the player sat facing an 8″ x 10″ playing board divided into 20 squares. A two-faced poker chip, white on one side, blue on the other, was on each square. All twenty chips were placed white side up at the start. Each player was also given a full matrix of outcomes showing the payoff to each player for every possible combination of choices by himself and by the other player. (A representation of this matrix, reduced to 5 x 5, is presented in Figure 1.) A play consisted of turning any number of discs (from 0 to 20) from white to blue.

The payoffs may be understood as rewarding each player one unit (2 monetary mills) for each blue side he exposes. If both players expose an identical number of blue tokens their payoffs are completely determined by this number. In the event of a disparity between the players in the number of blue chips exposed, the player showing *fewer* blue chips is given an additional payoff equal to twice the size of the disparity. For the player showing the larger number of blue tokens an amount equal to twice the disparity is subtracted from his total payoff. If players A and B expose Bl_a and Bl_b blue chips respectively and receive payoffs P_a and P_b

we felt that the individual's propensity to take risks might affect his play. Two measures were used to assess an individual's propensity to take risks. The first, a gambling task involving real monetary rewards, was followed by a task of social risk preference.

The monetary risk preference measure consists of a set of choices among actual monetary gambles which subjects make. (Copies are available.) The measure of social risk-taking was reported by Kogan and Wallach (1961). It investigates the chances which people would be willing to take in a series of life-like social situations.

respectively, then (1) $P_a = 2Bl_b - Bl_a$ and (2) $P_b = 2Bl_a - Bl_b$.

In other words, conversion to blue chips is rewarding when mutual but punishing to the degree that it is unilateral. Conversely, retention of white chips is nonrewarding if mutual, but rewarding to the extent that it is unilateral. Specifically: (1) if both players convert fully from white to blue chips, both win 20 units; (2) if neither player converts any tokens to their blue side, neither receives any units; (3) complete unilateral conversion to blue matched against an opposing player's complete retention of white results in a loss of 20 units to the cooperator and a gain of 40 units to the defector; and (4) payoffs between these extremes are determined by both the number of blue chips one exposes and the difference between that number and the number exposed by the other player. The extreme outcomes are identical to those shown in the illustrative two-choice payoff matrix given earlier. Some intermediate outcomes appear in Figure 1.

The game was played in two experimental settings, the *abstract* and the *simulated*. Sixty-four players, one-half the total, played only abstract games. The other half played simulated games exclusively. The abstract game has already been described. In it the tokens on the game board are merely tokens, i.e., poker chips which were blue on one side and white on the other. Instructions avoided such evaluative words as "cooperation or competition," "winning or losing," "contest," "opponent," and even "game." While these words were also omitted in the simulated condition, a new set of evaluative symbols was used. The simulated game was introduced with the terminology of an arms-race-

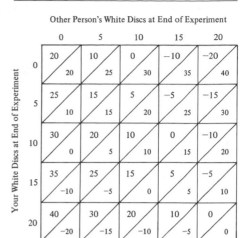

Other Person's White Discs at End of Experiment

Figure 1   Reduced form of payoff matrix shown to players. The actual matrix used showed all values from 0 to 20. The first figure in each box represents one's own payoff; the second figure, the payoff for the other player.

disarmament dilemma. A token with its white side showing was referred to as a weapon and contained a schematic picture of a missile upon it. Blue-side-up tokens were called economic units and contained schematic pictures of factories. A game board was a country. The simulated condition was intended to heighten the game's similarity to the arms race without expressing preference for either armament or disarmament.

Payoffs were identical in abstract and simulated conditions. After each play of the 55 plays of the game, a player was informed of his partner's choice by receipt of a note from the experimenter. From this he could refer to his matrix and keep informed of his payoffs.

The second experimental variation involved the manner in which players made their decision as to how far to cooperate or disarm, i.e., how many tokens to turn from white to blue. In the *short game* which has already been described, each player makes a single move converting from zero to twenty of his tokens. The single moves by the two players determine the payoffs to each and terminate that trial or play of the game.

The *long game* consisted of twenty separate moves. On a given move, white chips could be converted to blue, or blue chips could be converted back to white, provided only that a player might never turn more than two chips on any given move. No feedback was given prior to the twentieth (last) move. Since the intermediate moves of each player had no effect upon payoffs and were not made known to the other participant, the long game appears identical with the short. In fact, the long and short games are *logically* isomorphic. However, they may differ *psychologically*. Forcing players to enact their final decision in gradual steps could alter the decision.

All subjects played 40 short and 15 long games. Half of the subjects began with 40 short games and then played 15 long games. The other half reversed this order. A block design of the experimental variation is shown here:

	Abstract	Simulated
Long First	A_1	S_1
Short First	A_2	S_2

RESULTS[2]

A. Selection of Criterion Pairs

The data deal with characteristics of three types of pairs. The pairs were clas-

sified into discrete categories in accordance with the performance of both players during the last five games in an experimental session containing 55 games. The pair labels are Dove (cooperators), Hawk (noncooperators), and Mugwump (intermediate). A pair was labeled Dove if (1) both players turned 15 or more of their tokens from white to blue during *each* one of the last five games and (2) neither player turned over fewer than 17 tokens per trial, on an average, over these same trials. The Hawk criteria are completely symmetrical. A Hawk pair was so designated where (1) neither player turned more than 5 tokens to their blue side during the last five trials and (2) neither player turned over an average of three tokens or more per trial during these same games. The third and intermediate group, Mugwumps, contains all the remaining pairs which failed to meet the conditions for classification as either Dove or Hawk.

The grouping provides 26 pairs of Doves, 17 pairs of Hawks, and 21 Mugwump pairs. These criterion groups were used for the remainder of the analysis. The groupings, while arbitrary, provide for stringent differentiation between the cooperators (Doves) and the noncooperators (Hawks). (The probability that two players, making random choices, will fall into one of these two groups is less than 10^{-5}.) Some Mugwump pairs, however, were apparently moving toward greater cooperation during the final five trials and might

---

[2]Results contained here deal exclusively with the differentiation between criterion groups des-

ignated by performance during the last five plays of the game. The effects of experimental conditions on such gross indices of behavior as the average number of tokens turned over in all trials are discussed in Pilisuk and Rapoport (1963).

have met the Dove criterion had the experiment continued beyond 55 trials. Some Mugwumps, on the other hand, were showing essentially noncooperative behavior but not quite to the Hawk criterion. Even among the more homogeneous Dove and Hawk groups, pair histories display some interesting differences as well as similarities. For example, by applying the five-trial block criterion to trials earlier than the last five it is possible to split the Dove pairs into early and later cooperators. And it is possible to identify, among both Hawks and Doves, some few pairs who met the criterion and then lost it. By the end of an hour and a half of game play, however, the Doves were locked into the pattern of mutual cooperation, the Hawks were locked into a conflict of distrust, and the Mugwumps had achieved neither of these stable patterns.

B. The Influence of Personality Variables

Five personality variables were assessed. They were: (1) self-acceptance; (2) monetary risk preference; (3) tolerance for ambiguity; (4) internationalism; and (5) social risk preference. A brief rationale for the selection of these variables has been given in footnote 2.

We asked two questions about the differences in the personalities of the Doves, Hawks, and Mugwumps. First, we asked: Do the individual Doves, Hawks, and Mugwumps differ on the dimensions of personality we thought relevant to game behavior? That is, is the average Dove (or Hawk or Mugwump) different from members of the other two groups? Second, we asked: Do pair members among Dove, Hawk, or Mugwump pairs differ in the extent to which they are similar to their partners? The import of the second question may be seen in two variants of it. Do members of a pair of Doves resemble one another more closely or less closely than members of a typical Hawk or Mugwump pair? And does the instability of the Mugwumps' resolution reflect a greater personality disparity between partners than might be found among either Doves or Hawks?

Mean scores on each of the five individual difference measures are contrasted for Doves, Hawks, and Mugwumps in Table 1.

Examination of the differences between means on each variable presents a consistent and negative picture. The F values are not statistically significant. The variables selected here do not predict well to criterion group performance.

TABLE 1   Personality Differences among Doves, Hawks, and Mugwumps

Personality Measures	Means			$F_2/127$	p
	Doves	Hawks	Mugwumps		
Self-acceptance[a]	1.885	1.545	2.007	0.03	NS
Tolerance for Ambiguity[b]	−10.038	−3.618	−3.929	0.003	NS
Internationalism	21.558	25.235	24.262	0.01	NS
Monetary Risk Preference	45.154	47.029	45.905	0.003	NS
Social Risk Preference	45.250	45.353	43.619	0.003	NS

[a] Low scores indicate greater self-acceptance.
[b] Low scores indicate greater tolerance for ambiguity.

With the possible exception of tolerance for ambiguity, which may favor the potential for achievement of the Dove group criterion, there is little even to suggest that personality characteristics might be exerting a noticeable influence. This may appear in some contrast to the work of Deutsch (1960b) and Lutzker (1960) in the simpler two-choice games, but it must be recalled that they used total cooperation by an individual over all trials of a game.[3] Here, in addition to using a more complex game, the prediction is to the *terminal* behavior of the *pair* of players.[4] One negative finding which calls for special note is that internationalism scores did *not* predict significantly to criterion groups, even for those experimental groups playing under the simulated arms-race–disarmament condition. One highly internationalistic subject, an active advocate of disarmament and other liberal causes, displayed game behavior which was filled with unpredictable treachery and rearmament, at his opponent's expense. His comments on this performance were that while he felt he ought to move toward disarmament he also felt, at the same time, the challenge of the game. The

opportunity he perceived to make a killing was too great.

In one sense, it is not surprising that individual difference variables predict poorly to game outcomes. The very fact that Prisoner's Dilemma games so frequently result in "lock-ins" of either cooperation or noncooperation attests to the fact that randomly matched personalities do come to resemble one another in performance.

Such results suggest that individual personality has little effect on game behavior but do not rule out the possibility that personality characteristics of the pair, the match of traits between partners, may be effective. After all, the fact that diverse players come to resemble one another in game behavior does not explain why the resemblance is in cooperative (Dove-type) behavior in some cases and in much more competitive (Hawk-type) behavior in others. Similarity scores for a pair were obtained, using all personality measures in combination. Each measure was divided into thirds of high, medium, and low scores. When members of a pair both fell into the same third a score of 2 was entered, adjacent thirds were scored 1, and extreme thirds were scored 0. Summed over five variables this produced a possible range of similarity scores from 10 (very similar) to 0 (very dissimilar). Table 2 compares the more similar pairs (scores of 6 or more) with the less similar pairs (scores of 5 or less).

The data, again, show nothing of statistical significance and hardly anything in trends worthy of further examination. Refinement of similarity indices using actual numerical discrepancies and correcting for small intercorrelations among the separate measures would obviously contribute little to un-

---

[3]Actually the experimental situations are not strictly comparable. Deutsch predicted to the Prisoner's Dilemma game played once. Lutzker's payoff matrix presents the subject with an essentially different problem—the game of "chicken" rather than the Prisoner's Dilemma game. The two games are related, but in "chicken" unilateral cooperation is more rewarding than mutual defection and the motives for noncooperation are thus altered. The matrix shown on p. 301 above would be a "chicken" matrix if (0,0) were changed to, say, (−25, −25).

[4]Prediction from personality measures to gross levels of cooperation was only slightly more promising. No correlation as large as ± 0.4 was found.

TABLE 2   Personality Similarity of Doves, Hawks, and Mugwumps[a]

Similarity

	Low 5 or Less		High 6 or More		N
Doves	50%	(13)	50%	(13)	26
Hawks	41	(7)	59	(10)	17
Mugwumps	43	(9)	57	(12)	21
	45	(29)	55	(35)	64

[a]Entries are percentages over rows. Numbers in parenthesis are frequencies.

TABLE 3   Comparison of Dove Pairs High or Low on Tolerance for Ambiguity with Combined Hawk and Mugwump Pairs

Pair Rating on Tolerance for Ambiguity

	Hi-Hi or Hi-Med		Lo-Lo or Lo-Med		N
Doves	68.5%	(13)	31.5%	(6)	(19)
Hawks and Mugwumps	30.8	(8)	69.2	(18)	(26)
	46.6	(21)	53.4	(24)	(45)

χ^2: 16.00 $p < 0.01$

Note: Actual frequencies are given in parenthesis. N for this table is 45, i.e., 19 Dove pairs and 26 Hawk and Mugwump pairs. Pairs receiving Hi-Lo or Med–Med ratings are excluded from this analysis.

derstanding why some pairs become Doves, others Hawks, and others Mugwumps.

One single personality variable seemed to offer better differentiation of criterion groups than did the five-test battery. Pair members who were *both* high on tolerance for ambiguity were more likely to become Doves than were pairs lower on this variable ($p < 0.01$). Pair scores in tolerance for ambiguity are shown related to criterion groups in Table 3.

C. The Influence of the Experimental Setting

There were four experimental groups, as shown in the block design (see above, p. 302). Two groups, A_1 and A_2, played only abstract games. Groups S_1 and S_2 played only the simulated arms-race games. Groups A_1 and S_1 each started with fifteen long games followed by forty short games, whereas in groups A_2 and S_2 the forty short games came first. The number of pairs of Doves (cooperators), Hawks (defectors), and Mugwumps (in-betweens) in each of the four conditions is given in Table 4.

The findings in Table 4 can be summarized, but certain interactions between the effects of the two experimental conditions are difficult to interpret. A comparison of the conditions A_1 and S_1 (long first) with the A_2 and S_2 (short first) conditions in both the abstract and simulated forms would tend to indicate that playing the long game first pro-

TABLE 4   The Effect of Experimental Variations on Formation of Criterion Groups

	Doves		Hawks		Mugwumps		
Abstract—Long First (A_1)	68.8%	(11)	25.0%	(4)	6.2%	(1)	16
Abstract—Short First (A_2)	12.5	(2)	31.2	(5)	56.2	(9)	16
Simulated—Long First (S_1)	50.0	(8)	12.5	(2)	37.5	(6)	16
Simulated—Short First (S_2)	31.2	(5)	37.5	(6)	31.2	(5)	16
	40.6	(26)	26.5	(17)	32.8	(21)	64

χ^2 (total) 15.22; $p < 0.06$ (df: 2); χ^2 (interaction) 5.77; $p < 0.05$ (df: 2).

duces more Doves relative to the proportion of Hawks and Mugwumps. This long-short difference tends, however, to be muted in the simulated (S_1 and S_2) conditions. Hence, simulation makes the likelihood of becoming Doves or Mugwumps more nearly equal in the long-first and short-first conditions. However, the likelihood of becoming Hawks, while favored by the short-first conditions, shows this effect most markedly under simulated conditions. Arms-race labels, then, seem to be of secondary import and seem not to exert independent effects upon criterion groups. The labels do, however, show some effects in interaction with the other experimental condition.

The apparent conduciveness of long-first conditions A_1 and S_1 to the production of cooperating Doves may be seen in Table 5, which contrasts all long-first games with all short-first games.

This comparison shows, rather clearly, that partners who started by playing the slower long games and then switched to the rapid short ones were quite likely to turn into cooperating Doves. Conversely, those who began with the rapid short games were more likely to turn into either the undistinguished Mugwumps or the uncooperative Hawks. Whether this distinction is a function of boredom and/or need for activity is not known. Certainly, in starting from a fully armed position, twenty separate

opportunities to do something—in this case, to disarm—may be more difficult to resist than a single opportunity. Full control of this "mechanical" feature would require a reversal of the game with the initial level being the disarmed state. At this point, another hunch is that a cognitive reappraisal process quite apart from boredom is operating to induce cooperation (see discussion below).

When all players of abstract games are compared with all players in the arms-race-simulating games, the insignificance of simulation stands out clearly (see Table 6). Abstract games produce the same number of Doves, of Hawks, and of Mugwumps as do simulated games. In terms of final outcome for the pair, arms-race labels apparently make no difference.

One might argue that the absence of effects of the arms-race label should be expected, because the label does not affect the strategic structure of the game. However, the long and the short versions of the game are also strategically equivalent. Yet pronounced differences are observed in the two versions. Why? The authors suspect that something in the protracted nature of the long game permits more time for cognitive reappraisal of alternatives. Some yet unpublished results suggest that when the "player" is actually a team of three persons, a period of communication within the team (but not between teams) increases

TABLE 5   The Effect of Length of Initial 15 Games on Formation of Criterion Groups

	Doves		Hawks		Mugwumps		
Long First (A_1 & S_1)	59.4%	(19)	18.8%	(6)	21.9%	(7)	32
Short First (A_2 & S_2)	21.9	(7)	34.4	(11)	43.7	(14)	32
	31.2	(26)	26.5	(17)	32.8	(21)	64

$\chi^2 = 9.34$; $p < 0.01$ (df: 2).

TABLE 6   The Effect of Abstractness on Formation of Criterion Groups

	Doves		Hawks		Mugwumps		
Abstract (A_1 & A_2)	40.6%	(13)	28.1%	(9)	31.2%	(10)	32
Simulated (S_1 & S_2)	40.6	(13)	25.0	(8)	34.4	(11)	32
	31.2	(26)	26.5	(17)	32.8	(21)	64

χ^2: 0.11; NS (df: 2).

cooperation (Martin, 1964). Perhaps time favors such reappraisal by giving the individual player more chance to discuss alternatives with himself. Once begun, the rewards of the cooperative path tend to be reinforcing and self-perpetuating even if a switch is made to the short game.

D. Early Differences in Play

Criterion groups were distinguished, originally, by their performance on the last five of 55 consecutive games. Early experience in each of these criterion groups is defined by pair behavior during the first five games, in particular, but also by pair behavior in games six through ten.

Three measures of early game behavior were used: (1) *cooperativeness,* measured by the number of tokens turned from white to blue—the greater the number, the more cooperative; (2) *cooperative gesture,* defined as a play of the game in which a player converts 10 or more tokens, one-half or more of his total, from white to blue (in any given trial there may be a cooperative gesture by both, by one, or by neither player); (3) *discrepant outcome,* defined as a game in which one player converts five or more tokens from white to blue in excess of the number turned by his partner. The significance of discrepant outcomes, as a measure, is that they indicate an experience in which one player has gained at the other's expense. It means that one player on that trial was, unilaterally, cooperating more than his adversary. Over a period of five trials it is possible for both players to have both experiences—being at the short end and at the long end of the discrepant outcome. It is also possible that only one player experiences the short end; or discrepant outcomes may have been totally absent.

D-1. Some Indicators of Cooperativeness in Early Play   First let us consider each token turned from white to blue, from missile to factory, during any block of five trials of the game, to be a cumulative index of the cooperation achieved by that pair: i.e., the greater the number turned, the more the cooperation. Then, separating the Doves, Hawks, and Mugwumps according to their eventual performance as before, we find some very early differentiation between groups. During the first five trials the average Dove converted 8.5 tokens per game, the average Hawk 4.8 tokens, and the average Mugwump 4.2. (The Hawk–Mugwump difference is not statistically significant.) Fuller data are shown in Table 7.

The amount of cooperation for each of the three criterion groups may be calculated for every block of five non-overlapping trials, as shown in Figure 2.

TABLE 7   Cooperativeness in Early Games

Games	Doves	Hawks	Mug-wumps	$F_2/637$	p
1–5	8.5	4.8	4.2	26.66	<0.05
6–10	9.3	3.3	5.1	35.76	<0.05

The Dove group clearly retains its distinctiveness from the others. The Hawk group establishes itself below the Mugwumps on the seventh trial and remains there through all remaining trials. In sum, then, our findings show that Doves start higher on the cooperativeness index and ascend rapidly. Hawks start lower and decline, while Mugwumps start lower and ascend slowly.

The very fact that lock-ins (of Dove-like cooperation or Hawk-like defection) do occur suggests a degree to which partners come to play like each other. But how alike were partners during the first five games? Some insight into this question is given by calculating the performance of Dove members from each

Dove pair who cooperated less than their partners. Average cooperation for the more niggardly Doves was 6.6 tokens per games (first five games). This still exceeds the average Hawk player's 4.8 tokens and even exceeds the average of the more cooperative member of each Hawk pair, which was 5.6 tokens.

The finding suggests that the relatively high level of early cooperation by those who later proved themselves to be Doves was not the result of a single player extending himself unilaterally. However, other findings reopen the question. If we examine the case in which one *and only one* player converted more than 50 percent of his tokens from white to blue (disarmament), we find that 10 out of 26 Dove pairs met this criterion over the first five games. Meanwhile, only two out of 17 Hawk pairs and two out of 21 Mugwump pairs showed one and only one member cooperating more than halfway.

Again, if we examine the instances in which a disparity of 25 or more tokens (an average of five tokens or more per game) occurred over the first five games, the same pattern emerges. Seven out of 26 Dove pairs showed this disparity. However, only two out of 17 Hawk pairs

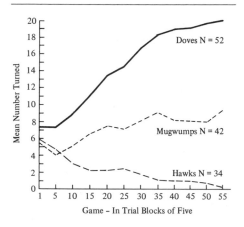

Figure 2 Comparison of time courses of cooperative moves between three criterion groups distinguished by pair performances on the last five trials.

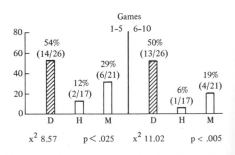

Figure 3 Percentage of pairs showing at least one mutual cooperative gesture. D: Doves; H: Hawks; M: Mugwumps.

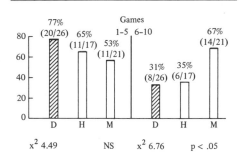

Figure 4   Percentage of pairs showing at least one unilateral cooperative gesture.

and three out of 21 Mugwump pairs showed this disparity. Obviously this does not resolve the case for or against the usefulness of early unilateral efforts in predicting ultimate criterion groups. But it does suggest the need for a finer analysis of game-by-game play, and such an analysis follows.

D-2. Early Cooperative Gestures as Predictors of Terminal Pair Performances   The data on cooperative gestures, converting 10 or more of one's white or weapon tokens to blue, are given in Figures 3 through 5.

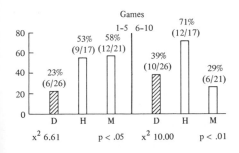

Figure 5   Percentage of pairs showing (four or more) mutual noncooperative gestures. Use of four or more as an index reflects an approximate median split.

Certain patterns emerge. First, if a pair had even a single early experience of mutual cooperation, i.e., both making cooperative gestures on the same trial, that pair was likely to become a Dove pair.

Second, we observe that instances of simultaneous gestures of cooperation were relatively infrequent during early play. The occurrence of unilateral gestures was more frequent among each of the three criterion groups.

Third, few of the Mugwump pairs were making cooperative gestures during the first five trials. The situation changed in the second five trials. Here numerous Mugwump pairs showed such gestures. But—as may be seen in Table 8—the gestures were not made simultaneously and, in fact, they tended to be made by only one player during the entire block of trials. By contrast, individual Hawks extended unilateral gestures of cooperation more often in the very first five trials. But, faced with nonreciprocation, these gestures became much less frequent in the second block of five trials. In sharp contrast, *both members* of Dove pairs tended to extend gestures during early play. In fact, by the second block of five trials those Dove pairs which were not demonstrating cooperative gestures by both members were likely to be demonstrating few unilateral gestures either. Some Dove pairs apparently showed mutual willingness to cooperate from the start. The other Dove pairs were apparently more like the Hawks than like the Mugwumps in their early play. This can be seen also in Table 8, which shows that both Dove and Hawk groups increased their frequency of mutually noncooperative, armed gestures from the first to the second block of five trials, while Mug-

TABLE 8   Effect of Reciprocation of Cooperative Gestures on Formation of Criterion Groups

Production of Cooperative Gestures

	Simultaneous and *mutual*		Unilateral		None		
			Games 1–5				
Doves	66%	(17)	23%	(6)	12%	(3)	26
Hawks	12	(2)	65	(11)	24	(4)	17
Mugwumps	29	(6)	29	(6)	43	(9)	21
	32.5	(25)	32.5	(23)	25	(16)	64
			Games 6–10				
Doves	54%	(14)	8%	(2)	34%	(10)	26
Hawks	12	(2)	12	(2)	77	(13)	17
Mugwumps	29	(6)	43	(9)	29	(6)	21
	35	(22)	20	(13)	45	(29)	64

Note: Figures given are for the occurrence of a single incident. None = mutual non-cooperative or armed gesture.

wumps reduced their frequency of mutual defection.

D-3. Early Discrepant Outcomes as Predictors of Terminal Pair Performance   A discrepant outcome, as noted earlier, means that one player has suffered and the other has benefited during a trial. What does such an experience do to the pair's future? Discrepant outcomes occurred in almost all pairs. Figure 6 compares the instances in which such

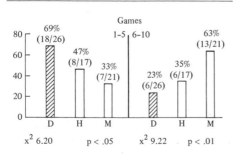

Figure 6   Percentage of pairs showing related (two or more) discrepant outcomes.

outcomes were repeated (occurred at least twice within a block of five trials).

During the first five trials, significantly more Doves than Hawks or Mugwumps experienced two or more discrepant outcomes. However, by the second block of five trials the Dove pairs were performing most congruently, showing fewest discrepant outcomes. Only the Mugwumps increased their frequency of discrepant outcomes during trials six through ten. This finding lends support to a conjecture introduced earlier—that even before the lock-in occurs, Dove and Hawk pairs tend to be moving toward greater symmetry (or sensitivity) in play than is true for the Mugwumps.

Figure 6 does not indicate whether the repeated occurrences of discrepant outcomes always favored the same player or whether both players had the experience of being both victor and vanquished. Table 9 contrasts relative frequencies with which the discrepant experiences were reciprocal, unidirec-

TABLE 9   Reciprocation of Discrepant Outcomes and the
Formation of Criterion Groups

Production of Discrepant Outcomes

		Reciprocal		*Unidirectional*		*None*		
				Games 1-5				
Doves	42%	(11)	50%	(13)	8%	(2)	26
Hawks	6	(1)	71	(12)	23	(4)	17
Mugwumps	14	(3)	53	(11)	33	(7)	21
	24	(15)	56	(36)	20	(13)	64
χ^2: 11.69; p < 0.025							
				Games 6-10				
Doves	62%	(16)	31%	(8)	8%	(2)	26
Hawks	12	(2)	71	(12)	17	(3)	17
Mugwumps	43	(9)	38	(8)	19	(4)	21
	42	(27)	44	(28)	14	(9)	64
χ^2: 6.87; p < 0.10							

tional, or entirely absent for the three criterion groups.

During the first five games, only the Dove pairs showed a high frequency of cases in which both players experienced the discrepancy from both directions. By the second block of five trials, the Doves and the Hawks showed the greatest number of pairs with no discrepant outcomes at all. The Mugwump pairs were still showing discrepancies during those trials. The data suggest that early experience of the good (and bad) effects of incongruent performance is an indication of future Dove-like cooperation—*if* each player has had a taste of the medicine of being caught disarmed and an opportunity of seeing the other player cooperate more than himself.

DISCUSSION AND CONCLUSIONS

The terminal states of Dove, Hawk, and Mugwump may be viewed as products of the forces that bring individuals into

social units which are either cohesive and facilitative, or divisive and despairing, or uncertain and unstable. Evidence from this experiment suggests that the locus of these forces lies primarily in the circumstances of the interaction rather than in such characteristics as personality traits brought to the situation. In addition, the early trials of interaction, like the early years, may have enduring effects upon later behavior.

From analysis of early interaction it seems clear that the interaction pattern which induces mutual cooperation is a two-party affair. For lasting cooperation, parties to a conflict situation do have to make overtures, for that is—in the last analysis—all they can do. But what also seems necessary is that cooperative gestures of the other are met with similar responses on one's own part at early stages in the conflict process.

Gestures of cooperation, whether or not they are defined as we have done here, are clearly both causes and effects of game performance. Our examination of the result of natural game conditions indicates that a unilateral initiative toward cooperation, if not quickly reciprocated (i.e., if it remains unilateral), does not lead to the development of a cooperative pair. On the other hand someone must initiate cooperative play, and it is relatively rare, in the absence of overt communication, that both players do this simultaneously. The findings on cooperative gestures (Table 8) and discrepant outcomes (Table 9) suggest that both unilateral and reciprocal elements are important in game performance. Their relative importance, however, would seem to be most readily determinable in a more structured experimental situation with stooges or a false feedback procedure.

At some point in the sequential moves and countermoves of a conflict situation it seems likely that a person takes cognizance of the intent which the other player is trying to communicate (or perhaps communicating without trying) through his moves. One subject, for example, offered the following comment after the experiment: "At first I thought he [the other player] was stupid letting me win like that. But after a while I saw that he was trying to get me to turn over more factories so we could both win." Obviously, there was a cost involved here in the signaling of intent. The authors are currently working on a modification of the game which permits signals of intention, in the form of inspections, without cost to either player.

The realization that behavior can be used to communicate one's hopes and expectations and threats to the other player raises the contest from what may be viewed initially as a game against nature, a game in which the other's moves are only partly predictable and

wholly out of reach of one's influence. A second realization, however, seems even more critical for enduring cooperation in a pair. It is the experience that both oneself and the other party are really part of the same system, unified by a common fate, and no longer independent decision-makers. Viewed from this perspective, the game does have a rational or strategic resolution which is easily found: cooperate fully on every trial. We have numerous instances of such comments as: "I could see from the start that turning them all over was the only thing for *us* to do." This perception of "we" or "us" is clearest if we look at some comments of Dove pairs whose cooperation came late and who played more like Hawks at the beginning. "I could see at this point that *we were both* in a rut and weren't going anyplace." The data we have showing more frequent early instances of mutual cooperative gestures by Dove pairs or more frequent reversing of roles in the case of discrepant outcomes suggest the very conditions which might teach the lesson of interdependence and common destiny.

Why a pair of potential antagonists seems better able to learn this during an early run of protracted decision games (long games) than during an equivalent run of short games is not entirely clear. At this point, our best guess seems to be that slowing the pace of the decision process, before the pattern of play has settled, enhances the opportunity for players to recast their concept of the conflict situation. Such cognitive recasting could then produce the realization that (1) communication through behavior is occurring, or (2) the two parties are really part of the same system, or both. From among five individual difference measures, only mutual tolerance for ambiguity seemed relevant to arriving at mutual cooperation. The ability to reframe old perceptions is a part of tolerance for ambiguity. The finding would seem consistent with the conclusion that a cognitive recasting which occurs during the moves and countermoves of an interpersonal conflict is necessary for the self-organization of the two parties into a single cohesive unit.

The most remarkable thing about the Hawks as a group is that they hardly ever tried to cooperate. Following a few unilateral and unreciprocated gestures at the very beginning, the frequency of cooperative gestures (either unilateral or reciprocal) becomes so low that one might conclude that one reason why Hawks never learned to cooperate is because they never experimented with or explored the communication channels that the game was structured to provide. One cannot say of them, as a group, that they are more deceitful or treacherous or aggressively competitive players. On the basis of game performance, what stands out is their conservatism, caution, and reluctance to try a new approach. This observation is also supported by the fact that the one personality indicator that did predict to game outcomes was tolerance for ambiguity. Players who were less tolerant of ambiguity seemed unwilling to explore the various potentials in the game situation.

In contrast, the Doves as a group were experimenting with cooperation from the start. Some tried and succeeded early, others failed but tried again later and were successful. Some of them use, and some of them report, interesting strategies of rewards and punishments intended to lure the other player toward mutual trust. The description of such strategies and the search for their determinants and their consequences make an intriguing problem for future research.

The Mugwump pairs probably represent several entities. Some may have contained a member who never changed his initial perception that success in the game depended solely upon outsmarting one's partner. Others may have rejected the formation of a predictable social unit because of fascination with gamesmanship—much like the Don Juans who enjoy the hunt but cannot stay with the marriage. One might argue that all individuals faced with sustained interaction do eventually develop stable and reciprocal behavior patterns—but our experiments were continued through only 55 trials.

We have stressed in our conclusions the theme that reciprocal behaviors at an early stage of the interaction process are of major importance in the development of later trust, and that personality indicators seem less relevant. Two alternative theories are brought to the fore by this. The first says that circumstances of play alone determine the resolution of conflict. By chance, this theory would state, certain moves made by one party meet moves made by the other, and the distribution of these random pairings provides the starting point for stochastic processes (probabilities of performance contingent on the prior happenings) which lead to the final outcomes.

The alternate theory is not that the player's cooperation is a product of some inherent propensity, a personal proclivity which he carries about either to cooperate or not. The extremely high correlation of cooperation rates found between randomly matched pair members seems adequate for rejection of such a theory. But the alternative to the random-start, stochastic-interaction theory is the view that players do bring to the game setting certain proclivities, not to act in a certain way, but rather to *react* in certain ways to the contingent circumstances presented by the other player's behavior. To test this latter theory one will have to think of personality traits as contingent reaction propensities; measure these propensities; and study their effects upon experimentally arranged contingencies of opponent's behavior. This is an important task for future research. What our present research has done is to help crystallize these alternative theories regarding the ways in which interaction synthesizes individuals into social units.

REFERENCES

Berger, E. M. "The Relation between Expressed Acceptance of Self and Expressed Acceptance of Others," *Journal of Abnormal and Social Psychology*, **47** (1952), 778–83.

Deutsch, M. "Trust and Suspicion," *Journal of Conflict Resolution*, **2**, 4 (Dec. 1958), 265–79.

———. "Trust, Trustworthiness, and the F Scale," *Journal of Abnormal and Social Psychology*, **61** (1960b), 138–40.

Kogan, N., and M. A. Wallach. "The Effect of Anxiety on Relations Between Subjective Age and Caution in an Older Sample." In P. H. Hoch and J. Zubin (eds.), *Psychopathology of Aging*. New York: Grune and Stratton, 1961.

Levinson, D. J. "Authoritarian Personality and Foreign Policy," *Journal of Conflict Resolution*, **1**, 1 (Mar. 1957), 37–57.

Lutzker, D. "Internationalism as a Predictor of Cooperative Game Behavior," *Journal of Conflict Resolution*, **4**, 4 (Dec. 1960), 426–35.

Martin, Niles W., Jr. "Some Effects of Communication of Group Behavior in Prisoner's Dilemma." Unpublished Ph.D. thesis, Case Institute of Technology, 1964.

O'Connor, Patricia. "Intolerance for Ambiguity and Abstract Reasoning Ability," *Journal of Abnormal and Social Psychology*, **47** (1952), Supplement.

Pilisuk, M., and A. Rapoport. "A Non-Zero-Sum Game Model of Some Disarmament Problems." Paper given at Peace Research Conference, University of Chicago, November 1963.

———, ———. "Stepwise Disarmament and Sudden Destruction in a Two-Person Game," *Journal of Conflict Resolution*, **8**, 1 (Mar. 1964), 36–49.

Rapoport, A. *Prisoner's Dilemma*. Ann Arbor, Mich.: University of Michigan Press, 1965.

Samson, P. L., and H. P. Smith. "A Scale to Measure World-Mindedness Attitudes," *Journal of Social Psychology*, **45** (1957), 99–106.

Webster, H., N. Sanford, and M. Freedman. "A New Instrument for Studying Authoritarianism," *Journal of Psychology*, **40** (1955), 73–84.

THIRTEEN
Research on Complex Human Behavior: II. Experiments in Quasi-Natural Settings

23

Some Conditions of Obedience and Disobedience to Authority

Stanley Milgram

In the following article, Stanley Milgram summarizes a series of studies he did on the subject of obedience. To what extent will people obey commands which require them to do seemingly reprehensible things? Milgram shows that the extent to which the typical subject will obey such commands is far greater than we would predict; in fact, their obedience is downright shocking! The results of his studies are very interesting, but from a methodological point of view they are an exceptionally fine illustration of the experimentalist's capacity for researching complex human phenomena in highly realistic settings. Most experimenters would have been likely either to research some other topic, regarding this one as too difficult for experimental investigation, or to do research on the topic by finding an analog—animal or other—of the behavior of interest. Milgram insisted on using an "ecologically valid" experimental arrangement, and found that he could do so with great success.

Reprinted from *Human Relations*, 1965, **18**, 57–75, by permission of the author and Plenum Publishing Company.

This research was supported by two grants from the National Science Foundation: NSF G-17916 and NSF G-24152. Exploratory studies carried out in 1960 were financed by a grant from the Higgins Funds of Yale University. I am grateful to John T. Williams, James J. McDonough, and Emil Elges for the important part they played in the project. Thanks are due also to Alan Elms, James Miller, Taketo Murata, and Stephen Stier for their aid as graduate assistants. My wife, Sasha, performed many valuable services. Finally, I owe a profound debt to the many people in New Haven and Bridgeport who served as subjects.

The situation in which one agent commands another to hurt a third turns up time and again as a significant theme in human relations. It is powerfully expressed in the story of Abraham, who is commanded by God to kill his son. It is no accident that Kierkegaard, seeking to orient his thought to the central themes of human experience, chose Abraham's conflict as the springboard to his philosophy.

War too moves forward on the triad of an authority which commands a person to destroy the enemy, and perhaps all organized hostility may be viewed as a theme and variation on the three elements of authority, executant, and victim.[1] We describe an experimental program, recently concluded at Yale University, in which a particular expression of this conflict is studied by experimental means.

In its most general form the problem may be defined thus: if X tells Y to hurt Z, under what conditions will Y carry out the command of X and under what conditions will he refuse. In the more limited form possible in laboratory research, the question becomes: if an experimenter tells a subject to hurt another person, under what conditions will the subject go along with this instruction, and under what conditions will he refuse to obey. The laboratory problem is not so much a dilution of the general statement as one concrete expression of the many particular forms this question may assume.

One aim of the research was to study behavior in a strong situation of deep consequence to the participants, for the psychological forces operative in powerful and lifelike forms of the conflict may not be brought into play under diluted conditions.

This approach meant, first, that we had a special obligation to protect the welfare and dignity of the persons who took part in the study; subjects were, of necessity, placed in a difficult predicament, and steps had to be taken to ensure their wellbeing before they were discharged from the laboratory. Toward this end, a careful, post-experimental treatment was devised and has been carried through for subjects in all conditions.[2]

---

[1]Consider, for example, J. P. Scott's analysis of war in his monograph on aggression:

". . . while the actions of key individuals in a war may be explained in terms of direct stimulation to aggression, vast numbers of other people are involved simply by being part of an organized society.

". . . For example, at the beginning of World War I an Austrian archduke was assassinated in Sarajevo. A few days later soldiers from all over Europe were marching toward each other, not because they were stimulated by the archduke's misfortune, but because they had been trained to obey orders." (Slightly rearranged from Scott (1958), *Aggression*, p. 103.)

[2]It consisted of an extended discussion with the experimenter and, of equal importance, a friendly reconciliation with the victim. It is made clear that the victim did not receive painful electric shocks. After the completion of the experimental series, subjects were sent a detailed report of the results and full purposes of the experimental program. A formal assessment of this procedure points to its overall effectiveness. Of the subjects, 83.7 per cent indicated that they were glad to have taken part in the study; 15.1 per cent reported neutral feelings; and 1.3 per cent stated that they were sorry to have participated. A large number of subjects spontaneously requested that they be used in further experimentation. Four-fifths of the subjects felt that more experiments of this sort should be carried out, and 74 per cent indicated that they had learned something of personal importance as a result of being in the study. Furthermore, a university psychiatrist, experienced in outpatient treatment, interviewed a sample of experimental subjects with the aim of

TERMINOLOGY

If Y follows the command of X we shall say that he has obeyed X; if he fails to carry out the command of X, we shall say that he has disobeyed X. The terms *to obey* and to *disobey,* as used here, refer to the subject's overt action only, and carry no implication for the motive or experiential states accompanying the action.[3]

---

uncovering possible injurious effects resulting from participation. No such effects were in evidence. Indeed, subjects typically felt that their participation was instructive and enriching. A more detailed discussion of this question can be found in Milgram (1964).

[3] *To obey* and *to disobey* are not the only terms one could use in describing the critical action of *Y*. One could say that *Y* is cooperating with *X*, or displays conformity with regard to *X*'s commands. However, *cooperation* suggests that *X* agrees with *Y*'s ends, and understands the relationship between his own behavior and the attainment of those ends. (But the experimental procedure, and, in particular, the experimenter's command that the subject shock the victim even in the absence of a response from the victim, preclude such understanding.) Moreover, cooperation implies status parity for the co-acting agents, and neglects the asymmetrical, dominance-subordination element prominent in the laboratory relationship between experimenter and subject. *Conformity* has been used in other important contexts in social psychology, and most frequently refers to imitating the judgments or actions of others when no explicit requirement for imitation has been made. Furthermore, in the present study there are two sources of social pressure: pressure from the experimenter issuing the commands, and pressure from the victim to stop the punishment. It is the pitting of a common man (the victim) against an authority (the experimenter) that is the distinctive feature of the conflict. At a point in the experiment the victim demands that he be let free. The experimenter insists that the subject continue to administer shocks. Which act of the subject can be interpreted as conformity? The subject may conform to the wishes of his peer or to the wishes

To be sure, the everyday use of the word *obedience* is not entirely free from complexities. It refers to action within widely varying situations, and connotes diverse motives within those situations: a child's obedience differs from a soldier's obedience, or the love, honor, and *obey* of the marriage vow. However, a consistent behavioral relationship is indicated in most uses of the term: in the act of obeying, a person does what another person tells him to do. Y obeys X if he carries out the prescription for action which X has addressed to him; the term suggests, moreover, that some form of dominance-subordination, or hierarchical element, is part of the situation in which the transaction between X and Y occurs.

A subject who complies with the entire series of experimental commands will be termed an *obedient* subject; one who at any point in the command series defies the experimenter will be called a *disobedient* or *defiant* subject. As used in this report, the terms refer only to the subject's performance in the experiment, and do not necessarily imply a general personality disposition to submit to or reject authority.

---

of the experimenter, and conformity in one direction means the absence of conformity in the other. Thus the word has no useful reference in this setting, for the dual and conflicting social pressures cancel out its meaning.

In the final analysis, the linguistic symbol representing the subject's action must take its meaning from the concrete context in which that action occurs; and there is probably no word in everyday language that covers the experimental situation exactly, without omissions or irrelevant connotations. It is partly for convenience, therefore, that the terms *obey* and *disobey* are used to describe the subject's actions. At the same time, our use of the words is highly congruent with dictionary meaning.

SUBJECT POPULATION

The subjects used in all experimental conditions were male adults, residing in the greater New Haven and Bridgeport areas, aged 20 to 50 years, and engaged in a wide variety of occupations. Each experimental condition described in this report employed 40 fresh subjects and was carefully balanced for age and occupational types. The occupational composition for each experiment was: workers, skilled and unskilled: 40 per cent; white collar, sales, business: 40 per cent; professionals: 20 per cent. The occupations were intersected with three age categories (subjects in 20s, 30s, and 40s, assigned to each condition in the proportions of 20, 40, and 40 per cent respectively).

THE GENERAL LABORATORY PROCEDURE[4]

The focus of the study concerns the amount of electric shock a subject is willing to administer to another person when ordered by an experimenter to give the 'victim' increasingly more severe punishment. The act of administering shock is set in the context of a learning experiment, ostensibly designed to study the effect of punishment on memory. Aside from the experimenter,

[4]A more detailed account of the laboratory procedure can be found in Milgram (1963). A similar and independently evolved experimental procedure, employing a shock generator, victim, and learning task, was reported by Buss (1961). Buss used the technique for studying aggression, not obedience, and did not make use of the fundamental measure employed in the present study: break-off points. His investigation promises to be a useful complement to the present research.

one naïve subject and one accomplice perform in each session. On arrival each subject is paid $4.50. After a general talk by the experimenter, telling how little scientists know about the effect of punishment on memory, subjects are informed that one member of the pair will serve as teacher and one as learner. A rigged drawing is held so that the naïve subject is always the teacher, and the accomplice becomes the learner. The learner is taken to an adjacent room and strapped into an "electric chair."

The naïve subject is told that it is his task to teach the learner a list of paired associates, to test him on the list, and to administer punishment whenever the learner errs in the test. Punishment takes the form of electric shock, delivered to the learner by means of a shock generator controlled by the naïve subject. The teacher is instructed to increase the intensity of electric shock one step on the generator on each error. The learner, according to plan, provides many wrong answers, so that before long the naïve subject must give him the strongest shock on the generator. Increases in shock level are met by increasingly insistent demands from the learner that the experiment be stopped because of the growing discomfort to him. However, in clear terms the experimenter orders the teacher to continue with the procedure in disregard of the learner's protests. *Thus, the naïve subject must resolve a conflict between two mutually incompatible demands from the social field. He may continue to follow the orders of the experimenter and shock the learner with increasing severity, or he may refuse to follow the orders of the experimenter and heed the learner's pleas. The experimenter's authority operates not in a free field, but against ever-mounting countervailing pressures from the person being punished.*

A few technical points need to be considered before the findings of the study are described. For the purpose of delivering shock, a simulated shock generator is used, with 30 clearly marked voltage levels that range from 15 to 450 volts (and each activated by one of 30 individual lever switches set in a horizontal line). The naïve subject is given a sample shock of 45 volts to convince him of the authenticity of the instrument. The generator bears verbal designations that range from "Slight Shock" to "Danger: Severe Shock."

The responses of the victim are standardized on tape, and each protest is coordinated to a particular voltage level on the shock generator. Starting with 75 volts the learner begins to grunt and moan. At 150 volts he demands to be let out of the experiment. At 180 volts he cries out that he can no longer stand the pain. At 300 volts he refuses to provide any more answers to the memory test, insisting that he is no longer a participant in the experiment and must be freed. In response to this last tactic, the experimenter instructs the naïve subject to treat the absence of an answer as equivalent to a wrong answer, and to follow the usual shock procedure. The experimenter reinforces his demand with the statement: "You have no other choice, you must go on!" (This imperative is used whenever the naïve subject tries to break off the experiment.) If the subject refuses to give the next higher level of shock, the experiment is considered at an end. A quantitative value is assigned to the subject's performance based on the maximum intensity shock he administered before breaking off. Thus any subject's score may range from zero (for a subject unwilling to administer the first shock level) to 30 (for a subject who proceeds to the highest voltage level on the board). For any particular subject and for any particular experimental condition the degree to which participants have followed the experimenter's orders may be specified with a numerical value, corresponding to the metric on the shock generator.

This laboratory situation gives us a framework in which to study the subject's reactions to the principal conflict of the experiment. Again, this conflict is between the experimenter's demands that he continue to administer the electric shock, and the learner's demands, which become increasingly more insistent, that the experiment be stopped. The crux of the study is to vary systematically the factors believed to alter the degree of obedience to the experimental commands, to learn under what conditions submission to authority is most probable, and under what conditions defiance is brought to the fore.

PILOT STUDIES

Pilot studies for the present research were completed in the winter of 1960; they differed from the regular experiments in a few details: for one, the victim was placed behind a silvered glass, with the light balance on the glass such that the victim could be dimly perceived by the subject (Milgram, 1961).

Though essentially qualitative in treatment, these studies pointed to several significant features of the experimental situation. At first no vocal feedback was used from the victim. It was thought that the verbal and voltage designations on the control panel would create sufficient pressure to curtail the subject's obedience. However, this was not the case. In the absence of protests from the learner, virtually all subjects, once commanded, went blithely to the end of the board, seemingly indifferent to the verbal designations ("Extreme Shock" and "Danger: Severe Shock"). This deprived us of an adequate basis for scaling obedient tendencies. A force had to be introduced that would strengthen the subject's resistance to the experimenter's commands, and reveal individual differences in terms of a distribution of break-off points.

This force took the form of protests from the victim. Initially, mild protests were used, but proved inadequate. Subsequently, more vehement protests were inserted into the experimental procedure. To our consternation, even the strongest protests from the victim did not prevent all subjects from administering the harshest punishment ordered by the experimenter; but the protests did lower the mean maximum shock somewhat and created some spread in the subject's performance; therefore, the victim's cries were standardized on tape and incorporated into the regular experimental procedure.

The situation did more than highlight the technical difficulties of finding a workable experimental procedure: it indicated that subjects would obey authority to a greater extent than we had supposed. It also pointed to the importance of feedback from the victim in controlling the subject's behavior.

One further aspect of the pilot study was that subjects frequently averted their eyes from the person they were shocking, often turning their heads in an awkward and conspicuous manner. One subject explained: "I didn't want to see the consequences of what I had done." Observers wrote:

. . . subjects showed a reluctance to look at the victim, whom they could see through the glass in front of them. When this fact was brought to their attention they indicated that it caused them discomfort to see the victim in agony. We note, however, that although the subject refuses to look at the victim, he continues to administer shocks.

This suggested that the salience of the victim may have, in some degree, regulated the subject's performance. If, in obeying the experimenter, the subject found it necessary to avoid scrutiny of the victim, would the converse be true? If the victim were rendered increasingly more salient to the subject, would obedience diminish? The first set of regular experiments was designed to answer this question.

IMMEDIACY OF THE VICTIM

This series consisted of four experimental conditions. In each condition the victim was brought "psychologically" closer to the subject giving him shocks.

In the first condition (Remote Feedback) the victim was placed in another room and could not be heard or seen by the subject, except that, at 300 volts, he pounded on the wall in protest. After 315 volts he no longer answered or was heard from.

The second condition (Voice Feedback) was identical to the first except that voice protests were introduced. As in the first condition the victim was placed in an adjacent room, but his complaints could be heard clearly through a door left slightly ajar, and through the walls of the laboratory.[5]

[5]It is difficult to convey on the printed page the full tenor of the victim's responses, for we have

The third experimental condition (Proximity) was similar to the second, except that the victim was now placed in the same room as the subject, and $1\frac{1}{2}$ feet from him. Thus he was visible as well as audible, and voice cues were provided.

The fourth, and final, condition of this series (Touch-Proximity) was identical to the third, with this exception: the victim received a shock only when his hand rested on a shockplate. At the 150-volt level the victim again demanded to be let free and, in this condition, refused to place his hand on the shockplate. The experimenter ordered the naïve subject to force the victim's hand onto the plate. Thus obedience in this condition required that the subject have physical contact with the victim

in order to give him punishment beyond the 150-volt level.

Forty adult subjects were studied in each condition. The data revealed that obedience was significantly reduced as the victim was rendered more immediate to the subject. The mean maximum shock for the conditions is shown in Figure 1.

Expressed in terms of the proportion of obedient to defiant subjects, the findings are that 34 percent of the subjects defied the experimenter in the Remote condition, 37.5 percent in Voice Feedback, 60 percent in Proximity, and 70 percent in Touch-Proximity.

How are we to account for this effect? A first conjecture might be that as the victim was brought closer the subject became more aware of the intensity of

---

no adequate notation for vocal intensity, timing, and general qualities of delivery. Yet these features are crucial to producing the effect of an increasingly severe reaction to mounting voltage levels. (They can be communicated fully only by sending interested parties the recorded tapes.) In general terms, however, the victim indicates no discomfort until the 75-volt shock is administered, at which time there is a light grunt in response to the punishment. Similar reactions follow the 90- and 105-volt shocks, and at 120 volts the victim shouts to the experimenter that the shocks are becoming painful. Painful groans are heard on administration of the 135-volt shock, and at 150 volts the victim cries out, "Experimenter, get me out of here! I won't be in the experiment any more! I refuse to go on!" Cries of this type continue with generally rising intensity, so that at 180 volts the victim cries out, "I can't stand the pain," and by 270 volts his response to the shock is definitely an agonized scream. Throughout, he insists that he be let out of the experiment. At 300 volts the victim shouts in desperation that he will no longer provide answers to the memory test; and at 315 volts, after a violent scream, he reaffirms with vehemence that he is no longer a participant. From this point on, he provides no

answers, but shrieks in agony whenever a shock is administered; this continues through 450 volts. Of course, many subjects will have broken off before this point.

A revised and stronger set of protests was used in all experiments outside the Proximity series. Naturally, new baseline measures were established for all comparisons using the new set of protests.

There is overwhelming evidence that the great majority of subjects, both obedient and defiant, accepted the victims' reactions as genuine. The evidence takes the form of: (a) tension created in the subjects (see discussion of tension); (b) scores on "estimated pain" scales filled out by subjects immediately after the experiment; (c) subjects' accounts of their feelings in post-experimental interviews; and (d) quantifiable responses to questionnaires distributed to subjects several months after their participation in the experiments. This matter will be treated fully in a forthcoming monograph.

(The procedure in all experimental conditions was to have the naïve subject announce the voltage level before administering each shock, so that—independently of the victim's responses—he was continually reminded of delivering punishment of ever-increasing severity.)

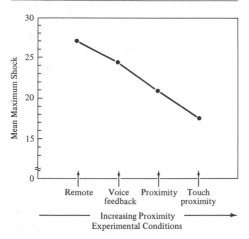

Figure 1   Mean maxima in proximity series.

his suffering and regulated his behavior accordingly. This makes sense, but our evidence does not support the interpretation. There are no consistent differences in the attributed level of pain across the four conditions (i.e. the amount of pain experienced by the victim as estimated by the subject and expressed on a 14-point scale). But it is easy to speculate about alternative mechanisms:

Empathic cues.   In the Remote and to a lesser extent the Voice Feedback condition, the victim's suffering possesses an abstract, remote quality for the subject. He is aware, but only in a conceptual sense, that his actions cause pain to another person; the fact is apprehended, but not felt. The phenomenon is common enough. The bombardier can reasonably suppose that his weapons will inflict suffering and death, yet this knowledge is divested of affect, and does not move him to a felt, emotional response to the suffering resulting from his actions. Similar observations have been made in

wartime. It is possible that the visual cues associated with the victim's suffering trigger empathic responses in the subject and provide him with a more complete grasp of the victim's experience. Or it is possible that the empathic responses are themselves unpleasant, possessing drive properties which cause the subject to terminate the arousal situation. Diminishing obedience, then, would be explained by the enrichment of empathic cues in the successive experimental conditions.

Denial and narrowing of the cognitive field.   The Remote condition allows a narrowing of the cognitive field so that the victim is put out of mind. The subject no longer considers the act of depressing a lever relevant to moral judgment, for it is no longer associated with the victim's suffering. When the victim is close it is more difficult to exclude him phenomenologically. He necessarily intrudes on the subject's awareness since he is continuously visible. In the Remote conditions his existence and reactions are made known only after the shock has been administered. The auditory feedback is sporadic and discontinuous. In the Proximity conditions his inclusion in the immediate visual field renders him a continuously salient element for the subject. The mechanism of denial can no longer be brought into play. One subject in the Remote condition said: "It's funny how you really begin to forget that there's a guy out there, even though you can hear him. For a long time I just concentrated on pressing the switches and reading the words."

If in the proximity condition the subject is in an improved position to observe the victim, the reverse is also true. The actions of the subject now come under proximal scrutiny by the victim. Possibly, it is easier to harm a person when he is unable to observe our action than when he can see what we are doing. His surveillance of the action directed against him may give rise to shame, or guilt, which may then serve to curtail the action. Many expressions of language refer to the discomfort or inhibitions that arise in face-to-face confrontation. It is often said that it is easier to criticize a man "behind his back" than to "attack him to his face." If we are in the process of lying to a person it is reputedly difficult to "stare him in the eye." We "turn away from others in shame" or in "embarrassment" and this action serves to reduce our discomfort. The manifest function of allowing the victim of a firing squad to be blindfolded is to make the occasion less stressful for him, but it may also serve a latent function of reducing the stress of the executioner. In short, in the Proximity conditions, the subject may sense that he has become more salient in the victim's field of awareness. Possibly he becomes more self-conscious, embarrassed, and inhibited in his punishment of the victim.

Phenomenal unity of act. In the Remote conditions it is more difficult for the subject to gain a sense of *relatedness* between his own actions and the consequences of these actions for the victim. There is a physical and spatial separation of the act and its consequences. The subject depresses a lever in one room, and protests and cries are heard from another. The two events are in correlation, yet they lack a compelling phenomenological unity. The structure of a meaningful act—*I am hurting a man*—breaks down because of the spatial arrangements, in a manner somewhat analogous to the disappearance of phi phenomena when the blinking lights are spaced too far apart. The unity is more fully achieved in the Proximity conditions as the victim is brought closer to the action that causes him pain. It is rendered complete in Touch-Proximity.

Incipient group formation. Placing the victim in another room not only takes him further from the subject, but the subject and the experimenter are drawn relatively closer. There is incipient group formation between the experimenter and the subject, from which the victim is excluded. The wall between the victim and the others deprives him of an intimacy which the experimenter and subject feel. In the Remote condition, the victim is truly an outsider, who stands alone, physically and psychologically.

When the victim is placed close to the subject, it becomes easier to form an alliance with him against the experimenter. Subjects no longer have to face the experimenter alone. They have an ally who is close at hand and eager to collaborate in a revolt against the experimenter. Thus, the changing set of spatial relations leads to a potentially shifting set of alliances over the several experimental conditions.

Acquired behavior dispositions. It is commonly observed that laboratory mice will rarely fight with their litter mates. Scott (1958) explains this in terms of passive inhibition. He writes: "By doing nothing under . . . circumstances [the animal] learns to do nothing, and this may be spoken of as passive inhibition . . . this principle has great importance in teaching an individual to be peaceful, for it means that he can learn not to fight simply by not fighting." Similarly, we may learn not to harm others simply by not harming them in everyday life. Yet this learning occurs in a context of proximal relations with others, and may not be generalized to that situation in which the person is physically removed from us. Or possibly, in the past, aggressive actions against others who were physically close resulted in retaliatory punishment which extinguished the original form of response. In contrast, aggression against others at a distance may have only sporadically led to retaliation. Thus the organism learns that it is safer to be aggressive toward others at a distance, and precarious to be so when the parties are within arm's reach. Through a pattern of rewards and punishments, he acquires a disposition to avoid aggression at close quarters, a disposition which does not extend to harming others at a distance. And this may account for experimental findings in the remote and proximal experiments.

Proximity as a variable in psychological research has received far less attention than it deserves. If men were sessile it would be easy to understand this neglect. But we move about; our spatial relations shift from one situation to the next, and the fact that we are near or remote may have a powerful effect on the psychological processes that mediate our behavior toward others. In the present situation, as the victim is brought closer to the man ordered to give him shocks, increasing numbers of subjects break off the experiment, refusing to obey. The concrete, visible, and proximal presence of the victim acts in an important way to counteract the experimenter's power and to generate disobedience.[6]

CLOSENESS OF AUTHORITY

If the spatial relationship of the subject and victim is relevant to the degree of obedience, would not the relationship of subject to experimenter also play a part?

There are reasons to feel that, on arrival, the subject is oriented primarily to the experimenter rather than to the victim. He has come to the laboratory to fit into the structure that the experimenter—not the victim—would provide. He has come less to understand his behavior than to *reveal* that behavior to

[6]Admittedly, the terms *proximity, immediacy, closeness,* and *salience-of-the-victim* are used in a loose sense, and the experiments themselves represent a very coarse treatment of the variable. Further experiments are needed to refine the notion and tease out such diverse factors as spatial distance, visibility, audibility, barrier interposition, etc. The Proximity and Touch-Proximity experiments were the only conditions where we were unable to use taped feedback from the victim. Instead, the victim was trained to respond in these conditions as he had in Experiment 2 (which employed taped feedback). Some improvement is possible here, for it should be technically feasible to do a proximity series using taped feedback.

a competent scientist, and he is willing to display himself as the scientist's purposes require. Most subjects seem quite concerned about the appearance they are making before the experimenter, and one could argue that this preoccupation in a relatively new and strange setting makes the subject somewhat insensitive to the triadic nature of the social situation. In other words, the subject is so concerned about the show he is putting on for the experimenter that influences from other parts of the social field do not receive as much weight as they ordinarily would. This overdetermined orientation to the experimenter would account for the relative insensitivity of the subject to the victim, and would also lead us to believe that alterations in the relationship between subject and experimenter would have important consequences for obedience.

In a series of experiments we varied the physical closeness and degree of surveillance of the experimenter. In one condition the experimenter sat just a few feet away from the subject. In a second condition, after giving initial instructions, the experimenter left the laboratory and gave his orders by telephone; in still a third condition the experimenter was never seen, providing instructions by means of a tape recording activated when the subjects entered the laboratory.

Obedience dropped sharply as the experimenter was physically removed from the laboratory. The number of obedient subjects in the first condition (Experimenter Present) was almost three times as great as in the second, where the experimenter gave his orders by telephone. Twenty-six subjects were fully obedient in the first condition, and only 9 in the second (Chi square obedient *vs.* defiant in the two conditions, 1 d.f. $= 14.7; p < \cdot 001$). Subjects seemed able to take a far stronger stand against the experimenter when they did not have to encounter him face to face, and the experimenter's power over the subject was severely curtailed.[7]

Moreover, when the experimenter was absent, subjects displayed an interesting form of behavior that had not occurred under his surveillance. Though continuing with the experiment, several subjects administered lower shocks than were required and never informed the experimenter of their deviation from the correct procedure. (Unknown to the subjects, shock levels were automatically recorded by an Esterline-Angus event recorder wired directly into the shock generator; the instrument provided us with an objective record of the subjects' performance.) Indeed, in telephone conversations some subjects specifically assured the experimenter that they were raising the shock level according to instruction, whereas in fact they were repeatedly using the lowest shock on the board. This form of behavior is particularly interesting: although these subjects acted in a way that clearly undermined the avowed purposes of the experiment, they found it easier to handle the conflict in this manner than to precipitate an open break with authority.

Other conditions were completed in which the experimenter was absent during the first segment of the experiment, but reappeared at the point that the subject definitely refused to give higher shocks when commanded by telephone.

[7]The third condition also led to significantly lower obedience than this first situation, in which the experimenter was present, but it contains technical difficulties that require extensive discussion.

Although he had exhausted his power via telephone, the experimenter could frequently force further obedience when he reappeared in the laboratory.

Experiments in this series show that the physical *presence* of an authority is an important force contributing to the subject's obedience or defiance. Taken together with the first experimental series on the proximity of the victim, it would appear that something akin to fields of force, diminishing in effectiveness with increasing psychological distance from their source, have a controlling effect on the subject's performance. As the victim is brought closer, the subject finds it harder to administer shocks to him. When the victim's position is held constant relative to the subject, and the authority is made more remote, the subject finds it easier to break off the experiment. This effect is substantial in both cases, but manipulation of the experimenter's position yielded the more powerful results. Obedience to destructive commands is highly dependent on the proximal relations between authority and subject.

TENSIONS

The description of final scores does not fully convey the character of the subjects' performance, and it would be useful to interrupt our reporting of quantitative relationships to remark on the subjects' general reaction to the situation.

One might suppose that a subject would simply break off or continue as his conscience and temperament dictated. Yet this is very far from what happened. There were powerful reactions of tension and emotional strain in a substantial proportion of the participants. Persons were observed to sweat, tremble, stutter, bite their lips, and groan as they found themselves increasingly implicated in the experimental conflict. Some sense of the subjects' mood can be gotten from a transcript of their remarks at break-off point. Here are the remarks of two defiant subjects:

> Is he banging? . . . Is he hurt out there? Well, I don't want to be responsible for anything that happens to him. No, I can't go on with it. I don't know whether he's all right or not. I mean he may have a heart condition or something; I wouldn't feel right doing it. He's banging for help. He's evidently in trouble or he wouldn't bang . . . I don't see any sense to this—to knocking him out or something. I just can't see it.
>
> (Subject refuses to administer shocks)
>
> [Subject 0108]
>
> The man is banging. He wants to get out . . . I'm sorry. If the man wants to get out I'd just as soon stop . . . I don't want to administer any more [extremely excited] . . . I will gladly refund the check, but I will not harm this man . . . I'm sorry, I will not give him any more if he obviously wants to get out. There is no money in the world that will make me hurt another individual.   [Subject 010X]

And here is a transcript from an obedient subject. He began the experiment calmly, but became increasingly tense as the experiment proceeded. After administering the 150-volt shock, he began to address the experimenter in agitated tones:

150 volts delivered. You want me to keep going?
165 volts delivered. That guy is hollering in there. There's a lot of them here. He's liable to have heart condition. You want me to go?
180 volts delivered. He can't stand it! I'm not going to kill that man in there! You hear him hollering? He's hollering. He can't stand it. What if something happens to him? . . . I'm not going to get that man sick in there. He's hollering in there. You know what I mean? I mean I refuse to take responsibility. He's getting hurt in there. He's in there hollering. Too many left here. Geez, if he gets them wrong. There's too many of them left. I mean who is going to take responsibility if anything happens to that gentleman?
[*The experimenter accepts responsibility.*] All right.
195 volts delivered. You see he's hollering. Hear that. Gee, I don't know. [*The experimenter says: "The experiment requires that you go on."*]—I know it does, sir, but I mean—hugh—he don't know what he's in for. He's up to 195 volts.
210 volts delivered
225 volts delivered
240 volts delivered. Aw, no. You mean I've got to keep going up with the scale? No sir. I'm not going to kill that man! I'm not going to give him 450 volts! [*The experimenter says: "The experiment requires that you go on."*]—I know it does, but that man is hollering in there, sir . . .

Despite his numerous, agitated objections, which were constant accompaniments to his actions, the subject unfailingly obeyed the experimenter, proceeding to the highest shock level on the generator. He displayed a curious dissociation between word and action. Although at the verbal level he had resolved not to go on, his actions were fully in accord with the experimenter's commands. This subject did not want to shock the victim, and he found it an extremely disagreeable task, but he was unable to invent a response that would free him from *E*'s authority. Many subjects cannot find the specific verbal formula that would enable them to reject the role assigned to them by the experimenter. Perhaps our culture does not provide adequate models for disobedience.

One puzzling sign of tension was the regular occurrence of nervous laughing fits. In the first four conditions 71 of the 160 subjects showed definite signs of nervous laughter and smiling. The laughter seemed entirely out of place, even bizarre. Full-blown, uncontrollable seizures were observed for 15 of these subjects. On one occasion we observed a seizure so violently convulsive that it was necessary to call a halt to the experiment. In the post-experimental interviews subjects took pains to point out that they were not sadistic types and that the laughter did not mean they enjoyed shocking the victim.

In the interview following the experiment subjects were asked to indicate on a 14-point scale just how nervous or tense they felt at the point of maximum tension (Figure 2). The scale ranged from "Not at all tense and nervous" to "Extremely tense and nervous." Self-reports of this sort are of limited precision, and at best provide only a rough indication of the subject's emotional response. Still, taking the reports for what they are worth, it can be seen that

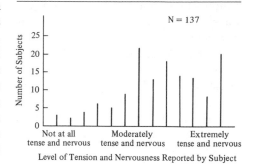

Figure 2 Level of tension and nervousness. Figure 2 shows the self-reports on "tension and nervousness" for 137 subjects in the Proximity experiments. Subjects were given a scale with 14 values ranging from "Not at all tense and nervous" to "Extremely tense and nervous." They were instructed: "Thinking back to that point in the experiment when you felt the most tense and nervous, indicate just how you felt by placing an X at the appropriate point on the scale." The results are shown in terms of midpoint values.

the distribution of responses spans the entire range of the scale, with the majority of subjects concentrated at the center and upper extreme. A further breakdown showed that obedient subjects reported themselves as having been slightly more tense and nervous than the defiant subjects at the point of maximum tension.

How is the occurrence of tension to be interpreted? First, it points to the presence of conflict. If a tendency to comply with authority were the only psychological force operating in the situation, all subjects would have continued to the end and there would have been no tension. Tension, it is assumed, results from the simultaneous presence of two or more incompatible response tendencies (Miller, 1944). If sympathetic concern for the victim were the exclusive force, all subjects would have calmly defied the experimenter. Instead, there were both obedient and defiant outcomes, frequently accompanied by extreme tension. A conflict develops between the deeply ingrained disposition not to harm others and the equally compelling tendency to obey others who are in authority. The subject is quickly drawn into a dilemma of a deeply dynamic character, and the presence of high tension points to the considerable strength of each of the antagonistic vectors.

Moreover, tension defines the strength of the aversive state from which the subject is unable to escape through disobedience. When a person is uncomfortable, tense, or stressed, he tries to take some action that will allow him to terminate this unpleasant state. Thus tension may serve as a drive that leads to escape behavior. But in the present situation, even where tension is extreme, many subjects are unable to perform the response that will bring about relief. Therefore there must be a competing drive, tendency, or inhibition that precludes activation of the disobedient response. The strength of this inhibiting factor must be of greater magnitude than the stress experienced, else the terminating act would occur. Every evidence of extreme tension is at the same time an indication of the strength of the forces that keep the subject in the situation.

Finally, tension may be taken as evidence of the reality of the situations for the subjects. Normal subjects do not tremble and sweat unless they are implicated in a deep and genuinely felt predicament.

BACKGROUND AUTHORITY

In psychophysics, animal learning, and other branches of psychology, the fact that measures are obtained at one institution rather than another is irrelevant to the interpretation of the findings, so long as the technical facilities for measurement are adequate and the operations are carried out with competence.

But it cannot be assumed that this holds true for the present study. The effectiveness of the experimenter's commands may depend in an important way on the larger institutional context in which they are issued. The experiments described thus far were conducted at Yale University, an organization which most subjects regarded with respect and sometimes awe. In postexperimental interviews several participants remarked that the locale and sponsorship of the study gave them confidence in the integrity, competence, and benign purposes of the personnel; many indicated that they would not have shocked the learner if the experiments had been done elsewhere.

This issue of background authority seemed to us important for an interpretation of the results that had been obtained thus far; moreover it is highly relevant to any comprehensive theory of human obedience. Consider, for example, how closely our compliance with the imperatives of others is tied to particular institutions and locales in our day-to-day activities. On request, we expose our throats to a man with a razor blade in the barber shop, but would not do so in a shoe store; in the latter setting we willingly follow the clerk's request to stand in our stockinged feet, but resist the command in a bank. In the laboratory of a great university, subjects may comply with a set of commands that would be resisted if given elsewhere. *One must always question the relationship of obedience to a person's sense of the context in which he is operating.*

To explore the problem we moved our apparatus to an office building in industrial Bridgeport and replicated experimental conditions, without any visible tie to the university.

Bridgeport subjects were invited to the experiment through a mail circular similar to the one used in the Yale study, with appropriate changes in letterhead, etc. As in the earlier study, subjects were paid $4.50 for coming to the laboratory. The same age and occupational distributions used at Yale, and the identical personnel, were employed.

The purpose in relocating in Bridgeport was to assure a complete dissociation from Yale, and in this regard we were fully successful. On the surface, the study appeared to be conducted by RE-SEARCH ASSOCIATES OF BRIDGEPORT, an organization of unknown character (the title had been concocted exclusively for use in this study).

The experiments were conducted in a three-room office suite in a somewhat run-down commercial building located in the downtown shopping area. The laboratory was sparsely furnished, though clean, and marginally respectable in appearance. When subjects inquired about professional affiliations, they were informed only that we were a private firm conducting research for industry.

Some subjects displayed skepticism concerning the motives of the Bridgeport experimenter. One gentleman gave us a written account of the thoughts he experienced at the control board:

> . . . Should I quit this damn test? Maybe he passed out? What dopes we were not to check up on this deal. How do we know that these guys are legit? No furniture, bare walls, no telephone. We could of called the Police up or the Better Business Bureau. I learned a lesson tonight. How do I know that Mr. Williams [the experimenter] is telling the truth . . . I wish I knew how many volts a person could take before lapsing into unconsciousness . . .   [*Subject 2424*]

Another subject stated:

> I questioned on my arrival my own judgment [about coming]. I had doubts as to the legitimacy of the operation and the consequences of participation. I felt it was a heartless way to conduct memory or learning processes on human beings and certainly dangerous without the presence of a medical doctor. [*Subject 2410 V*]

There was no noticeable reduction in tension for the Bridgeport subjects. And the subjects' estimation of the amount of pain felt by the victim was slightly, though not significantly, higher than in the Yale study.

A failure to obtain complete obedience in Bridgeport would indicate that the extreme compliance found in New Haven subjects was tied closely to the background authority of Yale University; if a large proportion of the subjects remained fully obedient, very different conclusions would be called for.

As it turned out, the level of obedience in Bridgeport, although somewhat reduced, was not significantly lower than that obtained at Yale. A large proportion of the Bridgeport subjects were fully obedient to the experimenter's commands (48 percent of the Bridgeport subjects delivered the maximum shock *vs.* 65 percent in the corresponding condition at Yale).

How are these findings to be interpreted? It is possible that if commands of a potentially harmful or destructive sort are to be perceived as legitimate they must occur within some sort of institutional structure. But it is clear from the study that it need not be a particularly reputable or distinguished institution. The Bridgeport experiments were conducted by an unimpressive firm lacking any credentials; the laboratory was set up in a respectable office building with title listed in the building directory. Beyond that, there was no evidence of benevolence or competence. It is possible that the *category* of institution, judged according to its professed function, rather than its qualitative position within that category, wins our compliance. Persons deposit money in elegant, but also in seedy-looking banks, without giving much thought to the differences in security they offer. Similarly, our subjects may consider one laboratory to be as competent as another, so long as it *is* a scientific laboratory.

It would be valuable to study the subjects' performance in other contexts which go even further than the Bridgeport study in denying institutional support to the experimenter. It is possible that, beyond a certain point, obedience disappears completely. But that point had not been reached in the Bridgeport office: almost half the subjects obeyed the experimenter fully.

FURTHER EXPERIMENTS

We may mention briefly some additional experiments undertaken in the Yale series. A considerable amount of obedience and defiance in everyday life occurs in connexion with groups. And we had reason to feel in the light of many group studies already done in psychology that group forces would have a profound effect on reactions to authority. A series of experiments was run to examine these effects. In all cases only one naïve subject was studied per hour, but he performed in the midst of actors who, unknown to him, were employed by the experimenter. In one experiment (Groups for Disobedience) two actors broke off in the middle of the experiment. When this happened 90 per cent of the subjects followed suit and defied the experimenter. In another condition the actors followed the orders obediently; this strengthened the experimenter's power only slightly. In still a third experiment the job of pushing the switch to shock the learner was given to one of the actors, while the naïve subject performed a subsidiary act. We wanted to see how the teacher would respond if he were involved in the situation but did not actually give the shocks. In this situation only three subjects out of forty broke off. In a final group experiment the subjects themselves determined the shock level they were going to use. Two actors suggested higher and higher shock levels; some subjects insisted, despite group pressure, that the shock level be kept low; others followed along with the group.

Further experiments were completed using women as subjects, as well as a set dealing with the effects of dual, unsanctioned, and conflicting authority. A final experiment concerned the personal relationship between victim and subject. These will have to be described elsewhere, lest the present report be extended to monographic length.

It goes without saying that future research can proceed in many different directions. What kinds of response from the victim are most effective in causing disobedience in the subject? Perhaps passive resistance is more effective than vehement protest. What conditions of entry into an authority system lead to greater or lesser obedience? What is the effect of anonymity and masking on the subject's behavior? What conditions lead to the subject's perception of responsibility for his own actions? Each of these could be a major research topic in itself, and can readily be incorporated into the general experimental procedure described here.

LEVELS OF OBEDIENCE AND DEFIANCE

One general finding that merits attention is the high level of obedience manifested in the experimental situation. Subjects often expressed deep disapproval of shocking a man in the face of his objections, and others denounced it as senseless and stupid. Yet many subjects complied even while they protested. The proportion of obedient subjects greatly exceeded the expectations of the experimenter and his colleagues. At the outset, we had conjectured that subjects would not, in general, go above the level of Strong Shock. In practice, many subjects were willing to administer the most

extreme shocks available when commanded by the experimenter. For some subjects the experiment provides an occasion for aggressive release. And for others it demonstrates the extent to which obedient dispositions are deeply ingrained, and are engaged irrespective of their consequences for others. Yet this is not the whole story. Somehow, the subject becomes implicated in a situation from which he cannot disengage himself.

The departure of the experimental results from intelligent expectation, to some extent, has been formalized. The procedure was to describe the experimental situation in concrete detail to a group of competent persons, and to ask them to predict the performance of 100 hypothetical subjects. For purposes of indicating the distribution of break-off points judges were provided with a diagram of the shock generator, and recorded their predictions before being informed of the actual results. Judges typically underestimated the amount of obedience demonstrated by subjects.

In Figure 3, we compare the predictions of forty psychiatrists at a leading medical school with the actual performance of subjects in the experiment. The psychiatrists predicted that most subjects would not go beyond the tenth shock level (150 volts; at this point the victim makes his first explicit demand to be freed). They further predicted that by the twentieth shock level (300 volts; the victim refuses to answer) 3.73 per cent of the subjects would still be obedient; and that only a little over one-tenth of one per cent of the subjects would administer the highest shock on the board. But, as the graph indicates, the obtained behavior was very different.

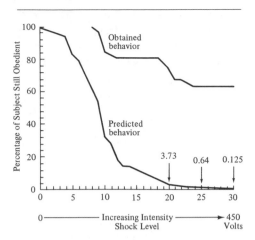

Figure 3 Predicted and obtained behavior in voice feedback.

Sixty-two per cent of the subjects obeyed the experimenter's commands fully. Between expectation and occurrence there is a whopping discrepancy.

Why did the psychiatrists underestimate the level of obedience? Possibly, because their predictions were based on an inadequate conception of the determinants of human action, a conception that focuses on motives *in vacuo*. This orientation may be entirely adequate for the repair of bruised impulses as revealed on the psychiatrist's couch, but as soon as our interest turns to action in larger settings, attention must be paid to the situations in which motives are expressed. A situation exerts an important press on the individual. It exercises constraints and may provide push. In certain circumstances it is not so much the kind of person a man is, as the kind of situation in which he is placed, that determines his actions.

Many people, not knowing much about the experiment, claim that subjects who go to the end of the board are sadistic. Nothing could be more foolish

as an overall characterization of these persons. It is like saying that a person thrown into a swift-flowing stream is necessarily a fast swimmer, or that he has great stamina because he moves so rapidly relative to the bank. The context of action must always be considered. The individual, upon entering the laboratory, becomes integrated into a situation that carries its own momentum. The subject's problem then is how to become disengaged from a situation which is moving in an altogether ugly direction.

The fact that disengagement is so difficult testifies to the potency of the forces that keep the subject at the control board. Are these forces to be conceptualized as individual motives and expressed in the language of personality dynamics, or are they to be seen as the effects of social structure and pressures arising from the situational field?

A full understanding of the subject's action will, I feel, require that both perspectives be adopted. The person brings to the laboratory enduring dispositions toward authority and aggression, and at the same time he becomes enmeshed in a social structure that is no less an objective fact of the case. From the standpoint of personality theory one may ask: What mechanisms of personality enable a person to transfer responsibility to authority? What are the motives underlying obedient and disobedient performance? Does orientation to authority lead to a short-circuiting of the shame-guilt system? What cognitive and emotional defenses are brought into play in the case of obedient and defiant subjects?

The present experiments are not, however, directed toward an exploration of the motives engaged when the subject obeys the experimenter's commands. Instead, they examine the situational variables responsible for the elicitation of obedience. Elsewhere, we have attempted to spell out some of the structural properties of the experimental situation that account for high obedience, and this analysis need not be repeated here (Milgram, 1963). The experimental variations themselves represent our attempt to probe that structure, by systematically changing it and noting the consequences for behavior. It is clear that some situations produce greater compliance with the experimenter's commands than others. However, this does not necessarily imply an increase or decrease in the strength of any single definable motive. Situations producing the greatest obedience could do so by triggering the most powerful, yet perhaps the most idiosyncratic, of motives in each subject confronted by the setting. Or they may simply recruit a greater number and variety of motives in their service. But whatever the motives involved—and it is far from certain that they can ever be known—action may be studied as a direct function of the situation in which it occurs. This has been the approach of the present study, where we sought to plot behavioral regularities against manipulated properties of the social field. Ultimately, social psychology would like to have a compelling *theory of situations* which will, first, present a language in terms of which situations can be defined; proceed to a typology of situations; and then point to the manner in which definable properties of situations are transformed into psychological forces in the individual.[8]

[8]My thanks to Professor Howard Leventhal of Yale for strengthening the writing in this paragraph.

POSTSCRIPT

Almost a thousand adults were individually studied in the obedience research, and there were many specific conclusions regarding the variables that control obedience and disobedience to authority. Some of these have been discussed briefly in the preceding sections, and more detailed reports will be released subsequently.

There are now some other generalizations I should like to make, which do not derive in any strictly logical fashion from the experiments as carried out, but which, I feel, ought to be made. They are formulations of an intuitive sort that have been forced on me by observation of many subjects responding to the pressures of authority. The assertions represent a painful alteration in my own thinking; and since they were acquired only under the repeated impact of direct observation, I have no illusion that they will be generally accepted by persons who have not had the same experience.

With numbing regularity good people were seen to knuckle under the demands of authority and perform actions that were callous and severe. Men who are in everyday life responsible and decent were seduced by the trappings of authority, by the control of their perceptions, and by the uncritical acceptance of the experimenter's definition of the situation, into performing harsh acts.

What is the limit of such obedience? At many points we attempted to establish a boundary. Cries from the victim were inserted; not good enough. The victim claimed heart trouble; subjects still shocked him on command. The victim pleaded that he be let free, and his answers no longer registered on the signal box; subjects continued to shock him. At the outset we had not conceived that such drastic procedures would be needed to generate disobedience, and each step was added only as the ineffectiveness of the earlier techniques became clear. The final effort to establish a limit was the Touch-Proximity condition. But the very first subject in this condition subdued the victim on command, and proceeded to the highest shock level. A quarter of the subjects in this condition performed similarly.

The results, as seen and felt in the laboratory, are to this author disturbing. They raise the possibility that human nature, or—more specifically—the kind of character produced in American democratic society, cannot be counted on to insulate its citizens from brutality and inhumane treatment at the direction of malevolent authority. A substantial proportion of people do what they are told to do, irrespective of the content of the act and without limitations of conscience, so long as they perceive that the command comes from a legitimate authority. If in this study an anonymous experimenter could successfully command adults to subdue a fifty-year-old man, and force on him painful electric shocks against his protests, one can only wonder what government, with its vastly greater authority and prestige, can command of its subjects. There is, of course, the extremely important question of whether malevolent political institutions could or would arise in American society. The present research contributes nothing to this issue.

In an article titled "The Dangers of Obedience," Harold J. Laski wrote:

. . . civilization means, above all, an unwillingness to inflict unnecessary pain. Within the ambit of that definition, those of us who heedlessly accept the commands of authority cannot yet claim to be civilized men.

. . . Our business, if we desire to live a life, not utterly devoid of meaning and significance, is to accept nothing which contradicts our basic experience merely because it comes to us from tradition or convention or authority. It may well be that we shall be wrong; but our self-expression is thwarted at the root unless the certainties we are asked to accept coincide with the certainties we experience. That is why the condition of freedom in any state is always a widespread and consistent skepticism of the canons upon which power insists.

REFERENCES

Buss, A. H. (1961). *The psychology of aggression.* New York and London: John Wiley.

Kierkegaard, S. (1843). *Fear and trembling.* English edition, Princeton: Princeton University Press, 1941.

Laski, H. J. (1929). The dangers of obedience. *Harper's Monthly Magazine* **159,** June, 1–10.

Milgram, S. (1961). Dynamics of obedience: Experiments in social psychology. Mimeographed report, *National Science Foundation,* January 25.

Milgram, S. (1963). Behavioral study of obedience. *J. abnorm. soc. Psychol.* **67,** 371–8.

Milgram, S. (1964). Issues in the study of obedience: A reply to Baumrind. *Amer. Psychol.* **19,** 848–52.

Miller, N. E. (1944). Experimental studies of conflict. In J. McV. Hunt (Ed.), *Personality and the behavior disorders.* New York: Ronald Press.

Scott, J. P. (1958). *Aggression.* Chicago: University of Chicago Press.

24

Bystander "Apathy"

Bibb Latané, and John M. Darley

The following article summarizes research on the phenomenon commonly known as "bystander apathy." There has been increasing concern in recent years over the fact that people seem willing to stand by and watch while others are injured or killed, and that the observers will do nothing to help the victim. It is as though something had happened to modern man, causing him to be unfeeling in the presence of suffering on the part of others. It has generally been assumed that the unresponsive bystander is *apathetic* (unfeeling), but this is really an interpretation of the *causes* of unresponsiveness, rather than a matter of direct observation. Unresponsiveness could be due to causes other than lack of feeling.

Does it seem possible that our understanding of bystander unresponsiveness could be enhanced by laboratory research? It seems hard to imagine how such research could be done, since it would be difficult to arrange situations of interest while staying within ethical limits. In the article which follows a number of ingenious tactics are described for doing experimental research on this topic. The article is of interest both because of the intrinsic interest value of the topic researched and because it shows once again how experimental psychologists have very great freedom to deal with socially relevant topics.

Do the work that's nearest
　Though it's dull at whiles,
Helping, when you meet them,
　Lame dogs over stiles.

Reprinted from *American Scientist*, 1969, **57**, 244–268, by permission of the authors and publisher.

The experiments reported in this paper were supported by National Science Foundation grants GS1238 and GS1239 and were conducted while the authors were at Columbia University and New York University, respectively. Their forthcoming book on this research (Latané and Darley, *The Unresponsive Bystander*, Appleton-Century-Crofts, 1970, won the 1968 Socio-Psychological Prize awarded by the American Association for the Advancement of Science and the Century Psychology Prize for 1968.

In the century since it was written, this minor bit of exhortatory doggerel has become sheer camp. We have become too sophisticated to appreciate the style—many believe that we have become too cynical to appreciate the moral. Working at dull tasks is now taken as a sign of dullness, and helping lame dogs is no longer much in vogue. At least, that is the impression we get from the newspapers.

On a March night in 1964, Kitty Genovese was set upon by a maniac as she came home from work at 3 A.M. Thirty-eight of her Kew Gardens neighbors came to their windows when she cried out in terror—none came to her assistance. Even though her assailant took over half an hour to murder her, no one even so much as called the police.

This story became the journalistic sensation of the decade. "Apathy," cried the newspapers. "Indifference," said the columnists and commentators. "Moral callousness," "dehumanization," "loss of concern for our fellow man," added preachers, professors, and other sermonizers. Movies, television specials, plays, and books explored this incident and many more like it. Americans became concerned about their lack of concern.

But can these epithets be correct? We think not. Although it is unquestionably true that witnesses in such emergencies have often done nothing to save the victims, "apathy," "indifference," and "unconcern" are not entirely accurate descriptions of their reactions. The 38 witnesses to Kitty Genovese's murder did not merely look at the scene once and then ignore it. Instead they continued to stare out their windows at what was going on. Caught, fascinated, distressed, unwilling to act but unable

to turn away, their behavior was neither helpful nor heroic; but it was not indifferent or apathetic either.

Actually, it was like crowd behavior in many other emergency situations; car accidents, drownings, fires, and attempted suicides all attract substantial numbers of people who watch the drama in helpless fascination without getting directly involved in the action. Are these people alienated and indifferent? Are the rest of us? Obviously not. It seems only yesterday we were being called overconforming. But why, then, don't we act?

There are certainly strong forces leading us to act. Empathy or sympathy, innate or learned, may cause us to share, at least in part, a victim's distress. If intervention were easy, most of us would be willing to relieve our own discomfort by alleviating another's suffering. As Charles Darwin put it some years ago, "As man is a social animal it is almost certain that . . . he would, from an inherited tendency, be willing to defend, in concert with others, his fellow men; and be ready to aid them in any way, which did not interfere too greatly with his own welfare or his own strong desires."

Even if empathy or sympathy were not strong enough to lead us to help in emergencies, there are a variety of social norms which suggest that each of us has a responsibility to each other, and that help is the proper thing to do. "Do unto others as you would have them do unto you," we hear from our earliest years. Although norms such as these may not have much influence on our behavior in specific situations, they may imbue us with a general predisposition to try to help others.

Indeed, in many non-emergency situations, people seem surprisingly willing to share their time and money with others. According to the Internal Revenue Service, Americans contribute staggering sums to a great variety of charitable organizations each year. Even when tax deductions don't fan the urge to help, people still help others. When Columbia students asked 2,500 people on the streets of New York for 10¢ or 20¢, over half of these people gave it.

If people are so willing to help in non-emergency situations, they should be even more willing to help in emergencies when the need is so much greater. Or should they? Emergencies differ in many ways from other types of situations in which people need help, and these differences may be important. The very nature of an emergency implies certain psychological consequences.

CHARACTERISTICS OF EMERGENCIES

Perhaps the most distinctive characteristic of an emergency is that it involves threat or harm. Life, well-being, or property is in danger. Even if an emergency is successfully dealt with, nobody is better off afterwards than before. Except in rare circumstances, the best that can be hoped for if an emergency occurs is a return to the status quo. Consequently, there are few positive rewards for successful action in an emergency. At worst, an emergency can claim the lives not only of those people who were initially involved in it, but also of anybody who intervenes in the situation. This fact puts pressures on individuals to ignore a potential emergency, to distort their perceptions of it, or to underestimate their responsibility for coping with it.

The second important feature of an emergency is that it is an unusual and rare event. Fortunately, although he may read about them in newspapers, or watch fictionalized accounts on television, the average person probably will encounter fewer than half a dozen serious emergencies in his lifetime. Unfortunately when he does encounter one, he will have had little direct personal experience in handling such a situation. Unlike the stereotyped patterns of his everyday behavior, an individual facing an emergency is untrained and unrehearsed.

In addition to being rare, emergencies differ widely, one from another. There are few common requirements for action between a drowning, a fire, or an automobile accident. Each emergency presents a different problem, and each requires a different type of action. Consequently, unlike other rare events, our culture provides us with little secondhand wisdom about how to deal with emergencies. An individual may cope with the rare event of a formal dinner party by using manners gleaned from late night Fred Astaire movies, but the stereotypes that the late movies provide for dealing with emergencies are much less accurate. "Charge!" "Women and children first!" "Quick, get lots of hot water and towels." This is about the extent of the advice offered for dealing with emergencies and it is singularly inappropriate in most specific real emergency situations.

The fourth basic characteristic of emergencies is that they are unforseen. They "emerge," suddenly and without warning. Being unexpected, emergencies must be handled without the benefit of forethought and planning and an individual does not have the opportunity to think through in advance what course of action he should take when faced with an emergency. He must do his thinking in the immediacy of the situation, and has no opportunity to consult others as to the best course of action or to alert others who are especially equipped to deal with emergencies. The individual confronted with an emergency is thrown on his own resources. We have already seen that he does not have much in the way of practiced responses or cultural stereotypes to fall back upon.

A final characteristic of an emergency is that it requires instant action. It represents a pressing necessity. If the emergency is not dealt with immediately, the situation will deteriorate. The threat will transform itself into damage; the harm will continue or spread. There are urgent pressures to deal with the situation at once. The requirement for immediate action prevents the individual confronted with an emergency from leisurely considering the possible courses of action open to him. It forces him to come to a decision before he has had time to consider his alternatives. It places him in a condition of stress.

The picture we have drawn is a rather grim one. Faced with a situation in which there is no benefit to be gained for himself, unable to rely on past experience, on the experience of others, or on forethought and planning, denied the opportunity to consider carefully his course of action, the bystander to an emergency is in an unenviable position. It is perhaps surprising that anyone should intervene at all.

A MODEL OF THE
INTERVENTION PROCESS

If an individual is to intervene in an emergency, he must make, not just one,

but a *series* of decisions. Only one particular set of choices will lead him to take action in the situation. Let us now consider the behavioral and cognitive processes that go on in an individual who is in the vicinity of an emergency. What must he do and decide before he actually intervenes? These may have important implications for predicting whether an individual will act.

Let us suppose that an emergency is actually taking place. A middle-aged man, walking down the street, has a heart attack. He stops short, clutches his chest, and staggers to the nearest building wall, where he slowly slumps to the sidewalk in a sitting position. What is the likelihood with which a passerby will come to his assistance? First, the bystander has to *notice* that something is happening. The external event has to break into his thinking and intrude itself on his conscious mind. He must tear himself away from his private thoughts or from the legs of the pretty girl walking down the street ahead of him and pay attention to this unusual event.

Once the person is aware of the event as something to be explained, it is necessary that he *interpret* the event. Specifically, he must decide that there is something wrong, that this ambiguous event is an emergency. It may be that the man slumped on the sidewalk is only a drunk, beyond any assistance that the passerby can give him. If the bystander decided that something is indeed wrong, he must next decide that he has a *responsibility* to act. Perhaps help is on the way or perhaps someone else might be better qualified to help. Even in an emergency, it is not clear that everybody should immediately intrude himself into the situation.

If the person does decide that he should help, he must decide what *form of assistance* he can give. Should he rush in directly and try to help the victim or should he detour by calling a doctor or the police? Finally, of course, he must decide how to *implement* his choice and form of intervention. Where is the nearest telephone? Is there a hospital nearby? At this point, the person may finally begin to act in the situation. The socially responsible act is the end point of a series of decisions that the person makes.

Obviously, this model is too rational. It seems unlikely that a bystander will run through the series of choice points in a strictly logical and sequential order. Instead, he may consider two or three of them simultaneously and "try on" various decisions and their consequences before he finally arrives at his overall assessment of the situation. Since he has no commitment to any intermediary decision until he has taken final action, he may cycle back and forth through the decision series until he comes up with a set which serves both his needs and the needs of "reality."

Second, the bystander in an emergency is not a detached and objective observer. His decisions have consequences for himself just as much as for the victim. Unfortunately, however, the rewards and penalties for action and inaction are biased in favor of inaction. All the bystander has to gain from intervention is a feeling of pride and the chance to be a hero. On the other hand, he can be made to appear a fool, sued, or even attacked and wounded. By leaving the situation, he has little to lose but his self-respect. There are strong pressures against deciding that an event is an emergency.

Intervention, then, requires choosing a single course of action through a rather complex matrix of possible ac-

tions. The failure to intervene may result from failing to notice an event, failing to realize that the event is an emergency, failing to feel personally responsible for dealing with the emergency, or failing to have sufficient skill to intervene.

SOCIAL DETERMINANTS OF BYSTANDER INTERVENTION, I

Most emergencies are, or at least begin as, ambiguous events. A quarrel in the street may erupt into violence, but it may be simply a family argument. A man staggering about may be suffering a coronary or an onset of diabetes; he may simply be drunk. Smoke pouring from a building may signal a fire; on the other hand, it may be simply steam or airconditioner vapor. Before a bystander is likely to take action in such ambiguous situations, he must first define the event as an emergency and decide that intervention is the proper course of action.

In the course of making these decisions, it is likely that an individual bystander will be considerably influenced by the decisions he perceives other bystanders to be taking. If everyone else in a group of onlookers seems to regard an event as nonserious and the proper course of action as non-intervention, this consensus may strongly affect the perceptions of any single individual and inhibit his potential intervention.

The definitions that other people hold may be discovered by discussing the situation with them, but they may also be inferred from their facial expressions or their behavior. A whistling man with his hands in his pockets obviously does not believe he is in the midst of a crisis. A bystander who does not respond to smoke obviously does not attribute it to fire. An individual, seeing the inaction of others, will judge the situation as less serious than he would if alone.

But why should the others be inactive? Unless there were some force inhibiting responses on the part of others, the kind of social influence process described would, by itself, only lead to a convergence of attitudes within a group. If each individual expressed his true feelings, then, even if each member of the group were entirely guided by the reactions of the others, the group should still respond with a likelihood equal to the average of the individuals.

An additional factor is involved, however. Each member of a group may watch the others, but he is also aware that others are watching him. They are an audience to his own reactions. Among American males, it is considered desirable to appear poised and collected in times of stress. Being exposed to the public view may constrain the actions and expressions of emotion of any individual as he tries to avoid possible ridicule and embarrassment. Even though he may be truly concerned and upset about the plight of a victim, until he decides what to do, he may maintain a calm demeanor.

The constraints involved with being in public might in themselves tend to inhibit action by individuals in a group, but in conjunction with the social influence process described above, they may be expected to have even more powerful effects. If each member of a group is, at the same time, trying to appear calm and also looking around at the other members to gauge their reactions, all members may be led (or misled) by each other to define the situation as less critical than they would if alone. Until someone acts, each person sees only other non-responding bystand-

ers, and is likely to be influenced not to act himself. A state of "pluralistic ignorance" may develop.

It has often been recognized (Brown, 1954, 1965) that a crowd can cause contagion of panic, leading each person in the crowd to over-react to an emergency to the detriment of everyone's welfare. What we suggest here is that a crowd can also force inaction on its members. It can suggest, implicitly but strongly, by its passive behavior that an event is not to be reacted to as an emergency, and it can make any individual uncomfortably aware of what a fool he will look for behaving as if it is.

This line of thought suggests that individuals may be less likely to intervene in an emergency if they witness it in the presence of other people than if they see it alone. It suggests that the presence of other people may lead each person to interpret the situation as less serious, and less demanding of action than he would if alone. The presence of other people may alter each bystander's perceptions and interpretations of the situation. We suspect that the presence of other people may also affect each individual's assessment of the rewards and costs involved in taking action, and indeed we will discuss this possibility in some detail later. First, however, let us look at evidence relevant to this initial process. The experiments reported below were designed to test the line of thought presented above.

EXPERIMENT 1
WHERE THERE'S SMOKE, THERE'S (SOMETIMES) FIRE[1]

In this experiment we presented an emergency to individuals either alone,

[1] A more detailed report of this experiment is given in: Latané, B., and Darley, J. M. Group

in the presence of two passive others (confederates of the experimenter who were instructed to notice the emergency but remain indifferent to it), or in groups of three. It was our expectation that individuals faced with the passive reactions of the confederates would be influenced by them and thus less likely to take action than single subjects. We also predicted that the constraints on behavior in public combined with social influence processes would lessen the likelihood that members of three-person groups would act to cope with the emergency.

Male Columbia students living in campus residences were invited to an interview to discuss "some of the problems involved in life at an urban university." As they sat in a small room waiting to be called for the interview and filling out a preliminary questionnaire, they faced an ambiguous but potentially dangerous situation as a stream of smoke began to puff into the room through a wall vent. Some subjects filled out the questionnaire and were exposed to this potentially critical situation while alone. Others were part of three-person groups consisting of one subject and two confederates acting the part of naive subjects. The confederates attempted to avoid conversation as much as possible. Once the smoke had been introduced, they stared at it briefly, made no comment, but simply shrugged their shoulders, returned to the questionnaires and continued to fill them out, occasionally waving away the smoke to do so. If addressed, they attempted to be as uncommunicative as possible and to show apparent indiffer-

ence to the smoke. "I dunno," they said, and no subject persisted in talking. In a final condition, three naive subjects were tested together. In general, these subjects did not know each other, although in two groups, subjects reported a nodding acquaintance with another subject. Since subjects arrived at slightly different times and since they each had individual questionnaires to work on, they did not introduce themselves to each other, or attempt anything but the most rudimentary conversation.

As soon as the subjects had completed two pages of their questionnaires, the experimenter began to introduce the smoke through a small vent in the wall. The "smoke" was finely divided titanium dioxide produced in a stoppered bottle and delivered under slight air pressure through the vent. It formed a moderately fine-textured but clearly visible stream of whitish smoke. For the entire experimental period, the smoke continued to jet into the room in irregular puffs. By the end of the experimental period, vision was obscured in the room by the amount of smoke present.

All behavior and conversation was observed and coded from behind a one-way window (largely disguised on the subject's side by a large sign giving preliminary instructions). When and if the subject left the experimental room and reported the smoke, he was told that the situation "would be taken care of." If the subject had not reported the smoke within six minutes of the time he first noticed it, the experiment was terminated.

The typical subject, when tested alone, behaved very reasonably. Usually, shortly after the smoke appeared, he would glance up from his questionnaire, notice the smoke, show a slight but distinct startle reaction, and

inhibition of bystander intervention in emergencies. *Journal of Personality and Social Psychology,* 1968, **10,** 215–221.

then undergo a brief period of indecision, and perhaps return briefly to his questionnaire before again staring at the smoke. Soon, most subjects would get up from their chairs, walk over to the vent, and investigate it closely, sniffing the smoke, waving their hands in it, feeling its temperature, etc. The usual Alone subject would hesitate again, but finally walk out of the room, look around outside, and, finding somebody there, calmly report the presence of the smoke. No subject showed any sign of panic; most simply said, "There's something strange going on in there, there seems to be some sort of smoke coming through the wall. . . ." The median subject in the Alone condition had reported the smoke within two minutes of first noticing it. Three-quarters of the 24 people run in this condition reported the smoke before the experimental period was terminated.

The behavior of subjects run with two passive confederates was dramatically different; of ten people run in this condition, only one reported the smoke. The other nine stayed in the waiting room as it filled up with smoke, doggedly working on their questionnaires and waving the fumes away from their faces. They coughed, rubbed their eyes, and opened the window—but they did not report the smoke. The difference between the response rate of 75% in the Alone condition and 10% in the Two Passive Confederates condition is highly significant ($p < .002$ by Fisher's Exact test, two-tailed).

Because there are three subjects present and available to report the smoke in the Three Naive Bystander condition as compared to only one subject at a time in the Alone condition, a simple comparison between the two conditions

is not appropriate. On the one hand, we cannot compare speeds in the Alone condition with the average speed of the three subjects in a group, since, once one subject in a group had reported the smoke, the pressures on the other two disappeared. They legitimately could feel that the emergency had been handled, and that any action on their part would be redundant and potentially confusing. Therefore, we used the speed of the *first* subject in a group to report the smoke as our dependent variable. However, since there were three times as many people available to respond in this condition as in the Alone condition, we would expect an increased likelihood that at least one person would report the smoke by chance alone. Therefore, we mathematically created "groups" of three scores from the Alone condition to serve as a baseline.[2]

In contrast to the complexity of this procedure, the results were quite simple. Subjects in the Three Naive Bystander condition were markedly inhibited from reporting the smoke. Since 75% of the Alone subjects reported the smoke, we would expect over 98% of the three-person groups to include at least one reporter. In fact, in only 38% of the eight groups in this condition did even one person report ($p < .01$). Of the twenty-four people run in these eight groups, only one person reported the smoke within the first four minutes before the room got noticeably unpleasant. Only three people reported the smoke within the entire experimental period. Social

---

[2] The formula for calculating the expected proportion of groups in which at least one person will have acted by a given time is $1-(1-p)^n$ where p is the proportion of single individuals who act by that time and n is the number of persons in the group.

inhibition of reporting was so strong that the smoke was reported quicker when only one person saw it than when groups of three were present ($p < .01$).

Subjects who had reported the smoke were relatively consistent in later describing their reactions to it. They thought the smoke looked somewhat "strange," they were not sure exactly what it was or whether it was dangerous, but they felt it was unusual enough to justify some examination. "I wasn't sure whether it was a fire, but it looked like something was wrong." "I thought it might be steam, but it seemed like a good idea to check it out."

Subjects who had not reported the smoke also were unsure about exactly what it was, but they uniformly said that they had rejected the idea that it was a fire. Instead, they hit upon an astonishing variety of alternative explanations, all sharing the common characteristic of interpreting the smoke as a nondangerous event. Many thought the smoke was either steam or airconditioning vapors, several thought it was smog, purposely introduced to simulate an urban environment, and two (from different groups) actually suggested that the smoke was a "truth gas" filtered in the room to induce them to answer the questionnaire accurately (surprisingly, they were not disturbed by this conviction). Predictably, some decided that "it must be some sort of experiment" and stoically endured the discomfort of the room rather than overreact.

Despite the obvious and powerful report-inhibiting effect of other bystanders, subjects almost invariably claimed that they had paid little or no attention to the reactions of the other people in the room. Although the presence of other people actually had a strong and pervasive effect on the subjects' reactions, they were either unaware of this or unwilling to admit it.

The results of this study clearly support the predictions. Individuals exposed to a room filling with smoke in the presence of passive others themselves remained passive, and groups of three naive subjects were less likely to report the smoke than solitary bystanders. Our predictions were confirmed—but this does not necessarily mean that our explanation for these results is the correct one. As a matter of fact several alternatives are available.

Two alternative explanations stem from the fact that the smoke represented a possible danger to the subject himself as well as to others in the building. Subjects' behavior might have reflected their fear of fire, with subjects in groups feeling less threatened by the fire than single subjects and thus less concerned to act. It has been demonstrated in studies with humans (Schachter, 1959) and with rats (Latané, 1969; Latané and Glass, 1968) that togetherness reduces fear, even in situations where it does not reduce danger. In addition, subjects may have felt that the presence of others increased their ability to cope with fire. For both these reasons, subjects in groups may have been less afraid of fire and thus less likely to report the smoke than solitary subjects.

A similar explanation might emphasize, not fearfulness, but the desire to hide fear. To the extent that bravery or stoicism in the face of danger or discomfort is a socially desirable trait (as it appears to be for American male undergraduates), we might expect individuals to attempt to appear more brave or more stoic when others are watching than when they are alone. It is possible that subjects in the Group condition saw themselves as engaged in a game of "Chicken," and thus did not react.

Although both of these explanations are plausible, we do not think that they provide an accurate account of subjects' thinking. In the post-experimental interviews, subjects claimed, *not* that they were unworried by the fire or that they were unwilling to endure the danger; but rather that they had decided that there was no fire at all and the smoke was caused by something else. They failed to act because they thought there was no reason to act. Their "apathetic" behavior was reasonable—given their interpretation of the circumstances.

EXPERIMENT 2.
A LADY IN DISTRESS[3]

Although it seems unlikely that the group inhibition of bystander intervention observed in Experiment 1 can be attributed entirely to the fact that smoke represents a danger to the individual bystander, it is certainly possible that this is so. Experiment 2 was designed to see whether similar group inhibition effects could be observed in situations where there is no danger to the individual himself for not acting. In addition, a new variable was included: whether the bystanders knew each other.

Male Columbia undergraduates waited either alone, with a friend, or with a stranger to participate in a market research study. As they waited, they

heard someone fall and apparently injure herself in the room next door. Whether they tried to help, and how long they took to do so were the main dependent variables of the study. Subjects were telephoned and offered $2 to participate in a survey of game and puzzle preferences conducted at Columbia by the Consumer Testing Bureau (CTB), a market research organization. Each person contacted was asked to find a friend who would also be interested in participating. Only those students who recommended friends, and the friends they suggested, were used as subjects.

Subjects were met at the door by the market research representative, an attractive young woman, and taken to the testing room. On the way, they passed the CTB office and through its open door they were able to see a desk and bookcases piled high with papers and filing cabinets. They entered the adjacent testing room which contained a table and chairs and a variety of games, and they were given a preliminary background information and game preference questionnaire to fill out. The representative told subjects that she would be working next door in her office for about 10 minutes while they completed the questionnaires, and left by opening the collapsible curtain which divided the two rooms. She made sure that subjects were aware that the curtain was unlocked and easily opened and that it provided a means of entry to her office. The representative stayed in her office, shuffling papers, opening drawers, and making enough noise to remind the subjects of her presence. Four minutes after leaving the testing area, she turned on a high fidelity stereophonic tape recorder.

[3] A more detailed description of this experiment is given in: Latané, B., and Rodin, J. A Lady in distress: Inhibiting effects of friends and strangers on bystander intervention, *Journal of Experimental Social Psychology*, 1969, **5**, 189–202.

The Emergency If the subject listened carefully, he heard the representative climb up on a chair to reach for a stack of papers on the bookcase. Even if he were not listening carefully, he heard a loud crash and a scream as the chair collapsed and she fell to the floor. "Oh, my God, my foot . . . I . . . can't move . . . it. Oh . . . my ankle," the representative moaned. "I . . . can't get this . . . thing . . . off me." She cried and moaned for about a minute longer, but the cries gradually got more subdued and controlled. Finally, she muttered something about getting outside, knocked over the chair as she pulled herself up, and thumped to the door, closing it behind her as she left. The entire incident took 130 seconds.

The main dependent variable of the study, of course, was whether the subjects took action to help the victim and how long it took him to do so. There were actually several modes of intervention possible: a subject could open the screen dividing the two rooms, leave the testing room and enter the CTB office by the door, find someone else, or, most simply, call out to see if the representative needed help. Four experimental conditions were run. In one condition (Alone, $n = 26$) each subject was by himself in the testing room while he filled out the questionnaire and heard the fall. In a second condition (Stooge, $n = 14$), a stranger, actually a confederate of the experimenter, was also present. The confederate had instructions to be as passive as possible and to answer questions put to him by the subjects with a brief gesture or remark. During the emergency, he looked up, shrugged his shoulders, and continued working on his questionnaire. Subjects in the third condition (Strangers, $n = 20$ pairs) were placed in the testing room in pairs. Each subject in the pair was unacquainted with the other before entering the room and they were not introduced. Only one subject in this condition spontaneously introduced himself to the other. In a final condition (Friends, $n = 20$ pairs), pairs of friends overheard the incident together.

Mode of Intervention Across all experimental groups, the majority of subjects who intervened did so by pulling back the room divider and coming into the CTB office (61%). Few subjects came the round-about way through the door to offer their assistance (14%), and a surprisingly small number (24%) chose the easy solution of calling out to offer help. No one tried to find someone else to whom to report the accident. Since experimental conditions did not differ in the proportions choosing various modes of intervention, the comparisons below will deal only with the total proportions of subjects offering help.

Alone vs. Stooge Conditions Seventy per cent of all subjects who heard the accident while alone in the waiting room offered to help the victim before she left the room. By contrast the presence of a non-responsive bystander markedly inhibited helping. Only 7% of subjects in the Stooge condition intervened. These subjects seemed upset and confused during the emergency and frequently glanced at the passive confederate who continued working on his questionnaire. The difference between the Alone and Stooge response rates is, of course, highly significant ($p < .001$).

Alone vs. Two Strangers Since 70% of Alone subjects intervened, we should expect that at least one person in 91%

of all two-person groups would offer help if members of a pair had no influence upon each other. In fact, members did influence each other. In only 40% of the groups did even one person offer help to the injured woman. Only 8 subjects of the 40 who were run in this condition intervened. This response rate is significantly below the hypothetical baseline ($p < .001$). Social inhibition of helping was so strong, that the victim was actually aided more quickly when only one person heard her distress than when two did ($p < .01$).

Strangers vs. Stooge   The response rate in the Two Strangers condition appears to be somewhat higher than the 7% rate in the Stooge condition. Making a correction similar to that used for the Alone scores, the expected response rate based on the Stooge condition is 13%. This is significantly lower than the response rate in the Strangers condition ($p < .05$).

Alone vs. Two Friends   Pairs of friends often talked about the questionnaire before the accident, and sometimes discussed a course of action after the fall. Even so, in only 70% of the pairs did even one person intervene. While, superficially, this appears as high as the Alone condition, there must again be a correction for the fact that twice as many people are free to act. When compared to the 91% hypothetical base rate, friends do inhibit each other from intervening ($p < .10$). They were also slower to intervene than would be expected from the Alone condition ($p < .05$).

Friends vs. Strangers   Although pairs of friends were inhibited from helping

when compared to the Alone condition, they were significantly faster to intervene than were pairs of strangers ($p < .01$). The median latency of the first response from pairs of friends was 36 seconds; the median pair of strangers did not respond at all within the arbitrary 130-second duration of the emergency.

Subjects who intervened usually claimed that they did so either because the fall sounded very serious or because they were uncertain what had occurred and felt they should investigate. Many talked about intervention as the "right thing to do" and asserted they would help again in any situation.

Many of the non-interveners also claimed that they were unsure what had happened (59%), but had decided that it was not too serious (46%). A number of subjects reported that they thought other people would or could help (25%), and three said they refrained out of concern for the victim—they did not want to embarrass her. Whether to accept these explanations as reasons or rationalizations is moot—they certainly do not explain the differences among conditions. The important thing to note is that non-interveners did not seem to feel that they had behaved callously or immorally. Their behavior was generally consistent with their interpretation of the situation. Subjects almost uniformly claimed that, in a "real" emergency, they would be among the first to help the victim.

Interestingly, when subjects were asked whether they had been influenced by the presence of action of their coworkers, they were either unwilling or unable to report that they had. Subjects in the passive confederate condition reported, on the average, that they were "very little" influenced by the stooge. Subjects in the Two Strangers condition claimed to have been only "a little bit" influenced by each other, and friends admitted to "moderate" influence. Put another way, only 14%, 30%, and 70% of the subjects in these three conditions admitted to at least a "moderate" degree of influence. These claims, of course, run directly counter to the experimental results, in which friends were the least inhibited and subjects in the Stooge condition most inhibited by the other's actions.

These results strongly replicate the findings of the Smoke study. In both experiments, subjects were less likely to take action if they were in the presence of passive confederates than if they were alone, and in both studies, this effect showed up even when groups of naive subjects were tested together. This congruence of findings from different experimental settings supports the validity and generality of the phenomenon: it also helps rule out a variety of alternative explanations suitable to either situation alone. For example, the possibility that smoke may have represented a threat to the subject's personal safety and that subjects in groups may have had a greater concern to appear "brave" than single subjects does not apply to the present experiment. In the present experiment, non-intervention cannot signify bravery. Comparison of the two experiments also suggests that the absolute number of non-responsive bystanders may not be a critical factor in producing social inhibition of intervention. One passive confederate in the present experiment was as effective as two in the smoke study; pairs of strangers in the present study inhibited each other as much as did trios in the former study.

How can we account for the differential social inhibition caused by friends and strangers? It may be that people are less likely to fear possible embarrassment in front of friends than before strangers, and that friends are less likely to misinterpret each other's inaction than are strangers. If so, social influence should be less likely to lead friends to decide there is no emergency than strangers. When strangers overheard the accident, they seemed noticeably concerned but confused. Attempting to interpret what they had heard and to decide upon a course of action, they often glanced furtively at one another, apparently anxious to discover the other's reaction yet unwilling to meet eyes and betray their own concern. Friends, on the other hand, seemed better able to convey their concern noverbally, and often discussed the incident and arrived at a mutual plan of action. Although these observations are admittedly impressionistic, they are consistent with other data. During the emergency, a record was kept of whether the bystanders engaged in conversation. Unfortunately, no attempt was made to code the amount or content of what was said, but it is possible to determine if there was any talking at all. Only 29% of subjects attempted any conversation with the stooge; while 60% of the pairs of strangers engaged in some conversation, it was mostly desultory and often unrelated to the accident. Although the latter rate seems higher than the former, it really is not, since there are two people free to initiate a conversation rather than just one. Friends, on the other hand, were somewhat more likely to talk than strangers—85% of the pairs did so. Friends, then, may show less mutual inhibition than strangers because they are less likely to develop a state of "pluralistic ignorance."

These first experiments show that in two, widely different types of emergency settings, the presence of other people inhibits intervention. Subjects were less likely to report a possible fire when together than alone, and they were less likely to go to the aid of the victim of an accident when others were present. Is this a general effect? Will it apply to all types of emergency? Are there situations in which the presence of other people might actually facilitate bystander intervention? One possible set of circumstances in which we might expect social facilitation of intervention is when an emergency is caused by a villain. People who fail to intervene in real emergencies sometimes claim they were afraid of the consequences of intervention—afraid of direct attack, afraid of later retribution, afraid of having to go to court. In situations involving a villain, even if one person is afraid to take action, the presence of other people as potential risk-sharing allies might embolden him to intervene. Under these circumstances, there might actually be a group facilitation of intervention. To test this possibility, two Columbia undergraduates, Paul Bonnarigo and Malcolm Ross, turned to a life of crime.

EXPERIMENT 3.
THE CASE OF THE STOLEN BEER

The Nu-Way Beverage Center in Suffern, New York, is a discount beer store. It sells beer and soda by the case, often to New Jerseyans who cross the state line to find both lowered prices and a lowered legal drinking age. During the spring of 1968 it was the scene of a minor crime wave—within one two-week period, it was robbed 96 times. The robbers followed much the same modus operandi on each occasion. Singly or in a pair, they would enter the store and ask the cashier at the checkout counter "What is the most expensive imported beer that you carry?" The cashier, in cahoots with the robbers, would reply "Lowenbrau. I'll go back and check how much we have." Leaving the robbers in the front of the store, the cashier would disappear into the rear to look for the Lowenbrau. After waiting for a minute, the robbers would pick up a case of beer near the front of the store, remark to nobody in particular, "They'll never miss this," walk out of the front door, put the beer in their car, and drive off. On 46 occasions, one robber carried off the theft; on 46 occasions, two robbers were present.

The robberies were always staged when there were either one or two people in the store, and the timing was arranged so that the one or both customers would be at the checkout counter at the time when the robbers entered. On 46 occasions, one customer was at the checkout counter during the theft; on 46 occasions, two customers were present. Although occasionally the two customers had come in together, more usually they were strangers to each other. Sixty-one per cent of the customers were male, 39% female. Since the checkout counter was about 20 feet from the front door, since the theft itself took less than a minute, and since the robbers were both husky young men, nobody tried directly to prevent the theft. There were, however, other courses of intervention available.

When the cashier returned from the rear of the store, he went to the checkout counter and resumed waiting on the customers there. After a minute, if nobody had spontaneously mentioned the theft, he casually inquired, "Hey, what happened to that man (those men) who was (were) in here? Did you see him (them) leave?" At this point the customer could either report the theft, say merely that he had seen the man or men leave, or disclaim any knowledge of the event whatsoever. Overall, 20% of the subjects reported the theft spontaneously, and 51% of the remainder reported it upon prompting. Since the results from each criterion followed an identical pattern, we shall indicate only the total proportion of subjects in each condition who reported the theft, whether spontaneously or not.

Results Whether there were one or two robbers present made little difference. Customers were somewhat but not significantly more likely to report the theft if there were two robbers (69%) than if there was only one (52%). Sex also made no difference; females were as likely to report as males. The number of customers, on the other hand, made a big difference. Thirty-one of the 48 single customers, or 65%, mentioned the theft. From this, we would expect that 87% of the two-person groups would include at least one reporter. In fact, in only 56% of the two-person groups did even one person report the theft ($p < .01$). Social inhibition of reporting was so strong that the theft was actually somewhat (though not significantly) less likely to be reported when two people saw it than when only one did.

In three widely differing situations the same effect has been observed. People are less likely to take a socially responsible action if other people are present than if they are alone. This effect has occurred in a situation involving general danger, in a situation where someone has been the victim of an accident, and in a situation involving one or more villains. The effect holds in real life as well as in the laboratory, and for members of the general population as well as college students. The results of each of these three experiments clearly support the line of theoretical argument advanced earlier. When bystanders to an emergency can see the reactions of other people, and when other people can see their own reactions, each individual may, through a process of social influence, be led to interpret the situation as less serious than he would if he were alone, and consequently be less likely to take action.

SOCIAL DETERMINANTS OF BYSTANDER INTERVENTION, II

So far we have devoted our attention exclusively to one stage of our hypothesized model of the intervention process: noticing the situation and interpreting it. Once an individual has noticed an emergency and interpreted it as being serious, he still has to decide what, if anything, he will do about it. He must decide that he has a responsibility to help, and that there is some form of assistance that he is in a position to give. He is faced with the choice of whether he himself will intervene. His decision will presumably be made in terms of the rewards and costs of the various alternative courses of action open to him.

In addition to affecting the interpretations that he places on a situation, the presence of other people can also alter the rewards and costs facing an individual bystander. Perhaps most importantly, the presence of other people can alter the cost of not acting. If only one bystander is present at an emergency, he carries all of the responsibility for dealing with it; he will feel all of the guilt for not acting; he will bear all of any blame others may level for non-intervention. If others are present, the onus of responsibility is diffused, and the individual may be more likely to resolve his conflict between intervening and not intervening in favor of the latter alternative.

When only one bystander is present at an emergency, if help is to come it must be from him. Although he may choose to ignore them (out of concern for his personal safety, or desire "not to get involved"), any pressures to intervene focus uniquely on him. When there are several observers present, however, the pressures to intervene do not focus on any one of the observers; instead the responsibility for intervention is shared among all the onlookers and is not unique to any one. As a result, each may be less likely to help.

Potential blame may also be diffused. However much we wish to think that an individual's moral behavior is divorced from considerations of personal punishment or reward, there is both theory and evidence to the contrary. It is perfectly reasonable to assume that, under circumstances of group responsibility for a punishable act, the punishment or blame that accrues to any one individual is often slight or nonexistent.

Finally, if others are known to be present, but their behavior cannot be closely observed, any one bystander may assume that one of the other observers is already taking action to end the emergency. If so, his own intervention would only be redundant—perhaps

harmfully or confusingly so. Thus, given the presence of other onlookers whose behavior cannot be observed, any given bystander can rationalize his own inaction by convincing himself that "somebody else must be doing something."

These considerations suggest that, even when bystanders to an emergency cannot see or be influenced by each other, the more bystanders who are present, the less likely any one bystander would be to intervene and provide aid. To test this suggestion, it would be necessary to create an emergency situation in which each subject is blocked from communicating with others to prevent his getting information about their behavior during the emergency. Experiment 4 attempted to fulfill this requirement.

EXPERIMENT 4.
A FIT TO BE TRIED[4]

Procedure Thirteen male and 104 female students in introductory psychology courses at New York University were recruited to take part in an unspecified experiment as part of their class requirement. When a subject arrived in the laboratory, he was ushered into an individual room from which a communication system would enable him to talk to the other participants (who were actually figments of the tape recorder). Over the intercom, the subject was told that the experimenter was concerned with the kinds of personal problems faced by normal college students in a

[4]Portions of these results have been reported in Darley, J. M., and Latané, B. Bystander intervention in emergencies: Diffusion of responsibility. *Journal of Personality and Social Psychology*, 1968, **8,** 377–383.

high-pressure, urban environment, and that he would be asked to participate in a discussion about these problems. To avoid possible embarrassment about discussing personal problems with strangers, the experimenter said, several precautions would be taken. First, subjects would remain anonymous, which was why they had been placed in individual rooms rather than face-to-face. Second, the experimenter would not listen to the initial discussion himself, but would only get the subjects' reactions later by questionnaire.

The plan for the discussion was that each person would talk in turn for two minutes, presenting his problems to the group. Next, each person in turn would comment on what others had said, and finally there would be a free discussion. A mechanical switching device regulated the discussion, switching on only one microphone at a time.

The Emergency The discussion started with the future victim speaking first. He said he found it difficult to get adjusted to New York and to his studies. Very hesitantly and with obvious embarrassment, he mentioned that he was prone to seizures, particularly when studying hard or taking exams. The other people, including the one real subject, took their turns and discussed similar problems (minus the proneness to seizures). The naive subject talked last in the series, after the last prerecorded voice.

When it was again the victim's turn to talk, he made a few relatively calm comments, and then, growing increasingly loud and incoherent, he continued:

I er um I think I I need er if if could er er somebody er er er er er er er give me a

little er give me a little help here because er I er I'm er er h-h-having a a a a real problem er right now and I er if somebody could help me out it would it would er er s-s-sure be sure be good . . . because er there er er a cause I er I uh I've got a a one of the er sei——er er things coming on and and and I could really er use some help so if somebody would er give me a little h-help uh er-er-er-er-er c-could somebody er er help er uh uh uh (choking sounds) . . . I'm gonna die er er I'm . . . gonna die er help er er seizure er (chokes, then quiet).

The major independent variable of the study was the number of people the subject believed also heard the fit. The subject was led to believe that the discussion group was one of three sizes: a two-person group consisting of himself and the victim; a three-person group consisting of himself, the victim and one other person; or a six-person group consisting of himself, the victim, and four other persons.

Varying the kind of bystanders present at an emergency as well as the number of bystanders should also vary the amount of responsibility felt by any single bystander. To test this, several variations of the three-person group were run. In one three-person condition, the other bystander was a female; in another, a male; and in a third, a male who said that he was a premedical student who occasionally worked in the emergency wards at Bellevue Hospital.

Subjects in the above conditions were female college students. To test whether there are sex differences in the likelihood of helping, males drawn from the same subject pool were tested in the three-person, female bystander condition.

Two final experimental variations concerned acquaintanceship relationships between the subject and other bystanders and between the subject and the victim. In one of these conditions, female subjects were tested in the three-person condition, but were tested with a friend that they had been asked to bring with them to the laboratory. In another, subjects were given prior contact with the victim before being run in the six-person group. Subjects underwent a very brief "accidental" encounter with an experimental confederate posing as the future victim. The two met for about a minute in the hall before the experiment began. During this time, they chatted about topics having nothing to do with the experiment.

The major dependent variable of the experiment was the time elapsed from the start of the victim's seizure until the subject left her experimental cubicle. When the subject left her room, she saw the experiment's assistant seated at the end of the hall, and invariably went to the assistant to report the seizure. If six minutes elapsed without the subject's having emerged from her room, the experiment was terminated.

Ninety-five per cent of all the subjects who ever responded did so within the first half of the time available to them. No subject who had not reported within three minutes after the fit ever did so. This suggests that even had the experiment been allowed to run for a considerably longer period of time, few additional subjects would have responded.

Eighty-five percent of the subjects who thought they alone knew of the victim's plight reported the seizure before the victim was cut off; only 31% of those who thought four other bystanders were present did so. Every one of the subjects in the two-person condition, but only 62% of the subjects in the six-person condition ever reported the emergency. To do a more detailed analysis of the results, each subject's time score was transformed into a "speed" score by taking the reciprocal of the response time in seconds and multiplying by 100. Analysis of variance of these speed scores indicates that the effect of group size was highly significant $(p < 01)$, and all three groups differed significantly one from another $(p < .05)$.

Effect of Group Composition and Sex of the Subject Several variations of the three-person group were run. In one pair of variations, the female subject thought the other bystander was either male or female, in another, she thought the other bystander was a premedical student who worked in the emergency ward at Bellevue Hospital. These variations in the sex and medical competence of the other bystander had no important or detectable effect on speed of response. Subjects responded equally frequently and fast whether the other bystander was female, male, or medically experienced.

Coping with emergencies is often thought to be the duty of males, especially when there are females present, but there was no evidence that this is the case in this study. Male subjects responded to the emergency with almost exactly the same speed as did females.

Effects of Friendship and Prior Acquaintance Friends responded considerably differently from strangers in the three-person condition. When two friends were each aware of the victim's distress, even though they could not see or be seen by each other, they responded significantly faster than subjects in the other three-person groups. In fact, the average speed of response by subjects who thought their friend was also present was not noticeably different from the average speed of response in the two-person condition, where subjects believed that they alone were aware of the emergency. This suggests that responsibility does not diffuse across friends.

The effects of prior acquaintance with the victim were also strong. Subjects who had met the victim, even though only for less than a minute, were significantly faster to report his distress than other subjects in the six-person condition. Subjects in this condition later discussed their reactions to the situation. Unlike subjects in any other group, some of those who had accidentally met the victim-to-be later reported that they had actually *pictured* him in the grip of the seizure. Apparently, the ability to *visualize* a specific, concrete, distressed individual increases the likelihood of helping that person.

Subjects, whether or not they intervened, believed the fit to be genuine and serious. "My God, he's having a fit," many subjects said to themselves (and we overheard via their microphones). Others gasped or simply said, "Oh." Several of the male subjects swore. One subject said to herself, "It's just my kind of luck, something has to happen to me!" Several subjects spoke aloud of their confusion about what course of action to take: "Oh, God, what should I do?"

When those subjects who intervened stepped out of their rooms, they found the experiment's assistant down the hall. With some uncertainty but without panic, they reported the situation. "Hey, I think Number 1 is very sick. He's having a fit or something." After ostensibly checking on the situation, the experimenter returned to report that "everything is under control." The subjects accepted these assurances with obvious relief.

Subjects who failed to report the emergency showed few signs of the apathy and indifference thought to characterize "unresponsive bystanders." When the experimenter entered her room to terminate the situation, the subject often asked if the victim were all right. "Is he being taken care of?" "He's all right, isn't he?" Many of these subjects showed physical signs of nervousness; they often had trembling hands and sweating palms. If anything, they seemed more emotionally aroused than did the subjects who reported the emergency.

Why, then, didn't they respond? It is not our impression that they had decided *not* to respond. Rather, they were still in a state of indecision and conflict concerning whether to respond or not. The emotional behavior of these non-responding subjects was a sign of their continuing conflict; a conflict that other subjects resolved by responding.

The fit created a conflict situation of the avoidance-avoidance type. On the one hand, subjects worried about the guilt and shame they would feel if they did not help the person in distress. On the other hand, they were concerned not to make fools of themselves by over-reacting, not to ruin the ongoing experiment by leaving their intercoms and not to destroy the anonymous nature of the situation, which the experimenter had earlier stressed as important. For subjects in the two-person condition, the obvious distress of the victim and his need for help were so important that their conflict was easily resolved. For the subjects who knew that there were other bystanders present, the cost of not helping was reduced and the conflict they were in was more acute. Caught between the two negative alternatives of letting the victim continue to suffer, or the costs of rushing in to help, the non-responding bystanders vacillated between them rather than choosing not to respond. This distinction may be academic for the victim, since he got no help in either case, but it is an extremely important one for understanding the causes of bystander's failures to help.

Although the subjects experienced stress and conflict during the emergency, their general reactions to it were highly positive. On a questionnaire administered after the experimenter had discussed the nature and purpose of the experiment, every single subject found the experiment either "interesting" or "very interesting" and was willing to participate in similar experiments in the future. All subjects felt they understood what the experiment was all about and indicated they thought the deceptions were necessary and justified. All but one felt they were better informed about the nature of psychological research in general.

We asked all subjects whether the presence or absence of other bystanders had entered their minds during the time that they were hearing the seizure. We asked the question every way we knew how: subtly, directly, tactfully, bluntly, and the answer was always the same. Subjects had been aware of the presence of other bystanders in the appropriate conditions, but they did not feel that they had been influenced in any way by their presence. As in our previous experiments, this denial occurred in the face of results showing that the presence of others did affect helping.

SOCIAL DETERMINANTS OF BYSTANDER INTERVENTION, III

We have suggested two distinct processes which might lead people to be less likely to intervene in an emergency if there are other people present than if they are alone. On the one hand, we have suggested that the presence of other people may affect the interpretations each bystander puts on an ambiguous emergency situation. If other people are present at an emergency, each bystander will be guided by their apparent reactions in formulating his own impressions. Unfortunately, their apparent reactions may not be a good indication of their true feelings. It is possible for a state of "pluralistic ignorance" to develop, in which each bystander is led by the *apparent* lack of concern of the others to interpret the situation as being less serious than he would if alone. To the extent that he does not feel the situation is an emergency, of course, he will be unlikely to take any helpful action.

Even if an individual does decide that an emergency is actually in process and that something ought to be done, he still is faced with the choice of whether he himself will intervene. Here again, the presence of other people may influence him—by reducing the costs associated with non-intervention. If a number of people witness the same event, the responsibility for action is diffused, and each may feel less necessity to help.

Both the "social influence" and the "diffusion of responsibility" explanations seem valid, and there is no reason why both should not be jointly operative. Neither alone can account for all the data. For example, the diffusion explanation cannot account for the significant difference in response rate between the Strangers and Stooge conditions in Experiment 2. There should be equal diffusion in either case. This difference can more plausibly be attributed to the fact that strangers typically did not show such complete indifference to the accident as did the stooge. The diffusion process also does not seem applicable to the results of Experiment 1. Responsibility for protecting oneself from fire should not diffuse. On the other hand, "social influence" processes cannot account for results in Experiment 4. Subjects in that experiment could not communicate with each other and thus could not be influenced by each other's reactions.

Although both processes probably operate, they may not do so at the same time. To the extent that social influence leads an individual to define the situation as non-serious and not requiring action, his responsibility is eliminated, making diffusion unnecessary. Only if social influence is unavailable or unsuccessful in leading subjects to misinterpret a situation, should diffusion play a role. Indirect evidence supporting this analysis comes from observation of non-intervening subjects in the various emergency settings. In settings involving face-to-face contact, as in Experiments 1 and 2, non-interveners typically redefined the situation and did not see it as a serious emergency. Consequently, they avoided the moral choice of whether or not to take action. During the post-experimental interviews, subjects in these experiments seemed relaxed and assured. They felt they had behaved reasonably and properly. In Experiment 4, on the other hand, face-to-face contact was prevented, social influence could not help subjects define the situation as non-serious, and they were faced with the moral dilemma of whether to intervene. Although the imagined presence of other people led many subjects to delay intervention, their conflict was exhibited in the post-experimental interviews. If anything, subjects who did not intervene seemed more emotionally aroused than did subjects who reported the emergency.

The results of these experiments suggest that social inhibition effects may be rather general over a wide variety of emergency situations. In four different experiments, bystanders have been less likely to intervene if other bystanders are present. The nature of the other bystander seems to be important: a non-reactive confederate provides the most inhibition, a stranger provides a moderate amount, and a friend, the least. Overall, the results are consistent with a multiprocess model of intervention; the effect of other people seems to be mediated both through the interpretations that bystanders place on the situation, and through the decisions they make once they have come up with an interpretation.

"There's safety in numbers," according to an old adage, and modern city dwellers seem to believe it. They shun deserted streets, empty subway cars, and lonely walks in dark parks, preferring instead to go where others are or to stay at home. When faced with stress, most individuals seem less afraid when they are in the presence of others than when they are alone. Dogs are less likely to yelp when they face a strange situation with other dogs; even rats are less likely to defecate and freeze when they are placed in a frightening open field with other rats.

A feeling so widely shared should have some basis in reality. Is there safety in numbers? If so, why? Two reasons are often suggested: Individuals are less likely to find themselves in trouble if there are others about, and even if they do find themselves in trouble, others are likely to help them deal with it. While it is certainly true that a victim is unlikely to receive help if nobody knows of his plight, the experiments above cast doubt on the suggestion that he will be more likely to receive help if more people are present. In fact, the opposite seems to be true. A victim may be more likely to get help, or an emergency be reported, the fewer people who are available to take action.

Although the results of these studies may shake our faith in "safety in numbers," they also may help us begin to understand a number of frightening incidents where crowds have listened to, but not answered, a call for help. Newspapers have tagged these incidents with the label "apathy." We have become indifferent, they say, callous to the fate of suffering others. Our society has become "dehumanized" as it has become urbanized. These glib phrases may contain some truth, since startling cases such as the Genovese murder often seem to occur in our large cities, but such terms may also be misleading. Our studies suggest a different conclusion. They suggest that situational factors, specifically factors involving the immediate social environment, may be of greater importance in determining an individual's reaction to an emergency than such vague cultural or personality concepts as "apathy" or "alienation due to urbanization." They suggest that the failure to intervene may be better understood by knowing the relationship among bystanders rather than that between a bystander and the victim.

Our results may explain why the failure to intervene seems to be more characteristic of large cities than rural areas. Bystanders to urban emergencies are more likely to be, or at least to think they are, in the presence of other bystanders than witnesses of non-urban emergencies. Bystanders to urban emergencies are less likely to know each other or to know the victim than are witnesses of non-urban emergencies. When an emergency occurs in a large city, a crowd is likely to gather; the crowd members are likely to be strangers; and it is likely that no one will be acquainted with the victim. These are exactly the conditions that made the helping response least likely in our experiments.

In a less sophisticated era, Rudyard Kipling prayed "That we, with Thee, may walk uncowed by fear or favor of the crowd; that, under Thee, we may possess man's strength to comfort man's distress." It appears that the latter hope may depend to a surprising extent upon the former.

REFERENCES

Brown, R. W. Mass Phenomena. In Lindzey, G. (ed.) *Handbook of Social Psychology*, Vol. 2, Cambridge, Addison-Wesley, 1954.

Brown, R. W. *Social Psychology*, New York, Free Press, 1965.

Darley, J. M., and Latané, B. Bystander intervention in emergencies: Diffusion of responsibility. *Journal of Personality and Social Psychology*, 1968, **8**, 377–383.

Latané, B. Gregariousness and fear in laboratory rats. *Journal of Experimental Social Psychology*, 1969, **5**, 61–69.

Latané, B., and Darley, J. M. Group inhibition of bystander intervention in emergencies. *Journal of Personality and Social Psychology,* 1968, **10,** 215–221.

Latané, B., and Glass, D. C. Social and non-social attraction in rats. *Journal of Personality and Social Psychology,* 1968, **9,** 142–146.

Latané, B., and Rodin, J. A lady in distress: Inhibiting effects of friends and strangers on bystander intervention. *Journal of Experimental Social Psychology,* 1969, **5,** 189–202.

Schachter, S. *The Psychology of Affiliation,* Stanford: Stanford University Press, 1959.

25

Eye Contact, Pupil Dilation, and Personal Preference

Jack W. Stass and Frank N. Willis

This article shows how experimental methods can be applied to the study of interpersonal attraction. Two simple independent variables—degree of eye contact and amount of pupillary dilation—were shown to have a marked influence on the degree to which individuals were preferred in a social interaction. Mere dilation of the pupils approximately doubled the frequency with which a given girl was chosen as a partner for intimate interaction! The technique of Stass and Willis provides a highly authentic method for evaluating variables that might influence interpersonal attractiveness.

The importance of visual contact in the interaction between animals has been described for many species in a variety of settings. The present study deals with the importance of visual contact for humans in their choice of partners for a future interaction.

Visual contact is not only important to human interaction but is also capable of being detected with extreme accuracy. Argyle & Dean (1965) investigated eye-contact and found that without it Ss did not feel that they were fully in communication. Gibson & Pick (1963)

found that considerable accuracy marks the reception of a glance from another at an angle of 70 degrees.

Exline (1960, 1963, 1965) has shown that eye-contact in interaction is related to affiliation, sex, topic of conversation, and role as speaker or listener.

A second area of visual communication that has received some attention is the effect of pupillary size. Hess (1965) reported that an increase in pupil size was related to interest in a viewed object. He found further that males were more attracted to a picture of a female with dilated pupils than they were to an identical picture with undilated pupils.

Reprinted from *Psychonomic Science*, 1967, **7**, 375–376, by permission of the authors and publisher.

There were two purposes for the present study. The first was to determine the effect of eye-contact on the choice of partners for a future interaction. The second was to examine the effect of pupil size on personal preference in an actual interaction as opposed to the response to photos as investigated by Hess.

SUBJECTS

The study was conducted in three phases. The first dealt with eye-contact and employed 37 male and 35 female Ss. The second dealt with pupil dilation and employed 54 male Ss. The third dealt with pupil size and employed 19 female Ss. All Ss were undergraduate students in three colleges in the greater Kansas City area.

APPARATUS

Pupillary dilation was achieved with a drug containing neo-synephrine 10% hydrochloride in a buffered low surface tension vehicle with sodium phosphate, sodium biphosphate and an antiseptic preservative, Zephiran chloride 1:10,000. This drug was selected because of its rapid effect, prolonged action, and lack of undesirable systemic side effects.

PROCEDURE

The Ss were told that they were to take part in an experiment that required an experimental partner. The Ss in phase I were told that the experiment involved the handling of money and that they should choose a partner they could trust. Ss in phases II and III were told that the experimental task required very intimate communication and that they should choose someone who was, in their opinion, pleasant and easy to talk to. Each S was taken to a room in which two available experimental partners were waiting. Ss were told that they would be introduced to two possible partners and that they were to inform E privately following the introduction as to their choice of partner. The available partners varied as follows: In phase I, one individual maintained eye-contact throughout the introduction while the other glanced away from the S during the introduction. In this phase both partners were male. They were similarly dressed. Their position in relation to the Ss was rotated (left-right) for each S. The partner giving eye-contact was rotated every fourth S. All partners in all phases were rehearsed by E so that their smile, casual posture, etc. were similar during the introduction. In phase II it was considered important that the partners be approximately equal in attractiveness, so two women were chosen from a group of 12 because they were rated as being most equal in attractiveness by a class of over 200 introductory psychology students. On the first day on which phase II was run, one of the two women had dilated pupils, and on the second day the other had dilated pupils. The dilation was obvious enough to permit identification of the dilated partner at a distance of four feet. An optometrist administered the drug and checked the size of pupils at 10-min. intervals throughout the experimental period. No changes in pupil size were noted after the original dilation. In phase III, procedures were identical to phase II except that male identical twins were employed as partners. The men and women serving as available experimental partners were not informed of the nature of the study until all Ss were run. All Ss were asked to give reasons for their choice of partners following the session.

pleasant, nice, etc. In phases II and III, no S reported a choice based upon pupil size. Ss either stated that they were unable to explain their choice or simply stated that their choice was good looking, appeared friendly, pleasant, etc.

RESULTS

Phase I   58 Ss chose the eye-contact partner and 14 chose the non-eye-contact partner. A chi-square test of goodness of fit yielded a $X^2 = 26.8$, with df = 1 and p < .01. The proportion of male and female Ss choosing the eye-contact partner were approximately equal. The men serving under the two conditions were chosen about equally often.

Phase II   36 Ss chose the dilated partner and 18 chose the non-dilated partner. A chi-square test of goodness of fit yielded a $X^2 = 6$, with df = 1, and p < .02. The two women chosen as available partners did not appear to be equally attractive to the Ss as planned since one was chosen twice as often as the other, but each girl was chosen approximately twice as often in the dilated condition as in the non-dilated condition.

Phase III   21 Ss chose the dilated partner and five chose the non-dilated partner. This resulted in a $X^2 = 9.8$, with df = 1, and p < .01. The men serving as available partners were chosen about equally often.

Reasons Given for Choice of Partners
Only eight of the 72 Ss in phase I mentioned eye-contact as being important in their choice. Other Ss stated that the partner appeared to be friendly,

DISCUSSION

All of the data from the present study support the generalization that visual contact may be quite important in forming initial impressions. This seems to be reflected in every day language in such expressions as "an honest face" and "shifty eyes." In view of Hess' finding that dilated pupils are an expression of interest, this study is significant in showing that women, like men, are attracted by others who appear to be interested in them.

A lack of eye-contact may, in our culture, be interpreted as an indication of dishonesty or may, in the words of Argyle & Dean (1965), indicate that channels for communication are closed.

It is interesting that although Ss may have a preference for others depending upon the appearance or behavior of the other's eyes, the Ss are not necessarily able to report the use of these cues.

In spite of the training and rehearsal of the partners aimed at controlling all behavior and appearance other than those being varied, it is possible that other differences existed at the time of the choice and influenced the choice. It should be noted, however, that the partners were not informed of the relationship being investigated, nor did they express an awareness of these relationships after the experiment was concluded. One might reason that an eye-contact partner could guess that he was to appear more attractive, but it does not follow that the partner in the dilated condition would make a similar guess.

REFERENCES

Argyle, M., & Dean, J. Eye-contact, distance, and affiliation. *Sociometry*, 1965, **28**, 289–304.

Exline, R. V. Effects of sex, norms, and affiliative motivation upon accuracy of interpersonal preferences. *J. Pers.*, 1960, **28**, 397–412.

Exline, R. V. Explorations in the process of persons perception: Visual interaction in relation to competition, sex, and need for affiliation. *J. Pers.*, 1963, **31**, 1–20.

Exline, R. V., et al. Visual behavior in a dyad as affected by interview content and sex of respondent. *J. Pers. soc. Psychol.*, 1965, **1**, 201–209.

Gibson, J. J., & Pick, A. D. Perception of another's looking behavior. *Amer. J. Psychol.*, 1963, **76**, 386–394.

Hess, E. H. Attitude and pupil size. *Scient. American*, 1965, **212**, 46–54.

FOURTEEN

*Research on Complex
Human Behavior: III.
Extending Understanding
and Control of
Psychological Events*

26

Electrophysiological Studies of Dreaming as the Prototype of a New Strategy in the Study of Consciousness

Johann Stoyva and Joe Kamiya

Experimental psychologists abandoned classical introspectionism largely because it proved to be an *unreliable* technique. The introspectionist had trouble being consistent with other introspectionists, and also had a difficult time being internally consistent. This ambiguity of subject matter was alleviated by shifting to the simple observational techniques of behaviorists or by modifying the introspective method so that naive, unanalyzed experiences were reported (the phenomenological method). Both types of methodological change improved observational reliability, but each of them had its inherent disadvantages. The phenomenological method had a "residual ambiguity," and tended to go hand in hand with a relative insensitivity to the problems involved in establishing the reliability of data. Though it was more reliable than analytic introspectionism, it was not reliable enough for many "hard-nosed" psychologists. The tough-minded tended to opt for behaviorism, because they regarded solid, scientific observation as of unparalleled importance. This led to a situation in which many, many important human problems were cast aside in favor of research on the details of albino rat behavior. Some psychologists insisted that the important problems of man must be dealt with, even if the methods were not entirely adequate. These men were in a kind of *therapeutic tradition* which has always placed its emphasis on dealing with the vital questions, usually with such inadequate

methods as intuition, uncontrolled observation, and armchair speculation. Yet, they made an important point in arguing that their scientific
counterparts—those in the *academic tradition*—were gathering more and
more information about "less and less"—about increasingly trivial matters.

Psychologists seemed to be in the awkward position of having
to choose between being scientifically pure but trivial and being socially
relevant but methodologically inadequate. Many forces have impinged
on us in recent times to resolve that dilemma. For example, the methods
of animal psychologists have proven their relevance to human problems
now that such things as behavior therapies and teaching machines have
come into vogue. Our society has become increasingly emphatic in its
demands for solutions to its problems, and psychologists are hard-
pressed to resist its threats and blandishments. Fortunately, it would be
out of the question for many of these scientists to abandon their rigor-
ousness. There is great hope that the academic and therapeutic traditions
will fuse into a truly adequate science of human behavior.

The following article illustrates one of the major breakthroughs
in bringing scientifically rigorous methods of measurement to bear on
subtle, normally inaccessible psychological events. Research on sleep
and dreaming has led to the realization that even the most private, inner
events can be measured rigorously. Not only has it been possible to get
objective measures of dream activity, but even the meditation states of
Zen disciples and masters and of yogis have been measured—and the
measures reflect their introspective reports quite accurately! Nothing
could have seemed more remote from accessibility to scientific investigation than these private, even mystical phenomena. These and many
other seemingly inaccessible phenomena will be treated by the methods
of experimental psychology in the future. And there is an important
"spin-off" from all this. If such events can be observed by an outsider,
they can be manipulated by such methods as those of respondent and
operant conditioning. Kamiya's technique of teaching people to control
their brain waves is discussed in the article. Since brain waves have
psychological counterparts such as relaxation, alertness, sleep, and so
forth, a method of controlling the psychological events is now available
to us.

A key concept in the article is that of multiple, converging operations. When something is defined operationally, it is defined in terms
of the procedures whereby it is measured. Many concepts seem to
include far more than can be expressed in terms of a single operation.
Take the case of dreaming. Operationally we might define a dream as
a verbal report which occurs when a subject is awakened from sleep.
This is a very commonly used operational definition of dreaming. Yet
the concept of "dream" includes the notion that some people dream
without being able to give a report of the dreams. Further, the ordinary

concept is one of something which occurs *while asleep*. Since the verbal report occurs while the subject is awake, we would be forced to say that dreams occur during waking hours and never during sleep if we were to take the simple operational view that the dream is *nothing but* the operation on which it is based (verbal report). Such paradoxes as these can be solved by the use of multiple, convergent operations.

An observation which has long impressed the authors is how the area of dream research suddenly became more acceptable—and interesting—to psychologists following the discovery of the rapid eye movement (REM) indicator by Aserinsky and Kleitman (1953). Why the sudden gain in respectability for this type of introspective evidence, a gain which was really quite striking when one considers the precarious position which reports of private events have long held in experimental psychology, in this country at least? Was the enthusiasm justified, or were the supposed benefits largely illusory?

The authors' position is that there were good reasons for the marked gain in the scientific status of dream studies.

Reprinted from *Psychological Review*, 1968, **75**, 192–205. Copyright 1968 by the American Psychological Association, and reproduced by permission.

The preparation of this paper and certain of the research projects described in it were supported partly by a National Institute of Mental Health Postdoctoral Fellowship to the first author in the Interdisciplinary Training Program at the University of California Medical Center, United States Public Health Service Grant Number 5T1MH-7082; by Grant Number MH-05069-03; and by United States Public Health Service National Institutes of Health Grant Number 5 RO 1 OHOO 213-02 and Office of Pesticides Program Contract Number 86-65-62.

The authors would like to express their gratitude to Allan Rechtschaffen, Donald Stilson, David Foulkes, Thomas Budzynski, and David Metcalf for their many valuable criticisms and suggestions.

Admittedly, not everyone would agree with this position. Hall (1966), for example, feels that we are in danger of physiologizing the dream out of existence. Malcolm (1959) also expresses dissenting views—he considers the electrophysiological studies of dreaming as largely irrelevant to the study of the dream as a psychological experience. Many others, as Fisher (1965) and Rechtschaffen (1964) point out, have concentrated purely on the physiology of the REM state, ignoring the experiential concomitants.

The authors differ from both of these positions, maintaining that a crucial point in the new status of dream studies is that the combined use of verbal report and physiological evidence has given renewed construct validity to the hypothetical internal state of dreaming. Subsequently—given the validity of REMs as an indicator of dreaming and of localizing the dream process in time—it has proved possible for researchers to bring to light a whole body of new findings about dreaming.

The authors also maintain that the combined use of verbal report and physiological measures is a method which need not be confined to dreaming but could—especially with the addition of information feedback procedures—be profitably extended to the study of certain types of waking mental activity as well. As an example of this extension of the basic method, the writers discuss some recent work on the operant control of the electroencephalographic (EEG) alpha rhythm. These studies employ electronic information feedback techniques which tell a subject (S) at once whether he is showing alpha or nonalpha. Such an approach may be useful in exploring the particular state of consciousness associated with alpha and may be applicable in the case of other EEG rhythms as well. This extension of the basic method is discussed in the final section of the paper.

THE BASIC LOGIC OF THE NEW STRATEGY

The gist of the authors' position is that there has evolved a new strategy in the study of certain conscious processes. This new approach involves a combination of verbal report and physiological measures, and may be best exemplified by the recent EEG studies of dreaming. The paper, therefore, is not so much about dreaming per se, as about a new methodology of which the current dream studies are the best example. In the authors' view, the electrophysiological studies of dreaming may be regarded as a prototype of a new strategy in the study of consciousness.

The development is surely something of a landmark in the troubled history of the introspective method and its place in psychology.[1] Though several writers

have spoken of a resurgence of interest in introspective data—Hebb (1960), Holt (1964), McClelland (1955)—the particular approach to private events described in this paper has not been explored elsewhere.

Indeed, the authors feel that certain basic points have suffered neglect. Specifically, no one seems to have asked: What is the fundamental logic underlying the combined use of physiological measures and verbal report in the study of dreaming? In the authors' estimation, it is the logic of converging operations, the essence of which is the selection or elimination of alternative hypotheses which might explain a given result. A consideration of the logic of converging operations and its relation to validating the hypothetical construct of dreaming follows in the next two sections.

In addition, when dreaming is conceptualized as a hypothetical construct (validated by certain converging operations) it becomes possible to restate the definition of dreaming in such a way as to clarify certain ambiguities which previous definitions of dream have left unresolved. The new definition and the advantages it offers in explicating the relations among the hypothetical experience of dreaming, the dream report,

---

[1] Very often the word *introspection* has been used to refer both to reports about *internal* events (e.g., imagery) and to reports about *external* events (e.g., perception). In the interests of clarity, however, the authors define *introspection* and *verbal reports of conscious processes* as being synonymous. The term introspection will be used chiefly in the interests of making clear certain historical continuities.

Though Boring (1953) has remarked that verbal report is simply introspection in a new guise, the

authors believe that *verbal reports of conscious processes* enjoys a number of advantages over the older term: (a) It underscores the fact that the primary datum available to the experimenter is what S says, that is, his verbal report. (b) It further serves to stress that anything said about conscious processes is made up of inferences from verbal report. Such inferences may be weak or strong depending upon the supporting evidence. (c) Also of some importance, the term verbal report is one less likely to raise hackles. It is a more neutral term than is introspection, and is less encumbered by the theoretical baggage of bygone controversies and REMs are discussed in a later section.

The REM Indicator and Its Validation

Though the discovery of the association between REMs and dreaming arose from a chance observation, it is worth noting that this relationship had been clearly anticipated by Max (1935) in his explorations of the motor theory of thinking. Max's major claim—that in deaf-mutes, there is a unique link between dreaming and finger electromyographic (EMG) activity—has since been disconfirmed by Stoyva (1965). But Max did offer a most intriguing speculation: He surmised that eye movements may be involved in those dreams which are visual in nature. Had he further pursued this remarkable conjecture, Max might very well have demonstrated the association between dreaming and eye movements some two decades prior to the unexpected discovery by the physiologists Aserinsky and Kleitman (1953).

Briefly, the latter found that bursts of eye movements occurred in cyclical fashion during sleep. These bursts of REMs regularly appeared during the periods of low voltage waves characteristic of activated EEG (Stage 1 sleep). Awakenings from Stage 1 REM periods produced a high frequency of dream recall; awakenings at other times (Stages 2, 3, and 4 sleep) yielded only a low incidence of recall. It seemed, therefore, that there might be at least two physiological indicators—REMs and low voltage EEG—which were closely related to the occurrence of dreaming.

But did REMs really represent dreaming? An alternative explanation might be that REM reports simply consisted of mental activity recalled from earlier stages of sleep. Troublesome questions of this nature raised the whole problem of how to validate REMs as an indicator of dreaming. This validation was subsequently accomplished in a series of related experiments in which: (a) Dement and Kleitman (1957) noted a positive correlation between the subjectively estimated length of a dream and the amount of REM time that had actually elapsed prior to a given awakening, (b) Berger and Oswald (1962) observed a relationship between the density of REM activity preceding a given awakening and the amount of physical activity reported in the dream narrative, (c) Dement and Kleitman (1957) also found a close relationship between the recorded direction of eye movement activity and the visual activity in the dream report. For example, from an awakening shortly after bursts of vertical eye movement, an S might report, "watching someone walking up a flight of stairs." (For a more detailed treatment of these REM validation experiments, see Dement, 1965.)

These last two observations (b and c above) suggested that there was more than a rough temporal correspondence between REMs and dreaming; and Dement and Kleitman (1957) formulated the hypothesis that REMs represent visual scanning—in the REM phase of sleep, Ss were "looking" at things. This surmise was confirmed in a more detailed study of Roffwarg, Dement, Muzio, and Fisher (1962), who deliberately attempted to improve the prospects for accurate recall by requesting their Ss to report in detail the visual imagery from the *final* 10–20 seconds prior to a given awakening.

Converging Operations

As emphasized in the preceding section, the REM indicator received an enthusiastic reception, and was assumed from the start to promise many advantages for the study of dreaming. But, oddly enough, these presumed advantages have never been explicitly examined by dream researchers. What, precisely, are the merits in having a physiological measure closely associated with verbal report? What, if anything, does the physiological indicator add to the report of S?

Probably the basic advantage is that the physiological measure serves to corroborate the verbal report, thereby strengthening the inference that certain conscious processes did, in fact, occur during sleep. It then becomes difficult to explain away the dream narrative as being merely a fabrication put together to please the experimenter, or the result of an awakening artifact. Thus, if S reports a dream episode involving vertical eye movements, and we also note corresponding vertical eye movements on the chart paper, then we feel more secure in inferring the mental process of dreaming. Moreover, since S's dream report has been confirmed in one particular, we are then inclined to accord credibility to the remainder of what he reports.

At first glance, such a correlation may not seem so important, but in the historical context of the many objections raised against introspective evidence—and which have shaken our faith in such evidence—the high measure of agreement between a report of a given conscious process and a concurrent physiological measure assumes considerable significance.

Moreover, when the electrophysiological studies of dreaming are viewed in a somewhat broader context, it becomes apparent that the basic strength of the new multidimensional approach lies in its consisting of a number of intersecting or *convergent indicators.* Thus, in the REM phase of sleep, there may be found, on the physiological level, the following linked indicators: REMs, low voltage EEG, marked cardiovascular irregularities, penile erections, pronounced drops in muscle tonus, and an increased firing rate in visual cortex neurons. On the verbal report level may be noted a high incidence of dream recall and frequent reports of vivid, bizarre, or emotion-charged events. On the behavioral level may be observed an increase in body movement frequency and an increased frequency of fine movements in the extremities (Fisher, 1965; Jouvet, 1967; Luce & Segal, 1966).

It is the authors' thesis that this intersecting evidence represents a type of convergent operationalism along the lines proposed by Garner, Hake, and Eriksen (1956), a formulation which Campbell and Fiske (1959) later elaborated and extended to psychological testing with their technique of convergent and discriminant validation. As Garner et al. (1956) described the procedure,

Converging operations may be thought of as any set of two or more experimental operations which allow the selection or elimination of alternative hypotheses or concepts which could explain an experimental result. They are called converging operations because they are not perfectly correlated and thus can converge on a single concept [pp. 150–151].

It should be emphasized that converging operations do not simply refer to the repetition of an experiment—this demonstrates only the reliability of an observation. Converging operations permit the selection or elimination of alternative hypotheses. Thus, with respect to the relation between REMs and the verbal report of dreaming, at least three hypotheses could be proposed:

1. Verbal reports of dreaming from Stage 1 REM sleep reflect a reasonably accurate recall of a genuine dream experience.
2. Verbal reports of dreaming from Stage 1 REM sleep reflect an inaccurate recall of a genuine dream experience.
3. Verbal reports of dreaming from Stage 1 REM sleep represent fabrications concocted subsequent to awakening.

Suppose the experiment of awakening Ss from Stage 1 REM sleep is repeated many times, and we regularly obtain recall in the order of 80–85% of the time. This still does not allow a decision as to which of the above three hypotheses is correct—although it does say something for the reliability of the observation. What does lead to a choice among the three hypotheses is the information presented in the previous section on "The REM Indicator and Its Validation." Positive correlations were noted between the density of REMs and the amount of physical activity in the dream report, REM duration and Ss' estimated length of the dream, direction of REMs and the direction of visual scanning movements recounted in verbal report. This agreement between the REM indicator and the verbal report permits the

elimination of Hypotheses 2 and 3, leaving Hypothesis 1 as the most probable interpretation. Thus, the verbal report of dreaming and the REM indicator support one another. They both point to the concept or the hypothetical construct of dreaming.

Though Garner et al. (1956) and Campbell and Fiske (1959) wrote with special reference to psychological research, it is intriguing to note that similar proposals have arisen in other disciplines. Feigl (1958), for example, in discussing how scientific concepts are tied to their operations, speaks of their being "fixed" by "triangulation in logical space." And Platt (1964), in examining the spectacular advances in molecular biology and in high-energy physics, argues that the main impetus behind these advances has been the use of "strong inference." Basically, this method involves: (a) the explicit formulation of alternative hypotheses, and ways of disproving them, and (b) "Recycling the procedure, making sub-hypotheses or sequential hypotheses to refine the possibilities that remain . . . [Platt, 1964, p. 347]."

Definitions of Dreaming

To summarize the argument so far: After the discovery of the REM indicator, it became possible to use the technique of converging operations in the study of dreams. Systematic application of this technique resulted in renewed validity for the hypothetical mental state of dreaming, and in subsequent experiments a wealth of new observations came to light.

There is little doubt, then, that the REM indicator has proved useful in the study of dreaming. Unfortunately, this very usefulness led to a common misconception; namely, the tendency to equate REMs and dreaming—dreaming being interpreted as any mental activity during sleep.

But what is the correct way to define dreaming? To date, sleep researchers have disagreed considerably among themselves on this issue. Two conflicting viewpoints have been dominant:

1. There is the position of the physiologically-oriented researchers who have preferred to define dreaming in terms of the Stage 1 REM indicator. This viewpoint, at least the most uncompromising version of it, was at its height in the late 1950s and the early 1960s. Among the proponents of this position have been Dement, 1955; Dement and Wolpert, 1958; Wolpert, 1960; Wolpert and Trosman, 1958. Adherents of this position would argue that if S shows recall from the REM phase of sleep 85% of the time, the remaining 15% of the time does not indicate an absence of dreaming, but rather a failure of recall.

2. The other major position on how to define dreaming—and the more formidable one logically—is that the ultimate criterion of dreaming is the verbal report of S. Thus, Malcolm (1959), in his analysis of the concept of dreaming, advocated ". . . holding firmly to waking testimony as the sole criterion of dreaming [p. 81]." Proponents of this view can argue that the REM indicator by itself tells us nothing about dreaming. Its usefulness is entirely dependent on its having been first of all validated against verbal report; the REM indicator is valuable to the extent it agrees with verbal report. Consequently, if S wakes up from a REM period and reports *no* dream, we are obliged to conclude that, indeed, he had *no* dream. When the REM indicator and the verbal report are in conflict, we are logically forced to accept the latter.

There are difficulties, however, with both of the above positions. Thus, a number of observations prove troublesome for the REM definition of dreaming:

1. Non-REM recall. Evidence for non-REM mental activity was first advanced by Foulkes (1962) who systematically awakened his Ss in sleep stages *outside* of REM periods. These non-REM reports were qualitatively different from REM reports; in comparison they were more thoughtlike, were closely related to everyday life, and often consisted only of static images.

However, this non-REM material, which is not closely coupled with any physiological indicator such as REMs, has been accorded a far less cordial reception than has REM recall. In the opinion of Foulkes and Rechtschaffen (1964),

. . . the authenticity of nonREM reports as reports of experience taking place during nonREM sleep will most likely remain in some doubt until preawakening physiological landmarks can be correlated with the content of subsequently elicited reports in the manner that Roffwarg, Dement, Muzio, and Fisher (1962) have associated preawakening eye movement patterns with visual imagery reported by Ss following REM period awakenings [p. 1003].

These last remarks underscore a major point of this paper: Verbal reports of conscious experience are far more readily accepted as valid if they are supported by correlated physiological measures. These correlated measures permit the elimination of alternative hypotheses.

In addition to the work on non-REM recall, there is other evidence of mental activity outside of REM periods. Foulkes and Vogel (1965), for example, in a study of the hypnagogic period—the time of falling asleep, and shortly thereafter—obtained a surprisingly high proportion of dreamlike reports. Experiments also show that both sleeptalking (Kamiya, 1961; Rechtschaffen, Goodenough, & Shapiro, 1962) and sleepwalking (Jacobson, Kales, Lehmann, & Zweizig, 1965) occur most often outside of REM periods. All this evidence, then, suggests that mental activity during sleep can occur in the absence of the REM indicator.

2. Extreme conditions. Most of the evidence accumulated for the REM-dreaming association has been obtained from young adults sleeping under more or less ordinary conditions. What if conditions are made extreme, or observations are taken on very young or very old Ss?

One such extreme condition has been the REM deprivation studies. In the course of these experiments, some investigators have noted a tendency for REMs to break through into other stages of sleep (Sampson, 1965). Is there any mental activity associated with these unusual REMs? So far, there is no experimental evidence on this point.

With respect to S age and REM activity, it may be noted that in the neonate, REMs occur in abundance, occupying something like 50% of the total sleep time (Roffwarg, Muzio, & Dement, 1966). Yet, it seems highly improbable that any associated dream experience occurs until a child is at least a few months old. Again, at the other

extreme of age, very old Ss fail to show as clear-cut sleep stages as do young adults (Krassoievitch, Weber, & Junod, 1965).

3. Failure of recall in REM awakenings. Something like 15–20% of REM awakenings fail to yield dream recall. Did S have a dream experience or not?

The other main position on how to define dreaming—which uses verbal report as the criterion—is not free of difficulties either. One problem is the need to invoke the concept of forgetting to account for the fact that persons awakened several minutes following the end of a REM period show a greatly reduced probability of dream reports (an observation reported in several electrophysiological studies of dreaming; e.g., Orlinsky, 1962; Wolpert & Trosman, 1958).

Another example underscores the same point. Suppose an S spends a night in the laboratory. Many REM periods are observed, but there are no awakenings and no dream reports. Suppose that in the morning S says that he had no dreams at all that night. In this instance we are likely to discount his verbal report. Instead, we give more credence to the REM indicator, and infer that he did dream, but forgot. We feel secure in making this inference because we know that if we were to run this S another night in the laboratory, and were to carry out REM awakenings, the probability of obtaining at least one dream report would be extremely high. Thus, we are here accepting the REM indicator as a more valid index of dreaming than S's verbal report. In other words, the verbal report criterion is not always the sole or the best indicator of dreaming.

Furthermore, two behavioral studies,

one from the human and one from the animal level, suggest that dreaming may be signaled without the medium of language. Antrobus, Antrobus, and Fisher (1965), for example, instructed human *S*s to signal dreaming sleep by pressing a thumbswitch. They noted a higher frequency of responding during REM periods.

Vaughan (1964), in an unusual experiment, taught monkeys to barpress as an indicator of the presence of imagery. A number of rhesus monkeys, housed in individual booths and seated in restraining chairs, were first taught by avoidance conditioning procedures to pull a lever whenever a visual image of any type appeared on the frosted glass screen mounted about 2 feet in front of their faces. When these trained monkeys fell asleep, they showed strikingly high rates of bar-pressing activity during REM periods, suggesting that they were reacting to the visual imagery of the dream in the same way that they had responded to the faint images physically present on the frosted glass screen. The fundamental logic in both of these last two studies is that inferences about private events are being made on the basis of nonverbal behavior.

Dreaming as a Hypothetical Construct

In view of the difficulties with both the REM criterion of dreaming and the verbal report criterion of dreaming, we propose a third position; namely, that dreaming—in the sense of any mental activity during sleep—is a hypothetical construct, not directly accessible to public observation. This hypothetical construct is indexed, but indexed in an imperfect way, by both REMs and verbal report.

When dreaming is conceptualized in this manner, an instructive comparison may be made with some instances of hypothetical constructs used in other sciences. In physics, for example, the atom has been employed as a hypothetical construct. Also, in biology, the gene is a postulated entity which is not directly observed, but is of an inferential nature. The important point is that neither of these concepts is fully indexed by any one operation, but is an inference built up on the basis of many intersecting and overlapping observations. Similarly we may conceive of dreaming as a hypothetical construct, and one which is indexed in a less than perfect way by *both* verbal reports and REMs. The specific logical structure of this position becomes apparent in the Venn diagram of Figure 1 which represents: (*a*) the dream experience (this is a hypothetical construct and is defined as all mental activity during sleep), (*b*) the verbal report of dreaming, and (*c*) the

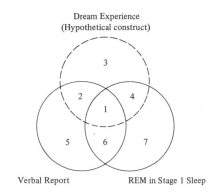

Dream Experience
(Hypothetical construct)

Verbal Report   REM in Stage 1 Sleep

Figure 1 Possible relationships among the hypothetical dream experience, the verbal report of dreaming, and Stage 1 REMs.

REM indicator of dreaming, as three overlapping circles.

A major advantage of this conceptualization is that it makes explicit the various logical possibilities relating the hypothetical construct of dreaming, verbal reports of dreaming, and the Stage 1 REM indicator. Support for this statement can be adduced by considering each of the following 7 regions shown in the Figure 1 Venn diagram:

Region 1   The intersection of the three circles represents the ideal case where the hypothesized dream activity, the verbal report of dreaming, and Stage 1 REMs occur congruently. It is in this instance that researchers have been able to apply the experimental logic of convergent operationalism; a technique which has resulted in the elimination of alternative hypotheses, thereby permitting the conclusion that verbal reports of dreaming from REM awakenings reflect a genuine dream experience. The evidence in support of this interpretation has been presented in earlier sections of this paper.

Region 2   This region represents the valid dream reports occurring from awakenings outside REM periods (e.g., non-REM reports, hypnagogic reports). This type of recall has been most systematically explored by Foulkes (1962, 1966).

Region 3   This region represents the dream experience that neither indicator detected; in other words, S forgot his non-REM dream. This possibility has been discussed by Kamiya (1961).

Region 4   This represents the occurrence of no dream reports despite the

occurrence of both the dream experience and REMs. In this region would fall the 15–20% of REM awakenings where there is no recall—at least this would be the interpretation expressed by Dement and Kleitman (1957).

Region 5   This represents the possibility that there are invalid dream reports from non-REM sleep. The possibility of such fabrication has been discussed by Kremen (1961), whose opinion was that most, if not all, of non-REM dream recall is made up of fabrications to please the experimenter. Let it be noted that it is difficult to discount such a view in the case of non-REM recall, since we lack the evidence for convergent validation that is available in the case of REM recall.

Region 6   This represents the possibility that invalid dream accounts may be reported from REM awakenings. For example, how do we know that reports from REM periods are not simply awakening artifacts, fabrications manufactured by S in the process of waking up? This possibility has generally been discounted as an explanation of REM dream reports following the discovery of the type of convergent validation discussed in the section on "The REM Indicator and Its Validation."

Region 7   This represents the possibility that REMs may occur in the absence of any dream experience and not be followed by dream reports. The absence of a dream report would in this case be valid. It will be noted that this interpretation is precisely opposed to the one offered in Region 4 in accounting for the 15–20% of REM awakenings which fail to yield dream recall. This would be the view espoused by the adherents of verbal report as the final criterion of dreaming; e.g., Malcolm (1959), Foulkes (1966).

Another pertinent example in this category is the case of the neonate. Here, there are REMs in abundance (approximately 50% of the time; Roffwarg, Muzio, & Dement, 1966), yet there are certainly no dream reports and, at this early age, any accompanying dream experience seems most unlikely.

From the foregoing discussion of the seven regions in the Figure 1 Venn diagram, it may be seen that though dream researchers have considered many of these categories, their examination has not taken place within any systematic framework. Making the logical possibilities explicit in the above manner should help in the clarification of conceptual issues in this field. Moreover, some previously neglected possibilities are brought to light. For example, Regions 3, 6, and 7 have seldom been discussed in the literature on sleep and dreaming. Furthermore, certain sleep experiences not associated with subsequent verbal reports of dreaming, such as sleepwalking and sleeptalking, are invited for consideration in Region 3, inasmuch as the postulated mental activity need not always imply reportability.

The type of conceptual framework proposed here may quite possibly be extended to some analogous situations where there is simultaneous use of physiological, behavioral, and verbal report indicators; for example, when inferring such states as arousal, anxiety, relaxation, or sleep. Take the example of sleep. How is this state to be defined; physiologically, behaviorally, or by means of

the sleeper's subsequent report? Suppose S shows the EEG and behavioral signs of sleep, yet when questioned, says that he was not asleep; how are we to judge his previous state?

In the authors' opinion, a Venn diagram similar to that of Figure 1 would be useful in examining the logical possibilities. Again, sleep can be regarded as a hypothetical construct; and it may be indexed physiologically, behaviorally, or by means of verbal reports.

Extending the New Strategy to Waking Mental Activity

To summarize what has been said so far: A confluence of verbal report and physiological evidence has given renewed construct validity to the hypothetical mental state of dreaming. The fundamental logic is that of converging operations.

The new strategy, however, need not be confined to the study of dreaming. Some recent work suggests that the general approach of combining verbal report and physiological measures could—especially with the addition of information feedback procedures—be expanded in order to explore and perhaps manipulate certain types of waking mental activity in addition to dreaming. This extension of the basic methodology will be described in the following section. The main focus will be on some recent work by Kamiya (cited in Luce & Segal, 1966) on the operant control of the EEG alpha rhythms which has not previously been discussed in the psychological literature.

The basic working assumption in the Kamiya alpha control studies and in similar experiments is this: If a measurable physiological event(s) is associated with a discriminable mental event(s), then it will be possible to reinforce in the presence of the physiological event, and in so doing: (*a*) enable *S* to discriminate better whether the physiological event and the associated mental event are present, (*b*) perhaps, also, enable *S* to acquire some degree of control over the physiological event and the associated mental event.

Kamiya's alpha experiments employed an operant conditioning paradigm, in which *S* not only learned to discriminate the presence or absence of EEG alpha, but in addition attempted to achieve control over the alpha rhythm. These experiments began with a study to see whether *S*s could be taught to identify the occurrence of their EEG alpha rhythm. An electrode was placed over the occipital (recording from occiput to left ear) area of a particular *S*, who lay on a bed in a quiet room. The *S* was told that a bell would ring, sometimes when alpha waves appeared, sometimes during other EEG patterns. He was asked to tell whether or not the bell rang during alpha and was always told whether he was right or wrong. With the first volunteer tested, the level of successful discriminations reached 100% by his fourth experimental session, and this *S* made 400 successful discriminations in a row. Six other *S*s achieved 70–100% accuracy on 50–100 trials.

The next phase of Kamiya's study explored the ability of *S*s to acquire control over their alpha rhythm. A band-pass filter was connected to the *S*s' occipital leads and calibrated to pass only a specific alpha range (9–11 cycles per second). When *S* was generating alpha frequencies within this desired range, a tone would sound. The tone started whenever alpha appeared and went off as soon as alpha vanished. The eight *S*s became quite adept at turning alpha on and off.

Postexperimental interviews indicated that when alpha was "on" *S*s felt relaxed and were not experiencing any visual imagery. (Some of Kamiya's *S*s also reported that long periods of time spent in the alpha state—20 minutes or more—were quite pleasant). On the other hand, during periods of alpha suppression, *S*s "saw" things, or exerted mental effort of some kind. Thus, not only was there a correlation between the private experience and the physiological event, but *S*s were also able to achieve some control over both the physiological event and its associated mental event.

Similar results were recently reported by Hart (1967), who used an experimental group receiving precise information feedback and a control group receiving no feedback. Experimentals showed greater increases in alpha than did the controls. Antrobus and Antrobus (1967), also using an information feedback paradigm, have trained *S*s to discriminate successfully between REM and non-REM sleep.

ALPHA CONTROL AS AN EXAMPLE OF CONVERGING OPERATIONS

The authors maintain that this type of research—which makes joint use of operant conditioning, verbal report, and physiological measures—can be subjected to the same analysis already proposed in the earlier section of this paper under "Dreaming as a Hypothetical Construct." As was the case with dreaming, we are dealing with the public accompaniments of an inferred mental state; that is, REMs are an indicator of dreaming; similarly, *alpha* is an indicator of a certain hypothetical Mental State X. This Mental State X may be thought of as an "absence of visual imagery"—a hypothetical construct—and in Figure 1 would be represented by the broken-edged circle.

As was the case with dreaming, we would feel most secure in inferring Mental State X when there is a congruence between the verbal report of Mental State X and the physiological indicator, alpha (cf. Region 1 of Figure 1).

But, as was noted with dreaming, there are other logical possibilities as to how the three classes of events may be related, and these possibilities cannot be ignored. For example, there is the possibility that alpha may be present in conjunction with invalid verbal reports of hypothetical Mental State X (cf. Region 6 in Figure 1). Also, there could be alpha together with a valid report of the absence of Mental State X (cf. Region 7 of Figure 1). As in Figure 1, there would be a total of seven ways of relating the three classes of events.

Additional evidence for the validation of the hypothetical construct, Mental State X, would be supplied by the operant conditioning procedure. Thus, if by means of the information feedback technique devised by Kamiya, S increases his percentage of time in alpha, and there is also an increase in the reported amount of Mental State X, this further corroborates the validity of alpha as an indicator of Mental State X. The use of such information feedback techniques to control the amount of alpha can be represented in a fashion analogous to Figure 1. A decrease in alpha could be similarly represented.

The major point to be made here is that the use of operant technique in combination with the physiological indicator (alpha) and the verbal report provides substantial construct validation for the hypothetical internal state by means of converging operations.

The authors feel that this type of research—which makes joint use of operant conditioning, verbal report, and physiological measures—raises a number of interesting theoretical and practical possibilities. For one thing, the procedure which has been described—with its use of more precise reinforcement contingencies for private events—could lead to a more precise reporting of many private events. For example, it may prove possible for Ss to discriminate and control other types of EEG waves in addition to the alpha rhythm; for instance, beta, delta, and theta waves, rhythms characteristic of alertness, rhythms characteristic of drowsiness. If such a degree of discrimination and control proves possible, it could give psychologists a means of exploring and mapping a variety of conscious states, thus providing a powerful tool for the introspective method. It may also develop that, if S's ability to report about a limited number of private events can be sharpened in this way, then this new skill may well transfer to other private events as well; so that S becomes more generally reliable—and sensitive—in the reporting of private events.

In conclusion: Although the methodological objections ascribed to introspective evidence have indeed been numerous, perhaps the most damning indictment of introspection was that it did not lead anywhere (Boring, 1953). The authors' thesis, however, is that this state of affairs has been considerably altered as a result of advances stemming from a confluence of methodologies: electrophysiological measurements on the intact human S (cf. Ax, 1964), information feedback procedures, and verbal report. The combined use of these three techniques suggests a fresh approach to introspection and its place in psychology.

As a consequence of the new developments, there would seem to be considerably less force than previously to the critical broadside Kety (1960) leveled at psychology. The latter, speaking for biologists, decried the behaviorists' ritualistic avoidance of "mentalisms." In his opinion:

By emphasizing the objective and measurable aspects of psychiatry and the behavioral sciences, they have demonstrated their kinship with medicine and the natural sciences and brought into them considerable rigor at the price of just a little rigidity. But in denying the existence or the importance of mental states merely because they are difficult to measure or because they cannot be directly observed in others is needlessly to restrict the field of the mental sciences and to curtail the opportunities for the discovery of new relationships. . . . Nature is an elusive quarry, and it is foolhardy to pursue her with one eye closed and one foot hobbled [p. 1862].

REFERENCES

Ax, A. Goals and methods of psychophysiology, *Psychophysiology*, 1964, **1**, 8–25.

Antrobus, J., & Antrobus, J. S. Discrimination of two sleep stages by human subjects. *Psychophysiology*, 1967, **4**, 48–55.

Antrobus, J., Antrobus, J. S., & Fisher, C. Discrimination of dreaming and nondreaming sleep. *Archives of General Psychiatry*, 1965, **12**, 395–401.

Aserinsky, E., & Kleitman, N. Regularly occurring periods of eye motility and concomitant phenomena during sleep. *Science*, 1953, **118**, 274–284.

Berger, R. J., & Oswald, I. Eye movements during active and passive dreams. *Science*, 1962, **137**, 601.

Boring, E. G. A history of introspection. *Psychological Bulletin*, 1953, **50**, 169–189.

Campbell, D. T., & Fiske, D. W. Convergent and discriminant validation by the multitrait-multimethod matrix. *Psychological Bulletin*, 1959, **56**, 82–105.

Dement, W. C. Dream recall and eye movements during sleep in schizophrenics and normals. *Journal of Nervous and Mental Disease*, 1955, **122**, 263–269.

Dement, W. C. An essay on dreams: The role of physiology in understanding their nature. In *New directions in psychology*. Vol. 2. New York: Holt, Rinehart & Winston, 1965, Pp. 135–257.

Dement, W., & Kleitman, N. The relation of eye movements during sleep to dream activity: An objective method for the study of dreaming. *Journal of Experimental Psychology*, 1957, **53**, 339–346.

Dement, W., & Wolpert, E. A. The relation of eye movements, body motility, and external stimuli to dream content. *Journal of Experimental Psychology*, 1958, **55**, 543–553.

Feigl, H. The mental and the physical. In H. Feigl, M. Scriven, & G. Maxwell (Eds.), *Minnesota studies in the philosophy of science*. Vol. II. *Concepts, theories and the mind-body problem*. Minneapolis: University of Minnesota Press, 1958.

Fisher, C. Psychoanalytic implications of recent research on sleep and dreaming. *Journal of American Psychoanalytic Association*, 1965, **8**, 197–303.

Foulkes, W. D. Dream reports from different stages of sleep. *Journal of Abnormal and Social Psychology*, 1962, **65**, 14–25.

Foulkes, D. *The psychology of sleep.* New York: Scribner, 1966.

Foulkes, D., & Rechtschaffen, A. Presleep determinants of dream content: The effects of two films. *Perceptual and Motor Skills*, 1964, **19**, 983–1005.

Foulkes, D., & Vogel, G. Mental activity at sleep onset. *Journal of Abnormal Psychology*, 1965, **70**, 231–243.

Garner, W. R., Hake, H. W., & Eriksen, C. W. Operationism and the concept of perception. *Psychological Review*, 1956, **63**, 149–159.

Hall, C. S. Processes of fantasy. *Science*, 1966, **153**, 626–627.

Hart, J. H. Autocontrol of EEG alpha. Paper presented at the meeting of the Society for Psychophysiological Research, San Diego, October 1967.

Hebb, D. O. The American revolution. *American Psychologist*, 1960, **15**, 735–745.

Holt, R. R. Imagery: The return of the ostracized. *American Psychologist*, 1964, **19**, 254–264.

Jacobson, A., Kales, A., Lehmann, D., & Zweizig, J. R. Somnambulism: Allnight electroencephalographic studies. *Science*, 1965, **148**, 975–977.

Jouvet, M. The states of sleep. *Scientific American*, 1967, **216**, 62–67.

Kamiya, J. Behavioral, subjective, and physiological aspects of drowsiness and sleep. In D. W. Fiske & S. R. Maddi (Eds.), *Functions of varied experience*. Homewood, Ill.: Dorsey, 1961. Pp. 145–174.

Kety, S. S. A biologist examines the mind and behavior. *Science*, 1960, **132**, 1861–1870.

Krassoievitch, M., Weber, K., & Junod, J. P. La désintégration du cycle du sommeil dans les démences du grand age. *Schweizer Archiv für Neurologie, Neurochirurgie, und Psychiatrie*, 1965, **96**, 170–179.

Kremen, I. Dream reports and rapid eye movements. Unpublished doctoral dissertation, Harvard University, 1961.

Luce, G. G., & Segal, J. *Sleep*. New York: Coward-McCann, 1966.

Malcolm, N. *Dreaming*. New York: Humanities Press, 1959.

Max, L. W. An experimental study of the motor theory of consciousness. III. Action-current responses in deaf-mutes during sleep, sensory stimulation and dreams. *Journal of Comparative Psychology*, 1935, **19**, 469–186.

McClelland, D. C. The psychology of mental content reconsidered. *Psychological Review*, 1955, **62**, 297–302.

Orlinsky, D. E. Psychodynamic and cognitive correlates of dream recall. Unpublished doctoral dissertation, University of Chicago, 1962.

Platt, J. R. Strong inference. *Science*, 1964, **146**, 347–353.

Rechtschaffen, A. Discussion of: Dement, W. Part III, Research studies: Dreams and communication. In *Science and Psychoanalysis*, Vol. VII. New York: Grune & Stratton, 1964. Pp. 162–170.

Rechtschaffen, A., Goodenough, D. R., & Shapiro, A. Patterns of sleeptalking. *Archives of General Psychiatry*, 1962, **7**, 418–426.

Roffwarg, H. P., Dement, W. C., Muzio, J. N., & Fisher, C. Dream imagery: Relationship to rapid eye movements of sleep. *Archives of General Psychiatry*, 1962, **7**, 235–258.

Roffwarg, H. P., Muzio, J. N., & Dement, W. C. Ontogenetic development of the human sleep-dream cycle. *Science*, 1966, **152**, 604–619.

Sampson, H. Deprivation of dreaming sleep by two methods. I. Compensatory REM time. *Archives of General Psychiatry*, 1965, **13**, 79–86.

Stoyva, J. M. Finger electromyographic activity during sleep: Its relation to dreaming in deaf and normal subjects. *Journal of Abnormal Psychology*, 1965, **70**, 343–349.

Vaughan, C. J. The development and use of an operant technique to provide evidence for visual imagery in the rhesus monkey under "sensory deprivation." Unpublished doctoral dissertation, University of Pittsburgh, 1964.

Wolpert, E. A. Studies in psychophysiology of dreams. II. An electromyographic study of dreaming. *Archives of General Psychiatry*, 1960, **2**, 231–241.

Wolpert, E. A., & Trosman, H. Studies in psychophysiology of dreams. I. Experimental evocation of sequential dream episodes. *Archives of Neurology and Psychiatry*, 1958, **70**, 603–606.

27

Learning of Visceral and Glandular Responses

Neal E. Miller

The article that follows is of special importance. For the most part we have defended the "relevance" of experimental psychology by showing that experimental techniques can be applied in complex situations. But it is also the case that basic research can prove to be of great importance to mankind. Many articles could have been chosen to illustrate this, but none of them could do the job better than Miller's article. He used a highly analytic strategy, exerting very heavy control from the outset rather than studying complex situations first and analyzing as the need arose. This strategy proved highly successful. It was possible to show that such responses as those of the heart and viscera can be brought under the control of reinforcement procedures. In other words, the heart and guts can "learn." This is of some academic interest, as Miller points out, because it runs in opposition to strongly held traditional views. However, the importance of these findings is far more global than that. In fact, it is quite possible to conceive of the development of a whole new branch of medicine based on the use of learning procedures rather than drugs or surgical devices to modify the activity of organs. For example, a heart that fails to beat in proper rhythm might be trained in proper behavior instead of being controlled by a cardiac pacemaker.

There is a strong traditional belief in the inferiority of the autonomic nervous system and the visceral responses that

Reprinted from *Science*, 1969, **163**, 434–445. Copyright 1969 by the American Association for the Advancement of Science, and reproduced by permission.

it controls. The recent experiments disproving this belief have deep implications for theories of learning, for individual differences in autonomic responses, for the cause and the cure of abnormal psychosomatic symptoms, and possibly also for the understanding of normal homeostasis. Their success encourages investigators to try other unconventional types of training. Before describing these experiments, let me briefly sketch some elements in the history of the deeply entrenched, false belief in the gross inferiority of one major part of the nervous system.

HISTORICAL ROOTS AND MODERN RAMIFICATIONS

Since ancient times, reason and the voluntary responses of the skeletal muscles have been considered to be superior, while emotions and the presumably involuntary glandular and visceral responses have been considered to be inferior. This invidious dichotomy appears in the philosophy of Plato (*1*), with his superior rational soul in the head above and inferior souls in the body below. Much later, the great French neuroanatomist Bichat (*2*) distinguished between the cerebrospinal nervous system of the great brain and spinal cord, controlling skeletal responses, and the dual chain of ganglia (which he called "little brains") running down on either side of the spinal cord in the body below and controlling emotional and visceral responses. He indicated his low opinion of the ganglionic system by calling it "vegetative": he also believed it to be largely independent of the cerebrospinal system, an opinion which is still reflected in our modern name for it, the autonomic nervous system. Considerably later, Cannon (*3*) studied the sympathetic part of the autonomic nervous system and concluded that the different nerves in it all fire simultaneously and are incapable of the finely differentiated individual responses possible for the cerebrospinal system, a conclusion which is enshrined in modern textbooks.

Many, though not all, psychiatrists have made an invidious distinction between the hysterical and other symptoms that are mediated by the cerebrospinal nervous system and the psychosomatic symptoms that are mediated by the autonomic nervous system. Whereas the former are supposed to be subject to a higher type of control that is symbolic, the latter are presumed to be only the direct physiological consequences of the type and intensity of the patient's emotions (see, for example, *4*).

Similarly, students of learning have made a distinction between a lower form, called classical conditioning and thought to be involuntary, and a superior form variously called trial-and-error learning, operant conditioning, type II conditioning, or instrumental learning and believed to be responsible for voluntary behavior. In classical conditioning, the reinforcement must be by an unconditioned stimulus that already elicits the specific response to be learned; therefore, the possibilities are quite limited. In instrumental learning, the reinforcement, called a reward, has the property of strengthening any immediately preceding response. Therefore, the possibilities for reinforcement are much greater; a given reward may reinforce any one of a number of different responses, and a given response may be reinforced by any one of a number of different rewards.

Finally, the foregoing invidious distinctions have coalesced into the strong traditional belief that the superior type of instrumental learning involved in the superior voluntary behavior is possible only for skeletal responses mediated by the superior cerebrospinal nervous system, while, conversely, the inferior classical conditioning is the only kind possible for the inferior, presumably involuntary, visceral and emotional responses mediated by the inferior autonomic nervous system. Thus, in a recent summary generally considered authoritative, Kimble (5) states the almost universal belief that "for autonomically mediated behavior, the evidence points unequivocally to the conclusion that such responses can be modified by classical, but not instrumental, training methods." Upon examining the evidence, however, one finds that it consists only of failure to secure instrumental learning in two incompletely reported exploratory experiments and a vague allusion to the Russian literature (6). It is only against a cultural background of great prejudice that such weak evidence could lead to such a strong conviction.

The belief that instrumental learning is possible only for the cerebrospinal system and, conversely, that the autonomic nervous system can be modified only by classical conditioning has been used as one of the strongest arguments for the notion that instrumental learning and classical conditioning are two basically different phenomena rather than different manifestations of the same phenomenon under different conditions. But for many years I have been impressed with the similarity between the laws of classical conditioning and those of instrumental learning, and with the fact that, in each of these two situations, some of the specific details of learning vary with the specific conditions of learning. Failing to see any clear-cut dichotomy, I have assumed that there is only one kind of learning (7). This assumption has logically demanded that instrumental training procedures be able to produce the learning of any visceral responses that could be acquired through classical conditioning procedures. Yet it was only a little over a dozen years ago that I began some experimental work on this problem and a somewhat shorter time ago that I first, in published articles (8), made specific sharp challenges to the traditional view that the instrumental learning of visceral responses is impossible.

SOME DIFFICULTIES

One of the difficulties of investigating the instrumental learning of visceral responses stems from the fact that the responses that are the easiest to measure—namely, heart rate, vasomotor responses, and the galvanic skin response—are known to be affected by skeletal responses, such as exercise, breathing, and even tensing of certain muscles, such as those in the diaphragm. Thus, it is hard to rule out the possibility that, instead of directly learning a visceral response, the subject has learned a skeletal response the performance of which causes the visceral change being recorded.

One of the controls I planned to use was the paralysis of all skeletal responses through administration of curare, a drug which selectively blocks the motor end plates of skeletal muscles without eliminating consciousness in human subjects or the neural control of visceral responses, such as the beating of the heart. The muscles involved in breathing are paralyzed, so the subject's breathing must be maintained through artificial respiration. Since it seemed unlikely that curarization and other rigorous control techniques would be easy to use with human subjects, I decided to concentrate first on experiments with animals.

Originally I thought that learning would be more difficult when the animal was paralyzed, under the influence of curare, and therefore I decided to postpone such experiments until ones on nonparalyzed animals had yielded some definitely promising results. This turned out to be a mistake because, as I found out much later, paralyzing the animal with curare not only greatly simplifies the problem of recording visceral responses without artifacts introduced by movement but also apparently makes it easier for the animal to learn, perhaps because paralysis of the skeletal muscles removes sources of variability and distraction. Also, in certain experiments I made the mistake of using rewards that induced strong unconditioned responses that interfered with instrumental learning.

One of the greatest difficulties, however, was the strength of the belief that instrumental learning of glandular and visceral responses is impossible. It was extremely difficult to get students to work on this problem, and when paid assistants were assigned to it, their attempts were so half-hearted that it soon became more economical to let them work on some other problem which they could attack with greater faith and enthusiasm. These difficulties and a few preliminary encouraging but inconclusive early results have been described elsewhere (9).

SUCCESS WITH SALIVATION

The first clear-cut results were secured by Alfredo Carmona and me in an experiment on the salivation of dogs. Initial attempts to use food as a reward for hungry dogs were unsuccessful, partly because of strong and persistent unconditioned salivation elicited by the food. Therefore, we decided to use water as a reward for thirsty dogs. Preliminary observations showed that the water had no appreciable effects one way or the other on the bursts of spontaneous salivation. As an additional precaution, however, we used the experimental design of rewarding dogs in one group whenever they showed a burst of spontaneous salivation, so that they would be trained to increase salivation, and rewarding dogs in another group whenever there was a long interval between spontaneous bursts, so that they would be trained to decrease salivation. If the reward had any unconditioned effect, this effect might be classically conditioned to the experimental situation and therefore produce a change in salivation that was not a true instance of instrumental learning. But in classical conditioning the reinforcement must elicit the response that is to be acquired. Therefore, conditioning of a response elicited by the reward could produce either an increase or a decrease in salivation, depending upon the direction of the unconditioned response elicited by the reward, but it could not produce a change in one direction for one group and in the opposite direction for the other group. The same type of logic applies for any unlearned cumulative aftereffects of the reward; they could not be in opposite directions for the two groups. With instrumental learning, however, the reward can reinforce any response that immediately precedes it; therefore, the same reward can be used to produce either increases or decreases.

The results are presented in Figure 1, which summarizes the effects of 40 days

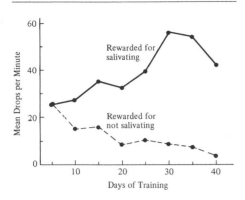

Figure 1 Learning curves for groups of thirsty dogs rewarded with water for either increases or decreases in spontaneous salivation. [From Miller and Carmona (10).]

of training with one 45-minute training session per day. It may be seen that in this experiment the learning proceeded slowly. However, statistical analysis showed that each of the trends in the predicted rewarded direction was highly reliable (10).

Since the changes in salivation for the two groups were in opposite directions, they cannot be attributed to classical conditioning. It was noted, however, that the group rewarded for increases seemed to be more aroused and active than the one rewarded for decreases. Conceivably, all we were doing was to change the level of activation of the dogs, and this change was, in turn, affecting the salivation. Although we did not observe any specific skeletal responses, such as chewing movements or panting, which might be expected to elicit salivation, it was difficult to be absolutely certain that such movements did not occur. Therefore, we decided to rule out such movements by paralyzing the dogs with curare, but we immediately found that curare had two effects which were disastrous for this experi-

ment: it elicited such copious and continuous salivation that there were no changes in salivation to reward, and the salivation was so viscous that it almost immediately gummed up the recording apparatus.

HEART RATE

In the meantime, Jay Trowill, working with me on this problem, was displaying great ingenuity, courage, and persistence in trying to produce instrumental learning of heart rate in rats that had been paralyzed by curare to prevent them from "cheating" by muscular exertion to speed up the heart or by relaxation to slow it down. As a result of preliminary testing, he selected a dose of curare (3.6 milligrams of d-tubocurarine chloride per kilogram, injected intraperitoneally) which produced deep paralysis for at least 3 hours, and a rate of artificial respiration (inspiration-expiration ratio 1:1; 70 breaths per minute; peak pressure reading, 20 cm-H_2O) which maintained the heart at a constant and normal rate throughout this time.

In subsequent experiments, DiCara and I have obtained similar effects by starting with a smaller dose (1.2 milligrams per kilogram) and constantly infusing additional amounts of the drug, through intraperitoneal injection, at the rate of 1.2 milligrams per kilogram per hour, for the duration of the experiment. We have recorded, electromyographically, the response of the muscles, to determine that this dose does indeed produce a complete block of the action potentials, lasting for at least an hour after the end of infusion. We have found that if parameters of respiration and the face mask are adjusted carefully, the procedure not only maintains the heart rate of a 500-gram control animal constant but also maintains the vital signs of temperature, peripheral vasomotor responses, and the pCO_2 of the blood constant.

Since there are not very many ways to reward an animal completely paralyzed by curare, Trowill and I decided to use direct electrical stimulation of rewarding areas of the brain. There were other technical difficulties to overcome, such as devising the automatic system for rewarding small changes in heart rate as recorded by the electrocardiogram. Nevertheless, Trowill at last succeeded in training his rats (11). Those rewarded for an increase in heart rate showed a statistically reliable increase, and those rewarded for a decrease in heart rate showed a statistically reliable decrease. The changes, however, were disappointingly small, averaging only 5 percent in each direction.

The next question was whether larger changes could be achieved by improving the technique of training. DiCara and I used the technique of shaping—in other words, of immediately rewarding first very small, and hence frequently occurring, changes in the correct direction and, as soon as these had been learned, requiring progressively larger changes as the criterion for reward. In this way, we were able to produce in 90 minutes of training changes averaging 20 percent in either direction (12).

KEY PROPERTIES OF LEARNING: DISCRIMINATION AND RETENTION

Does the learning of visceral responses have the same properties as the learning of skeletal responses? One of the important characteristics of the instrumental learning of skeletal responses is that a discrimination can be learned, so that the responses are more likely to be made in the stimulus situations in which they are rewarded than in those in which they are not. After the training of the first few rats had convinced us that we could produce large changes in heart rate, DiCara and I gave all the rest of the rats in the experiment described above 45 minutes of additional training with the most difficult criterion. We did this in order to see whether they could learn to give a greater response during a "time-in" stimulus (the presence of a flashing light and a tone) which indicated that a response in the proper direction would be rewarded than during a "time-out" stimulus (absence of light and tone) which indicated that a correct response would not be rewarded.

Figure 2 shows the record of one of the rats given such training. Before the beginning of the special discrimination training it had slowed its heart from an initial rate of 350 beats per minute to a rate of 230 beats per minute. From the top record of Figure 2 one can see that, at the beginning of the special discrimination training, there was no appreciable reduction in heart rate that was specifically associated with the time-in stimulus. Thus it took the rat considerable time after the onset of this stimulus to meet the criterion and get the reward. At the end of the discrimination training the heart rate during time-out remained approximately the same, but when the time-in light and tone came on, the heart slowed down and the criterion was promptly met. Although the other rats showed less change than this, by the end of the relatively short period of discrimination training their heart rate did change re-

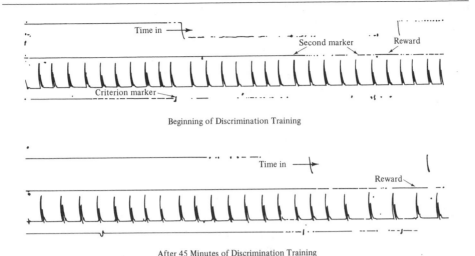

Figure 2 Electrocardiograms at the beginning and end of discrimination training of curarized rat rewarded for slow heart rate. Slowing of heart rate is rewarded only during a "time-in" stimulus (tone and light). [From Miller and DiCara (12).]

liably ($P < .001$) in the predicted direction when the time-in stimulus came on. Thus, it is clear that instrumental visceral learning has at least one of the important properties of instrumental skeletal learning—namely, the ability to be brought under the control of a discriminative stimulus.

Another of the important properties of the instrumental learning of skeletal responses is that it is remembered. DiCara and I performed a special experiment to test the retention of learned changes in heart rate (13). Rats that had been given a single training session were returned to their home cages for 3 months without further training. When curarized again and returned to the experimental situation for nonreinforced test trials, rats in both the "increase" and the "decrease" groups showed good retention by exhibiting reliable changes in the direction rewarded in the earlier training.

ESCAPE AND AVOIDANCE LEARNING

Is visceral learning by any chance peculiarly limited to reinforcement by the unusual reward of direct electrical stimulation of the brain, or can it be reinforced by other rewards in the same way that skeletal learning can be? In order to answer this question, DiCara and I (14) performed an experiment using the other of the two forms of thoroughly studied reward that can be conveniently used with rats which are paralyzed by curare—namely, the chance to avoid, or escape from, mild electric shock. A shock signal was turned on; after it had been on for 10 seconds it was accompanied by brief pulses of mild electric shock delivered to the rat's tail. During the first 10 seconds the rat could turn off the shock signal and avoid the shock by making the correct response of changing its heart rate in the required direction by the required amount. If it did not make the correct response in time, the shocks continued to be delivered until the rat escaped them by making the correct response, which immediately turned off both the shock and the shock signal.

For one group of curarized rats, the correct response was an increase in heart rate: for the other group it was a decrease. After the rats had learned to make small responses in the proper direction, they were required to make larger ones. During this training the shock signals were randomly interspersed with an equal number of "safe" signals that were not followed by shock; the heart rate was also recorded during so-called blank trials—trials without any signals or shocks. For half of the rats the shock signal was a tone and the "safe" signal was a flashing light: for the other half the roles of these cues were reversed.

The results are shown in Figure 3. Each of the 12 rats in this experiment changed its heart rate in the rewarded direction. As training progressed, the shock signal began to elicit a progressively greater change in the rewarded direction than the change recorded during the blank trials; this was a statistically reliable trend. Conversely, as training progressed, the "safe" signal came to elicit a statistically reliable change in the opposite direction, toward the initial base line. These results show learning when escape and avoidance are the rewards; this means that visceral responses in curarized rats can be reinforced by rewards other than direct electrical stimulation of the brain. These rats also discriminate between the shock and the "safe" signals. You will remember that, with noncurarized thirsty dogs, we were able to use yet another kind of reward, water, to produce learned changes in salivation.

TRANSFER TO NONCURARIZED STATE: MORE EVIDENCE AGAINST MEDIATION

In the experiments discussed above, paralysis of the skeletal muscles by curare

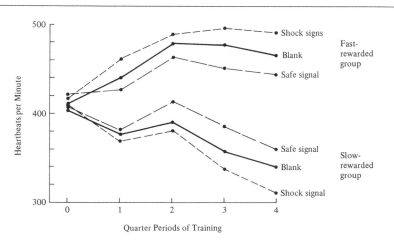

Figure 3   Changes in heart rate during avoidance training. [From DiCara and Miller (14).]

ruled out the possibility that the subjects were learning the overt performance of skeletal responses which were indirectly eliciting the changes in the heart rate. It is barely conceivable, however, that the rats were learning to send out from the motor cortex central impulses which would have activated the muscles had they not been paralyzed. And it is barely conceivable that these central impulses affected heart rate by means either of inborn connections or of classically conditioned ones that had been acquired when previous exercise had been accompanied by an increase in heart rate and relaxation had been accompanied by a decrease. But, if the changes in heart rate were produced in this indirect way, we would expect that, during a subsequent test without curare, any rat that showed learned changes in heart rate would show the movements in the muscles that were no longer paralyzed. Furthermore, the problem of whether or not visceral responses learned under curarization carry over to the noncurarized state is of interest in its own right.

In order to answer this question, DiCara and I (15) trained two groups of curarized rats to increase or decrease, respectively, their heart rate in order to avoid, or escape from, brief pulses of mild electric shock. When these rats were tested 2 weeks later in the noncurarized state, the habit was remembered. Statistically reliable increases in heart rate averaging 5 percent and decreases averaging 16 percent occurred. Immediately subsequent retraining without curare produced additional significant changes of heart rate in the rewarded direction, bringing the total overall increase to 11 percent and the decrease to 22 percent. While, at the beginning of the test in the noncurarized state, the two groups showed some differences in respiration and activity, these differences decreased until, by the end of the retraining, they were small and far from statistically reliable ($t = 0.3$ and 1.3, respectively). At the same time, the difference between the two groups with respect to heart rate was increasing, until it became large and thus extremely reliable ($t = 8.6$, d.f. $= 12$, $P < .001$).

In short, while greater changes in heart rate were being learned, the response was becoming more specific, involving smaller changes in respiration and muscular activity. This increase in specificity with additional training is another point of similarity with the instrumental learning of skeletal responses. Early in skeletal learning, the rewarded correct response is likely to be accompanied by many unnecessary movements. With additional training during which extraneous movements are not rewarded, they tend to drop out.

It is difficult to reconcile the foregoing results with the hypothesis that the differences in heart rate were mediated primarily by a difference in either respiration or amount of general activity. This is especially true in view of the research, summarized by Ehrlich and Malmo (16), which shows that muscular activity, to affect heart rate in the rat, must be rather vigorous.

While it is difficult to rule out completely the possibility that changes in heart rate are mediated by central impulses to skeletal muscles, the possibility of such mediation is much less attractive for other responses, such as intestinal contractions and the formation of urine by the kidney. Furthermore, if the learning of these different responses can be shown to be specific in enough visceral responses, one runs out of different skeletal movements each eliciting a specific different visceral response (*17*). Therefore, experiments were performed on the learning of a variety of different visceral responses and on the specificity of that learning. Each of these experiments was, of course, interesting in its own right, quite apart from any bearing on the problem of mediation.

SPECIFICITY: INTESTINAL VERSUS CARDIAC

The purpose of our next experiment was to determine the specificity of visceral learning. If such learning has the same properties as the instrumental learning of skeletal responses, it should be possible to learn a specific visceral response independently of other ones. Furthermore, as we have just seen, we might expect to find that, the better the rewarded response is learned, the more specific is the learning. Banuazizi and I worked on this problem (*18*). First we had to discover another visceral response that could be conveniently recorded and rewarded. We decided on intestinal contractions, and recorded them in the curarized rat with a little balloon filled with water thrust approximately 4 centimeters beyond the anal sphincter. Changes of pressure in the balloon were transduced into electric voltages which produced a record on a polygraph and also activated an automatic mechanism for delivering the reward, which was electrical stimulation of the brain.

The results for the first rat trained, which was a typical one, are shown in Figure 4. From the top record it may be seen that, during habituation, there were some spontaneous contractions. When the rat was rewarded by brain stimulation for keeping contractions below a certain amplitude for a certain time, the number of contractions was reduced and the base line was lowered. After the record showed a highly reliable change indicating that relaxation had been learned (Figure 4, second record from the top), the conditions of training were reversed and the reward was delivered whenever the amplitude of contractions rose above a certain level. From the next record (Figure 4, middle) it may be seen that this type of training increased the number of contractions and raised the base line. Finally (Figure 4, two bottom records) the reward was discontinued and, as would be expected, the response continued for a while but gradually became extinguished, so that the activity eventually returned to approximately its original base-line level.

After studying a number of other rats in this way and convincing ourselves that the instrumental learning of intestinal responses was a possibility, we designed an experiment to test specificity. For all the rats of the experiment, both intestinal contractions and heart rate were recorded, but half the rats were rewarded for one of these responses and half were rewarded for the other response. Each of these two groups of rats was divided into two subgroups, rewarded, respectively, for increased and decreased response. The rats were completely paralyzed by curare, maintained on artificial respiration, and rewarded by electrical stimulation of the brain.

The results are shown in Figures 5 and 6. In Figure 5 it may be seen that the group rewarded for increases in intestinal contractions learned an increase, the group rewarded for decreases learned a decrease, but neither of these groups showed an appreciable change in heart rate. Conversely (Figure 6), the group

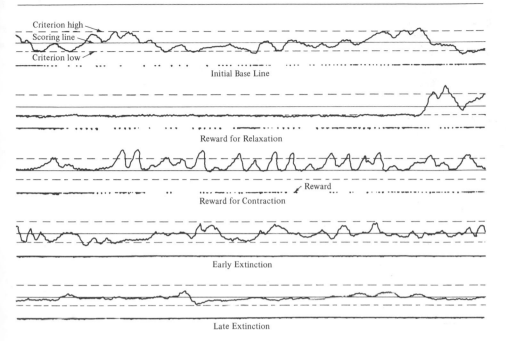

Criterion high

Scoring line

Criterion low

Initial Base Line

Reward for Relaxation

Reward

Reward for Contraction

Early Extinction

Late Extinction

Figure 4 Typical samples of a record of instrumental learning of an intestinal response by a curarized rat. (From top to bottom) Record of spontaneous contraction before training; record after training with reward for relaxation; record after training with reward for contractions; records during nonrewarded extinction trials. [From Miller and Banuazizi (18).]

rewarded for increases in heart rate showed an increase, the group rewarded for decreases showed a decrease, but neither of these groups showed a change in intestinal contractions.

The fact that each type of response changed when it was rewarded rules out the interpretation that the failure to secure a change when that change was not rewarded could have been due to either a strong and stable homeostatic regulation of that response or an inability of our techniques to measure changes reliably under the particular conditions of our experiment.

Each of the 12 rats in the experiment showed statistically reliable changes in the rewarded direction; for 11 the

changes were reliable beyond the $P < .001$ level, while for the 12th the changes were reliable only beyond the .05 level. A statistically reliable negative correlation showed that the better the rewarded visceral response was learned, the less change occurred in the other, nonrewarded response. This greater specificity with better learning is what we had expected. The results showed that visceral learning can be specific to an organ system, and they clearly ruled out the possibility of mediation by any single general factor, such as level of activation or central commands for either general activity or relaxation.

In an additional experiment, Banuazizi (19) showed that either increases

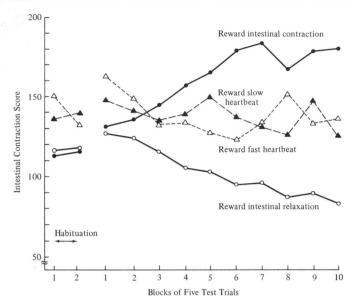

Figure 5 Graph showing that the intestinal contraction score is changed by rewarding either increases or decreases in intestinal contractions but is unaffected by rewarding changes in heart rate. [From Miller and Banuazizi (18).]

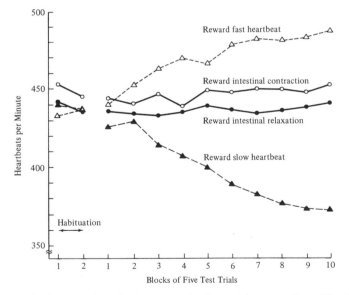

Figure 6 Graph showing that the heart rate is changed by rewarding either increases or decreases in heart rate but is unaffected by rewarding changes in intestinal contractions. Comparison with Figure 5 demonstrates the specificity of visceral learning. [From Miller and Banuazizi (18).]

or decreases in intestinal contractions can be rewarded by avoidance of, or escape from, mild electric shocks, and that the intestinal responses can be discriminatively elicited by a specific stimulus associated with reinforcement.

KIDNEY FUNCTION

Encouraged by these successes, DiCara and I decided to see whether or not the rate of urine formation by the kidney could be changed in the curarized rat rewarded by electrical stimulation of the brain (20). A catheter, permanently inserted, was used to prevent accumulation of urine by the bladder, and the rate of urine formation was measured by an electronic device for counting minute drops. In order to secure a rate of urine formation fast enough so that small changes could be promptly detected and rewarded, the rats were kept constantly loaded with water through infusion by way of a catheter permanently inserted in the jugular vein.

All of the seven rats rewarded when the intervals between times of urine-drop formation lengthened showed decreases in the rate of urine formation, and all of the seven rats rewarded when these intervals shortened showed increases in the rate of urine formation. For both groups the changes were highly reliable ($P < .001$).

In order to determine how the change in rate of urine formation was achieved, certain additional measures were taken. As the set of bars at left in Figure 7 shows, the rate of filtration, measured by means of ^{14}C-labeled inulin, increased when increases in the rate of urine formation were rewarded and decreased when decreases in the rate were rewarded. Plots of the correlations showed that the changes in the rates of filtration and urine formation were not related to changes in either blood pressure or heart rate.

The middle set of bars in Figure 7 shows that the rats rewarded for increases in the rate of urine formation had an increased rate of renal blood

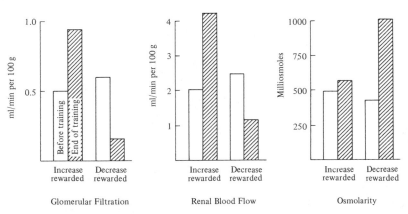

Figure 7   Effects of rewarding increased rate of urine formation in one group and decreased rate in another on measures of glomerular filtration, renal blood flow, and osmolarity. [From data in Miller and DiCara (20).]

flow, as measured by ^{3}H-p-aminohip-puric acid, and that those rewarded for decreases had a decreased rate of renal blood flow. Since these changes in blood flow were not accompanied by changes in general blood pressure or in heart rate, they must have been achieved by vasomotor changes of the renal arteries. That these vasomotor changes were at least somewhat specific is shown by the fact that vasomotor responses of the tail, as measured by a photoelectric plethys-mograph, did not differ for the two groups of rats.

The set of bars at right in Figure 7 shows that when decreases in rate of urine formation were rewarded, a more concentrated urine, having higher os-molarity, was formed. Since the slower passage of urine through the tubules would afford more opportunity for re-absorption of water, this higher concen-tration does not necessarily mean an increase in the secretion of antidiuretic hormone. When an increased rate of urine formation was rewarded, the urine did not become more diluted—that is, it showed no decrease in osmolarity; therefore, the increase in rate of urine formation observed in this experiment cannot be accounted for in terms of an inhibition of the secretion of antidiuretic hormone.

From the foregoing results it appears that the learned changes in urine for-mation in this experiment were pro-duced primarily by changes in the rate of filtration, which, in turn, were pro-duced primarily by changes in the rate of blood flow through the kidneys.

GASTRIC CHANGES

In the next experiment, Carmona, Demierre, and I used a photoelectric plethysmorgraph to measure changes, presumably in the amount of blood, in the stomach wall (21). In an operation performed under anesthesia, a small glass tube, painted black except for a small spot, was inserted into the rat's stomach. The same tube was used to hold the stomach wall against a small glass window inserted through the body wall. The tube was left in that position. After the animal had recovered, a bun-dle of optical fibers could be slipped snugly into the glass tube so that the light beamed through it would shine out through the unpainted spot in the tube inside the stomach, pass through the stomach wall, and be recorded by a photocell on the other side of the glass window. Preliminary tests indicated that, as would be expected, when the amount of blood in the stomach wall increased, less light would pass through. Other tests showed that stomach con-tractions elicited by injections of insulin did not affect the amount of light trans-mitted.

In the main experiment we rewarded curarized rats by enabling them to avoid or escape from mild electric shocks. Some were rewarded when the amount of light that passed through the stomach wall increased, while others were re-warded when the amount decreased. Fourteen of the 15 rats showed changes in the rewarded direction. Thus, we demonstrated that the stomach wall, under the control of the autonomic nervous system, can be modified by in-strumental learning. There is strong reason to believe that the learned changes were achieved by vasomotor responses affecting the amount of blood in the stomach wall or mucosa, or in both.

In another experiment, Carmona (22) showed that stomach contractions can be either increased or decreased by instrumental learning.

It is obvious that learned changes in the blood supply of internal organs can affect their functioning—as, for example, the rate at which urine was formed by the kidneys was affected by changes in the amount of blood that flowed through them. Thus, such changes can produce psychosomatic symptoms. And if the learned changes in blood supply can be specific to a given organ, the symptom will occur in that organ rather than in another one.

PERIPHERAL VASOMOTOR RESPONSES

Having investigated the instrumental learning of internal vasomotor responses, we next studied the learning of peripheral ones. In the first experiment, the amount of blood in the tail of a curarized rat was measured by a photoelectric plethysmograph, and changes were rewarded by electrical stimulation of the brain (23). All of the four rats rewarded for vasoconstriction showed that response, and, at the same time, their average core temperature, measured rectally, decreased from 98.9° to 97.9° F. All of the four rats rewarded for vasodilatation showed that response and, at the same time, their average core temperature increased from 99.9° to 101° F. The vasomotor change for each individual rat was reliable beyond the $P < .01$ level, and the difference in change in temperature between the groups was reliable beyond the .01 level. The direction of the change in temperature was opposite to that which would be expected from the heat conservation caused by peripheral vasoconstriction or the heat loss caused by peripheral vaso-

dilatation. The changes are in the direction which would be expected if the training had altered the rate of heat production, causing a change in temperature which, in turn, elicited the vasomotor response.

The next experiment was designed to try to determine the limits of the specificity of vasomotor learning. The pinnae of the rat's ears were chosen because the blood vessels in them are believed to be innervated primarily, and perhaps exclusively, by the sympathetic branch of the autonomic nervous system, the branch that Cannon believed always fired nonspecifically as a unit (3). But Cannon's experiments involved exposing cats to extremely strong emotion-evoking stimuli, such as barking dogs, and such stimuli will also evoke generalized activity throughout the skeletal musculature. Perhaps his results reflected the way in which sympathetic activity was elicited, rather than demonstrating any inherent inferiority of the sympathetic nervous system.

In order to test this interpretation, DiCara and I (24) put photocells on both ears of the curarized rat and connected them to a bridge circuit so that only differences in the vasomotor responses of the two ears were rewarded by brain stimulation. We were somewhat surprised and greatly delighted to find that this experiment actually worked. The results are summarized in Figure 8. Each of the six rats rewarded for relative vasodilatation of the left ear showed that response, while each of the six rats rewarded for relative vasodilatation of the right ear showed that response. Recordings from the right and left forepaws showed little if any change in vasomotor response.

It is clear that these results cannot be by-products of changes in either heart

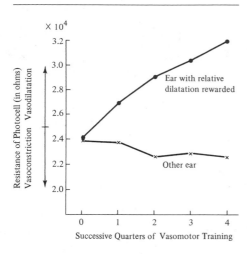

Figure 8 Learning a difference in the vasomotor responses of the two ears in the curarized rat. [From data in DiCara and Miller (24).]

rate or blood pressure, as these would be expected to affect both ears equally. They show either that vasomotor responses mediated by the sympathetic nervous system are capable of much greater specificity than has previously been believed, or that the innervation of the blood vessels in the pinnae of the ears is not restricted almost exclusively to sympathetic-nervous-system components, as has been believed, and involves functionally significant parasympathetic components. In any event, the changes in the blood flow certainly were surprisingly specific. Such changes in blood flow could account for specific psychosomatic symptoms.

BLOOD PRESSURE INDEPENDENT OF HEART RATE

Although changes in blood pressure were not induced as by-products of rewarded changes in the rate of urine formation, another experiment on curarized rats showed that, when changes in systolic blood pressure are specifically reinforced, they can be learned (25). Blood pressure was recorded by means of a catheter permanently inserted into the aorta, and the reward was avoidance of, or escape from, mild electric shock. All seven rats rewarded for increases in blood pressure showed further increases, while all seven rewarded for decreases showed decreases, each of the changes, which were in opposite directions, being reliable beyond the $P < .01$ level. The increase was from 139 mm-Hg, which happens to be roughly comparable to the normal systolic blood pressure of an adult man, to 170 mm-Hg, which is on the borderline of abnormally high blood pressure in man.

Each experimental animal was "yoked" with a curarized partner, maintained on artificial respiration and having shock electrodes on its tail wired in series with electrodes on the tail of the experimental animal, so that it received exactly the same electric shocks and could do nothing to escape or avoid them. The yoked controls for both the increase-rewarded and the decrease-rewarded groups showed some elevation in blood pressure as an unconditioned effect of the shocks. By the end of training, in contrast to the large difference in the blood pressures of the two groups specifically rewarded for changes in opposite directions, there was no difference in blood pressure between the yoked control partners for these two groups. Furthermore, the increase in blood pressure in these control groups was reliably less ($P < .01$) than that in the group specifically rewarded for increases. Thus, it is clear that the reward for an increase in blood pressure produced an additional increase over and above the effects of the shocks per se, while the reward for a decrease was able to overcome the unconditioned increase elicited by the shocks.

For none of the four groups was there a significant change in heart rate or in temperature during training; there were no significant differences in these measures among the groups. Thus, the learned change was relatively specific to blood pressure.

TRANSFER FROM HEART RATE TO SKELETAL AVOIDANCE

Although visceral learning can be quite specific, especially if only a specific response is rewarded, as was the case in the experiment on the two ears, under some circumstances it can involve a more generalized effect.

In handling the rats that had just recovered from curarization, DiCara noticed that those that had been trained, through the avoidance or escape reward, to increase their heart rate were more likely to squirm, squeal, defecate, and show other responses indicating emotionality than were those that had been trained to reduce their heart rate. Could instrumental learning of heart-rate changes have some generalized effects, perhaps on the level of emotionality, which might affect the behavior in a different avoidance-learning situation? In order to look for such an effect, DiCara and Weiss (26) used a modified shuttle avoidance apparatus. In this apparatus, when a danger signal is given, the rat must run from compartment A to compartment B. If he runs fast enough, he avoids the shock; if not, he must run to escape it. The next time the

danger signal is given, the rat must run in the opposite direction, from B to A.

Other work had shown that learning in this apparatus is an inverted U-shaped function of the strength of the shocks, with shocks that are too strong eliciting emotional behavior instead of running. DiCara and Weiss trained their rats in this apparatus with a level of shock that is approximately optimum for naive rats of this strain. They found that the rats that had been rewarded for decreasing their heart rate learned well, but that those that had been rewarded for increasing their heart rate learned less well, as if their emotionality had been increased. The difference was statistically reliable ($P < .001$). This experiment clearly demonstrates that training a visceral response can affect the subsequent learning of a skeletal one, but additional work will be required to prove the hypothesis that training to increase heart rate increases emotionality.

VISCERAL LEARNING WITHOUT CURARE

Thus far, in all of the experiments except the one on teaching thirsty dogs to salivate, the initial training was given when the animal was under the influence of curare. All of the experiments, except the one on salivation, have produced surprisingly rapid learning— definitive results within 1 or 2 hours. Will learning in the normal, noncurarized state be easier, as we originally thought it should be, or will it be harder, as the experiment on the noncurarized dogs suggests? DiCara and I have started to get additional evidence on this problem. We have obtained clear-cut evidence that rewarding (with the avoidance or escape reward) one group of freely moving rats for reducing heart rate and rewarding another group for increasing heart rate produces a difference between the two groups (27). That this difference was not due to the indirect effects of the overt performance of skeletal responses is shown by the fact that it persisted in subsequent tests during which the rats were paralyzed by curare. And, on subsequent retraining without curare, such differences in activity and respiration as were present earlier in training continued to decrease, while the differences in heart rate continued to increase. It seems extremely unlikely that, at the end of training, the highly reliable differences in heart rate ($t = 7.2$; $P < .0001$) can be explained by the highly unreliable differences in activity and respiration ($t = .07$ and 0.2, respectively).

Although the rats in this experiment showed some learning when they were trained initially in the noncurarized state, this learning was much poorer than that which we have seen in our other experiments on curarized rats. This is exactly the opposite of my original expectation, but seems plausible in the light of hindsight. My hunch is that paralysis by curare improved learning by eliminating sources of distraction and variability. The stimulus situation was kept more constant, and confusing visceral fluctuations induced indirectly by skeletal movements were eliminated.

LEARNED CHANGES IN BRAIN WAVES

Encouraged by success in the experiments on the instrumental learning of visceral responses, my colleagues and I have attempted to produce other unconventional types of learning. Electrodes placed on the skull or, better yet, touching the surface of the brain record summative effects of electrical activity over a considerable area of the brain. Such electrical effects are called brain waves, and the record of them is called an electroencephalogram. When the animal is aroused, the electroencephalogram consists of fast, low-voltage activity; when the animal is drowsy or sleeping normally, the electroencephalogram consists of considerably slower, higher-voltage activity. Carmona attempted to see whether this type of brain activity, and the state of arousal accompanying it, can be modified by direct reward of changes in the brain activity (28, 29).

The subjects of the first experiment were freely moving cats. In order to have a reward that was under complete control and that did not require the cat to move, Carmona used direct electrical stimulation of the medial forebrain bundle, which is a rewarding area of the brain. Such stimulation produced a slight lowering in the average voltage of the electroencephalogram and an increase in behavioral arousal. In order to provide a control for these and any other unlearned effects, he rewarded one group for changes in the direction of high-voltage activity and another group for changes in the direction of low-voltage activity.

Both groups learned. The cats rewarded for high-voltage activity showed more high-voltage slow waves and tended to sit like sphinxes, staring out into space. The cats rewarded for low-voltage activity showed much more low-voltage fast activity, and appeared to be aroused, pacing restlessly about, sniffing, and looking here and there. It was clear that this type of training had modified both the character of the electrical brain waves and the general level of the behavioral activity. It was not clear, however, whether the level of arousal of the brain was directly modified and hence modified the behavior; whether the animals learned specific items of behavior which, in turn, modified the arousal of the brain as reflected in the electroencephalogram; or whether both types of learning were occurring simultaneously.

In order to rule out the direct sensory consequences of changes in muscular tension, movement, and posture, Carmona performed the next experiment on rats that had been paralyzed by means of curare. The results, given in Figure 9, show that both rewarded groups showed changes in the rewarded direc-

tion; that a subsequent nonrewarded rest increased the number of high-voltage responses in both groups; and that, when the conditions of reward were reversed, the direction of change in voltage was reversed.

At present we are trying to use similar techniques to modify the functions of a specific part of the vagal nucleus, by recording and specifically rewarding changes in the electrical activity there. Preliminary results suggest that this is possible. The next step is to investigate the visceral consequences of such modification. This kind of work may open up possibilities for modifying the activity of specific parts of the brain and the functions that they control. In some cases, directly rewarding brain activity may be a more convenient or more powerful technique than rewarding skeletal or visceral behavior. It also may be a new way to throw light on the

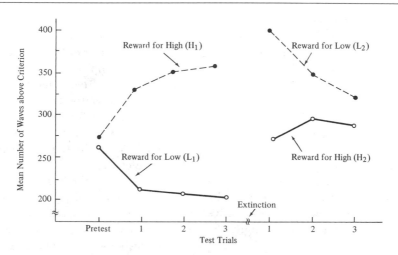

Figure 9 Instrumental learning by curarized rats rewarded for high-voltage or for low-voltage electroencephalograms recorded from the cerebral cortex. After a period of nonrewarded extinction, which produced some drowsiness, as indicated by an increase in voltage, the rats in the two groups were then rewarded for voltage changes opposite in direction to the changes for which they were rewarded earlier. [From Carmona (29).]

functions of specific parts of the brain (*30*).

HUMAN VISCERAL LEARNING

Another question is that of whether people are capable of instrumental learning of visceral responses. I believe that in this respect they are as smart as rats. But, as a recent critical review by Katkin and Murray (*31*) points out, this has not yet been completely proved. These authors have comprehensively summarized the recent studies reporting successful use of instrumental training to modify human heart rate, vasomotor responses, and the galvanic skin response. Because of the difficulties in subjecting human subjects to the same rigorous controls, including deep paralysis by means of curare, that can be used with animal subjects, one of the most serious questions about the results of the human studies is whether the changes recorded represent the true instrumental learning of visceral responses or the unconscious learning of those skeletal responses that can produce visceral reactions. However, the able investigators who have courageously challenged the strong traditional belief in the inferiority of the autonomic nervous system with experiments at the more difficult but especially significant human level are developing ingenious controls, including demonstrations of the specificity of the visceral change, so that their cumulative results are becoming increasingly impressive.

POSSIBLE ROLE IN HOMEOSTASIS

The functional utility of instrumental learning by the cerebrospinal nervous system under the conditions that existed during mammalian evolution is obvious. The skeletal responses mediated by the cerebrospinal nervous system operate on the external environment, so that there is survival value in the ability to learn responses that bring rewards such as food, water, or escape from pain. The fact that the responses mediated by the autonomic nervous system do not have such direct action on the external environment was one of the reasons for believing that they are not subject to instrumental learning. Is the learning ability of the autonomic nervous system something that has no normal function other than that of providing my students with subject matter for publications? Is it a mere accidental by-product of the survival value of cerebrospinal learning, or does the instrumental learning of autonomically mediated responses have some adaptive function, such as helping to maintain that constancy of the internal environment called homeostasis?

In order for instrumental learning to function homeostatically, a deviation away from the optimum level will have to function as a drive to motivate learning, and a change toward the optimum level will have to function as a reward to reinforce the learning of the particular visceral response that produced the corrective change.

When a mammal has less than the optimum amount of water in his body, this deficiency serves as a drive of thirst to motivate learning; the overt consummatory response of drinking functions as a reward to reinforce the learning of the particular skeletal responses that were successful in securing the water that restored the optimum level. But is the consummatory response essential? Can restoration of an optimum level by a glandular response function as a reward?

In order to test for the possible rewarding effects of a glandular response, DiCara, Wolf, and I (*32*) injected albino rats with antidiuretic hormone (ADH) if they chose one arm of a T-maze and with the isotonic saline vehicle if they chose the other, distinctively different, arm. The ADH permitted water to be reabsorbed in the kidney, so that a smaller volume of more concentrated urine was formed. Thus, for normal rats loaded in advance with H_2O, the ADH interfered with the excess-water excretion required for the restoration of homeostasis, while the control injection of isotonic saline allowed the excess water to be excreted. And, indeed, such rats learned to select the side of the maze that assured them an injection of saline so that their glandular response could restore homeostasis.

Conversely, for rats with diabetes insipidus, loaded in advance with hypertonic NaCl, the homeostatic effects of the same two injections were reversed; the ADH, causing the urine to be more concentrated, helped the rats to get rid of the excess NaCl, while the isotonic saline vehicle did not. And, indeed, a group of rats of this kind learned the opposite choice of selecting the ADH side of the maze. As a further control on the effects of the ADH per se, normal rats which had not been given H_2O or NaCl exhibited no learning. This experiment showed that an excess of either H_2O or NaCl functions as a drive and that the return to the normal concentration produced by the appropriate response of a gland, the kidney, functions as a reward.

When we consider the results of this experiment together with those of our experiments showing that glandular and

visceral responses can be instrumentally learned, we will expect the animal to learn those glandular and visceral responses mediated by the central nervous system that promptly restore homeostasis after any considerable deviation. Whether or not this theoretically possible learning has any practical significance will depend on whether or not the innate homeostatic mechanisms control the levels closely enough to prevent any deviations large enough to function as a drive from occurring. Even if the innate control should be accurate enough to preclude learning in most cases, there remains the intriguing possibility that, when pathology interferes with innate control, visceral learning is available as a supplementary mechanism.

IMPLICATIONS AND SPECULATIONS

We have seen how the instrumental learning of visceral responses suggests a new possible homeostatic mechanism worthy of further investigation. Such learning also shows that the autonomic nervous system is not as inferior as has been so widely and firmly believed. It removes one of the strongest arguments for the hypothesis that there are two fundamentally different mechanisms of learning, involving different parts of the nervous system.

Cause of Psychosomatic Symptoms

Similarly, evidence of the instrumental learning of visceral responses removes the main basis for assuming that the psychosomatic symptoms that involve the autonomic nervous system are fundamentally different from those functional symptoms, such as hysterical ones, that involve the cerebrospinal nervous system. Such evidence allows us to extend to psychosomatic symptoms the type of learning-theory analysis that Dollard and I (7, 33) have applied to other symptoms.

For example, suppose a child is terror-stricken at the thought of going to school in the morning because he is completely unprepared for an important examination. The strong fear elicits a variety of fluctuating autonomic symptoms, such as a queasy stomach at one time and pallor and faintness at another; at this point his mother, who is particularly concerned about cardiovascular symptoms, says, "You are sick and must stay home." The child feels a great relief from fear, and this reward should reinforce the cardiovascular responses producing pallor and faintness. If such experiences are repeated frequently enough, the child, theoretically, should learn to respond with that kind of symptom. Similarly, another child whose mother ignored the vasomotor responses but was particularly concerned by signs of gastric distress would learn the latter type of symptom. I want to exphasize, however, that we need careful clinical research to determine how frequently, if at all, the social conditions sufficient for such theoretically possible learning of visceral symptoms actually occur. Since a given instrumental response can be reinforced by a considerable variety of rewards, and by one reward on one occasion and a different reward on another, the fact that glandular and visceral responses can be instrumentally learned opens up many new theoretical possibilities for the reinforcement of psychosomatic symptoms.

Furthermore, we do not yet know how severe a psychosomatic effect can be produced by learning. While none of the 40 rats rewarded for speeding up their heart rates have died in the course of training under curarization, 7 of the 40 rats rewarded for slowing down their heart rates have died. This statistically reliable difference (chi square = 5.6, $P < .02$) is highly suggestive, but it could mean that training to speed up the heart helped the rats resist the stress of curare rather than that the reward for slowing down the heart was strong enough to overcome innate regulatory mechanisms and induce sudden death. In either event the visceral learning had a vital effect. At present, DiCara and I are trying to see whether or not the learning of visceral responses can be carried far enough in the noncurarized animal to produce physical damage. We are also investigating the possibility that there may be a critical period in early infancy during which visceral learning has particularly intense and long-lasting effects.

Individual and Cultural Differences

It is possible that, in addition to producing psychosomatic symptoms in extreme cases, visceral learning can account for certain more benign individual and cultural differences. Lacey and Lacey (34) have shown that a given individual may have a tendency, which is stable over a number of years, to respond to a variety of different stresses with the same profile of autonomic responses, while other individuals may have statistically reliable tendencies to respond with different profiles. It now seems possible that differential conditions of learning may account for at least some of these individual differences in patterns of autonomic response.

Conversely, such learning may account also for certain instances in which the same individual responds to the same stress in different ways. For example, a small boy who receives a severe bump in rough-and-tumble play may learn to inhibit the secretion of tears in this situation since his peer group will punish crying by calling it "sissy." But the same small boy may burst into tears when he gets home to his mother, who will not punish weeping and may even reward tears with sympathy.

Similarly, it seems conceivable that different conditions of reward by a culture different from our own may be responsible for the fact that Homer's adult heroes so often "let the big tears fall." Indeed, a former colleague of mine, Herbert Barry III, has analyzed cross-cultural data and found that the amount of crying reported for children seems to be related to the way in which the society reacts to their tears (35).

I have emphasized the possible role of learning in producing the observed individual differences in visceral responses to stress, which in extreme cases may result in one type of psychosomatic symptom in one person and a different type in another. Such learning does not, of course, exclude innate individual differences in the susceptibility of different organs. In fact, given social conditions under which any form of illness will be rewarded, the symptoms of the most susceptible organ will be the most likely ones to be learned. Furthermore, some types of stress may be so strong that the innate reactions to them produce damage without any learning. My colleagues and I are currently investi-

gating the psychological variables involved in such types of stress (36).

Therapeutic Training

The experimental work on animals has developed a powerful technique for using instrumental learning to modify glandular and visceral responses. The improved training technique consists of moment-to-moment recording of the visceral function and immediate reward, at first, of very small changes in the desired direction and then of progressively larger ones. The success of this technique suggests that it should be able to produce therapeutic changes. If the patient who is highly motivated to get rid of a symptom understands that a signal, such as a tone, indicates a change in the desired direction, that tone could serve as a powerful reward. Instruction to try to turn the tone on as often as possible and praise for success should increase the reward. As patients find that they can secure some control of the symptom, their motivation should be strengthened. Such a procedure should be well worth trying on any symptom, functional or organic, that is under neural control, that can be continuously monitored by modern instrumentation, and for which a given direction of change is clearly indicated medically— for example, cardiac arrhythmias, spastic colitis, asthma, and those cases of high blood pressure that are not essential compensation for kidney damage (37). The obvious cases to begin with are those in which drugs are ineffective or contraindicated. In the light of the fact that our animals learned so much better when under the influence of curare and transferred their training so well to the normal, nondrugged state, it should be worth while to try to use hypnotic suggestion to achieve similar results by enhancing the reward effect of the signal indicating a change in the desired direction, by producing relaxation and regular breathing, and by removing interference from skeletal responses and distraction by irrelevant cues.

Engel and Melmon (*38*) have reported encouraging results in the use of instrumental training to treat cardiac arrhythmias of organic origin. Randt, Korein, Carmona, and I have had some success in using the method described above to train epileptic patients in the laboratory to suppress, in one way or another, the abnormal paroxysmal spikes in their electroencephalogram. My colleagues and I are hoping to try learning therapy for other symptoms—for example, the rewarding of high-voltage electroencephalograms as a treatment for insomnia. While it is far too early to promise any cures, it certainly will be worth while to investigate thoroughly the therapeutic possibilities of improved instrumental training techniques.

REFERENCES AND NOTES

1. *The Dialogues of Plato,* B. Jowett, Transl., (Univ. of Oxford Press, London, ed. 2, 1875), vol. 3, "Timaeus."

2. X. Bichat, *Recherches Physiologiques sur la Vie et le Mort* (Brosson, Gabon, Paris, 1800).

3. W. B. Cannon, *The Wisdom of the Body* (Norton, New York, 1932).

4. F. Alexander, *Psychosomatic Medicine: Its Principles and Applications* (Norton, New York, 1950), pp. 40–41.

5. G. A. Kimble, *Hilgard and Marquis' Conditioning and Learning* (Appleton-Century-Crofts, New York, ed. 2, 1961), p. 100.

6. B. F. Skinner, *The Behavior of Organisms* (Appleton-Century, New York, 1938); O. H. Mowrer, *Harvard Educ. Rev.* **17,** 102 (1947).

7. N. E. Miller and J. Dollard, *Social Learning and Imitation* (Yale Univ. Press, New Haven, 1941); J. Dollard and N. E. Miller, *Personality and Psychotherapy* (McGraw-Hill, New York, 1950); N. E. Miller, *Psychol. Rev.* **58,** 375 (1951).

8. N. E. Miller, *Ann. N.Y. Acad. Sci.* **92,** 830 (1961); ———, in *Nebraska Symposium on Motivation,* M. R. Jones, Ed. (Univ. of Nebraska Press, Lincoln, 1963); ———, in *Proc. 3rd World Congr. Psychiat., Montreal, 1961* (1963), vol. 3, p. 213.

9. ———, in "Proceedings, 18th International Congress of Psychology, Moscow, 1966," in press.

10. ——— and A. Carmona, *J. Comp. Physiol. Psychol.* **63,** 1 (1967).

11. J. A. Trowill, *ibid.,* p. 7.

12. N. E. Miller and L. V. DiCara, *ibid.,* p. 12.

13. L. V. DiCara and N. E. Miller, *Commun. Behav. Biol.* **2,** 19 (1968).

14. ———, *J. Comp. Physiol. Psychol.* **65,** 8 (1968).

15. ———, *ibid.,* in press.

16. D. J. Ehrlich and R. B. Malmo, *Neuropsychologia* **5,** 219 (1967).

17. "It even becomes difficult to postulate enough different thoughts each arousing a different emotion, each of which in turn innately elicits a specific visceral response. And if one assumes a more direct specific connection between different thoughts and different visceral responses, the notion becomes indistinguishable from the ideo-motor hypothesis of the voluntary movement of skeletal muscles." [W. James, *Principles of Psychology* (Dover, New York, new ed., 1950), vol. 2, chap. 26].

18. N. E. Miller and A. Banuazizi, *J. Comp. Physiol. Psychol.* **65,** 1 (1968).

19. A. Banuazizi, thesis, Yale University (1968).
20. N. E. Miller and L. V. DiCara, *Amer. J. Physiol.* **215**, 677 (1968).
21. A. Carmona, N. E. Miller, T. Demierre, in preparation.
22. A. Carmona, in preparation.
23. L. V. DiCara and N. E. Miller, *Commun. Behav. Biol.* **1**, 209 (1968).
24. ———, *Science* **159**, 1485 (1968).
25. ———, *Psychosom. Med.* 30, 489 (1968).
26. L. V. DiCara and J. M. Weiss, *J. Comp. Physiol. Psychol.,* in press.
27. L. V. DiCara and N. E. Miller, *Physiol. Behav.,* in press.
28. N. E. Miller, *Science* **152**, 676 (1966).
29. A. Carmona, thesis, Yale University (1967).
30. For somewhat similar work on the single-cell level, see J. Olds and M. E. Olds, *in Brain Mechanisms and Learning,* J. Delafresnaye, A. Fessard, J. Konorski, Eds. (Blackwell, London, 1961).
31. E. S. Katkin and N. E. Murray, *Psychol.*

Bull. **70,** 52 (1968); for a reply to their criticisms see A. Crider, G. Schwartz, S. Shnidman, *ibid.,* in press.
32. N. E. Miller, L. V. DiCara, G. Wolf, *Amer. J. Physiol.* **215,** 684 (1968).
33. N. E. Miller, in *Personality Change,* D. Byrne and P. Worchel, Eds. (Wiley, New York, 1964), p. 149.
34. J. I. Lacey and B. C. Lacey, *Amer. J. Psychol.* **71,** 50 (1958); *Ann. N.Y. Acad. Sci.* **71,** 50 (1958); *Ann. N.Y. Acad. Sci.* **98,** 1257 (1962).
35. H. Barry III, personal communication.
36. N. E. Miller, *Proc. N.Y. Acad. Sci.,* in press.
37. Objective recording of such symptoms might be useful also in monitoring the effects of quite different types of psychotherapy.
38. B. T. Engel and K. T. Melmon, personal communication.
39. The work described is supported by U.S. Public Health Service grant MH 13189.

28

Hemisphere Disconnection and Unity in Conscious Awareness

Roger W. Sperry

The article by Sperry, like that of Miller, shows how important basic research can be to mankind, but it does so in a different way. The article reviews work that has been done on human subjects with their cerebral hemispheres disconnected at the midline. The disconnection procedure in humans has not only proven of therapeutic value for certain patients, but as the article shows, has revealed a great deal about the nature and location of conscious processes in man. Men have always tried to understand the phenomenon of consciousness, and this work seems to be helping them to do so in very important ways. Yet it all began with basic animal research. It was not really very many years ago when it was discovered that cats after hemisphere disconnection behaved as though there were two separate learning systems in the two disconnected hemispheres. Work such as this should lead us to be very cautious about accusing the basic researcher of "ivory towerism." The satisfaction of human curiosity should be of value in its own right. Jay Boyd Best (1963) has shown that even the lowly flatworm needs novel stimulation if he is to function well, so why should we hold human curiosity in contempt? Yet it is possible to insist on practical application of experimental discoveries and still to see great value in the work of experimental psychologists—even in the work of those doing "basic" research.

Reprinted from *American Psychologist,* 1968, **23,** 723–733. Copyright 1968 by the American Psychological Association, and reproduced by permission.

Invited address presented to the American Psychological Association in Washington, D.C., September 1967, and to the Pan American Congress of Neurology in San Juan, Puerto Rico, October 1967. Original work referred to in the text by the writer and his co-workers was supported by Grant MH–03372 from the National Institute of Mental Health, United States Public Health Service, and by the Hixon Fund of the California Institute of Technology.

The following article is a result of studies my colleagues and I have been conducting with some neurosurgical patients of Philip J. Vogel of Los Angeles. These patients were all advanced epileptics in whom an extensive midline section of the cerebral commissures had been carried out in an effort to contain severe epileptic convulsions not controlled by medication. In all these people the surgical sections included division of the corpus callosum in its entirety, plus division also of the smaller anterior and hippocampal commissures, plus in some instances the massa intermedia. So far as I know, this is the most radical disconnection of the cerebral hemispheres attempted thus far in human surgery. The full array of sections was carried out in a single operation.

No major collapse of mentality or personality was anticipated as a result of this extreme surgery: earlier clinical observations on surgical section of the corpus callosum in man, as well as the results from dozens of monkeys on which I had carried out this exact same surgery, suggested that the functional deficits might very likely be less damaging than some of the more common forms of cerebral surgery, such as frontal lobotomy, or even some of the unilateral lobotomies performed more routinely for epilepsy.

The first patient on whom this surgery was tried had been having seizures for more than 10 years with generalized convulsions that continued to worsen despite treatment that had included a sojourn in Bethesda at the National Institutes of Health. At the time of the surgery, he had been averaging two major attacks per week, each of which left him debilitated for another day or

so. Episodes of *status epilepticus* (recurring seizures that fail to stop and represent a medical emergency with a fairly high mortality risk) had also begun to occur at 2- to 3-month intervals. Since leaving the hospital following his surgery over 5½ years ago, this man has not had, according to last reports, a single generalized convulsion. It has further been possible to reduce the level of medication and to obtain an overall improvement in his behavior and well being (see Bogen & Vogel, 1962).

The second patient, a housewife and mother in her 30s, also has been seizure-free since recovering from her surgery, which was more than 4 years ago (Bogen, Fisher, & Vogel, 1965). Bogen related that even the EEG has regained a normal pattern in this patient. The excellent outcome in the initial, apparently hopeless, last-resort cases led to further application of the surgery to some nine more individuals to date, the majority of whom are too recent for therapeutic evaluation. Although the alleviation of the epilepsy has not held up 100% throughout the series (two patients are still having seizures, although their convulsions are much reduced in severity and frequency and tend to be confined to one side), the results on the whole continue to be predominantly beneficial, and the overall outlook at this time remains promising for selected severe cases.

The therapeutic success, however, and all other medical aspects are matters for our medical colleagues, Philip J. Vogel and Joseph E. Bogen. Our own work has been confined entirely to an examination of the functional outcome, that is, the behavioral, neurological, and psychological effects of this surgical disruption of all direct cross-talk between the hemispheres. Initially we were concerned as to whether we would be able to find in these patients any of the numerous symptoms of hemisphere deconnection that had been demonstrated in the so-called "split-brain" animal studies of the 1950s (Myers, 1961; Sperry, 1967a, 1967b). The outcome in man remained an open question in view of the historic Akelaitis (1944) studies that had set the prevailing doctrine of the 1940s and 1950s. This doctrine maintained that no important functional symptoms are found in man following even complete surgical section of the corpus callosum and anterior commissure, provided that other brain damage is excluded.

These earlier observations on the absence of behavioral symptoms in man have been confirmed in a general way to the extent that it remains fair to say today that the most remarkable effect of sectioning the neocortical commissures is the apparent lack of effect so far as ordinary behavior is concerned. This has been true in our animal studies throughout, and it seems now to be true for man also, with certain qualifications that we will come to later. At the same time, however—and this is in contradiction to the earlier doctrine set by the Akelaitis studies—we know today that with appropriate tests one can indeed demonstrate a large number of behavioral symptoms that correlate directly with the loss of the neocortical commissures in man as well as in animals (Gazzaniga, 1967; Sperry, 1967a, 1967b; Sperry, Gazzaniga, & Bogen, 1968). Taken collectively, these symptoms may be referred to as the syndrome of the neocortical commissures or the syndrome of the forebrain commissures or, less specifically, as the syndrome of hemisphere deconnection.

One of the more general and also more interesting and striking features of this syndrome may be summarized as an apparent doubling in most of the realms of conscious awareness. Instead of the normally unified single stream of consciousness, these patients behave in many ways as if they have two independent streams of conscious awareness, one in each hemisphere, each of which is cut off from and out of contact with the mental experiences of the other. In other words, each hemisphere seems to have its own separate and private sensations; its own perceptions; its own concepts; and its own impulses to act, with related volitional, cognitive, and learning experiences. Following the surgery, each hemisphere also has thereafter its own separate chain of memories that are rendered inaccessible to the recall processes of the other.

This presence of two minds in one body, as it were, is manifested in a large number and variety of test responses which, for the present purposes, I will try to review very briefly and in a somewhat streamlined and simplified form. First, however, let me take time to emphasize that the work reported here has been very much a team project. The surgery was performed by Vogel at the White Memorial Medical Center in Los Angeles. He has been assisted in the surgery and in the medical treatment throughout by Joseph Bogen. Bogen has also been collaborating in our behavioral testing program, along with a number of graduate students and postdoctoral fellows, among whom M. S. Gazzaniga, in particular, worked closely with us during the first several years and managed much of the testing during that period. The patients and their families have been most cooperative, and the whole project gets its primary funding from the National Institute of Mental Health.

Most of the main symptoms seen after hemisphere deconnection can be described for convenience with reference to a single testing setup—shown in Figure 1. Principally, it allows for the lateralized testing of the right and left halves of the visual field, separately or together, and the right and left hands and legs with vision excluded. The tests can be arranged in different combinations and in association with visual, auditory, and other input, with provisions for eliminating unwanted stimuli. In testing vision, the subject with one eye covered centers his gaze on a designated fixation point on the upright translucent screen. The visual stimuli on 35-millimeter transparencies are arranged in a standard projector equipped with a shutter and are then back-projected at $\frac{1}{10}$ of a second or less—too fast for eye movements to get the material into the wrong half of the visual field. Figure 2 is merely a reminder that everything seen to the left of the vertical meridian through either eye is projected

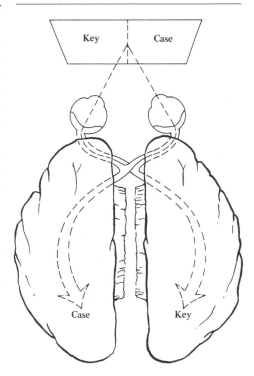

Figure 2   Things seen to the left of a central fixation point with either eye are projected to the right hemisphere and vice-versa.

to the right hemisphere and vice versa. The midline division along the vertical meridian is found to be quite precise without significant gap or overlap (Sperry, 1968).

When the visual perception of these patients is tested under these conditions the results indicate that these people have not one inner visual world any longer, but rather two separate visual inner worlds, one serving the right half of the field of vision and the other the left half—each, of course, in its respective hemisphere. This doubling in the visual sphere shows up in many ways: For example, after a projected picture of an object has been identified and responded to in one half field, we find

Figure 1   Apparatus for studying lateralization of visual, tactual, lingual, and associated functions in the surgically separated hemispheres.

that it is recognized again only if it reappears in the same half of the field of vision. If the given visual stimulus reappears in the opposite half of the visual field, the subject responds as if he had no recollection of the previous exposure. In other words, things seen through the right half of the visual field (i.e., through the left hemisphere) are registered in mental experience and remembered quite separately from things seen in the other half of the field. Each half of the field of vision in the commissurotomized patient has its own train of visual images and memories.

This separate existence of two visual inner worlds is further illustrated in reference to speech and writing, the cortical mechanisms for which are centered in the dominant hemisphere. Visual material projected to the right half of the field—left-hemisphere system of the typical right-handed patient—can be described in speech and writing in an essentially normal manner. However, when the same visual material is projected into the left half of the field, and hence to the right hemisphere, the subject consistently insists that he did not see anything or that there was only a flash of light on the left side. The subject acts as if he were blind or agnostic for the left half of the visual field. If, however, instead of asking the subject to tell you what he saw, you instruct him to use his left hand to point to a matching picture or object presented among a collection of other pictures or objects, the subject has no trouble as a rule in pointing out consistently the very item that he has just insisted he did not see.

We do not think the subjects are trying to be difficult or to dupe the examiner in such tests. Everything indicates that the hemisphere that is talking to

the examiner did in fact not see the left-field stimulus and truly had no experience with, nor recollection of, the given stimulus. The other, the right or nonlingual hemisphere, however, did see the projected stimulus in this situation and is able to remember and recognize the object and can demonstrate this by pointing out selectively the corresponding or matching item. This other hemisphere, like a deaf mute or like some aphasics, cannot talk about the perceived object and, worse still, cannot write about it either.

If two different figures are flashed simultaneously to the right and left visual fields, as for example a "dollar sign" on the left and a "question mark" on the right and the subject is asked to draw what he saw using the left hand out of sight, he regularly reproduces the figure seen on the left half of the field, that is, the dollar sign. If we now ask him what he has just drawn, he tells us without hesitation that the figure he drew was the question mark, or whatever appeared in the right half of the field. In other words, the one hemisphere does not know what the other hemisphere has been doing. The left and the right halves of the visual field seem to be perceived quite separately in each hemisphere with little or no crossinfluence.

When words are flashed partly in the left field and partly in the right, the letters on each side of the midline are perceived and responded to separately. In the "key case" example shown in Figure 2 the subject might first reach for and select with the left hand a key from among a collection of objects indicating perception through the minor hemisphere. With the right hand he might then spell out the word "case" or he might speak the word if verbal response is in order. When asked what kind of "case" he was thinking of here, the answer coming from the left hemisphere might be something like "in *case* of fire" or "the *case* of the missing corpse" or "a *case* of beer," etc., depending upon the particular mental set of the left hemisphere at the moment. Any reference to "key case" under these conditions would be purely fortuitous, assuming that visual, auditory, and other cues have been properly controlled.

A similar separation in mental awareness is evident in tests that deal with stereognostic or other somesthetic discriminations made by the right and left hands, which are projected separately to the left and right hemispheres, respectively. Objects put in the right hand for identification by touch are readily described or named in speech or writing, whereas, if the same objects are placed in the left hand, the subject can only make wild guesses and may often seem unaware that anything at all is present. As with vision in the left field, however, good perception, comprehension, and memory can be demonstrated for these objects in the left hand when the tests are so designed that the subject can express himself through nonverbal responses. For example, if one of these objects which the subject tells you he cannot feel or does not recognize is taken from the left hand and placed in a grab bag or scrambled among a dozen other test items, the subject is then able to search out and retrieve the initial object even after a delay of several minutes is deliberately interposed. Unlike the normal subject, however, these people are obliged to retrieve such an object with the same hand with which it was initially identified. They fail at cross-retrieval. That is, they cannot recognize with one hand something identified only moments before with the other hand. Again, the second hemisphere does not know what the first hemisphere has been doing.

When the subjects are first asked to use the left hand for these stereognostic tests they commonly complain that they cannot "work with that hand," that the hand "is numb," that they "just can't feel anything or can't do anything with it," or that they "don't get the message from that hand." If the subjects perform a series of successful trials and correctly retrieve a group of objects which they previously stated they could not feel, and if this contradiction is then pointed out to them, we get comments like "Well, I was just guessing," or "Well, I must have done it unconsciously."

With other simple tests a further lack of cross-integration can be demonstrated in the sensory and motor control of the hands. In a "symmetric handpose" test the subject holds both hands out of sight symmetrically positioned and not in contact. One hand is then passively placed by the examiner into a given posture, such as a closed fist, or one, two, or more fingers extended or crossed or folded into various positions. The subject is then instructed verbally or by demonstration to form the same pose with the other hand, also excluded from vision. The normal subject does this quite accurately, but the commissurotomy patient generally fails on all but the very simplest hand postures, like the closed fist or the fully extended hand.

In a test for crossed topognosis in the hands, the subject holds both hands out of sight, forward and palm up with the fingers held apart and extended. The examiner then touches lightly a point on one of the figures or at the base of the fingers. The subject responds by touching the same target point with the tip of the thumb of the same hand. Cross-integration is tested by requiring the patient to use the opposite thumb to find the corresponding mirror point on the opposite hand. The commissurotomy patients typically perform well within either hand, but fail when they attempt to cross-locate the corresponding point on the opposite hand. A crude cross-performance with abnormally long latency may be achieved in some cases after practice, depending on the degree of ipsilateral motor control and the development of certain strategies. The latter breaks down easily under stress and is readily distinguished from the natural performance of the normal subject with intact callosum.

In a related test the target point is presented visually as a black spot on an outline drawing of the hand. The picture is flashed to the right or left half of the visual field, and the subject then attempts as above to touch the target spot with the tip of the thumb. The response again is performed on the same side with normal facility but is impaired in the commissurotomy patient when the left visual field is paired with a right-hand response and vice versa. Thus the duality of both manual stereognosis and visuognosis is further illustrated; each hemisphere perceives as a separate unit unaware of the perceptual experience of the partner.

If two objects are placed simultaneously, one in each hand, and then are removed and hidden for retrieval in a scrambled pile of test items, each hand will hunt through the pile and search out selectively its own object. In the process each hand may explore, identify, and reject the item for which the other hand is searching. It is like two separate individuals working over the collection of test items with no cooperation between them. We find the interpretation of this and of many similar performances to be less confusing if we do not try to think of the behavior of the commissurotomy patient as that of a single individual, but try to think instead in terms of the mental faculties and performance capacities of the left and the right hemispheres separately. Most of the time it appears that the major, that is, the left, hemisphere is in control. But in some tasks, particularly when these are forced in testing procedures, the minor hemisphere seems able to take over temporarily.

It is worth remembering that when you split the brain in half anatomically you do not divide in half, in quite the same sense, its functional properties. In some respects cerebral functions may be doubled as much as they are halved because of the extensive bilateral redundancy in brain organization, wherein most functions, particularly in subhuman species, are separately and rather fully organized on both sides. Consider for example the visual inner world of either of the disconnected hemispheres in these patients. Probably neither of the separated visual systems senses or perceives itself to be cut in half or even incomplete. One may compare it to the visual sphere of the hemianopic patient who, following accidental destruction of an entire visual cortex of one hemisphere, may not even notice the loss of the whole half sphere of vision until this has been pointed out to him in specific optometric tests. These commissurotomy patients continue to watch television and to read the paper and books with no complaints about peculiarities in the perceptual appearance of the visual field.

At the same time, I want to caution against any impression that these patients are better off mentally without their cerebral commissures. It is true that if you carefully select two simple tasks, each of which is easily handled by a single hemisphere, and then have the two performed simultaneously, there is a good chance of getting better than normal scores. The normal interference effects that come from trying to attend to two separate right and left tasks at the same time are largely eliminated in the commissurotomized patient. However, in most activities that are at all complex the normally unified cooperating hemispheres still appear to do better than the two disconnected hemispheres. Although it is true that the intelligence, as measured on IQ tests, is not much affected and that the personality comes through with little change, one gets the impression in working with these people that their intellect is nevertheless handicapped in ways that are probably not revealed in the ordinary tests. All the patients have marked short-term memory deficits, which are especially pronounced during the first year, and it is open to question whether this memory impairment ever clears completely. They also have orientation problems, fatigue more quickly in reading and in other tasks requiring mental concentration, and presumably have various other impairments that reduce the upper limits of performance in functions that have yet to be investigated. The patient that has shown the best recovery, a boy of 14, was able to return to public school and was doing passing work with B to D grades, except for an F in math, which

he had to repeat. He was, however, a D student before the surgery, in part, it would seem, for lack of motivation. In general, our tests to date have been concerned mostly with basic cross-integrational deficits in these patients and the kind of mental capacities preserved in the subordinate hemisphere. Studied comparisons of the upper limits of performance before and after surgery are still needed.

Much of the foregoing is summarized schematically in Figure 3. The left hemisphere in the right-handed patients is equipped with the expressive mechanisms for speech and writing and with the main centers for the comprehension

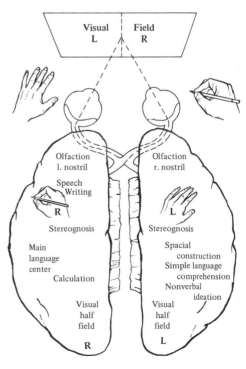

Figure 3 Schematic outline of the functional lateralization evident in behavioral tests of patients with forebrain commissurotomy.

and organization of language. This "major" hemisphere can communicate its experiences verbally and in an essentially normal manner. It can communicate, that is, about the visual experiences of the right half of the optic field and about the somesthetic and volitional experiences of the right hand and leg and right half of the body generally. In addition, and not indicated in the figure, the major hemisphere also communicates, of course, about all of the more general, less lateralized cerebral activity that is bilaterally represented and common to both hemispheres. On the other side we have the mute aphasic and agraphic right hemisphere, which cannot express itself verbally, but which through the use of nonverbal responses can show that it is not agnostic; that mental processes are indeed present centered around the left visual field, left hand, left leg, and left half of the body; along with the auditory, vestibular, axial somatic, and all other cerebral activities that are less lateralized and for which the mental experiences of the right and left hemispheres may be characterized as being similar but separate.

It may be noted that nearly all of the symptoms of cross-integrational impairment that I have been describing are easily hidden or compensated under the conditions or ordinary behavior. For example, the visual material has to be flashed at $1/10$ of a second or less to one half of the field in order to prevent compensation by eye movements. The defects in manual stereognosis are not apparent unless vision is excluded; nor is doubling in olfactory perception evident without sequential occlusion of right and left nostril and elimination of visual cues. In many tests the major hemisphere must be prevented from talking to the minor hemisphere and thus giving away the answer through auditory channels. And, similarly, the minor hemisphere must be prevented from giving nonverbal signals of various sorts to the major hemisphere. There is a great diversity of indirect strategies and response signals, implicit as well as overt, by which the informed hemisphere can be used to cue-in the uninformed hemisphere (Levy-Agresti, 1968).

Normal behavior under ordinary conditions is favored also by many other unifying factors. Some of these are very obvious, like the fact that these two separate mental spheres have only one body, so they always get dragged to the same places, meet the same people, and see and do the same things all the time and thus are bound to have a great overlap of common, almost identical, experience. Just the unity of the optic image—and even after chiasm section in animal experiments, the conjugate movements of the eyes—means that both hemispheres automatically center on, focus on, and hence probably attend to, the same items in the visual field all the time. Through sensory feedback a unifying body schema is imposed in each hemisphere with common components that similarly condition in parallel many processes of perception and motor action onto a common base. To get different activities going and different experiences and different memory chains built up in the separated hemispheres of the bisected mammalian brain, as we do in the animal work, requires a considerable amount of experimental planning and effort.

In motor control we have another important unifying factor, in that either hemisphere can direct the movement of both sides of the body, including to some extent the movements of the ipsilateral hand (Hamilton, 1967). Insofar as a response involves mainly the axial parts and proximal limb segments, these patients have little problem in directing overall response from sensory information restricted to either single hemisphere. Control of the distal limb segments and especially of the finer finger movements of the hand ipsilateral to the governing hemisphere, however, are borderline functions and subject to considerable variation. Impairments are most conspicuous when the subject is given a verbal command to respond with the fingers of the left hand. The absence of the callosum, which normally would connect the language processing centers in the left hemisphere to the

main left-hand motor controls in the opposite hemisphere, is clearly a handicap, especially in the early months after surgery. Cursive writing with the left hand presents a similar problem. It may be accomplished in time by some patients using shoulder and elbow rather than finger movement. At best, however, writing with the left hand is not as good after as before the surgery. The problem is not in motor coordination per se, because the subject can often copy with the left hand a word already written by the examiner when the same word cannot be written to verbal command.

In a test used for more direct determination of the upper limits of this ipsilateral motor control, a simple outline sketch of a finger posture (see Figure 4) is flashed to a single hemisphere, and

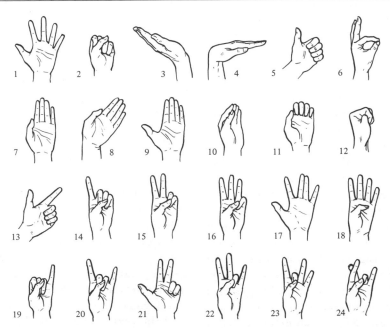

Figure 4 In tests for ipsilateral motor control, different hand postures in outline drawing are projected one at a time to left or right visual field (see Figure 1). Subject attempts to copy sample hand pose with the homolateral and the contralateral hand.

the subject then tries to mimic the posture with the same or the opposite hand. The sample posture can usually be copied on the same side (i.e., through the main, contralateral control system) without difficulty, but the performance does not go so easily and often breaks down completely when the subject is obliged to use the opposite hand. The closed fist and the open hand with all fingers extended seem to be the two simplest responses, in that these can most often be copied with the ipsilateral hand by the more adept patients.

The results are in accord with the thesis (Gazzaniga, Bogen, & Sperry, 1967) that the ipsilateral control systems are delicate and marginal and easily disrupted by associated cerebral damage and other complicating factors. Preservation of the ipsilateral control system in varying degree in some patients and not in others would appear to account for many of the discrepancies that exist in the literature on the symptoms of hemisphere deconnection, and also for a number of changes between the present picture and that described until 2 years ago. Those acquainted with the literature will notice that the present findings on dyspraxia come much closer to the earlier Akelaitis observations than they do to those of Liepmann or of others expounded more recently (see Geschwind, 1965).

To try to find out what goes on in that speechless agraphic minor hemisphere has always been one of the main challenges in our testing program. Does the minor hemisphere really possess a true stream of conscious awareness or is it just an agnostic automaton that is carried along in a reflex or trancelike state? What is the nature, the quality, and the level of the mental life of this isolated subordinate unknown half of the human brain—which, like the animal mind, cannot communicate its experiences? Closely tied in here are many problems that relate to lateral dominance and specialization in the human brain, to the functional roles mediated by the neocortical commissures, and to related aspects of cerebral organization.

With such in mind, I will try to review briefly some of the evidence obtained to date that pertains to the level and nature of the inner mental life of the disconnected minor hemisphere. First, it is clear that the minor hemisphere can perform intermodal or cross-modal transfer of perceptual and mnemonic information at a characteristically human level. For example, after a picture of some object, such as a cigarette, has been flashed to the minor hemisphere through the left visual field, the subject can retrieve the item pictured from a collection of objects using blind touch with the left hand, which is mediated through the right hemisphere. Unlike the normal person, however, the commissurotomy patient is obliged to use the corresponding hand (i.e., the left hand, in this case) for retrieval and fails when he is required to search out the same object with the right hand (see Figure 5): Using the right hand the subject recognizes and can call off the names of each object that he comes to if he is allowed to do so, but the right hand or its hemisphere does not know what it is looking for, and the hemisphere that can recognize the correct answer gets no feedback from the right hand. Hence, the two never get together, and the performance fails. Speech and other auditory cues must be controlled.

It also works the other way around: that is, if the subject is holding an object

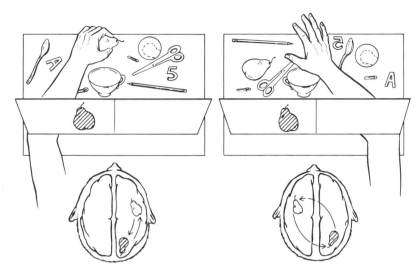

Figure 5 Visuo-tactile associations succeed between each half of the visual field and the corresponding hand. They fail with crossed combinations in which visual and tactual stimuli are projected into opposite hemispheres.

in the left hand, he can then point out a picture of this object or the printed name of the object when these appear in a series presented visually. But again, these latter must be seen through the corresponding half of the visual field; an object identified by the left hand is not recognized when seen in the right half of the visual field. Intermodal associations of this sort have been found to work between vision, hearing and touch, and, more recently, olfaction in various combinations within either hemisphere but not across from one hemisphere to the other. This perceptual or mnemonic transfer from one sense modality to another has special theoretical interest in that it is something that is extremely difficult or impossible for the monkey brain. The right hemisphere, in other words, may be animallike in not being able to talk or write, but in performances like the foregoing and in a number

of other respects it shows mental capacities that are definitely human.

Other responses from the minor hemisphere in this same testing situation suggest the presence of ideas and a capacity for mental association and at least some simple logic and reasoning. In the same visuo-tactual test described above, the minor hemisphere, instead of selecting objects that match exactly the pictured item, seems able also to select related items or items that "go with" the particular visual stimulus, if the subject is so instructed. For example, if we flash a picture of a wall clock to the minor side and the nearest item that can be found tactually by the left hand is a toy wrist watch, the subjects significantly select the watch. It is as if the minor hemisphere has an idea of a timepiece here and is not just matching sensory outlines. Or, if the picture of a dollar sign is flashed to the minor side, the subject searches through the list of items with the left hand and finally selects a coin such as a quarter or a 50¢ piece. If a picture of a hammer is presented, the subject may come up with a nail or a spike after checking out and rejecting all other items.

The capacity to think abstractly with symbols is further indicated in the ability of the minor hemisphere to perform simple arithmetical problems. When confronted with two numerals each less than 10, the minor hemisphere was able in four of six subjects so tested to respond with the correct sum or product up to 20 or so. The numbers were flashed to the left half of the visual field or presented as plastic block numerals to the left hand for identification. The answer was expressed by pointing to the correct number in columns of seen figures, or by left-hand signals in which the fingers were extended out of the subject's sight, or by writing the numerals with the left hand out of sight. After a correct left-hand response had been made by pointing or by writing the numeral, the major hemisphere could then report the same answer verbally, but the verbal report could not be made prior to the left-hand response. If an error was made with the left hand, the verbal report contained the same error. Two different pairs of numerals may be flashed to right and left fields simultaneously and the correct sum or products signaled separately by right and left hands. When verbal confirmation of correct left-hand signals is required under these conditions, the speaking hemisphere can only guess fortuitously, showing again that the answer must have been obtained from the minor and not from the major hemisphere. This has been demonstrated re-

cently in a study still in progress by Biersner and the present writer. The findings correct an earlier impression (Gazzaniga & Sperry, 1967) in which we underestimated the capacity for calculation on the minor side. Normal subjects and also a subject with agenesis of the callosum (Saul & Sperry, 1968) were able to add or to multiply numerals shown one in the left and one in the right field under these conditions. The commissurotomy subjects, however, were able to perform such calculations only when both numerals appeared in the same half of the visual field.

According to a doctrine of long standing in the clinical writings on aphasia, it is believed that the minor hemisphere, when it has been disconnected by commissural or other lesions from the language centers on the opposite side, becomes then "word blind," "word deaf," and "tactually alexic." In contradiction to this, we find that the disconnected minor hemisphere in these commissurotomy patients is able to comprehend both written and spoken words to some extent, although this comprehension cannot be expressed verbally (Gazzaniga & Sperry, 1967; Sperry, 1966; Sperry & Gazzaniga, 1967). If the name of some object is flashed to the left visual field, like the word "eraser," for example, the subject is able then to search out an eraser from among a collection of objects using only touch with the left hand. If the subject is then asked what the item is after it has been selected correctly, his replies show that he does not know what he is holding in his left hand—as is the general rule for left-hand stereognosis. This means of course that the *talking* hemisphere does not know the correct answer, and we concluded accordingly that the minor hemisphere must, in this situation, have read and understood the test word.

These patients also demonstrate comprehension of language in the minor hemisphere by being able to find by blind touch with the left hand an object that has been named aloud by the examiner. For example, if asked to find a "piece of silverware," the subject may explore the array of test items and pick up a fork. If the subject is then asked what it is that he has chosen, he is just as likely in this case to reply "spoon" or "knife" as fork. Both hemispheres have heard and understood the word "silverware," but only the minor hemisphere knows what the left hand has actually found and picked up. In similar tests for comprehension of the spoken word, we find that the minor hemisphere seems able to understand even moderately advanced definitions like "shaving instrument" for razor or "dirt remover" for soap and "inserted in slot machines" for quarter.

Work in progress shows that the minor hemisphere can also sort objects into groups by touch on the basis of shape, size, and texture. In some tests the minor hemisphere is found to be superior to the major, for example, in tasks that involve drawing spatial relationships and performing block design tests. Perceptive mental performance in the minor hemisphere is also indicated in other situations in which the two hemispheres function concurrently in parallel at different tasks. It has been found, for example, that the divided hemispheres are capable of perceiving different things occupying the same position in space at the same time, and of learning mutually conflicting discrimination habits, something of which the normal brain is not capable. This was shown in the monkey work done some years ago by Trevarthen (1962) using a system of polarized light filters. It also required section of the optic chiasm, which of course is not included in the human surgery. The human patients, unlike normal subjects, are able to carry out a double voluntary reaction-time task as fast as they carry out a single task (Gazzaniga & Sperry, 1966). Each hemisphere in this situation has to perform a separate and different visual discrimination in order to push with the corresponding hand the correct one of a right and left pair of panels. Whereas interference and extra delay are seen in normal subjects with the introduction of the second task, these patients with the two hemispheres working in parallel simultaneously perform the double task as rapidly as the single task.

The minor hemisphere is also observed to demonstrate appropriate emotional reactions as, for example, when a pinup shot of a nude is interjected by surprise among a series of neutral geometric figures being flashed to the right and left fields at random. When the surprise nude appears on the left side the subject characteristically says that he or she saw nothing or just a flash of light. However, the appearance of a sneaky grin and perhaps blushing and giggling on the next couple of trials or so belies the verbal contention of the speaking hemisphere. If asked what all the grinning is about, the subject's replies indicate that the conversant hemisphere has no idea at this stage what it was that had turned him on. Apparently, only the emotional effect gets across, as if the cognitive component of the process cannot be articulated through the brainstem.

Emotion is also evident on the minor side in a current study by Gordon and Sperry (1968) involving olfaction. When odors are presented through the right nostril to the minor hemisphere the subject is unable to name the odor but can frequently tell whether it is pleasant or unpleasant. The subject may even grunt, make aversive reactions or exclamations like "phew!" to a strong unpleasant smell, but not be able to state verbally whether it is garlic, cheese, or some decayed matter. Again it appears that the affective component gets across to the speaking hemisphere, but not the more specific information. The presence of the specific information within the minor hemisphere is demonstrated by the subject's correct selection through left-hand stereognosis of corresponding objects associated with the given odor. The minor hemisphere also commonly triggers emotional reactions of displeasure in the course of ordinary testing. This is evidenced in the frowning, wincing, and negative head shaking in test situations where the minor hemisphere, knowing the correct answer but unable to speak, hears the major hemisphere making obvious verbal mistakes. The minor hemisphere seems to express genuine annoyance at the erroneous vocal responses of its better half.

Observations like the foregoing lead us to favor the view that in the minor hemisphere we deal with a second conscious entity that is characteristically human and runs along in parallel with the more dominant stream of consciousness in the major hemisphere (Sperry, 1966). The quality of mental awareness present in the minor hemisphere may be comparable perhaps to that which survives in some types of aphasic patients following losses in the motor and main language centers. There is no indication that the dominant mental system of the left hemisphere is concerned about or even aware of the presence of the minor system under most ordinary conditions except quite indirectly as, for example, through occasional responses triggered from the minor side. As one patient remarked immediately after seeing herself make a left-hand response of this kind, "Now I know it wasn't me did that!"

Let me emphasize again in closing that the foregoing represents a somewhat abbreviated and streamlined account of the syndrome of hemisphere deconnection as we understand it at the present time. The more we see of these patients and the more of these patients we see, the more we become impressed with their individual differences, and with the consequent qualifications that must be taken into account. Although the general picture has continued to hold up in the main as described, it is important to note that, with respect to many of the deconnection symptoms mentioned, striking modifications and even outright exceptions can be found among the small group of patients examined to date. Where the accumulating evidence will settle out with respect to the extreme limits of such individual variations and with respect to a possible average "type" syndrome remains to be seen.

REFERENCES

Akelaitis, A. J. A study of gnosis, praxis, and language following section of the corpus callosum and anterior commissure. *Journal of Neurosurgery*, 1944, **1**, 94–102.

Bogen, J. E., Fisher, E. D., & Vogel, P. J.

Cerebral commissurotomy: A second case report. *Journal of the American Medical Association*, 1965, **194,** 1328–1329.

Bogen, J. E., & Vogel, P. J. Cerebral commissurotomy: A case report. *Bulletin of the Los Angeles Neurological Society*, 1962, **27,** 169.

Gazzaniga, M. S. The split brain in man. *Scientific American*, 1967, **217,** 24–29.

Gazzaniga, M. S., Bogen, J. E., & Sperry, R. W. Dyspraxia following division of the cerebral commissures. *Archives of Neurology*, 1967, **16,** 606–612.

Gazzaniga, M. S., & Sperry, R. W. Simultaneous double discrimination following brain bisection. *Psychonomic Science*, 1966, **4,** 262–263.

Gazzaniga, M. S., & Sperry, R. W. Language after section of the cerebral commissures. *Brain*, 1967, **90,** 131–148.

Geschwind, N. Disconnexion syndromes in animals and man. *Brain*, 1965, **88,** 237–294, 584–644.

Gordon, H. W., & Sperry, R. W. Olfaction following surgical disconnection of the hemispheres in man. In, *Proceedings of the Psychonomic Society*, 1968, in press.

Hamilton, C. R. Effects of brain bisection on eye-hand coordination in monkeys wearing prisms. *Journal of Comparative and Physiological Psychology*, 1967, **64,** 434–443.

Levy-Agresti, J. Ipsilateral projection systems and minor hemisphere function in man after neocommissurotomy. *Anatomical Record*, 1968, **160,** 384.

Myers, R. E. Corpus callosum and visual gnosis. In J. F. Delafresnaye (Ed.), *Brain mechanisms and learning*. Oxford: Blackwell, 1961.

Saul, R., & Sperry, R. W. Absence of commissurotomy symptoms with agenesis of the corpus callosum. *Neurology*, 1968, **17,** in press.

Sperry, R. W. Brain bisection and mechanisms of consciousness. In J. C. Eccles (Ed.), *Brain and conscious experience*. New York: Springer-Verlag, 1966.

Sperry, R. W. Mental unity following surgical disconnection of the hemispheres. *The Harvey lectures*. Series 62. New York: Academic Press, 1967. (a)

Sperry, R. W. Split-brain approach to learning problems In G. C. Quarton, T. Melncchuk, & F. O. Schmitt (Eds.), *The neurosciences: A study program*. New York: Rockefeller University Press, 1967. (b)

Sperry, R. W. Apposition of visual half-fields after section of neocortical commissures. *Anatomical Record*, 1968, **160,** 498–499.

Sperry, R. W., & Gazzaniga, M. S. Language following surgical disconnection of the hemispheres. In C. H. Milikan (Ed.), *Brain mechanisms underlying speech and language*. New York: Grune & Stratton, 1967.

Sperry, R. W., Gazzaniga, M. S., & Bogen, J. E. Function of neocortical commissures: Syndrome of hemisphere deconnection. In P. J. Vinken & G. W. Bruyn (Eds.), *Handbook of neurology*. Amsterdam: North Holland, 1968, in press.

Trevarthen, C. B. Double visual learning in split-brain monkeys. *Science*, 1962, **136,** 258–259.

29

Pain as a Puzzle for Psychology and Physiology

Ernest R. Hilgard

In this article, Hilgard summarizes a research program on the hypnotic modification of pain. Pain has generally been either allowed to persist, modified by drugs, or alleviated surgically. The effects of psychological factors on pain (for example, placebo effects) have been regarded as somehow illegitimate. Yet it would seem that it matters very little how pain is alleviated, as long as it is alleviated without untoward side effects. The psychological approach to pain reduction holds very great promise, and Hilgard's research in this area has been outstanding. Note his attempts to reduce variability by selecting subjects according to a scale of suggestibility, and in particular note his use of multiple methods of inducing and of measuring pain. His research shows with particular emphasis the value of such multiple operations in psychological research.

Pain is so familiar that we take it for granted, but this does not lessen its importance. Pain reduction is a primary task of the physician, second only to the preservation of life. The ubiquity of pain is clear enough from the many advertisements which pit one pain killer against another. Because pain is so important, and interest in pain is so great, it is surprising how little firm knowledge there is about pain.

Reprinted from *American Psychologist,* 1969, **24,** 103–113. Copyright 1969 by the American Psychological Association, and reproduced by permission.

The preparation of this article and the investigations here reported have been supported by the National Institute of Mental Health, Public Health Service, Grant MH–3859, and by a contract with the United States Air Force Office of Research (Contract AF 49 [638] –1436). Requests for reprints should be sent to Hilgard, Department of Psychology, Stanford University, Stanford, California 94305.

WHAT IS PUZZLING ABOUT PAIN?

The very familiarity of pain may cause us to acknowledge it without questioning it. Pain appears to warn us of tissue damage, and it is easy to assign a superficial interpretation that it is merely "the cry of an injured nerve." When one does begin to question pain, however, there are many mysteries that remain to be unraveled. I wish to mention some of these before reporting some of our own experiments on pain and its reduction.

1. Is Pain a Sensory Modality? The first question is this: Shall we consider pain to be a sensory modality like vision or audition? If you cut your finger or stub your toe, pain behaves very much as if it were an ordinary sensory modality. That is, there is a stimulus, there are receptors in the fingers and toes, there is an afferent transmission of impulses, a central processing of data, a perceptual response appropriate to the stimulus, and perhaps some verbal accompaniment, such as "Ouch." The perceptual response of felt pain localized in a finger or a toe is analogous to seeing a light off to the left or of hearing a sound off to your right. Perceptual responses give knowledge of environmental events, and you guide your actions accordingly. Furthermore, the stimulus to pain can be graduated, as by an electric shock of varying intensity, or by water at different degrees of hot or cold, with subsequent changes in felt pain. All that I have said thus far qualifies pain as a sensory modality.

But there are other considerations which make it less easy to assign pain the status of a sensory modality. Most defined sensory modalities have definite stimuli, definite receptors, specific sensory tracts, and localized receptive areas within the cortex. Not so for pain. Any stimulus can qualify to produce pain if it is intense enough; loud sounds and very bright lights are painful. The receptors are unspecified, despite the role traditionally assigned to free nerve endings. While there are pathways for cutaneous pain, there are at least two afferent systems, and they operate quite differently (Melzack & Wall, 1965). And there is no one pain center that has been localized in the brain.

A further problem arises in that there are so many differences in the quality of felt pain that it may be as dubious to consider pain a single sense as to consider all cutaneous experiences as belonging to a single sense of touch. Even the attempt to define pain has met numerous obstacles (e.g., Beecher, 1959; Melzack, 1968). One of the puzzles is how to deal with the distinction between mild sensory pain and the intense pains that are described as suffering or anguish; under frontal lobe operations, for example, the anguish may be reduced even though the pain remains.

We must therefore give a qualified answer to the question whether or not pain can be counted as a sensory modality.

2. Are There Any Satisfactory Physiological Indicators of Pain? We know about pain through a subject's verbal reports, but if we expect to objectify the amount of pain he feels we would be happy to have some physiological indicators by which to compare his pain with that of others who suffer. Our second question is, then: Do satisfactory indicators exist?

A satisfactory physiological indicator of pain is one which is present (or increased) when pain is felt, and absent (or reduced) when pain is not felt. The correlation between the physiological indicator and the verbal report has to be established both positively and negatively if the indicator is to be used in confidence in the absence of supplementary verbal report. Without attempting at this time a literature review, may I simply summarize the state of our knowledge of the physiological correlates of pain by saying that there is at present *no single accepted indicator of pain* that can be counted to vary in an orderly way with degrees of pain and absence of pain.[1] While in many experiments some kind of average difference in a physiological response can be detected with increase in pain, individual differences in the patterning of responses, and some individual response stereotypy to different kinds of stress, complicate the problem.

3. Where Is the Pain that Is Felt? My third question about the puzzle of pain is this: Where is the pain that the subject reports? A subject locates the pain of an injury at the site of the injury or noxious stimulation by the same sorts of local signs and environmental references that he uses in localizing other sources of stimulation. I say: "I feel pain in my finger." My listener sees that the finger is bleeding, and replies: "No wonder you feel pain in your finger; you cut it." The pain is in my finger just as the word I read is on the printed page. The psychoneural *conditions* of feeling pain and of seeing words are within me, but it would be as uninformative to say that the pain is in my head as to say that the word I read is in my head. We have to distinguish between the *conditions* of the perception and the *informative aspect*

of the perception itself. The *information* is of a pain in my finger and of a word on the printed page.

The trouble about pain as informative is that there are at least three kinds of pain which make us wonder whether or not to accept information conferred by the localized pain. The first of these is *referred* pain, in which the source of irritation is one place and the pain is felt at another place, as in heartburn as the result of indigestion. The second is *psychosomatic* pain, in which the stimulus conditions may be vague, as in a headache following a political argument. The third kind is *phantom-limb* pain, where the pain is felt in a part of the body which has been amputated from it. Of these, phantom-limb pain is particularly interesting. Our tendency to revert to a strict sensory analogy is very strong; hence we would expect phantom-limb pain to be the result of referring the stimulation of a cut nerve in the stump to the limb from which it originally received its impulses. However, phantom-limb pain probably has more to do with body image than with local signs (Melzack, 1968; Sternbach, 1968; Szasz, 1967). The reply to our question must then be that, *as information* (even if it be false), the best we can do is to accept that the pains are where they are felt, including the phantom-limb pains; as *conditions* for pain, there are many complex events within the nervous system.

4. How Account for the Great Individual Differences in Felt Pain? My fourth and final question about the puzzle of pain has to do with the *lack* of relationship between the conditions of noxious stimulation and the amount of pain that is felt. This is primarily a matter of individual differences, but they are very impressive. I am not talking about the extreme cases of people who are born with practically complete lack of sensitivity to cutaneous or other pains. These people correspond in their own way to the totally blind or the totally deaf. Within the normal population, however, there are widespread differences, and it is these which concern us now.

In the relief of postsurgical pain through morphine, Beecher (1959) and his associates have found results that may be summarized roughly as follows: about a third of the patients gain relief of pain through morphine that is greater than the relief following a placebo; about a third get as much relief from a placebo as they do from morphine; the final third are relieved neither by placebo nor by morphine in doses considered safe to use.

Differences in pain responses are found to be related to cognitive styles by Petrie (1967). She reports that subjects selected on the basis of a test of kinesthetic aftereffects can be classified as *augmenters* or *reducers:* The augmenters exaggerate their pain responses and the reducers tend to inhibit theirs.

Differences in pain responsiveness, particularly complaints about pain, have been found to be associated with social class, ethnic groups, and family constellation. For example, Gonda (1962a, 1962b) found that those from the working class complain more to the nurses in hospitals than do those from white-collar classes, an observation confirmed in England as well as in the United States.

Finally, pain responses in the laboratory appear to follow some of the theories of cognitive consistency, in that the pain corresponds to the amount of re-

ward offered for participating in pain experiments—the greater the reward the greater the pain—as though some suffering is consistent with the higher pay for participation (Lewin, 1965; Zimbardo, Cohen, Weisenberg, Dworkin, & Firestone, 1966; Zimbardo, 1969).

By raising these four questions, about pain as a sensory modality, about the physiological indicators of pain, about where pain is felt, and about individual differences in pain responsiveness, I hope that you will now agree that there are sufficient unsolved problems to make a concerned attack on pain a fruitful scientific enterprise.

PAIN AS A SENSORY MODALITY: COLD PRESSOR RESPONSE AND ISCHEMIC PAIN IN THE NORMAL WAKING STATE[2]

We have used two sources of noxious stimulation in the experiments I am about to report. In the first of these pain is produced by placing the subject's hand and forearm in circulating cold water at several temperatures. This arrangement is commonly referred to as the *cold pressor test* (Greene, Boltax, Lustig, & Rogow, 1965; Hines & Brown, 1932; Wolf & Hardy, 1941). In

[2] Among the professional workers in the Laboratory of Hypnosis Research who have contributed most directly to the pain studies reported here the author wishes to mention Leslie M. Cooper, Arthur F. Lange, John R. Lenox, Arlene H. Morgan, Lewis B. Sachs, Toshimasa Saito, and John Voevodsky. A number of others have assisted in the record reading and data analysis. The author wishes to express his appreciation to these co-workers for permitting him to make use of the results of joint efforts as they have appeared in reports already published, and as they will appear in other reports in which the participants will be coauthors.

the second method pain is produced by first placing a tourniquet just above the elbow, and then asking the subject to squeeze a dynamometer a standard number of times. After he quits working and is quiet, the pain begins to mount. This we call *ischemic pain,* following the practice of Beecher and his associates (Beecher, 1966; Smith, Lawrence, Markowitz, Mosteller, & Beecher, 1966). Their method is a modification of the method initiated by Lewis, Pickering, and Rothschild (1931).

First, the cold pressor test. I shall not report here the details of experimental arrangements, which will appear in due course in the form of journal articles. Suffice it to say that there are base-line conditions: first, a *vigilance* condition, in which the subject keeps alert by pressing the appropriate one of a pair of buttons, to turn off that one of two discriminable sounds which happens to be sounding; this is followed by a condition of *relaxation* for several minutes prior to the immersion of the hand and forearm in the cold water; the *immersion period,* usually of 40 seconds; then, after the hand and arm are removed from the water and dried, a repetition of the vigilance and relaxation conditions. Except as part of the situational background, the base-line conditions are not important for the present psychophysical account, but they are important for the physiological measures which were taken concomitantly with the verbal reports. While the hand and forearm are immersed in the cold water, the subject reports his felt pain on a scale of 0 to 10, 0 being no pain, and 10 being a pain so severe that he would wish to remove his hand. We refer to this as a *critical level,* for it is the tolerance level for the pain, without special encouragement to

continue to suffer. If a subject has reached the pain level of 10 before the immersion period is over, he is persuaded to keep his hand in the water a little longer and to keep on counting. This he is able to do, and the result is of course a pain report beyond 10.

That such verbal pain reports yield an orderly relationship to the conditions of stimulation, both to the temperature of the water, and to the time in the water, is shown by the mean results for 0, 5, 10, and 15 degrees Centigrade as plotted in Figure 1. The means of the pain-state reports in each of the temperatures differ significantly from each of the other temperatures by t tests, with significances of at least $p = .05$.

These data appear orderly enough to provide a test of standard psychophysical models. The model chosen is Stevens'

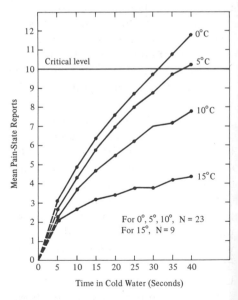

Figure 1 Reported pain as a function of time in water at temperatures of 0, 5, 10, and 15 degrees Centigrade.

(1966) power function because it proves to fit better than the standard Fechner logarithmic function. The test is quite simple. If both the numerical pain report and some measure of the intensity of stimulation are plotted logarithmically, the power function fits if a straight-line function results.

There is the single scale for verbal pain reports, but there are two possibilities for describing the intensity of stimulation: one, the *temperature* of the water, on the simple assumption that the colder the water the greater the pain; two, the *time* in the water, on the assumption that the pain mounts the longer the hand and forearm are exposed to the cold. The two measures have a common intermediary, which is the relationship between cold and pain, but there is no a priori reason for both of them to fit the same mathematical function.

Let us first see how pain varies as a function of water temperature. Other workers have found that the threshold for cold pressor pain is near 18 degrees Centigrade. This is well below skin temperature, but water can feel cold without feeling painful. If we then plot the average pain-state reports at 15, 10, 5, and 0 degrees on a scale which assumes that as the water gets colder the pain will be a power function of the difference in water temperature from the threshold value of 18 degrees we get the plot shown in Figure 2. The four plotted points fall quite well along a straight line, and the line projects to a threshold value of pain near 18 degrees.

Now we may ask whether a similar result will be obtained if we plot pain as a power function of the time in water of a given temperature. Because we have four temperatures, we have a family of

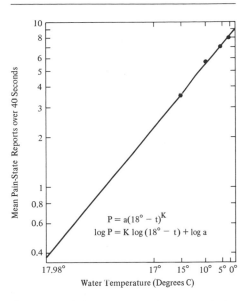

Figure 2 Pain as a power function of the differences in water temperature from the threshold value of 18 degrees Centigrade.

four lines, as shown in Figure 3. Again the straight lines fit well enough to indicate the appropriateness of the power function.[3]

Turning now to ischemia, as our second form of laboratory pain, and using the same scale of pain reports, we again find a power function with time, although now the time units are in minutes rather than in seconds (Figure 4).

[3] There are limitations in the fit of the power functions for both the cold pressor response and the ischemic response, when the stimulating conditions endure too long. In the cold pressor response numbing begins to set in at about 60 seconds for 0 degrees Centigrade water; in the case of ischemia there may be a sudden upturn of pain as the critical tolerance level is passed. We have elsewhere proposed a more complex function which can be used when there are inflections in the rate of change of pain or when the pain change is not monotonic (Voevodsky, Cooper, Morgan, & Hilgard, 1967).

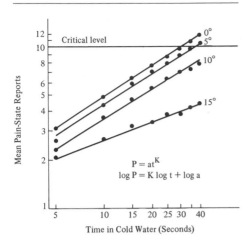

Figure 3 Pain as a power function of time in cold water.

Thus far I have shown that pain reported verbally on a simple numerical scale yields not only orderly results, but valid results, in the sense that the pain reported bears a systematic relationship to the temperature of the water and to the time of exposure to the noxious stimulus. The lawfulness is supported by the fit of the power function which holds within so many other perceptual modalities.

I emphasize these findings as a reply to those who would degrade the subject's statements as being "merely" verbal reports, as though some sort of physiological response would be sounder. I wish to assert flatly that there is no physiological measure of pain which is either as discriminating of fine differences in stimulus conditions, as reliable upon repetition, or as lawfully related to changed conditions, as the subject's verbal report.

PHYSIOLOGICAL ACCOMPANIMENTS OF PAIN

If I seem to disparage physiological indicators of pain, it is not because we have not studied them, nor indeed because results are negative, for I shall have some positive results to report. We have studied a number of measures, but I shall confine my discussion to one indicator, systolic blood pressure as measured from a finger on the hand opposite to that which is suffering the pain. We place a small inflatable cuff around one finger, with a plethysmographic transducer on the finger tip to indicate when the pulse is occluded. Another plethysmograph on an adjacent finger helps us to monitor heart responses. An automatically operated air pump inflates the finger cuff until the circulation is cut off, as indicated by the record from the plethysmograph on that finger, and then a device automatically

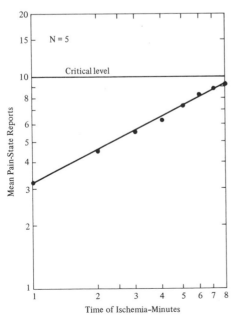

Figure 4 Pain as a function of time of ischemia.

releases the air from the cuff until the pulse again appears and is restored to normal, when the cycle automatically repeats itself. Thus a record is obtained on the polygraph of the systolic blood pressure every 10 seconds or so. By connecting these measurements as they appear on the polygraph we have an essentially continuous record of the blood pressure.

The rise in pain in the cold water is accompanied by a rise in blood pressure, and the rise in ischemic pain is also accompanied by a rise in blood pressure. Thus, under appropriate conditions, blood pressure appears to be the kind of indicator of pain for which we have been searching. A record of the blood pressure rise within cold water at four temperatures is given in Figure 5, which corresponds closely to the verbal pain reports earlier shown in Figure 1. The average results hold also for individual subjects. That is, those who suffer less at a given temperature also show less rise in blood pressure. Thus, for water at 0 degrees Centigrade, a correlation between mean pain reports and blood pressure rise for 22 subjects reaches $r = .53$, a satisfactorily significant correlation ($p = .02$). Others have reported similar findings (e.g., Tétreault, Panisset, & Gouger, 1964).

Blood pressure also rises as pain rises in ischemia. Rise in pain reports and rise in blood pressure yield the curves shown in Figure 6. These are means for 11 subjects. The abscissa has been converted to ratios of time in ischemia in order to plot the several subjects in comparable units. The time to maximum tolerable pain (at which the tourniquet had to be removed) fell between 12 and 32 minutes, by contrast with the water pain which was measured over a fraction of a minute only.

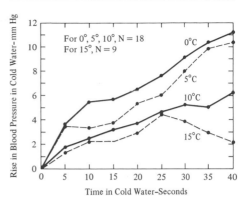

Figure 5 Blood pressure as a function of time in water at temperatures of 0, 5, 10, and 15 degrees Centigrade.

Thus we have established blood pressure as a candidate to serve as an indicator of pain. At least, in two stressful situations, it mounts as the pain mounts. As we shall see later, this does not satisfy all the requisites for a physiological pain indicator.

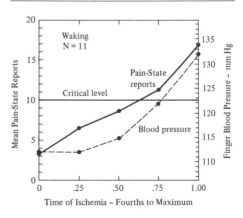

Figure 6 Pain reports and blood pressure as a function of time in ischemia. (The tourniquet was removed when pain became intolerable, which varied from 12 to 32 minutes for these 11 subjects. Hence the time to intolerable pain was divided into fourths for purposes of obtaining the means that are plotted.)

PAIN REDUCTION UNDER HYPNOSIS: COLD PRESSOR RESPONSE

Now I wish to turn to the reduction of pain, under the identical physical conditions of stressful stimulation, when that reduction is by way of hypnosis.[4] First we shall consider reduction of cold pressor pain.

College students or high school students who come to the laboratory for their first experience of hypnosis differ widely in their responses to a standard induction procedure followed by a standard list of suggestions. By making use of some scales earlier standardized in our laboratory (Weitzenhoffer & Hilgard, 1959, 1962, 1967) we are able to sort our subjects according to their degree of hypnotic susceptibility before they take part in the experiments concerned with pain. Then, at some later time, they experience the cold pressor pain in the waking condition, and learn to use the verbal pain report to indicate how much pain they feel. On a subsequent occasion we may hypnotize them, without suggesting any pain reduction, and then expose them to immersion in

the cold water, or we may hypnotize them and tell them that they will feel no pain in the cold water. This is the condition which we call attempted hypnotic analgesia. The subjects who entered the ice water experiments had had very little experience of hypnosis, and they were not trained in pain reduction. Our purpose was not to see how completely we could wipe out pain, but rather to see what individual differences in pain reduction would appear under standard conditions.

Because we did not have blood pressure measures on the subjects of our first reported experiment,[5] I shall turn to our second experiment which was partially a replication of the first one, but also introduced some modifications. We used high school students as subjects in this second investigation, instead of college students, largely because they were conveniently available in large numbers during the summer when the experiment was conducted. The subjects had already served in the experiment with water at different temperatures, in the normal waking state, so that they came to the hypnotic portion of the experiment well familiar with reports of pain on the verbal pain-state scale. They served three days, one in the normal waking condition, one in hypnosis without analgesia, and one in hypnosis with suggested analgesia; the orders of the latter two days were randomized, to

---

[4] The experimental literature on pain reduction (and pain production) in hypnosis is very confused, despite the well-established clinical successes in childbirth, dentistry, major surgery, and the successful relief of pain through hypnosis in severe burns and terminal cancer. A few of the major reports from other laboratories of experimental studies are listed here for the benefit of those who may care to explore this literature: Barber and Hahn (1962, 1964), Brown and Vogel (1938), Doupe, Miller, and Keller (1939), Dudley, Holmes, Martin, and Ripley (1964, 1966), Dynes (1932), Levine (1930), Sears (1932), Shor (1962), Sutcliffe (1961), West, Neill, and Hardy (1952), Wolff and Goodell (1943).

[5] Hilgard (1967). In this first experiment of the series with the cold pressor response, reactions from 55 college students were reported. The correlation between the amount of pain reduction under hypnotic analgesia and susceptibility to hypnosis was reported as $r = .37$ ($p = .01$). If one very discordant subject is eliminated, this rises to $r = .46$. See also Hilgard, Cooper, Lenox, Morgan, and Voevodsky (1967).

correct for any demand characteristics associated with having the hand in ice water in the midst of hypnosis. The advantages of comparing a day of hypnosis *without* suggested analgesia and hypnosis *with* analgesia are twofold. In the first place, this arrangement separates out any physiological effects that are attributable to the hypnosis as distinct from those associated with the stressful stimulus, and, in the second place, it rules out the effect upon pain of whatever relaxation is associated with hypnotic induction. It is well known that relaxation may itself reduce pain. The results for the three days are shown in Figure 7, plotted separately for the subjects low in hypnotic susceptibility and for those high in susceptibility. What we see from the figure is that hypnosis alone did not reduce pain appreciably for either group, but the suggested analgesia did indeed produce a reduction in verbally reported pain, slightly for the low hypnotizables, more for the high hypnotizables. In Figure 7 the high and low susceptibles are the extremes of a larger distribution, so that a correlational analysis is not appropriate. For a smaller group of 19 subjects, unselected for hypnosis, and including moderates as well as highs and lows, the correlation between hypnotic susceptibility as tested prior to the pain experiment and the pain reduction under hypnosis turned out to be $r = .60$ ($p = .01$).

The verbal pain reports thus yield an orderly picture of pain reduction under hypnotic analgesia, with the greatest reduction found for those who are the most hypnotizable. Now what of the blood pressure measures? Will they continue to correlate with pain reports under these conditions? To our surprise,

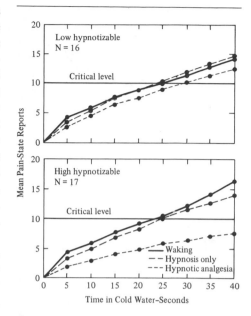

Figure 7 Pain as a function of time in water of 0 degrees Centigrade in waking state, and following attempted hypnotic induction without analgesia instructions and with analgesia instructions. (Low subjects, scores of 0–9 on combined Forms A and C—Mean = 7.1; High subjects, scores of 18–24 on combined Forms A and C—Mean = 21.6.)

the blood pressure *rises* under hypnosis and is highest under the analgesic condition, for both high and low hypnotizable subjects (Figure 8). It may be noted that, particularly for the high hypnotizable subjects, the blood pressure rises before the hands are placed in the ice water, so that the initial readings are above those of the less hypnotizable.[6]

We are thus led to two propositions

[6]The initial differences in blood pressure between waking and hypnosis days were not found in ischemia (Figure 9), and this discrepancy sets problems for further investigation. The conclusion holds, however, that blood pressure rises in the cold pressor test even when no pain is felt.

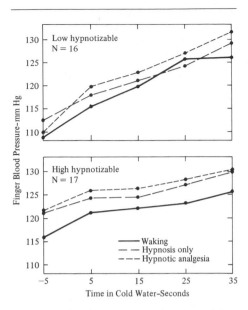

Figure 8 Blood pressure as a function of time in water of 0 degrees Centigrade in waking state, and following attempted hypnotic induction without analgesia instructions and with analgesia instructions. (Same subjects as in Figure 7.)

about the relationship between blood pressure and pain:

1. When pain is felt there is a tendency for blood pressure to rise in an amount correlated with the amount of experienced pain.

2. Blood pressure may rise in a stressful situation independent of the amount of felt pain.

The second of these statements is my reason for asserting that blood pressure is not a completely satisfactory physiological indicator of pain. It works in some situations, but not in others. There is nothing very surprising about this, because we know that there are many controls over blood pressure of which pain is but one. The two propositions, taken together, show that we have to be careful not to identify a *correlate* of pain, found in some special arrangement, with the pain itself. We may note also that we have to avoid a superficial interpretation of pain reduction under hypnosis by claiming that the effects of hypnotic analgesia rest entirely on the reduction of anxiety; it appears that excitation, possibly with some anxiety over the impending stress, may keep the blood pressure high, even while the pain is reduced.

PAIN REDUCTION UNDER HYPNOSIS: ISCHEMIC PAIN

The relationship between blood pressure and pain reduction under hypnosis turned out quite differently in ischemia. It is fortunate that we performed both experiments, for had we performed only one of them we might have produced misleading generalizations. There are several differences in the experiments to be noted. First, the cold water has the stress of cold, in addition to pain, while the cold is lacking in the ischemia experiment. Second, ischemic pain tends to mount very slowly at first, so that there is time for the hypnotic subject to achieve a confident analgesic state, while the shock of the ice water is immediate. Third, in the experiments to be reported the subjects were much more highly selected for their ability to reduce pain in hypnosis than they were in the cold pressor experiment, in which they were not selected at all. Still, the subjects in the ischemia experiments were selected from those in the cold pressor experiment, so we are not dealing with idiosyncrasies that can be accounted for on the basis of subject differences. These subjects behaved differently in ischemia from the way that they themselves had behaved in the ice water experiment.

It turns out that in the ischemia experiment these highly responsive subjects were able not only to rid themselves completely of pain for a matter of 18–45 minutes, but their blood pressure, which rose sharply in the waking state, *did not rise in ischemia or rose very little* even though the stressful condition was continued for many minutes beyond the time, in the waking condition, when the pain was too severe to be further endured. Results for six subjects, all of whom suffered greatly in the waking state but were able to maintain their analgesia throughout in the hypnotic state, are shown in Figure 9. The time to unbearable pain in the waking state is taken as unity; under hypnotic analgesia the tourniquet was kept on well beyond the time at which the intolerable pain would have been found in the waking state. Two subjects were unable to remain analgesic throughout; their blood pressures showed changes beyond

the subjects reported in Figure 9. While they were eliminated from Figure 9, statistical treatment with them left in shows a significant difference ($t = 3.12$, $df = 7$, $p = .01$) between the rise in blood pressure in the waking state over hypnotic analgesia for the whole group of subjects tested.

The three additional subjects, whose responses to ischemia in the waking state were reported earlier (in Figure 6), were subjects refractory to hypnosis, who were intended to be used as simulators in the hypnotic analgesia experiment, according to the experimental design recommended by Orne (1959, 1962). It turned out that the stress was too great, however, and none of them could tolerate the pain for the time required to parallel the behavior of the "true" hypnotic analgesia subjects. While this in some respects spoiled the experimental design, the conclusions are the same regarding the reality of the hypnotic analgesia for the "true" subjects, substantiated by the lack of any appreciable rise in blood pressure.

We are now prepared to add a third proposition regarding the relationship between blood pressure and pain:

3. When stressful conditions which normally lead both to reported pain and to an increase in blood pressure do not lead to an increase in blood pressure, it may be assumed that pain is absent.

This now brings us to a conclusion regarding the reality of hypnotic analgesia and to a summary assertion about the role of blood pressure. The absence of pain, reported by the hypnotically analgesia subject, is confirmed by the absence of a rise in blood pressure. Thus we have a physiological validation for the reality of hypnotic analgesia, but the validator works in one direction only.

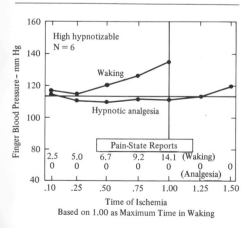

Figure 9 Blood pressure in ischemia, in waking state and in hypnotic analgesia (Mean, 6 subjects).

That is, *absence* of the blood pressure rise may be taken as an indication of absent pain under specified conditions, but pain may be absent *even if blood pressure rises*. This is a logical problem which has caused a good deal of confusion in earlier efforts to deal with the question of pain reduction under hypnotic analgesia (see especially Barber, 1963; Barber & Hahn, 1962; Sutcliffe, 1961).

CLINICAL RELEVANCE OF THE LABORATORY STUDY OF PAIN AND HYPNOTIC ANALGESIA

I wish to close my remarks with a few comments on the practical implications of the kind of experiments I have reported. There are continuing arguments over the relative amounts of money and energy to be expended on basic research and on research aimed at the applications of science. There are those who take the position that basic research is an end in itself, designed to satisfy curiosity, to seek the truth, to discover and order knowledge for its own sake. There are others who take the position that basic science will ultimately pay off in its contributions to society, although immediate payoff is not to be expected; this is the essence of the position that "there is nothing so practical as a good theory." On the more general issues, I take a moderate position: I believe that science has multiple aims, that there is a division of labor along the spectrum from pure science to the arts of practice, that there should be mutual respect and encouragement for those who work at any point along this spectrum, so long as their work is imaginative and sound.

When, however, there is an evident application for laboratory results I believe there is an obligation on the scientific enterprise as a whole to provide the bridging investigations that move from the laboratory to the real world. Thus the psychology of learning is incomplete if it is not reflected in educational practices, and the study of pain is incomplete if it does not contribute to the relief of pain outside the laboratory.

One may well ask how the experiments which I have reported bear upon the relief of pain through hypnosis by dentists, obstetricians, surgeons, and others who are confronted with the practical problems of suffering people. The answer is that the studies alone will not make much of a contribution unless they are extended to deal with the practical problems, either by those within laboratories such as ours, or by others who build upon our findings.

The potential contributions fall along the following lines:

1. First, our hypnotic susceptibility scales make it possible to determine what kinds of responsiveness to hypnosis are essential if a patient is to profit from the use of hypnosis in pain reduction. Not all people can be helped, and one obligation upon science is to be diagnostic regarding those who can be served by particular applications. It must be pointed out, however, that until normative data are obtained in the practical setting, the scales cannot be used effectively.

2. Second, the further study of the physiological consequences of pain, and the alterations of these consequences by hypnotic analgesia, can yield better understanding of what is happening in otherwise stressful conditions, such as the preparation for surgery or surgery itself. If hypnosis can reduce surgical pain or postoperative shock, it is impor-

tant to know what is happening inside the body. Again, unless these studies are carried out eventually in the hospital, the information gained in the laboratory will tend to be idle and useless.

We have accepted this as part of the responsibility of our own laboratory, and have undertaken studies of some patients suffering the pains of terminal cancer, others with migraine headaches. Clinicians are at present far ahead of our laboratories in the hypnotic reduction of pain, but the laboratory worker has a contribution to make. The contribution will be made, however, only if he takes his obligation seriously, and goes to the necessary trouble to tailor his findings to the needs of the world outside the laboratory.

REFERENCES

Barber, T. X. The effects of "hypnosis" on pain: A critical review of experimental and clinical finding. *Psychosomatic Medicine,* 1963, **24,** 303–333.

Barber, T. X., & Hahn, K. W., Jr. Physiological and subjective responses to pain-producing stimulation under hypnotically suggested and waking-imagined "analgesia." *Journal of Abnormal and Social Psychology,* 1962, **65,** 411–418.

Barber, T. X., & Hahn, K. W., Jr. Experimental studies in "hypnotic" behavior: Physiologic and subjective effects of imagined pain. *Journal of Nervous and Mental Disease,* 1964, **139,** 416–425.

Beecher, H. K. *Measurement of subjective responses.* New York: Oxford University Press, 1959.

Beecher, H. K. Pain: One mystery solved. *Science,* 1966, **151,** 840–841.

Brown, R. R., & Vogel, V. H. Psychophysiological reactions following painful stimuli under hypnotic analgesia contrasted with gas anesthesia and Novocain block. *Journal of Applied Psychology,* 1938, **22,** 408–420.

Doupe, J., Miller, W. R., & Keller, W. K. Vasomotor reactions in the hypnotic state. *Journal of Neurology and Psychiatry,* 1939, **2,** 97–106.

Dudley, D. L., Holmes, T. H., Martin, C. J., & Ripley, H. S. Changes in respiration associated with hypnotically induced emotion, pain, and exercise. *Psychosomatic Medicine,* 1964, **24,** 46–57.

Dudley, D. L., Holmes, T. H., Martin, C. J., & Ripley, H. S. Hypnotically induced facsimile of pain. *Archives of General Psychiatry,* 1966, **15,** 198–204.

Dynes, J. B. Hypnotic analgesia. *Journal of Abnormal and Social Psychology,* 1932, **27,** 79–88.

Gonda, T. A. The relation between complaints of persistent pain and family size. *Journal of Neurology, Neurosurgery, and Psychiatry,* 1962, **25,** 277–281. (a)

Gonda, T. A. Some remarks on pain. *Bulletin, British Psychological Society,* 1962, **47,** 29–35. (b)

Greene, M. A., Boltan, A. J., Lustig, G. A., & Rogow, E. Circulatory dynamics during the cold pressor test. *American Journal of Cardiology,* 1965, **16,** 54–60.

Hilgard, E. R. A quantitative study of pain and its reduction through hypnotic suggestion. *Proceedings of the National Academy of Sciences,* 1967, **57,** 1581–1586.

Hilgard, E. R., Cooper, L. M., Lenox, J., Morgan, A. H., & Voevodsky, J. The use of pain-state reports in the study of hypnotic analgesia to the pain of ice water. *Journal of Nervous and Mental Disease,* 1967, **144,** 506–513.

Hines, E. A., & Brown, G. E. A standard stimulus for measuring vasomotor reactions: Its application in the study of hypertension. *Proceedings of Staff Meetings, Mayo Clinic,* 1932, **7,** 332.

Levine, M. Psychogalvanic reaction to painful stimuli in hypnotic and hysterical anesthesia. *Bulletin Johns Hopkins Hospital,* 1930, **46,** 331–339.

Lewin, I. The effect of reward on the experience of pain. In, *Dissertations in cognitive processes.* Detroit, Mich.: Center for Cognitive Processes, Wayne State University, 1965.

Lewis, T., Pickering, G. W., & Rothschild, P. Observations upon muscular pain in intermittent claudication. *Heart,* 1931, **15**, 359–383.

Melzack, R. Pain. *International Encyclopedia of the Social Sciences.* Vol. 11. New York: Macmillan and Free Press, 1968. Pp. 357–363.

Melzack, R., & Wall, P. D. Pain mechanisms: A new theory. *Science,* 1965, **150**, 971–979.

Orne, M. T. The nature of hypnosis: Artifact and essence. *Journal of Abnormal and Social Psychology,* 1959, **58**, 277–299.

Orne, M. T. On the social psychology of the psychological experiment: With particular reference to demand characteristics and their implications. *American Psychologist,* 1962, **17**, 776–783.

Petrie, A. *Individuality in pain and suffering.* Chicago: University of Chicago Press, 1967.

Sears, R. R. Experimental study of hypnotic anesthesia. *Journal of Experimental Psychology,* 1932, **15**, 1–22.

Shor, R. E. Physiological effects of painful stimulation during hypnotic analgesia under conditions designed to minimize anxiety. *International Journal of Clinical and Experimental Hypnosis,* 1962, **8**, 151–163.

Smith, G. M., Lawrence, D. E., Markowitz, R. A., Mosteller, F., & Beecher, H. K. An experimental pain method sensitive to morphine in man: The submaximum effort tourniquet technique. *Journal of Pharmacology and Experimental Therapeutics,* 1966, **154**, 324–332.

Sternbach, R. A. *Pain: A psychophysiological analysis.* New York: Academic Press, 1968.

Stevens, S. S. Matching functions between loudness and ten other continua. *Perception and Psychophysics,* 1966, **1**, 5–8.

Sutcliffe, J. P. "Credulous" and "skeptical"

views of hypnotic phenomena: Experiments on esthesia, hallucination, and delusion. *Journal of Abnormal and Social Psychology,* 1961, **62**, 189–200.

Szasz, T. S. *Pain and pleasure.* New York: Basic Books, 1967.

Tétreault, L., Panisset, A., & Gouger, P. Étude des facteurs, émotion et douleur dans la réponse tensionnelle au "cold pressor test." *L'Union Médicale du Canada,* 1964, **93**, 177–180.

Voevodsky, J., Cooper, L. M., Morgan, A. H., & Hilgard, E. R. The measurement of suprathreshold pain. *American Journal of Psychology,* 1967, **80**, 124–128.

Weitzenhoffer, A. M., & Hilgard, E. R. *Stanford Hypnotic Susceptibility Scales, Forms A and B.* Palo Alto, Calif.: Consulting Psychologists Press, 1959.

Weitzenhoffer, A. M., & Hilgard, E. R. *Stanford Hypnotic Susceptibility Scales, Form C.* Palo Alto, Calif.: Consulting Psychologists Press, 1962.

Weitzenhoffer, A. M., & Hilgard, E. R. *Revised Stanford Profile Scales of Hypnotic Susceptibility, Forms I and II.* Palo Alto, Calif.: Consulting Psychologists Press, 1967.

West, L. J., Neill, K. C., & Hardy, J. D. Effects of hypnotic suggestions on pain perception and galvanic skin response. *Archives of Neurology and Psychiatry,* 1952, **68**, 549–560.

Wolf, S., & Hardy, J. D. Studies on pain: Observations on pain due to local cooling and on factors involved in the "cold pressor" effect. *Journal of Clinical Investigation,* 1941, **20**, 521–533.

Wolff, H. G., & Goodell, H. The relation of attitude and suggestion to the perception of and reaction to pain. *Proceedings of the Association for Research in Nervous and Mental Disease,* 1943, **23**, 434–448.

Zimbardo, P. G. *Cognitive control of motivation.* Chicago: Scott, Foresman, 1969.

Zimbardo, P. G., Cohen, A. R., Weisenberg, M., Dworkin, L., & Firestone, I. Control of pain motivation by cognitive dissonance. *Science,* 1966, **151**, 217–219.

30

Intracerebral Radio Stimulation and Recording in Completely Free Patients

José M. R. Delgado, Vernon Mark,
William Sweet, Frank Ervin, Gerhard Weiss,
George Bach-y-Rita, and Rioji Hagiwara

The following article shows in a particularly striking—even a frightening—way how powerful the techniques of experimental psychology have become. A technique is described for submitting human subjects to procedures which permit access to the depths of the brain so that EEG recordings can be made and the brain areas of interest can be stimulated or destroyed. All of this can be done while a subject moves about freely because the apparatus has been miniaturized, and both recording and stimulation can take place through a telemetering system capable of transmission over considerable distances without having wires attached to the subject. This is hardly a procedure to be used lightly, but it has its special uses, as the article reveals. The important point from our present perspective is that there is at least some set of circumstances in which these very powerful experimental control procedures can be applied to human subjects behaving freely in their natural habitat.

Reprinted from *Journal of Nervous and Mental Disease,* 1968, **147,** 329–340. Copyright 1968, The Williams & Wilkins Company, Baltimore, Maryland 21202 U.S.A.

Research and instrumental development for the construction of the stimoceiver was supported by the United States Air Force 6571st Aeromedical Research Laboratory F 29600–67–C–0058. Additional support for our research was provided by the United States Public Health Service, M 2004, and the Office of Naval Research, 609 (48).

The circuit for EEG recording is a modified version of the unit described by Meehan (21), and his help in providing us with information and with one of his units is gratefully acknowledged. The help of Mr. Per Hals in developing telestimulation instrumentation is also gratefully acknowledged.

Diagnosis and treatment of focal brain dysfunction associated with behavioral abnormalities are complex tasks which require more effective exploratory techniques. Intracerebral electrodes, electrocorticographical studies, and subsequent discrete neurosurgery have given the epileptologist and stereotaxic surgeon new possibilities for clinical investigation which as yet have been applied to only a small percentage of the patients suffering from neurological disorders including temporal lobe epilepsy and related episodic behavior problems. In these therapeutic studies, recordings and stimulations of any chosen cerebral structure can be performed over a period of days or weeks, and neuronal sites identified as triggers for abnormal electrical patterns associated with behavioral disturbances can be destroyed by electrolysis or resection. Unfortunately, in some patients episodic behavior disorders may be more disabling than their epileptic seizures, and focal lesions may improve one syndrome without modifying the other. Furthermore, recording and stimulation are usually performed under conditions which qualify their usefulness, because the patients' mobility is limited by connecting leads, and their behavior is likewise altered by the stressful and artificial environment of the recording room.

During the last few years, methodology has been developed to stimulate and record the electrical activity of the brain in completely unrestrained monkeys and chimpanzees (10, 13). This procedure should be of considerable clinical interest because it permits exploration of the brain for unlimited periods in patients without disturbing their rest or normal spontaneous activities. This paper reports instrumentation used and clinical application in four patients with psychomotor epilepsy in whom electrodes had been implanted in the temporal lobes. To our knowledge, this is the first clinical use of intracerebral radio stimulation and recording in man.

METHODS

Implantation of Electrodes

Electrodes were constructed and stereotaxically implanted according to methods previously described (20). The electrode assemblies, which were connected to a McPherson skull plug, consisted of a plastic stylet, 1.2 mm in diameter, with 15 stainless steel 3 mm wide contacts attached at 3-mm intervals, plus one thermistor and three other contacts at the tip. Using a McPherson type 2 stereotaxic machine (20), electrode assemblies were implanted bilaterally into the anterior medial amygdala of each patient.

Radio Stimulation

This system consists of two instruments: (1) the RF transmitter which measures 30 by 25 by 15 cm and includes the circuitry for controlling the repetition rate, duration and amplitude (intensity) of the stimulating pulse. The repetition rate may be varied in steps between 10 and 200 Hz and the duration between 0.1 and 1.5 msec. Single pulses may also be generated. Intensity control is accomplished by varying the frequency of the three subcarrier oscillators which operate in the 100 to 500 kHz frequency range. A 100 MHz oscillator is turned on and off by the pulse train from the subcarrier oscillators. The duration of this pulse train is determined by the pulse duration switch. These bursts of 100 MHz RF energy are received by (2) the receiver-stimulator which is carried by the subject, measures 3.7 by 3.0 by 1.4 cm, and weighs 20 g. The solid state circuitry is encapsulated in epoxy resin which provides it with very good mechanical strength and makes it waterproof. Space for the 7-volt Mercury battery is included in the size mentioned above. After RF detection, the resulting subcarrier frequency is demodulated into an amplitude. This amplitude controls the current intensity of the stimulation pulse by means of a constant current transistor in the output circuit of the receiver. This method makes the pulse intensity independent of biological impedance changes over a wide range. Under average stimulation conditions, the battery life is approximately 1 week. Operating range is up to 100 ft. Three channels of stimulation are available. The pulse intensity of each channel can be controlled individually from the transmitter. The pulse duration and repetition rate are the same for all three channels.

Electroencephalographic (EEG) Telemetry

A miniature FM-FM amplifier-transmitter combination and a telemetry receiver are used for this purpose. (1) The transmitting circuitry, carried by the subject, consists of an EEG amplifier with a gain of 100, input impedance of 2 MegaOhms, frequency response from 2 to 200 Hz, and a voltage-controlled oscillator (VCO) for each channel. The VCO operates in one of the frequency bands assigned for subcarrier oscillators

by the IRIG standards. In these studies, a three-channel system was used which operated on IRIG channels 11, 13 and 14. The outputs of all three subcarrier oscillators were summed and connected to the single RF transmitter module. The miniaturized RF transmitter operates at 216 MHz and its range is 50 to 200 ft, depending on the environment. The size of the three-channel unit, including the battery, is 4.5 by 4.5 by 1.5 cm, and it weighs 50 g. The signals from the depth electrodes are received by the amplifier. The output signal of the amplifier controls the frequency of the subcarrier oscillator, and the oscillator output in turn controls the frequency of the transmitter. (2) After amplification of the received signal from the transmitter has been demodulated, the composite subcarrier signals are connected to the inputs of the three discriminators which then separate and demodulate their respective subcarriers to obtain the telemetered analogue information. In the instrumentation used in this instance, a 100-μv signal at the input of the EEG amplifier resulted in a 1-volt output from the corresponding discriminator in the receiver.

The analogue output signals from the receiver were connected to the inputs of an EEG recorder and a magnetic tape recorder. A microphone was also mounted in the room with the subjects and conversation was recorded along with the EEG on magnetic tape.

Stimoceiver

The integration of the three-channel units for radio stimulation and EEG telemetry constitutes the stimoceiver (*stimu*lator and EEG re*ceiver*). Several tests were conducted to ensure proper

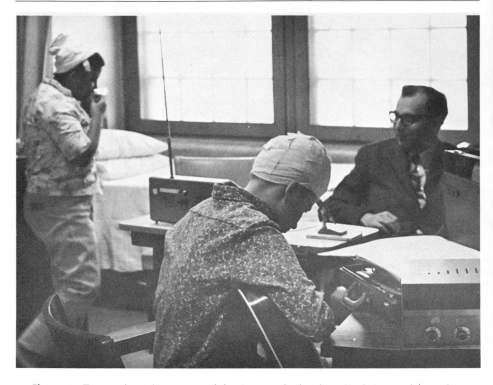

Figure 1 Two patients instrumented for intracerebral radio stimulation and recording engage in spontaneous activities (one is playing the guitar) in the psychiatric ward in the presence of the doctor (VM). Explorations of the brain can be performed for as long as necessary without disturbing the patients.

electronic and biological operation, as explained later. The complete instrument, which weighs only 70 g, can easily be taped onto the patient's head bandage (Figure 1). During part of her treatment, one patient wore a wig which covered her stimoceiver and all evidence of instrumentation.

Additional Equipment

Conversations with the patients were tape-recorded and synchronized with the EEG recordings and moments of stimulation. During interviews with the first two patients, time lapse photog-raphy was used to record possible changes in facial expression or behavior, according to a method employed for studies in monkey colonies (9).

Physical Location of the Studies

The first two patients were under treatment at the Boston General Hospital, and radio stimulations and recordings were performed in a curtained, shielded 12 by 12 ft room in which the patients could walk around or remain seated. The other two cases were studied in their customary quarters within a closed psychiatric ward at Massachusetts General

Hospital, and they could move freely around their bedrooms, bathroom, sitting room or dining room. Nurses and other patients were present during some of the recording and stimulation sessions, as seen in Figure 1.

Experimental Design

The purpose of this study was to identify sites of abnormal intracerebral electrical activity and to test brain excitability in order to guide contemplated therapeutic surgery. Patterns of electrical activity were correlated with behavioral performance, and alterations of conduct evoked by brain stimulation were evaluated. Many hours of EEG recordings were taped and analyzed to determine the frequency, severity and propagation of spontaneous electrical discharges which could have pathological significance. Interviews were structured in order to elicit the patient's verbal expression without unduly influencing the ideological content. During these sessions, two intracerebral points were selected for more extensive study, and they were randomly stimulated at 3- to 5-min intervals according to a predetermined schedule. Neither the patient nor the therapist was informed of the exact moments of stimulation, and each point was stimulated seven times during three 60- to 90-min sessions. Tape-recorded conversations were transcribed, analyzed for number of words per minute and for ideological and emotional content, and correlated with the EEG activity recorded continuously during control periods and stimulations (17, 19).

Instrumenting the patient for telestimulation and recording is a simple and rapid procedure requiring only connection of the stimoceiver to the electrode assembly plug. The stimoceiver is so small and light that it can be concealed within the head bandage, as shown in Figure 1. The patient is thus continuously available, day and night, for brain exploration, and there is no interference with spontaneous behavior.

The entire instrumentation for these studies consisted of the stimoceiver, radiotransmitter, FM receiver, electroencephalograph, tape recorder and oscilloscope. This equipment could be rapidly assembled in a small space and operates without any special physical or electrical requirements. These aspects are emphasized to indicate the feasibility of this type of research within minimum facilities of a hospital ward.

Controls and Functional Characteristics of the Stimoceiver

Fidelity of Recording As demonstrated in previous animal experimentation (13), the traces obtained by means of direct wire connection with the brain were identical with tracings obtained from the same points by telemetry. In the present study this fact was also confirmed.

Noise of Open Input Tests were made by disconnecting the instrumentation from the terminals of the implanted electrodes on the patient's head without removing the instrumentation. In this electrically adverse situation of open input, the noise level was below 15 μv. When the input of the EEG transmitter was connected with the calibrator, the noise level was below 5 μv, as shown in Figure 2I.

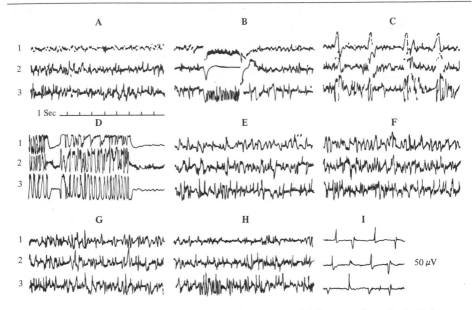

Figure 2 *A,* Control. Recordings from the left temporal lobe in patient G. C. Linkages are: channel 1: 3–4 (amygdala); channel 2: 8–10; (hippocampus); and channel 3: 15–16 (optic radiation). Observe the lack of poststimulation disturbance. *B,* Artifact of stimulation through contact 9 with 0.8 mA, which was below the AD threshold, demonstrating the brief duration of blocking time for telemetric transmission. *C,* Single pulses of 1 ma applied through contact 9 (hippocampus) induced high voltage activity in links 16–17 and the perception of funny feelings. *D,* Electrical seizure evoked by radio stimulation of contact 9 with 1 ma caused a complete behavioral inhibition without observable motor manifestations. *E,* Sixty seconds after stimulation, slow activity is prominent, especially in channel 1, while the patient thinks she is going to faint (she did not). *F,* One hundred seconds after stimulation, high voltage sharp waves dominate the three channels and the patient feels frightened. *G,* One hundred forty seconds after stimulation, abnormal high voltage is still present in channel 1, and the patient reports a sensation of "floating around." *H,* Five minutes after stimulation, spontaneous activity is similar to controls, and the patient behaves and speaks normally. *I,* Telemetric calibration with 50 μV was applied to each channel independently.

Movement Artifacts The leads connecting the terminal plug of the intracerebral electrodes with the telemetric unit were multistrand, Teflon-covered, unshielded copper wires about 80 mm long, attached to the patient's bandage. Normal activities including walking around did not produce observable artifacts.

Interference by Extraneous Noise Most of the recordings, as in Figures 2, 3, and 4, were reasonably free of electrical interference in spite of the fact that no special precautions had been taken in the ward, and the rooms were unshielded. From time to time, however, brief periods of electrical noise appeared in the telemetric recordings, probably related to motors or other instrumentation in use at the hospital. These disturbances sometimes lasted for 10 to 15 sec.

Walls and Obstacles Suitable tests demonstrated that radio stimulation and telemetry could be performed through walls and closed doors which did not obstruct the transmission of RF energy. As an added precaution, receiving and emitting antennae were attached to the ceiling of the ward.

Cross-talk Tests were performed to ensure the lack of cross-talk between the telemetric recording channels, and also between the channels of radio stimulation. During application of radio stimulations, however, artifacts appeared in the recordings, as seen in Figure 2*B*.

Blocking Time after Stimulation The amplifiers of the telemetric units recovered from the over-voltage block immediately after stimulation, and the delay in onset of EEG recording was very brief, as shown in Figure 2*B*. In general, recordings were obtained from points adjacent to the stimulated leads to avoid direct interference between input and outputs in the instrumentation. One cerebral contact could be shared by recording and stimulating units.

Monitoring of Stimulation In animal experimentation, prior to releasing the subject for telestimulation, we always monitor on the oscilloscope the voltage and milliamperage of cerebral radio stimulations. In two patients we performed similar oscillographic monitoring. It should be clarified that in the completely free situation there is no direct monitoring of the actual intensity

used, but as the output is constant current, reliability of electrical parameters is ensured.

Safety in Stimulations In patients walking around while instrumented with stimoceivers, there is a theoretical risk that they might receive extraneous electrical signals. In our stimulators this risk is avoided because of the specificity of the frequency-modulated coding needing to activate them. In addition, by construction the maximum amount of current that the stimoceiver can deliver is 2 ma.

Clinical Applications of the Stimoceiver

1. L.K. This 35-year old white male design engineer had experienced attacks of staring and automatisms for 10 to 12 years. He also had frequent episodes of rage during which he assaulted and injured his wife and children. His driving was precarious because he became enraged if other cars cut in front of him and he would go miles out of his way to force them off the road.

The EEG revealed temporal lobe spiking more prominent on the right side. Pneumoencephalogram disclosed dilatation of the right lateral ventricle, and recording from inlying temporal lobe electrodes showed marked EEG abnormalities. Telemetered recordings were done to correlate the results of amygdala stimulation, EEG recording, and behavior without risking the danger of displacing the intracerebral electrodes by sudden, untoward movements of the patient which could not be compensated for with the usual method of EEG recording by means of direct leads.

2. M.R. This 25-year-old white male

suffered from encephalitis as an infant and a severe head injury in the Navy. Following this he had 4 years of staring spells and automatisms. He was the driver of a car involved in a serious accident and had a police record for vagrancy and violence. He began assaulting his medical attendants on the neurology service of a local veterans' hospital and had to be confined in a mental institution while awaiting surgical evaluation.

The EEG showed bilateral temporal lobe abnormalities. Electrodes were implanted in both amygdalas and depth recordings revealed abnormalities particularly prominent on the right side. The clinical problem here was to decide if and where in the amygdala a focal destructive lesion should be made. The telemetered recording and stimulation allowed us to correlate the patient's behavior and electrical abnormalities without the structured rigidity of the EEG recording room.

3. J.P. This 20-year-old white female had a history of encephalitis at the age of 18 months. In addition, she had experienced temporal lobe seizures and occasional grand mal seizures for 10 years. She also had frequent rage attacks which on more than a dozen occasions resulted in an assault on another person. On one occasion she inserted a knife into a stranger's myocardium, and another time she inserted scissors into the pleural cavity of a nurse.

The EEG showed occasional temporal lobe spikes and depth recordings revealed dramatic electrical abnormalities in both amygdala and hippocampus. The use of stimoceivers proved to be of crucial importance in selection of the temporal lobe site for a destructive lesion because it was difficult to confine the patient in the EEG recording room

during a rage attack while recordings were easily made by telemetry.

4. G.C. This 14-year-old Negro girl was brought up in a foster home and was of borderline intelligence. On two separate occasions her violent behavior resulted in the death of a young foster sibling, and she subsequently assaulted a 7-year-old child at the state hospital where she was confined.

The EEGs, ventriculograms and arteriograms appeared normal, and extradural plates beneath the temporal lobes recorded normal brain waves. Depth electrodes were placed in each amygdala through the posterior approach. Recordings from the hippocampus showed marked focal electrical abnormalities. Telerecordings and telestimulations were used because of this patient's unpredictable behavior. She could not be relied on to sit quietly with the conventional EEG recording system. Stimulation in her right hippocampus produced a clinical and electrical temporal lobe seizure. In retrospect, the patient claimed to have had a number of these before electrode implantation but she had not communicated this information to her physicians.

RECORDING AND STIMULATION

In the four patients, recording of spontaneous electrical activity showed typical patterns which in general permitted the identification of each linkage in different recordings, indicating the reliability of the information. The activity of each linkage indicated the existence of autochthonous electrical generators rather than the predominance of widespread pacemakers. This fact is demonstrated in Figures 2, 3 and 4, which show

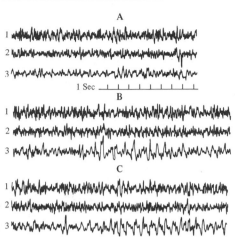

Figure 3   Recording from the right side in patient J. P. Linkages are: channel 1: 2–5 (amygdala); channel 2: 6–9 (anterior part optic radiation); channel 3: 15–17 (posterior part optic radiation). A, Control; B, Spontaneous aimless walking around the room for several minutes coincided with high voltage sharp waves in channel 3; C, Similar high voltage activity appeared in channel 3 when a flashlight was waved in front of the patient's eyes. Calibration as in Figure 2.

patterns and behavioral manifestations. Computer analysis of the tape-recorded information is the best method for this purpose, and its results will be reported in the future. Visual inspection of ink writing recording may also give valuable data, as indicated in the following examples.

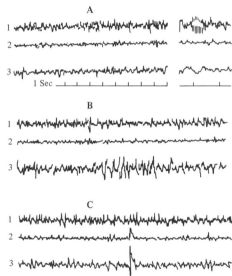

Figure 4   Recording from the right side in patient J. P. Linkages are: channel 1: 3–4 (amygdala); channel 2: 6–7 (anterior part optic radiation); channel 3: 15–16 (posterior part optic radiation). A, Spontaneous bursts of about 16 cps appeared in channel 1 and were more prominent when the patient was psychologically excited. The upper right insert shows similar bursts recorded at greater speed. B, Sudden spontaneous arrest of speech coincided with bursts of spike activity in channel 3. C, Spontaneous over-friendliness of the patient culminated in an attempt to kiss the therapist. No correlation with electrical changes in the brain was detected. In spite of the considerable motor activity of the patient, the recording is almost free of artifacts. Observe also the increase in bursts of rapid activity in channel 1. Calibration as in Figure 2.

the lack of synchrony among the waves in the three channels, contrasting with the simultaneous detection of single shock stimulus artifact which appeared in Figure 2C and also contrasting with the correlation of patterns during the evoked after-discharges which spread to the three channels (Figure 2D). We do not know the extension of the electrical fields generated within each cerebral structure but recordings indicate that the localization is rather precise because a clear pattern, such as the 12-cps bursts in Figure 4A, was detected exclusively in channel 1.

One of the main objectives in telemetric recording of intracerebral activity is the search for correlations between electrical

In patient J.P., spontaneous, brief periods of aimless walking around the room coincided with an increase in high voltage sharp waves, as shown in Figure 3B. At other times, spontaneous inhibition of speech lasting for several minutes was accompanied by a burst of spike activity localized to contacts 15–16, as seen in Figure 4B. Psychological excitement of the same patient was related with an increase in the number and duration of 16-cps bursts (see Figure 4). Emotionally charged conversation often modified the recordings from the amygdala, but this result was not as evident as the above mentioned changes. The possible significance of these correlations was increased by the fact that other behavioral manifestations did not produce detectable electrical changes. The patient walked around the room, used the toilet, read papers, and conversed without visible alterations in the telemetered depth recordings.

Radio stimulation of different points in the amygdala and hippocampus in the four patients produced a variety of effects including pleasant sensations, elation, deep thoughtful concentration, odd feelings, super relaxation, colored visions and other responses. In this article we will discuss only the following selected results:

During a recorded interview in patient G.C., point 9, located in the left hippocampus, was radio-stimulated for 5 sec with 100 cps, 0.5 msec, and 1 ma, resulting in an electrical after-discharge (Figure 2D) involving the amygdala, hippocampus and optic radiation, which lasted for 25 sec. During this time the patient's conversation stopped completely and she was unresponsive, without exhibiting motor convulsions, automatisms or other visible disturbances. When the after-discharge was over, the patient resumed conversation, remembered her speech arrest, but was not able to explain it. Spontaneous electrical activity of the brain was considerably modified for more than 2 min after stimulation, as shown in Figure 2 (E, F, G). During this period, the patient expressed the successive sensations of fainting, fright and floating around. These "floating" feelings were repeatedly evoked on different days by stimulation of the same point even in the absence of after-discharges. Single shocks applied to the hippocampus induced bursts of high voltage activity in the optic radiation and were accompanied by the perception of "funny feelings."

In patient J.P., crises of assaultive behavior reminiscent of her spontaneous bursts of anger could be elicited by radio stimulation of contact 3 in the right amygdala. Seven seconds after the onset of radio stimulation with 50 cps, 1.0 msec, and l.2 ma, the patient interrupted spontaneous activities such as guitar playing, and in a fit of rage threw herself against the wall (never attacking the interviewer), paced around the room for several minutes, and then gradually reassumed her normal behavior. This effect was repeated on 2 days with similar results. During this elicited rage, no seizure activity was evident in the depth recording. The fact that only one contact gave this type of response suggested that the surrounding neuronal field was involved in the behavioral problems of the patient.

DISCUSSION

Important limitations of standard electroencephalographic recordings are as follows: (1) psychological stress of the recording room; (2) time required to attach leads to the patients; (3) restrictions imposed on individual mobility by the connecting leads; (4) limited period for the acquisition of data; and (5) the slim likelihood of taking recordings during spontaneous electrical or behavioral crises, which could provide the most important information for the patient's diagnosis and treatment.

These handicaps are eliminated by using telemetry. Extensive information has been published about different systems for radio telemetry in biological studies (4, 7, 15, 24). The disparity between the large number of technical papers and the few reports of results indicates the existence of methodological problems. There is some data on telemetered EEG obtained during space flights (1, 23); preliminary descriptions of scalp EEG studies in humans have been reported (6, 18); and there is also a technical paper on telemetered scalp EEG in disturbed children (25). Data is presented here to demonstrate that telemetry of EEG has already attained a degree of sophistication, miniaturization and reliability that render it suitable for widespread clinical application in both standard scalp and intracerebral electrical studies.

In the last decade, depth recording in man has become a major therapeutic tool in various medical centers (2, 3, 5, 16, 22, 26–28). The usefulness of intracerebral electrodes would be significantly increased if stimulations and recordings were performed by remote control. This technique, in addition to being more comfortable for the patients, would permit more detailed exploration and prolonged studies including periods of normal sleep.

Electrical stimulation of the brain, which is a standard procedure in neurosurgery, has been proposed by some authors as a therapeutic technique (16, 22, 27). For this purpose, programmed radio stimulation of ambulatory patients would be obviously advantageous.

The combination of both stimulation and EEG recording by radio telemetry offers a new tool for two-way clinical exploration of the brain, and it may be predicted that in the near future microminiaturization and more refined methodology will permit the construction of instruments without batteries and small enough to be permanently implanted underneath the patient's skin, for transdermal reception and transmission of signals through several channels. Part of the basic circuitry for this purpose has already passed satisfactory testing in our laboratory. While the use of cardiac pacemakers is well established in clinical medicine, methodological problems in the development of a similar instrument for cerebral pacemaking are far more difficult because of the requirements of multichanneling, external control of several parameters of stimulation, and the far greater functional complexity of the brain in comparison with the heart. These technical problems, however, are soluble, and the possibility of clinical application should attract the interest of more electronic and medical investigators.

Experimentation in animals has demonstrated the practicality of long term, programmed stimulation of the brain to inhibit episodes of assaultive behavior (8), to increase or decrease appetite (14), to modify drives (10) and to modulate intracerebral reactivity (9). Some of these findings may be applicable to the treatment of cerebral disturbances in man.

With respect to the electrical information obtained in our four patients, analysis of their telemetered EEG supports the assumption that depth recordings reveal local activity rather than diffuse volume conductor fields in the brain, in agreement with previous work obtained by direct leads (12). The considerable independence of the electrical activity of different intracerebral points indicates that this electrographic information has anatomical significance. Caution is necessary, however, in a calculation of the origin of apparently abnormal waves, such as the burst recorded from channel 1 in Figure 2A, which could originate in the neuronal field around the contacts or could reflect merely the activity transmitted from a distant cerebral area, as demonstrated in animal experiments (11). The distinction between reactive and propagated activity which can be made by studying recorded electrical patterns may help to evaluate the origin of abnormal intracerebral activity.

SUMMARY

A new instrument called "stimoceiver" has been developed for the simultaneous multichannel recording and stimulation of the brain by FM radio waves in completely unrestrained subjects. This instrument is small enough to be worn comfortably and permanently by the patient.

Clinical application of the stimoceiver is reported in four patients with psychomotor epilepsy who had electrodes implanted in the amygdala and hippocampus for therapeutical reasons. The advantages of this methodology are: (1) the patient is instrumented for telestimulation and recording simply by plugging the stimoceiver into the electrode socket on the head; (2) the instrumentation does not limit or modify spontaneous behavior; (3) the patient is continuously available, day and night, for intracerebral recording or treatment; (4) studies are performed, without introducing factors of anxiety or stress, in the relatively normal environment of the hospital ward and during spontaneous social interactions; (5) cerebral explorations may be conducted in severely disturbed patients who would not tolerate the confinement of the recording room; (6) the lack of connecting wires eliminates the risk that during unpredictable behavior or convulsive episodes the patient may dislodge or even pull out the implanted electrodes; (7) programmed stimulation of the brain for therapeutic reasons may be continued for as long as necessary.

In four patients telemetric information obtained supports the following conclusions: (1) depth recordings reveal local activity rather than diffuse volume conductor fields, giving anatomical significance to the data; (2) abnormality in spontaneous behavior, including aimless walking, speech inhibition, and psychological excitement, coincided with abnormal EEG patterns: (3) arrest reaction accompanied by an afterdischarge was evoked in one patient by radio stimulation of the hippocampus, and during the subsequent 2 min, abnormalities in brain waves coincided with successive sensations of fainting, fright and floating around; (4) assaultive behavior, reminiscent of spontaneous crises, was elicited in another patient by radio stimulation of the amygdala, and this fact was important in orienting therapeutic surgery.

REFERENCES

1. Adey, W. R. Potential for telemetry in the recording of brain waves from animals and men exposed to the stresses of space flight. In Slater, L., ed. *Bio-Telemetry* pp. 289–300. Pergamon Press, New York, 1963.
2. Alberts, W. W., Feinstein, B., Levin, G., and Wright, E. W., Jr. Electrical stimulation of therapeutic targets in waking dyskinetic patients. EEG Clin. Neurophysiol., **20**:559–566, 1966.
3. Ajmone Marsan, C., and Van Buren, J. Functional relationship between frontal cortex and subcortical structures in man. EEG Clin. Neurophysiol., **16**:80–87, 1964.
4. Barwick, R. E., and Fullagar, P. J. A bibliography of radio telemetry in biological studies. Proc. Ecol. Soc. Aust., **2**:27, 1967.
5. Bickford, R. G., Dodge, H. W., Jr., and Uihlein, A. Electrographic and behavioral effects related to depth stimulation in human patients. In Ramey, E. R. and O'Doherty, D. S., eds. *Electrical Studies on the Unanesthetized Brain* pp. 248–259. Hoeber, New York, 1960.
6. Breakell, C. C., Parker, C. S., and Christopherson, F. Radio transmission of the human electroencephalogram and other electrophysiological data. EEG Clin. Neurophysiol., **1**:243–244, 1949.
7. Caceres, C. A., ed. *Biomedical Telemetry.* Academic Press, New York, 1965.
8. Delgado, J. M. R. Aggression and defense under cerebral radio control. In Clemente, C. D. and Lindsley, D. B., eds. *Aggression and Defense. Neural Mechanisms and Social Patterns* [Brain Function, vol. V], pp. 171–193. University of California Press, Berkeley, 1967.
9. Delgado, J. M. R. Free behavior and brain stimulation. In Pfeiffer, C. C. and Smythies, J. R., eds. *International Review of Neurobiology*, vol. 6, pp. 349–449. Academic Press, New York, 1964.
10. Delgado, J. M. R. Man's intervention in intracerebral functions. IEEE Int. Conv. Rec., **9**:143–150, 1967.
11. Delgado, J. M. R., and Hamlin, H. Depth electrography. Confin. Neurol., **22**:228–235, 1962.
12. Delgado, J. M. R., and Hamlin, H. Direct recording of spontaneous and evoked seizures in epileptics. EEG Clin. Neurophysiol., **10**:463–486, 1958.
13. Delgado, J. M. R., and Mir, D. Fragmental organization of emotional behavior in the monkey brain. N.Y. Acad. Sci. In press.
14. Fonberg, E., and Delgado, J. M. R. Avoidance and alimentary reactions during amygdala stimulation. J. Neurophysiol., **24**:651–664, 1961.
15. Geddes, L. A. A bibliography of biological telemetry. Amer. J. Med. Electronics, **1**:294–298, 1962.
16. Heath, R. G. Electrical self-stimulation of the brain in man. Amer. J. Psychiat., **120**:571–577, 1963.
17. Higgins, J. W., Mahl, G. F., Delgado, J. M. R., and Hamlin, H. Behavioral changes during intracerebral electrical stimulation. Arch. Neurol. Psychiat. (Chicago), **76**:399–419, 1956.
18. Kamp, A., and Van Leeuwen, W. S. A two-channel EEG radio telemetering system. EEG Clin. Neurophysiol., **13**:803–806, 1961.
19. Mahl, G. F., Rothenberg, A., Delgado, J. M. R. and Hamlin, H. Psychological responses in the human to intracerebral electrical stimulation. Psychosom. Med., **26**:337–368, 1964.
20. Mark, V. H., and Ervin, F. The relief of chronic severe pain by stereotactic surgery. In White, J. C. and Sweet, W. H., eds. *Pain and the Neurosurgeon: A Forty Years' Experience.* Thomas, Springfield, Ill. In press.
21. Meehan, J. P., and Rader, R. D. Multiple channel physiological data acquisition system for restrained and mobile

subjects. Report to Air Force Systems Command on Contact AF 04(695)–178, 1965.

22. Sem-Jacobsen, C. W. Electrical stimulation of the human brain. EEG Clin. Neurophysiol., **17**:211, 1964.

23. Simmons, D. G., and Prather, W. A personalised radio telemetry system for monitoring central nervous system arousal in aerospace flight. IEEE Trans. Biomed. Engin., **11**:40, 1964.

24. Slater, L., ed. *Bio-Telemetry.* Pergamon Press, New York, 1963.

25. Vreeland, R., Collins, C., Williams, L., Yeager, C., Gianascol, A., and Henderson, J., Jr. A subminiature radio EEG telemeter for studies of disturbed children. EEG Clin. Neurophysiol., **15**:327–329, 1963.

26. Walker, A. E. and Marshall, C. The contribution of depth recording to clinical medicine. EEG Clin. Neurophysiol., **16**:88–99, 1964.

27. Walter, W. G. and Crow, H. J. Depth recording from the human brain. EEG Clin. Neurophysiol., **16**:68–72, 1964.

28. White, J. C. and Sweet, W. H., eds. *Pain and the Neurosurgeon: A Forty Years' Experience.* Thomas, Springfield, Ill. In press.

EDITOR'S REFERENCES

Anderson, B. F., *The psychology experiment*. Belmont, Calif.: Brooks/Cole, 1966.

Bachrach, A. J., *Psychological research*. New York: Random House, 1962.

Barber, T. X., & Silver, M. J. Pitfalls in data analysis and interpretation: A reply to Rosenthal. *Psychological Bulletin Monograph*, 1968, **70,** 48–62.

Berne, E. *The games people play: The psychology of human relations*. New York: Grove Press, 1964.

Best, J. B. Protopsychology. *Scientific American*, 1963, **208** (2), 55–62.

Beveridge, W. I. B. *The art of scientific investigation*. New York: Vintage, 1950.

Caws, P. The structure of discovery. *Science*, 1969, **166,** 1375–1380.

Craik, K. *The nature of explanation*. Cambridge: Cambridge University Press, 1943.

Ebbinghaus, H. *Memory, A contribution to experimental psychology*. (1885) H. A. Ruger and C. E. Bussenius (Trans.). New York: Teachers College, Columbia University, 1913.

Hanson, N. R. *Patterns of discovery*. Cambridge: Cambridge University Press, 1965.

Koffka, K. *Principles of gestalt psychology*. New York: Harcourt, Brace, & Jovanovich, 1935.

Lashley, K. S. The mechanism of vision I: A method for rapid analysis of pattern-vision in the rat. *Journal of Genetic Psychology*, 1930, **37,** 453–460.

Platt, J. R. *The excitement of science*. Boston: Houghton Mifflin, 1962.

Rosenthal, R. Experimenter expectancy and the reassuring nature of the null hypothesis decision procedure. *Psychological Bulletin Monograph*, 1968, **70,** 30–47.

Selye, H. *From dream to discovery*. New York: McGraw-Hill, 1964.

Skinner, B. F. Are theories of learning necessary? *Psychological Review*, 1950, **57,** 193–216.

Toulmin, S. *The philosophy of science*. New York: Harper & Row, 1960.

White, M. *Toward reunion in philosophy*. New York: Atheneum, 1963.

Wilson, E. B. *An introduction to scientific research*. New York: McGraw-Hill, 1952.

Zaffron, R. Understanding what we don't know how we know. *Science*, 1970, **168,** 1440–1492.

AUTHOR INDEX

Goodenough, A., 375
Goodman, L., 258
Gordon, H., 422
Gordon, K., 234
Gouger, P., 431
Graham, C., 101, 144
Graham, S., 212
Green, D., 96, 103, 104
Greene, M., 427
Greenspoon, J., 53, 202, 214
Griffith, R., 213
Griffiths, W., 242
Gruehl, H., 252
Gruenberg, B., 208
Guilford, J., 124, 126
Gustav, A., 270
Guthrie, E., 217

H

Hadamard, J., 84
Hagiwara, R., 439
Hahn, K., 436
Haigh, G., 62
Hake, H., 372
Halas, E., 208, 217
Hale, E., 243
Hall, C., 369
Hall, G., 266
Hamilton, C., 417
Hamlin, H., 187
Hammer, E., 213
Hanson, N., 53
Hardy, J., 427
Harris, H., 209
Harter, N., 140
Hart, J., 379
Hayes, K., 144
Head, H., 7
Heath, R., 187
Hebb, D., 234, 370
Heinemann, E., 143
Helmholtz, H., 10, 76, 77, 132
Hempel, C., 83
Hering, E., 10
Heron, W. T., 170, 171
Herrnstein, R., 174
Hess, E., 187, 360, 361, 362
Higgins, J., 184
Hilgard, E., 290, 424, 434
Hines, E., 427
Hinton, M., 239, 241
Hipparchus, 154
Hively, W., 202
Hodges, J., 127
Hogben, L., 111
Holmes, D., 271
Holt, R., 370
Holz, W., 202
Hsia, Y., 144

Hull, C., 56, 67, 149, 217, 267, 290
Hume, D., 27, 77
Hunt, H., 174
Hunter, W., 163

I

Innes, I., 254, 255
Irion, A., 140
Ison, J., 208, 217

J

Jackson, C., 269, 274
Jackson, H., 252
Jacobson, A., 375
Jacobson, E., 141
Jaffe, J., 190
James, W., 39, 48, 141
Jarrett, R., 209, 215
Jasper, H., 183
Jastak, J., 190
Jensen, M., 144
Johnson, H., 56, 63
Jones, M., 141
Jourard, S., 264, 280
Jouvet, M., 372
Junod, J., 375
Justesen, D., 251, 252

K

Kaiser, H., 119, 122
Kales, A., 375
Kallos, P., 252
Kamiya, J., 132, 367, 368, 375, 377, 378, 379, 380
Kanger, F., 65, 209, 216
Kant, E., 81
Karlin, J., 96
Katkin, E., 402
Katz, D., 140, 186
Keeler, C., 242
Keller, F., 164, 170, 173
Kellog, L., 140
Kellog, W., 140
Kelman, H., 271, 275, 279, 280
Kepler, J., 69, 70, 82, 88, 140
Kety, S., 381
Keynes, J., 113
Kierkegaard, S., 318
Kimble, G., 385
King, H., 241
Kintz, B., 207
Kipling, R., 358
Kirk, S., 202
Kleitman, N., 369, 371, 377
Kline, L., 240
Klüver, H., 184
Knight, J., 251

SUBJECT INDEX